# Intro to Business Tech

## Sixth Edition

R. KELLY RAINER JR. • BRAD PRINCE

**Intro to Business Technology BA 131**
**Portland Community College**

**Wiley Custom Learning Solutions**

To order books or for customer service, please call 1(800)-CALL-WILEY (225-5945).

Printed in the United States of America.

ISBN 978-1-119-33428-6
Printed and bound by Sheridan Books.

10 9 8 7 6 5 4 3 2

| | |
|---|---|
| t & Director | George Hoffman |
| itor | Lisé Johnson |
| arketing Manager | Christopher DeJohn |
| ign Manager | Allison Morris |
| Editor | Jennifer Manias |
| tions Assistant | Amanda Dallas |
| ent Manager | Dorothy Sinclair |
| uction Editor | Jane Lee |
| ector | Harry Nolan |
| igner | Wendy Lai |
| o Editor | Billy Ray |
| Management Services | Thomson Digital |
| er Image | A-Digit/Getty Images, Inc. |
| er Image | Pedro Castellano/Getty Images, Inc. |

was set in 9.5/11.5 Electra LT Std by Thomson Digital, and printed and bound by Donnelley/Von Hoffman.
was printed by Donnelley/Von Hoffman. This book is printed on acid free paper.

in 1807, John Wiley & Sons, Inc. has been a valued source of knowledge and understanding for more than 200 years,
eople around the world meet their needs and fulfill their aspirations. Our company is built on a foundation of principles
de responsibility to the communities we serve and where we live and work. In 2008, we launched a Corporate Citizenship
, a global effort to address the environmental, social, economic, and ethical challenges we face in our business. Among the
are addressing are carbon impact, paper specifications and procurement, ethical conduct within our business and among
ors, and community and charitable support. For more information, please visit our website: www.wiley.com/go/citizenship.

N  978-1-119-10800-9 (Binder-Ready Version)

er, R. Kelly, Jr., 1949–
ntroduction to Information Systems : Supporting and Transforming Business / R. Kelly Rainer Jr., Brad Prince. — Sixth edition.
1 online resource.
ncludes index.
Description based on print version record and CIP data provided by publisher; resource not viewed.
ISBN 978-1-119-10799-6 (pdf) – ISBN 978-1-119-10800-9 (looseleaf)
1.  Information technology.  2.   Computer networks.  3.   Management information systems.
I.  Prince, Brad, 1978-   II.  Title.
T58.5
658.4'038011—dc23

2015025301

Printed in the United States of America
10 9 8 7 6 5 4 3 2 1

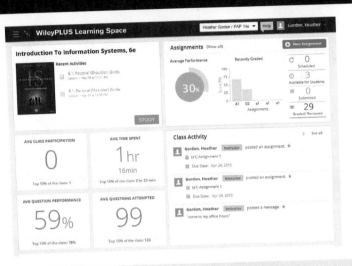

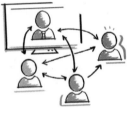

# Introduction to
# Information Systems

Supporting and Transforming Business

**Sixth Edition**

**R. Kelly Rainer Jr.**
**Brad Prince**

WILEY

# Preface

## What Do Information Systems Have to Do with Business?

This edition of Rainer and Prince's *Introduction to Information Systems* will answer this question for you. In every chapter, you will see how real global businesses use technology and information systems to increase their profitability, gain market share, improve their customer service, and manage their daily operations. In other words, you will learn how information systems provide the foundation for modern business enterprises.

Our goal is to teach all business majors, especially undergraduates, how to use IT to master their current or future jobs and to help ensure the success of their organization. Our focus is not on merely *learning* the concepts of information technology but rather on *applying* those concepts to perform business processes more efficiently and effectively. We concentrate on placing information systems in the context of business, so that you will more readily grasp the concepts presented in the text.

The theme of this book, *What's in IT for Me?*, is a question asked by most students who take this course. Our book will show you that IT is the backbone of any business, whether you're majoring in Accounting, Finance, Marketing, Human Resources, Operations Management, or MIS.

## New to This Edition

The sixth edition contains many exciting additions and changes. These elements make the text more interesting and readable for students of all majors, while still providing the most current information possible in the rapidly changing field of information systems.

### Overall

- A new section on Relational Database Operations in Chapter 5 (Data and Knowledge Management).
- Expanded coverage on Big Data in Chapter 5 (Data and Knowledge Management).
- A new section on The Internet of Things in Chapter 8 (Wireless, Mobile Computing, and Mobile Commerce).
- All new or updated chapter-opening and closing cases.
- All new or updated *IT's About Business* boxes in every chapter.

# Key Features

We have been guided by the following goals that we believe will enhance the teaching and learning experience.

## "What's in IT for Me?" theme

- We show why IT is important by calling attention in each chapter to how that chapter's IT topic relates to students in each major.
  - A feature of this edition is chapter-opening "teasers" that list specific tasks for each major that the chapter will help prepare students to do.
  - Throughout each chapter, icons guide the reader to relevant issues for their specific functional area—Accounting (ACC), Finance (FIN), Marketing (MKT), Operations Management (POM), Management Information Systems (MIS), and Human Resources Management (HRM).
  - Every chapter concludes with a summary of how the concepts relate to each functional area ("What's in IT for Me?").

## Active Learning

We recognize the need to actively involve students in problem solving, creative thinking, and capitalizing on opportunities. Therefore, we have included in every chapter a variety of hands-on exercises, activities, and mini-cases, including exercises that require students to use software application tools. Through these activities and an interactive Web site, we enable students to apply the concepts they learn.

## Diversified and Unique Examples from Different Industries

Extensive use of vivid examples from large corporations, small businesses, and government and not-for-profit organizations helps to enliven concepts by demonstrating the capabilities of IT, its cost and justification, and innovative ways in which real corporations are using IT in their operations. Each chapter constantly highlights the integral connection between IT and business. This is especially evident in the "IT's About Business" boxes.

## Misuse of IS

Like other textbooks, this text presents many examples of IS success. But we also provide numerous examples of IS failures, in the context of lessons that can be learned from such failures. Misuse of IS can be very expensive, as we illustrate.

## Innovation and Creativity

In today's rapidly changing environment, creativity and innovation are essential for a business to operate effectively and profitably. Throughout the text we demonstrate how IT facilitates these concepts.

## Global Focus

Because an understanding of global competition, partnerships, and trading is essential to success in business, we provide a broad selection of international cases and examples. We discuss how IT facilitates export and import, the management of multinational companies, and electronic trading around the globe.

## Focus on Ethics

With corporate scandals appearing daily in the news, ethics and ethical questions have come to the forefront of business people's minds. In addition to a chapter that concentrates on ethics and privacy (Chapter 3), we have included examples and cases that focus on business ethics throughout the chapters.

# Pedagogical Structure

Other pedagogical features provide a structured learning system that reinforces the concepts through features such as chapter-opening organizers, section reviews, frequent applications, and hands-on exercises and activities.

*Chapter-opening organizers* include the following pedagogical features:

- The *Learning Objectives* provide an overview of the key concepts students should come away with after reading the chapter.
- *Web Resources* highlight ancillary materials available on the book companion site and within *WileyPLUS* for both instructors and students.
- The *Chapter Outline* lists the major chapter headings.
- An opening *case* identifies a business problem faced by an actual company, describes the IT solution applied to the business problem, presents the results of the IT solution, and summarizes what students can learn from the case.
- New "What's in IT for Me?" "teasers" give students a quick hint about skills in their majors for which this chapter will help prepare them.

*Study aids* are provided throughout each chapter. These include the following:

- *IT's About Business* cases provide real-world applications, with questions that relate to concepts covered in the text. Icons relate these sections to the specific functional areas.
- Highlighted *Examples* interspersed throughout the text illustrate the use (and misuse) of IT by real-world organizations, thus making the conceptual discussion more concrete.
- *Tables* list key points or summarize different concepts.
- End-of-section reviews (*Before You Go On . . .*) prompt students to pause and test their understanding of basic concepts before moving on to the next section.

*End-of-chapter study aids* provide extensive opportunity for the reader to review and actually "do something" with the concepts they have just studied:

- *What's in IT for Me?* is a unique chapter summary section that demonstrates the relevance of topics for different functional areas (accounting, finance, marketing, production/operations management, and human resources management).
- The *Chapter Summary*, keyed to learning objectives listed at the beginning of the chapter, enables students to review the major concepts covered in the chapter.
- The end-of-chapter *Glossary* facilitates studying by listing and defining all of the key terms introduced in the chapter.
- *Discussion Questions* and *Problem-Solving Activities* provide practice through active learning. These exercises are hands-on opportunities to use the concepts discussed in the chapter.
- A *Case* presents a brief case study organized around a business problem and explains how IT helped to solve it. Questions at the end of the case relate it to concepts discussed in the chapter.

# Online Resources

**www.wiley.com/college/rainer**

This text also facilitates the teaching of an introductory IS course by providing extensive support materials for instructors and students. Go to *www.wiley.com/college/rainer* to access the Student and Instructor Web Sites.

## Instructor's Manual

The *Instructor's Manual*, created by Bob Gehling of Auburn University at Montgomery, includes a chapter overview, teaching tips and strategies, answers to all end-of-chapter questions, supplemental mini-cases with essay questions and answers, and experiential exercises that relate to particular topics.

## Test Bank

The *Test Bank*, written by Jennifer Gerow of Virginia Military Institute, is a comprehensive resource for test questions. It contains multiple-choice, true/false, short answer, and essay questions for each chapter. The multiple-choice and true/false questions are labeled according to difficulty: easy, medium, or hard.

The test bank is available for use in Respondus' easy-to-use software. Respondus is a powerful tool for creating and managing exams that can be printed to paper or published directly to Blackboard, WebCT, Desire2Learn, eCollege, ANGEL, and other eLearning systems. For more information on Respondus and the Respondus Test Bank Network, please visit *www.respondus.com*.

## PowerPoint Presentations

The *PowerPoint Presentations* consist of a series of slides for each chapter of the text that are designed around the text content, incorporating key points from the text and all text illustrations as appropriate.

## Wiley Information Systems Hub

http://wileyiscommunity.ning.com/

This is a new online, interactive community designed to support the teaching of the Intro IS course. The Hub will allow IS faculty to explore a centralized and constantly updated set of current articles for use in class, connect with IS colleagues for help and advice about upcoming course topics, and share course materials with other IS faculty. The Community Manager is David Firth of the University of Montana

## Weekly Updates

Weekly updates, harvested from around the web by David Firth of the University of Montana, provide you with the latest IT news and issues. These are posted every Monday morning throughout the year at *http://wileyinformationsystemsupdates.com/* and include links to articles and videos as well as discussion questions to assign or use in class.

## Image Library

All textbook figures are available for download from the Web site. These figures can easily be added to PowerPoint presentations.

## OfficeGrader

OfficeGrader™ is an Access-based VBA macro that enables automatic grading of Office assignments. The macros compare Office files and grade them against a master file. OfficeGrader™ is available for Word, Access, Excel, and PowerPoint for Office 2010 and Office 2013. For more information, contact your Wiley sales representative or visit www.wiley.com/college/microsoft and click on "OfficeGrader."

# WileyPlus Learning Space

What is *WileyPLUS Learning Space*? It's a place where students can learn, collaborate, and grow. Through a personalized experience, students create their own study guide while they interact with course content and work on learning activities.

*WileyPLUS Learning Space* combines adaptive learning functionality with a dynamic new e-textbook for your course—giving you tools to quickly organize learning activities, manage student collaboration, and customize your course so that you have full control over content as well as the amount of interactivity between students.

You can:

- Assign activities and add your own materials
- Guide students through what's important in the e-textbook by easily assigning specific content
- Set up and monitor collaborative learning groups
- Assess student engagement
- Benefit from a sophisticated set of reporting and diagnostic tools that give greater insight into class activity

Learn more at www.wileypluslearningspace.com. If you have questions, please contact your Wiley representative.

# Wiley Flex

Wiley provides a wide variety of printed and electronic formats that provide many choices to your students at a range of price points. Contact your Wiley sales representative for more details on any of the below.

## Wiley E-Textbook

E-Textbooks are complete digital versions of the text that help students study more efficiently as they:

- Access content online and offline on your desktop, laptop and mobile device
- Search across the entire book content
- Take notes and highlight
- Copy and paste or print key sections

*Wiley E-Text: Powered by VitalSource (available for all titles) Ask your sales representative about other available formats.*

## Wiley Custom

This group's services allow you to:

- Adapt existing Wiley content and combine texts
- Incorporate and publish your own materials
- Collaborate with our team to ensure your satisfaction

## Wiley Custom Select

Wiley Custom Select allows you to build your own course materials using selected chapters of any Wiley text and your own material if desired. For more information, contact your Wiley sales representative or visit http://customselect.wiley.com/.

# Acknowledgments

Creating, developing, and producing a text for an introduction to information technology course is a formidable undertaking. Along the way, we were fortunate to receive continuous evaluation, criticism, and direction from many colleagues who regularly teach this course. We would like to acknowledge the contributions made by the following individuals.

We would like thank the Wiley team: Lisé Johnson, Executive Editor; Jennifer Manias, Sponsoring Editor; Allison Morris, Product Design Manager; Chris DeJohn, Executive Marketing Manager; and Amanda Dallas, Market Solutions Assistant. We also thank the production team, including Dorothy Sinclair, Senior Content Manager; Jane Lee, Senior Production Editor; and Gaurav Uppal of Thomson Digital. And thanks to Harry Nolan, Design Director; Wendy Lai, Senior Designer; and Billy Ray, Senior Photo Editor. We also would like to thank Robert Weiss for his skillful and thorough editing of the manuscript.

We also acknowledge and appreciate Bob Gehling and Jennifer Gerow for their work on the supplements, and David Firth for his work on the Weekly Updates and the new Faculty Hub. Many thanks also to Alina M. Chircu and Marco Marabelli of Bentley University for developing material that enhances our coverage of business processes and ERP. Finally, we thank all the faculty listed below who have generously shared their varied opinions by reviewing the manuscript and/or completing our user surveys.

KELLY RAINER
BRAD PRINCE

## Reviewers

Ahlam Alhweiti, *Southern New Hampshire University*
Barbara Gordon, *Seminole State College of Florida*
Milele Hallingquest, *Iowa State University*
Sandy Keeter, *Southern New Hampshire University*
Nicole Lytle-Kosola, *California State University, San Bernardino*
Joe Parker, *Southern New Hampshire University*
Melissa Ray, *University of Phoenix*
Donna Rex, *York University*
Kevin Scheibe, *Iowa State University*
Kevin Wilhelmsen, *University of Phoenix*
Gaya P. Agrawal, *Rutgers University*
Ihssan Alkadi, *South Louisiana Community College*
Mary Baldwin-Grimes, *Gateway Technical College*
Mary Barnard, *IUPUI*
Nicholas Barnes, *Nichols College*
Lisa Reeves Bertin, *Penn State University Shenango Campus*
Mark Best, *The University of Kansas*
Neelima Bhatnagar, *University of Pittsburgh at Johnstown*
Dan Brandon, *Christian Brothers University*
Fredrick Bsharah, *Cape Cod Community College*
Jessie Brown, *Macquarie City Campus*
Patrick Browning, *The University of Southern Mississippi*
Trini Callava, *University of Miami*
Pam Carter, *North Carolina A&T State University*
Antoinette Cevenini, *Macquarie City Campus*
Lewis Chasalow, *The University of Findlay*
H. Michael Chung, *California State University Long Beach*
Ken Corley, *Appalachian State University*
Jose Cruz, *University of Puerto Rico - Mayaguez*
Barry Cumbie, *University of Southern Mississippi*
Subhasish Dasgupta, *George Washington University*

Lauren Eder, *Rider University*
Greg Foudray, *Salem State University*
Bob Gehling, *Auburn University Montgomery*
Cody Gray, *Portland Community College*
Eileen Griffin, *Canisius College*
Heather Griffo, *Portland Community College*
Joseph Harder, *Indiana State University*
Jeff Harper, *Indiana State University*
Jim Howatt, *Luther College*
Chang-tseh Hsieh, *University of Southern Mississippi*
Scott Hunsinger, *Appalachian State University*
Micki Hyde, *Indiana University of Pennsylvania*
Jinman Kim, *University of Sydney*
Richard Klein, *Florida International University*
Dana Ladd, *University of Findlay*
Faith Lamprey, *Rhode Island College*
Christine Lazaro, *Gateway Technical College*
Mark Lewis, *Alfred University*
Susan Li, *Adelphi University*
Thomas Long, *DePaul University*
James Scott Magruder, *The University of Southern Mississippi*
Kalana Malimage, *Mississippi State University*
Efrem Mallach, *Rhode Island College*
Steven Mandelbaum, *George Washington University*
Nichelle Manuel, *IADT*
Stanley Marcinczyk, *Central Connecticut State University*
Robert Marmelstein, *East Stroudsburg University*
Tom Mattson, *University of Hawaii*
Lee McClain, *Western Washington University*
Rodger Morrison, *Troy University*
Mahdi Nasereddin, *Penn State University*

Bill Neumann, *University of Arizona*
Cynthia Nitsch, *University of San Diego*
Anthony Offor, *Sanford-Brown College*
Jim Ott, *Fontbonne University*
Neal Parker, *Appalachian State University*
Sheila Pearson, *Southern Arkansas University*
Jennifer Percival, *University of Ontario Institute of Technology*
Olga Petkova, *Central Connecticut State University*
Sean Piotrowski, *Rider University*
Robert Plant, *University of Miami*
Carol Pollard, *Appalachian State University*
Simon Poon, *University of Sydney*
Drew Procaccino, *Rider University*
Carl Rebman, *University of San Diego*
Howard D Rees, *Rider University*
Lisa Rich, *Athens State University*
Jim Ryan, *Troy University*
Anselm Sequeira, *University of Southern Mississippi*

Linda Spauldig, *Gateway Technical College*
Suneel Sharma, *GDGWI-Lancaster University*
Troy Strader, *Drake University*
Sharon Tabor, *Boise State University*
Zaiyong Tang, *Salem State University*
Christopher Taylor, *Appalachian State University*
Gary Templeton, *Mississippi State University*
Cheryl Ucakar, *Gateway Technical College*
Michael Waclawiczek, *Salem State University*
Shouhong Wang, *University of Massachusetts Dartmouth*
John Wee, *University of Mississippi*
Brian West, *University of Louisiana at Lafayette*
Paul Wheatcraft, *Portland Community College*
Melody White, *University of North Texas*
Dezhi Wu, *Southern Utah University*
Carol Wysocki, *Columbia Basin College*
Li Richard Ye, *Carlifornia State University, Northridge*
Saad Yousuf, *Gateway Technical College*

# Brief Contents

# Contents

# 1 Introduction to Information Systems

| [ LEARNING OBJECTIVES ] | [ CHAPTER OUTLINE ] | [ WEB RESOURCES ] |
|---|---|---|
| 1. Identify the reasons why being an informed user of information systems is important in today's world. | 1.1 Why Should I Study Information Systems? | • Student PowerPoints for note taking |
| 2. Describe the various types of computer-based information systems in an organization. | 1.2 Overview of Computer-Based Information Systems | **WileyPLUS Learning Space** • E-book • Author video lecture for each chapter section |
| 3. Discuss ways in which information technology can affect managers and nonmanagerial workers. | 1.3 How Does IT Impact Organizations? | • Practice quizzes • Flash Cards for vocabulary review |
| 4. Identify positive and negative societal effects of the increased use of information technology. | 1.4 Importance of Information Systems to Society | • Additional "IT's About Business" cases • Video interviews with managers • Lab Manuals for Microsoft Office 2010 and 2013 |

## What's In IT For Me?

This Chapter Will Help Prepare You To...

| ACCT | FIN | MKT | POM | HRM | MIS |
|---|---|---|---|---|---|
| ACCOUNTING | FINANCE | MARKETING | PRODUCTION OPERATIONS MANAGEMENT | HUMAN RESOURCES MANAGEMENT | MIS |
| Monitor social media for compliance | Collaborate with external financial experts | Receive real-time feedback from customers | Partners/ customers collaborate on product development | Enhance recruiting efforts | Develop internal company social networks |

# [AngelList Helps Entrepreneurs Build Companies]

Fundraising is a difficult and time-consuming process that diverts entrepreneurs from building their companies. For decades, entrepreneurs who sought to obtain funding from Silicon Valley's small, wealthy group of angel investors found the process similar to breaking into an exclusive club. (An angel investor is an individual who provides capital for a startup, usually in exchange for convertible debt or ownership equity.) They had to work with their personal networks to set up meetings with financiers and then negotiate privately, with little awareness of fair market value or better opportunities elsewhere.

To assist these individuals, AngelList (*https://angel.co*), founded in 2010 in San Francisco, has created an online forum where founders of early-stage companies—called *startups*—post their ideas and meet investors who fund these often risky ventures. AngelList's mission is to make startup investing transparent and efficient.

How does AngelList work? Basically, startups access the site and create profiles that list information such as their previous financial backers (if any) and the amount of capital they have already raised. They then utilize those profiles to make their "pitch" to hundreds of certified investors—financial firms as well as wealthy individuals and companies. To avoid fraud, AngelList vets its investors by requiring them to provide a track record of their prior investments. At the same time, the company thoroughly researches any startups that it lists on its Web site.

AngelList restricts its services to startups that are trying to obtain funding for the first time. For example, the company handles the regulatory paperwork to help startups complete the relevant forms. One feature on the company's Web site, called "Syndicates," lets investors pool their money under the direction of a single, wealthy investor known as a "lead." Then, whenever the lead decides to back a startup, so do the other investors, or "backers." Leads set their own terms. For example, one lead investor collects up to a 20 percent "carry" fee from his backers, plus a portion of any positive return they receive if the startup is acquired or goes public. AngelList takes a 5 percent cut on any such paydays. In 2014, some $87 million worth of deals were transacted via AngelList's syndicates.

Startups such as the private taxi service Uber (*www.uber.com*) and babysitting-jobs Web site Urbansitter (*www.urbansitter.com*) have used AngelList to make contact with new investors and quickly finalize their funding deals. In another example, Sprig (*www.eatsprig.com*), a San Francisco-based dinner delivery service, raised most of the money it needed for a new kitchen in a single day on AngelList.

At the end of 2013, AngelList added startup job listings to its Web site. In addition, it was lobbying the U.S. government to further relax fundraising restrictions contained in the JOBS Act, the 2012 Federal law that lowered regulatory requirements for startups. The company's goal is for the public—rather than simply accredited investors—to use the site to provide funding for promising startups.

And the bottom line? By early 2015, AngelList featured tens of thousands of businesses, and it had provided entrepreneurs with thousands of introductions to potential investors. Also in early 2015, AngelList expanded its investor syndicates to the United Kingdom.

*Sources:* Compiled from K. Collins, "AngelList Syndicates to Bring Investment to UK Startups," *Wired*, February 13, 2015; D. Primack, "A Disrupter Shakes Up Angel Investing," *Fortune*, December 1, 2014; B. Stone, "The Social Network for Startups," *Bloomberg BusinessWeek*, January 20–26, 2014; F. Lardinois, "OnTheGo Raises $700K Seed Round from Foundry Group's AngelList Syndicate and Others to Improve Smart Glasses," *TechCrunch*, January 6, 2014; L. Rao, "Kima Ventures Will Allow Startups to Raise $150K Within 15 Days via AngelList," *TechCrunch*, December 4, 2013; N. Hughes, "Will AngelList Help or Hurt Startup Fundraising," *GeekWire*, October 12, 2013; A. Davidson, "Follow the Money: AngelList Has Blown Open Early-Stage Investments," *Wired*, May 17, 2013; P. Sloan, "AngelList Attacks Another Startup Pain Point: Legal Fees," *CNET News*, September 5, 2012; L. Rao, "AngelList Launches Docs to Help Startups Sign and Close Seed Rounds Online with Low Legal Fees," *TechCrunch*, September 5, 2012; *www.angellist.com*, accessed January 20, 2015.

### Questions

1. What are the advantages that AngelList offers to entrepreneurs?
2. What are potential disadvantages that entrepreneurs might encounter by using AngelList? (*Hint:* What if you listed your company profile on AngelList and no investor provided funding?)

# Introduction

Before we proceed, we need to define **information technology** (IT) and **information systems** (IS). Information technology refers to any computer-based tool that people use to work with information and to support the information and information-processing needs of an organization. An information system collects, processes, stores, analyzes, and disseminates information for a specific purpose.

IT has far-reaching effects on individuals, organizations, and our planet. Although this text is largely devoted to the many ways in which IT has transformed modern organizations, you will also learn about the significant impacts of IT on individuals and societies, the global economy, and our physical environment. In addition, IT is making our world smaller, enabling more and more people to communicate, collaborate, and compete, thereby leveling the digital playing field.

When you graduate, you will either start your own business or work for an organization, whether it is public sector, private sector, for-profit, or not-for-profit. Your organization will have to survive and compete in an environment that has been radically transformed by information technology. This environment is global, massively interconnected, intensely competitive, 24/7/365, real-time, rapidly changing, and information-intensive. To compete successfully, your organization must use IT effectively.

As you read this chapter and this text, keep in mind that the information technologies you will learn about are important to businesses of all sizes. No matter what area of business you major in, what industry you work for, or the size of your company, you will benefit from learning about IT. Who knows? Maybe you will use the tools you learn about in this class to make your great idea a reality by becoming an entrepreneur and starting your own business! In fact, as you see in the chapter opening case, you can use information technology (in the form of AngelList.com) to help you raise the necessary funds to successfully grow your business.

The modern environment is intensely competitive not only for your organization, but for you as well. You must compete with human talent from around the world. Therefore, you will also have to make effective use of IT.

Accordingly, this chapter begins with a discussion of why you should become knowledgeable about IT. It also distinguishes among data, information, and knowledge, and it differentiates computer-based information systems (CBIS) from application programs. Finally, it considers the impacts of information systems on organizations and on society in general.

# Why Should I Study Information Systems? 1.1

You are part of the most connected generation in history: You have grown up online; you are, quite literally, never out of touch; you use more information technologies (in the form of digital devices), for more tasks, and are bombarded with more information than any generation in history. The MIT Technology Review refers to you as *Homo conexus*. Information technologies are so deeply embedded in your lives that your daily routines would be almost unrecognizable to a college student just 20 years ago.

Essentially, you practice continuous computing, surrounded by a movable information network. This network is created by constant cooperation between the digital devices you carry (e.g., laptops, tablets, and smartphones), the wired and wireless networks that you access as you move about, and Web-based tools for finding information and communicating and collaborating with other people. Your network enables you to pull information about virtually anything from anywhere, at any time, and to push your own ideas back to the Web, from wherever you are, via a mobile device. Think of everything you do online, often with your smartphone: register for classes; take classes (and not just at your university); access class syllabi, information, PowerPoints, and lectures; research class papers and presentations; conduct banking; pay your bills; research, shop, and buy products from companies or other people; sell your "stuff"; search for, and apply for, jobs; make your travel reservations (hotel, airline, rental car); create your own blog and post your own podcasts and videocasts to it; design your own page on

Facebook; make and upload videos to YouTube; take, edit, and print your own digital photographs; "burn" your own custom-music CDs and DVDs; use RSS feeds to create your personal electronic newspaper; text and tweet your friends and family throughout your day; send Snaps; and many other activities. (Note: If any of these terms are unfamiliar to you, don't worry. You will learn about everything mentioned here in detail later in this text.)

## The Informed User—You!

So, the question is: Why you should learn about information systems and information technologies? After all, you can comfortably use a computer (or other electronic devices) to perform many activities, you have been surfing the Web for years, and you feel confident that you can manage any IT application that your organization's MIS department installs.

The answer lies in your becoming an **informed user**; that is, a person knowledgeable about information systems and information technology. There are several reasons why you should be an informed user.

In general, informed users tend to get more value from whatever technologies they use. You will enjoy many benefits from being an informed user of IT.

- First, you will benefit more from your organization's IT applications because you will understand what is "behind" those applications (see Figure 1.1). That is, what you see on your computer screen is brought to you by your MIS department, which is operating "behind" your screen.

- Second, you will be in a position to enhance the quality of your organization's IT applications with your input.

- Third, even as a new graduate, you will quickly be in a position to recommend—and perhaps help select—the IT applications that your organization will use.

- Fourth, being an informed user will keep you abreast of both new information technologies and rapid developments in existing technologies. Remaining "on top of things" will help you to anticipate the impacts that "new and improved" technologies will have on your organization and to make recommendations on the adoption and use of these technologies.

**FIGURE 1.1** MIS provides what users see on their computer screens.

USERS    MIS

@ Slaomir Fajer/iStockphoto

- Fifth, you will understand how using IT can improve your organization's performance and teamwork as well as your own productivity.
- Finally, if you have ideas of becoming an entrepreneur, then being an informed user will help you use IT when you start your own business.

Going further, managing the IS function within an organization is no longer the exclusive responsibility of the IS department. Rather, users now play key roles in every step of this process. The overall objective in this text is to provide you with the necessary information to contribute immediately to managing the IS function in your organization. In short, the goal is to help you become a very informed user!

## IT Offers Career Opportunities

Because information technology is vital to the operation of modern businesses, it offers many employment opportunities. The demand for traditional IT staff—programmers, business analysts, systems analysts, and designers—is substantial. In addition, many well-paid jobs exist in areas such as the Internet and electronic commerce (e-commerce), mobile commerce (m-commerce), network security, telecommunications, and multimedia design.

The information systems field includes the people in various organizations who design and build information systems, the people who use those systems, and the people responsible for managing those systems. At the top of the list is the chief information officer (CIO).

The CIO is the executive who is in charge of the IS function. In most modern organizations, the CIO works with the chief executive officer (CEO), the chief financial officer (CFO), and other senior executives. Therefore, he or she actively participates in the organization's strategic planning process. In today's digital environment, the IS function has become increasingly strategic within organizations. As a result, although most CIOs still rise from the IS department, a growing number are coming up through the ranks in the business units (e.g., marketing and finance). So, regardless of your major, you could become the CIO of your organization one day. This is another reason to be an informed user of information systems!

Table 1.1 provides a list of IT jobs, along with a description of each one. For further details about careers in IT, see *www.computerworld.com/careertopics/careers* and *www.monster.com*.

Career opportunities in IS are strong and are projected to remain strong over the next 10 years. In fact, *Forbes* listed its "12 top jobs" for 2014, the *U.S. News & World Report and Money* listed their "100 top jobs" for 2014, and *Money* listed its "top jobs" for 2014. Let's take a look at these rankings. (Note that the rankings differ because the magazines used different criteria in their research.) As you can see, jobs suited for MIS majors rank extremely high in all three lists. The magazines with their job rankings are as follows:

**Forbes** (out of 12)
#1 Software developer
#6 Web developer
#8 Database administrators
#12 Information security analysts

**U.S. News & World Report** (out of 100)
#3 Software Developer
#7 Computer System Analyst
#8 Information Security Analyst
#11 Web developer
#21 IT manager

**Money**
#1 Software architect
#8 Database administrator
#11 Clinical applications specialist (IT in healthcare)
#14 User experience designer
#17 IT program manager

**Table**

**1.1**

**Information Technology Jobs**

| Position | Job Description |
|---|---|
| Chief Information Officer | Highest-ranking IS manager; is responsible for all strategic planning in the organization |
| IS Director | Manages all systems throughout the organization and the day-to-day operations of the entire IS organization |
| Information Center Manager | Manages IS services such as help desks, hot lines, training, and consulting |
| Applications Development Manager | Coordinates and manages new systems development projects |
| Project Manager | Manages a particular new systems development project |
| Systems Manager | Manages a particular existing system |
| Operations Manager | Supervises the day-to-day operations of the data and/or computer center |
| Programming Manager | Coordinates all applications programming efforts |
| Systems Analyst | Interfaces between users and programmers; determines information requirements and technical specifications for new applications |
| Business Analyst | Focuses on designing solutions for business problems; interfaces closely with users to demonstrate how IT can be used innovatively |
| Systems Programmer | Creates the computer code for developing new systems software or maintaining existing systems software |
| Applications Programmer | Creates the computer code for developing new applications or maintaining existing applications |
| Emerging Technologies Manager | Forecasts technology trends; evaluates and experiments with new technologies |
| Network Manager | Coordinates and manages the organization's voice and data networks |
| Database Administrator | Manages the organization's databases and oversees the use of database-management software |
| Auditing or Computer Security Manager | Oversees the ethical and legal use of information systems |
| Webmaster | Manages the organization's World Wide Web site |
| Web Designer | Creates World Wide Web sites and pages |

Going further, the *U.S. News & World Report* picked technology as the #1 career choice for 2014. Not only do IS careers offer strong job growth, but also the pay is excellent. The Bureau of Labor Statistics, an agency within the Department of Labor that is responsible for tracking and analyzing trends relating to the labor market, notes that the median salary in 2014 for "computer and information systems managers" was approximately $121,000, and predicted that the profession would grow by an average of 15 percent per year through 2022.

## Managing Information Resources

Managing information systems in modern organizations is a difficult, complex task. Several factors contribute to this complexity. First, information systems have enormous strategic value to organizations. Firms rely on them so heavily that, in some cases, when these systems are not working (even for a short time), the firm cannot function. (This situation is called "being hostage to information systems.") Second, information systems are very expensive to acquire, operate, and maintain.

A third factor contributing to the difficulty in managing information systems is the evolution of the management information systems (MIS) function within the organization. When businesses first began to use computers in the early 1950s, the MIS department "owned" the only computing resource in the organization, the mainframe. At that time, end users did not interact directly with the mainframe.

In contrast, in the modern organization, computers are located in all departments, and almost all employees use computers in their work. This situation, known as *end user computing*, has led to a partnership between the MIS department and the end users. The MIS department now acts as more of a consultant to end users, viewing them as customers. In fact, the main function of the MIS department is to use IT to solve end users' business problems.

As a result of these developments, the responsibility for managing information resources is now divided between the MIS department and the end users. This arrangement raises several important questions: Which resources are managed by whom? What is the role of the MIS department, its structure, and its place within the organization? What is the appropriate relationship between the MIS department and the end users? Regardless of who is doing what, it is essential that the MIS department and the end users work in close cooperation.

There is no standard way to divide responsibility for developing and maintaining information resources between the MIS department and the end users. Instead, that division depends on several factors: the size and nature of the organization, the amount and type of IT resources, the organization's attitudes toward computing, the attitudes of top management toward computing, the maturity level of the technology, the amount and nature of outsourced IT work, and even the countries in which the company operates. Generally speaking, the MIS department is responsible for corporate-level and shared resources, and the end users are responsible for departmental resources. Table 1.2 identifies both the traditional functions and various new, consultative functions of the MIS department.

So, where do the end users come in? Take a close look at Table 1.2. Under the traditional MIS functions, you will see two functions for which you provide vital input: managing systems development and infrastructure planning. Under the consultative MIS functions, in contrast, you exercise the primary responsibility for each function, while the MIS department acts as your advisor. IT's About Business 1.1 illustrates how the University System of Georgia (USG) manages its IT resources across its 31 member higher education institutions.

MIS

---

**Table 1.2 The Changing Role of the Information Systems Department**

**Traditional Functions of the MIS Department**
- Managing systems development and systems project management
  - As an end user, you will have critical input into the systems development process. You will learn about systems development in Chapter 13.
- Managing computer operations, including the computer center
- Staffing, training, and developing IS skills
- Providing technical services
- Infrastructure planning, development, and control
  - As an end user, you will provide critical input about the IS infrastructure needs of your department.

**New (Consultative) Functions of the MIS Department**
- Initiating and designing specific strategic information systems
  - As an end user, your information needs will often mandate the development of new strategic information systems.
- You will decide which strategic systems you need (because you know your business needs better than the MIS department does), and you will provide input into developing these systems.

**Table 1.2** (continued)

- Incorporating the Internet and electronic commerce into the business
  - As an end user, you will be primarily responsible for effectively using the Internet and electronic commerce in your business. You will work with the MIS department to accomplish this task.
- Managing system integration, including the Internet, intranets, and extranets
  - As an end user, your business needs will determine how you want to use the Internet, your corporate intranets, and extranets to accomplish your goals. You will be primarily responsible for advising the MIS department on the most effective use of the Internet, your corporate intranets, and extranets.
- Educating the non-MIS managers about IT
  - Your department will be primarily responsible for advising the MIS department on how best to educate and train your employees about IT.
- Educating the MIS staff about the business
  - Communication between the MIS department and the business units is a two-way street. You will be responsible for educating the MIS staff on your business, its needs, and its goals.
- Partnering with business unit executives
  - Essentially, you will be in a partnership with the MIS department. You will be responsible for seeing that this partnership is one "between equals" and ensuring its success.
- Managing outsourcing
  - Outsourcing is driven by business needs. Therefore, the outsourcing decision resides largely with the business units (i.e., with you). The MIS department, working closely with you, will advise you on technical issues such as communications bandwidth and security.
- Proactively using business and technical knowledge to seed innovative ideas about IT
  - Your business needs will often drive innovative ideas about how to effectively use information systems to accomplish your goals. The best way to bring these innovative uses of IS to life is to partner closely with your MIS department. Such close partnerships have amazing synergies!
- Creating business alliances with business partners
  - The needs of your business unit will drive these alliances, typically along your supply chain. Again, your MIS department will act as your advisor on various issues, including hardware and software compatibility, implementing extranets, communications, and security.

# IT's [about business]

## 1.1 Information Technology Supports Students in Georgia   MIS

There are two major drivers for change in U.S. higher education: lowering costs and improving performance. Lowering costs is necessary because the expenses associated with higher education have been rapidly increasing for many years, leading to concerns that higher education is out of reach for low- and increasingly middle-income families. Improving performance is necessary because there is pressure on universities to graduate more students while at the same time maintaining a high-quality educational experience. In essence, colleges and universities are under increasing pressure to accomplish more with less.

To achieve these seemingly contradictory goals, the University System of Georgia (*www.usg.edu*) has employed several cutting-edge information technologies. USG is the organizational body that includes 31 public institutions of higher learning in the state of Georgia. The system, which is governed by the Georgia Board of Regents, establishes goals and dictates general policy to its member institutions.

These policies require universities to deliver learning using new technologies—for example, delivering lectures via video— to stay current. In addition, university IT organizations must devise innovative strategies to reduce costs and increase effi-ciencies both within and among universities. This requirement has become vital as state funding shrinks and students struggle under the escalating costs of higher education. To satisfy this requirement, university IT departments have to be flexible and entrepreneurial.

The individual who bears the major responsibility for imple-menting these policies is Board of Regents Vice Chancellor and CIO Curtis Carver. Significantly, Carver has to collaborate with 31 independent-minded university CIOs. This position requires him to sell services. USG institutions can pursue technology contracts on their own. So, Carver looks for scenarios where three to five universities are planning to purchase the same product and there-fore can consolidate their buying or centralize the service. This approach not only reduces costs but also helps alleviate staff shortages in some areas, such as database administration and analytics. The central IT organization's vision statement asserts, "If our customers can choose anyone to provide them IT services, they would choose us." Let's take a look at a specific example of how Carver utilized his strategy to resolve a problem.

The problem involves situations where a class is overbooked at one member university while the same class at other schools has empty seats. To manage such situations, the universities offered a number of such classes across institutions via videoconferenc-ing. However, the registration process posed a serious problem for students.

In addition to constituting a major inconvenience, overbooked classes and waiting lists can cause students to take longer to graduate, adding to their loan debt and delaying their entry into the workforce. Although a few vendors sell software to facilitate cross-institution registration, Carver considered those products too complex and costly. As an alternative, USG system develop-ers wrote custom computer code to handle cross-registration. This software integrated student information systems to create a total headcount of registrants in each course across all USG universities. The system provides an interface for each student that exactly resembles the user interface at his or her home insti-tution. Therefore, if a student at Coastal Georgia University reg-isters for a course at the University of Georgia, the system looks exactly like the Coastal Georgia system, with no need to register or pay fees to another university. Thousands of students now sign up for courses through this cross-registration system, known as the Intra-Georgia Registration Sharing System, or Ingress (not to be confused with the open-source Ingres database).

After the developers had created Ingress, Carver had to con-vince member universities that this system was really the way to go. University CIOs often have the option to use or not to use a shared service. As of this writing, 22 of the 31 USG universities use or are implementing Ingress. Carver takes the same approach with shared data center services, which the central group offers via a private cloud. The USG has also centralized the operation of its Desire2Learn learning management system, used by 300,000 students statewide. Finally, Carver is exploring whether the USG can sell Ingress to other institutions. We discuss cloud computing in Technology Guide 3.

*Sources:* Compiled from C. Murphy, "Chiefs of the Year," *InformationWeek,* December 16, 2013; K. Flinders, "Universities Investing in Back-Office IT Systems," *Computer Weekly,* March 2, 2012; "University IT Departments Can Drive Efficiencies and Modernisation," *The Guardian,* June, 2011; "Information Technology in Higher Education: Survey of Chief Informa-tion Officers," *The Chronicle of Higher Education,* 2010; *www.usg.edu,* accessed January 25, 2015.

**Questions**

1. Describe how the University System of Georgia manages its information resources vis-à-vis the individual universities in the system.
2. What are the advantages of central management of information systems in the University System of Georgia?
3. What are the disadvantages of central management of informa-tion systems in the University System of Georgia?

# before you go on...

1. Rate yourself as an informed user. (Be honest; this isn't a test!)
2. Explain the benefits of being an informed user of information systems.
3. Discuss the various career opportunities offered in the IT field.

# Overview of Computer-Based Information Systems

## 1.2

Organizations refer to their management information systems functional area by several names, including the MIS Department, the Information Systems (IS) Department, the Infor-mation Technology Department, and the Information Services Department. Regardless of the name, however, this functional area deals with the planning for—and the development, management, and use of—information technology tools to help people perform all the tasks related to information processing and management. Recall that information technology relates to any computer-based tool that people use to work with information and to support the information and information-processing needs of an organization.

As previously stated, an information system collects, processes, stores, analyzes, and disseminates information for a specific purpose. The purpose of information systems has been defined as getting the right information to the right people, at the right time, in the right amount, and in the right format. Because information systems are intended to supply useful information, we need to differentiate between information and two closely related terms: data and knowledge (see Figure 1.2).

**Data items** refer to an elementary description of things, events, activities, and transactions that are recorded, classified, and stored but are not organized to convey any specific meaning. Data items can be numbers, letters, figures, sounds, and images. Examples of data items are collections of numbers (e.g., 3.11, 2.96, 3.95, 1.99, 2.08) and characters (e.g., B, A, C, A, B, D, F, C).

**Information** refers to data that have been organized so that they have meaning and value to the recipient. For example, a grade point average (GPA) by itself is data, but a student's name coupled with his or her GPA is information. The recipient interprets the meaning and draws conclusions and implications from the information. Consider the examples of data provided in the preceding paragraph. Within the context of a university, the numbers could be grade point averages, and the letters could be grades in an Introduction to MIS class.

**Knowledge** consists of data and/or information that have been organized and processed to convey understanding, experience, accumulated learning, and expertise as they apply to a current business problem. For example, suppose that a company recruiting at your school has

**FIGURE 1.2** Data, information, and knowledge.

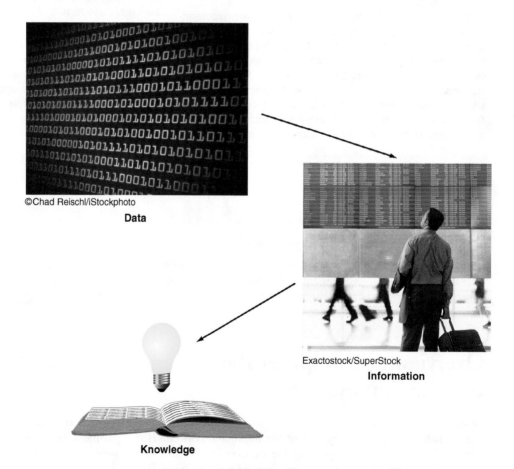

©Chad Reischl/iStockphoto
**Data**

Exactostock/SuperStock
**Information**

**Knowledge**

found over time that students with grade point averages over 3.0 have experienced the greatest success in its management program. Based on this accumulated knowledge, that company may decide to interview only those students with GPAs over 3.0. This example presents an example of knowledge because the company utilizes information—GPAs—to address a business problem—hiring successful employees. As you can see from this example, organizational knowledge, which reflects the experience and expertise of many people, has great value to all employees.

Consider this example:

| Data | Information | Knowledge |
|---|---|---|
| **[No context]** | **[University context]** | |
| 3.16 | 3.16 + John Jones = GPA | * Job prospects |
| 2.92 | 2.92 + Sue Smith = GPA | * Graduate school prospects |
| 1.39 | 1.39 + Kyle Owens = GPA | * Scholarship prospects |
| 3.95 | 3.95 + Tom Elias = GPA | |
| **[No context]** | **[Professional baseball pitcher context]** | |
| 3.16 | 3.16 + Ken Rice = ERA | |
| 2.92 | 2.92 + Ed Dyas = ERA | * Keep pitcher, trade pitcher, or send pitcher to minor leagues |
| 1.39 | 1.39 + Hugh Carr = ERA | * Salary/contract negotiations |
| 3.95 | 3.95 + Nick Ford = ERA | |

GPA = grade point average (higher is better).
ERA = earned run average (lower is better); ERA is the number of runs per nine innings that a pitcher surrenders.

You see that the same data items, with no context, can mean entirely different things in different contexts.

Now that you have a clearer understanding of data, information, and knowledge, let's shift our focus to computer-based information systems. As you have seen, these systems process data into information and knowledge that you can use.

A **computer-based information system** is an information system that uses computer technology to perform some or all of its intended tasks. Although not all information systems are computerized, today most are. For this reason, the term "information system" is typically used synonymously with "computer-based information system." The basic components of computer-based information systems are listed below. The first four are called **information technology components**. Figure 1.3 illustrates how these four components interact to form a CBIS.

- **Hardware** consists of devices such as the processor, monitor, keyboard, and printer. Together, these devices accept, process, and display data and information.
- **Software** is a program or collection of programs that enable the hardware to process data.
- A **database** is a collection of related files or tables containing data.
- A **network** is a connecting system (wireline or wireless) that permits different computers to share resources.
- **Procedures** are the instructions for combining the above components to process information and generate the desired output.
- *People* are those individuals who use the hardware and software, interface with it, or utilize its output.

Figure 1.4 illustrates how these components are integrated to form the wide variety of information systems found within an organization. Starting at the bottom of the figure, you see that the IT components of hardware, software, networks (wireline and wireless), and databases form the **information technology platform**. IT personnel use these components to develop information systems, oversee security and risk, and manage data. These activities cumulatively

**FIGURE 1.3** Computer-based information systems consist of hardware, software, databases, networks, procedures, and people.

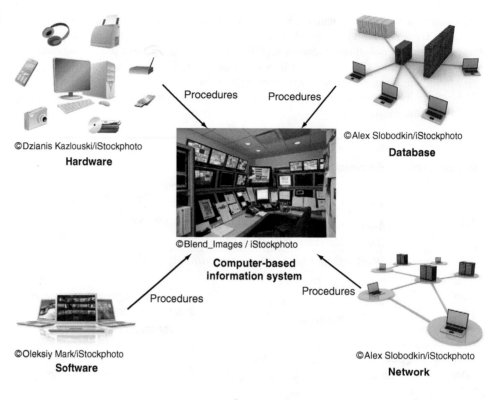

©Dzianis Kazlouski/iStockphoto
**Hardware**

©Alex Slobodkin/iStockphoto
**Database**

©Blend_Images / iStockphoto
**Computer-based information system**

©Oleksiy Mark/iStockphoto
**Software**

©Alex Slobodkin/iStockphoto
**Network**

Procedures

Procedures

Procedures

Procedures

**FIGURE 1.4** Information technology inside your organization.

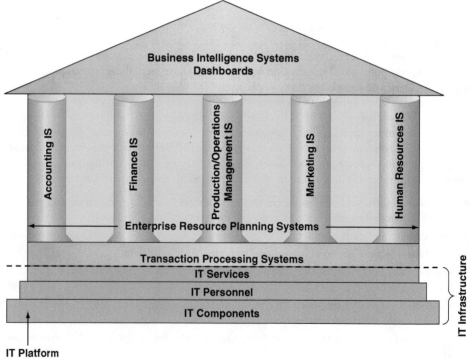

**Business Intelligence Systems Dashboards**

Accounting IS

Finance IS

Production/Operations Management IS

Marketing IS

Human Resources IS

**Enterprise Resource Planning Systems**

**Transaction Processing Systems**

**IT Services**

**IT Personnel**

**IT Components**

IT Infrastructure

**IT Platform**

are called **information technology services**. The IT components plus IT services comprise the organization's **information technology infrastructure**. At the top of the pyramid are the various organizational information systems.

Computer-based information systems have many capabilities. Table 1.3 summarizes the most important ones.

- Perform high-speed, high-volume numerical computations.
- Provide fast, accurate communication and collaboration within and among organizations.
- Store huge amounts of information in an easy-to-access, yet small space.
- Allow quick and inexpensive access to vast amounts of information worldwide.
- Interpret vast amounts of data quickly and efficiently.
- Automate both semiautomatic business processes and manual tasks.

**Table 1.3**
**Major Capabilities of Information Systems**

Information systems perform these various tasks via a wide spectrum of applications. An **application (or app)** is a computer program designed to support a specific task or business process. (A synonymous term is *application program*.) Each functional area or department within a business organization uses dozens of application programs. For instance, the human resources department sometimes uses one application for screening job applicants and another for monitoring employee turnover. The collection of application programs in a single department is usually referred to as a *departmental information system* (also known as a *functional area information system* (FAIS)). For example, the collection of application programs in the human resources area is called the *human resources information system* (HRIS). There are collections of application programs—that is, departmental information systems—in the other functional areas as well, such as accounting, finance, marketing, and production/operations.

## Types of Computer-Based Information Systems

Modern organizations employ many different types of information systems. Figure 1.4 illustrates the different types of information systems that function *within* a single organization, and Figure 1.5 shows the different types of information systems that function *among* multiple organizations. You will study transaction processing systems (TPSs), management information systems, and enterprise resource planning (ERP) systems in Chapter 10. You will learn about customer relationship management (CRM) systems and supply chain management (SCM) systems in Chapter 11.

**FIGURE 1.5** Information systems that function among multiple organizations.

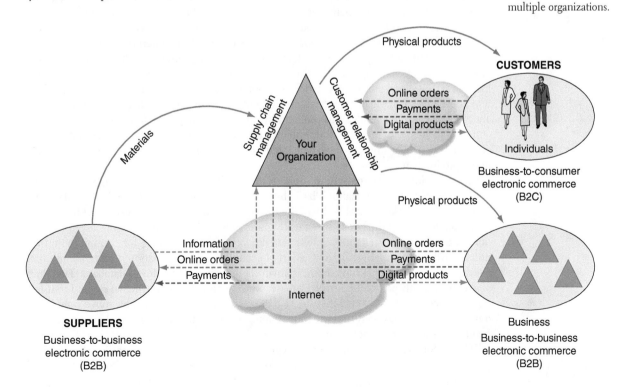

In the next section, you will learn about the numerous and diverse types of information systems employed by modern organizations. You will also read about the types of support these systems provide.

**Breadth of Support of Information Systems.** Certain information systems support parts of organizations, others support entire organizations, and still others support groups of organizations. This section addresses all of these systems.

Recall that each department or functional area within an organization has its own collection of application programs, or information systems. These **functional area information systems** are supporting pillars for the information systems located at the top of Figure 1.4, namely, business intelligence (BI) systems and dashboards. As the name suggests, each FAIS supports a particular functional area within the organization. Examples are accounting IS, finance IS, production/operations management (POM) IS, marketing IS, and human resources IS.

Consider these examples of IT systems in the various functional areas of an organization. In finance and accounting, managers use IT systems to forecast revenues and business activity, to determine the best sources and uses of funds, and to perform audits to ensure that the organization is fundamentally sound and that all financial reports and documents are accurate.

In sales and marketing, managers use information technology to perform the following functions:

- *Product analysis:* developing new goods and services
- *Site analysis:* determining the best location for production and distribution facilities
- *Promotion analysis:* identifying the best advertising channels
- *Price analysis:* setting product prices to obtain the highest total revenues

Marketing managers also use IT to manage their relationships with their customers. In *manufacturing*, managers use IT to process customer orders, develop production schedules, control inventory levels, and monitor product quality. They also use IT to design and manufacture products. These processes are called *computer-assisted design* (CAD) and *computer-assisted manufacturing* (CAM).

Managers in *human resources* use IT to manage the recruiting process, analyze and screen job applicants, and hire new employees. They also employ IT to help employees manage their careers, to administer performance tests to employees, and to monitor employee productivity. Finally, they rely on IT to manage compensation and benefits packages.

Two information systems that support the entire organization, enterprise resource planning systems and transaction processing systems, are designed to correct a lack of communication among the functional area ISs. For this reason, Figure 1.4 shows ERP systems spanning the FAISs. ERP systems were an important innovation because the various functional area ISs were often developed as standalone systems and did not communicate effectively (if at all) with one another. ERP systems resolve this problem by tightly integrating the functional area ISs via a common database. In doing so, they enhance communications among the functional areas of an organization. For this reason, experts credit ERP systems with greatly increasing organizational productivity.

**A transaction processing system** supports the monitoring, collection, storage, and processing of data from the organization's basic business transactions, each of which generates data. When you are checking out at Walmart, for example, a transaction occurs each time the cashier swipes an item across the bar code reader. Significantly, within an organization, different functions or departments can define a transaction differently. In accounting, for example, a transaction is anything that changes a firm's chart of accounts. The information system definition of a transaction is broader: A transaction is anything that changes the firm's database. The chart of accounts is only part of the firm's database. Consider a scenario in which a student transfers from one section of an Introduction to MIS course to another section. This move would be a transaction to the university's information system, but not to the university's accounting department (the tuition would not change).

The TPS collects data continuously, typically in *real time*—that is, as soon as the data are generated—and it provides the input data for the corporate databases. TPSs are considered critical to the success of any enterprise because they support core operations. Significantly, nearly all ERP systems are also TPSs, but not all TPSs are ERP systems. In fact, modern ERP systems incorporate many functions that previously were handled by the organization's functional area information systems. You will study both TPSs and ERP systems in detail in Chapter 10.

ERP systems and TPSs function primarily within a single organization. Information systems that connect two or more organizations are referred to as **interorganizational information systems (IOSs)**. IOSs support many interorganizational operations, of which *supply chain management* is the best known. An organization's **supply chain** is the flow of materials, information, money, and services from suppliers of raw materials through factories and warehouses to the end customers.

Note that the supply chain in Figure 1.5 shows physical flows, information flows, and financial flows. Digitizable products are those that can be represented in electronic form, such as music and software. Information flows, financial flows, and digitizable products go through the Internet, whereas physical products are shipped. For example, when you order a computer from *www.dell.com*, your information goes to Dell via the Internet. When your transaction is completed (i.e., your credit card is approved and your order is processed), Dell ships your computer to you. (We will discuss supply chains in more detail in Chapter 11.)

**Electronic commerce systems** are another type of interorganizational information system. These systems enable organizations to conduct transactions, called business-to-business (B2B) electronic commerce, and customers to conduct transactions with businesses, called business-to-consumer (B2C) electronic commerce. E-commerce systems typically are Internet based. Figure 1.5 illustrates B2B and B2C electronic commerce. Electronic commerce systems are so important that we discuss them in detail in Chapter 7, with additional examples interspersed throughout the text. IT's About Business 1.2 shows how information systems have enabled Warby Parker to grow rapidly via e-commerce.

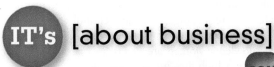

## 1.2 Warby Parker

Warby Parker (Warby; *www.warbyparker.com*) is an online eyewear retailer founded in 2010. The idea for the company was conceived when the firm's founders (MBA students at the time) wondered why glasses—uncomplicated, easily breakable, and mass produced—cost so much ($500 or more, for example). The students were convinced they knew why. The optical industry is an oligopoly, meaning that a small number of companies monopolize the business and are making large margins.

Consider, for example, Luxottica (*www.luxottica.com*), based in Milan, Italy. Luxottica runs the eyewear business for most major fashion houses, including Armani, Chanel, Prada, and Ralph Lauren. Luxottica also markets its own frames as well: Oakley, Oliver-Peoples, Persol, and Ray-Ban are all Luxottica brands. Further, LensCrafters, Pearle Vision, and Sunglass Hut are Luxottica subsidiaries. Luxottica also owns EyeMed, a leading vision insurance company.

Warby's founders realized that Luxottica had created "the illusion of choice," while in fact they monopolized the eyewear industry. Warby uses the same materials and the same Chinese factories as Luxottica. It then sells its glasses at a lower price because it does not have to pay licensing fees, which can amount to as much as 15 percent of the $100 wholesale cost of a pair of glasses.

Warby also does not have to deal with retailers, whose markups can double prices.

Warby's business model allows customers to test the company's retro-style glasses via a mail order, try-it-at-home program. The glasses cost only $95, and customers may test up to five frames at a time. The price includes prescription lenses, shipping, and a donation to its not-for-profit organization, VisionSpring (*www.visionspring.org*).

VisionSpring has a market-based approach to philanthropy. Rather than simply give away free eyeglasses, the organization supplies frames to entrepreneurs to sell to their neighbors.

On its Web site, Warby even offers a way to upload photos and "try on" frames virtually. Such large-scale individualized shopping experiences have attracted a devoted following among young, trendy professionals and have made the firm a commercial success.

In addition to enjoying great commercial success, Warby also has a social mission. For every pair of glasses it sells, it provides subsidies to help someone in need buy a pair—although not one—of Warby's creations.

By July 2014, Warby had distributed their millionth pair of glasses for that year, up from 500,000 during all of 2013. Analysts estimate that the company's annual revenue in 2014 exceeded

$100 million. By early 2015, Warby had opened 10 retail stores around the United States. Warby plans to open additional stores and to increase their product offerings—for example, thinner lenses for customers with extreme prescriptions and even clip-on sunglasses. Significantly, Warby does *not* plan to offer contact lenses in the near future because lens prescriptions tend to be brand specific, and that market is dominated by 1-800-Contacts (*www.1800contacts.com*).

Warby does face intense competition from companies such as EyeFly (*www.eyefly.com*), Made Eyewear (*www.madeeye-wear.com*), and Jimmy Fairly (*www.jimmyfairly.com/fr*). In addition, Luxottica has not been standing still. In January 2015, the company acquired Glasses.com, which mimics many of Warby's features and offers some additional ones, including a three-dimensional virtual try-on app that is similar to Warby's virtual try-on app. Around the same time, it has made its brand, Pearle Vision, "look and feel" much like Warby.

*Sources*: Compiled from "For Building the First Great Made-on-the-Internet Brand," *FastCompany*, March, 2015; M. Fox, "Who Says Glasses Can't Be Edgy? Warby Parker Out-Innovates Tech Giants," *CNBC*, February 15, 2015; "Warby Parker Named Most Innovative Company," *CBS News*, February 9, 2015; J. Avins, "Warby Parker Proves Customers Don't Have to Care About Your Social Mission," *qz.com*, December 29, 2014; M. Fitzgerald, "Warby Parker: Buy One, Give One Pair of Trendy Eyeglasses," *Impact Alpha*, November 30, 2014; C. Peterson-Withorn, "Warby Parker CEO Is Building a Brand That Gives Back," *Forbes*, September 8, 2014; J. Chokkattu, "Warby Parker Hits One Million Glasses Sold, Distributed," *TechCrunch*, June 25, 2014; *www.warbyparker.com*, accessed February 20, 2015.

### Questions

1. Provide two examples of how Warby Parker uses information technology to support its business model.
2. How might Warby Parker further use information technology to counter major competitors who want to emulate Warby's business model? Support your answer.

---

**Support for Organizational Employees.** So far, you have concentrated on information systems that support specific functional areas and operations. Now you will learn about information systems that typically support particular employees within the organization.

*Clerical workers*, who support managers at all levels of the organization, include bookkeepers, secretaries, electronic file clerks, and insurance claim processors. *Lower level managers* handle the day-to-day operations of the organization, making routine decisions such as assigning tasks to employees and placing purchase orders. *Middle managers* make tactical decisions, which deal with activities such as short-term planning, organizing, and control.

**Knowledge workers** are professional employees such as financial and marketing analysts, engineers, lawyers, and accountants. All knowledge workers are experts in a particular subject area. They create information and knowledge, which they integrate into the business. Knowledge workers, in turn, act as advisors to middle managers and executives. Finally, *executives* make decisions that deal with situations that can significantly change the manner in which business is done. Examples of executive decisions are introducing a new product line, acquiring other businesses, and relocating operations to a foreign country.

**Office automation systems (OASs)** typically support the clerical staff, lower and middle managers, and knowledge workers. These employees use OASs to develop documents (word processing and desktop publishing software), schedule resources (electronic calendars), and communicate (e-mail, voice mail, videoconferencing, and groupware).

**Functional area information systems** summarize data and prepare reports, primarily for middle managers, but sometimes for lower level managers as well. Because these reports typically concern a specific functional area, report generators (RPGs) are an important type of functional area IS.

**Business intelligence systems** provide computer-based support for complex, nonroutine decisions, primarily for middle managers and knowledge workers. (They also support lower level managers, but to a lesser extent.) These systems are typically used with a data warehouse, and they enable users to perform their own data analysis. You learn about BI systems in Chapter 12.

**Expert systems (ES)** attempt to duplicate the work of human experts by applying reasoning capabilities, knowledge, and expertise within a specific domain. They have become valuable in many application areas, primarily but not exclusively areas involving decision making. For example, navigation systems use rules to select routes, but we do not typically think of these systems as expert systems. Significantly, expert systems can operate as

| Type of System | Function | Example |
|---|---|---|
| Functional area IS | Supports the activities within specific functional area | System for processing payroll |
| Transaction processing system | Processes transaction data from terminal | Walmart checkout point-of-sale business events |
| Enterprise resource planning | Integrates all functional areas of the organization | Oracle, SAP system |
| Office automation system | Supports daily work activities of individuals and groups | Microsoft® Office |
| Management information system | Produces reports summarized from transaction data, usually in one functional area | Report on total sales for each customer |
| Decision support system | Provides access to data and analysis tools | "What–if" analysis of changes in budget |
| Expert system | Mimics human expert in a particular area and makes decisions | Credit card approval analysis |
| Executive dashboard | Presents structured, summarized information about aspects of business important to executives | Status of sales by product |
| Supply chain management system | Manages flows of products, services, and information among organizations | Walmart Retail Link system connecting suppliers to Walmart |
| Electronic commerce system | Enables transactions among organizations and between organizations and customers | *www.dell.com* |

**Table**

# 1.4

**Types of Organizational Information Systems**

standalone systems or be embedded in other applications. We examine ESs in greater detail in Technology Guide 4.

**Dashboards** (also called **digital dashboards**) are a special form of IS that support all managers of the organization. They provide rapid access to timely information and direct access to structured information in the form of reports. Dashboards that are tailored to the information needs of executives are called *executive dashboards*. Chapter 12 provides a thorough discussion of dashboards.

Table 1.4 provides an overview of the different types of information systems used by organizations.

# before you go on...

1. What is a computer-based information system?
2. Describe the components of computer-based information systems.
3. What is an application program?
4. Explain how information systems provide support for knowledge workers.
5. As we move up the organization's hierarchy from clerical workers to executives, how does the type of support provided by information systems change?

## 1.3 How Does IT Impact Organizations?

Throughout this text you will encounter numerous examples of how IT affects various types of organizations. This section provides an overview of the impact of IT on modern organizations. As you read this section, you will learn how IT will affect you as well.

### IT Impacts Entire Industries

As of early 2015, the technology required to transform industries through software had been developed and integrated and could be delivered globally. In addition, software tools and Internet-based services enabled companies in many industries to launch new software-powered startups without investing in new infrastructure or training new employees. For example, in 2000, operating a basic Internet application cost businesses approximately $150,000 per month. In early 2015, operating that same application in Amazon's cloud cost less than $1,000 per month.

In essence, software is impacting every industry, and every organization must prepare for these impacts. Let's examine a few examples of software disruption across several industries. Many of these examples focus on two scenarios: (1) industries where software disrupted the previous market-leading companies and (2) industries where a new company (or companies) used software to achieve a competitive advantage.

- *The book industry*: Which is the largest book publisher and bookseller in the United States today? Would it surprise you to learn that the answer is Amazon, a software company? Amazon's core capability is its software engine, which can sell virtually anything online without building or maintaining any retail stores. Now, even the books themselves have become software products, known as electronic (or digital) books, or eBooks. (In early 2015, electronic books were gaining in popularity, but approximately 80 percent of book sales were still for print books.)

   Consider the Borders bookstore chain. In 2001, Borders agreed to hand over its online business to Amazon because Borders was convinced that online book sales were nonstrategic and unimportant. Ten years later, Borders filed for bankruptcy.

- *The music industry*: Today's dominant music companies are also software companies: Apple's iTunes (*www.apple.com/itunes*), Spotify (*www.spotify.com*), and Pandora (*www.pandora.com*). Traditional record labels now exist largely to provide these software companies with content. Meanwhile, the Recording Industry Association of America (RIAA) continues to fight battles over copyright infringement and the illegal download and sharing of digital music files.

- *The video industry*: Blockbuster—which rented and sold videos and ancillary products through its chain of stores—was the industry leader until it was disrupted by a software company Netflix (*www.netflix.com*). In early 2015, Netflix had the largest subscriber base of any video service with millions of subscribers. Meanwhile, Blockbuster declared bankruptcy in February 2011 and was acquired by satellite television provider Dish Networks a month later.

- *The software industry*: Incumbent software companies such as Oracle and Microsoft are increasingly threatened by software-as-a-service (SaaS) products (e.g., Salesforce.com) and Android, an open-source operating system developed by the Open Handset Alliance (*www.openhandsetalliance.com*). (We discuss operating systems in Technology Guide 2 and SaaS in Technology Guide 3.)

- *The videogame industry*: Today, the fastest-growing entertainment companies are videogame makers—again, software. Examples are Zynga (*www.zynga.com*), the creator of FarmVille; Rovio (*www.rovio.com*), the maker of Angry Birds; and Minecraft (*www.minecraft.net*).

- *The photography industry*: This industry was disrupted by software years ago. Today it is virtually impossible to buy a mobile phone that does not include a software-powered camera. In addition, people can upload photos automatically to the Internet for permanent archiving and global sharing. Leading photography companies include Shutterfly (*www.shutterfly.com*), Snapfish (*www.snapfish.com*), Flickr (*www.flickr.com*), and Instagram (*www.instagram.com*). Meanwhile, the longtime market leader, Kodak—whose name was almost synonymous with cameras—declared bankruptcy in January 2012.

- *The marketing industry:* Today's largest direct marketing companies include Facebook (*www.facebook.com*), Google (*www.google.com*), and Foursquare (*www.foursquare.com*). All of these companies are using software to disrupt the retail marketing industry.

- *The recruiting industry:* LinkedIn (*www.linkedin.com*) is a fast-growing company that is disrupting the traditional job recruiting industry. For the first time, employees and job searchers can maintain their resumes on a publicly accessible Web site that interested parties can search in real time.

- *The financial services industry:* Software has transformed the financial services industry. Practically every financial transaction (e.g., buying and selling stocks) is now performed by software. Also, many of the leading innovators in financial services are software companies. For example, Square (*https://squareup.com*) allows anyone to accept credit card payments with a mobile phone.

- *The motion picture industry:* The process of making feature-length computer-generated films has become incredibly IT intensive. Studios require state-of-the-art information technologies, including massive numbers of servers (described in Technology Guide 1), sophisticated software (described in Technology Guide 2), and an enormous amount of storage (described in Technology Guide 1).

Consider DreamWorks Animation (*www.dreamworksanimation.com*), a motion picture studio that creates animated feature films, television programs, and online virtual worlds. For a single motion picture, the studio manages more than 500,000 files and 300 terabytes (a terabyte is 1 trillion bytes) of data, and it uses about 80 million central processing unit (CPU) (described in Technology Guide 1) hours. As DreamWorks executives state, "In reality, our product is data that looks like a movie. We are a digital manufacturing company."

Software is also disrupting industries that operate primarily in the physical world. Consider these examples:

- *The automobile industry:* In modern cars, software is responsible for running the engines, controlling safety features, entertaining passengers, guiding drivers to their destinations, and connecting the car to mobile, satellite, and GPS networks. Other software functions in modern cars include Wi-Fi receivers, which turn your car into a mobile hot spot; software, which helps maximize fuel efficiency; and ultrasonic sensors, which enable some models to parallel-park automatically.

The next step is to network all vehicles together, a necessary step toward the next major breakthrough: self-driving or driverless cars. The creation of software-powered driverless cars is already being undertaken at Google as well as at several major car companies, and interestingly, Apple.

- *The agriculture industry:* Agriculture is increasingly powered by software, including satellite analysis of soils linked to per-acre seed selection software algorithms. In addition, precision agriculture makes use of automated, driverless tractors controlled by global positioning systems and software. (Precision agriculture is based on observing, measuring, and responding to inter- and intrafield variability.)

- *National defense:* Even national defense is increasingly software based. The modern combat soldier is embedded in a web of software that provides intelligence, communications, logistics, and weapons guidance. Software-powered drone aircraft launch airstrikes without placing human pilots at risk. Intelligence agencies perform large-scale data mining with software to uncover and track potential terrorist plots.

- *The fashion industry:* Women have long "borrowed" special-occasion dresses from department stores, buying them and then returning them after wearing them for one evening.

Now, Rent the Runway (*www.renttherunway.com*) has redefined the fashion business, making expensive clothing available to more women than ever before. The firm is also disrupting traditional physical retailers. After all, why buy a dress when you can rent one for a very low price? Some department stores feel so threatened by Rent the Runway that they have reportedly told vendors that they will remove floor merchandise if it ever shows up on that company's Web site.

Rent the Runway employs 200 people, including one of the nation's largest dry cleaning operations. Their Web site has more than 3 million members, and it features 35,000 dresses and 7,000 accessories created by 170 designers.

- *Education:* College graduates owe approximately $1 trillion in student debt, a crippling burden for many recent graduates. UniversityNow (*www.unow.com*) was founded to make college more accessible to working adults by offering online, self-paced degrees. Two key characteristics distinguish UniversityNow from an increasing number of rivals: (1) very low fees (as little as $2,600, which includes tuition and books for as many courses as students can complete in one year) and (2) fully accredited degrees, from an associate's degree to an MBA.

- *The legal profession:* Today, electronic discovery (e-discovery) software applications can analyze documents in a fraction of the time that human lawyers would take, at a fraction of the cost. For example, Blackstone Discovery (*www.blackstonediscovery.com*) helped one company analyze 1.5 million documents for less than $100,000. That company estimated that the process would have cost $1.5 million had it been performed by lawyers.

## IT Reduces the Number of Middle Managers

IT makes managers more productive, and it increases the number of employees who can report to a single manager. Thus, IT ultimately decreases the number of managers and experts. It is reasonable to assume, therefore, that in coming years organizations will have fewer managerial levels and fewer staff and line managers. If this trend materializes, promotional opportunities will decrease, making promotions much more competitive. Bottom line: Pay attention in school!

## IT Changes the Manager's Job

One of the most important tasks of managers is making decisions. A major consequence of IT has been to change the manner in which managers make their decisions. In this way, IT ultimately has changed managers' jobs.

IT often provides managers with near-real-time information, meaning that managers have less time to make decisions, making their jobs even more stressful. Fortunately, IT also provides many tools—for example, business analytics applications such as dashboards, search engines, and intranets—to help managers handle the volumes of information they must deal with on an ongoing basis.

So far in this section, we have been focusing on managers in general. Now, let's focus on you. Due to advances in IT, you will increasingly supervise employees and teams who are geographically dispersed. Employees can work from anywhere at any time, and teams can consist of employees who are literally dispersed throughout the world. Information technologies such as telepresence systems (discussed in Chapter 6) can help you manage these employees even though you do not often see them face-to-face. For these employees, electronic or "remote" supervision will become the norm. Remote supervision places greater emphasis on completed work and less emphasis on personal contacts and office politics. You will have to reassure your employees that they are valued members of the organization, thereby diminishing any feelings they might have of being isolated and "out of the loop."

## Will IT Eliminate Jobs?

One major concern of every employee, part-time or full-time, is job security. Relentless cost-cutting measures in modern organizations often lead to large-scale layoffs. Put simply, organizations are responding to today's highly competitive environment by doing more with less. Regardless of your position, then, you consistently will have to add value to your organization and to make certain that your superiors are aware of this value.

Many companies have responded to difficult economic times, increased global competition, demands for customization, and increased consumer sophistication by increasing their investments in IT. In fact, as computers continue to advance in terms of intelligence and capabilities, the competitive advantage of replacing people with machines is increasing rapidly. This process frequently leads to layoffs. At the same time, however, IT creates entirely new categories of jobs, such as electronic medical record-keeping and nanotechnology.

## IT Impacts Employees at Work

Many people have experienced a loss of identity because of computerization. They feel like "just another number" because computers reduce or eliminate the human element present in noncomputerized systems.

The Internet threatens to exert an even more isolating influence than have computers and television. Encouraging people to work and shop from their living rooms could produce some unfortunate psychological effects, such as depression and loneliness.

**IT Impacts Employees' Health and Safety.**   Although computers and information systems are generally regarded as agents of "progress," they can adversely affect individuals' health and safety. To illustrate this point, we consider two issues associated with IT: job stress and long-term use of the keyboard.

HRM

An increase in an employee's workload and/or responsibilities can trigger *job stress*. Although computerization has benefited organizations by increasing productivity, it also has created an ever-expanding workload for some employees. Some workers feel overwhelmed and have become increasingly anxious about their job performance. These feelings of stress and anxiety can actually diminish rather than improve workers' productivity while jeopardizing their physical and mental health. Management can help alleviate these problems by providing training, redistributing the workload among workers, and hiring more workers.

On a more specific level, the long-term use of keyboards can lead to *repetitive strain injuries* such as backaches and muscle tension in the wrists and fingers. *Carpal tunnel syndrome* is a particularly painful form of repetitive strain injury that affects the wrists and hands.

Designers are aware of the potential problems associated with the prolonged use of computers. To address these problems, they continually attempt to design a better computing environment. The science of designing machines and work settings that minimize injury and illness is called ergonomics. The goal of ergonomics is to create an environment that is safe, well lit, and comfortable. Examples of ergonomically designed products are antiglare screens that alleviate problems of fatigued or damaged eyesight and chairs that contour the human body to decrease backaches. Figure 1.6 displays some sample ergonomic products.

**IT Provides Opportunities for People with Disabilities.**   Computers can create new employment opportunities for people with disabilities by integrating speech-recognition and vision-recognition capabilities. For example, individuals who cannot type can use a voice-operated keyboard, and individuals who cannot travel can work at home.

Going further, adaptive equipment for computers enables people with disabilities to perform tasks they normally would not be able to do. For example, the Web and graphical user interfaces (GUIs) (e.g., Windows) can be difficult for people with impaired vision to use. To address this problem, manufacturers have added audible screen tips and voice interfaces, which essentially restore the functionality of computers to the way it was before GUIs became standard.

Other devices help improve the quality of life in more mundane, but useful, ways for people with disabilities. Examples are a two-way writing telephone, a robotic page turner, a hair brusher, and a hospital-bedside video trip to the zoo or the museum. Several organizations specialize in IT designed for people with disabilities.

**FIGURE 1.6** Ergonomic products protect computer users. (a) Wrist support. (b) Back support. (c) Eye-protection filter (optically coated glass). (d) Adjustable foot rest.

(a)
Media Bakery

(b)
Media Bakery

(c)
Media Bakery

(d)
Media Bakery

**before you go on...**

**1.** Why should employees in all functional areas become knowledgeable about IT?

**2.** Describe how IT might change the manager's job.

**3.** Discuss several ways in which IT impacts employees at work.

## 1.4 Importance of Information Systems to Society

This section explains in greater detail why IT is important to society as a whole. Other examples of the impact of IT on society appear throughout the text.

### IT Affects Our Quality of Life

IT has significant implications for our quality of life. The workplace can be expanded from the traditional 9-to-5 job at a central location to 24 hours a day at any location. IT can provide employees with flexibility that can significantly improve the quality of leisure time, even if it doesn't increase the total amount of leisure time.

From the opposite perspective, however, IT also can place employees on "constant call," which means they are never truly away from the office, even when they are on vacation. In fact, surveys reveal that the majority of respondents take their laptops and smartphones on their vacations, and 100 percent took their cell phones. Going further, the majority of respondents did some work while vacationing, and almost all of them checked their e-mail regularly.

## The Robot Revolution Is Here Now

Once restricted largely to science fiction movies, robots that can perform practical tasks are becoming more common. In fact, "cyberpooches," "nursebots," and other mechanical beings may be our companions before we know it. Around the world, quasi-autonomous devices have become increasingly common on factory floors, in hospital corridors, and in farm fields. For home use, iRobot (*www.irobot.com*) produces the Roomba to vacuum our floors, the Scooba to wash our floors, the Dirt Dog to sweep our garages, the Verro to clean our pools, and the Looj to clean our gutters.

Robots are increasingly being utilized in a variety of areas. For example, take a look at the commercial use of drones in the chapter closing case. Further, IT's About Business 1.3 illustrates the use of social, collaborative robots in the workplace.

 **IT's [about business]**

### 1.3 Social, Collaborative Robots

Manufacturing constitutes a $2 trillion sector of the U.S. economy. In the past, the United States retained higher-value-added manufacturing jobs while allowing lower-value-added jobs to go elsewhere. However, the world will eventually run out of places where low-cost labor is available. Therefore, the question is: "What will it take to break out of the cycle of making inexpensive goods by hand with unskilled, inexpensive labor?" Perhaps robots are the answer.

Today's *industrial robots* perform well on very narrowly defined, repetitive tasks. However, they are not adaptable, flexible, or easy to use, and they are very expensive. In addition, most industrial robots are not safe for people to be around. Moreover, it typically takes 18 months to integrate an industrial robot into a factory operation.

As of early 2015, about 70 percent of all industrial robots in the United States were being utilized in automobile factories. The cost to integrate one of today's industrial robots into a factory operation is often three to five times the cost of the robot itself. Such integration requires the services of computer programmers and machine specialists. In addition, companies must place safety cages around the robots so that they do not strike people while they are operating. Further, most industrial robots have no sensors or means to detect what is happening in their environment.

There are roughly 300,000 small manufacturing companies in the United States that have fewer than 500 employees. Almost none of these firms utilizes industrial robots, for the reasons we just discussed. In addition, almost all of these firms have relatively small production runs, meaning that they are constantly changing the design and manufacturing procedures for their products. Some of these companies, called "job shops," produce a wide variety of goods for other companies. They specialize in manufacturing a type of product that can be highly customized to an individual client's needs. In a typical factory that uses an industrial robot, a production run is rarely less than four months long. For a job shop, a production run can be as short as one hour. Clearly, then, small manufacturing firms need a different kind of robot.

Rethink Robotics (*www.rethinkrobotics.com*) is putting these technological developments to work with Baxter, a new kind of industrial robot that sells for $25,000. Baxter is very different from existing industrial robots. It does not need an expensive or elaborate safety cage, and factory operators do not need to segregate it from human workers. In fact, humans actually share a workspace with Baxter, making it an excellent example of a social, collaborative robot.

Baxter also works right out of the box. It can be integrated into a factory's workflow in about one hour. Baxter also requires no special programming.

Interacting with Baxter is more like working with a person than operating a traditional industrial robot. If Baxter picks up something it shouldn't on the assembly line, for instance, workers can take its arm and move the robot to put the object down.

Baxter also contains a variety of sensors, including depth sensors as well as cameras in its wrists, so it "sees" with its hands. It is constantly building and adjusting a mathematical model of the world in front of it, enabling it to recognize different objects.

Another benefit of Baxter is that other factory workers can train it. In fact, a factory worker who has never seen a robot before can learn to train Baxter to perform simple tasks in five minutes. For example, a worker can show Baxter a part of the task she is asking the robot to perform, and Baxter can infer the rest of the task. Also, if a human is interacting with Baxter or doing part of the task, the robot can figure out how to perform the rest of the task.

In November 2014, Rethink Robotics announced its new Robot Positioning System for Baxter. This system enables Baxter to adapt to changing, real-world environments, such as tables and benches being moved. As a result, manufacturers can now deploy Baxter in flexible manufacturing environments, such as short production runs.

The new system highlights a huge advantage for companies that acquire Baxter. Because so much of Baxter's capabilities are contained in its software, when the robot is upgraded it tends to *increase in value*.

Rethink Robotics asserts that Baxter empowers factory workers by providing them with user-friendly machines they can manage themselves. In fact, Rethink claims it is on a mission to rescue U.S. manufacturing through technological innovation. That is, Baxter can help U.S. manufacturers lower costs sufficiently to compete with manufacturers overseas who employ low-cost labor.

However, Baxter does raise the question of the future of low-skilled labor in the United States: How fast will Baxter replace these workers, and what will they do after they are replaced?

*Sources:* Compiled from J. Green, "Collaborative Robotics, Job Security, and ROI," *Rethink Robotics Press Release*, February 12, 2015; J. Barnes, "Rethink Robotics Turns Robots into Better Co-Workers," *InformationWeek*, November 28, 2014; "Rethink Robotics Introduces Industry-First Robot Positioning System," *Rethink Robotics Press Release*, November 3, 2014; J. Guinto, "Machine Man," *Boston Magazine*, November 2014; T. Green, "Building the Factory of the Future at RoboBusiness," *Robotics Business Review*, October 17, 2014; J. Morton, "Baxter the Robot Rolls On In," *The New Zealand Herald*, January 21, 2014; B. Trebilcock, "Is There a Robot in Your Distribution Future?" *Modern Materials Handling*, December 1, 2013; S. Castellanos, "Rethink Robotics to Distribute Baxter in Japan," *Boston Business Journal*, November 6, 2013; M. Naitove, "'Collaborative' Robot Works Safely, Comfortably Alongside Human Workers," *Plastics*

*Technology*, November 2013; J. Markoff, "Making Robots More Like Us," *The New York Times*, October 28, 2013; K. Alspach, "New Brain for Baxter: Rethink Robotics Releases Baxter 2.0 Software," *Boston Business Journal*, September 23, 2013; B. Jackson, "Baxter the Friendly Robot," *Yale Daily News Magazine*, September 8, 2013; R. Brooks, "Robots at Work: Toward a Smarter Factory," *The Futurist*, May–June, 2013; G. Anderson, "Help Wanted: Robots to Fill Service Jobs," *Retail Wire*, April 10, 2013; J. Young, "The New Industrial Revolution," *The Chronicle of Higher Education*, March 25, 2013; L. Kratochwill, "Rethink's Baxter Robot Got a Job Packaging Toys and Sending Them to China," *Fast Company*, February 26, 2013; A. Regalado, "Small Factories Give Baxter the Robot a Cautious Once-Over," *MIT Technology Review*, January 16, 2013; www.rethinkrobotics.com, accessed April 4, 2015.

**Questions**
1. Rethink Robotics claims that Baxter will not necessarily replace workers, rather it will enable workers to transition into higher paying jobs (e.g., programming Baxter robots and supervising Baxter robots). Will Baxter replace workers in small manufacturing companies? Why or why not? Support your answer.
2. Discuss the possible reactions of labor unions to Baxter.
3. Identify and discuss additional potential applications for Baxter.

It will probably be a long time before we see robots making decisions by themselves, handling unfamiliar situations, and interacting with people. Nevertheless, robots are extremely helpful in various environments, particularly those that are repetitive, harsh, or dangerous to humans.

### Improvements in Healthcare

IT has brought about major improvements in healthcare delivery. Medical personnel use IT to make better and faster diagnoses and to monitor critically ill patients more accurately. IT has also streamlined the process of researching and developing new drugs. Expert systems now help doctors diagnose diseases, and machine vision is enhancing the work of radiologists. Surgeons use virtual reality to plan complex surgeries. They also employ surgical robots to perform long-distance surgery. Finally, doctors discuss complex medical cases via videoconferencing. New computer simulations recreate the sense of touch, allowing doctors-in-training to perform virtual procedures without risking harm to an actual patient.

Information technology can be applied to improve the efficiency and effectiveness of healthcare. In IT's About Business 1.4 you will see how Apricot Forest is using information technology to improve healthcare in China.

 **IT's [about business]**

### 1.4 Apricot Forest Helps China's Physicians

Most physicians in China work for state-operated hospitals, where entry-level physicians earn about $500 per month. This amount is roughly equivalent to what taxi drivers make. In addition, China's physicians have a potentially overwhelming caseload, typically treating 50–60 patients per day. This situation is causing problems.

One of these problems is violence perpetrated by patients against health providers. Chinese hospitals experienced an average of 27 assaults in 2012, as angry patients beat, stabbed, and even killed the physicians who failed to meet their expectations. These problems have created a need for software tools that improve the efficiency and effectiveness of patient care.

Essentially, these tools must provide China's physicians with more data—about patients, their records, and their illnesses—as well as easier access to those data. Further, the tools must allow physicians and their patients to communicate seamlessly.

Apricot Forest (*http://www.xingshulin.com*) is a Beijing-based startup company that offers three applications that address the problems in China's medical system. The primary app is MedClip, an all-in-one patient service system. Physicians can photograph, store, and organize patient records; dictate notes directly into a patient's chart; send patients reminders and educational materials via China's popular Weixin (aka WeChat) messaging system; and consult with other physicians on difficult cases. The second app, e-Pocket, contains reference materials, such as drug formularies and specialized calculators. The third app, Medical Journals, helps physicians stay current on the latest research literature.

Apricot Forest's clients are China's physicians who, as we discussed, earn little money. The company compensates for this problem by making money in other areas. Pharmaceutical companies place ads inside the apps to reach doctors. The company takes a cut of the sales of books and other publications made accessible through e-Pocket and Medical Journals. Further, Apricot Forest plans to charge patients for follow-up phone calls with their physicians via MedClip. Both physicians and patients agree to this arrangement because patients cannot currently connect easily with their doctors, and the app lets doctors keep their phone numbers private and control the amount of contact with patients. Apricot Forest also plans to aggregate the data that physicians upload to MedClip, analyze them, and sell the reports to companies that research, design, and market medical products. Finally, the Apricot Forest apps can also become a mobile office for physicians, enabling them to treat patients in the patients' homes.

And the results? By early 2015, roughly 25 percent of China's 2.5 million physicians were using at least one of Apricot Forest's apps.

*Sources*: Compiled from "The Healthcare System and Medical Device Market in China," *PR Newswire,* February 17, 2015; J. Makinen, "The World's 50 Most Innovative Companies," *FastCompany*, March 2015; L. Qi and L. Burkitt, "Falling through the Cracks of China's Health-Care System," *The Wall Street Journal*, January 4, 2015; S. Shankar, "Hospital Attack in Northern China's Beidaihe Town Kills 7 People, Including 6 Nurses," *International Business Times*, November 20, 2014; C. Beam, "Under the Knife," *The New Yorker*, August 25, 2014; E. Rauhala, "Why China's Doctors Are Getting Beaten Up," *Time*, March 7, 2014; P. Bischoff, "Apricot Forest Wants to Streamline Your Hospital Visits," *TechinAsia*, June 7, 2013; *www.xingshulin.com*, accessed February 25, 2015.

## Questions

1. Explain how Apricot Forest's apps will help improve the relationship between physicians and patients in China.
2. Explain how Apricot Forest's apps will help improve overall healthcare in China.
3. Discuss potential disadvantages of Apricot Forest's apps to patients.
4. Discuss potential disadvantages of Apricot Forest's apps to physicians.

---

Among the thousands of other healthcare applications, administrative systems are critically important. These systems perform functions ranging from detecting insurance fraud to creating nursing schedules, to financial and marketing management.

The Internet contains vast amounts of useful medical information (see, for example, *www.webmd.com*). In an interesting study, researchers at the Princess Alexandra Hospital in Brisbane, Australia, identified 26 difficult diagnostic cases published in the *New England Journal of Medicine*. They selected three to five search terms from each case and then conducted a Google search. Next, they recorded the three diagnoses that Google ranked most prominently and that appeared to fit the symptoms and signs. Finally, they compared these results with the correct diagnoses as published in the journal. The researchers discovered that their Google searches had found the correct diagnosis in 15 of the 26 cases, a success rate of 57 percent. Despite these results, the research team cautions against self-diagnosis. They maintain that people should use diagnostic information gained from Google and medical Web sites such as WebMD (*www.webmd.com*) only to ask questions of their physicians.

# before you go on...

1. What are some of the quality-of-life improvements made possible by IT? Has IT any negative effects on our quality of life? If so, explain and provide examples.
2. Describe the robotic revolution and consider its implications for humans.
3. Explain how IT has improved healthcare practices.

# What's In IT For Me?

In Section 1.2, we discussed how IT supports each of the functional areas of the organization. Here we examine the MIS function.

### For the MIS Major

The MIS function directly supports all other functional areas in an organization. That is, the MIS function is responsible for providing the information that each functional area needs in order to make decisions. The overall objective of MIS personnel is to help users improve performance and solve business problems using IT. To accomplish this objective, MIS personnel must understand both the information requirements and the technology associated with each functional area. Given their position, however, they must think "business needs" first and "technology" second.

## [ Summary ]

1. **Identify the reasons why being an informed user of information systems is important in today's world.**

   The benefits of being an informed user of IT include the following:

   - You will benefit more from your organization's IT applications because you will understand what is "behind" those applications.
   - You will be able to provide input into your organization's IT applications, thus improving the quality of those applications.
   - You will quickly be in a position to recommend or participate in the selection of IT applications that your organization will use.
   - You will be able to keep up with rapid developments in existing information technologies, as well as with the introduction of new technologies.
   - You will understand the potential impacts that "new and improved" technologies will have on your organization and therefore will be qualified to make recommendations concerning their adoption and use.
   - You will play a key role in managing the information systems in your organization.
   - You will be in a position to use IT if you decide to start your own business.

2. **Describe the various types of computer-based information systems in an organization.**

   - Transaction processing systems support the monitoring, collection, storage, and processing of data from the organization's basic business transactions, each of which generates data.
   - Functional area information systems support a particular functional area within the organization.
   - Interorganizational information systems support many interorganizational operations, of which supply chain management is the best known.
   - Enterprise resource planning systems correct a lack of communication among the FAISs by tightly integrating the functional area ISs via a common database.
   - Electronic commerce systems enable organizations to conduct transactions with other organizations (called business-to-business electronic commerce) and with customers (called business-to-consumer electronic commerce).
   - Office automation systems typically support the clerical staff, lower and middle managers, and knowledge workers by enabling them to develop documents (word processing and desktop publishing software), schedule resources (electronic calendars), and communicate (e-mail, voice mail, videoconferencing, and groupware).

- Business intelligence systems provide computer-based support for complex, nonroutine decisions, primarily for middle managers and knowledge workers.
- Expert systems attempt to duplicate the work of human experts by applying reasoning capabilities, knowledge, and expertise within a specific domain.

3. **Discuss ways in which information technology can affect managers and nonmanagerial workers.**

Potential IT impacts on managers:

- IT may reduce the number of middle managers.
- IT will provide managers with real-time or near-real-time information, meaning that managers will have less time to make decisions.
- IT will increase the likelihood that managers will have to supervise geographically dispersed employees and teams.

Potential IT impacts on nonmanagerial workers:

- IT may eliminate jobs.
- IT may cause employees to experience a loss of identity.
- IT can cause job stress and physical problems, such as repetitive stress injury.

4. **List positive and negative societal effects of the increased use of information technology.**

Positive societal effects:

- IT can provide opportunities for people with disabilities.
- IT can provide people with flexibility in their work (e.g., work from anywhere, anytime).
- Robots will take over mundane chores.
- IT will enable improvements in healthcare.

Negative societal effects:

- IT can cause health problems for individuals.
- IT can place employees on constant call.
- IT can potentially misinform patients about their health problems.

## [ Chapter Glossary ]

**application (or app)** A computer program designed to support a specific task or business process.

**business intelligence systems** Provide computer-based support for complex, nonroutine decisions, primarily for middle managers and knowledge workers.

**computer-based information system** An information system that uses computer technology to perform some or all of its intended tasks.

**dashboards** A special form of IS that support all managers of the organization by providing rapid access to timely information and direct access to structured information in the form of reports.

**data items** An elementary description of things, events, activities, and transactions that are recorded, classified, and stored but are not organized to convey any specific meaning.

**database** A collection of related files or tables containing data.

**electronic commerce systems** A type of interorganizational information system that enables organizations to conduct transactions, called business-to-business electronic commerce, and customers to conduct transactions with businesses, called business-to-consumer electronic commerce.

**enterprise resource planning systems** Information systems that correct a lack of communication among the functional area ISs by tightly integrating the functional area ISs via a common database.

**ergonomics** The science of adapting machines and work environments to people; focuses on creating an environment that is safe, well lit, and comfortable.

**expert systems** Attempt to duplicate the work of human experts by applying reasoning capabilities, knowledge, and expertise within a specific domain.

**functional area information systems** ISs that support a particular functional area within the organization.

**hardware** A device such as a processor, monitor, keyboard, or printer. Together, these devices accept, process, and display data and information.

**information** Data that have been organized so that they have meaning and value to the recipient.

**information system** Collects, processes, stores, analyzes, and disseminates information for a specific purpose.

**information technology** Relates to any computer-based tool that people use to work with information and support the information and information-processing needs of an organization.

**information technology components** Hardware, software, databases, and networks.

**information technology infrastructure** IT components plus IT services.

**information technology platform** Formed by the IT components of hardware, software, networks (wireline and wireless), and databases.

**information technology services** IT personnel use IT components to perform these IT services: develop information systems, oversee security and risk, and manage data.

**informed user** A person knowledgeable about information systems and information technology.

**interorganizational information systems** Information systems that connect two or more organizations.

**knowledge** Data and/or information that have been organized and processed to convey understanding, experience, accumulated learning, and expertise as they apply to a current problem or activity.

**knowledge workers** Professional employees such as financial and marketing analysts, engineers, lawyers, and accountants, who are experts in a particular subject area and create information and knowledge, which they integrate into the business.

**network** A connecting system (wireline or wireless) that permits different computers to share resources.

**procedures** The set of instructions for combining hardware, software, database, and network components in order to process information and generate the desired output.

**software** A program or collection of programs that enable the hardware to process data.

**supply chain** The flow of materials, information, money, and services from suppliers of raw materials through factories and warehouses to the end customers.

**transaction processing system** Supports the monitoring, collection, storage, and processing of data from the organization's basic business transactions, each of which generates data.

# [ Discussion Questions ]

1. Describe a business that you would like to start. Discuss how information technology could help you (a) find and research an idea for a business, (b) formulate your business plan, and (c) finance your business.

2. Your university wants to recruit high-quality high school students from your state. Provide examples of (a) the data that your recruiters would gather in this process, (b) the information that your recruiters would process from these data, and (c) the types of knowledge that your recruiters would infer from this information.

3. Can the terms data, information, and knowledge have different meanings for different people? Support your answer with examples.

4. Information technology makes it possible to "never be out of touch." Discuss the pros and cons of always being available to your employers and clients (regardless of where you are or what you are doing).

5. Robots have the positive impact of being able to relieve humans from working in dangerous conditions. What are some negative impacts of robots in the workplace?

6. Is it possible to endanger yourself by accessing too much medical information on the Web? Why or why not? Support your answer.

7. Describe other potential impacts of IT on societies as a whole.

8. What are the major reasons why it is important for employees in all functional areas to become familiar with IT?

9. Given that information technology is impacting every industry, what does this mean for a company's employees? Provide specific examples to support your answer.

10. Given that information technology is impacting every industry, what does this mean for students attending a college of business? Provide specific examples to support your answer.

11. Refer to the study at Princess Alexandra Hospital (in the "Improvements in Healthcare" section). How do you feel about Google searches finding the correct diagnosis in 57 percent of the cases? Are you impressed with these results? Why or why not? What are the implications of this study for self-diagnosis?

12. Is the vast amount of medical information on the Web a good thing? Answer from the standpoint of a patient and from the standpoint of a physician.

## [ Problem-Solving Activities ]

1. Visit some Web sites that offer employment opportunities in IT. Prominent examples are *www.dice.com, www.monster.com, www.collegerecruiter.com, www.careerbuilder.com, www.jobcentral.com, www.job.com, www.career.com, www.simplyhired.com,* and *www.truecareers.com.* Compare the IT salaries with salaries offered to accountants, marketing personnel, financial personnel, operations personnel, and human resources personnel. For other information on IT salaries, check *Computerworld*'s annual salary survey.

2. Enter the Web site of UPS (*www.ups.com*).

    a. Find out what information is available to customers before they send a package.

    b. Find out about the "package tracking" system.

    c. Compute the cost of delivering a 10″ × 20″ × 15″ box, weighing 40 pounds, from your hometown to Long Beach, California (or to Lansing, Michigan, if you live in or near Long Beach). Compare the fastest delivery against the least cost. How long did this process take? Look into the business services offered by UPS. How do they make this process easier when you are a business customer?

3. Surf the Internet for information about the Department of Homeland Security (DHS). Examine the available information and comment on the role of information technologies in the department.

4. Access *www.irobot.com*, and investigate the company's Education and Research Robots. Surf the Web for other companies that manufacture robots, and compare their products with those of iRobot.

## [ Closing Case **What to Do About Commercial Drones** ]

### The Problem

A drone is an unmanned aerial vehicle (UAV) that either is controlled by pilots from the ground or autonomously follows a preprogrammed mission. Commercial drones are used for a wide variety of business purposes, in contrast to drones used by hobbyists for recreational purposes. In 2010, commercial drones (drones outside the military) did not really exist. By early 2015, analysts estimated the global market for commercial drones to be approximately $2.5 billion annually. In addition, that number is growing by 15–20 percent each year. During this period, the costs of producing drones decreased rapidly, and drone capabilities increased just as rapidly.

Commercial drones are very useful. They can fly lower than manned aircraft and higher than cranes and other ground-based vehicles can reach. They offer film producers, civil engineers, open-air mining operations, and individual photographers (to name but a few examples) a new perspective on the world. Using sophisticated sensors, drones can capture data that are impossible for the human eye to see—such as gas leaking from a pipeline and food crops suffering from lack of nitrogen—faster and in far greater volumes than previously was possible. Utilizing cloud computing, the data from drones can quickly produce high-resolution, three-dimensional maps of large geographical areas.

The problem is that, as of February 2015, one of the largest potential markets for commercial drones, the United States, was not open for commercial drone business. In fact, in December 2014, the U.S. Government Accounting Office (GAO) stated that Japan, Australia, the United Kingdom, and Canada had "progressed further than the United States with regulations supporting drone integration." U.S. businesses had been waiting for the FAA's regulations on the commercial use of drones for years. The FAA claimed that it was moving carefully on drone regulations out of concern for potential collisions with other aircraft as well as injuries to people and damage to structures on the ground.

### An Interim Solution

The FAA initially instituted a blanket ban on the commercial use of drones. (The agency did not restrict the recreational use of drones.) Then the agency decided to grant exemptions on a case-by-case basis to organizations that wanted to use drones for commercial purposes. (Interestingly, the FAA had been granting exemptions for drone use to public agencies such as local police departments for years.)

In September 2014, the FAA issued exceptions to six film companies to use drones. It has also approved their use to monitor oil operations in Alaska. As a result of these exemptions, various other organizations began to utilize drones. Let's examine five industries that are currently employing this technology.

**Agriculture**. Sensors on drones, coupled with data analytics (see Chapter 12), are extending precision agriculture beyond simply monitoring crops. Drones help farmers increase crop yields by optimizing the fertilizer mix for different parts of a field down to the square meter. They similarly help winemakers increase yields by precisely controlling drip irrigation down to the individual vine.

**Construction**. On large-scale construction sites, envisioning the overall "picture" presents a major challenge for contractors. Drones enable project managers from construction giants such as Bechtel (*www.bechtel.com*) and DPR (*www.dpr.com*) to monitor progress and supply stockpiles on a real-time basis.

**Energy**. The energy industry uses drones for applications beyond monitoring and inspecting pipelines. In Alaska, BP (*www.bp.com*) uses drones to monitor its gravel-extraction operations to comply with environmental guidelines. ConocoPhillips (*www.conocophillips.com*) and Chevron (*www.chevron.com*) use drones in the Arctic to help search for new sources of oil. First Solar (*www.firstsolar.com*) uses drones to inspect for faulty solar panels.

**Mining**. Large mining companies such as Rio Tinto (*www.riotinto.com*) are reducing risk to their workers by using drones to detect potential landslides and to inspect safety infrastructure, as well as to more accurately monitor how much mineral their workers are extracting.

**Film and Television**. American film and television studios, such as 20th Century Fox (*www.foxmovies.com*) and Warner Bros (*www.warnerbros.com*), have been using drones in their overseas productions because they were allowed to do so by foreign governments. When the FAA allowed them to use drones in U.S. airspace, these studios began to move their operations back to the United States.

As of February 15, 2015, the FAA had granted a total of 24 exemptions for the commercial use of drones. At that time, the FAA had received 342 requests for exemptions from commercial organizations and individuals.

## The Next Step in the Solution

On January 26, 2015, a drone crashed at the White House, dramatically highlighting the need for drone regulations. Although the incident is under investigation as of February 15, 2015, indications are that the incident involved a recreational user who lost control of the aircraft.

On February 15, 2015, the FAA issued its proposal for regulating small commercial drones. The proposal would allow drones weighing up to 55 pounds to fly within sight of their remote pilots during daylight hours. This line-of-sight requirement prohibits operators from utilizing on-board cameras to fly greater distances.

The proposals further stipulate that the drones must stay below 500 feet in the air and fly less than 100 miles per hour. The people operating the drones would need to be at least 17 years old, pass an aeronautics test, and be cleared by the Transportation Security Administration (TSA). However, a certificate to fly drones would not require the flight hours or medical rating required to obtain a private pilot's license.

Significantly, the new FAA proposal does not apply to hobbyists. The agency had already issued a policy for recreational use. This policy requires drones to fly less than 400 feet high and within sight of the operator, while keeping clear of other aircraft. In addition, operators must notify air traffic control when a drone is flying within five miles of an airport.

Also on February 15, 2015, President Obama signed a presidential memorandum regulating how federal agencies would use drones of all sizes. The memorandum requires agencies, within one year, to publish how citizens can access their policies about drones, particularly policies about the collection, retention, and dissemination of information. The goal is to ensure that drones and the information they capture do not violate the First Amendment or discriminate against people based on ethnicity, race, gender, religion, or sexual orientation. The Commerce Department will begin developing a framework for privacy and transparency regarding the commercial use of drones.

The certification requirement for flying commercial drones has already encountered opposition. From one perspective, the Air Line Pilots Association, a union representing 50,000 commercial pilots, argued that this requirement was not sufficiently stringent. The group has urged that drone pilots be highly trained and monitored to prevent midair collisions. From the opposite perspective, Amazon maintained that the FAA rules are too restrictive and would ground its drone delivery plans.

## The Very Early Results

The Association for Unmanned Vehicle Systems International (*www.auvsi.org*), a trade group, projects that the drone industry will create 70,000 jobs and generate almost $14 billion in economic activity during the first three years after drones fully share the skies with other aircraft.

Meanwhile, the drone industry continues to expand. Amazon, Google, and German shipping company DHL (*www.dhl.com*) are experimenting with drones for delivery. In addition, Facebook announced it is developing a drone the size of a 747 that could fly for months at a time, beaming down wireless signals.

*Sources*: Compiled from S. Shane, "FAA Acts to Regulate Commercial Drone Use," *The Wall Street Journal*, February 16, 2015; B. Jansen, "Drone Rules Dismay Amazon," *USA Today*, February 16, 2015; B. Jansen, "FAA Unveils Drone Rules; Obama Orders Policy for Agencies," *USA Today*, February 15, 2015; A. Cooper, "Commercial Drone Permission Comes with Strings Attached," *CNN*, February 13, 2015; S. Shankland, "FAA Eases Barrier to Commercial Drone Use," *CNET*, February 4, 2015; L. Wheeler, "FAA Clears More Commercial Drones for Takeoff," *The Hill*, February 3, 2015; D. Kravets, "Pilot, FAA Settle Test Case About Legality of Commercial Use of Drones," *Ars Technica*, January 22, 2015; J. Goglia, "Sad, but True: Report Finds U.S. Lags Behind Other Countries in Commercial Drone Use," *Forbes*, December 20, 2014; B. Jansen, "FAA Lets 4 Companies Fly Commercial Drones," *USA Today*, December 10, 2014; J. Nicas and A. Pasztor, "Drone Flights Face FAA Hit," *The Wall Street Journal*, November 24, 2014; C. Osborne, "FAA to Impose Restrictions on Commercial Drone Use," *ZDNet*, November 24, 2014; C. Dillow, "Get Ready for Drone Nation," *Fortune*, October 8, 2014; J. Aschbrenner, "Real Estate Agents Pushing Legal Limits with Drone Use," *The Des Moines Register*, July 7, 2014.

**Questions**

1. Why do you think the FAA took six years to issue regulations on the commercial use of drones? Support your answer.

2. What are the advantages of commercial drones (in general)?

3. What are the disadvantages of commercial drones (in general)?

4. Do you think the advantages outweigh the disadvantages, or vice versa? Support your answer.

# Organizational Strategy, Competitive Advantage, and Information Systems

**2**

| [ LEARNING OBJECTIVES ] | [ CHAPTER OUTLINE ] | [ WEB RESOURCES ] |
|---|---|---|
| 1. Discuss ways in which information systems enable cross-functional business processes and business processes for a single functional area. | 2.1 Business Processes | • Student PowerPoints for note taking |
| 2. Differentiate between business process reengineering, business process improvement, and business process management. | 2.2 Business Process Reengineering, Business Process Improvement, and Business Process Management | **WileyPLUS Learning Space** |
| 3. Identify effective IT responses to different kinds of business pressures. | 2.3 Business Pressures, Organizational Responses, and Information Technology Support | • E-book<br>• Author video lecture for each chapter section<br>• Practice quizzes<br>• Flash Cards for vocabulary review |
| 4. Describe the strategies that organizations typically adopt to counter Porter's five competitive forces. | 2.4 Competitive Advantage and Strategic Information Systems | • Additional "IT's About Business" cases<br>• Video interviews with managers<br>• Lab Manuals for Microsoft Office 2010 and 2013 |

## What's In IT For Me?

### This Chapter Will Help Prepare You To...

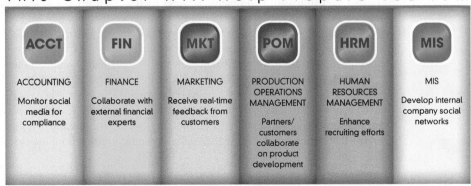

| ACCT | FIN | MKT | POM | HRM | MIS |
|---|---|---|---|---|---|
| ACCOUNTING | FINANCE | MARKETING | PRODUCTION OPERATIONS MANAGEMENT | HUMAN RESOURCES MANAGEMENT | MIS |
| Monitor social media for compliance | Collaborate with external financial experts | Receive real-time feedback from customers | Partners/customers collaborate on product development | Enhance recruiting efforts | Develop internal company social networks |

# [GrubHub]

I n August 2013, two formerly separate companies—Seamless (*www.seamless.com*) and GrubHub (*www.grubhub.com*)—merged to form a combined organization, called Grub-Hub, Inc. The new organization, which has retained both brands, is the leading company in food delivery. The two brands offer similar products.

- GrubHub's diner products include the GrubHub.com Web site and the mobile app Track Your Grub, which is GrubHub's system for providing diners with real-time notifications and order tracking. GrubHub's restaurant products include OrderHub, an in-restaurant tablet that helps streamline the order confirmation process, and DeliveryHub, an app that helps delivery drivers plan their routes more efficiently. These two products collaborate to provide real-time updates to GrubHub diners through Track Your Grub.

- Seamless's diner products include the Seamless.com Web site and the mobile app Food Tracker, which is Seamless's system for providing diners with real-time order tracking. Seamless's restaurant product is Boost, an in-restaurant tablet that helps streamline the order-confirmation process. Seamless allows businesses to consolidate all food ordering and subsequent billing into a single account. It provides three ordering options: individual meals, group ordering, and corporate catering.

Visitors to GrubHub begin by entering their physical address. The service then returns a list of restaurants that deliver to that address, as well as takeout restaurants situated within a pre-determined radius. Users are also able to browse restaurants in their city or search by cuisine, restaurant name, or specific item. Once users make their selection, they can place their order either through the GrubHub Web site or over the phone. GrubHub also provides its users with access to reviews, coupons, special deals, and a 24/7 customer service team that tracks and monitors each order.

GrubHub's expertise is concentrated primarily on the technical side of the industry. Though the company employs many former servers, it has not focused on recruiting people with high-level restaurant expertise. Therefore, since late 2013, GrubHub has been sending employees from its headquarters to work in kitchens and to accompany drivers on deliveries.

GrubHub provides restaurants with tablets to manage orders. The company also employs account managers to advise restaurants based on industry sales data. For example, sports bars know they will sell more hot wings during National Football League games than at other times. In addition, GrubHub claims it can accurately predict how much chicken the restaurants in a particular neighborhood will need. In fact, GrubHub maintains that, when restaurants run out of an item on the menu, employees can instantly adjust their online menus using the tablets. Half of all GrubHub orders are now processed on the tablets.

GrubHub's strategy is to integrate itself into restaurants' operations to justify its commissions, which range from 10 to more than 20 percent of the food order. Small businesses in particular are typically skeptical of companies that offer data services, especially when their commissions are as high as GrubHub's. Convenient tablets may not be enough to offset a 10–20 percent revenue cut. Industry analysts note that the primary value of OrderHub is to GrubHub, not the restaurants. In fact, these analysts claim it is in the restaurants' best interests to play GrubHub against competing services such as Delivery (*www.delivery.com*) and Eat24 (*www.eat24.com*).

Despite these problems and a competitive marketplace, by early 2015 GrubHub was filling an average of 174,000 online orders per day from almost 30,000 restaurants in more than 700 U.S. cities as well as London. The company served more than 4 million unique diners in 2014.

In 2014, GrubHub filed an initial public offering (IPO) and raised nearly $200 million. In early 2015, GrubHub entered the delivery business. Delivery will benefit restaurants that do not currently offer this service. To accomplish this new venture, GrubHub acquired two restaurant delivery services—Restaurants on the Run (*www.rotr.com*) and DiningIn (*www.diningin .com*)—that currently serve more than 3,000 restaurants throughout the country.

*Sources:* Compiled from D. Smith, "How GrubHub Seamless Will Capture a Bigger Bite of the $70 Billion Takeout Market," *Business Insider*, February 12, 2015; L. Picker, "Seamless.com Owner GrubHub Surges After $192 Million IPO," *Bloomberg BusinessWeek*, April 3, 2014; S. Kim, "GrubHub, in IPO Filing, Reveals Too Lazy to Cook Site Is Profitable," *ABC News*,

February 28, 2014; J. Brustein, "GrubHub Puts Data on Its Menu," *Bloomberg BusinessWeek*, December 23, 2013–January 5, 2014; L. Lazare, "GrubHub and Seamless Complete Merger," *Chicago Business Journal*, August 9, 2013; A. Moscaritolo, "Grub-Hub 'Track Your Grub' Lets You Keep Tabs on Your Order," *PC Magazine*, November 13, 2012; A. Shontell, "The Digital 100: The World's Most Valuable Private Tech Companies," *Business Insider*, November 7, 2012; *www.grubhub.com*, *www.seamless.com*, accessed February 14, 2015.

### Questions

1. Look ahead in this chapter. Which one of Porter's strategies for competitive advantage is GrubHub pursuing? Explain your answer.

2. Propose additional applications that GrubHub could develop to gain a competitive advantage in the marketplace.

# Introduction

Organizations operate in the incredible complexity of the modern high-tech world. As a result, they are subject to a myriad of business pressures. Information systems (ISs) are critically important in helping organizations respond to business pressures and in supporting organizations' global strategies. As you study this chapter, you will see that any information system can be *strategic*, meaning that it can provide a competitive advantage if it is used properly.

Competitive advantage refers to any assets that provide an organization with an edge against its competitors in some measure such as cost, quality, or speed. A competitive advantage helps an organization to control a market and to accrue larger-than-average profits. Significantly, both strategy and competitive advantage take many forms.

Although there are many companies that use technology in more expensive ways, Grub-Hub, discussed in the chapter opening case, demonstrates that an entrepreneurial spirit coupled with a solid understanding of what IT can do for you will provide competitive advantages to entrepreneurs just as it does for Wall Street CIOs. As you study this chapter, think of the small businesses in your area that are utilizing popular technologies in interesting and novel ways. Have any of them found an innovative use for Twitter? Facebook? Amazon? PayPal? If not, then can you think of any businesses that would benefit from employing these technologies?

This chapter is important for you for several reasons. First, the business pressures we address in the chapter will affect your organization. Just as important, however, they also will affect *you*. Therefore, you must understand how information systems can help you—and eventually your organization—respond to these pressures.

In addition, acquiring competitive advantage is essential for your organization's survival. Many organizations achieve competitive advantage through the efforts of their employees. Therefore, becoming knowledgeable about strategy and how information systems affect strategy and competitive position will help you throughout your career.

This chapter encourages you to become familiar with your organization's strategy, mission, and goals and to understand its business problems and how it makes (or loses) money. It will help you understand how information technology contributes to organizational strategy. Further, you likely will become a member of business/IT committees that decide (among many other things) how to use existing technologies more effectively and whether to adopt new ones. After studying this chapter, you will be able to make immediate contributions to these committees when you join your organizations.

Information systems can be just as strategic to a small- or medium-sized company as they are to a large firm. The chapter opening case illustrates how information systems are strategically important to GrubHub, an online food ordering service.

In this chapter, you will see how information systems enable organizations to respond to business pressures. Next, you will learn how information systems help organizations gain competitive advantages in the marketplace.

# 2.1 Business Processes

A **business process** is an ongoing collection of related activities that create a product or a service of value to the organization, its business partners, and/or its customers. The process involves three fundamental elements:

- *Inputs:* Materials, services, and information that flow through and are transformed as a result of process activities
- *Resources:* People and equipment that perform process activities
- *Outputs:* The product or a service created by the process

If the process involves a customer, then that customer can be either internal or external to the organization. A manager who is the recipient of an internal reporting process is an example of an internal customer. In contrast, an individual or a business that purchases the organization's products is the external customer of the fulfillment process.

Successful organizations measure their process activities to evaluate how well they are executing these processes. Two fundamental metrics that organizations employ in assessing their processes are efficiency and effectiveness. *Efficiency* focuses on doing things well in the process; for example, progressing from one process activity to another without delay or without wasting money or resources. *Effectiveness* focuses on doing the things that matter; that is, creating outputs of value to the process customer—for example, high-quality products.

Many processes cross functional areas in an organization. For example, product development involves research, design, engineering, manufacturing, marketing, and distribution. Other processes involve only a single functional area. Table 2.1 identifies the fundamental business processes performed in an organization's functional areas.

## Cross-Functional Processes

All of the business processes in Table 2.1 fall within a single functional area of the company. However, many other business processes, such as procurement and fulfillment, cut across multiple functional areas; that is, they are **cross-functional business processes**, meaning that no single functional area is responsible for their execution. Rather, multiple functional areas collaborate to perform the process. For a cross-functional process to be successfully completed, each functional area must execute its specific process steps in a coordinated, collaborative way. To clarify this point, let's take a look at the procurement and fulfillment cross-functional processes. We discuss these processes in greater detail in Chapter 10.

The *procurement process* includes all of the tasks involved in acquiring needed materials externally from a vendor. Procurement comprises five steps that are completed in three different functional areas of the firm: warehouse, purchasing, and accounting.

The process begins when the warehouse recognizes the need to procure materials, perhaps due to low inventory levels. The warehouse documents this need with a purchase requisition, which it sends to the purchasing department (step 1). In turn, the purchasing department identifies a suitable vendor, creates a purchase order based on the purchase requisition, and sends the order to the vendor (step 2). When the vendor receives the purchase order, it ships the materials, which are received in the warehouse (step 3). The vendor then sends an invoice,  which is received by the accounting department (step 4). Accounting sends payment to the vendor, thereby completing the procurement process (step 5).

The *fulfillment process* is concerned with processing customer orders. Fulfillment is triggered by a customer purchase order that is received by the sales department. Sales then validates the purchase order and creates a sales order. The sales order communicates data related to the order to other functional areas within the organization, and it tracks the progress of the order. The warehouse prepares and sends the shipment to the customer. Once accounting is  notified of the shipment, it creates an invoice and sends it to the customer. The customer then makes a payment, which accounting records.

Table **2.1**
**Examples of Business Processes**

Accounting Business Processes
- Managing accounts payable
- Managing accounts receivable
- Reconciling bank accounts
- Managing cash receipts
- Managing invoice billings
- Managing petty cash
- Producing month-end close
- Producing virtual close

**ACCT**

Finance Business Processes
- Managing account collection
- Managing bank loan applications
- Producing business forecasts
- Applying customer credit approval and credit terms
- Producing property tax assessments
- Managing stock transactions
- Generating financial cash flow reports

**FIN**

Marketing Business Processes
- Managing post-sale customer follow-up
- Collecting sales taxes
- Applying copyrights and trademarks
- Using customer satisfaction surveys
- Managing customer service
- Handling customer complaints
- Handling returned goods from customers
- Producing sales leads
- Entering sales orders
- Training sales personnel

**MKT**

Production/Operations Management Business Processes
- Processing bills of materials
- Processing manufacturing change orders
- Managing master parts list and files
- Managing packing, storage, and distribution
- Processing physical inventory
- Managing purchasing
- Managing quality control for finished goods
- Auditing for quality assurance
- Receiving, inspecting, and stocking parts and materials
- Handling shipping and freight claims
- Handling vendor selection, files, and inspections

**POM**

Human Resources Business Processes
- Applying disability policies
- Managing employee hiring
- Handling employee orientation
- Managing files and records
- Applying healthcare benefits
- Managing pay and payroll
- Producing performance appraisals and salary adjustments
- Managing resignations and terminations
- Applying training/tuition reimbursement
- Managing travel and entertainment
- Managing workplace rules and guidelines
- Overseeing workplace safety

**HRM**

Management Information Systems Business Processes
- Antivirus control
- Computer security issues incident reporting
- Training computer users
- Computer user/staff training
- Applying disaster recovery procedures
- Applying electronic mail policy
- Generating Internet use policy
- Managing service agreements and emergency services
- Applying user workstation standards
- Managing the use of personal software

**MIS**

An organization's business processes can create a **competitive advantage** if they enable the company to innovate or to execute more effectively and efficiently than its competitors. They can also be liabilities, however, if they make the company less responsive and productive. Consider the airline industry. It has become a competitive necessity for all of the airlines to offer electronic ticket purchases via their Web sites. To provide competitive advantage, however, these sites must be highly responsive and they must provide both current and accurate information on flights and prices. An up-to-date, user-friendly site that provides fast answers to user queries will attract customers and increase revenues. In contrast, a site that provides outdated or inaccurate information, or has a slow response time, will hurt rather than improve business.

Clearly, good business processes are vital to organizational success. But how can organizations determine if their business processes are well designed? The first step is to document the process by describing its steps, its inputs and outputs, and its resources. The organization can then analyze the process and, if necessary, modify it to improve its performance.

To understand this point, let's consider the e-ticketing process. E-ticketing consists of four main process activities: searching for flights, reserving a seat, processing payment, and issuing an e-ticket. These activities can be broken down into more detailed process steps. The result may look like the process map in Figure 2.1. Note that different symbols correspond to different types of process steps. For instance, rectangles (steps) are activities that are performed by process resources (reserve seats, issue e-ticket). Diamond-shaped boxes indicate decisions that need to be made (seats available?). Arrows are used as connectors between steps; they indicate the sequence of activities.

**FIGURE 2.1** Business process for ordering e-ticket from airline Web site.

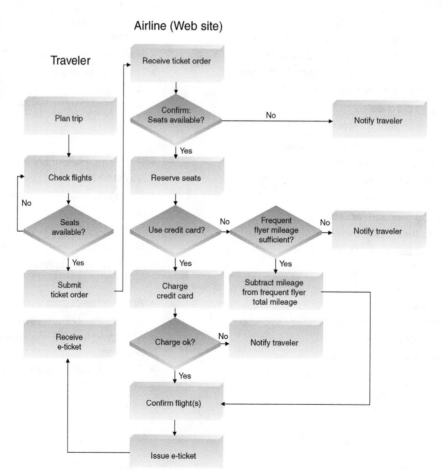

These symbols are important in the process flowchart (which is similar to a programming flowchart). Other symbols may be used to provide additional process details. For example, D-shaped boxes are used instead of rectangles when a waiting period is part of a process; ovals can show start and stop points; and process resources can be attached to activities with resource connector lines, or included as an annotation or property for each activity box.

The customers of the process are travelers planning a trip, and the process output is an e-ticket. Travelers provide inputs to the process: the desired travel parameters to begin the search, the frequent flyer miles number, and their credit card information. In addition, a computerized reservation system that stores information for many airlines also provides some of the process inputs—such as the seat availability and prices. The resources used in the process are the airline Web site, the computerized reservation system, and, if the customer calls the airline call center at any time during the process, the call center system and the human travel agents. The process creates customer value by efficiently generating an output that meets the customer search criteria—dates and prices. The performance of the process depends on efficiency metrics such as the time required to purchase an e-ticket, from the moment the customer initiates the ticket search until he or she receives the e-ticket. Effectiveness metrics include customer satisfaction with the airline Web site. Finally, the performance of the process may be affected if the quality or the timeliness of the inputs is low—for example, if the customer enters the wrong dates—or if the process resources are not available—for example, if the Web site crashes before the purchase is finalized.

## Information Systems and Business Processes

An information system is a critical enabler of an organization's business processes. Information systems facilitate communication and coordination among different functional areas, and allow easy exchange of, and access to, data across processes. Specifically, ISs play a vital role in three areas:

- Executing the process
- Capturing and storing process data
- Monitoring process performance

In this section, you will learn about each of these roles. In some cases the role is fully automated—that is, it is performed entirely by the IS. In other cases, the IS must rely on the manager's judgment, expertise, and intuition. IT's About Business 2.1 shows how NASCAR uses information technology to streamline its pre-race process.

 **[about business]**

### 2.1 NASCAR Uses IT in Its Pre-Race Inspection

The National Association for Stock Car Auto Racing (NASCAR) (*www.nascar.com*) is a family-owned-and-operated business that governs multiple auto racing sports events. One of NASCAR's key business processes occurs before each race: specifically, the pre-race inspection of the cars. The rationale for pre-race inspection is to ensure that all cars are as evenly matched as possible.

Pre-race inspection is a thorough process that begins two days before a race. Each car on the entry list for a particular race must pass inspection to compete. Here is how the process works.

In the first inspection, NASCAR officials assess whether a car meets NASCAR requirements—for example, height off the ground at the front of the car, height off the ground at the back of the car,

weight, fuel tank capacity, and many other factors. Cars that meet these requirements are cleared to practice, and they qualify for the race.

If a car does not pass inspection on the first try, then NASCAR allows that team to fix the problem and undergo a second inspection. However, the team has to go to the back of the line. This process can create a backup as the qualifying time approaches. In past years, NASCAR would allow a team with a violation to fix its issue and then get back in line, cutting in front of teams that had not undergone the initial inspection. That situation allowed crew chiefs to do the minimum when trying to repair violations. If the repair did not fix the violation, they would simply try again.

After the initial inspection, each team has two days before the race to work on their cars. After each team qualifies, NASCAR conducts a post-qualifying inspection. On race morning, all cars are inspected one final time.

Historically, NASCAR officials performed the pre-race inspection process by walking to each inspection station and visually observing each car. Moreover, they conducted the inspections using paper forms. These forms contained more than 100 individual items clustered in categories based on the type of inspection. The form would stay with each vehicle and follow it through the inspection process. This process used 25,000 sheets of paper in a single NASCAR season.

In September 2014, NASCAR implemented an app from Microsoft that incorporates all of the items on the paper-based form, but in a more informative format. A dashboard view displays each vehicle, along with its progress through the inspection process. The dashboard also uses color-coded flags to highlight violations. NASCAR officials can drill down on any vehicle to review details about any pending issues. The app has a button to open up a digital copy of the NASCAR rulebook to verify any issues. Officials can also annotate violations with digital notes and photographs. In addition, the app enables officials to determine whether pre-race inspections are on time. Finally, the race director can use his tablet to monitor each inspection station, identify which cars have been cited for infractions, and track the individual progress of every car.

The Microsoft app has simplified the pre-race inspection process. Consider, for instance, that the paper form required a NASCAR official's signature on every item. In contrast, the app uses a "default good" approach, in which officials have to note only those areas where they find violations.

One interesting benefit of the app is the cumulative value of the collected data. Information on the pre-race inspections of all vehicles is collected and stored in real time. Consequently, NASCAR executives can identify trends and patterns to help maintain a level playing field for all racers.

*Sources:* Compiled from N. Linhart, "NASCAR App Improves Inspection Efficiency," *Charlotte Sun Times*, February 10, 2015; J. Gluck, "App Improves NASCAR Inspections," *USA Today*, February 9, 2015; "Going through Inspections," *NASCAR.com*, January 5, 2015; "A Day at the Track for a NASCAR Race," *NASCAR.com*, January 5, 2015; J. Richter, "NASCAR Pre-Race Inspection? There's an App for That," *Fox Sports*, October 23, 2014; T. Bradley, "NASCAR Turns to Microsoft and Windows 8 to Streamline Race Operations," *Forbes*, October 21, 2014; J. Hammond, "NASCAR Inspections a Work in Progress," *Fox Sports*, June 6, 2014; *www.nascar.com*, accessed March 2, 2015.

**Questions**

1. Describe why pre-race inspection is a business process for NASCAR.
2. Describe the various benefits that the app provides NASCAR.
3. Look ahead to Section 2.4. Is the app a strategic information system (SIS) for NASCAR? Why or why not? Support your answer.

**Executing the Process.** An IS helps organizations execute processes efficiently and effectively. ISs are typically embedded into the processes, and they play a critical role in executing the processes. In other words, an IS and the processes are usually intertwined. If the IS does not work, the process cannot be executed. IS helps execute processes by informing people when it is time to complete a task, by providing the necessary data to complete the task, and, in some cases, by providing the means to complete the task.

In the procurement process, for example, the IS generates the purchase requisitions and then informs the purchasing department that action on these requisitions is needed. The accountant will be able to view all shipments received to match an invoice that has been received from a supplier and verify that the invoice is accurate. Without the IS, these steps, and therefore the process, cannot be completed. For example, if the IS is not available, how will the warehouse know which orders are ready to pack and ship?

In the fulfillment process, the IS will inform people in the warehouse that orders are ready for shipment. It also provides them with a listing of what materials must be included in the order and where to find those materials in the warehouse.

**Capturing and Storing Process Data.** Processes create data such as dates, times, product numbers, quantities, prices, and addresses, as well as who did what, when, and where. ISs capture and store these data, commonly referred to as *process data* or *transaction data*. Some of these data are generated and automatically captured by the IS. These are data related to who completes an activity, when, and where. Other data are generated outside the IS and must be entered into it. This data entry can occur in various ways, ranging from manual entry to automated methods involving data in forms such as bar codes and RFID tags that can be read by machines.

In the fulfillment process, for example, when a customer order is received by mail or over the phone, the person taking the order must enter data such as the customer's name, what the customer ordered, and how much he or she ordered. Significantly, when a customer order is received via the firm's Web site, then all customer details are captured by the IS. Data such as the name of the person entering the data (who), at which location the person is completing the task (where), and the date and time (when) are automatically included by the IS when it creates the order. The data are updated as the process steps are executed. When the order is shipped, the warehouse will provide data about which products were shipped and in what quantities, and the IS will automatically include data related to who, when, and where.

An important advantage of using an IS compared to a manual system or multiple functional area information systems is that the data need to be entered into the system only once. Further, once they are entered, other people in the process can easily access them, and there is no need to reenter them in subsequent steps.

The data captured by the IS can provide immediate feedback. For example, the IS can use the data to create a receipt or to make recommendations for additional or alternative products.

**Monitoring Process Performance.** A third contribution of IS is to help monitor the state of the various business processes. That is, the IS indicates how well a process is executing. The IS performs this role by evaluating information about a process. This information can be created either at the *instance level* (i.e., a specific task or activity) or at the *process level* (i.e., the process as a whole).

For example, a company might be interested in the status of a particular customer order. Where is the order within the fulfillment process? Was the complete order shipped? If so, when? If not, then when can we expect it to be shipped? Or, for the procurement process, when was the purchase order sent to the supplier? What will be the cost of acquiring the material? At the process level, the IS can evaluate how well the procurement process is being executed by calculating the lead time, or the time between sending the purchase order to a vendor and receiving the goods, for each order and each vendor over time.

Not only can the IS help monitor a process, but it can also detect problems with the process. The IS performs this role by comparing the information with a standard—that is, what the company expects or desires—to determine if the process is performing within expectations. Management establishes standards based on organizational goals.

If the information provided by the IS indicates that the process is not meeting the standards, then the company assumes that some type of problem exists. Some problems can be routinely and automatically detected by the IS, whereas others require a person to review the information and make judgments. For example, the IS can calculate the expected date that a specific order will be shipped and determine whether this date will meet the established standard. Or, the IS can calculate the average time taken to fill all orders over the last month and compare this information with the standard to determine if the process is working as expected.

Monitoring business processes, then, helps detect problems with these processes. Very often these problems are really symptoms of a more fundamental problem. In such cases, the IS can help diagnose the cause of the symptoms by providing managers with additional, detailed information. For example, if the average time to process a customer order appears to have increased over the previous month, this problem could be a symptom of a more basic problem.

A manager can then drill down into the information to diagnose the underlying problem. To accomplish this task, the manager can request a breakdown of the information by type of product, customer, location, employees, day of the week, time of day, and so on. After reviewing this detailed information, the manager might determine that the warehouse has experienced an exceptionally high employee turnover rate over the last month and that the delays are occurring because new employees are not sufficiently familiar with the process. The manager might conclude that this problem will work itself out over time, in which case there is nothing more to be done. Alternatively, the manager could conclude that the new employees are not being adequately trained and supervised. In this case, the company must take actions to correct the problem. The following section discusses several methodologies that managers can use to take corrective action when process problems are identified.

# before you go on...

**1.** What is a business process?

**2.** Describe several business processes carried out at your university.

**3.** Define a cross-functional business process, and provide several examples of such processes.

**4.** Pick one of the processes described in question 2 or 3 above, and identify its inputs, outputs, customer(s), and resources. How does the process create value for its customer(s)?

## 2.2 Business Process Reengineering, Business Process Improvement, and Business Process Management

Excellence in executing business processes is widely recognized as the underlying basis for all significant measures of competitive performance in an organization. Consider the following measures, for example:

- *Customer satisfaction:* The result of optimizing and aligning business processes to fulfill customers' needs, wants, and desires.
- *Cost reduction:* The result of optimizing operations and supplier processes.
- *Cycle and fulfillment time reduction:* The result of optimizing the manufacturing and logistics processes.
- *Quality:* The result of optimizing the design, development, and production processes.
- *Differentiation:* The result of optimizing the marketing and innovation processes.
- *Productivity:* The result of optimizing each individual's work processes.

The question is: How does an organization ensure business process excellence?

In their book *Reengineering the Corporation*, first published in 1993, Michael Hammer and James Champy argued that to become more competitive, American businesses needed to radically redesign their business processes to reduce costs and increase quality. The authors further asserted that information technology is the key enabler of such change. This radical redesign, called **business process reengineering (BPR)**, is a strategy for making an organization's business processes more productive and profitable. The key to BPR is for enterprises to examine their business processes from a "clean sheet" perspective and then determine how they can best reconstruct those processes to improve their business functions. BPR's popularity was propelled by the unique capabilities of information technology, such as automation and standardization of many process steps and error reduction due to improved communication among organizational information silos.

Although some enterprises have successfully implemented BPR, many organizations found this strategy too difficult, too radical, too lengthy, and too comprehensive. The impact on employees, on facilities, on existing investments in information systems, and even on organizational culture was overwhelming. Despite the many failures in BPR implementation, however, businesses increasingly began to organize work around business processes rather than individual tasks. The result was a less radical, less disruptive, and more incremental approach, called **business process improvement (BPI)**.

BPI focuses on reducing variation in the process outputs by searching for root causes of the variation in the process itself (e.g., a broken machine on an assembly line) or among the process inputs (e.g., a decline in the quality of raw materials purchased from a certain supplier).

BPI is usually performed by teams of employees that include a process expert—usually the process owner (the individual manager who oversees the process)—as well as other individuals who are involved in the process. These individuals can be involved directly; for example, the workers who actually perform process steps. Alternatively, these individuals can be involved indirectly; for example, customers who purchase the outputs from the process.

Six Sigma is a popular methodology for BPI initiatives. Its goal is to ensure that the process has no more than 3.4 defects per million outputs by using statistical methods to analyze the process. (A defect is defined as a faulty product or an unsatisfactory service.) Six Sigma was developed by Motorola in the 1980s, and it is now used by companies worldwide, thanks in part to promotional efforts by early adopters such as GE. Six Sigma is especially appropriate for manufacturing environments, where product defects can be easily defined and measured. Over the years, the methodology has been modified so that it focuses less on defects and more on customer value. As a result, it can now be applied to services as well as to products. Today, Six Sigma tools are widely used in financial services and healthcare institutions as components of process-improvement initiatives.

Regardless of the specific methodology you use, a successful BPI project generally follows five basic phases: define, measure, analyze, improve, and control (DMAIC).

- In the *define phase*, the BPI team documents the existing "as is" process activities, process resources, and process inputs and outputs, usually as a graphical process map or diagram. The team also documents the customer and the customer's requirements for the process output, together with a description of the problem that needs to be addressed.

- In the *measure phase*, the BPI team identifies relevant process metrics, such as time and cost to generate one output (product or service), and collects data to understand how the metrics evolve over time. Sometimes the data already exist, in which case they can be extracted from the IS that supports the process, as described in the previous section. Many times, however, the BPI team needs to combine operational process data already stored in the company's IS systems with other data sources, such as customer and employee observations, interviews, and surveys.

- In the *analysis phase*, the BPI team examines the "as is" process map and the collected data to identify problems with the process (e.g., decreasing efficiency or effectiveness) and their root causes. If possible, the team should also benchmark the process; that is, compare its performance with that of similar processes in other companies, or other areas of the organization. The team can employ IT applications such as statistical analysis software or simulation packages in this phase.

  It is often valuable to use process simulation software during the analysis phase. Utilizing this software provides two benefits. First, it enables a process manager to quickly simulate a real situation (e.g., with a certain number of people undertaking activities) for a specific amount of time (e.g., a working day, a week, or a month). The manager can then estimate the process performance over time without having to observe the process in practice. Second, it allows the manager to create multiple scenarios; for instance, using a different number of resources in the process and/or using a different configuration for the process steps. In addition, process simulation software can provide a number of outputs regarding a process, including the time used by all resources to execute specific activities, the overall cycle time of a process, the identification of resources that are infrequently used, and the bottlenecks in the process. Simulating a process is extremely valuable for process managers because it is a risk-free and inexpensive test of an improvement solution that does not need to be conducted with real resources.

- In the *improve phase*, the BPI team identifies possible solutions for addressing the root causes, maps the resulting "to be" process alternatives, and selects and implements the most appropriate solution. Common ways to improve processes are eliminating process activities that do not add value to the output and rearranging activities in a way that reduces delays or improves resource utilization. The organization must be careful, however, not to eliminate internal *process controls*—those activities that safeguard company resources, guarantee the accuracy of its financial reporting, and ensure adherence to rules and regulations.

- In the *control phase*, the team establishes process metrics and monitors the improved process after the solution has been implemented to ensure the process performance remains stable. An IS system can be very useful for this purpose.

Although BPI initiatives do not deliver the huge performance gains promised by BPR, many organizations prefer them because they are less risky and less costly. BPI focuses on delivering quantifiable results—and if a business case cannot be made, the project is not continued. All employees can be trained to apply BPI techniques in their own work to identify opportunities for improvement. Thus, BPI projects tend to be performed more from the bottom-up, in contrast to BPR projects that involve top-down change mandates. BPI projects take less time overall, and even if they are unsuccessful, they consume fewer organizational resources than BPR projects. However, if incremental improvements through BPI are no longer possible, or if significant changes occur in the firm's business environment, then the firm should consider BPR projects. One final consideration is that over time, employees can become overstretched or lose interest if the company undertakes too many BPI projects and does not have an effective system to manage and focus the improvement efforts.

To sustain BPI efforts over time, organizations can adopt **business process management (BPM)**, a management system that includes methods and tools to support the design, analysis, implementation, management, and continuous optimization of core business processes throughout the organization. BPM integrates disparate BPI initiatives to ensure consistent strategy execution.

Important components of BPM are process modeling, Web-enabled technologies, and business activity monitoring (BAM). BPM begins with *process modeling*, which is a graphical depiction of all of the steps in a process. Process modeling helps employees understand the interactions and dependencies among the people involved in the process, the information systems they rely on, and the information they require to optimally perform their tasks. Process modeling software can support this activity. IT's About Business 2.2 shows how Chevron has employed BPR, BPI, and BPM.

# IT's [about business]

## 2.2 BPR, BPI, and BPM at Chevron

Chevron (*www.chevron.com*), one of the world's largest oil and gas companies, and its subsidiaries are involved in exploring and producing oil and natural gas, as well as in manufacturing, transporting, and distributing petrochemical products, including gasoline and refined products. In 2013, Chevron employed more than 60,000 people worldwide, produced the equivalent of more than 2.6 million barrels of oil every day, and reported more than $230 billion in sales. Chevron has been involved in several process-reengineering and improvement efforts over the years, evolving from BPR to BPI and eventually to BPM, as described below.

In 1995, Chevron was less than half of its current size, producing roughly 1 million barrels of oil per day across six plants. The company was divided into three major departments: Refining, Marketing, and Supply and Distribution (S&D). Management determined that they needed to improve their supply chain (see Chapter 11) to better integrate their multiple internal processes. A key figure in decision making related to process management was Vice President Peter McCrea. McCrea was convinced that the best strategy to dramatically improve performance at Chevron was to reengineer the company's end-to-end core processes,

from the acquisition of crude oil through the distribution of final products to Chevron customers.

To accomplish this task, the Chevron team collaborated with a consultant company to create a model of the existing processes. The objective was to radically improve these processes to reflect Chevron's business goals. In other words, Chevron's strategy was not to analyze the existing processes to identify specific areas to improve. Rather, the project identified the desired outputs and then examined the supporting processes, utilizing BPR. As an added benefit, this holistic approach led the company to examine the interdependencies among processes executed in different business units. Adopting this holistic perspective ultimately improved the company's overall performance. In a 1996 report, Chevron claimed the BPR project saved the company $50 million.

This complex BPR effort was initially followed by several smaller, employee-driven BPI initiatives. For example, in 1998, six Chevron employees initiated a project to improve water treatment processes at a company plant in California. Their efforts reduced operating costs by 30 percent. Their success inspired other employees to initiate BPI projects in Indonesia, Angola, and other locations around the globe by employing Six Sigma improvement techniques. Although some managers were able to demonstrate the benefits of BPI at the local level, these efforts did not achieve companywide recognition and corporate backing until 2006. In that year, Lean Six Sigma, a methodology that combines statistical process analysis with techniques to eliminate waste and improve process flow, became the preferred improvement methodology at Chevron. Since Chevron implemented that methodology, company employees have executed hundreds of BPI projects worldwide, generating significant financial benefits. From 2008 to 2010 alone, Chevron reported more than $1 billion in BPI benefits. To support these internal improvement efforts, Chevron engaged its suppliers in BPI initiatives as well.

To coordinate these various BPI efforts, Chevron has adopted a unified BPM approach that involves standardizing processes across the entire company and consolidating process information within a central repository. Chevron estimates that only 20 percent of its processes can be fully automated—the rest involve a combination of manual and automated steps. Thus, process standardization involves not only supporting processes through integrated information systems but also ensuring that relevant employees are familiar with the standards for manual activities. To facilitate this task, Chevron implemented Nimbus (nimbus.tibco.com), a BPMS that acts as an intelligent repository of standard, companywide business rules and procedures. In addition, Nimbus can provide employees with detailed work instructions.

Consider, for example, Chevron's shipping process that experienced efficiency and risk problems due to its different execution in locations throughout Asia, Europe, and the United States. To establish uniform company standards, Chevron employed a BPI approach. The company analyzed "as is" operations across different geographical locations, identified best practices, and combined these practices into a common "to be" process. It then created documents that detailed these policies and procedures, which it distributed to managers through the company's Web-based BPMS.

Chevron's BPM strategy is part of a larger companywide management system that focuses on operational excellence. The program requires all Chevron operating companies and business units to adopt a continuous improvement perspective, directed by carefully defined guidelines, metrics, and targets that are reviewed and adapted every year. Apart from process efficiency, Chevron focuses on metrics related to safety, risk, and the environment. All employees participate in operational excellence activities, and managers receive specific operational excellence training to support the continuous improvement culture.

For 2014, Chevron reported more than $19 billion in net earnings. For the fourth quarter, however, the company's net income was $3.5 billion, down nearly 30 percent from $4.9 billion for the same period in 2013. This decline resulted primarily from the steep drop in crude oil prices. Chevron's CEO noted that increased operational efficiency in the company's downstream operations—that is, refining oil products and delivering them to customers—partially offset the effect of lower crude oil prices. This increased efficiency was a product of the company's ongoing BPR, BPI, and BPM efforts.

*Sources:* Compiled from "Operational Excellence," *chevron.com*, March 2012; "Chevron: Using Nimbus Control Software to Manage Processes," *Finding FindingPetroleum.com*, September 23, 2010; "Chevron Wins Boston Strategies International's 2010 Award for Lean Six Sigma Implementation in Oil and Gas Operations," *www.bostonstrategies.com*, September 22, 2010; "From the Bottom Up: Grassroots Effort Finds Footing at Chevron," *isixsigma.com*, March 1, 2010; "Business Process Improvement: A Talk with Chevron's Jim Boots," *Ebizq.net*, August 26, 2009; P. Harmon, *Business Process Management*, Elsevier, Burlington, MA, 2007; *www.chevron.com*, accessed February 22, 2015.

**Questions**
1. Describe the main advantages of BPR at Chevron.
2. Why did Chevron adopt BPI?
3. How does Chevron apply BPM in its operations today?

---

*Web-enabled technologies* display and retrieve data via a Web browser. They enable an organization to integrate the necessary people and applications into each process, across functional areas and geographical locations.

Finally, *business activity monitoring* is a real-time approach for measuring and managing business processes. Companies use BAM to monitor their business processes, identify failures or exceptions, and address these failures in real time. Further, because BAM tracks process operations and indicates whether they will succeed or fail, it creates valuable records of process behaviors that organizations can use to improve their processes.

BPM activities are often supported by *business process management suites* (BPMS). A BPMS is an integrated set of applications that include a repository of process information, such as process maps and business rules; tools for process modeling, simulation, execution, coordination across functions, and reconfiguration in response to changing business needs; as well as process-monitoring capabilities.

BPM is growing in business value. In 2012, Capgemini (*www.capgemini.com*), an international consulting firm, surveyed more than 1,000 senior business executives. The majority of the respondents indicated that BPM would play a more prominent role in their organizations in 2013 and 2014.

Further, Gartner (*www.gartner.com*), a leading IT research and advisory firm, stated that companies need to focus on developing and mastering BPM skills throughout the organization.

Gartner predicts that by 2016, high-performing companies will use BPM technologies such as real-time process monitoring, visualization, analytics, and intelligent automated decision making—all of them integrated in second-generation BPMS—to support intelligent business operations.

Another promising emerging trend is *social BPM*. This technology enables employees to collaborate, using social media tools on wired and mobile platforms, both internally across functions and externally with stakeholders (e.g., customers or experts), to exchange process knowledge and improve process execution.

BPM initially helps companies improve profitability by decreasing costs and increasing revenues. Over time, BPM can create a competitive advantage by improving organizational flexibility—making it easy to adapt to changing business conditions and to take advantage of new opportunities. For many companies, BPM can reduce costs, increase customer satisfaction, and ensure compliance with rules and regulations. In all cases, the company's strategy should drive the BPM effort. The following example illustrates these benefits.

## before you go on...

1. What is business process reengineering?
2. What is business process improvement?
3. What is business process management?

## 2.3 Business Pressures, Organizational Responses, and Information Technology Support

Modern organizations compete in a challenging environment. To remain competitive, they must react rapidly to problems and opportunities that arise from extremely dynamic conditions. In this section, you examine some of the major pressures confronting modern organizations and the strategies that organizations employ to respond to these pressures.

### Business Pressures

The **business environment** is the combination of social, legal, economic, physical, and political factors in which businesses conduct their operations. Significant changes in any of these factors are likely to create business pressures on organizations. Organizations typically respond to these pressures with activities supported by IT. Figure 2.2 illustrates the relationships among business pressures, organizational performance and responses, and IT support. You will learn about three major types of business pressures: market, technology, and societal pressures.

Market Pressures.    Market pressures are generated by the global economy, intense competition, the changing nature of the workforce, and powerful customers. Let's look more closely at each of these factors.

**Globalization.**    Globalization is the integration and interdependence of economic, social, cultural, and ecological facets of life, made possible by rapid advances in information technology. Today, individuals around the world are able to connect, compute, communicate, collaborate, and compete everywhere and anywhere, anytime and all the time; to access limitless amounts of information, services, and entertainment; to exchange knowledge; and to produce and sell goods and services. People and organizations can now operate without regard to geography, time, distance, or even language barriers. The bottom line? Globalization is markedly increasing competition.

These observations highlight the importance of market pressures for you. Simply put, you and the organizations you join will be competing with people and organizations from all over a flat world.

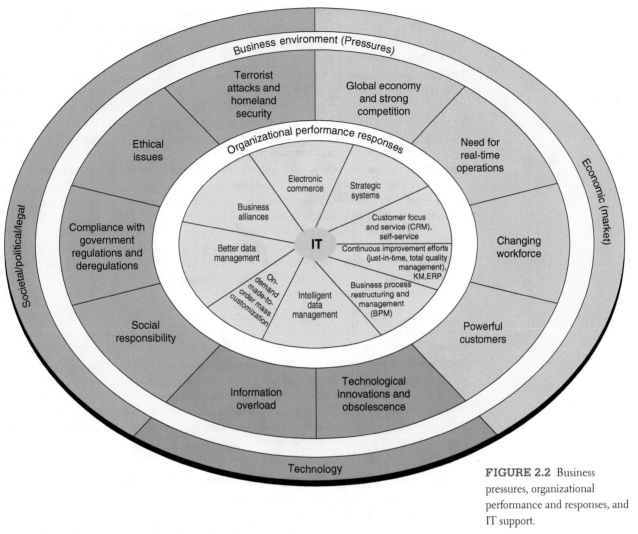

**FIGURE 2.2** Business pressures, organizational performance and responses, and IT support.

Let's consider some examples of globalization:

- Multinational corporations operate on a global scale, with offices and branches located worldwide.
- Many automobile manufacturers use parts from other countries, such as a car being assembled in the United States with parts coming from Japan, Germany, or Korea.
- The World Trade Organization (*www.wto.org*) supervises international trade.
- Regional agreements such as the North American Free Trade Agreement (NAFTA), which includes the United States, Canada, and Mexico, have contributed to increased world trade and increased competition.
- The European Union is an economic and political union of 28 countries that are located primarily in Europe.
- The rise of India and China as economic powerhouses has increased global competition.

One important pressure that businesses in a global market must contend with is the cost of labor, which varies widely among countries. In general, labor costs are higher in developed countries such as the United States and Japan than in developing countries such as China and El Salvador. Also, developed countries usually offer greater benefits, such as healthcare, to employees, driving the cost of doing business even higher. Therefore, many labor-intensive industries have moved their operations to countries with low labor costs. IT has made such moves much easier to implement.

However, manufacturing overseas is no longer the bargain it once was, and manufacturing in the United States is no longer as expensive. For example, manufacturing wages in China have more than doubled between 2002 and 2015, and they continue to rise. Meanwhile, the value of China's currency has steadily risen.

**The Changing Nature of the Workforce.** The workforce, particularly in developed countries, is becoming more diversified. Increasing numbers of women, single parents, minorities, and persons with disabilities are now employed in all types of positions. IT is easing the integration of these employees into the traditional workforce. IT is also enabling people to work from home, which can be a major benefit for parents with young children and for people confronted with mobility and/or transportation issues.

**Powerful Customers.** Consumer sophistication and expectations increase as customers become more knowledgeable about the products and services they acquire. Customers can use the Internet to find detailed information about products and services, to compare prices, and to purchase items at electronic auctions.

Organizations recognize the importance of customers and they have increased their efforts to acquire and retain them. Modern firms strive to learn as much as possible about their customers to better anticipate and address their needs. This process, called *customer intimacy*, is an important component of *customer relationship management* (CRM), an organization-wide effort toward maximizing the customer experience. You will learn about CRM in Chapter 11.

**Technology Pressures.** The second category of business pressures consists of those pressures related to technology. Two major technology-related pressures are technological innovation and information overload.

**Technological Innovation and Obsolescence.** Few and improved technologies rapidly create or support substitutes for products, alternative service options, and superb quality. As a result, today's state-of-the-art products may be obsolete tomorrow. For example, how fast are new versions of your smartphone being released? How quickly are electronic versions of books, magazines, and newspapers replacing traditional hard copy versions? These changes force businesses to keep up with consumer demands.

Consider the rapid technological innovation of the Apple iPad (*www.apple.com/ipad*):

- Apple released the first iPad in April 2010 and sold 3 million devices in just 80 days.
- Apple released the iPad 2 on March 11, 2011, only 11 months later.
- Apple released the iPad 3 on March 7, 2012.
- Apple released its fourth-generation iPad on November 2, 2012, along with the iPad mini.
- On November 1, 2013, Apple released the fifth generation of its iPad, called the iPad Air.
- On November 12, 2013, Apple released its iPad mini 2 with Retina Display.
- In October 2014, Apple released the iPad Air 2.

One manifestation of technological innovation is "bring your own device" (BYOD). BYOD refers to the policy of permitting employees to bring personally owned mobile devices (laptops, tablet computers, and smartphones) to the workplace and to use those devices to connect to the corporate network as well as for personal use. The academic version of BYOD involves students' utilizing personally owned devices in educational settings to connect to their school's network.

The rapid increase in BYOD represents a huge challenge for IT departments. Not only has IT lost the ability to fully control and manage these devices, but also employees are now demanding that they should be able to conduct company business from multiple personal devices.

The good news is that BYOD has increased worker productivity and satisfaction. In fact, some employees with BYOD privileges actually work longer hours with no additional pay.

The bad news is security concerns. Many companies with BYOD policies have experienced an increase in malware (malicious software, discussed in Chapter 4). Further, there is an increased risk of losing sensitive, proprietary information. Such information might not be securely stored on a personal, mobile device, which can be lost or stolen.

**Information Overload.** The amount of information available on the Internet doubles approximately every year, and much of it is free. The Internet and other telecommunications networks are bringing a flood of information to managers. To make decisions effectively and efficiently, managers must be able to access, navigate, and utilize these vast stores of data, information, and knowledge. Information technologies, such as search engines (discussed in Chapter 6) and data mining (Chapter 12), provide valuable support in these efforts.

**Societal/Political/Legal Pressures.** The third category of business pressures includes social responsibility, government regulation/deregulation, spending for social programs, spending to protect against terrorism, and ethics. This section will explain how all of these elements affect modern businesses. We start with social responsibility.

**Social Responsibility.** Social issues that affect businesses and individuals range from the state of the physical environment to company and individual philanthropy, to education. Some corporations and individuals are willing to spend time and/or money to address various social problems. These efforts are known as organizational social responsibility or individual social responsibility.

One critical social problem is the state of the physical environment. A growing IT initiative, called *green IT*, is addressing some of the most pressing environmental concerns. IT is instrumental in organizational efforts to "go green" in three areas.

- *Facilities design and management.* Organizations are creating more environmentally sustainable work environments. Many organizations are pursuing Leadership in Energy and Environmental Design (LEED) certification from the U.S. Green Building Council, a nonprofit group that promotes the construction of environmentally-friendly buildings. One impact of this development is that IT professionals are expected to help create green facilities.

- *Carbon management.* As companies try to reduce their carbon footprints, they are turning to IT executives to develop the systems needed to monitor carbon throughout the organization and its supply chain, which can be global in scope. Therefore, IT employees need to become knowledgeable about embedded carbon and how to measure it in the company's products and processes.

- *International and U.S. environmental laws.* IT executives must deal with federal and state laws and international regulations that impact everything, from the IT products they buy to how they dispose of them, to their company's carbon footprint.

Continuing our discussion of social responsibility, social problems all over the world may be addressed through corporate and individual philanthropy. In some cases, questions arise as to what percentage of contributions actually goes to the intended causes and recipients and what percentage goes to the charity's overhead. Another problem that concerns contributors is that they often exert little influence over the selection of projects their contributions will support. The Internet can help address these concerns and facilitate generosity and connection. Consider the following examples:

- *PatientsLikeMe* (*www.patientslikeme.com*), or any of the thousands of message boards dedicated to infertility, cancer, and various other ailments. People use these sites and message boards to obtain information about healthcare decisions based on volunteered information, while also receiving much-needed emotional support from strangers.

- *Collaborative Consumption* (*www.collaborativeconsumption.com*): This Web site is an online hub for discussions about the growing business of sharing, resale, reuse, and barter (with many links to Web sites engaged in these practices).

- *Kiva* (*www.kiva.org*): Kiva is a nonprofit enterprise that provides a link between lenders in developed countries and entrepreneurs in developing countries. Users pledge interest-free loans rather than tax-deductible donations. Kiva directs 100 percent of the loans to borrowers.

- *DonorsChoose* (*www.donorschoose.org*): DonorsChoose is an education-oriented Web site that functions entirely within the United States. Users make donations rather than loans. The Web site addresses the huge problem of underfunded public schools.

Still another social problem that affects modern business is the digital divide. The **digital divide** refers to the wide gap between those individuals who have access to information and communications technology and those who do not. This gap exists both within and among countries.

Many government and international organizations are trying to close the digital divide. As technologies develop and become less expensive, the speed at which the gap can be closed will accelerate. On the other hand, the rapid pace of technological development can make it more difficult for groups with few resources to keep up with more affluent groups.

One well-known project to narrow the divide is the One Laptop per Child (OLPC) project (*http://one.laptop.org*). OLPC is a nonprofit association dedicated to developing a very inexpensive laptop—a technology that aims to revolutionize how the world can educate its children. In early 2015, the price of OLPC's laptop remains approximately $200. We should note, however, that this price includes educational software loaded on the laptop. IT's About Business 2.3 discusses an interesting experiment by the OLPC in the East African nation of Ethiopia.

# IT's [about business]

## 2.3 Solar-Powered Tablets in Ethiopia  MIS

Nearly 100 million children throughout the world never make it to first grade. This tragedy occurs not only because there are no schools but also because there are very few literate adults to educate the children. To address this problem, the OLPC designed an experiment.

The experiment took place in two Ethiopian villages: Wonchi and Wolonchete. The literacy rate in these two villages was very close to zero. In fact, the children—as well as most of the adults— had never even seen a written word. They had no books, no newspapers, no street signs, and no labels on packaged foods or goods.

The OLPC set out to determine whether children with no previous exposure to written words could learn to read all by themselves, without intervention by teachers or other adults. In early 2013, the organization delivered approximately 1,000 solar-powered tablet computers (Motorola Xoom) to the children in the two villages. Each tablet was preloaded with alphabet-training games, electronic books, movies, cartoons, paintings, and many other applications—a total of 500 for each tablet. Each tablet also contained a memory card with tracking software to record how it was being used. Significantly, the OLPC team left the boxes containing the tablets in each village closed and taped shut. The team offered no instructions to either the adults or the children.

The results were amazing. Within four minutes, one child not only had opened the box containing the tablets but had also found the on/off switch and turned the tablet on. This feat was very impressive, considering he had never before seen an on/off switch. Within five days, the children were using an average of 47 apps each per day. Within two weeks, they were singing ABC songs in English. Within five months, the children had accessed the Android operating system. The OLPC had disabled the cameras in the tablets, and the children turned them back on and began taking pictures of themselves. The OLPC had also frozen the tablets' desktop settings. So, the children disabled the OLPC's settings, and each child customized his or her desktop.

The early results were promising. Within one year, the children had learned the alphabet, could recognize some words by sight, and had figured out how to use applications that would help them learn even more. One of the apps that was particularly successful, TinkrBook presents an interactive story that invites children to "tinker" with the text and graphics to explore how these changes affect the narrative.

The OLPC plans to bring tablets to India, Bangladesh, and Uganda, as well as to rural U.S. communities that have no preschools. Interestingly, the experiment produced a significant and unexpected benefit: The children were teaching their parents what they had learned, and the adults were moving toward literacy along with their children.

*Sources:* Compiled from C. Shahan, "Solar + Tablets to Improve Global Literacy," *Clean Technica*, May 22, 2014; M. Howard, "Tablet Computers for Global Literacy," *Tufts Now*, April 30, 2014; J. Brakel, "Tablets Without Teachers Improving Literacy in Ethiopia," *Gulf Times*, September 28, 2013; "Tablet as Teacher: Poor Ethiopian Kids Learn ABCs," *Associated Press*, December 24, 2012; E. Ackerman, "Ethiopian Kids, Hack OLPCs in 5 Months with Zero Instruction," *DVICE*, October 30, 2012; D. Talbot, "Given Tablets but No Teachers, Ethiopian Children Teach Themselves," *MIT Technology Review*, October 29, 2012.

### Questions

1. What advantages could result from increasing the literacy of 100 million children around the world? Be specific.
2. In this experiment, the tablets were not connected to the Internet. Discuss the advantages and disadvantages to the children if the tablets were connected.

**Compliance with Government Regulations.** Another major source of business pressures is government regulations regarding health, safety, environmental protection, and equal opportunity. Businesses tend to view government regulations as expensive constraints on their activities. In general, government deregulation intensifies competition.

In the wake of 9/11 and numerous corporate scandals, the U.S. government passed many new laws, including the Sarbanes–Oxley Act, the USA PATRIOT Act, the Gramm–Leach–Bliley Act, and the Health Insurance Portability and Accountability Act (HIPAA). Organizations must be in compliance with the regulations contained in these statutes. The process of becoming and remaining compliant is expensive and time consuming. In almost all cases, organizations rely on IT support to provide the necessary controls and information for compliance.

**Protection against Terrorist Attacks.** Since September 11, 2001, organizations have been under increased pressure to protect themselves against terrorist attacks. In addition, employees who are in the military reserves have been called up for active duty, creating personnel problems. Information technology can help protect businesses by providing security systems and possibly identifying patterns of behavior associated with terrorist activities, including cyberattacks (discussed in Chapter 4). For a good example of a firm that provides this protection, see Palantir (*www.palantir.com*).

An example of protection against terrorism is the Department of Homeland Security's (DHS) Office of Biometric Identity Management (OBIM) program. (We discuss biometrics in Chapter 4.) OBIM is a network of biometric screening systems, such as fingerprint and iris and retina scanners, that ties into government databases and watch lists to check the identities of millions of people entering the United States. The system is now operational in more than 300 locations, including major international ports of entry by air, sea, and land.

**Ethical Issues.** Ethics relates to general standards of right and wrong. Information ethics relates specifically to standards of right and wrong in information processing practices. Ethical issues are very important because, if handled poorly, they can damage an organization's image and destroy its employees' morale. The use of IT raises many ethical issues, ranging from monitoring e-mail to invading the privacy of millions of customers whose data are stored in private and public databases. Chapter 3 covers ethical issues in detail.

Clearly, then, the pressures on organizations are increasing, and organizations must be prepared to take responsive actions if they are to succeed. You will learn about these organizational responses in the next section.

## Organizational Responses

Organizations are responding to the various pressures just discussed by implementing IT such as strategic systems, customer focus, make-to-order and mass customization, and e-business. This section explores each of these responses.

**Strategic Systems.** Strategic systems provide organizations with advantages that enable them to increase their market share and/or profits, to better negotiate with suppliers, and to prevent competitors from entering their markets. IT's About Business 2.4 provides another example of how strategically important information systems can be by examining The Weather Channel (TWC).

 **IT's [about business]**

### 2.4 The Weather Channel

The Weather Channel (*www.weather.com*) is a cable and satellite television channel that is owned as a joint venture by NBC Universal (*www.nbcuniversal.com*) and two investment firms: The Blackstone Group (*www.blackstone.com*) and Bain Capital (*www.bain.com*). The channel broadcasts weather forecasts along with weather-related news, documentaries, and entertainment. In addition to its programming on the cable channel, TWC provides forecasts for terrestrial and satellite radio stations, newspapers, and Web sites. TWC maintains its online presence at *www.weather.com* as well as via a set of mobile smartphone and tablet applications.

Despite its powerful and well-known brand, however, TWC is losing viewers. According to Nielsen, TWC viewership has declined by 20 percent since 2013.

One reason for this decline is that viewers have been complaining about TWC airing reality TV programs (e.g., *Fat Guys in the Woods*, *Prospectors*, and many others) for large amounts of time, rather than straight weather coverage. In addition, TWC viewers are increasingly using mobile devices instead of television as their primary source of weather information. According to the analytics firm Distimo (*www.distimo.com*), more than 10,000 weather apps have been developed for the iPhone and Android devices.

TWC also has to contend with changing user expectations about what a weather forecast should be. "Nowcasting"—highly accurate short-term weather predictions for a specific location—is becoming increasingly popular among weather watchers who dislike semireliable five-day forecasts. TWC has typically relied on methods that can actually delay forecasts, such as having meteorologists interpret data for longer term predictions over a broader geographical area.

Despite these competitive pressures, thanks largely to its brand recognition, TWC's mobile app is the category's most popular, with approximately 100 million users. However, a group of startup companies, including Dark Sky (*www.darkskyapp.com*), Sky Motion (*www.skymotion.com*), and WeatherSphere (*www.weathersphere.com*), are beginning to cut into TWC's lead.

Whereas TWC's app can present conditions in 15-minute intervals, Dark Sky, for example, predicts to the minute—often with startling precision—when it is going to start raining or snowing within the next hour. Sky Motion does the same for the upcoming two hours. WeatherSphere's product, Radar Cast, can navigate drivers around oncoming storms.

These startups can predict the weather with such accuracy because they integrate and analyze data from National Weather Service radar, satellites, and personal weather stations to improve short-term forecasting. Interestingly, Dark Sky's $3.99 app has been downloaded about 400,000 times since 2012.

Another competitor, IBM (*www.ibm.com*), has been in the weather forecasting arena since it initiated its Deep Thunder project in 1996. Deep Thunder provides local, high-resolution weather predictions, customized to weather-sensitive specific business operations. For example, the system could predict up to 84 hours in advance the wind velocity at an Olympic diving platform or which locations are at risk for flooding or damaged power lines.

To combat viewer migration, TWC revamped its TV channel in November 2013, implementing major changes to both its appearance and its coverage. The channel now supports a graphic display on the bottom third of the television screen that displays local hourly weather conditions 24/7, even during commercials. The channel is also deploying technology that enables it to televise location-specific information to a defined geographical area, called "hyperlocal" forecasting. Using this technology, TWC's 220 meteorologists divide the country into 4,000 geographical zones. Viewers can watch weather forecasts pertinent to their zone.

TWC is also developing mobile projects to compete with the startups. For example, the company created an app called Radius that lets weather watchers share user-generated photos with other people in their areas.

Another new technology, called Forecast on Demand, could be transformative. Forecast on Demand incorporates elements of nowcasting, but it can also create a detailed forecast, at the request of a user, for more than 2 billion points around the globe. The application runs on a Web site that features a world map. As the user clicks on a location, Forecast on Demand instantly generates real-time forecasts for that specific geographical point. This technology disrupts traditional forecasting, which relies on pregenerated predictions.

Not surprisingly, the competition is not standing still. Dark Sky, for example, has created a service that makes short-term and long-term forecasts available to other up-and-coming companies, encroaching even further into TWC's territory. In addition, the company is negotiating with auto companies to install its technology in their vehicles, which could dramatically expand its user base.

Meanwhile, DirecTV (*www.directv.com*) dropped the TWC for about three months in 2014 after failing to come to an agreement about how much DirecTV should be paid in affiliate fees. To reach an agreement with DirecTV, TWC agreed to reduce its reality programming to include more local weather updates. If the two sides had not resolved this dispute, then TWC would have lost approximately 20 million of its 100 million viewers. Despite this agreement, in November 2014, TWC laid off approximately 6 percent of its workforce. These layoffs indicate that TWC is still having problems.

*Sources:* Compiled from D. Mersereau, "The Weather Channel Lays Off Six Percent of Its Staff as Ratings Slide," *The Vane*, November 6, 2014; A. Watts, "The Weather Channel Is Losing Viewers to Global Warming and Other Pointless Programming," *Watts Up With That?*, September 13, 2014; A. Sherman, D. Banerjee, and L. Shaw, "Weather Channel Said to Talk to Banks on Options Including Sale," *Bloomberg BusinessWeek*, September 12, 2014; J. McCorvey, "A Storm Brews over Weather," *Fast Company*, February, 2014; K. Bell, "Hyperlocal Weather App Dark Sky Gets 24-Hour and 7-Day Forecasts," *Mashable*, January 27, 2014; J. Samenow, "Soul Searching Time for The Weather Channel," *The Washington Post*, January 16, 2014; D. Lu, "13 Best Weather Apps to Take Your Day by Storm," *Mashable*, August 12, 2013; S. Gallagher, "How IBM's Deep Thunder Delivers 'Hyper-Local' Forecasts 3½ Days Out," *Arstechnica*, March 14, 2012; "Dark Sky Reinvents Weather Apps with Hyper-Local Forecasts," *Fast Company*, November 8, 2011; H. Czerski, "150 Years Since the First UK Weather 'Forecast'," *BBC*, August 1, 2011; *www.twc.com*, *www.darksky.com*, *www.ibm.com*, accessed February 6, 2015.

## Questions

1. Identify several reasons (not discussed in the case) why accurate weather predictions are so important. Can an accurate weather prediction be considered a competitive advantage for an organization that receives this information? Why or why not? Support your answer with specific examples.

2. Will Dark Sky, Sky Motion, and WeatherSphere enjoy a lasting competitive advantage over The Weather Channel? Why or why not? Support your answer.

**Customer Focus.**    Organizational attempts to provide superb customer service can make the difference between attracting and retaining customers versus losing them to competitors. Numerous IT tools and business processes have been designed to keep customers happy. (Recall that a *business process* is a collection of related activities that produce a product or a service of value to the organization, its business partners, and/or its customers.) Consider Amazon, for example. When you visit Amazon's Web site anytime after your first visit, the site welcomes you back by name and it presents you with information about items that you might like, based on your previous purchases. In another example, Dell guides you through the process of purchasing a computer by providing information and choices that help you make an informed buying decision.

**Make-to-Order and Mass Customization.**    **Make-to-order** is a strategy of producing customized (made to individual specifications) products and services. The business problem is how to manufacture customized goods efficiently and at a reasonably low cost. Part of the solution is to change manufacturing processes from mass production to mass customization. In mass production, a company produces a large quantity of identical items. An early example of mass production was Henry Ford's Model T, where buyers could pick any color—as long as it was black.

Ford's policy of offering a single product for all of its customers eventually gave way to *consumer segmentation*, in which companies provided standard specifications for different consumer groups, or segments. Clothes manufacturers, for example, designed their products in different sizes and colors to appeal to different customers. The next step was *configured mass customization*, in which companies offer features that allow each shopper to customize his or her product or service with a range of components. Examples are ordering a car, a computer, or a smartphone, where the customer can specify which features he or she wants.

In the current strategy, known as **mass customization**, a company produces a large quantity of items, but it customizes them to match the needs and preferences of individual customers. Mass customization is essentially an attempt to perform make-to-order on a large scale. Bodymetrics (*www.bodymetrics.com*) is an excellent example of mass customization that involves men's and women's jeans and swimsuits. Bodymetrics provides a "body scanner" that customers can access either at home or in a store. This technology scans the customer's body, captures more than 150 measurements, and produces a digital replica of the customer's size and shape. This scan is then used to provide made-to-measure jeans and swimsuits. The following are other examples:

- NikeID (*www.nikeid.com*): Allows customers to design their footwear.
- M&M candies: My M&Ms (*www.mymms.com*) allows customers to add photos, art, and messages to candy.
- Dell (*www.dell.com*) and HP (*www.hp.com*): Allow customers to exactly specify the computer that they want.

**E-Business and E-Commerce.**    Conducting business electronically is an essential strategy for companies that are competing in today's business environment. *Electronic commerce* (EC or e-commerce) describes the process of buying, selling, transferring, or exchanging products, services, or information via computer networks, including the Internet. *E-business* is a somewhat broader concept. In addition to the buying and selling of goods and services, e-business also refers to servicing customers, collaborating with business partners, and performing electronic transactions within an organization. Chapter 7 focuses extensively on this topic. In addition, e-commerce applications appear throughout the text.

You now have a general overview of the pressures that affect companies in today's business environment and the responses that they choose to manage these pressures. To plan for the most effective responses, companies formulate strategies. In the new digital economy, these strategies rely heavily on information technology, especially strategic information systems. You examine these topics in the next section.

# before you go on...

**1.** What are the characteristics of the modern business environment?

**2.** Discuss some of the pressures that characterize the modern global business environment.

**3.** Identify some of the organizational responses to these pressures. Are any of these responses specific to a particular pressure? If so, which ones?

## 2.4 Competitive Advantage and Strategic Information Systems

A *competitive strategy* is a statement that identifies a business's approach to compete, its goals, and the plans and policies that will be required to carry out those goals (Porter, 1985).[1] A strategy, in general, can apply to a desired outcome, such as gaining market share. A competitive strategy focuses on achieving a desired outcome when competitors want to prevent you from reaching your goal. Therefore, when you create a competitive strategy, you must plan your own moves, but you must also anticipate and counter your competitors' moves.

Through its competitive strategy, an organization seeks a competitive advantage in an industry. That is, it seeks to outperform its competitors in a critical measure such as cost, quality, and time-to-market. Competitive advantage helps a company function profitably with a market and generate larger-than-average profits.

Competitive advantage is increasingly important in today's business environment, as you will note throughout the text. In general, the *core business* of companies has remained the same. That is, information technologies simply offer tools that can enhance an organization's success through its traditional sources of competitive advantage, such as low cost, excellent customer service, and superior supply chain management. **Strategic information systems** provide a competitive advantage by helping an organization implement its strategic goals and improve its performance and productivity. Any information system that helps an organization either achieve a competitive advantage or reduce a competitive disadvantage qualifies as a strategic information system.

### Porter's Competitive Forces Model

The best-known framework for analyzing competitiveness is Michael Porter's **competitive forces model** (Porter, 1985). Companies use Porter's model to develop strategies to increase their competitive edge. Porter's model also demonstrates how IT can make a company more competitive.

Porter's model identifies five major forces that can endanger or enhance a company's position in a given industry. Figure 2.3 highlights these forces. Although the Web has changed the nature of competition, it has not changed Porter's five fundamental forces. In fact, what makes these forces so valuable as analytical tools is that they have not changed for centuries. Every competitive organization, no matter how large or small, or what business it is in, is driven by these forces. This observation applies even to organizations that you might not consider competitive, such as local governments. Although local governments are not for-profit enterprises, they compete for businesses to locate in their districts, for funding from higher levels of government, for employees, and for many other things.

Significantly, Porter (2001)[2] concludes that the *overall* impact of the Web is to increase competition, which generally diminishes a firm's profitability. Let's examine Porter's five forces and the ways that the Web influences them.

**1.** *The threat of entry of new competitors.* The threat that new competitors will enter your market is high when entry is easy and low when there are significant barriers to entry. An **entry**

[1] Porter, M.E. (1985) *Competitive Advantage*, Free Press, New York.
[2] Porter, M.E. (2001) "Strategy and the Internet," *Harvard Business Review*, March.

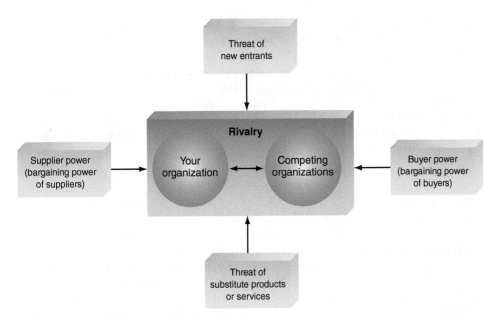

**FIGURE 2.3** Porter's competitive forces model.

**barrier** is a product or service feature that customers have learned to expect from organizations in a certain industry. A competing organization must offer this feature in order to survive in the marketplace. There are many types of entry barriers. Consider, for example, legal requirements such as admission to the bar to practice law or a license to serve liquor, where only a certain number of licenses are available.

Suppose you want to open a gasoline station. In order to compete in that industry, you would have to offer pay-at-the-pump service to your customers. Pay-at-the-pump is an IT-based barrier to entering this market because you must offer it for free. The first gas station that offered this service gained first-mover advantage and established barriers to entry. This advantage did not last, however, because competitors quickly offered the same service and thus overcame the entry barrier.

For most firms, the Web *increases* the threat that new competitors will enter the market because it sharply reduces traditional barriers to entry, such as the need for a sales force or a physical storefront. Today, competitors frequently need only to set up a Web site. This threat of increased competition is particularly acute in industries that perform an *intermediation role*, which is a link between buyers and sellers (e.g., stock brokers and travel agents), as well as in industries where the primary product or service is digital (e.g., the music industry). In addition, the geographical reach of the Web enables distant competitors to compete more directly with an existing firm.

In some cases, the Web increases barriers to entry. This scenario occurs primarily when customers have come to expect a nontrivial capability from their suppliers. For example, the first company to offer Web-based package tracking gained a competitive advantage from that service. Competitors were forced to follow.

2. *The bargaining power of suppliers.* Supplier power is high when buyers have few choices from whom to buy and low when buyers have many choices. Therefore, organizations would rather have more potential suppliers so that they will be in a stronger position to negotiate price, quality, and delivery terms.

   The Internet's impact on suppliers is mixed. On the one hand, it enables buyers to find alternative suppliers and to compare prices more easily, thereby reducing the supplier's bargaining power. On the other hand, as companies use the Internet to integrate their supply chains, participating suppliers prosper by locking in customers.

3. *The bargaining power of customers (buyers).* Buyer power is high when buyers have many choices from whom to buy and low when buyers have few choices. For example, in the past, there were few locations where students could purchase textbooks (typically, one or two campus bookstores). In this situation, students had low buyer power. Today, the Web

provides students with access to a multitude of potential suppliers as well as detailed information about textbooks. As a result, student buyer power has increased dramatically.

In contrast, *loyalty programs* reduce buyer power. As their name suggests, loyalty programs reward customers based on the amount of business they conduct with a particular organization (e.g., airlines, hotels, and rental car companies). Information technology enables companies to track the activities and accounts of millions of customers, thereby reducing buyer power. That is, customers who receive "perks" from loyalty programs are less likely to do business with competitors. (Loyalty programs are associated with customer relationship management, which you will study in Chapter 11.)

4. *The threat of substitute products or services.* If there are many alternatives to an organization's products or services, then the threat of substitutes is high. If there are few alternatives, then the threat is low. Today, new technologies create substitute products very rapidly. For example, customers today can purchase wireless telephones instead of landline telephones, Internet music services instead of traditional CDs, and ethanol instead of gasoline in cars.

Information-based industries experience the greatest threat from substitutes. Any industry in which digitized information can replace material goods (e.g., music, books, and software) must view the Internet as a threat because the Internet can convey this information efficiently and at low cost and high quality.

Even when there are many substitutes for their products, however, companies can create a competitive advantage by increasing switching costs. *Switching costs* are the costs, in money and time, imposed by a decision to buy elsewhere. For example, contracts with smartphone providers typically include a substantial penalty for switching to another provider until the term of the contract expires (quite often, two years). This switching cost is monetary.

As another example, when you buy products from Amazon, the company develops a profile of your shopping habits and recommends products targeted to your preferences. If you switch to another online vendor, that company will need time to develop a profile of your wants and needs. In this case, the switching cost involves time rather than money.

5. *The rivalry among existing firms in the industry.* The threat from rivalry is high when there is intense competition among many firms in an industry. The threat is low when the competition is among fewer firms and is not as intense.

In the past, proprietary information systems—systems that belong exclusively to a single organization—have provided strategic advantage to firms in highly competitive industries. Today, however, the visibility of Internet applications on the Web makes proprietary systems more difficult to keep secret. In simple terms, when I see my competitor's new system online, I will rapidly match its features to remain competitive. The result is fewer differences among competitors, which leads to more intense competition in an industry.

To understand this concept, consider the highly competitive grocery industry, where Walmart, Kroger, Safeway, and other companies compete essentially on price. Some of these companies have IT-enabled loyalty programs in which customers receive discounts and the store gains valuable business intelligence on customers' buying preferences. Stores use this business intelligence in their marketing and promotional campaigns. (You will learn about business intelligence in Chapter 12.)

Grocery stores are also experimenting with wireless technologies such as *radio-frequency identification* (RFID, discussed in Chapter 8) to speed up the checkout process, track customers through the store, and notify customers of discounts as they pass by certain products. Grocery companies also use IT to tightly integrate their supply chains for maximum efficiency and thus reduce prices for shoppers.

Competition also is being affected by the extremely low variable cost of digital products. That is, once a digital product has been developed, the cost of producing additional "units" approaches zero. Consider the music industry as an example. When artists record music, their songs are captured in digital format. Physical products, such as CDs or DVDs of the songs for sale in music stores, involve costs. The costs of a physical distribution channel are much higher than those involved in delivering the songs digitally over the Internet.

In fact, in the future companies might give away some products for free. For example, some analysts predict that commissions for online stock trading will approach zero because investors can search the Internet for information to make their own decisions regarding buying and selling stocks. At that point, consumers will no longer need brokers to give them information that they can obtain themselves, virtually for free.

## Porter's Value Chain Model

Organizations use Porter's competitive forces model to design general strategies. To identify specific activities where they can use competitive strategies for greatest impact, they use his value chain model (1985). A **value chain** is a sequence of activities through which the organization's inputs, whatever they are, are transformed into more valuable outputs, whatever they are. The **value chain model** identifies points where an organization can use information technology to achieve competitive advantage (see Figure 2.4).

According to Porter's value chain model, the activities conducted in any organization can be divided into two categories: primary activities and support activities. **Primary activities** relate to the production and distribution of the firm's products and services. These activities create value for which customers are willing to pay. The primary activities are buttressed by **support activities**. Unlike primary activities, support activities do not add value directly to the firm's products or services. Rather, as their name suggests, they contribute to the firm's competitive advantage by supporting the primary activities.

Next, you will see examples of primary and support activities in the value chain of a manufacturing company. Keep in mind that other types of firms, such as transportation, healthcare, education, retail, and others, have different value chains. The key point is that *every* organization has a value chain.

**FIGURE 2.4** Porter's value chain model.

**SUPPORT ACTIVITIES**

| Administration and management | Legal, accounting, finance management | Electronic scheduling and message systems; collaborative workflow intranet |
| Human resource management | Personnel, recruiting, training, career development | Workforce planning systems; employee benefits intranet |
| Product and technology development | Product and process design, production engineering, research and development | Computer-aided design systems; product development extranet with partners |
| Procurement | Supplier management, funding, subcontracting, specification | E-commerce Web portal for suppliers |

**PRIMARY ACTIVITIES**

| Inbound logistics | Operations | Outbound logistics | Marketing and sales | Customer service |
|---|---|---|---|---|
| Quality control; receiving; raw materials control; supply schedules | Manufacturing; packaging; production control; quality control; maintenance | Finishing goods; order handling; dispatch; delivery; invoicing | Customer management; order taking; promotion; sales analysis; market research | Warranty; maintenance; education and training; upgrades |
| Automated warehousing systems | Computer-controlled machining systems; computer-aided flexible manufacturing | Automated shipment scheduling systems; online point of sale and order processing | Computerized ordering systems; targeted marketing | Customer relationship management systems |

**FIRM ADDS VALUE**

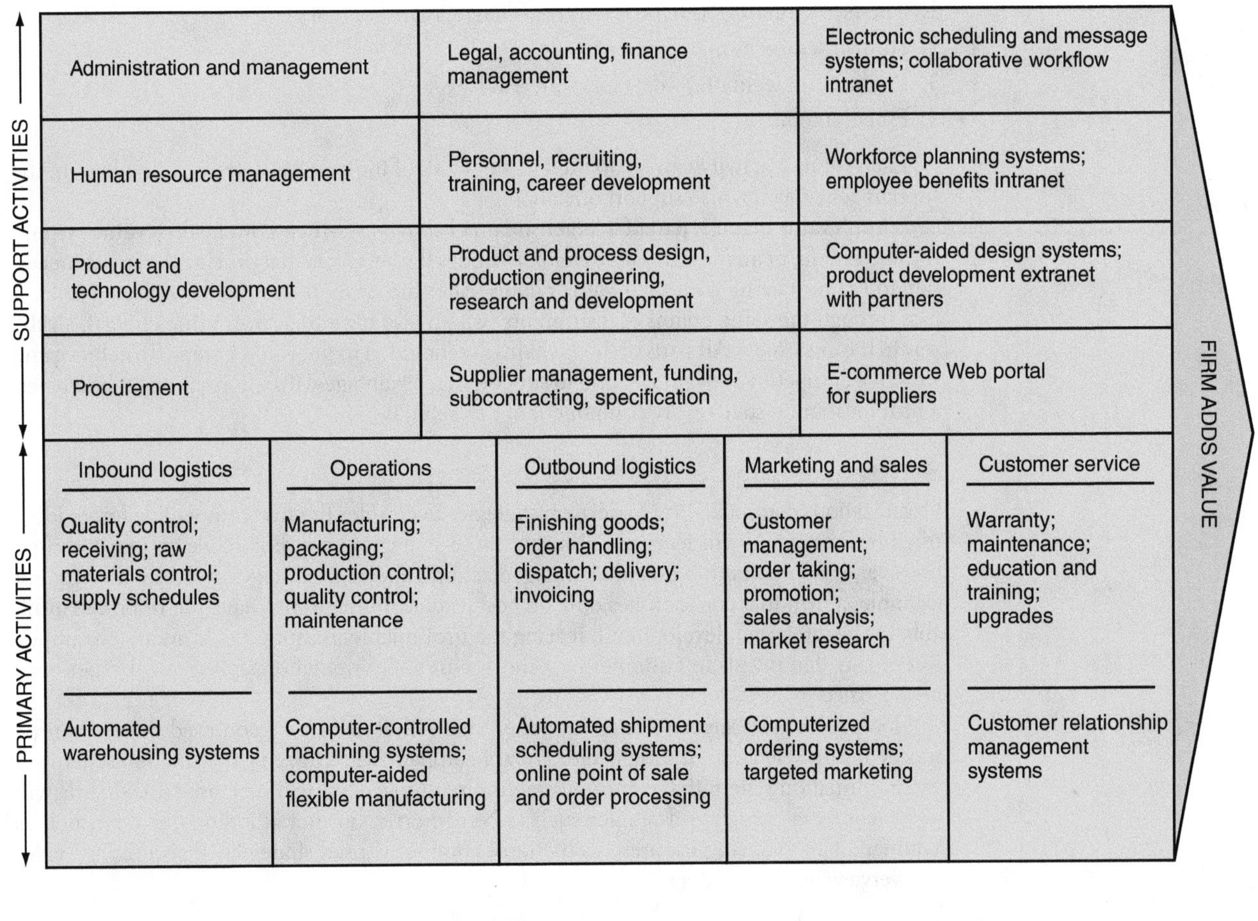

In a manufacturing company, primary activities involve purchasing materials, processing the materials into products, and delivering the products to customers. Manufacturing companies typically perform five primary activities in the following sequence:

1. Inbound logistics (inputs)
2. Operations (manufacturing and testing)
3. Outbound logistics (storage and distribution)
4. Marketing and sales
5. Services

As work progresses in this sequence, value is added to the product in each activity. Specifically, the following steps occur:

1. The incoming materials are processed (in receiving, storage, and so on) in activities called *inbound logistics*.
2. The materials are used in operations, where value is added by turning raw materials into products.
3. These products are prepared for delivery (packaging, storing, and shipping) in the outbound logistics activities.
4. Marketing and sales sell the products to customers, increasing product value by creating demand for the company's products.
5. Finally, the company performs after-sales service for the customer, such as warranty service or upgrade notification, adding further value.

As noted above, the primary activities are buttressed by support activities. Support activities consist of the following:

1. The firm's infrastructure (accounting, finance, management)
2. Human resources management
3. Product and technology development (R&D)
4. Procurement

Each support activity can be applied to any or all of the primary activities. In addition, the support activities can also support one another.

A firm's value chain is part of a larger stream of activities, which Porter calls a **value system**. A value system, or an *industry value chain*, includes the suppliers that provide the inputs necessary to the firm along with their value chains. After the firm creates products, these products pass through the value chains of distributors (which also have their own value chains), all the way to the customers. All parts of these chains are included in the value system. To achieve and sustain a competitive advantage, and to support that advantage with information technologies, a firm must understand every component of this value system.

## Strategies for Competitive Advantage

Organizations continually try to develop strategies to counter the five competitive forces identified by Porter. You will learn about five of those strategies here. Before we go into specifics, however, it is important to note that an organization's choice of strategy involves trade-offs. For example, a firm that concentrates only on cost leadership might not have the resources available for research and development, leaving the firm unable to innovate. As another example, a company that invests in customer happiness (customer orientation strategy) will experience increased costs.

Companies must select a strategy and then stay with it, because a confused strategy cannot succeed. This selection, in turn, decides how a company will utilize its information systems. A new information system that can improve customer service but will increase costs slightly will be welcomed at a high-end retailer such as Nordstrom's, but not at a discount store such as Walmart. The following list presents the most commonly used strategies. Figure 2.5 provides an overview of these strategies.

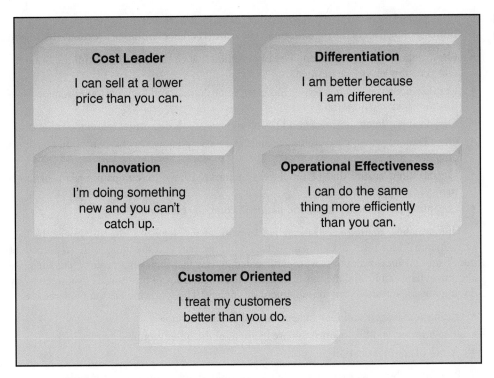

**FIGURE 2.5** Strategies for competitive advantage.

1. *Cost leadership strategy*. Produce products and/or services at the lowest cost in the industry. An example is Walmart's automatic inventory replenishment system, which enables Walmart to reduce inventory storage requirements. As a result, Walmart stores use floor space only to sell products, and not to store them, thereby reducing inventory costs.

2. *Differentiation strategy*. Offer different products, services, or product features than your competitors. Southwest Airlines, for example, has differentiated itself as a low-cost, short-haul, express airline. This has proved to be a winning strategy for competing in the highly competitive airline industry.

3. *Innovation strategy*. Introduce new products and services, add new features to existing products and services, or develop new ways to produce them. A classic example is the introduction of automated teller machines (ATMs) by Citibank. The convenience and cost-cutting features of this innovation gave Citibank a huge advantage over its competitors. Like many innovative products, the ATM changed the nature of competition in the banking industry. Today, an ATM is a competitive *necessity* for any bank. Another excellent example is Apple's rapid introduction of innovative products.

4. *Operational effectiveness strategy*. Improve the manner in which a firm executes its internal business processes so that it performs these activities more effectively than its rivals. Such improvements increase quality, productivity, and employee and customer satisfaction while decreasing time to market.

5. *Customer orientation strategy*. Concentrate on making customers happy. Web-based systems are particularly effective in this area because they can create a personalized, one-to-one relationship with each customer. Amazon (*www.amazon.com*), Apple (*www.apple.com*), and Starbucks (*www.starbucks.com*) are classical examples of companies devoted to customer satisfaction.

## Business–Information Technology Alignment

The best way for organizations to maximize the strategic value of IT is to achieve business–information technology alignment. In fact, the "holy grail" of organizations is business–information technology alignment, or strategic alignment (which we will call simply *alignment*). **Business–information technology alignment** is the tight integration of the IT function with the organization's strategy, mission, and goals. That is, the IT function directly supports the business objectives of the organization. There are six characteristics of excellent alignment:

- Organizations view IT as an engine of innovation that continually transforms the business, often creating new revenue streams.
- Organizations view their internal and external customers and their customer service function as supremely important.
- Organizations rotate business and IT professionals across departments and job functions.
- Organizations provide overarching goals that are completely clear to each IT and business employee.
- Organizations ensure that IT employees understand how the company makes (or loses) money.
- Organizations create a vibrant and inclusive company culture.

Unfortunately, many organizations fail to achieve this type of close alignment. In fact, according to a McKinsey & Company survey on IT strategy and spending, only 16 percent of the IT and business executives who participated agreed that their organization had adequate alignment between IT and the business. Given the importance of business–IT alignment, why do so many organizations fail to implement this policy? The following are the major reasons:

- Business managers and IT managers have different objectives.
- The business and IT departments are ignorant of the other group's expertise.
- A lack of communication.

Put simply, business executives often know little about information technology, and IT executives understand the technology but may not understand the real needs of the business. One solution to this problem is to foster a collaborative environment in organizations so that business and IT executives can communicate freely and learn from each other.

Businesses can also utilize enterprise architecture to foster alignment. Originally developed as a tool to organize a company's IT initiatives, the enterprise architecture concept has evolved to encompass both a technical specification (the information and communication technologies and the information systems used in an organization) and a business specification (a collection of core business processes and management activities). IT's About Business 2.5 illustrates effective business–IT alignment at the University of Pittsburgh Medical Center (UPMC).

# IT's [about business]

## 2.5 The University of Pittsburgh Medical Center Makes Effective Use of IT

The University of Pittsburgh Medical Center (www.upmc.com) is one of the country's largest nonprofit healthcare organizations. Its revenues for fiscal year 2013 totaled more than $10 billion. UPMC operates more than 20 hospitals and 400 physician offices and outpatient sites in Pennsylvania. It is also one of the state's largest health insurance plans. In its dual role of provider and payer, UPMC services more than 2 million customers. The center has implemented an aggressive approach to implementing and developing information technology to make healthcare more effective and efficient.

UPMC's IT organization performs several major roles. For example, it must improve the operations of the company's hospitals and health insurance plan, enhance patient care, and drive down the company's costs. In addition, it should be profitable for UPMC rather than function as a cost center. Finally, it has the mandate to develop unique technologies that the company can sell to other healthcare providers and insurers.

UPMC's IT initiatives are developed at its Technology Development Center (TDC), a business incubator and laboratory located in Pittsburgh. The TDC's mission is to develop new healthcare technologies and then to provide resources for startup companies to develop these technologies. (A business incubator is an organization that speeds up the growth and success of startup and early-stage companies. Just a few of the services provided by incubators are help with business basics, marketing assistance, high-speed Internet access, help with accounting and financial management, and help with bank loans.)

The TDC initially attempts to use off-the-shelf technology to meet the needs of its clinicians, insurance teams, and other business groups. (Off-the-shelf technology are products that are ready-made and available for sale to the public.) For example, it uses electronic health record (EHR) systems from Cerner (*www.cerner.com*) and Epic (*www.epic.com*). If it cannot find the technology it needs, then it will look to develop that technology, often in a joint venture with a large vendor. Another strategy is to purchase a stake in a startup, in which case it can influence the development process.

One example of a technology that TDC is developing is a telemedicine system called Virtual Care Collaboration (VCC). VCC combines videoconferencing with medical records. The greatest obstacle to telemedicine is not the technology, but the business model. For example, health insurance plans often will not pay for telemedicine consultations, and licensing rules can prevent doctors from treating patients across state lines. To combat these problems and to provide impetus for the practice of telemedicine, the UPMC health plan and some other insurers are starting to cover telemedicine appointments.

UPMC's IT group is also utilizing cloud computing, a system in which tasks are performed by networked computers in remote locations (the cloud). (We discuss cloud computing in Technology Guide 3.) Cloud computing presents problems for the healthcare industry because it typically requires patient data to leave the healthcare providers' data centers. In early 2015, UPMC had more than 5 petabytes of data, and that volume was doubling every 18 months. These data include medical images, genomic data (data about the complete set of genetic information for each patient which is encoded in the patient's chromosomes), and remote patient monitoring data. UPMC could not afford to spend tens of millions of dollars to build data centers with the capacity to store all of that data. Therefore, the center turned to the cloud. Specifically, it rents storage infrastructure from cloud computing vendors such as Amazon and IBM.

UPMC's IT group is also creating a data warehouse that combines clinical, genomic, insurance, financial, and other information from more than 200 data sources. (We discuss data warehouses in detail in Chapter 5.) This initiative ties into the aspect of the U.S. healthcare reform that intends to change how healthcare is delivered and paid for. Providers will be paid to keep a group of people—for example, all the employees at a company—healthy rather than treat them after they become ill. This arrangement creates a financial incentive for providers to increase their preventive care efforts and to minimize mishaps that lead to hospital readmissions.

UPMC cannot accomplish its goals without analytics. Consider a recent UPMC study of the use of a particular catheter. The study revealed that the catheter was not used consistently, although on average it led to better outcomes. The study also found that the catheter was more expensive than other similar catheters. These findings led to the next analysis that examined which patients benefited from the catheter and under which circumstances. The findings were presented to doctors to help them make decisions about the use of the catheter. Ongoing projects include analyzing patients' individual genomes so that health providers can personalize their treatments.

UPMC has experienced some IT problems. For example, problems occurred in the implementation of electronic health records that were needed to comply with government mandates and financial incentives. As one example, new technologies allow physicians to cut-and-paste electronic records. As a result, an in-hospital progress note that used to present the patient's daily status in less than 1 page can now total 19 pages.

*Sources:* Compiled from B. Toland, "Pitt, UPMC Reach Commercialization Agreement," *Pittsburgh Post-Gazette*, February 20, 2015; K. Mamula, "Pitt, UPMC to Speed Commercialization Push," *Pittsburgh Business Times*, February 20, 2015; N. Versel, "The Evolution of Health IT Continues," *U.S. News & World Report*, February 6, 2014; "Information Technology Is Changing the Healthcare System," *The Washington Post*, January 12, 2014; D. Gardner, "Healthcare Turns to Big Data Analytics for Improved Patient Outcomes," *ZDNet*, December 12, 2013; C. Murphy, "UPMC Plays to Win in the Tech Game," *InformationWeek*, September 9, 2013; E. McCann, "Clinical Data Analytics Next Big Thing," *Healthcare IT News*, August 27, 2013; V. Ramachandran, "How Is Information Technology Changing Healthcare?" *Mashable*, August 15, 2013; S. Tibkin, "Numbers, Numbers, and More Numbers," *The Wall Street Journal*, February 14, 2013; E. Topol, "The Future of Healthcare: Information Technology," *Modern Healthcare*, July 25, 2011; *www.upmc.com*, accessed February 20, 2015.

**Questions**

1. Describe the strategic advantages that IT provides to UPMC.
2. Which of Porter's competitive strategies is UPMC employing? Support your answer.
3. Describe how UPMC illustrates effective business–IT alignment.

# before you go on...

1. What are strategic information systems?
2. According to Porter, what are the five forces that could endanger a firm's position in its industry or marketplaces?
3. Describe Porter's value chain model. Differentiate between Porter's competitive forces model and his value chain model.
4. What strategies can companies use to gain competitive advantage?
5. What is business–IT alignment?
6. Give examples of business–IT alignment at your university, regarding student systems. (Hint: What are the "business" goals of your university with regard to student registration, fee payment, grade posting, etc.?)

# What's In IT For Me?

## For All Business Majors

All functional areas of any organization are literally composed of a variety of business processes, as we can see from the examples in this chapter. Regardless of your major, you will be involved in a variety of business processes from your first day on the job. Some of these processes you will do by yourself, some will involve only your group, team, or department, while others will involve several (or all) functional areas of your organization.

It is important for you to be able to visualize processes, understand the inputs and outputs of each process, and know the "customer" of each process. If you can do these things, you will contribute to making processes more efficient and effective, which often means incorporating information technology in the process. It is also important for you to know how each process fits into your organization's strategy.

All functional areas in any organization must work together in an integrated fashion in order for the firm to respond adequately to business pressures. These responses typically require each functional area to utilize a variety of information systems to support, document, and manage cross-functional business processes. In today's competitive global marketplace, the timeliness and accuracy of these responses are even more critical.

Closely following this discussion, all functional areas must work together for the organization to gain competitive advantage in its marketplace. Again, the functional areas use a variety of strategic information systems to achieve this goal. BPR and BPI process change efforts contribute to the goal as well.

You have seen why companies must be concerned with strategic advantage. But why is this chapter so important for you? There are several reasons. First, the business pressures you have learned about have an impact on your organization, but they also affect you as an individual. So, it is critical that you understand how information systems can help you, and eventually your organization, respond to these pressures.

In addition, achieving competitive advantage is essential for your organization's survival. In many cases, you, your team, and all your colleagues will be responsible for creating a competitive advantage. Therefore, having general knowledge about strategy and about how information systems affect the organization's strategy and competitive position will help you in your career.

You also need a basic knowledge of your organization's strategy, mission, and goals, as well as its business problems and how it makes (or loses) money. You now know how to analyze your organization's strategy and value chain, as well as the strategies and value chains of your competitors. You also have acquired a general knowledge of how information technology contributes to organizational strategy. This knowledge will help you to do your job better, to be promoted more quickly, and to contribute significantly to the success of your organization.

## [ Summary ]

1. **Discuss ways in which information systems enable cross-functional business processes and processes for a single functional area.**

   A business process is an ongoing collection of related activities that produce a product or a service of value to the organization, its business partners, and/or its customers. Examples of business processes in the functional areas include managing accounts payable, managing accounts receivable, managing after-sale customer follow-up, managing bills of materials, managing manufacturing change orders, applying disability policies, employee hiring, computer user/staff training, and applying Internet use policy. The procurement and fulfillment processes are examples of cross-functional business processes.

2. **Compare and contrast business process reengineering and business process management to determine the different advantages and disadvantages of each.**

Business process reengineering is a radical redesign of business processes that is intended to improve the efficiency and effectiveness of an organization's business processes. The key to BPR is for enterprises to examine their business processes from a "clean sheet" perspective and then determine how they can best reconstruct those processes to improve their business functions. Because BPR proved difficult to implement, organizations have turned to business process management. Business process management is a management technique that includes methods and tools to support the design, analysis, implementation, management, and optimization of business processes.

3. **Identify effective IT responses to different kinds of business pressures.**

*Market pressures:* An example of a market pressure is powerful customers. Customer relationship management is an effective IT response that helps companies achieve customer intimacy.

*Technology pressures:* An example of a technology pressure is information overload. Search engines and business intelligence applications enable managers to access, navigate, and utilize vast amounts of information.

*Societal/political/legal pressures:* An example of a societal/political/legal pressure is social responsibility, such as the state of the physical environment. Green IT is one response that is intended to improve the environment.

4. **Describe the strategies that organizations typically adopt to counter Porter's five competitive forces.**

Porter's five competitive forces:

*The threat of entry of new competitors:* For most firms, the Web increases the threat that new competitors will enter the market by reducing traditional barriers to entry. Frequently, competitors need only to set up a Web site to enter a market. The Web can also increase barriers to entry, as when customers come to expect a nontrivial capability from their suppliers.

*The bargaining power of suppliers:* The Web enables buyers to find alternative suppliers and to compare prices more easily, thereby reducing suppliers' bargaining power. From a different perspective, as companies use the Web to integrate their supply chains, participating suppliers can lock in customers, thereby increasing suppliers' bargaining power.

*The bargaining power of customers (buyers):* The Web provides customers with incredible amounts of choices for products, as well as information about those choices. As a result, the Web increases buyer power. However, companies can implement loyalty programs in which they use the Web to monitor the activities of millions of customers. Such programs reduce buyer power.

*The threat of substitute products or services:* New technologies create substitute products very rapidly, and the Web makes information about these products available almost instantly. As a result, industries (particularly information-based industries) are in great danger from substitutes (e.g., music, books, newspapers, magazines, and software). However, the Web can also enable a company to build in switching costs, so that it will cost customers time and/or money to switch from your company to a competitor.

*The rivalry among existing firms in the industry:* In the past, proprietary information systems provided strategic advantage for firms in highly competitive industries. The visibility of Internet applications on the Web makes proprietary systems more difficult to keep secret. Therefore, the Web makes strategic advantage more short-lived.

The five strategies are as follows:

*Cost leadership strategy*: produce products and/or services at the lowest cost in the industry.

*Differentiation strategy*: offer different products, services, or product features.

*Innovation strategy*: introduce new products and services, put new features in existing products and services, or develop new ways to produce them.

*Operational effectiveness strategy*: improve the manner in which internal business processes are executed so that a firm performs similar activities better than its rivals.

*Customer orientation strategy*: concentrate on making customers happy.

# [ Chapter Glossary ]

**business environment** The combination of social, legal, economic, physical, and political factors in which businesses conduct their operations.

**business–information technology alignment** The tight integration of the IT function with the strategy, mission, and goals of the organization.

**business process** A collection of related activities that create a product or a service of value to the organization, its business partners, and/or its customers.

**business process management** A management technique that includes methods and tools to support the design, analysis, implementation, management, and optimization of business processes.

**business process reengineering** A radical redesign of a business process that improves its efficiency and effectiveness, often by beginning with a "clean sheet" (i.e., from scratch).

**competitive advantage** An advantage over competitors in some measure such as cost, quality, or speed; leads to control of a market and to larger-than-average profits.

**competitive forces model** A business framework devised by Michael Porter that analyzes competitiveness by recognizing five major forces that could endanger a company's position.

**cross-functional processes** No single functional area is responsible for a process's execution.

**digital divide** The gap between those who have access to information and communications technology and those who do not.

**entry barrier** Product or service feature that customers expect from organizations in a certain industry; an organization trying to enter this market must provide this product or service at a minimum to be able to compete.

**globalization** The integration and interdependence of economic, social, cultural, and ecological facets of life, enabled by rapid advances in information technology.

**individual social responsibility** See **organizational social responsibility**.

**make-to-order** The strategy of producing customized products and services.

**mass customization** A production process in which items are produced in large quantities but are customized to fit the desires of each customer.

**organizational social responsibility (also individual social responsibility)** Efforts by organizations to solve various social problems.

**primary activities** Those business activities related to the production and distribution of the firm's products and services, thus creating value.

**strategic information systems (SISs)** Systems that help an organization gain a competitive advantage by supporting its strategic goals and/or increasing performance and productivity.

**support activities** Business activities that do not add value directly to a firm's product or service under consideration but support the primary activities that do add value.

**value chain** A sequence of activities through which the organization's inputs, whatever they are, are transformed into more valuable outputs, whatever they are.

**value chain model** Model that shows the primary activities that sequentially add value to the profit margin; also shows the support activities.

**value system** Includes the producers, suppliers, distributors, and buyers, all with their value chains.

# [ Discussion Questions ]

1. Consider the student registration process at your university:
   - Describe the steps necessary for you to register for your classes each semester.
   - Describe how information technology is used (or is not used) in each step of the process.

2. Why is it so difficult for an organization to actually implement business process reengineering?

3. Explain why IT is both a business pressure and an enabler of response activities that counter business pressures.

4. What does a flat world mean to you in your choice of a major? In your choice of a career? Will you have to be a "lifelong learner"? Why or why not?

5. What might the impact of a flat world be on your standard of living?

6. Is IT a strategic weapon or a survival tool? Discuss.

7. Why might it be difficult to justify a strategic information system?

8. Describe the five forces in Porter's competitive forces model, and explain how increased access to high-speed Internet has affected each one.

9. Describe Porter's value chain model. What is the relationship between the competitive forces model and the value chain model?

10. Describe how IT can be used to support different value chains for different companies.

11. Discuss the idea that an information system by itself can rarely provide a sustainable competitive advantage.

## [ Problem-Solving Activities ]

1. Surf the Internet for information about the Department of Homeland Security. Examine the available information, and comment on the role of information technologies in the department.

2. Experience mass customization by designing your own shoes at *www.nike.com*, your car at *www.jaguar.com*, your CD at *www.easternrecording.com*, your business card at *www.iprint.com*, and your diamond ring at *www.bluenile.com*. Summarize your experiences.

3. Access *www.go4customer.com*. What does this company do and where is it located? Who are its customers? Which of Friedman's flatteners does this company fit? Provide examples of how a U.S. company would use its services.

4. Enter Walmart China (*www.wal-martchina.com/english/index.htm*). How does Walmart China differ from your local Walmart (consider products, prices, services, etc.)? Describe these differences.

5. Apply Porter's value chain model to Costco (*www.costco.com*). What is Costco's competitive strategy? Who are Costco's major competitors? Describe Costco's business model. Describe the tasks that Costco must accomplish for each primary value chain activity. How would Costco's

information systems contribute to Costco's competitive strategy, given the nature of its business?

6. Apply Porter's value chain model to Dell (*www.dell.com*). What is Dell's competitive strategy? Who are Dell's major competitors? Describe Dell's business model. Describe the tasks that Dell must accomplish for each primary value chain activity. How would Dell's information systems contribute to Dell's competitive strategy, given the nature of its business?

7. The market for optical copiers is shrinking rapidly. It is estimated that 90 percent of all duplicated documents are generated by computer printers. Can a company such as Xerox Corporation survive?

   a. Read about the problems and solutions of Xerox from 2000 to 2010 at *www.fortune.com*, *www.findarticles.com*, and *www.google.com*.

   b. Identify all the business pressures on Xerox.

   c. Find some of Xerox's response strategies (see *www.xerox.com*, *www.yahoo.com*, and *www.google.com*).

   d. Identify the role of IT as a contributor to the business technology pressures (e.g., obsolescence).

   e. Identify the role of IT as a facilitator of Xerox's critical response activities.

## [ Closing Case IBM's Watson ]

### The Problem

Computer scientists have long sought to design computer-based information systems (CBISs) that interact in natural human terms across a range of applications and processes, comprehending the questions that humans ask and providing answers that humans can understand. A major step toward achieving this goal is the development of the IBM Watson system.

### An Interesting IT Solution

IBM (*www.ibm.com*) has developed an artificial intelligence CBIS capable of answering questions posed in natural language.

(We discuss artificial intelligence in Technology Guide 4.) IBM named the system "Watson," after the company's founder, Thomas J. Watson, Sr. IBM asserts that Watson processes information more like a computer than a human. In fact, Watson is an application of advanced natural language processing, information retrieval, knowledge representation and reasoning, and machine learning technologies to the field of open-domain (general) question answering. IBM has labeled the type of processing demonstrated by Watson as *cognitive computing*.

IBM developed Watson specifically to answer questions on the quiz show *Jeopardy!*. In February 2011, Watson competed on *Jeopardy!* against former winners Brad Rutter and Ken

Jennings. Watson won the game series and received the first prize of $1 million. (In *Jeopardy!*, the host reads the answer, and the contestants must then provide the correct question.)

# The Results

Following the television performance, IBM executives immediately turned their attention to commercializing Watson. Today, Watson is being employed by a wide variety of organizations, to address a diverse set of problems.

One of Watson's earliest applications was in the field of medicine. IBM executives chose medicine because Watson could have a distinctive social impact while also proving its ability to master a complex body of knowledge.

- *Medicine* was a logical choice. Although some health data are structured—for example, blood pressure readings and cholesterol counts—the vast majority are unstructured. These data include textbooks, medical journals, patient records, and nurse and physician notes. In fact, modern medicine entails so much unstructured data that its rapid growth has surpassed the ability of healthcare practitioners to keep up. It is important to note here that IBM has made it clear that Watson is *not* intended to replace doctors. Rather, its purpose is to assist them in avoiding medical errors and sharpening their medical diagnoses.

  Enter Watson. Watson can read all of the world's medical journals in seconds. The system can read, and remember, patient histories, monitor the latest drug trials, examine the potency of new therapies, and closely follow state-of-the-art guidelines that help doctors choose the best treatments. Watson can also analyze images such as MRIs and EKGs.

  In early 2015, the three top-ranked *U.S. News & World Report for Health* 2014–2015 hospitals in cancer care were working with Watson: Memorial Sloan Kettering (*www.mskcc.org*), MD Anderson Cancer Center (*www.mdanderson.org*), and the Mayo Clinic (*www.mayoclinic.org*). In addition, the Cleveland Clinic and the New York Genome Center are using Watson in the new field of genomic-based medicine. Similarly, Pathway Genomics (*www.pathway.com*) employs Watson to provide personalized options to help patients and their physicians make informed decisions about living a healthier life.

- *Customer service.* The Watson Engagement Advisor is designed to help customer-facing personnel assist consumers with deeper insights more quickly than was previously possible. Engagement Advisor's "Ask Watson" feature can quickly address customers' questions, offer feedback to guide their purchase decisions, and troubleshoot their problems. Companies employing the Advisor include USAA (*www.usaa.com*), Genesys (*www.genesys.com*), DBS Bank of Singapore (*www.dbs.com.sg*), and many others.

  - USAA is also using Watson to assist military personnel in transitioning from the military to civilian life.

  - RedAnt (*www.redant.com*) uses Watson to transform how consumers shop. It also used Watson to develop a retail sales trainer that lets employees easily identify individual customers' buying preferences by analyzing demographics, purchase history, and wish lists, as well as product information, local pricing, customer reviews, and tech specs.

  - MD Buyline (*www.mdbuyline.com*) uses Watson to help hospitals procure medical devices.

  - Welltok (*www.welltok.com*) uses Watson to enable health plans to more effectively engage their members.

- *Financial services.* Many financial organizations have integrated Watson into their business processes. As one example, Citigroup (*www.citigroup.com*) employs Watson to analyze financial, regulatory, economic, and social data across financial exchanges, currencies, and funds to help simplify and improve the bank's digital interactions with its customers.

- *Travel services.* Terry Jones, founder of Travelocity (*www.travelocity.com*) and Kayak (*www.kayak.com*), has launched WayBlazer (*www.wayblazer.com*), a new travel company powered by Watson. Watson engages, learns, and advises users through a natural language interface to help create the best travel experience.

- *Other interesting applications*:

  - Macy's (*www.macys.com*) uses Watson to better target Millennials by interpreting their social signals on social media.

  - BNSF Railway (*www.bnsf.com*) is using Watson to help detect faulty sections in the company's 32,500 miles of track before they break.

  - Repsol (*www.repsol.com*) is using Watson to improve its strategic decision making in the optimization of oil reservoir production and in the discovery of new oilfields.

In February 2014, IBM announced that it was deploying Watson to Africa to encourage business opportunities across the world's fastest-growing continent. Watson eventually will be available for use in key areas such as education, water and sanitation, and agriculture.

One year later, IBM announced an alliance with Japanese telecommunications giant SoftBank (*www.softbank.jp/en*). As part of the deal, Watson is learning to speak and think in Japanese, one of the most challenging languages for a computer system because it relies on a pictorial alphabet known as kanji.

By early 2015, hundreds of IBM clients and partners across 6 continents, 25 countries, and 12 industries had projects underway with Watson. IBM executives asserted that Watson was 24 times faster, 2400 percent more powerful, and less than 10 percent the size of the system that won *Jeopardy!*. In fact, Watson has shrunk from the size of a master bedroom to that of three stacked pizza boxes.

*Sources:* Compiled from "IBM Watson Group Invests in Pathway Genomics to Help Personalize Consumer Health," *IBM News Release*, November 2014; "IBM's $100M 'Project Lucy' Brings Watson to Africa," *KurzweilAI.net*, February 7, 2014;

D. Henschen, "With Watson, Is IBM Riding the Right Wave?" *InformationWeek*, January 10, 2014; A. Regalado, "Facing Doubters, IBM Expands Plans for Watson," *MIT Technology Review*, January 9, 2014; L. Dignan, "IBM Form Watson Business Group: Will Commercialization Follow?" *ZDNet*, January 9, 2014; J. Best, "IBM Watson: How the Jeopardy-Winning Supercomputer Was Born and What It Wants to Do Next," *TechRepublic*, November 4, 2013; "MD Anderson Cancer Center Taps IBM Watson to Power Its Mission to Eradicate Cancer," *KurzweilAI.net*, October 20, 2013; "IBM Research Unveils Two New Watson-Related Projects from Cleveland Clinic Collaboration," *KurzweilAI.net*, October 20, 2013; J. Hempel, "IBM's Massive Bet on Watson," *Fortune*, October 7, 2013; T. Simonite, "Trained on Jeopardy, Watson Is Headed for Your Pocket," *MIT Technology Review*, May 28, 2013; "IBM Watson Engagement Advisor Hopes to Improve Customer Service," *KurzweilAI.net*, May 22, 2013; "Watson Provides Cancer Treatment Options to Doctors in Seconds," *KurzweilAI.net*, February 11, 2013; N. Leske, "Doctors Seek Help on Cancer Treatment from IBM Supercomputer," *Reuters*, February 8, 2013; B. Upbin, "IBM's Watson Gets Its First Piece of Business in Healthcare," *Forbes*, February 8, 2013; J. Fitzgerald, "Watson Supercomputer Offers Medical Expertise," *USA Today*, February 8, 2013; *www.ibm.com/watson*, accessed February 22, 2015.

## Questions

1. What applications can you think of for Watson in a university setting?

2. What are potential disadvantages of using Watson in healthcare settings?

3. Would you consider being diagnosed only by Watson? Why or why not?

4. Would you consider being diagnosed by your personal physician, if he or she consulted Watson? Why or why not?

# 3 Ethics and Privacy

| [ LEARNING OBJECTIVES ] | [ CHAPTER OUTLINE ] | [ WEB RESOURCES ] |
|---|---|---|

**[ LEARNING OBJECTIVES ]**

1. Define ethics, list and describe the three fundamental tenets of ethics, and describe the four categories of ethical issues related to information technology.

2. Identify three places that store personal data, and for each one, discuss at least one potential threat to the privacy of the data stored there.

**[ CHAPTER OUTLINE ]**

3.1 Ethical Issues

3.2 Privacy

**[ WEB RESOURCES ]**

- Student PowerPoints for note taking

**WileyPLUS Learning Space**

- E-book
- Author video lecture for each chapter section
- Practice quizzes
- Flash Cards for vocabulary review
- Additional "IT's About Business" cases
- Video interviews with managers
- Lab Manuals for Microsoft Office 2010 and 2013

## What's In IT For Me?

**This Chapter Will Help Prepare You To...**

| ACCT | FIN | MKT | POM | HRM | MIS |
|---|---|---|---|---|---|
| ACCOUNTING | FINANCE | MARKETING | PRODUCTION OPERATIONS MANAGEMENT | HUMAN RESOURCES MANAGEMENT | MIS |
| Monitor social media for compliance | Collaborate with external financial experts | Receive real-time feedback from customers | Partners/ customers collaborate on product development | Enhance recruiting efforts | Develop internal company social networks |

## The Huge Problem

The National Security Agency (NSA) (*www.nsa.gov*), officially formed in 1952, is a U.S. intelligence agency responsible for global monitoring, collection, decoding, translation, and analysis of information and data for foreign intelligence and counterintelligence purposes. The NSA is also charged with protecting the U.S. government communications and information systems against penetration and network warfare. The NSA is part of the Department of Defense and simultaneously reports to the Director of National Intelligence.

The surveillance efforts of the NSA expanded dramatically under laws passed following the September 11, 2001 terrorist attacks. In 2006, the U.S. Congress approved changes to the Patriot Act that made it easier for the government to collect phone subscriber data under the Foreign Intelligence Surveillance Act (FISA), passed by Congress in 1978. These changes helped the NSA collection programs become institutionalized, rather than being conducted only under the authority of the president. At the same time, advances in information technology have enabled the agency to accumulate and analyze far larger volumes of phone, Internet, social, and financial data to search for potential terrorist activities.

In 2007, the NSA launched another data collection effort, called PRISM, that obtains stored Internet communications from companies such as Google and Apple. These companies are legally required to turn over any data that match search terms approved by the U.S. Foreign Intelligence Surveillance Court (FISC). In addition, the nation's leading Internet firms (Comcast (*www.comcast.com*), Time Warner (*www.timewarnercable.com*), Charter (*www.charter.com*), AT&T (*www.att.com*), and Verizon (*www.verizon.com*)) provided the NSA and the FBI with direct access to their servers and thus to the e-mails, photos, and other private information of hundreds of millions of users both within the United States and around the world. The NSA developed similar relationships with credit card companies.

The NSA's data collection programs had attracted very limited public scrutiny until June 2013 when a computer expert named Edward Snowden, who had previously worked for Booz Allen Hamilton, a major NSA contractor, leaked numerous classified NSA documents. Snowden maintained that he disclosed details of the programs in the hopes of initiating a debate over the U.S. surveillance policies. On June 6, 2013, *The Washington Post* (*www.washingtonpost.com*) and the British newspaper *The Guardian* (*www.theguardian.com*) published Snowden's disclosures.

The public release of these documents forced the Obama administration to acknowledge that it had been collecting many billions of U.S. phone records and monitoring the Internet communications of foreign individuals and organizations that are conducted through Microsoft, Google, Facebook, Apple, and other U.S. technology companies. These revelations immediately generated a storm of controversy.

In fact, the NSA possesses only limited legal authority to spy on U.S. citizens. Nevertheless, the agency has created a surveillance network that covers the Internet communications of more Americans than officials had publicly disclosed. The system has the capacity to reach roughly 75 percent of all the U.S. Internet traffic in the search for foreign intelligence, including a wide array of communications by foreigners and Americans. In some cases, the NSA retains the written content of e-mails sent between citizens within the United States. It also filters domestic phone calls made with Internet technology.

The NSA's filtering process, carried out with the cooperation of the telecommunications companies, is designed to search for communications that either originate or end abroad, or are entirely foreign but happen to be passing through the United States. In its first analysis of the data, the NSA requires telecommunications companies to submit various streams of Internet traffic it believes most likely to contain foreign intelligence. The telecommunications companies must hand over any data the NSA requests under orders from the FISC. This initial step does not involve all Internet traffic. Rather, it focuses on certain areas of interest. In its second analysis, the NSA briefly copies the traffic and decides which communications to retain based on criteria the agency has identified as "strong selectors." A strong selector could be an e-mail address or a large block of computer addresses that correspond to an organization the NSA is monitoring. The NSA examines the content of the communications as well as the ancillary information concerning who is sending and receiving the communications.

According to the documents released by Snowden, the NSA logs almost 5 billion mobile phone location records around the world *every day*, via its CO-TRAVELER system. The agency obtains these data by tapping into the cables that connect mobile networks globally. These cables serve both the U.S. and foreign mobile phones.

The NSA's monitoring of Americans includes customer records from the three major phone networks (Verizon, AT&T, and Sprint Nextel) as well as e-mails and Web searches. In addition, the agency cataloged credit card transactions. As a consequence of the arrangement with the phone companies, every time the majority of Americans make a call, the NSA obtains a record of the location, the number called, the time of the call, and the length of the conversation. This practice, which evolved from warrantless wiretapping programs implemented after 2001, was approved by all three branches of the U.S. government. Telephone and Internet companies find themselves in the uncomfortable position of balancing extensive government demands for information against the need to maintain their customers' trust.

The NSA surveillance programs are not limited to private citizens. Rather, the agency collects data from foreign governments and other targets by accessing thousands of classified documents. Significantly, the NSA routinely spies on allies as well as on foes. The agency's official mission list includes using its surveillance powers to achieve "diplomatic advantage" over such allies as France and Germany and "economic advantage" over Japan and Brazil, among other countries. In just one instance, in September 2013 President Obama was standing uncomfortably beside Brazilian President Dilma Rousseff at an economic conference in Russia. Rousseff was furious when she learned she was a target of NSA eavesdropping. In response to this revelation, she canceled a trip to Washington, and she publicly criticized the NSA program in a speech delivered at the United Nations. Mexico, France, Germany, Spain, and the European Union have also issued protests.

Encryption methods (explained in Chapter 4) are essential to securing personal and corporate information around the world. Encryption technology is considered the backbone of modern digital security, and it is used to protect e-mail systems, personal data, Internet searching, and banking information. However, Snowden also revealed that the U.S. and British intelligence agencies have cracked encryption designed to provide online privacy and security. In a secret effort to defeat encryption, the NSA, along with its British counterpart, the Government Communications Headquarters (GCHQ), have used supercomputers to crack encryption codes and have inserted secret "back doors" (explained in Chapter 4) into software with the help of technology companies.

The NSA went even further. According to a report by Reuters, the NSA paid $10 million to vendor RSA in a secret deal to incorporate a deliberately flawed encryption algorithm into widely used security software. The contract was a part of a NSA campaign to weaken encryption standards in an effort to aid the agency's surveillance programs.

## The Reaction

Critics contend that neither the FISC nor the Congress has made a serious effort to restrict the NSA's data-gathering efforts. They emphasize, for example, that from 1979 through 2012, the FISC rejected only 11 of the more than 33,900 surveillance applications submitted by the U.S. government—roughly 0.03 percent—according to the annual Justice Department reports to Congress.

From its perspective, the NSA defends its practices as legal and respectful of Americans' privacy. In an attempt to ensure privacy, NSA programs employ complex software algorithms that, in effect, operate like filters placed over a stream with holes designed to allow only certain pieces of information flow through. After 9/11, the NSA widened the holes to capture more information when the government broadened its definition of what constitutes "reasonable" data collection.

## The Results

U.S. intelligence officials and the White House argue that the NSA's surveillance programs provide early warnings of terror threats that do not respect geographical boundaries. Nevertheless, in response to the public outcry, in August 2013 President Obama announced plans to overhaul key aspects of the NSA's surveillance programs. The most significant proposal would restructure the FISC by adding an advocate for privacy concerns.

The fallout from Snowden's revelations continues. Technology companies that pass data to the NSA under the PRISM program could face legal actions in the European Union. Companies that operate within the European Union and serve citizens of EU countries are subject to its relatively strict data-protection laws. These laws limit the actions of companies that collect data, and they require these companies to be transparent about how they will use this information and to whom they will disclose it.

In addition, in November 2014 the Obama administration endorsed a legislative proposal to drastically overhaul the NSA's once-secret phone data collection program. The president asserted he wanted to get the NSA out of the business of collecting call records in bulk, while preserving the program's capabilities.

And Edward Snowden? In early 2015, he was granted asylum in Russia.

*Sources:* Compiled from D. Volz, "Edward Snowden: Living in Russia Is 'Great'," *National Journal*, January 8, 2015; S. Dinan, "White House Backs Bill to End NSA Snooping," *The Washington Times*, November 17, 2014; C. Savage, "Obama Is Set to Curb NSA on Call Data," *New York Times*, March 25, 2014; N. Avellana, "FISC Okays Two of President Barack Obama's Proposed Changes to NSA Surveillance," *Venture Capital Post*, February 8, 2014; M. Ferranti, "Report on NSA 'Secret' Payments to RSA Fuels Encryption Controversy," *Network World*, December 22, 2013; B. Gellman and A. Soltani, "NSA Tracking Cellphone Locations Worldwide, Snowden Documents Show," *The Washington Post*, December 4, 2013; S. Shane, "No Morsel Too Minuscule for All-Consuming NSA," *New York Times*, November 2, 2013; November 6–8, 2013; M. Winter, "NSA Cracks Internet Privacy," *USA Today*, September 6, 2013; S. Gorman and J. Valentino-DeVries, "NSA's Reach into U.S. Net Is Deep, Wide," *The Wall Street Journal*, August 21, 2013; S. Gorman, C. Lee, and J. Hook, "Obama Vows Spying Overhaul," *The Wall Street Journal*, August 10–11, 2013; B. Stone and J. Brustein, "This Prism Isn't Reflecting Much Light," *Bloomberg BusinessWeek*, June 24–30, 2013; G. Greenwald and J. Ball, "The Top Secret Rules That Allow NSA to Use US Data Without a Warrant," *The Guardian*, June 20, 2013; G. Greenwald and E. MacAskill, "Boundless Informant: The NSA's Secret Tool to Track Global Surveillance Data," *The Guardian*, June 11, 2013; S. Gorman, A. Entous, and A. Dowell, "Technology Emboldened NSA," *The Wall Street Journal*, June 10, 2013; D. Barrett and D. Yadron, "Contractor Says He Is Source of NSA Leak," *The Wall Street Journal*, June 10, 2013; G. Greenwald, E. MacAskill, and L. Poitras, "Edward Snowden: The Whistleblower behind the NSA Surveillance Revelations," *The Guardian*, June 9, 2013; S. Gorman, E. Perez, and J. Hook, "U.S. Collects Vast Data Trove," *The Wall Street Journal*, June 7, 2013; N. Hopkins, "UK Gathering Secret Intelligence via Covert NSA Operation," *The Guardian*, June 7, 2013; G. Greenwald and E. MacAskill, "NSA Prism Program Taps in to User Data of Apple, Google, and Others," *The Guardian*, June 6, 2013; G. Greenwald, "NSA Collecting Phone Records of Millions of Verizon Customers Daily," *The Guardian*, June 5, 2013; www.nsa.gov, accessed March 29, 2015.

### Questions

1. Present the pros and cons of the NSA's actions.
2. Present the pros and cons of Edward Snowden's actions.
3. Are the NSA's actions legal? Support your answer with specific examples.
4. Are the NSA's actions ethical? Support your answer with specific examples.
5. Were Edward Snowden's actions legal? Support your answer with specific examples.
6. Were Edward Snowden's actions ethical? Support your answer with specific examples.

# Introduction

The chapter opening case about surveillance programs at the National Security Agency addresses the two major issues you will study in this chapter: ethics and privacy. The two issues are closely related to each other and also to IT, and both raise significant questions involving access to information in the digital age. For example: Are the actions of the NSA ethical? Does the NSA violate the privacy of governments, organizations, and individuals? The answers to these questions are not straightforward. In fact, IT has made finding answers to these questions even more difficult.

You will encounter numerous ethical and privacy issues in your career, many of which will involve IT in some manner. This chapter will provide insights into how to respond to these issues. Furthermore, it will help you to make immediate contributions to your company's code of ethics and its privacy policies. You will also be able to provide meaningful input concerning the potential ethical and privacy impacts of your organization's information systems on people within and outside the organization.

For example, suppose your organization decides to adopt social computing technologies (which you will study in Chapter 9) to include business partners and customers in new product development. You will be able to analyze the potential privacy and ethical implications of implementing these technologies.

All organizations, large and small, must be concerned with ethics. In particular, small business (or startup) owners face a very difficult situation when their employees have access to sensitive customer information. There is a delicate balance between access to information and the appropriate use of that information. This balance is best maintained by hiring honest and trustworthy employees who abide by the organization's code of ethics. Ultimately this issue leads to another question: Does the small business, or a startup, even have a code of ethics to fall back on in this type of situation?

# 3.1 Ethical Issues

**Ethics** refers to the principles of right and wrong that individuals use to make choices that guide their behavior. Deciding what is right or wrong is not always easy or clear-cut. Fortunately, there are many frameworks that can help us make ethical decisions.

## Ethical Frameworks

There are many sources for ethical standards. Here we consider four widely used standards: the utilitarian approach, the rights approach, the fairness approach, and the common good approach. There are many other sources, but these four are representative.

The *utilitarian approach* states that an ethical action is the one that provides the most good or does the least harm. The ethical corporate action would be the one that produces the greatest good and does the least harm for all affected parties—customers, employees, shareholders, the community, and the physical environment.

The *rights approach* maintains that an ethical action is the one that best protects and respects the moral rights of the affected parties. Moral rights can include the rights to make one's own choices about what kind of life to lead, to be told the truth, not to be injured, and to enjoy a degree of privacy. Which of these rights people are actually entitled to—and under what circumstances—is widely debated. Nevertheless, most people acknowledge that individuals are entitled to some moral rights. An ethical organizational action would be one that protects and respects the moral rights of customers, employees, shareholders, business partners, and even competitors.

The *fairness approach* posits that ethical actions treat all human beings equally, or, if unequally, then fairly, based on some defensible standard. For example, most people might believe it is fair to pay people higher salaries if they work harder or if they contribute a greater amount to the firm. However, there is less certainty regarding CEO salaries that are hundreds or thousands of times larger than those of other employees. Many people question whether this huge disparity is based on a defensible standard or whether it is the result of an imbalance of power and hence is unfair.

Finally, the *common good approach* highlights the interlocking relationships that underlie all societies. This approach argues that respect and compassion for all others is the basis for ethical actions. It emphasizes the common conditions that are important to the welfare of everyone. These conditions can include a system of laws, effective police and fire departments, healthcare, a public educational system, and even public recreation areas.

If we combine these four standards, we can develop a general framework for ethics (or ethical decision making). This framework consists of five steps:

- Recognize an ethical issue:
  - Could this decision or situation damage someone or some group?
  - Does this decision involve a choice between a good and a bad alternative?
  - Does this issue involve more than simply legal considerations? If so, then in what way?
- Get the facts:
  - What are the relevant facts of the situation?
  - Do I have sufficient information to make a decision?

- ○ Which individuals and/or groups have an important stake in the outcome?
- ○ Have I consulted all relevant persons and groups?
- Evaluate alternative actions:
  - ○ Which option will produce the most good and do the least harm? (the utilitarian approach)
  - ○ Which option best respects the rights of all stakeholders? (the rights approach)
  - ○ Which option treats people equally or proportionately? (the fairness approach)
  - ○ Which option best serves the community as a whole, and not just some members? (the common good approach)
- Make a decision and test it:
  - ○ Considering all the approaches, which option best addresses the situation?
- Act and reflect on the outcome of your decision:
  - ○ How can I implement my decision with the greatest care and attention to the concerns of all stakeholders?
  - ○ How did my decision turn out, and what did I learn from this specific situation?

Now that we have created a general ethical framework, we will focus specifically on ethics in the corporate environment.

## Ethics in the Corporate Environment

Many companies and professional organizations develop their own codes of ethics. A **code of ethics** is a collection of principles intended to guide decision making by members of the organization. For example, the Association for Computing Machinery (*www.acm.org*), an organization of computing professionals, has a thoughtful code of ethics for its members (see *www.acm.org/constitution/code.html*).

Keep in mind that different codes of ethics are not always consistent with one another. Therefore, an individual might be expected to conform to multiple codes. For example, a person who is a member of two large professional computing-related organizations may be simultaneously required by one organization to comply with all applicable laws and by the other organization to refuse to obey unjust laws.

Fundamental tenets of ethics include responsibility, accountability, and liability:

**Responsibility** means that you accept the consequences of your decisions and actions.
**Accountability** refers to determining who is responsible for actions that were taken.
**Liability** is a legal concept that gives individuals the right to recover the damages done to them by other individuals, organizations, or systems.

Before you go any further, it is critical that you realize that what is *unethical* is not necessarily *illegal*. For example, a bank's decision to foreclose on a home can be technically legal, but it can raise many ethical questions. In many instances, then, an individual or organization faced with an ethical decision is not considering whether to break the law. As the foreclosure example illustrates, however, ethical decisions can have serious consequences for individuals, organizations, and society at large.

We have witnessed a large number of extremely poor ethical decisions, not to mention outright criminal behavior, at many organizations. During 2001 and 2002, three highly publicized fiascos occurred at Enron, WorldCom, and Tyco. At each company, executives were convicted of various types of fraud for using illegal accounting practices. These actions led to the passage of the Sarbanes-Oxley Act in 2002. Sarbanes-Oxley requires publicly held companies to implement financial controls and company executives to personally certify financial reports.

FIN

Then, the subprime mortgage crisis exposed unethical lending practices throughout the mortgage industry. The crisis also highlighted pervasive weaknesses in the regulation of the U.S. financial industry as well as the global financial system. It ultimately contributed to a deep recession in the global economy. Along these same lines, financier Bernie Madoff was convicted in 2009 of operating a Ponzi scheme and sentenced to 150 years in federal prison. In addition, several of Madoff's employees were convicted in 2014.

Advancements in information technologies have generated a new set of ethical problems. Computing processing power doubles roughly every 18 months, meaning that organizations are more dependent than ever on their information systems. Organizations can store increasing amounts of data at decreasing costs. As a result, they can maintain more data on individuals for longer periods of time. Going further, computer networks, particularly the Internet, enable organizations to collect, integrate, and distribute enormous amounts of information on individuals, groups, and institutions. These developments have created numerous ethical problems concerning the appropriate collection and use of customer information, personal privacy, and the protection of intellectual property.

These developments affect the academic world as well. For example, vast amounts of information on the Internet make it easier for students to plagiarize papers and essays. IT's About Business 3.1 addresses the plagiarism problem.

 **IT's [about business]**

### 3.1 Cheating Is Risky for Business Students

For $29.99, an MBA applicant can access the Web site Wordprom (*http://wordprom.com*) and purchase an admissions essay that another student used to gain admission to a different university. If that applicant is daring, he or she might even try to pass off parts of that essay as his or her own.

Unfortunately, cheating has become more common at business schools. Between 2002 and 2004, Rutgers Business School professor Don McCabe surveyed 5,000 graduate students and discovered that MBA students confessed to cheating more than their nonbusiness peers. In fact, the managing director of the MBA program at Pennsylvania State University's Smeal College of Business claims that recycled essays are the school's most serious problem.

However, it is becoming much more difficult to fool admissions staff and instructors. To combat the increasing reliance on recycled essays and papers, a growing number of schools use plagiarism-detection software such as Turnitin (*www.turnitin.com*). For years, classroom instructors have employed Turnitin, which crawls the Web to identify plagiarized passages on term papers. Today, essays submitted through online admission portals at business schools are passed through Turnitin as well. The software has matched material to *Wikipedia* and *Bloomberg Business-Week*, among many other sites. Turnitin's database also includes academic research papers and a growing repository of college papers. The software issues an alert when substantial parts of an essay match an entry by a different author stored in the system.

Smeal College provides an excellent illustration of this process. Since the school began to use Turnitin in 2010, it has rejected 85 applicants for plagiarizing their admissions essays, including 40 in 2013 alone. Overall, the number of MBA admissions offices using Turnitin continues to increase now that the tool is being marketed as an add-on to a widely used software suite (see *www.iparadigms.com*) for processing applications. Significantly, Turnitin keeps its client roster private, and most business schools do not disclose whether they are using the service, either for applications or for term papers. Among those that do, Smeal College is the only one that has notified suspected plagiarizers. All other

schools have rejected applicants without offering any explanation. Wordprom's CEO maintains that its Web site is intended to give applicants samples of effective work so that they can get a feel for structure and style when drafting original essays. The site does warn users that it has an agreement to provide Turnitin with access to its database.

Some experts contend that tools like Turnitin are a deterrent but not a cure, because applicants can still hire someone to write their essays for them. Moreover, even cheaters are turning to content-tracking services such as Turnitin. They want to make certain that the authors they hire to write their essays are not plagiarizing themselves or selling the essays to multiple customers.

A Ukraine-based competitor of Turnitin, Plagtracker (*www.plagtracker.com*), reports that its client base is growing rapidly. The site claims that 60 percent of its customers are either students or prospective students.

*Sources:* Compiled from "Turnitin Spring Webcasts Focus on Strategies for Educators to Improve Student Outcomes," *Turnitin Press Release*, January 27, 2015; C. Straumsheim, "Turnitin Put to the Test," *Inside Higher Ed*, February 6, 2014; J. Bailey, "New Turnitin Study on the Impact of Plagiarism Detection in Higher Education," *Plagiarism Today*, February 5, 2014; M. Saltzman, "Turnitin: Plagiarizing Students Beware New App for iPad," *USA Today*, September 17, 2013; E. Zlomek, "Master's in Plagiarism," *Bloomberg BusinessWeek*, April 22–28, 2013; N. Heckler, M. Rice, and C. Bryan, "Turnitin Systems: A Deterrent to Plagiarism in College Classrooms," *Journal of Research on Technology in Education*, March 6, 2013; "Why Students Cheat, and What To Do About It," *Hult Labs*, February 9, 2013; D. McCabe, "MBAs Cheat. But Why?" *Harvard Business Review blog*, April 13, 2009; *www.turnitin.com*, *www.iparadigms.com*, *www.plagtracker.com*, accessed March 30, 2015.

**Questions**

1. As the Turnitin database expands rapidly by incorporating a growing number of papers and essays, what will be the impact on subsequent papers submitted to it?

2. Discuss the ethical implications of writing a paper yourself that you know contains some plagiarized material and then using Turnitin's service yourself.

## Ethics and Information Technology

All employees have a responsibility to encourage ethical uses of information and information technology. Many of the business decisions you will face at work will have an ethical dimension. Consider the following decisions that you might have to make:

- Should organizations monitor employees' Web surfing and e-mail?
- Should organizations sell customer information to other companies?
- Should organizations audit employees' computers for unauthorized software or illegally downloaded music or video files?

The diversity and ever-expanding use of IT applications have created a variety of ethical issues. These issues fall into four general categories: privacy, accuracy, property, and accessibility.

1. *Privacy issues* involve collecting, storing, and disseminating information about individuals.
2. *Accuracy issues* involve the authenticity, fidelity, and correctness of information that is collected and processed.
3. *Property issues* involve the ownership and value of information.
4. *Accessibility issues* revolve around who should have access to information and whether they should pay a fee for this access.

Table 3.1 lists representative questions and issues for each of these categories. In addition, Online Ethics Cases presents 14 scenarios that raise ethical issues. These scenarios will provide a context for you to consider situations that involve ethical or unethical behavior.

Many of the issues and scenarios discussed in this chapter involve privacy as well as ethics. In the next section, you will learn about privacy issues in more detail.

**Table**

# 3.1

**A Framework for Ethical Issues**

### Privacy Issues
What information about oneself should an individual be required to reveal to others?

What kinds of surveillance can an employer use on its employees?

What types of personal information can people keep to themselves and not be forced to reveal to others?

What information about individuals should be kept in databases, and how secure is the information there?

### Accuracy Issues
Who is responsible for the authenticity, fidelity, and accuracy of the information collected?

How can we ensure that the information will be processed properly and presented accurately to users?

How can we ensure that errors in databases, data transmissions, and data processing are accidental and not intentional?

Who is to be held accountable for errors in information, and how should the injured parties be compensated?

### Property Issues
Who owns the information?

What are the just and fair prices for its exchange?

How should we handle software piracy (illegally copying copyrighted software)?

Under what circumstances can one use proprietary databases?

Can corporate computers be used for private purposes?

How should experts who contribute their knowledge to create expert systems be compensated?

How should access to information channels be allocated?

<table>
<tr><td>Table<br>3.1 (continued)</td><td>Accessibility Issues<br>Who is allowed to access information?<br>How much should companies charge for permitting access to information?<br>How can access to computers be provided for employees with disabilities?<br>Who will be provided with the equipment needed for accessing information?<br>What information does a person or an organization have a right to obtain, under what conditions, and with what safeguards?</td></tr>
</table>

## before you go on...

1. What does a code of ethics contain?
2. Describe the fundamental tenets of ethics.

## 3.2 Privacy

In general, **privacy** is the right to be left alone and to be free of unreasonable personal intrusions. **Information privacy** is the right to determine when, and to what extent, information about you can be gathered and/or communicated to others. Privacy rights apply to individuals, groups, and institutions. The right to privacy is recognized today in all the U.S. states and by the federal government, either by statute or in common law.

Privacy can be interpreted quite broadly. However, court decisions in many countries have followed two rules fairly closely:

1. The right of privacy is not absolute. Privacy must be balanced against the needs of society.
2. The public's right to know supersedes the individual's right of privacy.

These two rules illustrate why determining and enforcing privacy regulations can be difficult.

As we discussed earlier, rapid advances in information technologies have made it much easier to collect, store, and integrate vast amounts of data on individuals in large databases. On an average day, data about you are generated in many ways: surveillance cameras located on toll roads, on other roadways, in busy intersections, in public places, and at work; credit card transactions; telephone calls (landline and cellular); banking transactions; queries to search engines; and government records (including police records). These data can be integrated to produce a **digital dossier**, which is an electronic profile of you and your habits. The process of forming a digital dossier is called **profiling**.

Data aggregators, such as LexisNexis (*www.lexisnexis.com*), ChoicePoint (*www.choicepoint.com*), and Acxiom (*www.acxiom.com*), are prominent examples of profilers. These companies collect public data such as real estate records and published telephone numbers, in addition to nonpublic information such as Social Security numbers; financial data; and police, criminal, and motor vehicle records. They then integrate these data to form digital dossiers on most adults in the United States. They ultimately sell these dossiers to law enforcement agencies and companies that conduct background checks on potential employees. They also sell them to companies that want to know their customers better, a process called *customer intimacy*.

Data on individuals can also be used in more controversial manners. For example, a controversial map in California identifies the addresses of donors who supported Proposition 8, the referendum approved by California voters in the 2008 election that outlawed same-sex marriage in that state (see *www.eightmaps.com*). Gay activists created the map by combining

Google's satellite mapping technology with publicly available campaign records that listed Proposition 8 donors who contributed $100 or more. These donors were outraged, claiming that the map invaded their privacy.

## Electronic Surveillance

According to the American Civil Liberties Union (ACLU), tracking people's activities with the aid of information technology has become a major privacy-related problem. The ACLU notes that this monitoring, or **electronic surveillance**, is rapidly increasing, particularly with the emergence of new technologies. Electronic surveillance is conducted by employers, the government, and other institutions.

Americans today live with a degree of surveillance that would have been unimaginable just a few years ago. For example, surveillance cameras track you at airports, subways, banks, and other public venues. In addition, inexpensive digital sensors are now everywhere. They are incorporated into laptop webcams, video-game motion sensors, smartphone cameras, utility meters, passports, and employee ID cards. Step out your front door and you could be captured in a high-resolution photograph taken from the air or from the street by Google or Microsoft, as they update their mapping services. Drive down a city street, cross a toll bridge, or park at a shopping mall, and your license plate will be recorded and time-stamped.

Emerging technologies such as low-cost digital cameras, motion sensors, and biometric readers are helping to increase the monitoring of human activity. In addition, the costs of storing and using digital data are rapidly decreasing. The result is an explosion of sensor data collection and storage.

In fact, your smartphone has become a sensor. The average price of a smartphone has increased 17 percent since 2000. However, the phone's processing capability has increased by *13,000 percent* during that time, according to technology market research firm ABI Research (*www.abiresearch.com*). As you will study in Chapter 8, smartphones can now record video, take pictures, send and receive e-mail, search for information, access the Internet, and locate you on a map, among many other things. Your phone also stores large amounts of information about you that can be collected and analyzed. A special problem arises with smartphones that are equipped with global positioning system (GPS) sensors. These sensors routinely *geotag* photos and videos, embedding images with the longitude and latitude of the location shown in the image. Thus, you could be inadvertently supplying criminals with useful intelligence by posting personal images on social networks or photo-sharing Web sites. These actions would show the criminals exactly where you live.

Another example of how new devices can contribute to electronic surveillance is facial recognition technology. Just a few years ago, this software worked only in very controlled settings such as passport checkpoints. However, this technology can now match faces even in regular snapshots and online images. For example, Intel and Microsoft have introduced in-store digital billboards that can recognize your face. These billboards can keep track of the products you are interested in based on your purchases or browsing behavior. One marketing analyst has predicted that your experience in every store will soon be customized.

Google and Facebook are using facial-recognition software—Google Picasa and Facebook Photo Albums—in their popular online photo-editing and sharing services. Both companies encourage users to assign names to people in photos, a practice referred to as *photo tagging*. Facial-recognition software then indexes facial features. Once an individual in a photo is tagged, the software searches for similar facial features in untagged photos. This process allows the user to quickly group photos in which the tagged person appears. Significantly, the individual is not aware of this process.

Why is tagging important? The reason is that once you are tagged in a photo, that photo can be used to search for matches across the entire Internet or in private databases, including databases fed by surveillance cameras. How could this type of surveillance affect you? As one example, a car dealer can take a picture of you when you step onto the car lot. He or she could then quickly profile you (find out information about where you live, your employment, etc.) on the Web to achieve a competitive edge in making a sale. Even worse, a stranger in a restaurant could photograph you with a smartphone and then go online to profile you for reasons of his or her own. One privacy attorney has asserted that losing your right to anonymity would have a chilling effect on where you go, whom you meet, and how you live your life. IT's About Business 3.2 illustrates another type of surveillance technology employed by retailers.

The scenarios we just considered deal primarily with your personal life. However, electronic surveillance has become a reality in the workplace as well. In general, employees have very limited legal protection against surveillance by employers. The law supports the right of employers to read their employees' e-mail and other electronic documents and to monitor their employees' Internet use. Today, more than three-fourths of organizations routinely monitor their employees' Internet usage. In addition, two-thirds use software to block connections to inappropriate Web sites, a practice called *URL filtering*. Furthermore, organizations are installing monitoring and filtering software to enhance security by blocking malicious software and to increase productivity by discouraging employees from wasting time.

# IT's [about business]

## 3.2 Those Mannequins Are Watching You

Store mannequin maker Almax (*www.almax-italy.com*) is deploying the EyeSee, a mannequin equipped with technology that is typically used to identify criminals at airports. The mannequins allow retailers to gather demographic data and shopping patterns from customers as they move through stores. Although retailers are reluctant to discuss the mannequins' use, Almax claims that several companies are using them in three European countries and the United States.

From the outside the EyeSee looks like an ordinary mannequin. Internally, however, a camera in one eye feeds data into demographic-profiling software to determine each customer's age, gender, and race. To give the EyeSee ears as well as eyes, Almax is developing technology that recognizes words. This feature will allow retailers to eavesdrop on shoppers' comments regarding the mannequins' attire.

The EyeSee is designed for merchants who increasingly use technology to help personalize their product offerings. Merchants are enthusiastic over technology that can help profile customers while keeping their customers' identities anonymous.

Whereas some stores deploy similar technology to watch shoppers from overhead security cameras, Almax contends that the EyeSee provides better data because it stands at eye level and thus invites customer attention. The mannequin revealed to one store that men who shopped in the first two days of a sale spent more money than women did. Another store discovered that one in three visitors who accessed one of its doors after 4 p.m. were Asian, prompting the store to place Chinese-speaking staff by that entrance.

Regulations imposed by the United States and Europe permit the use of cameras for security purposes, but they also require retailers to place signs in their stores warning customers that they may be filmed. Watching people solely for commercial gain could be construed as gathering personal data without consent. One legal expert notes that when you access Facebook, before you start the registration process, you can see exactly what information the site will collect and what the site will do with that information. In contrast, with the EyeSee, what can customers do? Almax counters that because the EyeSee does not store any images, retailers can use it as long as they have a closed-circuit television license.

*Sources:* Compiled from L. Clark, "Mannequins Are Now Digitally Tracking UK Shoppers," *Wired*, August 12, 2014; "Retailers Are Watching: The EyeSee Mannequin," *The Barcoding Blog*, January 2, 2014; "Retailers Go High-Tech to Track Shoppers," *CBS News*, December 11, 2013; "EyeSee Mannequins Monitor Footfall Traffic," *Fashion United*, December 9, 2013; A. Roberts, "In Some Stores, All Eyes Are on You," *Bloomberg BusinessWeek*, December 10–16, 2012; K. Hill, "Why Do Mannequins That Spy on Us Creep Us Out?" *Forbes*, November 28, 2012; J. Stern, "Department Store Mannequins Are Watching You. No, Really." *ABC News*, November 26, 2012; L. Clark, "Mannequins Are Spying on Shoppers for Market Analysis," *Wired*, November 23, 2012; *www.almax-italy.com*, accessed March 30, 2015.

**Questions**

1. Is using EyeSee mannequins in stores an ethical practice? Why or why not? Support your answer.

2. If stores notify people that they may be filmed, do the stores have to indicate how they might be filmed (i.e., by mannequins)? What are the ethical implications of how stores make these notifications?

3. Would knowing that the mannequins may be watching you change your shopping behavior? Why or why not? Explain your answer.

4. What are the privacy implications of the EyeSee mannequins, given that stores already have security cameras placed in strategic locations?

In one organization, the chief information officer (CIO) monitored roughly 13,000 employees for three months to determine the type of traffic they engaged in on the network. He then forwarded the data to the chief executive officer (CEO) and the heads of the human resources and legal departments. These executives were shocked at the questionable Web sites the employees were visiting, as well as the amount of time they were spending on those sites. The executives quickly decided to implement a URL filtering product.

In general, surveillance is a concern for private individuals regardless of whether it is conducted by corporations, government bodies, or criminals. As a nation, the United States is still struggling to define the appropriate balance between personal privacy and electronic surveillance, especially in situations that involve threats to national security.

## Personal Information in Databases

Modern institutions store information about individuals in many databases. Perhaps the most visible locations of such records are credit-reporting agencies. Other institutions that store personal information include banks and financial institutions; cable TV, telephone, and utilities companies; employers; mortgage companies; hospitals; schools and universities; retail establishments; government agencies (Internal Revenue Service, your state, your municipality); and many others.

There are several concerns about the information you provide to these record keepers. Some of the major concerns are as follows:

- Do you know where the records are?
- Are the records accurate?
- Can you change inaccurate data?
- How long will it take to make a change?
- Under what circumstances will the personal data be released?
- How are the data used?
- To whom are the data given or sold?
- How secure are the data against access by unauthorized people?

## Information on Internet Bulletin Boards, Newsgroups, and Social Networking Sites

Every day we see more and more *electronic bulletin boards, newsgroups, electronic discussions* such as chat rooms, and *social networking sites* (discussed in Chapter 9). These sites appear on the Internet, within corporate intranets, and on blogs. A *blog*, short for "Weblog," is an informal, personal journal that is frequently updated and is intended for general public reading. How does society keep owners of bulletin boards from disseminating information that may be offensive to readers or simply untrue? This is a difficult problem because it involves the conflict between freedom of speech on the one hand and privacy on the other. This conflict is a fundamental and continuing ethical issue in the United States and throughout the world.

There is no better illustration of the conflict between free speech and privacy than the Internet. Many Web sites contain anonymous, derogatory information on individuals, who typically have little recourse in the matter. The vast majority of the U.S. firms use the Internet in examining job applications, including searching on Google and on social networking sites. Consequently, derogatory information contained on the Internet can harm a person's chances of being hired.

New information technologies can also present serious privacy concerns. IT's About Business 3.3 shows how Tapad can track you across various devices.

# IT's [about business]

## **3.3** Tapad Can Track You across Devices

Targeting potential customers is a simple operation to perform on a desktop. Just add cookies—bits of code that tag visitors—to a Web site, and advertisers can follow prospects with ads as they surf the Web. Visit a Web site for your university's football team, for instance, and you might see ads for team paraphernalia. Because these ads appear only to people who have visited a brand's Web site, their click-through rate is up to three times that of banner ads, notes AdRoll, a San Francisco-based digital advertising company.

Cookies, however, can track on only one device. Therefore, the trail goes cold when, for example, you leave your desktop and use your phone. Today, it is not unusual for users to switch devices many times within just one hour, leaving marketers in the dark. Tapad (*www.tapad.com*), a rapidly growing digital advertising startup, claims that it can track and target the same consumer across multiple devices—desktop computers, laptops, smartphones, and tablets—using software algorithms.

Tapad analyzes 150 billion data points—from cookies, smartphone IDs (which link individual phones to app downloads and Web browsing), Wi-Fi connections, Web site registrations, browsing history, and other inputs that it will not reveal. In essence, Tapad is searching for commonalities that link one device with another.

For instance, if a tablet and a laptop share the same Wi-Fi network, it is an indication that one person is using both devices. In a similar fashion, browsing patterns are also important—say, two devices that share a history of visiting sports Web sites. Each correlation increases the likelihood that the same person owns both devices. Based on these probabilities, Tapad clients serve ads to potential customers across devices. Thus, the same customer might see one ad on a work computer, another ad on the mobile Web on the commute home, and a third ad while sitting with a tablet on the couch.

Significantly, Tapad encountered a major problem right from the start. Agencies and marketing departments are often divided into mobile, desktop, and television advertising divisions. Tapad had to sell its product to all three groups.

In August 2011, Tapad secured its first client, a U.S. wireless network. The startup ran a month-long campaign that increased the network's click-through rates by 300 percent. That higher rate enabled the network to fine-tune its marketing budget, because it knew which devices, when used at key times, correlated with a specific transaction.

By mid-2014, Tapad had acquired 160 clients, including Audi, American Airlines, and TurboTax, serving 2 billion ads each month. Tapad revenues increased to $34 million in 2014, a 48 percent increase over 2013. However, the company's success is running the risk of irritating Congress, regulators, and privacy advocates.

Success breeds scrutiny, and not just from competitors such as Drawbridge (*http://drawbrid.ge*). The U.S. Senate Commerce Committee may force advertisers to adopt "Do Not Track" technology, which requires Web browsers to offer an easy opt-out. (We will discuss opt-out and opt-in in the next section.) Tapad protests that it does not collect data that can be used to pinpoint users by name. Furthermore, the company includes opt-out buttons in all of its ads. Tapad employs a privacy lawyer in Washington to ensure that the company is functioning within the law while it continues to expand rapidly.

*Sources:* Compiled from "America's Most Promising Companies," *Forbes*, January, 2015; T. Peterson, "Google Tests Desktop-to-Mobile Retargeting with Brand Data," *Advertising Age*, March 12, 2014; "Introducing AdRoll Retargeting for Mobile: A New Way to Retarget across Devices," *PR Newswire*, February 20, 2014; J. Colao, "The Stalker," *Forbes*, June 10, 2013; N. Dujnic, "Tapad & the Multiscreen World," *Live Intent*, June 5, 2013; J. McDermott, "Can Mobile Targeting Ever Be as Accurate as Cookies on the Desktop?" *Advertising Age*, March 21, 2013; "Tapad and TRUSTe Forge Partnership," *TRUSTe.com*, March 12, 2013; J. Del Rey, "Tapad Brings Retargeting to Phones, Tablets, But Marketers Aren't Talking," *Advertising Age*, March 7, 2012; *www.tapad.com*, accessed March 29, 2015.

**Questions**

1. Is Tapad's business model ethical? Why or why not?
2. What is the relationship between Tapad's business model and your privacy? Provide specific examples to support your answer.

---

## Privacy Codes and Policies

**Privacy policies** or **privacy codes** are an organization's guidelines for protecting the privacy of its customers, clients, and employees. In many corporations, senior management has begun to understand that when they collect vast amounts of personal information, they must protect it. In addition, many organizations give their customers some voice in how their information is used by providing them with opt-out choices. The **opt-out model** of informed consent permits the company to collect personal information until the customer specifically requests that the data not be collected. Privacy advocates prefer the **opt-in model** of informed consent, which prohibits an organization from collecting any personal information unless the customer specifically authorizes it.

One privacy tool available to consumers is the *Platform for Privacy Preferences* (P3P), a protocol that automatically communicates privacy policies between an electronic commerce Web site and the visitors to that site. P3P enables visitors to determine the types of personal data that can be extracted by the sites they visit. It also allows visitors to compare a site's privacy policy with the visitors' preferences or with other standards, such as the Federal Trade Commission's (FTC) Fair Information Practices Standard or the European Directive on Data Protection.

Table 3.2 provides a sampling of privacy policy guidelines. The last section, "Data Confidentiality," refers to security, which we consider in Chapter 4. All of the good privacy intentions in the world are useless unless they are supported and enforced by effective security measures.

Despite privacy codes and policies, and despite opt-out and opt-in models, guarding whatever is left of your privacy is becoming increasingly difficult. However, several companies are providing help in maintaining your privacy, as you see in the chapter closing case.

## International Aspects of Privacy

As the number of online users has increased globally, governments throughout the world have enacted a large number of inconsistent privacy and security laws. This highly complex global legal framework is creating regulatory problems for companies. Approximately 50 countries have some form of data protection laws. Many of these laws conflict with those of other countries, or they require specific security measures. Other countries have no privacy laws at all.

The absence of consistent or uniform standards for privacy and security obstructs the flow of information among countries (*transborder data flows*). The European Union, for one, has taken steps to overcome this problem. In 1998, the European Community Commission (ECC) issued guidelines to all of its member countries regarding the rights of individuals to access information about themselves. The EU data protection laws are stricter than the U.S. laws and

| **Table 3.2** Privacy Policy Guidelines: A Sampler |
| --- |
| **Data Collection** |
| Data should be collected on individuals only for the purpose of accomplishing a legitimate business objective. |
| Data should be adequate, relevant, and not excessive in relation to the business objective. |
| Individuals must give their consent before data pertaining to them can be gathered. Such consent may be implied from the individual's actions (e.g., applications for credit, insurance, or employment). |
| **Data Accuracy** |
| Sensitive data gathered on individuals should be verified before they are entered into the database. |
| Data should be kept current, where and when necessary. |
| The file should be made available so that the individual can ensure that the data are correct. |
| In any disagreement about the accuracy of the data, the individual's version should be noted and included with any disclosure of the file. |
| **Data Confidentiality** |
| Computer security procedures should be implemented to ensure against unauthorized disclosure of data. These procedures should include physical, technical, and administrative security measures. |
| Third parties should not be given access to data without the individual's knowledge or permission, except as required by law. |
| Disclosures of data, other than the most routine, should be noted and maintained for as long as the data are maintained. |
| Data should not be disclosed for reasons incompatible with the business objective for which they are collected. |

therefore could create problems for the U.S.-based multinational corporations, which could face lawsuits for privacy violations.

The transfer of data into and out of a nation without the knowledge of either the authorities or the individuals involved raises a number of privacy issues. Whose laws have jurisdiction when records are stored in a different country for reprocessing or retransmission purposes? For example, if data are transmitted by a Polish company through a U.S. satellite to a British corporation, which country's privacy laws control the data, and at what points in the transmission? Questions like these will become more complicated and frequent as time goes on. Governments must make an effort to develop laws and standards to cope with rapidly changing information technologies to solve some of these privacy issues.

The United States and the European Union share the goal of privacy protection for their citizens, but the United States takes a different approach. To bridge the different privacy approaches, the U.S. Department of Commerce, in consultation with the European Union, developed a "safe harbor" framework to regulate the way that the U.S. companies export and handle the personal data (e.g., names and addresses) of European citizens. See *www.export.gov/safeharbor* and *http://ec.europa.eu/justice_home/fsj/privacy/index_en.htm.*

## before you go on...

**1.** Describe the issue of privacy as it is affected by IT.

**2.** Discuss how privacy issues can impact transborder data flows.

# What's In IT For Me?

### For the Accounting Major

Public companies, their accountants, and their auditors have significant ethical responsibilities. Accountants now are being held professionally and personally responsible for increasing the transparency of transactions and ensuring compliance with Generally Accepted Accounting Principles (GAAP). In fact, regulatory agencies such as the SEC and the Public Company Accounting Oversight Board (PCAOB) require accounting departments to adhere to strict ethical principles.

### For the Finance Major

As a result of global regulatory requirements and the passage of Sarbanes-Oxley, financial managers must follow strict ethical guidelines. They are responsible for full, fair, accurate, timely, and understandable disclosure in all financial reports and documents that their companies submit to the Securities and Exchange Commission (SEC) and in all other public financial reports. Furthermore, financial managers are responsible for compliance with all applicable governmental laws, rules, and regulations.

### For the Marketing Major

Marketing professionals have new opportunities to collect data on their customers, for example, through business-to-consumer electronic commerce (discussed in Chapter 7). Business ethics clearly mandate that these data should be used only within the company and should not be sold to anyone else. Marketers do not want to be sued for invasion of privacy over data collected for the marketing database.

Customers expect their data to be properly secured. However, profit-motivated criminals want that data. Therefore, marketing managers must analyze the risks of their operations. Failure to protect corporate and customer data will cause significant public relations problems and outrage customers. Customer relationship management (discussed in Chapter 11) operations and tracking customers' online buying habits can expose unencrypted data to misuse or result in privacy violations.

### For the Production/Operations Management Major

POM professionals decide whether to outsource (or offshore) manufacturing operations. In some cases, these operations are sent overseas to countries that do not have strict labor laws. This situation raises serious ethical questions. For example: Is it ethical to hire employees in countries with poor working conditions in order to reduce labor costs?

### For the Human Resource Management Major

Ethics is critically important to HR managers. HR policies explain the appropriate use of information technologies in the workplace. Questions such as the following can arise: Can employees use the Internet, e-mail, or chat systems for personal purposes while at work? Is it ethical to monitor employees? If so, how? How much? How often? HR managers must formulate and enforce such policies while at the same time maintaining trusting relationships between employees and management.

### For the MIS Major

Ethics might be more important for MIS personnel than for anyone else in the organization, because these individuals have control of the information assets. They also have control over a huge amount of the employees' personal information. As a result, the MIS function must be held to the highest ethical standards.

## [ Summary ]

1. **Define ethics, list and describe the three fundamental tenets of ethics, and describe the four categories of ethical issues related to information technology.**

   Ethics refers to the principles of right and wrong that individuals use to make choices that guide their behavior.

   Fundamental tenets of ethics include responsibility, accountability, and liability. Responsibility means that you accept the consequences of your decisions and actions. Accountability refers to determining who is responsible for actions that were taken. Liability is a legal concept that gives individuals the right to recover the damages done to them by other individuals, organizations, or systems.

   The major ethical issues related to IT are privacy, accuracy, property (including intellectual property), and access to information. Privacy may be violated when data are held in databases or transmitted over networks. Privacy policies that address issues of data collection, data accuracy, and data confidentiality can help organizations avoid legal problems.

2. **Identify three places that store personal data, and for each one, discuss at least one personal threat to the privacy of the data stored there.**

   Privacy is the right to be left alone and to be free of unreasonable personal intrusions. Threats to privacy include advances in information technologies, electronic surveillance, personal information in databases, Internet bulletin boards, newsgroups, and social networking sites. The privacy threat in Internet bulletin boards, newsgroups, and social networking sites is that you might post too much personal information that many unknown people can see.

# [ Chapter Glossary ]

**accountability** A tenet of ethics that refers to determining who is responsible for actions that were taken.

**code of ethics** A collection of principles intended to guide decision making by members of an organization.

**digital dossier** An electronic description of an individual and his or her habits.

**electronic surveillance** Tracking people's activities with the aid of computers.

**ethics** The principles of right and wrong that individuals use to make choices to guide their behaviors.

**information privacy** The right to determine when, and to what extent, personal information can be gathered by and/or communicated to others.

**liability** A legal concept that gives individuals the right to recover the damages done to them by other individuals, organizations, or systems.

**opt-in model** A model of informed consent in which a business is prohibited from collecting any personal information unless the customer specifically authorizes it.

**opt-out model** A model of informed consent that permits a company to collect personal information until the customer specifically requests that the data not be collected.

**privacy** The right to be left alone and to be free of unreasonable personal intrusions.

**privacy codes** See privacy policies.

**privacy policies** (also known as **privacy codes**) An organization's guidelines for protecting the privacy of customers, clients, and employees.

**profiling** The process of forming a digital dossier.

**responsibility** A tenet of ethics in which you accept the consequences of your decisions and actions.

# [ Discussion Questions ]

1. In 2008, the Massachusetts Bay Transportation Authority (MBTA) obtained a temporary restraining order barring three Massachusetts Institute of Technology (MIT) students from publicly displaying what they claimed to be a way to get "free subway rides for life." Specifically, the 10-day injunction prohibited the students from revealing vulnerabilities of the MBTA's fare card. The students were scheduled to present their findings in Las Vegas at the DEFCON computer hacking conference. Were the students' actions legal? Were their actions ethical? Discuss your answer from the students' perspective and then from the perspective of the MBTA.

2. Frank Abagnale, the criminal played by Leonardo DiCaprio in the motion picture *Catch Me If You Can*, ended up in prison. After he left prison, however, he worked as a consultant to many companies on matters of fraud.

   a. Why do these companies hire the perpetrators (if caught) as consultants? Is this a good idea?
   b. You are the CEO of a company. Discuss the ethical implications of hiring Frank Abagnale as a consultant.

3. Access various search engines to find information relating to the use of drones (unmanned aerial vehicles (UAVs)) for electronic surveillance purposes in the United States.

   a. Take the position favoring the use of drones for electronic surveillance.
   b. Take the position against the use of drones for electronic surveillance.

# [ Problem-Solving Activities ]

1. An information security manager routinely monitored Web surfing among her company's employees. She discovered that many employees were visiting the "sinful six" Web sites. (Note: The "sinful six" are Web sites with material related to pornography, gambling, hate, illegal activities, tastelessness, and violence.) She then prepared a list of the employees and their surfing histories and gave the list to management. Some managers punished their employees. Some employees, in turn, objected to the monitoring, claiming that they should have a right to privacy.

   a. Is monitoring of Web surfing by managers ethical? (It is legal.) Support your answer.
   b. Is employee Web surfing on the "sinful six" ethical? Support your answer.
   c. Is the security manager's submission of the list of abusers to management ethical? Why or why not?
   d. Is punishing the abusers ethical? Why or why not? If yes, then what types of punishment are acceptable?
   e. What should the company do in this situation? (*Note:* There are a variety of possibilities here.)

2. Access the Computer Ethics Institute's Web site at *www. cpsr.org/issues/ethics/cei*. The site offers the "Ten Commandments of Computer Ethics." Study these rules and decide whether any others should be added.

3. Access the Association for Computing Machinery's code of ethics for its members (see *www.acm.org/constitution/ code.html*). Discuss the major points of this code. Is this code complete? Why or why not? Support your answer.

4. Access *www.eightmaps.com*. Is the use of data on this Web site illegal? Unethical? Support your answer.

5. The Electronic Frontier Foundation (*www.eff.org*) has a mission of protecting rights and promoting freedom in the "electronic frontier." Review the organization's suggestions about how to protect your online privacy, and summarize what you can do to protect yourself.

6. Access your university's guidelines for ethical computer and Internet use. Are there limitations as to the types of Web sites that you can visit and the types of material you can view? Are you allowed to change the programs on the lab computers? Are you allowed to download software from the lab computers for your personal use? Are there rules governing the personal use of computers and e-mail?

7. Access *http://www.albion.com/netiquette/corerules.html*. What do you think of this code of ethics? Should it be expanded? Is it too general?

8. Access *www.cookiecentral.com* and *www.epubliceye.com*. Do these sites provide information that helps you protect your privacy? If so, then explain how.

9. Do you believe that a university should be allowed to monitor e-mail sent and received on university computers? Why or why not? Support your answer.

# [ Closing Case **Protecting Your Privacy** ]

## The Problem

Competition is intense for the control of personal data, which some observers call the "new oil" of the twenty-first century. Facebook's market value illustrates the value of maintaining detailed data about more than 1 billion people. Companies constantly seek to obtain increasing amounts of data on all of us so that they can more precisely target advertising messages to each of us. For example, the ubiquitous "Like" and "Share" buttons deployed by Web sites to make it easier to promote their content enable Facebook (via Facebook Connect) to track people online.

However, the National Security Agency spying scandal has generated new fears on the part of Web surfers of being tracked and traced by countless ad networks, data miners, and data brokers. The Federal Trade Commission (FTC) is pressuring browser companies, consumer advocates, and advertisers to establish a "Do Not Track" option for Internet users. Negotiations have broken down, however, because advertisers and privacy advocates cannot agree on how much protection consumers are entitled to.

## A Variety of Solutions

As a result of the privacy problem, in recent years a number of companies have launched that provide privacy and software tools. Let's take a closer look at some of them.

- Snapchat (*www.snapchat.com*): This smartphone app is a picture and video viewer that allows users to send pictures or videos that self-destruct after a few seconds. The app also contains a notification feature that lets you know if someone performs a "screen grab" of any photos that you send.

- Wickr (*https://www.mywickr.com*): This smartphone app allows users to send military-grade encrypted texts, photos, and videos to other Wickr users. In addition, it deletes information such as location and type of device from files before sending them. Nothing is stored on Wickr's servers that could be used to track (or subpoena) the sender.

- Burn Note (*https://burnnote.com*): This smartphone app sends encrypted notes that self-destruct after a set amount of time. The notes are deleted from the recipient's computer, and they are not stored on Burn Note servers. Burn Note also displays only a specific highlighted area of a note as the recipient mouses over it. As a result, it is difficult for a screenshot to capture an entire note.

- TigerText (*www.tigertext.com*): This app is marketed to businesses—particularly healthcare—that require a secure messaging system. For example, your physician can use TigerText to securely text X-rays of your knee to a colleague. TigerText also allows senders to retrieve messages that they have already sent.

- Reputation (*www.reputation.com*): This company manages its clients' online reputation by making individuals and businesses look their best on the Internet. Reputation will search for damaging content online and destroy it. In addition, it helps its clients prevent private information from being made public.

- Silent Circle (*https://silentcircle.com*): This company produces a smartphone app that allows people to easily make secure, encrypted phone calls and send secure, encrypted texts. In addition, the sender can specify a time period after which the file will automatically be deleted from both devices (sending and receiving). Silent Circle makes life easier and safer for journalists, political dissidents, diplomats, and companies that are trying to evade state surveillance or corporate espionage.

As one example, in early 2013 a reporter in South Sudan used Silent Circle to record a video of brutality that occurred at a vehicle checkpoint. He then encrypted the video and sent it to Europe. Within a few minutes, the video was automatically deleted from the sender's device. This way, even if authorities had arrested and searched the sender, they would not have found the footage on his phone. Meanwhile, the film, which included location data indicating exactly where it was taken, was already in safe hands. It was eventually used to build a case documenting human rights abuses.

From a different perspective, law enforcement agencies have expressed concerns that criminals will use the Silent Circle app. The FBI, for instance, wants all communications providers to build in back doors (discussed in Chapter 4) so that the agency can secretly spy on suspects. Silent Circle, however, has implemented an explicit policy that it will not comply with eavesdropping requests from law enforcement entities.

- Personal (*www.personal.com*) provides users with personal data lockers in which they store information about themselves in a single account. Businesses would pay for these data because the data enable them to offer personalized products and advertising. Further, people retain control over the data in their lockers, so they can demand something of value in return, such as cash or discounts on products.
- iPredator (*https://www.ipredator.se*) is a virtual private networking service (discussed in Chapter 4) whose stated goal is to provide Internet privacy.
- Disconnect (*https://disconnect.me*) is a shareware tool that places a green "D" next to the search bar and displays the number of requests for your personal data that are being made on that Web site, as well as the companies requesting the data. Disconnect then blocks those requests, thereby dramatically speeding up surfing. (Shareware is software that is available free of charge and is often distributed for consumer evaluation, after which the provider might request a fee for continued use.) The most current version

of Disconnect blocks more than 2,000 parties from collecting your data.

- Burner (*http://burnerapp.com*) is an iPhone app that provides temporary phone numbers, so you can send and receive calls and texts from disposable digits. After you have finished your business, you "nuke" the number so that it cannot be easily traced back to you. Unlike Silent Circle, Burner complies with law enforcement requests.

## The Results

Ultimately, the results for each of us will be different, depending on our Web presence (or our digital footprint), how much information we share on social media, and many other factors. Therefore, as you try any or all of these privacy products, you will be able to determine the impact(s) on your privacy.

*Sources:* Compiled from "What's the Point of SnapChat and How Does It Work? *Pocket-Lint*, January 29, 2015; "How to Protect Your Privacy Online," *The Wall Street Journal*, October 21, 2013; M. Carney, "TigerText Takes Its Secure Messaging Platform Freemium, Targeting Both Enterprises and Consumers," *Pando Daily*, October 3, 2013; K. Hill, "Track Me If You Can," *Forbes*, August 12, 2013; B. Tekspert, "How Can I Protect My Privacy Online?" *Senior Planet*, August 6, 2013; M. Lee, "Encryption Works: How to Protect Your Privacy in the Age of NSA Surveillance," *Freedom of the Press Foundation*, July 2, 2013; R. Gallagher, "The Threat of Silence," *Slate*, February 4, 2013; J. Brustein, "Start-Ups Seek to Help Users Put a Price on Their Personal Data," *New York Times*, February 12, 2012; *www.snapchat.com*, https://www.mywickr.com, https://burnnote.com, www.tigertext.com, www.reputation.com, https://silentcircle.com, www.personal.com, www.ipredator.se, https://disconnect.me, http://burnerapp.com, accessed March 29, 2015.

### Questions

1. Describe how each of the companies discussed above can protect your privacy in some way.
2. Describe the disadvantages to you from using any of the services described in this case.

# Chapter

# 4 Information Security

## What's In IT For Me?

This Chapter Will Help Prepare You To...

| ACCT | FIN | MKT | POM | HRM | MIS |
|------|-----|-----|-----|-----|-----|
| ACCOUNTING | FINANCE | MARKETING | PRODUCTION OPERATIONS MANAGEMENT | HUMAN RESOURCES MANAGEMENT | MIS |
| Monitor social media for compliance | Collaborate with external financial experts | Receive real-time feedback from customers | Partners/ customers collaborate on product development | Enhance recruiting efforts | Develop internal company social networks |

# [The Sony Pictures Entertainment Hack]

## The Problem

On November 24, 2014, a hacker group called the "Guardians of Peace" or "GOP" successfully attacked Sony Pictures Entertainment (SPE) (*www.sonypictures.com*). The attackers obtained personally identifiable information about 47,000 current and former SPE employees and their dependents, numerous sensitive e-mails, executive salaries, complete copies of unreleased Sony films, and other information. The personally identifiable information included names, addresses, social security numbers, driver's license numbers, passport numbers, bank account information, credit card information used for corporate travel and expenses, usernames and passwords, and compensation and other employment-related information. The hackers claimed to have stolen more than 100 terabytes of data from SPE.

The GOP initially released the most damaging information over the Internet. This information consisted of digital copies of SPE films that had been released (e.g., Fury) or were yet to be released (e.g., *Annie*). In addition, the attackers announced they would continue to release more interesting SPE information.

Although the specific motives for the attack had not been revealed by early 2015, the hack has been linked to the planned release of the film *The Interview*. In this movie, producers of a tabloid television show learn that North Korea's leader, Kim Jong Un, is a big fan of the show, and they set up an interview with him. While the show's team is preparing for the interview, the CIA recruits them to assassinate Kim Jong Un.

Prior to the Sony hack, North Korean officials had expressed concerns about the film to the United Nations. The officials stated that "to allow the production and distribution of such a film on the assassination of an incumbent head of a sovereign state should be regarded as the most undisguised sponsoring of terrorism as well as an act of war."

On December 16, 2014, the GOP mentioned *The Interview* by name, and they threatened to take terrorist actions against the film's New York City premiere at Sunshine Cinema on December 18. The GOP also threatened similar actions on the film's America-wide release date of December 25.

On December 18, 2014, two messages allegedly from the GOP appeared. The first claimed that the GOP would not release any further information if SPE agreed not to release the film and to remove it completely from the Internet. The second stated that SPE had "suffered enough" and could release *The Interview*, but only if Kim Jong Un's death scene was not "too happy."

## The Law Enforcement Response

Meanwhile, the Federal Bureau of Investigation (FBI) launched an investigation into the incident. In 2014 the agency announced it had connected the North Korean government to the attack. The FBI's statement was based on intelligence gathered during a U.S. hack of North Korea's networks in 2010. In that action, the U.S. tracked the internal operations of North Korean computers and networks. In turn, North Korea denied any responsibility for the Sony hack. Although most of the speculation about the attack has focused on North Korea, the authorities are investigating alternative scenarios, including the possibility that the attack involved a SPE employee or a former employee.

## The Sony Response

As a result of the attack, SPE shut down its entire network on November 25, and it pulled the theatrical release of *The Interview* on December 17. Two days later, President Obama labeled the attack as "cybervandalism" and not an act of war. He charged that that Sony's decision to pull the film from release rather than defy the hackers was a mistake.

Following initial threats made toward theaters that showed *The Interview*, several cinema chains, including Carmike Cinemas, Bow Tie Cinemas, Regal Entertainment Group, AMC Theaters, and Cinemark Theaters, announced that they would not screen *The Interview*. On December 23, 2014, SPE authorized some 300 largely independent theaters to show the movie on Christmas Day. The following day SPE released *The Interview* to Google Play, Xbox Video, and YouTube.

# The Results

Beginning on December 22, 2014, North Korea experienced an Internet failure, for which the government blamed the United States, identifying the disruptions as an attack in retaliation for the SPE hack. The U.S. government denied having any role in the disruptions.

Interestingly, North Korea's Internet connections run through servers only in China. Therefore, China could interdict any hacking attempts originating in North Korea. However, China and the United States are embroiled in a dispute over bilateral hacking, so it does not seem likely that China will police North Korean hacking attempts.

The SPE attack had serious repercussions for Sony, for the U.S. government, and for every organization. Consider the damage to SPE. Analysts estimate that the costs of the attack could exceed $150 million. However, the damage done to SPE's reputation (via very sensitive e-mails) could be incalculable. In fact, several former SPE employees are suing the company for failure to adequately protect their personal data. (SPE offered one year of free credit monitoring and fraud protection to current and former employees.)

The U.S. government is faced with a serious problem. By presidential directive, the U.S. military has the responsibility to help protect and defend the nation's critical infrastructure, such as its power grid, banking system, and communications networks. However, the U.S. and international entertainment companies are not part of that infrastructure. The question is: If a foreign government is attacking U.S. corporations, what is the federal government's responsibility? A related question is: Why didn't the U.S. government warn SPE?

SPE's inability to protect its information from hackers serves as a reminder to corporations and individuals that if you are connected to the Internet, your information is simply not safe. Further, no one should commit anything on e-mail that he or she would not want to see on the front page of a newspaper. The likelihood of serious breaches is increasing, as is the damage these breaches can cause. Therefore the time, effort, and money that organizations spend on information security need to increase as well.

One final note: As of early 2015, any North Korean involvement in the SPE attack had not been proved. In fact, some security analysts doubt that North Korea had anything to do with the attack.

*Sources*: Compiled from W. Ashford, "U.S. Blamed North Korea for Sony Attack Based on Data from 2010 U.S. Hack," *Computer Weekly*, January 20, 2015; "North Korea Slams 'Hostile' U.S. Sanctions over Sony Cyber Attack," *Computer Weekly*, January 5, 2015; M. Fackler, "North Korea Accuses U.S. of Staging Internet Failure," *The New York Times*, December 27, 2014; "Sony Hack: The Consequences of Mocking Kim Jong Un," *The Week*, December 26, 2014; B. Barnes and M. Cieply, "Sony, in About-Face, Will Screen 'The Interview' in a Small Run," *The New York Times*, December 23, 2014; M. Williams, "Sony Looking for Ways to Distribute 'The Interview' Online," *IDG News Service*, December 21, 2014; B. Tau, "Obama Calls Sony Hack 'Cybervandalism' Not Act of War," *Washington Wire*, December 21, 2014; M. Elgan, "The Sony Pictures Hack Changes Everything," *Baseline Magazine*, December 19, 2014; A. Bacle, "White House Is Treating Sony Hack as 'Serious National Security Matter'," *Entertainment Weekly*, December 18, 2014; D. Yadron, D. Barrett, and J. Barnes, "U.S. Struggles for Response to Sony Hack," *The Wall Street Journal*, December 18, 2014; T. Greene, "U.S. on Sony Breach: North Korea Did It," *Network World*, December 18, 2014; J. Kwaak, "Sony Hack Shines Light on North Korea Cyber Attackers," *The Wall Street Journal*, December 18, 2014; E. Weise, "Experts: Sony Hackers 'Have Crossed the Line'," *USA Today*, December 17, 2014; D. Sanger and N. Perlroth, "U.S. Links North Korea to Sony Hacking," *The New York Times*, December 17, 2014; M. Williams, "Sony Hackers Release More Data, Promise 'Christmas Gift'," *IDG News Service*, December 14, 2014; B. Child, "Hackers Demand Sony Cancel Release of Kim Jong-un-Baiting Comedy," *The Guardian*, December 9, 2014; W. Ashford, "North Korea Denies Sony Hack That Exposed 47,000 Personal Records," *Computer Weekly*, December 5, 2014; B. Fritz and D. Yadron, "Sony Hack Exposed Personal Data of Hollywood Stars," *The Wall Street Journal*, December 5, 2014; B. Barnes and N. Perlroth, "Sony Pictures and F.B.I. Widen Hack Inquiry," *The New York Times*, December 3, 2014; W. Ashford, "Films Leaked Online After Sony Pictures Hack," *Computer Weekly*, December 1, 2014; "Sony's New Movies Leak Online Following Hack Attack," *Variety*, November 29, 2014; *www.sonypictures.com*, accessed February 10, 2015.

## Questions

1. Was Sony's response to the breach adequate? Why or why not?
2. Should the U.S. government help private organizations that are attacked (or allegedly attacked) by foreign governments? Why or why not?

# Introduction

The opening case provides several lessons. First, it is difficult, if not impossible, for organizations to provide perfect security for their data. Second, there is a growing danger that countries are engaging in economic cyberwarfare among themselves. Third, it appears that it is impossible to secure the Internet. The answer to this question impacts each and every one of us. In essence, our personally identifiable, private data are not secure.

The answers to these issues and others are not clear. As you learn about information security in the context of information technology, you will acquire a better understanding of these issues, their importance, their relationships, and their trade-offs. Keep in mind that the issues involved in information security impact individuals and small organizations as well as large companies.

Information security is especially important to small businesses. Large organizations that experience an information security problem have greater resources to both resolve and survive the problem. In contrast, small businesses have fewer resources and therefore can be destroyed by a data breach.

When properly used, information technologies can have enormous benefits for individuals, organizations, and entire societies. In Chapters 1 and 2, you read about diverse ways in which IT has made businesses more productive, efficient, and responsive to consumers. You also explored fields such as medicine and philanthropy in which IT has improved people's health and well-being. Unfortunately, information technologies can also be misused, often with devastating consequences. Consider the following scenarios:

- Individuals can have their identities stolen.
- Organizations can have customer information stolen, leading to financial losses, erosion of customer confidence, and legal action.
- Countries face the threats of *cyberterrorism* and *cyberwarfare*, terms for Internet-based attacks. Cyberwarfare is a critical problem for the U.S. government. In fact, President Obama signed a cyberwarfare directive in October 2012. In that directive, the White House, for the first time, laid out specific ground rules for how and when the U.S. military can carry out offensive and defensive cyber operations against foreign threats. The directive emphasizes the Obama administration's focus on cybersecurity as a top priority.

Clearly, the misuse of information technologies has come to the forefront of any discussion of IT. Studies have revealed that each security breach costs an organization millions of dollars. For example, consider the Target breach described in this chapter's closing case. The direct costs of a data breach include hiring forensic experts, notifying customers, setting up telephone hotlines to field queries from concerned or affected customers, offering free credit monitoring, and providing discounts for future products and services. The more intangible costs of a breach include the loss of business from increased customer turnover—called *customer churn*—and decreases in customer trust.

Unfortunately, employee negligence caused many of the data breaches, meaning that organizational employees are a weak link in information security. It is therefore very important for you to learn about information security so that you will be better prepared when you enter the workforce.

# 4.1 Introduction to Information Security

**Security** can be defined as the degree of protection against criminal activity, danger, damage, and/or loss. Following this broad definition, **information security** refers to all of the processes and policies designed to protect an organization's information and information systems (IS) from unauthorized access, use, disclosure, disruption, modification, or destruction. You have seen that information and information systems can be compromised by deliberate criminal actions and by anything that can impair the proper functioning of an organization's information systems.

Before continuing, let's consider these key concepts. Organizations collect huge amounts of information and employ numerous information systems that are subject to myriad threats. A **threat** to an information resource is any danger to which a system may be exposed. The **exposure** of an information resource is the harm, loss, or damage that can result if a threat compromises that resource. An information resource's **vulnerability** is the possibility that the system will be harmed by a threat.

Today, five key factors are contributing to the increasing vulnerability of organizational information resources, making it much more difficult to secure them:

- Today's interconnected, interdependent, wirelessly networked business environment
- Smaller, faster, cheaper computers and storage devices
- Decreasing skills necessary to be a computer hacker
- International organized crime taking over cybercrime
- Lack of management support

The first factor is the evolution of the IT resource from mainframe-only to today's highly complex, interconnected, interdependent, wirelessly networked business environment. The Internet now enables millions of computers and computer networks to communicate freely and seamlessly with one another. Organizations and individuals are exposed to a world of untrusted networks and potential attackers. A *trusted network*, in general, is any network within your organization. An *untrusted network*, in general, is any network external to your organization. In addition, wireless technologies enable employees to compute, communicate, and access the Internet anywhere and anytime. Significantly, wireless is an inherently nonsecure broadcast communications medium.

The second factor reflects the fact that modern computers and storage devices (e.g., thumb drives or flash drives) continue to become smaller, faster, cheaper, and more portable, with greater storage capacity. These characteristics make it much easier to steal or lose a computer or storage device that contains huge amounts of sensitive information. Also, far more people are able to afford powerful computers and connect inexpensively to the Internet, thus raising the potential of an attack on information assets.

The third factor is that the computing skills necessary to be a hacker are *decreasing*. The reason is that the Internet contains information and computer programs called *scripts* that users with few skills can download and use to attack any information system connected to the Internet. (Security experts can also use these scripts for legitimate purposes, such as testing the security of various systems.)

The fourth factor is that international organized crime is taking over cybercrime. **Cybercrime** refers to illegal activities conducted over computer networks, particularly the Internet. iDefense (*http://labs.idefense.com*), a company that specializes in providing security information to governments and Fortune 500 companies, maintains that groups of well-organized criminal organizations have taken control of a global billion-dollar crime network. The network, powered by skillful hackers, targets known software security weaknesses. These crimes are typically nonviolent, but quite lucrative. Consider, for example, that losses from armed robberies average hundreds of dollars, and those from white-collar crimes average tens of thousands of dollars. In contrast, losses from computer crimes average hundreds of thousands of dollars. Also, computer crimes can be committed from anywhere in the world, at any time, effectively providing an international safe haven for cybercriminals. Computer-based crimes cause billions of dollars in damages to businesses each year, including the costs of both repairing information systems and lost business.

The fifth, and final, factor is lack of management support. For the entire organization to take security policies and procedures seriously, senior managers must set the tone. Unfortunately, senior managers often do not do so. Ultimately, however, lower level managers may be even more important. These managers are in close contact with employees every day and thus are in a better position to determine whether employees are following security procedures.

# before you go on...

1. Define information security.
2. Differentiate among a threat, an exposure, and a vulnerability.
3. Why are the skills needed to be a hacker decreasing?

# 4.2 Unintentional Threats to Information Systems

Information systems are vulnerable to many potential hazards and threats, as you can see in Figure 4.1. The two major categories of threats are unintentional threats and deliberate threats. This section discusses unintentional threats, and the next section addresses deliberate threats.

**FIGURE 4.1** Security threats.

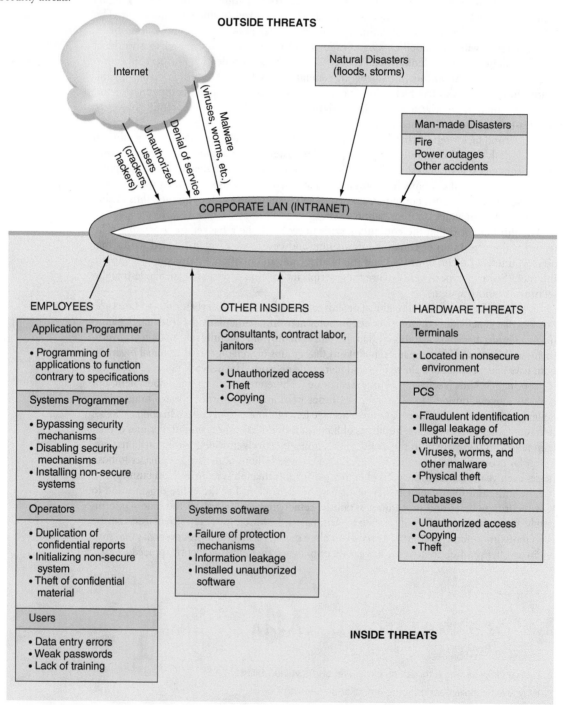

Unintentional threats are acts performed without malicious intent that nevertheless represent a serious threat to information security. A major category of unintentional threats is human error.

## Human Errors

Organizational employees span the breadth and depth of the organization, from mail clerks to the CEO, and across all functional areas. There are two important points to be made about employees. First, the higher the level of employee, the greater the threat he or she poses to information security. This is true because higher level employees typically have greater access to corporate data, and they enjoy greater privileges on organizational information systems. Second, employees in two areas of the organization pose especially significant threats to information security: human resources and information systems. Human resources employees generally have access to sensitive personal information about all employees. Likewise, IS employees not only have access to sensitive organizational data but also often control the means to create, store, transmit, and modify those data. IT's About Business 4.1 describes how a relatively simple, unintentional programming mistake led to the Heartbleed "bug."

 # IT's [about business]

### 4.1 The Heartbleed Bug    MIS

### What Is Heartbleed?

OpenSSL, an open-source software package, is a popular type of transport layer security (TLS) software (discussed later in this chapter) that secures numerous Internet Web sites worldwide. Web servers use OpenSSL to offer encrypted TLS connections that appear to users as a "lock" and the "https" prefix in the browser's address bar. The encryption provides protection for online banking, shopping, e-mail, and other private communications. OpenSSL software is built into Apache, the server software used by about two-thirds of the world's Web sites to deliver Web pages to your computer. When OpenSSL is working properly, data traveling between the two computers looks like gibberish to anyone except to the authorized computers, which have keys for decoding the information being transmitted.

OpenSSL is vital to Internet commerce, making it safe to move information online. It is widely used in software that connects devices in homes, offices, and industrial settings to the Internet.

The Heartbleed bug is an encryption security flaw in the OpenSSL software package that was reported by the Google security team in 2014. The flaw resulted from an unintended coding mistake by a German researcher three years earlier.

Attackers can exploit Heartbleed to crack encrypted connections and steal user passwords as well as a company's encryption keys. The bug can let attackers eavesdrop on Web, e-mail, and some VPN communications. It can be found not only in servers using OpenSSL but also in network equipment from Cisco and Juniper Networks. When exploited by attackers, Heartbleed leaks data from a server's memory, which could include SSL digital keys, usernames and passwords, and even personal user data such as e-mail, instant messages, and files.

### Attacks Using Heartbleed

Many attacks exploiting the Heartbleed bug have been reported. Consider these examples:

- The Canadian Revenue Agency reported a theft of social insurance numbers belonging to 900 taxpayers. The agency stated that the attackers exploited the Heartbleed bug.
- A parenting Web site in the United Kingdom, Mumsnet (*www.mumsnet.com*), had several user accounts hijacked, and its CEO was impersonated.
- Interestingly, anti-malware researchers also exploited Heartbleed to access secret online forums used by cybercriminals.
- Attackers used Heartbleed to steal security keys from Community Health Systems (*www.chs.net*), the second-largest for-profit U.S. hospital chain.

### Repairing Heartbleed

The Google security team created a code fix for Heartbleed. Even after organizations install the fix, however, they have to take further measures. The reason is that a system attacked via Heartbleed may remain at risk after the vulnerability itself has been repaired. To regain confidentiality and authenticity, organizations must create new private key–public key pairs, and they have to revoke and replace all digital certificates linked to these pairs. In addition, they need to replace all compromised authentication material (e.g., passwords).

### The Results

The Heartbleed flaw could persist for years in devices such as networking software, home automation systems, and even critical industrial control systems, because these devices are updated only infrequently. Among the major classes of devices likely to be affected are cable boxes and home Internet routers.

The Heartbleed bug highlights a fundamental weakness in overall Internet security. Much of this security is managed by four European computer programmers and a former military consultant in Maryland. Most of the 11-member team are volunteers, and only one works full time. Their budget is less than $1 million per year.

And the final word? As of June 2014, more than 300,000 TLS-enabled Web sites remained vulnerable to Heartbleed. And the problem continues. In April 2015, security firm Venafi (*www.venafi.com*) found that more than 1,200 of the Forbes Global 2000 companies had not taken the steps necessary to repair Heartbleed vulnerabilities in all their servers.

*Sources*: C. Cerrudo, "Why the Shellshock Bug Is Worse Than Heartbleed," *MIT Technology Review*, September 30, 2014; B. Blevins, "Community Health Breach Shows Detecting Heartbleed Exploits a Struggle," *TechTarget*, August 22, 2014; W. Ashford, "Heartbleed Bug Linked to U.S. Hospital Group Attack," *Computer Weekly*, August 21, 2014; B. Blevins, "Heartbleed Scan Shows Majority of Global 2000 Still Vulnerable," *TechTarget*, July 30, 2014; B. Blevins, "Successful Heartbleed Response

Still Raises Important Questions," *TechTarget*, July 11, 2014; F. Trotter, "Heartbleed Bodes Ill for Sensitive Health Data," *MIT Technology Review*, April 22, 2014; J. Perlow, "Heartbleed's Lesson: Passwords Must Die," *ZDNet*, April 11, 2014; E. Messmer, "Heartbleed Bug Hits at Heart of Many Cisco, Juniper Products," *Network World*, April 10, 2014; M. Wood, "Flaw Calls for Altering Passwords, Experts Say," *The New York Times*, April 10, 2014; "3 Questions About Tricky Heartbleed," *USA Today*, April 10, 2014; S. Vaughan-Nichols, "How to Protect Yourself in Heartbleed's After-shocks," *ZDNet*, April 10, 2014; "The Under-Funded Project Keeping the Web Secure," *MIT Technology Review*, April 9, 2014; N. Perlroth, "Thought Safe, Websites Find the Door Ajar," *The New York Times*, April 9, 2014; H. Bray, "'Heartbleed' Internet Security Bug Is As Bad As It Sounds," *The Boston Globe*, April 9, 2014; I. Paul, "The Critical, Widespread Heartbleed Bug and You: How to Keep Your Private Info Safe," *Network World*, April 9, 2014; T. Simonite, "Many Devices Will Never Be Patched to Fix Heartbleed Bug," *MIT Technology Review*, April 9, 2014; D. Talbot, "What Should You Do About Heartbleed? Excellent Question." *MIT Technology Review*, April 9, 2014.

### Questions

1. What are two lessons we can learn from the Heartbleed bug?
2. What actions should you (personally) take to combat the Heartbleed bug?

---

Other employees include contract labor, consultants, and janitors and guards. Contract labor, such as temporary hires, may be overlooked in information security arrangements. However, these employees often have access to the company's network, information systems, and information assets. Consultants, although technically not employees, perform work for the company. Depending on the nature of their work, they may also have access to the company's network, information systems, and information assets.

Finally, janitors and guards are the most frequently ignored people in information security systems. Companies frequently outsource their security and janitorial services. As with contractors, then, these individuals work for the company, although they technically are not employees. Moreover, they are usually present when most—if not all—other employees have gone home. They typically have keys to every office, and nobody questions their presence in even the most sensitive parts of the building. In fact, an article from 2600: *The Hacker Quarterly* described how to get a job as a janitor for the purpose of gaining physical access to an organization.

Human errors or mistakes by employees pose a serious problem. These errors are typically the result of laziness, carelessness, or a lack of awareness concerning information security. This lack of awareness arises from poor education and training efforts by the organization. Human mistakes manifest themselves in many different ways, as illustrated in Table 4.1.

The human errors you have just studied, although unintentional, are committed entirely by employees. However, employees can also make unintentional mistakes in response to actions by an attacker. Attackers often employ social engineering to induce individuals to make unintentional mistakes and disclose sensitive information.

### Social Engineering

**Social engineering** is an attack in which the perpetrator uses social skills to trick or manipulate legitimate employees into providing confidential company information such as passwords. The most common example of social engineering occurs when the attacker impersonates someone else on the telephone, such as a company manager or an information systems employee. The attacker claims he forgot his password and asks the legitimate employee to give him a password to use. Other common ploys include posing as an exterminator, an air-conditioning technician, or a fire marshal. Examples of social engineering abound.

Table
# 4.1
Human Mistakes

| Human Mistake | Description and Examples |
|---|---|
| Carelessness with laptops | Losing or misplacing laptops, leaving them in taxis, and so on. |
| Carelessness with computing devices | Losing or misplacing these devices, or using them carelessly so that malware is introduced into an organization's network. |
| Opening questionable e-mails | Opening e-mails from someone unknown, or clicking on links embedded in e-mails (see *phishing attack* in Table 4.2). |
| Careless Internet surfing | Accessing questionable Web sites; can result in malware and/or alien software being introduced into the organization's network. |
| Poor password selection and use | Choosing and using weak passwords (see *strong passwords* in the "Authentication" section later in this chapter). |
| Carelessness with one's office | Leaving desks and filing cabinets unlocked when employees go home at night; not logging off the company network when leaving the office for any extended period of time. |
| Carelessness using unmanaged devices | Unmanaged devices are those outside the control of an organization's IT department and company security procedures. These devices include computers belonging to customers and business partners, computers in the business centers of hotels, and so on. |
| Carelessness with discarded equipment | Discarding old computer hardware and devices without completely wiping the memory; includes computers, smartphones, BlackBerry® units, and digital copiers and printers. |
| Careless monitoring of environmental hazards | These hazards, which include dirt, dust, humidity, and static electricity, are harmful to the operation of computing equipment. |

In one company, a perpetrator entered a company building wearing a company ID card that looked legitimate. He walked around and put up signs on bulletin boards reading "The help desk telephone number has been changed. The new number is 555-1234." He then exited the building and began receiving calls from legitimate employees thinking they were calling the company help desk. Naturally, the first thing the perpetrator asked for was user-name and password. He now had the information necessary to access the company's information systems.

Two other social engineering techniques are tailgating and shoulder surfing. *Tailgating* is a technique designed to allow the perpetrator to enter restricted areas that are controlled with locks or card entry. The perpetrator follows closely behind a legitimate employee and, when the employee gains entry, the attacker asks him or her to "hold the door." *Shoulder surfing* occurs when a perpetrator watches an employee's computer screen over the employee's shoulder. This technique is particularly successful in public areas such as in airports and on commuter trains and airplanes.

# before you go on...

**1.** What is an unintentional threat to an information system?

**2.** Provide examples of social engineering attacks other than the ones just discussed.

# 4.3 Deliberate Threats to Information Systems

There are many types of deliberate threats to information systems. We provide a list of 10 common types for your convenience.

- Espionage or trespass
- Information extortion
- Sabotage or vandalism
- Theft of equipment or information
- Identity theft
- Compromises to intellectual property
- Software attacks
- Alien software
- Supervisory control and data acquisition (SCADA) attacks
- Cyberterrorism and cyberwarfare

## Espionage or Trespass

Espionage or trespass occurs when an unauthorized individual attempts to gain illegal access to organizational information. It is important to distinguish between competitive intelligence and industrial espionage. Competitive intelligence consists of legal information-gathering techniques such as studying a company's Web site and press releases, attending trade shows, and similar actions. In contrast, industrial espionage crosses the legal boundary.

## Information Extortion

Information extortion occurs when an attacker either threatens to steal or actually steals information from a company. The perpetrator demands payment for not stealing the information, for returning stolen information, or for agreeing not to disclose the information.

## Sabotage or Vandalism

Sabotage and vandalism are deliberate acts that involve defacing an organization's Web site, potentially damaging the organization's image and causing its customers to lose faith. One form of online vandalism is a hacktivist or cyberactivist operation. These are cases of high-tech civil disobedience to protest the operations, policies, or actions of an organization or government agency. For example, the English Twitter account for the Arabic news network Al Jazeera was subject to hacktivism. The Associated Press reported that supporters of Syrian President Bashar Assad used the account to tweet pro-Assad links and messages.

## Theft of Equipment or Information

Computing devices and storage devices are becoming smaller yet more powerful with vastly increased storage (e.g., laptops, personal digital assistants, smartphones, digital cameras, thumb drives, and iPods). As a result, these devices are becoming easier to steal and easier for attackers to use to steal information.

Table 4.1 points out that one type of human mistake is carelessness with laptops. In fact, many laptops have been stolen due to such carelessness. The cost of a stolen laptop includes the loss of data, the loss of intellectual property, laptop replacement, legal and regulatory costs, investigation fees, and lost productivity.

One form of theft, known as *dumpster diving*, involves rummaging through commercial or residential trash to find discarded information. Paper files, letters, memos, photographs, IDs, passwords, credit cards, and other forms of information can be found in dumpsters. Unfortunately, many people never consider that the sensitive items they throw in the trash might be recovered. When this information is recovered, it can be used for fraudulent purposes.

Dumpster diving is not necessarily theft, because the legality of this act varies. Because dumpsters are usually located on private premises, dumpster diving is illegal in some parts of the United States. Even in these cases, however, these laws are enforced with varying degrees of rigor.

## Identity Theft

**Identity theft** is the deliberate assumption of another person's identity, usually to gain access to his or her financial information or to frame him or her for a crime. Techniques for illegally obtaining personal information include the following:

- Stealing mail or dumpster diving
- Stealing personal information in computer databases
- Infiltrating organizations that store large amounts of personal information (e.g., data aggregators such as Acxiom) (*www.acxiom.com*)
- Impersonating a trusted organization in an electronic communication (phishing)

Recovering from identity theft is costly, time consuming, and burdensome.

Victims also report problems in obtaining credit and obtaining or holding a job, as well as adverse effects on insurance or credit rates. In addition, victims state that it is often difficult to remove negative information from their records, such as their credit reports.

Your personal information can be compromised in other ways. For example, your identity can be uncovered just by examining your searches in a search engine. The ability to analyze all searches by a single user can enable a criminal to identify who the user is and what he or she is doing. To demonstrate this fact, *The New York Times* tracked down a particular individual based solely on her AOL searches.

## Compromises to Intellectual Property

Protecting intellectual property is a vital issue for people who make their livelihood in knowledge fields. **Intellectual property** is the property created by individuals or corporations that is protected under *trade secret, patent,* and *copyright* laws.

A **trade secret** is an intellectual work, such as a business plan, that is a company secret and is not based on public information. An example is the formula for Coca-Cola. A **patent** is an official document that grants the holder exclusive rights on an invention or a process for a specified period of time. **Copyright** is a statutory grant that provides the creators or owners of intellectual property with ownership of the property, for a designated period. Current U.S. laws award patents for 20 years and copyright protection for the life of the creator plus 70 years. Owners are entitled to collect fees from anyone who wants to copy their creations. It is important to note that these are definitions under U.S. law. There is some international standardization of copyrights and patents, but it is far from total. Therefore, there can be discrepancies between U.S. law and other countries' laws.

The most common intellectual property related to IT deals with software. In 1980, the U.S. Congress amended the Copyright Act to include software. The amendment provides protection for the *source code* and *object code* of computer software, but it does not clearly identify what is eligible for protection. For example, copyright law does not protect fundamental concepts, functions, and general features such as pull-down menus, colors, and icons. However, copying a software program without making payment to the owner—including giving a disk to a friend to install on his or her computer—is a copyright violation. Not surprisingly, this practice, called **piracy**, is a major problem for software vendors. The BSA (*www.bsa.org*) Global Software Piracy Study found that the commercial value of software theft totals billions of dollars per year.

## Software Attacks

Software attacks have evolved from the early years of the computer era, when attackers used malicious software to infect as many computers worldwide as possible, to the profit-driven,

**Table 4.2**

**Types of Software Attacks**

| Type | Description |
|---|---|
| **(1) Remote Attacks Requiring User Action** | |
| Virus | Segment of computer code that performs malicious actions by attaching to another computer program. |
| Worm | Segment of computer code that performs malicious actions and will replicate, or spread, by itself (without requiring another computer program). |
| Phishing attack | Phishing attacks use deception to acquire sensitive personal information by masquerading as official-looking e-mails or instant messages. |
| Spear phishing | Phishing attacks target large groups of people. In spear phishing attacks, the perpetrators find out as much information about an individual as possible to improve their chances that phishing techniques will obtain sensitive, personal information. |
| **(2) Remote Attacks Needing No User Action** | |
| Denial-of-service attack | An attacker sends so many information requests to a target computer system that the target cannot handle them successfully and typically crashes (ceases to function). |
| Distributed denial-of-service attack | An attacker first takes over many computers, typically by using malicious software. These computers are called **zombies** or **bots**. The attacker uses these bots—which form a **botnet**—to deliver a coordinated stream of information requests to a target computer, causing it to crash. |
| **(3) Attacks by a Programmer Developing a System** | |
| Trojan horse | Software programs that hide in other computer programs and reveal their designed behavior only when they are activated. |
| Back door | Typically a password, known only to the attacker, that allows him or her to access a computer system at will, without having to go through any security procedures (also called a **trap door**). |
| Logic bomb | A segment of computer code that is embedded within an organization's existing computer programs and is designed to activate and perform a destructive action at a certain time or date. |

Web-based attacks of today. Modern cybercriminals use sophisticated, blended malware attacks, typically via the Web, to make money. Table 4.2 displays a variety of software attacks. These attacks are grouped into three categories: remote attacks requiring user action, remote attacks requiring no user action, and software attacks initiated by programmers during the development of a system. The chapter's opening and closing cases provide excellent examples of software attacks.

Not all cybercriminals are sophisticated, however. For example, a student at a U.S. university was sentenced to one year in prison for using keylogging software (discussed later in this chapter) to steal 750 fellow students' passwords and vote himself and four of his fraternity brothers into the student government's president and four vice president positions. The five positions would have combined to bring the students a combined $36,000 in stipends.

The student was caught when university security personnel noticed strange activity on the campus network. Authorities identified the computer used in the activity from its IP address. On this computer, which belonged to the student in question, authorities found a PowerPoint presentation detailing the scheme. Authorities also found research on his computer, with queries such as "how to rig an election" and "jail time for keylogger."

Once the university caught onto the scheme, the student reportedly turned back to hacking to try to get himself out of trouble. He created new Facebook accounts in the names of actual classmates, going as far as conducting fake conversations between the accounts to try to deflect the blame. Those actions contributed to the one-year prison sentence, which the judge imposed even after the student pleaded guilty and requested probation.

## Alien Software

Many personal computers have alien software, or *pestware*, running on them that the owners are unaware of. **Alien software** is clandestine software that is installed on your computer through duplicitous methods. It is typically not as malicious as viruses, worms, or Trojan horses, but it does use up valuable system resources. In addition, it can enable other parties to track your Web surfing habits and other personal behaviors.

The vast majority of pestware is **adware**—software that causes pop-up advertisements to appear on your screen. Adware is common because it works. According to advertising agencies, for every 100 people who close a pop-up ad, 3 click on it. This "hit rate" is extremely high for Internet advertising.

**Spyware** is software that collects personal information about users without their consent. Two common types of spyware are keystroke loggers and screen scrapers.

Keystroke loggers, also called *keyloggers*, record both your individual keystrokes and your Internet Web browsing history. The purposes range from criminal—for example, theft of passwords and sensitive personal information such as credit card numbers—to annoying—for example, recording your Internet search history for targeted advertising.

Companies have attempted to counter keyloggers by switching to other forms of identifying users. For example, at some point all of us have been forced to look at wavy, distorted letters and type them correctly into a box. That string of letters is called a *CAPTCHA*, and it is a test. The point of CAPTCHA is that computers cannot (yet) accurately read those distorted letters. Therefore, the fact that you can transcribe them means that you are probably not a software program run by an unauthorized person, such as a spammer. As a result, attackers have turned to *screen scrapers*, or *screen grabbers*. This software records a continuous "movie" of a screen's contents rather than simply recording keystrokes.

**Spamware** is pestware that uses your computer as a launch pad for spammers. **Spam** is an unsolicited e-mail, usually advertising for products and services. When your computer is infected with spamware, e-mails from spammers are sent to everyone in your e-mail address book, but they appear to come from you.

Not only is spam a nuisance, but it wastes time and money. Spam costs U.S. companies billions of dollars every year. These costs arise from productivity losses, clogged e-mail systems, additional storage, user support, and antispam software. Spam can also carry viruses and worms, making it even more dangerous.

**Cookies** are small amounts of information that Web sites store on your computer, temporarily or more or less permanently. In many cases, cookies are useful and innocuous. For example, some cookies are passwords and user IDs that you do not want to retype every time you access the Web site that issued the cookie. Cookies are also necessary for online shopping because merchants use them for your shopping carts.

*Tracking cookies*, however, can be used to track your path through a Web site, the time you spend there, what links you click on, and other details that the company wants to record, usually for marketing purposes. Tracking cookies can also combine this information with your name, purchases, credit card information, and other personal data to develop an intrusive profile of your spending habits.

Most cookies can be read only by the party that created them. However, some companies that manage online banner advertising are, in essence, cookie-sharing rings. These companies can track information such as which pages you load and which ads you click on. They then share this information with their client Web sites, which may number in the thousands.

## Supervisory Control and Data Acquisition Attacks

*SCADA* refers to a large-scale, distributed measurement and control system. SCADA systems are used to monitor or to control chemical, physical, and transport processes such as those used in oil refineries, water and sewage treatment plants, electrical generators, and nuclear power plants. Essentially, SCADA systems provide a link between the physical world and the electronic world.

SCADA systems consist of multiple sensors, a master computer, and communications infrastructure. The sensors connect to physical equipment. They read status data such as the open/closed status of a switch or a valve, as well as measurements such as pressure, flow, voltage, and current. They control the equipment by sending signals to it, such as opening or closing a switch or a valve or setting the speed of a pump.

The sensors are connected in a network, and each sensor typically has an Internet address (Internet Protocol, or IP, address, discussed in Chapter 6). If attackers gain access to the network, they can cause serious damage, such as disrupting the power grid over a large area or upsetting the operations of a large chemical or nuclear plant. Such actions could have catastrophic results. IT's About Business 4.2 illustrates a SCADA attack on a simple home device.

## IT's [about business]

### 4.2  Shodan: Good Tool or Bad Tool?    MIS

Jim Smith got a terrible surprise from a stranger on his birthday. After the celebration, he heard an unfamiliar voice coming from his daughter's room. The person was telling his sleeping 2-year-old, "Wake up." When Smith rushed into her bedroom, he discovered that the voice was coming from his baby monitor and that whoever had taken control of the monitor was also able to manipulate the camera. Significantly, the baby monitor enables users to monitor audio and video over the Internet from anywhere in the world. Smith immediately unplugged the monitor, which is made by Foscam (*www.foscam.us*) of Shenzhen, China. Smith was the victim of a SCADA attack, albeit on a simple, inexpensive home device used by millions of families.

Months before Smith's experience, security researchers had discovered software flaws in the monitor that enabled attackers to take control of the monitor remotely if they entered the username "admin." Foscam had already developed a fix, but it had not aggressively informed users about it. When Smith checked his Foscam account, he discovered that the hacker had added his own username so that he could sign in whenever he wanted to. Smith is now considering initiating a class action against Foscam. He could find other plaintiffs by using a search engine called Shodan (*www.shodanhq.com*). In fact, Shodan is probably the tool that the attacker used to find Smith!

Shodan crawls the Internet searching for devices, many of which are programmed to answer. It has discovered a broad array of systems, including cars, fetal heart monitors, office building heating control systems, water treatment facilities, power plant controls, traffic lights, and glucometers. A search for the type of baby monitor used by the Smiths reveals that more than 40,000 other people are using the monitor—and all of them may be vulnerable to hackers!

Shodan has become a critical tool for security researchers, law enforcement officials, and hackers searching for devices that should not be on the Internet or that are vulnerable to being hacked. An industry report from the Swedish technology company Ericsson estimated that by 2020 some 50 billion devices will be networked into an "Internet of Things." (We discuss the Internet of Things in Chapter 8.)

Hackers have used Shodan to find Webcams whose security is so poor that the hackers only needed to type an Internet Protocol (IP) address into their browser to look into people's homes, security offices, hospital operating rooms, childcare centers, and drug dealer operations. Shodan has also targeted banks, apartment buildings, convention centers, and even Google's headquarters in Australia, in which the security, lights, and heating and cooling systems operated online and therefore could be controlled by a hacker. In 2014, one security analyst noted that there were 2,000 facilities on the Internet that hackers could take control of if they could determine the IP address. The Department of Homeland Security (DHS) has revealed that hackers had used Shodan to virtually break into the energy management systems of a "state government facility" and a "New Jersey manufacturing company."

Shodan's freemium model allows users to obtain 10 search results for free. Approximately 10,000 users pay a nominal one-time fee of up to $20 to obtain 10,000 results per search. A dozen institutional users, all of them cybersecurity firms, pay five figures annually for access to Shodan's entire database of 1.5 billion connected devices.

Shodan is extremely valuable for calling attention to the mistakes that gadget companies make when they configure their products as well as consumers' inattention to the security of the products they buy. Every device that connects to the Internet should be password-protected, although many are not. Nor should these devices ship with a default username and password, although many do. How vulnerable are these devices to attacks? Consider that in 2013 an anonymous user took control of more than 400,000 Internet-connected devices using just four default passwords.

*Sources:* Compiled from D. Pauli, "Shodan Boss Finds 250,000 Routers Have Common Keys," *The Register*, February 20, 2015; P. Nelson, "Security Flaw Search Engine Shodan Adds Reports," *Network World*, October 7, 2014; "Locating ICS and SCADA Systems on .EDU Networks with Shodan,"

*Tripwire*, May 14, 2014; A. Stern, "Getting Rid of Shady Toolbars," *Kaspersky Labs Daily*, March 27, 2014; A. Grau, "Shutting the Door on Shodan," *Manufacturing.net*, December 16, 2013; K. Hill, "A Google for Hackers," *Forbes*, September 23, 2013; A. Couts, "Shodan, the Search Engine That Points Hackers Directly to Your Webcam," *Digital Trends*, September 5, 2013; R. McMillan, "The Internet of Things: Shodan," *Wired*, July 8, 2013; D. Goldman, "Shodan: The Scariest Search Engine on the Internet," *CNN Money*, April 8, 2013; *www.shodanhq.com*, accessed March 27, 2015.

**Questions**

1. Is Shodan more useful for hackers or for security defenders? Provide specific examples to support your choice.
2. What impact should Shodan have on the manufacturers of devices that connect to the Internet?
3. As an increasingly large number of devices are connected to the Internet, what will Shodan's impact be? Provide examples to support your answer.
4. Explain how Shodan can be used to conduct a SCADA attack.

## Cyberterrorism and Cyberwarfare

**Cyberterrorism** and **cyberwarfare** refer to malicious acts in which attackers use a target's computer systems, particularly via the Internet, to cause physical, real-world harm or severe disruption, often to carry out a political agenda. Although not proven in early 2015, the U.S. government considers the Sony hack (see chapter opening case) to be an example of cyberwarfare committed by North Korea. These actions range from gathering data to attacking critical infrastructure (e.g., via SCADA systems). We treat the two types of attacks as synonymous here, even though cyberterrorism is typically carried out by individuals or groups, whereas cyberwarfare is carried out by nation states.

# before you go on...

1. Why has the theft of computing devices become more serious over time?
2. What are the three types of software attacks?
3. Define alien software, and explain why it is a serious problem.
4. What is a SCADA system? Why can attacks against SCADA system have catastrophic consequences?

# What Organizations Are Doing to Protect Information Resources

4.4

Why is stopping cybercriminals such a challenge? Table 4.3 illustrates the many major difficulties involved in protecting information. Because organizing an appropriate defense system is so important to the entire enterprise, it is one of the major responsibilities of any prudent CIO as well as of the functional managers who control information resources. In fact, IT security is the business of *everyone* in an organization.

In addition to the problems listed in Table 4.3, another reason why information resources are difficult to protect is that the online commerce industry is not particularly willing to

| **Table 4.3** The Difficulties in Protecting Information Resources | • Hundreds of potential threats exist.<br>• Computing resources may be situated in many locations.<br>• Many individuals control or have access to information assets.<br>• Computer networks can be located outside the organization, making them difficult to protect.<br>• Rapid technological changes make some controls obsolete as soon as they are installed.<br>• Many computer crimes are undetected for a long period of time, so it is difficult to learn from experience.<br>• People tend to violate security procedures because the procedures are inconvenient.<br>• The amount of computer knowledge necessary to commit computer crimes is usually minimal. As a matter of fact, a potential criminal can learn hacking, for free, on the Internet.<br>• The costs of preventing hazards can be very high. Therefore, most organizations simply cannot afford to protect themselves against all possible hazards.<br>• It is difficult to conduct a cost–benefit justification for controls before an attack occurs because it is difficult to assess the impact of a hypothetical attack. |
|---|---|

install safeguards that would make completing transactions more difficult or complicated. As one example, merchants could demand passwords or personal identification numbers for all credit card transactions. However, these requirements might discourage people from shopping online. For credit card companies, it is cheaper to block a stolen credit card and move on than to invest time and money prosecuting cybercriminals.

And the final reason why information resources are difficult to protect is that it is extremely difficult to catch perpetrators. However, IT's About Business 4.3 shows that it is possible to catch attackers, albeit with great effort, time, and expense.

# IT's [about business]

### 4.3 Catching a Hacker

To be a hacker, all you really need is a computer and an Internet connection. Aleksandr Panin is a Russian hacker who created SpyEye, one of the most sophisticated and destructive malicious software programs ever developed. According to court documents, SpyEye appeared on January 10, 2010, when Panin placed it for sale on *www.darkode.com*, an underground hacker marketplace. A basic SpyEye package sold for $1,000, while a top-of-the-line version cost up to $8,500.

SpyEye automates the collection of confidential personal and financial information. The malware can hijack Web browsers and/or present fake bank Web pages that prompt users to enter their login information. SpyEye also scans infected computers for credit card credentials.

The FBI estimates that Panin had some 150 clients. Panin allegedly provided his clients with SpyEye updates and security patches as well as after-sale maintenance, updates, and technical support.

SpyEye systematically infected nearly 1.5 million computers around the world, creating a massive botnet. SpyEye penetrated computers at multinational corporations, financial institutions, and governments. The malware collected bank account credentials, credit card numbers, passwords, and personal identification numbers. The damage from thefts conducted using SpyEye totals $500 million, according to the U.S. Justice Department.

### The Chase

To catch Panin, FBI agents traveled the world, hacked into computers, and posed as cybercrooks. They examined millions of lines of computer code; argued with law enforcement officials in Thailand, Bulgaria, and Britain; and finally waited patiently for Panin to leave Russia before they could arrest him. Let's see how Panin was brought to justice.

In February 2011, the FBI seized and searched a SpyEye command-and-control server located near Atlanta, Georgia. (Note: A command-and-control server is a computer that controls a botnet.) The agency alleges that Hamza Bendelladj, Panin's online collaborator, operated this server remotely from his home in Algeria. That server controlled more than 200 computers infected with SpyEye, including computers connected to 253 banks in North Carolina, New York, California, and Virginia.

In the summer of 2011, FBI informants, posing as cybercriminals, communicated with Panin on *www.darkode.com* to purchase a SpyEye package costing $8,500. Following his instructions, they paid for the malware with money electronically transferred to a digital account at Liberty Reserve, a Costa Rica-based money processor that subsequently was shut down by federal agents in 2012. By December, agents had collected enough evidence of criminal acts (two hard drives and more than 1 terabyte of data) to secure a 23-count indictment against Bendelladj. However, they still did not know the creator of SpyEye. As a result, a grand jury indicted "John Doe."

Federal agents then sought the assistance of white-hat hackers. This term refers to ethical computer system hackers who specialize in testing organizational information systems to identify weaknesses and thus improve security. In the SpyEye case, the FBI and the Justice Department cited the work of TrendMicro (*www.trendmicro.com*), a computer security firm based in Dallas, Texas, that employs 1,200 white-hat hackers who identify and stop malware attacks.

TrendMicro's initial step was to identify the digital characteristics of SpyEye's computer code and map the malware's infrastructure (i.e., IP addresses and the location of command-and-control computers). The company then infiltrated an underground forum frequently visited by Panin and his customers.

Fortunately for the investigators, Panin and a computer programmer he worked with who was known online as "bx1" demonstrated occasionally poor operational security. Specifically, they let slip e-mail addresses and information about instant messenger accounts, which TrendMicro used to find actual identities.

For instance, on one SpyEye server, TrendMicro analysts analyzed the computer code and discovered an online name, "bx1," and an e-mail address and login credentials for virtest, a detection-testing service used by cybercriminals. The researchers matched that information with names used in the underground criminal forum to link the computer code to one of Panin's online collaborators. TrendMicro turned over this information to law enforcement officials.

Even after federal investigators collected the evidence, however, the new indictment remained sealed for two years so that Panin would not know he had been identified. Russia does not have an extradition treaty with the United States, so federal agents had to wait until Panin left Russia.

## The Capture

Thai authorities arrested Bendelladj on January 5, 2013, at the airport in Bangkok as he traveled from Malaysia to Egypt. He was extradited in May, 2013 to face U.S. charges. He has pleaded not guilty.

FBI agents arrested Panin on July 1, 2013, when he flew through Hartsfield–Jackson Atlanta International Airport. Panin had been visiting a friend in the Dominican Republic and was flying back to Russia. As of early 2015, Panin faced 30 years in a U.S. prison after pleading guilty in January 2014 to bank and wire fraud.

Panin's capture was one of law enforcement's great successes in the war on cybercrime. However, efforts to catch cybercriminals are often stymied by layers of encryption, anonymous online names, and uncooperative foreign governments. Panin's case illustrates the intricate, widespread puzzle that U.S. law enforcement must solve in their efforts to find and prosecute hackers who attack U.S. consumers, banks, and retailers. In essence, law enforcement officials must chase digital footprints.

*Sources*: "Russian National To Be Sentenced in SpyEye Malware Case in March 2015," *Russian Legal Information Agency*, November 14. 2014; "SpyEye Hacker Arrested," *CyberWarZone*, May 24, 2014; "SpyEye-Using Cybercriminal Arrested in Britain," *TrendMicro Blog*, May 22, 2014; K. Eichenwald, "The $500,000,000 Cyber-Heist," *Newsweek*, March 13, 2014; D. Leger and A. Arutunyan, "How the Feds Brought Down a Notorious Russian Hacker," *USA Today*, March 5, 2014; D. Neal, "FBI Bests SpyEye Banking Botnet Coder," *The Inquirer*, January 29, 2014; A. Grossman and D. Yadron, "Island Vacation Costs Russian Hacker Aleksandr Panin," *The Wall Street Journal*, January 28, 2014; "Cyber Criminal Pleads Guilty to Developing and Distributing Notorious SpyEye Malware," *U.S. Department of Justice News*, January 28, 2014; D. Kerr, "SpyEye Malware Inventor Pleads Guilty to Bank Fraud," *CNET News*, January 28, 2014.

### Questions

1. Why did the FBI need to "argue with law enforcement officials in various countries"?
2. Describe the difficulties that investigators encounter in bringing cybercriminals to justice.

---

Organizations spend a great deal of time and money protecting their information resources. Before doing so, they perform risk management.

A **risk** is the probability that a threat will impact an information resource. The goal of **risk management** is to identify, control, and minimize the impact of threats. In other words, risk management seeks to reduce risk to acceptable levels. Risk management consists of three processes: risk analysis, risk mitigation, and controls evaluation.

Organizations perform risk analyses to ensure that their IS security programs are cost-effective. **Risk analysis** involves three steps: (1) assessing the value of each asset being protected, (2) estimating the probability that each asset will be compromised, and (3) comparing the probable costs of the asset's being compromised with the costs of protecting that asset. The organization then considers how to mitigate the risk.

In **risk mitigation**, the organization takes concrete actions against risks. Risk mitigation has two functions: (1) implementing controls to prevent identified threats from occurring, and (2) developing a means of recovery if the threat becomes a reality. There are several risk mitigation strategies that organizations can adopt. The three most common are risk acceptance, risk limitation, and risk transference.

- *Risk acceptance*: Accept the potential risk, continue operating with no controls, and absorb any damages that occur.
- *Risk limitation*: Limit the risk by implementing controls that minimize the impact of the threat.
- *Risk transference*: Transfer the risk by using other means to compensate for the loss, such as by purchasing insurance.

Finally, in controls evaluation, the organization examines the costs of implementing adequate control measures against the value of those control measures. If the costs of implementing a control are greater than the value of the asset being protected, the control is not cost-effective. In the next section, you will study the various controls that organizations use to protect their information resources.

# before you go on...

**1.** Describe several reasons why it is difficult to protect information resources.

**2.** Compare and contrast risk management and risk analysis.

## 4.5 Information Security Controls

To protect their information assets, organizations implement **controls**, or defense mechanisms (also called *countermeasures*). These controls are designed to protect all of the components of an information system, including data, software, hardware, and networks. Because there are so many diverse threats, organizations utilize layers of controls, or *defense-in-depth*.

Controls are intended to prevent accidental hazards, deter intentional acts, detect problems as early as possible, enhance damage recovery, and correct problems. Before you study controls in more detail, it is important to emphasize that the single most valuable control is user education and training. Effective and ongoing education makes every member of the organization aware of the vital importance of information security.

In this section, you will learn about three major types of controls: physical controls, access controls, and communications controls. Figure 4.2 illustrates these controls. In addition to applying controls, organizations plan for business continuity in case of a disaster, and they periodically audit their information resources to detect possible threats. You will study these topics in this section as well.

### Physical Controls

**Physical controls** prevent unauthorized individuals from gaining access to a company's facilities. Common physical controls include walls, doors, fencing, gates, locks, badges, guards, and alarm systems. More sophisticated physical controls include pressure sensors, temperature sensors, and motion detectors. One shortcoming of physical controls is that they can be inconvenient to employees.

Guards deserve special mention because they have very difficult jobs, for at least two reasons. First, their jobs are boring and repetitive and generally do not pay well. Second, if guards

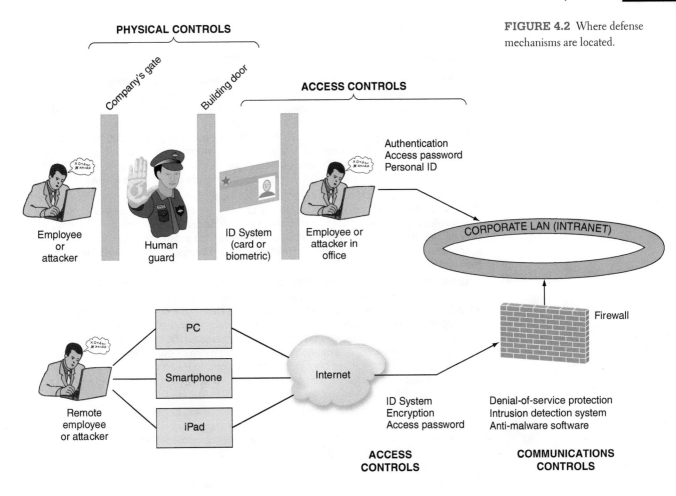

**FIGURE 4.2** Where defense mechanisms are located.

perform their jobs thoroughly, the other employees harass them, particularly if they slow up the process of entering the facility.

Organizations also implement physical security measures that limit computer users to acceptable login times and locations. These controls also limit the number of unsuccessful login attempts, and they require all employees to log off their computers when they leave for the day. In addition, they set the employees' computers to automatically log off the user after a certain period of disuse.

## Access Controls

**Access controls** restrict unauthorized individuals from using information resources. These controls involve two major functions: authentication and authorization. **Authentication** confirms the identity of the person requiring access. After the person is authenticated (identified), the next step is authorization. **Authorization** determines which actions, rights, or privileges the person has, based on his or her verified identity. Let's examine these functions more closely.

Authentication.    To authenticate (identify) authorized personnel, an organization can use one or more of the following methods: something the user is, something the user has, something the user does, and/or something the user knows.

Something the user *is*, also known as **biometrics**, is an authentication method that examines a person's innate physical characteristics. Common biometric applications are fingerprint scans, palm scans, retina scans, iris recognition, and facial recognition. Of these applications, fingerprints, retina scans, and iris recognition provide the most definitive identification. The following example shows how powerful biometrics can be for identification purposes.

Consider this example:

## The Biometric Identification Project of India

India has vast numbers of anonymous poor citizens. To address this problem, the nation instituted its Unique Identification Project, also known as Aadhaar, which means "the foundation" in several Indian languages. The goal of the project is to issue identification numbers linked to the fingerprints and iris scans of every individual in India. This process will ultimately encompass some 1.2 billion people who speak more than 300 languages and dialects. The biometrics and the Aadhaar identification number will serve as a verifiable, portable, and unique national ID. The Aadhaar project should enable millions of poor Indian citizens to access government services that previously were out of reach to them.

Aadhaar seeks to remedy a critical problem that afflicts poor people. The Indian government does not officially acknowledge the existence of many impoverished citizens because these individuals do not possess birth certificates and other official documentation. Therefore, they cannot access government services to which they are entitled, nor can they open bank accounts. When the project started, many Indian households were "unbanked," meaning they had to stash their savings in cash around their homes.

Aadhaar went into operation in September 2010, when officials armed with iris scanners, fingerprint scanners, digital cameras, and laptops began to register the first few villagers as well as slum dwellers in the country's capital city, Delhi. One of the most daunting challenges confronting the project is to ensure that each individual's record in the database is matched to one and only one person. For this process, Aadhaar must check all 10 fingerprints and both irises of each person against those of everyone else in the country. Using 10 prints and both irises boosts the accuracy rate to 99 percent. However, in a country the size of India, 99 percent accuracy means that 12 million people could end up with faulty records.

Additionally, Aadhaar faces enormous physical and technical challenges: reaching millions of illiterate Indians who have never seen a computer, persuading them to have their irises scanned, ensuring that their scanned information is accurate, and safeguarding the resulting massive amounts of data. In addition, civil libertarians object to the project on privacy grounds.

Further, a number of people have complained that the Aadhaar cards they have received contain errors in their names, addresses, and other personal information. One newspaper reported that an Aadhaar recipient received a card that had the face of a dog in place of his photograph.

As of early 2015, Aadhaar had enrolled some 850 million people (8.5 billion fingerprints, 1.7 billion iris images, 850 million facial photos), comprising 10 petabytes of data. At the current rate of enrollment, Aadhaar planners hope to reach the entire population of India by mid-2016.

*Sources:* Compiled from V. Dhoot and M. Raishekhar, "Nandan Nilekani Impresses Narendra Modi & Arun Jaitley, Gets Aadhaar a Lifeline," *The Economic Times*, July 24, 2014; S. Bhattacharjee, "Aadhaar Future at Stake, Govt Seeks Meeting with States," *The Indian Express*, June 17, 2014; B. Rohith, "Aadhaar Drive Loses Its Pace," *The Times of India*, March 15, 2014; J. Ribeiro, "Indian Biometric ID Project Faces Court Hurdle," *PC World*, September 24, 2013; S. Rai, "Why India's Identity Scheme Is Groundbreaking," *BBC News*, June 5, 2012; E. Hannon, "For India's Undocumented Citizens, an ID at Last," *NPR.org*, March 1, 2012; "World's Biggest Biometric ID Scheme Forges Ahead," *BBC News India*, February 12, 2012; M. Magnier, "India's Biometric ID Number Plan Divided by Bureaucracy," *Los Angeles Times*, January 28, 2012; B. Turbeville, "Cashless Society: India Implements First Biometric ID Program for All of Its 1.2 Billion Residents," *Infowars.com*, January 12, 2012; V. Beiser, "Identified," *Wired*, September 2011; *www.iaadhaar.com*, accessed April 25, 2015.

### Questions

1. Describe the problems that India is facing in implementing this biometric identification system.
2. Describe the benefits that India hopes to achieve in implementing the biometric identification system.
3. Describe the benefits that the biometric identification system should provide to India's impoverished citizens.

Something the user *has* is an authentication mechanism that includes regular identification (ID) cards, smart ID cards, and tokens (see IT's About Business 4.4). *Regular ID cards*, or *dumb cards*, typically have the person's picture and often his or her signature. *Smart ID cards* have an embedded chip that stores pertinent information about the user. (Smart ID cards used for identification differ from smart cards used in electronic commerce, which you learn about in Chapter 7. Both types of card have embedded chips, but they are used for different purposes.) *Tokens* have embedded chips and a digital display that presents a login number that the employees use to access the organization's network. The number changes with each login.

Something the user *does* is an authentication mechanism that includes voice and signature recognition. In *voice recognition*, the user speaks a phrase (e.g., his or her name and department) that has been previously recorded under controlled conditions. The voice recognition system matches the two voice signals. In *signature recognition*, the user signs his or her name, and the system matches this signature with one previously recorded under controlled, monitored conditions. Signature recognition systems also match the speed and the pressure of the signature.

Something the user *knows* is an authentication mechanism that includes passwords and passphrases. **Passwords** present a huge information security problem in all organizations. Most of us have to remember numerous passwords for different online services, and we typically must choose complicated strings of characters to make them harder to guess. Security experts examined the frequency and usage of passwords belonging to 500,000 computer users. They found that each person had an average of 6.5 passwords that he or she used for 25 different online accounts. Unfortunately, as you see in IT's About Business 4.4, passwords (even strong passwords) are terribly vulnerable to attack.

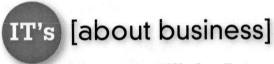

## IT's [about business]

### 4.4 Let's Kill the Password!

We bank online, track our finances online, fill out our tax returns online, and store our photos, our documents, and our data online. As a result, the amount of personal information being stored online has exploded. Further, we typically link our various online accounts, using our e-mail addresses as universal usernames, a problem that becomes worse as the number of our online accounts increases. The combination of our e-mail address as username and a password creates a single point of failure that attackers can exploit with devastating results. In fact, according to a Verizon report, 76 percent of organizational breaches exploit weak or stolen user credentials.

How did this problem start? Companies that conduct business over the Internet had to devise a method to make people feel secure about conducting online transactions and storing personal information on merchants' Web sites. To function in the real world, the security systems provided by online merchants must effectively manage the trade-off between convenience and security. The most secure system is useless if it is too difficult for users to access. For example, if the merchant requires customer passwords to be 50 characters in length and to include special symbols, these passwords might keep their customers' accounts safe, but they would be impossible to remember.

We have all bought into the idea that a password is sufficient to protect our data, as long as it is sufficiently elaborate. In reality, however, passwords by themselves can no longer protect us, regardless of how unique or complex we make them.

Attackers employ a number of strategies to obtain our passwords, no matter how strong they are. Among the most common methods are the following:

- Attackers can steal them because many people still use weak, predictable passwords such as birthdays.

- Attackers can crack them. With modern computers, cracking passwords utilizing brute-force computation takes just a few seconds.

- Attackers can obtain them online. Hackers have dumped hundreds of millions of "hashes"—that is, encrypted but readily crackable passwords—online for everyone to see.

- Attackers can discover them through phishing and spear phishing attacks.

The ultimate problem with passwords is that it is impossible for any password-based authentication system to be memorable enough to allow multiple online logins, flexible enough to vary from Web site to Web site, convenient enough to be easily reset, and yet also secure against brute-force hacking. So, what are users and businesses supposed to do?

Several initiatives are underway to improve the authentication process under the auspices of the Fast Identity Online (FIDO) Alliance (*https://fidoalliance.org*). FIDO is an industry consortium launched in February 2013 to address the lack of interoperability among strong authentication devices and the problems that users face in creating and remembering multiple usernames and passwords. Google, Microsoft, PayPal, and Lenovo were among the founding members.

The concept underlying all of these products is that identifiers such as a person's fingerprint, iris scan, and the unique identifier of any USB device or contactless ring will not be sent over the Internet. Rather, they will be checked locally. The only data that will be transferred over the Internet are cryptographic keys that cannot be reverse-engineered to steal a person's identify. Let's consider a few examples.

- Nok Nok Labs (*www.noknok.com*) employs tools on user devices, such as a camera, touchscreen, and microphone to provide biometric authentication. Users store both their login data and their biometric data—voice, facial features, and fingerprints—on their personal computers, smartphones, and tablets. When companies employ the Nok Nok protocol, their customers have the option of using these authentication methods instead of a password on their devices. When the user provides a valid match, his or her device connects securely to the desired Web site. This process provides strong multifactor authentication.

- Bionym (*www.bionym.com*) manufactures a wristband called the Nymi that verifies users' identities by the unique signals generated by their heartbeat. The Nymi has many potential uses. For example, it can open a car door, authenticate a mobile payment, and unlock your phone.

- Eyelock (*www.eyelock.com*) manufactures the Myris, a device that scans the iris of users' eyes for authentication.

- Yubico (*www.yubico.com*) manufactures the YubiKey, a physical token used in combination with a username and password for two-factor authentication. Users insert the YubiKey into a USB port or tap it against a mobile device when they need to log into an app or a Web service.

- Apple (*www.apple.com*) provides its TouchID feature on the iPhone 6 and iPhone 6 Plus, the iPad Air 2, and the iPad Mini 3. TouchID uses biometric authentication by scanning and recognizing users' fingerprints.

- Hoyos Labs (*www.hoyoslabs.com*) has developed the 1U, an app and subscription-based service that employs biometric authentication in the form of facial recognition. For example, when users access 1U on their smartphones to access their bank accounts, the app instructs them to hold the selfie camera to their faces, quickly verifies their identities, launches a new tab in their browsers, and logs in to their bank accounts automatically. In this entire process, users never touch the keyboard or keypad.

- Twitter (*http://twitter.com*) enables users to replace passwords with a text message-based one-time passcode service, called Digits. Digits enables users to log in using their mobile phone number as an identifier. Digits then sends users a one-time passcode by text message to access an app.

- Barclays (*www.barclaysus.com*) is implementing biometric authentication in the form of voice recognition for its 12 million retail banking customers.

- The NFC Ring (*http://nfcring.com*) contains contactless RFID technology that can automatically unlock an NFC-capable phone when a person picks it up. In addition, the ring can operate other RFID devices such as door locks.

- The Google security key (*www.google.com*) is a physical USB device that users insert into their computers. Users then tap the key when prompted by Chrome.

In the future, online identity verification will no longer be a password-based system. Instead, the password, if used at all, will be a less significant component of a multifactor process. Each online account will have to integrate many pieces of information: who we are and what we do; where we go and when; what we have with us; and how we act when we are there—true multifactor authentication. Biometrics will undoubtedly play an important role in future authentication systems.

Of course, as measures such as these are implemented, future security systems will require significant sacrifices to our privacy. These systems will need to draw upon our location and habits, and perhaps even our speech patterns or our DNA. The only path to improved security is to allow our movements to be tracked in all sorts of ways and to have those movements and metrics tied to our actual identity. This shift will involve significant investments and inconvenience. Also, it will likely raise concerns among privacy advocates.

*Sources:* Compiled from A. Diallo, "Why Hackers Love Passwords," *Forbes*, December 15, 2014; A. Diallo, "1U App Replaces Passwords with Your Face," *Forbes*, December 4, 2014; I. Urbina, "The Secret Life of Passwords," *The New York Times*, November 19, 2014; T. Simonite, "Unlock Your Computer and Websites with a Glance," *MIT Technology Review*, November 13, 2014; "The Power of Your Fingerprint to Change the World of Smartphones," *Pocket-Lint.com*, November 13, 2014; W. Ashford, "Twitter Announces Text Message-Based Password Initiative," *Computer Weekly*, October 23, 2014; T. Simonite, "A Physical Key to Your Google Account," *MIT Technology Review*, October 21, 2014; "Millions of Voiceprints Quietly Being Harvested as Latest Identification Tool," *The Guardian*, October 13, 2014; E. Weise, "Passwords: A Weak Link in Your Security," *USA Today*, September 9, 2014; M. Williams, "Seven Ways DARPA Is Trying to Kill the Password," *IDG News Service*, August 8, 2014; M. Dickey, "This Startup Lets You Use Your Heartbeat as a Password, and It's Awesome," *Business Insider*, January 9, 2014; T. Simonite, "CES 2014: A Technological Assault on the Password," *MIT Technology Review*, January 8, 2014; M. Flores, "Eyelock's Myris: You'll Never Have to Enter Another Password Again," *Tech Radar*, January 7, 2014; "FPC and Nok Nok Labs Deliver Infrastructure for Fingerprint-Based Strong Authentication," *PR Newswire*, November 26, 2013; M. Flacy, "NFC Ring Can Unlock Your Smartphone or Front Door," *Digital Trends*, August 8, 2013.

**Questions**

1. What are the advantages, if any, of any of our FIDO examples over strong passwords?

2. Examine the strength of the passwords you use. How vulnerable are your passwords to guessing? To brute-force hacking?

3. Does the security burden fall primarily on the user? On the company that the user is doing business with? On both? Support your answer.

4. Is it possible to ever have complete security in your online transactions? Why or why not? Explain your answer.

All users should use *strong passwords*, which are difficult for hackers to discover. The basic guidelines for creating strong passwords are the following:

- They should be difficult to guess.
- They should be long rather than short.
- They should have uppercase letters, lowercase letters, numbers, and special characters.
- They should not be recognizable words.
- They should not be the name of anything or anyone familiar, such as family names or names of pets.
- They should not be a recognizable string of numbers, such as a Social Security number or a birthday.

Unfortunately, strong passwords are more difficult to remember than weak ones. Consequently, employees frequently write them down, which defeats their purpose. The ideal solution to this dilemma is to create a strong password that is also easy to remember. To achieve this objective, many people use passphrases.

A *passphrase* is a series of characters that is longer than a password but is still easy to memorize. Examples of passphrases are "maytheforcebewithyoualways" and "goaheadmakemyday." A passphrase can serve as a password itself, or it can help you create a strong password. You can turn a passphrase into a strong password in this manner. Starting with the last passphrase above, take the first letter of each word. You will have "gammd." Then, capitalize every other letter to create "GaMmD". Finally, add special characters and numbers to create "9GaMmD//*." You now have a strong password that you can remember.

To identify authorized users more efficiently and effectively, organizations frequently implement more than one type of authentication, a strategy known as *multifactor authentication*. This system is particularly important when users log in from remote locations.

Single-factor authentication, which is notoriously weak, commonly consists simply of a password. Two-factor authentication consists of a password plus one type of biometric identification (e.g., a fingerprint). Three-factor authentication is any combination of three authentication methods. In most cases, the more factors the system utilizes, the more reliable it is. However, stronger authentication is also more expensive, and, as with strong passwords, it can be irritating to users.

**Authorization.** After users have been properly authenticated, the rights and privileges to which they are entitled on the organization's systems are established in a process called *authorization*. A **privilege** is a collection of related computer system operations that a user is authorized to perform. Companies typically base authorization policies on the principle of **least privilege**, which posits that users be granted the privilege for an activity only if there is a justifiable need for them to perform that activity.

## Communications Controls

**Communications controls** (also called **network controls**) secure the movement of data across networks. Communications controls consist of firewalls, anti-malware systems, whitelisting and blacklisting, encryption, virtual private networks (VPNs), transport layer security, and employee monitoring systems.

**Firewalls.** A **firewall** is a system that prevents a specific type of information from moving between untrusted networks, such as the Internet, and private networks, such as your company's network. Put simply, firewalls prevent unauthorized Internet users from accessing private networks. All messages entering or leaving your company's network pass through a firewall. The firewall examines each message and blocks those that do not meet specified security rules.

Firewalls range from simple, for home use, to very complex for organizational use. Figure 4.3a illustrates a basic firewall for a home computer. In this case, the firewall is implemented as software on the home computer. Figure 4.3b shows an organization that has implemented an external firewall, which faces the Internet, and an internal firewall, which faces the company network. Corporate firewalls typically consist of software running on a computer

**FIGURE 4.3** (a) Basic firewall for home computer. (b) Organization with two firewalls and demilitarized zone.

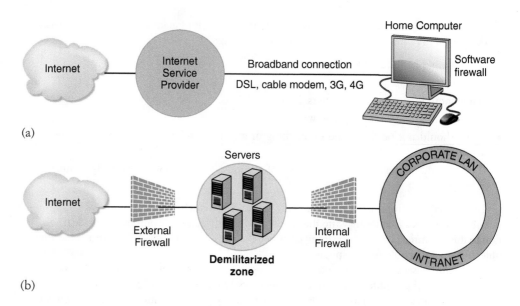

(a)

(b)

dedicated to the task. A **demilitarized zone (DMZ)** is located between the two firewalls. Messages from the Internet must first pass through the external firewall. If they conform to the defined security rules, they are then sent to company servers located in the DMZ. These servers typically handle Web page requests and e-mail. Any messages designated for the company's internal network (e.g., its intranet) must pass through the internal firewall, again with its own defined security rules, to gain access to the company's private network.

The danger from viruses and worms is so severe that many organizations are placing firewalls at strategic points *inside* their private networks. In this way, if a virus or worm does get through both the external and internal firewalls, then the internal damage may be contained.

**Anti-malware Systems.**   Anti-malware systems, also called *antivirus*, or *AV*, software, are software packages that attempt to identify and eliminate viruses and worms, and other malicious software. AV software is implemented at the organizational level by the IS department. Hundreds of AV software packages are currently available. Among the best known are Norton AntiVirus (*www.symantec.com*), McAfee VirusScan (*www.mcafee.com*), and Trend Micro PC-cillin (*www.trendmicro.com*).

Anti-malware systems are generally reactive. Whereas firewalls filter network traffic according to categories of activities that are likely to cause problems, anti-malware systems filter traffic according to a database of specific problems. These systems create definitions, or signatures, of various types of malware and then update these signatures in their products. The anti-malware software then examines suspicious computer code to determine whether it matches a known signature. If the software identifies a match, then it removes the code. For this reason, organizations regularly update their malware definitions.

Because malware is such a serious problem, the leading vendors are rapidly developing anti-malware systems that function proactively as well as reactively. These systems evaluate behavior rather than relying entirely on signature matching. In theory, therefore, it is possible to catch malware before it can infect systems.

**Whitelisting and Blacklisting.**   A report by the Yankee Group (*www.yankeegroup.com*), a technology research and consulting firm, stated that 99 percent of organizations had installed anti-malware systems, but 62 percent still suffered malware attacks. As we have seen, anti-malware systems are usually reactive, and malware continues to infect companies.

One solution to this problem is **whitelisting**. Whitelisting is a process in which a company identifies the software that it will allow to run on its computers. Whitelisting permits acceptable software to run, and it either prevents any other software from running or lets new software run only in a quarantine environment until the company can verify its validity.

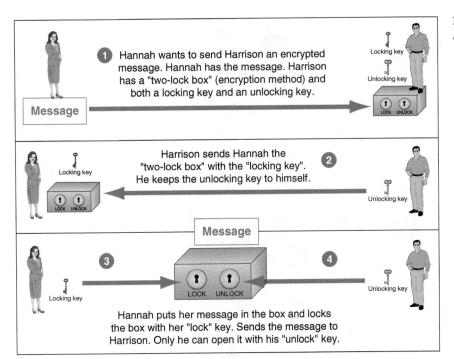

**FIGURE 4.4** How public key encryption works.

① Hannah wants to send Harrison an encrypted message. Hannah has the message. Harrison has a "two-lock box" (encryption method) and both a locking key and an unlocking key.

Message

Locking key
Unlocking key

② Harrison sends Hannah the "two-lock box" with the "locking key". He keeps the unlocking key to himself.

Locking key
Unlocking key

Message

③ ④

Locking key
LOCK UNLOCK
Unlocking key

Hannah puts her message in the box and locks the box with her "lock" key. Sends the message to Harrison. Only he can open it with his "unlock" key.

Whereas whitelisting allows nothing to run unless it is on the whitelist, **blacklisting** allows everything to run unless it is on the blacklist. A blacklist, then, includes certain types of software that are not allowed to run in the company environment. For example, a company might blacklist peer-to-peer file sharing on its systems. In addition to software, people, devices, and Web sites can also be whitelisted and blacklisted.

Encryption.    Organizations that do not have a secure channel for sending information use encryption to stop unauthorized eavesdroppers. **Encryption** is the process of converting an original message into a form that cannot be read by anyone except the intended receiver.

All encryption systems use a key, which is the code that scrambles and then decodes the messages. The majority of encryption systems use public-key encryption. **Public-key encryption**—also known as *asymmetric encryption*—uses two different keys: a public key and a private key (see Figure 4.4). The public key (locking key) and the private key (the unlocking key) are created simultaneously using the same mathematical formula or algorithm. Because the two keys are mathematically related, the data encrypted with one key can be decrypted by using the other key. The public key is publicly available in a directory that all parties can access. The private key is kept secret, never shared with anyone, and never sent across the Internet. In this system, if Hannah wants to send a message to Harrison, she first obtains Harrison's public key (locking key), which she uses to encrypt her message (put the message in the "two-lock box"). When Harrison receives Hannah's message, he uses his private key to decrypt it (open the box).

Although this arrangement is adequate for personal information, organizations that conduct business over the Internet require a more complex system. In these cases, a third party, called a **certificate authority**, acts as a trusted intermediary between the companies. The certificate authority issues digital certificates and verifies the integrity of the certificates. A **digital certificate** is an electronic document attached to a file that certifies that the file is from the organization it claims to be from and has not been modified from its original format. As you can see in Figure 4.5, Sony requests a digital certificate from VeriSign, a certificate authority, and it uses this certificate when it conducts business with Dell. Note that the digital certificate contains an identification number, the issuer, validity dates, and the requester's public key. For examples of certificate authorities, see *www.entrust.com, www.verisign.com, www.cybertrust. com, www.secude.com,* and *www.thawte.com.*

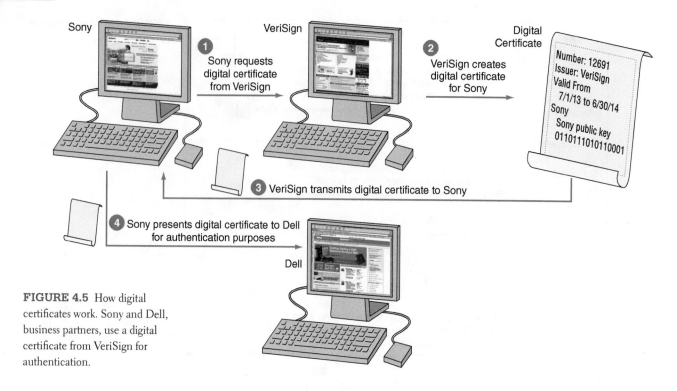

**FIGURE 4.5**  How digital certificates work. Sony and Dell, business partners, use a digital certificate from VeriSign for authentication.

**Virtual Private Networking.**  A **virtual private network** is a private network that uses a public network (usually the Internet) to connect users. VPNs essentially integrate the global connectivity of the Internet with the security of a private network and thereby extend the reach of the organization's networks. VPNs are called *virtual* because they have no separate physical existence. They use the public Internet as their infrastructure. They are created by using logins, encryption, and other techniques to enhance the user's *privacy*, which we defined in Chapter 3 as the right to be left alone and to be free of unreasonable personal intrusion.

VPNs have several advantages. First, they allow remote users to access the company network. Second, they provide flexibility. That is, mobile users can access the organization's network from properly configured remote devices. Third, organizations can impose their security policies through VPNs. For example, an organization may dictate that only corporate e-mail applications are available to users when they connect from unmanaged devices.

To provide secure transmissions, VPNs use a process called tunneling. **Tunneling** encrypts each data packet to be sent and places each encrypted packet inside another packet. In this manner, the packet can travel across the Internet with confidentiality, authentication, and integrity. Figure 4.6 illustrates a VPN and tunneling.

**Transport Layer Security.**  **Transport layer security**, formerly called **secure socket layer**, is an encryption standard used for secure transactions such as credit card purchases and online banking. TLS encrypts and decrypts data between a Web server and a browser end to end.

TLS is indicated by a URL that begins with "https" rather than "http," and it often displays a small padlock icon in the browser's status bar. Using a padlock icon to indicate a secure connection and placing this icon in a browser's status bar are artifacts of specific browsers. Other browsers use different icons (e.g., a key that is either broken or whole). The important thing to remember is that browsers usually provide visual confirmation of a secure connection.

**Employee Monitoring Systems.**  Many companies are taking a proactive approach to protecting their networks against what they view as one of their major security threats, namely, employee mistakes. These companies are implementing **employee monitoring systems**, which scrutinize their employees' computers, e-mail activities, and Internet surfing activities.

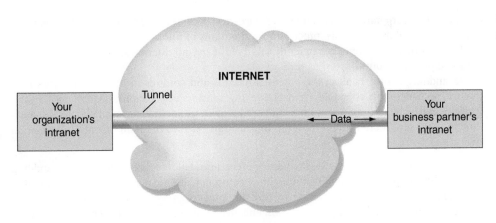

**FIGURE 4.6** Virtual private network and tunneling.

These products are useful to identify employees who spend too much time surfing on the Internet for personal reasons, who visit questionable Web sites, or who download music illegally. Vendors that provide monitoring software include SpectorSoft (*www.spectorsoft.com*) and Websense (*www.websense.com*).

## Business Continuity Planning

A basic security strategy for organizations is to be prepared for any eventuality. A critical element in any security system is a *business continuity plan*, also known as a *disaster recovery plan*.

**Business continuity** is the chain of events linking planning to protection and to recovery. The purpose of the business continuity plan is to provide guidance to people who keep the business operating after a disaster occurs. Employees use this plan to prepare for, react to, and recover from events that affect the security of information assets. The objective is to restore the business to normal operations as quickly as possible following an attack. The plan is intended to ensure that critical business functions continue.

In the event of a major disaster, organizations can employ several strategies for business continuity. These strategies include hot sites, warm sites, and cold sites. A *hot site* is a fully configured computer facility with all of the company's services, communications links, and physical plant operations. A hot site duplicates computing resources, peripherals, telephone systems, applications, and workstations. A *warm site* provides many of the same services and options as the hot site. However, it typically does not include the actual applications the company needs. A warm site includes computing equipment such as servers, but it often does not include user workstations. A *cold site* provides only rudimentary services and facilities, such as a building or a room with heating, air conditioning, and humidity control. This type of site provides no computer hardware or user workstations.

Hot sites reduce risk to the greatest extent, but they are the most expensive option. Conversely, cold sites reduce risk the least, but they are the least expensive option.

## Information Systems Auditing

Companies implement security controls to ensure that information systems function properly. These controls can be installed in the original system, or they can be added after a system is in operation. Installing controls is necessary but not sufficient to provide adequate security. In addition, people responsible for security need to answer questions such as: Are all controls installed as intended? Are they effective? Has any breach of security occurred? If so, what actions are required to prevent future breaches?

These questions must be answered by independent and unbiased observers. Such observers perform the task of *information systems auditing*. In an IS environment, an **audit** is an examination of information systems, their inputs, outputs, and processing.

**Types of Auditors and Audits.**    There are two types of auditors and audits: internal and external. IS auditing is usually a part of accounting *internal auditing*, and it is frequently performed by corporate internal auditors. An *external auditor* reviews the findings of the internal audit as well as the inputs, processing, and outputs of information systems. The external audit of information systems is frequently a part of the overall external auditing performed by a certified public accounting (CPA) firm.

IS auditing considers all of the potential hazards and controls in information systems. It focuses on issues such as operations, data integrity, software applications, security and privacy, budgets and expenditures, cost control, and productivity. Guidelines are available to assist auditors in their jobs, such as those from the Information Systems Audit and Control Association (*www.isaca.org*).

**How Is Auditing Executed?** IS auditing procedures fall into three categories: (1) auditing around the computer, (2) auditing through the computer, and (3) auditing with the computer.

*Auditing around the computer* means verifying processing by checking for known outputs using specific inputs. This approach is most effective for systems with limited outputs. In *auditing through the computer*, auditors check inputs, outputs, and processing. They review program logic, and they test the data contained within the system. *Auditing with the computer* means using a combination of client data, auditor software, and client and auditor hardware. This approach enables the auditor to perform tasks such as simulating payroll program logic using live data.

# before you go on...

1. What is the single most important information security control for organizations?
2. Differentiate between authentication and authorization. Which of these processes is always performed first?
3. Compare and contrast whitelisting and blacklisting.
4. What is the purpose of a disaster recovery plan?
5. What is information systems auditing?

# What's In IT For Me?

### For the Accounting Major

**ACCT**

Public companies, their accountants, and their auditors have significant information security responsibilities. Accountants are now being held professionally responsible for reducing risk, assuring compliance, eliminating fraud, and increasing the transparency of transactions according to Generally Accepted Accounting Principles (GAAP). The SEC and the Public Company Accounting Oversight Board (PCAOB), among other regulatory agencies, require information security, fraud prevention and detection, and internal controls over financial reporting. Forensic accounting, a combination of accounting and information security, is one of the most rapidly growing areas in accounting today.

### For the Finance Major

Because information security is essential to the success of organizations today, it is no longer just the concern of the CIO. As a result of global regulatory requirements and the passage of Sarbanes–Oxley Act, responsibility for information security lies with the CEO and CFO. Consequently, all aspects of the security audit, including the security of information and information systems, are a key concern for financial managers.

In addition, CFOs and treasurers are increasingly involved with investments in information technology. They know that a security breach of any kind can have devastating financial effects on a company. Banking and financial institutions are prime targets for computer criminals. A related problem is fraud involving stocks and bonds that are sold over the Internet. Finance personnel must be aware of both the hazards and the available controls associated with these activities.

### For the Marketing Major

Marketing professionals have new opportunities to collect data on their customers, for example, through business-to-consumer electronic commerce. Customers expect their data to be properly secured. However, profit-motivated criminals want those data. Therefore, marketing managers must analyze the risk of their operations. Failure to protect corporate and customer data will cause significant public relations problems, make customers very angry, may lead to lawsuits, and may result in losing customers to competitors. CRM operations and tracking customers' online buying habits can expose data to misuse (if they are not encrypted) or result in privacy violations.

### For the Production/Operations Management Major

Every process in a company's operations—inventory purchasing, receiving, quality control, production, and shipping—can be disrupted by an information technology security breach or an IT security breach at a business partner. Any weak link in supply chain management or enterprise resource management systems puts the entire chain at risk. Companies may be held liable for IT security failures that impact other companies.

### For the Human Resources Management Major

HR managers have responsibilities to secure confidential employee data. In addition, they must ensure that all employees explicitly verify that they understand the company's information security policies and procedures.

### For the MIS Major

The MIS function provides the security infrastructure that protects the organization's information assets. This function is critical to the success of the organization, even though it is almost invisible until an attack succeeds. All application development, network deployment, and introduction of new information technologies have to be guided by IT security considerations. MIS personnel must customize the risk exposure security model to help the company identify security risks and prepare responses to security incidents and disasters.

Senior executives of publicly held companies look to the MIS function for help in meeting Sarbanes–Oxley Act requirements, particularly in detecting "significant deficiencies" or "material weaknesses" in internal controls and remediating them. Other functional areas also look to the MIS function to help them meet their security responsibilities.

## [ Summary ]

1. **Identify the five factors that contribute to the increasing vulnerability of information resources, and provide a specific example of each one.**

   The five factors are the following:

   - Today's interconnected, interdependent, wirelessly networked business environment. Example: The Internet.

- Smaller, faster, cheaper computers and storage devices.

    Examples: Netbooks, thumb drives, iPads.
- Decreasing skills necessary to be a computer hacker.

    Example: Information system hacking programs circulating on the Internet.
- International organized crime taking over cybercrime.

    Example: Organized crime has formed transnational cybercrime cartels. Because it is difficult to know exactly where cyberattacks originate, these cartels are extremely hard to bring to justice.
- Lack of management support.

    Example: Suppose that your company spent $10 million on information security countermeasures last year, and they did not experience any successful attacks on their information resources. Short-sighted management might conclude that the company could spend less during the next year and obtain the same results. Bad idea.

**2. Compare and contrast human mistakes and social engineering, and provide a specific example of each one.**

*Human mistakes* are unintentional errors. However, employees can also make unintentional mistakes as a result of actions by an attacker, such as social engineering. *Social engineering* is an attack where the perpetrator uses social skills to trick or manipulate a legitimate employee into providing confidential company information.

An example of a human mistake is tailgating. An example of social engineering is when an attacker calls an employee on the phone and impersonates a superior in the company.

**3. Discuss the 10 types of deliberate attacks.**

The 10 types of deliberate attacks are the following:

*Espionage or trespass* occurs when an unauthorized individual attempts to gain illegal access to organizational information.

*Information extortion* occurs when an attacker either threatens to steal, or actually steals, information from a company. The perpetrator demands payment for not stealing the information, for returning stolen information, or for agreeing not to disclose the information.

*Sabotage and vandalism* are deliberate acts that involve defacing an organization's Web site, possibly causing the organization to lose its image and experience a loss of confidence by its customers.

*Theft of equipment and information* is becoming a larger problem because computing devices and storage devices are becoming smaller yet more powerful with vastly increased storage, making these devices easier and more valuable to steal.

*Identity theft* is the deliberate assumption of another person's identity, usually to gain access to his or her financial information or to frame him or her for a crime.

Preventing *compromises to intellectual property* is a vital issue for people who make their livelihood in knowledge fields. Protecting intellectual property is particularly difficult when that property is in digital form.

*Software attacks* occur when malicious software penetrates an organization's computer system. Today, these attacks are typically profit-driven and Web-based.

*Alien software* is clandestine software that is installed on your computer through duplicitous methods. It typically is not as malicious as viruses, worms, or Trojan horses, but it does use up valuable system resources.

*Supervisory control and data acquisition* refers to a large-scale, distributed measurement and control system. SCADA systems are used to monitor or control chemical, physical, and transport processes. A *SCADA attack* attempts to compromise such a system in order to cause damage to the real-world processes that the system controls.

With both *cyberterrorism* and *cyberwarfare*, attackers use a target's computer systems, particularly via the Internet, to cause physical, real-world harm or severe disruption, usually to carry out a political agenda.

4. **Define the three risk mitigation strategies, and provide an example of each one in the context of owning a home.**

The three risk mitigation strategies are the following:

*Risk acceptance*, where the organization accepts the potential risk, continues operating with no controls, and absorbs any damages that occur. If you own a home, you may decide not to insure it. Thus, you are practicing risk acceptance. Clearly, this is a bad idea.

*Risk limitation*, where the organization limits the risk by implementing controls that minimize the impact of threats. As a homeowner, you practice risk limitation by putting in an alarm system or cutting down weak trees near your house.

*Risk transference*, where the organization transfers the risk by using other means to compensate for the loss, such as by purchasing insurance. The vast majority of homeowners practice risk transference by purchasing insurance on their houses and other possessions.

5. **Identify the three major types of controls that organizations can use to protect their information resources, and provide an example of each one.**

*Physical controls* prevent unauthorized individuals from gaining access to a company's facilities. Common physical controls include walls, doors, fencing, gates, locks, badges, guards, and alarm systems. More sophisticated physical controls include pressure sensors, temperature sensors, and motion detectors.

*Access controls* restrict unauthorized individuals from using information resources. These controls involve two major functions: authentication and authorization. Authentication confirms the identity of the person requiring access. An example is biometrics. After the person is authenticated (identified), the next step is authorization. Authorization determines which actions, rights, or privileges the person has, based on his or her verified identity. Authorization is generally based on least privilege.

*Communications (network) controls* secure the movement of data across networks. Communications controls consist of firewalls, anti-malware systems, whitelisting and blacklisting, encryption, virtual private networking, secure socket layer, and vulnerability management systems.

## [ Chapter Glossary ]

**access controls** Controls that restrict unauthorized individuals from using information resources and are concerned with user identification.

**adware** Alien software designed to help pop-up advertisements appear on your screen.

**alien software** Clandestine software that is installed on your computer through duplicitous methods.

**anti-malware systems (antivirus software)** Software packages that attempt to identify and eliminate viruses, worms, and other malicious software.

**audit** An examination of information systems, their inputs, outputs, and processing.

**authentication** A process that determines the identity of the person requiring access.

**authorization** A process that determines which actions, rights, or privileges the person has, based on verified identity.

**back door** Typically a password, known only to the attacker, that allows the attacker to access the system without having to go through any security procedures.

**biometrics** The science and technology of authentication (i.e., establishing the identity of an individual) by measuring the subject's physiological or behavioral characteristics.

**blacklisting** A process in which a company identifies certain types of software that are not allowed to run in the company environment.

**bot** A computer that has been compromised by, and under the control of, a hacker.

**botnet** A network of computers that have been compromised by, and under control of, a hacker, who is called the botmaster.

**business continuity** The chain of events linking planning to protection and to recovery.

**certificate authority** A third party that acts as a trusted intermediary between computers (and companies) by issuing digital certificates and verifying the worth and integrity of the certificates.

**communications controls (also network controls)** Controls that deal with the movement of data across networks.

**controls** Defense mechanisms (also called *countermeasures*).

**cookie** Small amounts of information that Web sites store on your computer, temporarily or more or less permanently.

**copyright** A grant that provides the creator of intellectual property with ownership of it for a specified period of time, currently the life of the creator plus 70 years.

**cybercrime** Illegal activities executed on the Internet.

**cyberterrorism** Can be defined as a premeditated, politically motivated attack against information, computer systems, computer programs, and data that results in violence against noncombatant targets by subnational groups or clandestine agents.

**cyberwarfare** War in which a country's information systems could be paralyzed from a massive attack by destructive software.

**demilitarized zone (DMZ)** A separate organizational local area network that is located between an organization's internal network and an external network, usually the Internet.

**denial-of-service attack** A cyberattack in which an attacker sends a flood of data packets to the target computer, with the aim of overloading its resources.

**digital certificate** An electronic document attached to a file certifying that this file is from the organization it claims to be from and has not been modified from its original format or content.

**distributed denial-of-service (DDoS) attack** A denial of-service attack that sends a flood of data packets from many compromised computers simultaneously.

**employee monitoring systems** Systems that monitor employees' computers, e-mail activities, and Internet surfing activities.

**encryption** The process of converting an original message into a form that cannot be read by anyone except the intended receiver.

**exposure** The harm, loss, or damage that can result if a threat compromises an information resource.

**firewall** A system (either hardware, software, or a combination of both) that prevents a specific type of information from moving between untrusted networks, such as the Internet, and private networks, such as your company's network.

**identity theft** Crime in which someone uses the personal information of others to create a false identity and then uses it for some fraud.

**information security** Protecting an organization's information and information systems from unauthorized access, use, disclosure, disruption, modification, or destruction.

**intellectual property** The intangible property created by individuals or corporations, which is protected under trade secret, patent, and copyright laws.

**least privilege** A principle that users be granted the privilege for some activity only if there is a justifiable need to grant this authorization.

**logic bombs** Segments of computer code embedded within an organization's existing computer programs.

**malware** Malicious software such as viruses and worms.

**network controls** See communications controls.

**password** A private combination of characters that only the user should know.

**patent** A document that grants the holder exclusive rights on an invention or process for a specified period of time, currently 20 years.

**phishing attack** An attack that uses deception to fraudulently acquire sensitive personal information by masquerading as an official-looking e-mail.

**physical controls** Controls that restrict unauthorized individuals from gaining access to a company's computer facilities.

**piracy** Copying a software program (other than freeware, demo software, etc.) without making payment to the owner.

**privilege** A collection of related computer system operations that can be performed by users of the system.

**public-key encryption** (also called *asymmetric encryption*) A type of encryption that uses two different keys, a public key and a private key.

**risk** The likelihood that a threat will occur.

**risk acceptance** A strategy in which the organization accepts the potential risk, continues to operate with no controls, and absorbs any damages that occur.

**risk analysis** The process by which an organization assesses the value of each asset being protected, estimates the probability that each asset might be compromised, and compares the probable costs of each being compromised with the costs of protecting it.

**risk limitation** A strategy in which the organization limits its risk by implementing controls that minimize the impact of a threat.

**risk management** A process that identifies, controls, and minimizes the impact of threats, in an effort to reduce risk to manageable levels.

**risk mitigation** A process whereby the organization takes concrete actions against risks, such as implementing controls and developing a disaster recovery plan.

**risk transference** A process in which the organization transfers the risk by using other means to compensate for a loss, such as by purchasing insurance.

**secure socket layer (SSL)** (also known as transport layer security) An encryption standard used for secure transactions such as credit card purchases and online banking.

**security** The degree of protection against criminal activity, danger, damage, and/or loss.

**social engineering** Getting around security systems by tricking computer users inside a company into revealing sensitive information or gaining unauthorized access privileges.

**spam** Unsolicited e-mail.

**spamware** Alien software that uses your computer as a launch platform for spammers.

**spyware** Alien software that can record your keystrokes and/or capture your passwords.

**threat** Any danger to which an information resource may be exposed.

**trade secret** Intellectual work, such as a business plan, that is a company secret and is not based on public information.

**transport layer security (TLS)** See secure socket layer.

**trap doors** See back door.

**Trojan horse** A software program containing a hidden function that presents a security risk.

**tunneling** A process that encrypts each data packet to be sent and places each encrypted packet inside another packet.

**virtual private network (VPN)** A private network that uses a public network (usually the Internet) to securely connect users by using encryption.

**viruses** Malicious software that can attach itself with (or "infect") other computer programs without the owner of the program being aware of the infection.

**vulnerability** The possibility that an information resource will be harmed by a threat.

**whitelisting** A process in which a company identifies acceptable software and permits it to run, and either prevents anything else from running or lets new software run in a quarantined environment until the company can verify its validity.

**worms** Destructive programs that replicate themselves without requiring another program to provide a safe environment for replication.

**zombie computer** See bot.

## [ Discussion Questions ]

1. Why are computer systems so vulnerable?
2. Why should information security be a prime concern to management?
3. Is security a technical issue? A business issue? Both? Support your answer.
4. Compare information security in an organization with insuring a house.
5. Why are authentication and authorization important to e-commerce?
6. Why is cross-border cybercrime expanding rapidly? Discuss possible solutions.
7. Discuss why the Sarbanes–Oxley Act is having an impact on information security.
8. What types of user authentication are used at your university and/or place of work? Do these measures seem to be effective? What if a higher level of authentication were implemented? Would it be worth it, or would it decrease productivity?
9. Why are federal authorities so worried about SCADA attacks?

## [ Problem-Solving Activities ]

1. A critical problem is assessing how far a company is legally obligated to go in order to secure personal data. Because there is no such thing as perfect security (i.e., there is always more that you can do), resolving this question can significantly affect cost.
   a. When are security measures that a company implements sufficient to comply with its obligations?
   b. Is there any way for a company to know if its security measures are sufficient? Can you devise a method for any organization to determine if its security measures are sufficient?
2. Assume that the daily probability of a major earthquake in Los Angeles is 0.07 percent. The chance that your computer center will be damaged during such a quake is 5 percent. If the center is damaged, the estimated damage to the computer center will be $4.0 million.
   a. Calculate the expected loss in dollars.
   b. An insurance agent is willing to insure your facility for an annual fee of $25,000. Analyze the offer, and discuss whether to accept it.
3. Enter *www.scambusters.org*. Find out what the organization does. Learn about e-mail scams and Web site scams. Report your findings.
4. Visit *www.dhs.gov/dhspublic* (Department of Homeland Security). Search the site for "National Strategy to Secure Cyberspace" and write a report on their agenda and accomplishments to date.

5. Enter *www.alltrustnetworks.com* and other vendors of biometrics. Find the devices they make that can be used to control access into information systems. Prepare a list of products and major capabilities of each vendor.

6. Software piracy is a global problem. Access the following Web sites: *www.bsa.org* and *www.microsoft.com/piracy/*. What can organizations do to mitigate this problem? Are some organizations dealing with the problem better than others?

7. Investigate the Sony PlayStation Network hack that occurred in April 2011.

a. What type of attack was it?

b. Was the success of the attack due to technology problems at Sony, management problems at Sony, or a combination of both? Provide specific examples to support your answer.

c. Which Sony controls failed?

d. Could the hack have been prevented? If so, how?

e. Discuss Sony's response to the hack.

f. Describe the damages that Sony incurred from the hack.

# [ Closing Case  Lessons Learned from the Target Data Breach ]

## The Business Problem

Target Corporation (Target) (*www.target.com*) is the second-largest discount retailer in the United States, after Walmart. In late 2013, Target disclosed that it had been the victim of a massive data breach. The breach has been compared with the 2009 non-retail Heartland Payment Systems breach, which affected 130 million card holders, and with the 2007 retail TJX Companies breach, which affected 90 million card holders.

Let's take a closer look at the attack. Just prior to Thanksgiving 2013, an unknown individual or group installed malware in Target's security and payments system. The malware was designed to steal every credit card used at the company's nearly 1,800 U.S. stores.

Amazingly, Target was prepared for the attack. Six months prior to Thanksgiving, the company had installed a malware detection tool manufactured by the computer security firm FireEye (www.fireeye.com). In addition, Target had assembled a team of security specialists in Bangalore, India, to monitor its computers around the clock. If the team noticed anything suspicious, they would notify Target's security operations center in Minneapolis.

Around Thanksgiving, Target's antivirus system, Symantec Endpoint Protection (www.symantec.com), identified suspicious behavior over several days. Target management ignored the system's warnings.

On November 30, 2013, the attackers loaded malware to transfer stolen credit card numbers—first to computers around the United States to cover their tracks and then into their computers in Russia. FireEye spotted the attackers and alerted Bangalore. In turn, Bangalore alerted the Target security team in Minneapolis. And … nothing happened. For some reason, Minneapolis did not respond to the alert. Even worse, the FireEye system includes an option to automatically delete malware as it is detected. Target's security team had turned off the option.

On December 18, 2013, security expert Brian Krebs (see http://krebsonsecurity.com) broke the news that Target was investigating a major data breach. On December 19, Target confirmed the incident via a press release, revealing that the attack took place between November 27 and December 15. Eventually, Target acknowledged that attackers had stolen personal data from 110 million customers including customer names, addresses, phone numbers, e-mail addresses, credit and debit card numbers, card expiration dates, credit card security codes (also called card verification codes), and debit card PIN data. The attackers sent 11 gigabytes of data to a Moscow-based hosting service called vpsville.ru. A Target spokesman defended the company by arguing it has too many clients to monitor all of them effectively.

Investigators from the U.S. Secret Service, the agency leading the government's investigation into the Target breach, visited the offices of Fazio Mechanical Services (www.fazio-mechanical.com), a refrigeration and HVAC (heating, ventilation, and air conditioning) systems provider. The investigators believe that Target's attackers initially accessed the retailer's network on November 15, 2013, using access credentials they had stolen from Fazio in a phishing attack. The attackers then used those credentials to access Target's payment processing and point-of-sale (POS) systems. (It is important to note that as of early 2015, none of these points had been proved, and the investigation was ongoing.)

Fazio purportedly used a free version of an antivirus software product called Malwarebytes (www.malwarebytes.com) for protection. Significantly, this version is intended for consumer use only. Therefore, if Fazio had used this version, then the company would be in violation of Malwarebytes's license. Further, the free version of Malwarebytes does not provide real-time scanning of files for malware, meaning that free antivirus software is not an industry best practice. Fazio responded that "our IT system and security measures are in full compliance with industry practices."

Fazio had access to Target's network because Target relies on HVAC systems with IP addresses that can be remotely monitored and adjusted by Fazio to manage store environments. (Note: This practice is standard for retailers, supermarkets, and similar businesses.)

Target's system, like any standard corporate network, is segmented so that the most sensitive areas—including customer payments and personal data—are walled off from other parts of the network, particularly the Internet. Clearly, Target's internal walls had holes. As a result, the attackers could proceed from the part of the network that its vendors could access to more sensitive parts of the network where customer data were located.

Questions involving the Target breach focused on the security processes in place at Fazio, as well as the controls in place at Target. Target is liable, per Payment Card Industry Data Security Standards (PCI-DSS), for any of its third-party contractors' security faults. Notably, PCI-DSS requires that merchants "incorporate two-factor authentication for remote access to the network by employees, administrators, and third parties." However, one challenge when granting remote access to a third party (e.g., a contractor) is that multiple employees of that contractor may have access to those credentials. For example, a contractor may have many technicians who require access on a revolving basis.

Among the most pertinent questions regarding the Target attack are the following:

- Did Target secure Fazio's access to its network using two-factor authentication?
- What level of network access did Target grant to Fazio?
- Was Target actively monitoring Fazio's access?
- Were Target's HVAC appliances located on an isolated network segment that should have prevented attackers from accessing other network systems?

## Target's Response

Target encouraged customers who shopped at its U.S. stores (online orders were not affected) during the specified time frame to closely monitor their credit and debit cards for irregular activity. The retailer cooperated with law enforcement agencies to bring the responsible parties to justice.

Gregg Steinhafel, Target's CEO, apologized to the retailer's customers in a press release. As a further apology to the public, all Target stores in the United States awarded retail shoppers a 10 percent storewide discount for the weekend of December 21–22, 2013. Finally, Target offered free credit monitoring via Experian to affected customers.

## The Results from the Breach

Security analysts at the technology research firm Gartner (www.gartner.com) estimated that the cost of the breach will eventually exceed $1 billion. These costs include paying card networks to cover losses and expenses in reissuing cards,

lawsuits, government investigations, and enforcement proceedings. Target's net income for the fourth quarter of 2013 fell 46 percent.

A consolidated class action lawsuit for negligence and compensatory damages was filed against Target by customers as well as the banks that issued the credit cards. In December 2014, a federal judge denied a motion by Target to dismiss the lawsuit, meaning that the lawsuit will move forward and will probably be tried in 2016.

Target also announced that it was implementing encrypted "chip and PIN" credit card technology, to be completed by the first quarter of 2015. The retailer will reissue its store credit cards with this technology, and it plans to deploy new card readers in all of its U.S. stores.

On March 6, 2014, Target's chief information officer resigned, and the company began an overhaul of its information security practices. In a further step to restore customer faith, the retailer announced it would search outside the company for a new CIO. Target also announced an external search for a newly created position, chief compliance officer. On May 5, 2014, Target's CEO, Gregg Steinhafel, resigned. He had been with the company for 35 years.

Ultimately, if the company's security team had responded appropriately when it was supposed to, then the theft might not have occurred.

And the breaches continue. In fact, 2014 was an extremely bad year for data breaches. Other companies reporting data breaches include Domino's (www.dominos.com), Lowe's (www.lowes.com), eBay (www.ebay.com), Neiman Marcus (www.neimanmarcus.com), Sony (www.sony.com; see this chapter's opening case), and Home Depot (www.homedepot.com). With regard to the Home Depot breach, the attackers gained access by using a third-party vendor's stolen credentials. This attack is very similar to the attack on Target.

*Sources:* Compiled from N. Raymond, "Consumers Can Sue Target Corp Over Data Breach: Judge," *Reuters*, December 19, 2014; "A Year After Target Data Breach, Aftershocks Finally End," *Tribune News Service*, November 25, 2014; R. Abrams, "Target Puts Data Breach Costs at $148 Million, and Forecasts Profit Drop," *The New York Times*, August 5, 2014; A. Levin, After the Big Data Breach, Has Target Learned Its Lesson?" *ABC News*, June 15, 2014; P. Sheridan, "Target Breach: How Things Stand," *CNN Money*, May 5, 2014; M. Schwartz, "Target Ignored Data Breach Alarms," *InformationWeek*, March 14, 2014; M. Riley, B. Elgin, D. Lawrence, and C. Matlack, "The Epic Hack," *Bloomberg BusinessWeek*, March 13, 2014; A. Shrivastava and M. Thomas, "Target Announces Technology Overhaul, CIO Departure," *Reuters*, March 5, 2014; B. Horovitz, "Breach Takes Toll on Target," *USA Today*, February 27, 2014; E. Harris, "Data Breach Hurts Profit at Target," *The New York Times*, February 27, 2014; J. Pagliery, "Why Retailers Aren't Protecting You from Hackers," *CNN Money*, February 18, 2014; A. Gonsalves, "Experts Question Security Used in Target Breach," *CSO Online*, February 13, 2014; M. Schwartz, "Target Breach: Phishing Attack Implicated," *InformationWeek*, February 13, 2014; L. MacVittie, "Target Breach Takeaway: Secure Your Remote Access," *InformationWeek*, February 10, 2014; M. Schwartz, "Target Breach: HVAC Contractor Systems Investigated," *InformationWeek*, February 6, 2014; D. Leger, "Target to Rush Card Chip Security," *USA Today*, February 5, 2014; H. Stout, "Target Vows to Speed Anti-Fraud Technology," *The New York Times*, February 5, 2014; E. Harris, N. Periroth, and N. Popper, "Neiman Marcus Data Breach Worse Than First Said," *The New York Times*, January 24, 2014; M. Feibus, "A Tale of Two Cyberheists," *InformationWeek*, January 22, 2014; "Why the Target Data Hack Is Just the Beginning," *Bloomberg BusinessWeek*, January 16, 2014; M. Schwartz, "Target Breach: 8 Facts on Memory-Scraping Malware," *InformationWeek*, January 14, 2014; A. d'Innocenzio and M. Chapman, "Target: Breach Affected Millions More Customers," *Associated Press*, January 10, 2014; P. McNamara, "Target Confesses: Breach Victim Total Soars to 70 Million," *Network World*, January 10, 2014; D. Goldman, "Target Confirms PIN Data Was Stolen in Breach," *CNN Money*, December 27, 2013; C. Woodyard, "Target Offers 10% Off as Credit Fraud Apology," *USA Today*, December 22, 2013; J. Ribeiro, "Target Says 40 Million Cards Likely Skimmed in Security Breach," *Network World*, December 19, 2013; "Target Confirms Unauthorized Access to Payment Card Data in U.S. Stores," *Target Pressroom*, December 19, 2013; B. Krebs, "Sources: Target Investigating Data Breach," *Krebs on Security*, December 18, 2013; *www.target.com, www.krebsonsecurity.com*, accessed March 10, 2015.

## Questions

1. Describe the flaws in Target's security system that enabled the breach.

2. Was Target's response to the breach appropriate? Why or why not?

3. What should you do as a consumer to protect yourself against losing your personal data from establishments where you shop?

# 5 Data and Knowledge Management

| [ LEARNING OBJECTIVES ] | [ CHAPTER OUTLINE ] | [ WEB RESOURCES ] |
|---|---|---|

**[ LEARNING OBJECTIVES ]**

1. Discuss ways that common challenges in managing data can be addressed using data governance.

2. Discuss the advantages and disadvantages of relational databases.

3. Define *Big Data*, and discuss its basic characteristics.

4. Explain the elements necessary to successfully implement and maintain data warehouses.

5. Describe the benefits and challenges of implementing knowledge management systems in organizations.

6. Understand the processes of querying a relational database, entity-relationship modeling, and normalization and joins.

**[ CHAPTER OUTLINE ]**

**[ WEB RESOURCES ]**

- Student PowerPoints for note taking

**WileyPLUS Learning Space**

- E-book
- Author video lecture for each chapter section
- Practice quizzes
- Flash Cards for vocabulary review
- Additional "IT's About Business" cases
- Video interviews with managers
- Lab Manuals for Microsoft Office 2010 and 2013

# What's In **IT** For **Me?**

## This Chapter Will Help Prepare You To...

| ACCT | FIN | MKT | POM | HRM | MIS |
|------|-----|-----|-----|-----|-----|
| ACCOUNTING | FINANCE | MARKETING | PRODUCTION OPERATIONS MANAGEMENT | HUMAN RESOURCES MANAGEMENT | MIS |
| Cost justify firm's databases | Use data for internal investment decisions | Use customer data to plan marketing campaigns | Analyze data for quality control | Use employee data for performance evaluations | Provide infrastructure to store firm's data |

## [ Database Saves the State of Washington Medicaid Dollars ]

When a patient is admitted to the emergency room (ER) of a hospital, his physician may never have seen him before and must diagnose his problem very quickly. If the physician already knew the patient's medical history, then her examination and subsequent diagnosis would be faster, less expensive, and more accurate.

As the Affordable Care Act expands Medicaid to an increasing number of patients, the need for states to control ER costs becomes more critical. Many Medicaid patients visit hospital ERs too many times. In fact, in the state of Washington, patients who went to the ER more than four times in one year comprise some 20 percent of all ER visits paid for by Medicaid.

To address this problem, the State of Washington implemented the Emergency Department Information Exchange (EDIE), a database that contains the records of each patient treated in every hospital ER in the state. The database allows physicians to track patients' ER visits to multiple hospitals.

The state experienced some difficulties implementing the database. In the past, some state hospitals had attempted to create regional databases. However, many hospitals did not join these efforts, fearing they would lose both patients and Medicaid dollars.

In response, the state announced that it would no longer reimburse hospitals for more than three non-emergency ER visits by a Medicaid recipient each year. Physicians and hospitals successfully sued the state, claiming the policy was arbitrary and would increase the hospitals' costs.

The state's Medicaid office responded by creating a list of 500 medical problems—for example, acute bronchitis, urinary tract infections, and headaches—that it would no longer reimburse as emergency care. The state argued that those complaints could be treated in doctors' offices or clinics.

Hospitals objected to this list because patients who were not treated in hospitals would reduce hospitals' income. As a result, the state adopted the database as a compromise. The EDIE database meets federal health privacy laws by allowing only approved medical staff members to access data on patients under their care. When a patient registers at an ER anywhere in the state of Washington, the attending physician and nurses immediately receive a fax (some hospitals still use fax machines) or e-mail from the database. The report lists all of the patient's recent ER admissions, diagnoses, and treatments.

Further, when patients leave the ER, the database helps physicians track their care. One hospital sends paramedics to check on high-risk patients. Other hospitals hire care coordinators to ensure that patients make appointments with a family doctor or specialist. Rural hospitals discovered that many of their ER patients needed help managing pain, so they set up a pain-management clinic.

In addition, the database has helped reduce the prescription of narcotics in the state's ERs by 24 percent in its first year of use in large part because patients cannot visit multiple health

MIS

facilities to obtain prescriptions. More than 400 primary care physicians have signed up to receive automatic notifications when one of their patients is admitted to the ER. The state is signing up more family doctors as well as community and mental health clinics.

Physicians can now send many of their patients to clinics or other less expensive care centers. Data released in March 2014 indicate that ER visits by Medicaid patients dropped 10 percent in the 2013 fiscal year, and the rate of ER visits that resulted in a nonacute diagnosis decreased more than 14 percent. The state credits the database for a substantial amount of the state's $33.7 million reduction in 2013 Medicaid costs.

*Sources:* Compiled from "How Big Data Can Reduce ER Visits," *Real Business,* October 23, 2014; J. Creswell, "Doctors Find Barriers to Sharing Digital Medical Records," *The New York Times,* September 30, 2014; T. Bannow, "Oregon Hospitals Begin Sharing ER Data," *The Bend Bulletin,* September 18, 2014; "Report Finds Data Sharing Popular Among Hospitals," *ClinicalKey,* September 12, 2014; R. Daly, "EHR Data Sharing Challenges Hospitals," *Healthcare Financial Management Association,* August 7, 2014; D. Gorenstein, "Data: The Secret Ingredient in Hospital Cooperation," *Marketplace.org,* June 5, 2014; K. Weise, "Hospitals Share Data to Stop ER Abusers," *Bloomberg BusinessWeek,* April 7–13, 2014; "Emergency Department Partnership Is Improving Care and Saving Medicaid Funds," *Washing State Hospital Association,* March 20, 2014; E. Rizzo, "When Hospitals Share Data, Who Benefits?" *Becker's Hospital Review,* March 12, 2014; "When Hospitals Share Patient Records, Emergency Patients Benefit, Study Suggests," *University of Michigan Health System,* January 24, 2014.

### Questions

1. Describe additional benefits (beyond those discussed in the case) of the State of Washington's EDIE database.
2. Describe potential disadvantages of the State of Washington's EDIE database.

## What We Learned from This Case

Information technologies and systems support organizations in managing—that is, acquiring, organizing, storing, accessing, analyzing, and interpreting—data. As you noted in Chapter 1, when these data are managed properly, they become *information* and then *knowledge.* (Recall our discussion of data, information, and knowledge in Section 1.2). As you see in the chapter's opening case, information and knowledge are invaluable organizational resources that can provide any organization with a competitive advantage.

So, just how important are data and data management to organizations? From confidential customer information, to intellectual property, to financial transactions, to social media posts, organizations possess massive amounts of data that are critical to their success. Of course, to benefit from these data, they need to manage them effectively. This type of management, however, comes at a huge cost. According to Symantec's (*www.symantec.com*) State of Information Survey, digital information costs organizations worldwide $1.1 trillion annually, and it makes up roughly *half* of an organization's total value. The survey found that large organizations spend an average of some $40 million annually to maintain and utilize data, and small-to-medium-sized businesses spend almost $350,000.

This chapter will examine the processes whereby data are transformed first into information and then into knowledge. Managing data is critically important in all organizations. Few business professionals are comfortable making or justifying business decisions that are not based on solid information. This is especially true today, when modern information systems make access to that information quick and easy. For example, we have information systems that format data in a way that managers and analysts can easily understand. Consequently, these professionals can access these data themselves and then analyze them according to their needs. The result is useful *information.* Managers can then apply their experience to use this information to address a business problem, thereby producing *knowledge.* Knowledge management (KM), enabled by information technology, captures and stores knowledge in forms that all organizational employees can access and apply, thereby creating the flexible, powerful "learning organization."

Organizations store data in databases. Recall from Chapter 1 that a *database* is a collection of related data files or tables containing data. We discuss databases in Section 5.2.

Clearly, data and knowledge management are vital to modern organizations. But, why should *you* learn about them? The reason is that you will play an important role in the development of database applications. The structure and content of your organization's database depend on how users (you) define your business activities. For example, when database developers in the firm's MIS group build a database, they use a tool called entity-relationship modeling. This tool creates a model of how users view a business activity. When you understand how to create and interpret an entity-relationship model, then you can evaluate whether the developers have captured your business activities correctly.

Keep in mind that decisions about data last longer, and have a broader impact, than decisions about hardware or software. If decisions concerning hardware are wrong, then the equipment can be replaced relatively easily. If software decisions turn out to be incorrect, they can be modified, though not always painlessly or inexpensively. Database decisions, in contrast, are much harder to undo. Database design constrains what the organization can do with its data for a long time. Remember that business users will be stuck with a bad database design, while the programmers who created the database will quickly move on to their next projects. This is why it is so important to get database designs right the first time—and you will play a key role in these designs.

In addition, you might want to create a small, personal database using a software product such as Microsoft Access. In that case, you will need to be familiar with at least the basics of the product.

After the data are stored in your organization's databases, they must be accessible to users in a form that helps them make decisions. Organizations accomplish this objective by developing *data warehouses*. You should become familiar with data warehouses because they are invaluable decision-making tools. We discuss data warehouses in Section 5.4.

You will also make extensive use of your organization's knowledge base to perform your job. For example, when you are assigned a new project, you will likely research your firm's knowledge base to identify factors that contributed to the success (or failure) of previous, similar projects. We discuss knowledge management in Section 5.5.

You begin this chapter by examining the multiple problems involved in managing data. You then study the database approach that organizations use to help solve these problems. You turn your attention to Big Data, which organizations must manage in today's business environment. Next, you study data warehouses and data marts, and you learn how to utilize them for decision making. You finish the chapter by examining knowledge management.

## 5.1 Managing Data

All IT applications require data. These data should be of high quality, meaning that they should be accurate, complete, timely, consistent, accessible, relevant, and concise. Unfortunately, the process of acquiring, keeping, and managing data is becoming increasingly difficult.

### The Difficulties of Managing Data

Because data are processed in several stages and often in multiple locations, they are frequently subject to problems and difficulties. Managing data in organizations is difficult for many reasons.

First, the amount of data increases exponentially with time. Much historical data must be kept for a long time, and new data are added rapidly. For example, to support millions of customers, large retailers such as Walmart have to manage petabytes of data. (A petabyte is approximately 1,000 terabytes, or trillions of bytes; see Technology Guide 1.)

In addition, data are also scattered throughout organizations, and they are collected by many individuals using various methods and devices. These data are frequently stored in numerous servers and locations and in different computing systems, databases, formats, and human and computer languages.

Another problem is that data are generated from multiple sources: internal sources (for example, corporate databases and company documents); personal sources (for example, personal thoughts, opinions, and experiences); and external sources (for example, commercial databases, government reports, and corporate Web sites). Data also come from the Web, in the form of clickstream data. **Clickstream data** are those data that visitors and customers produce when they visit a Web site and click on hyperlinks (described in Chapter 6). Clickstream data provide a trail of the users' activities in the Web site, including user behavior and browsing patterns.

Adding to these problems is the fact that new sources of data, such as blogs, podcasts, videocasts, and RFID tags and other wireless sensors, are constantly being developed and the data these technologies generate must be managed. In addition, data degrade over time. For example, customers move to new addresses or change their names, companies go out of business or are bought, new products are developed, employees are hired or fired, and companies expand into new countries.

Data are also subject to *data rot*. Data rot refers primarily to problems with the media on which the data are stored. Over time, temperature, humidity, and exposure to light can cause physical problems with storage media and thus make it difficult to access the data. The second aspect of data rot is that finding the machines needed to access the data can be difficult. For example, it is almost impossible today to find 8-track players. Consequently, a library of 8-track tapes has become relatively worthless, unless you have a functioning 8-track player or you convert the tapes to a modern medium such as CDs.

Data security, quality, and integrity are critical, yet they are easily jeopardized. In addition, legal requirements relating to data differ among countries as well as among industries, and they change frequently.

Another problem arises from the fact that, over time, organizations have developed information systems for specific business processes, such as transaction processing, supply chain management, and customer relationship management. Information systems that specifically support these processes impose unique requirements on data, which results in repetition and conflicts across the organization. For example, the marketing function might maintain information on customers, sales territories, and markets. These data might be duplicated within the billing or customer service functions. This situation can produce inconsistent data within the enterprise. Inconsistent data prevent a company from developing a unified view of core business information—data concerning customers, products, finances, and so on—across the organization and its information systems.

Two other factors complicate data management. First, federal regulations—for example, the Sarbanes–Oxley Act of 2002—have made it a top priority for companies to better account for how they are managing information. Sarbanes–Oxley requires that (1) public companies evaluate and disclose the effectiveness of their internal financial controls and (2) independent auditors for these companies agree to this disclosure. The law also holds CEOs and CFOs personally responsible for such disclosures. If their companies lack satisfactory data management policies and fraud or a security breach occurs, the company officers could be held liable and face prosecution.

Second, companies are drowning in data, much of which is unstructured. As you have seen, the amount of data is increasing exponentially. To be profitable, companies must develop a strategy for managing these data effectively.

An additional problem with data management is Big Data. Big Data is so important that we devote the entire Section 5.3 to this topic.

## Data Governance

To address the numerous problems associated with managing data, organizations are turning to data governance. **Data governance** is an approach to managing information across an entire organization. It involves a formal set of business processes and policies that are designed to ensure that data are handled in a certain, well-defined fashion. That is, the organization follows unambiguous rules for creating, collecting, handling, and protecting its information. The objective is to make information available, transparent, and useful for the people who are authorized to access it, from the moment it enters an organization until it is outdated and deleted.

One strategy for implementing data governance is master data management. **Master data management** is a process that spans all organizational business processes and applications. It provides companies with the ability to store, maintain, exchange, and synchronize a consistent, accurate, and timely "single version of the truth" for the company's master data.

**Master data** are a set of core data, such as customer, product, employee, vendor, geographic location, and so on, that span the enterprise information systems. It is important to distinguish between master data and transaction data. *Transaction data*, which are generated and captured by operational systems, describe the business's activities, or transactions. In contrast, master data are applied to multiple transactions and are used to categorize, aggregate, and evaluate the transaction data.

Let's look at an example of a transaction: You (Mary Jones) purchase one Samsung 42-inch plasma television, part number 1234, from Bill Roberts at Best Buy, for $2,000, on April 20, 2014. In this example, the master data are "product sold," "vendor," "salesperson," "store," "part number," "purchase price," and "date." When specific values are applied to the master data, then a transaction is represented. Therefore, transaction data would be, respectively, "42-inch plasma television," "Samsung," "Best Buy," "Bill Roberts," "1234," "$2,000," and "April 20, 2014."

An example of master data management is Dallas, Texas, which implemented a plan for digitizing the city's public and private records, such as paper documents, images, drawings, and video and audio content. The master database can be utilized by any of the 38 government departments that have appropriate access. The city is also integrating its financial and billing processes with its customer relationship management program. (You will learn about customer relationship management in Chapter 11.)

How will Dallas utilize this system? Imagine that the city experiences a water-main break. Before it implemented the system, repair crews had to search City Hall for records that were filed haphazardly. Once the workers found the hard-copy blueprints, they would take them to the site and, after examining them manually, would decide on a plan of action. In contrast, the new system delivers the blueprints wirelessly to the laptops of crews in the field, who can magnify or highlight areas of concern to generate a rapid response. This process reduces the time it takes to respond to an emergency by several hours.

Along with data governance, organizations use the database approach to efficiently and effectively manage their data. We discuss the database approach in the Section 5.2.

## before you go on...

1. What are some of the difficulties involved in managing data?
2. Define *data governance, master data,* and *transactional data.*

## 5.2 The Database Approach

From the mid-1950s, when businesses first adopted computer applications, until the early 1970s, organizations managed their data in a *file management environment*. This environment evolved because organizations typically automated their functions one application at a time. Therefore, the various automated systems developed independently from one another, without any overall planning. Each application required its own data, which were organized in a data file.

A **data file** is a collection of logically related records. In a file management environment, each application has a specific data file related to it. This file contains all of the data records the application requires. Over time, organizations developed numerous applications, each with an associated, application-specific data file.

For example, imagine that most of your information is stored in your university's central database, but a club to which you belong maintains its own files, the athletics department has separate files for student athletes, and your instructors maintain grade data on their personal computers. It is easy for your name to be misspelled in one of these databases or files but not in others. Similarly, if you move, then your address might be updated correctly in one database or file but not in others.

Using databases eliminates many problems that arose from previous methods of storing and accessing data, such as file management systems. Databases are arranged so that one set of software programs—the database management system—provides all users with access to all of

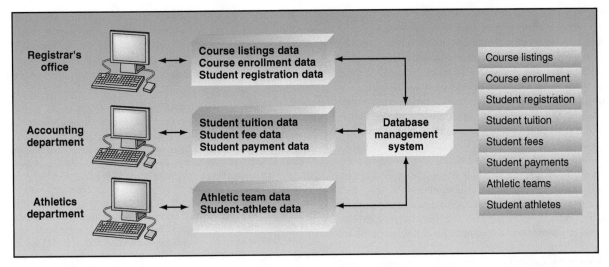

**FIGURE 5.1** Database management system.

the data. (You will study database management systems later in this chapter.) Database systems minimize the following problems:

- *Data redundancy*: The same data are stored in multiple locations.
- *Data isolation*: Applications cannot access data associated with other applications.
- *Data inconsistency*: Various copies of the data do not agree.

In addition, database systems maximize the following:

- *Data security*: Because data are "put in one place" in databases, there is a risk of losing a lot of data at one time. Therefore, databases must have extremely high security measures in place to minimize mistakes and deter attacks.
- *Data integrity*: Data meet certain constraints; for example, there are no alphabetic characters in a Social Security number field.
- *Data independence*: Applications and data are independent of one another; that is, applications and data are not linked to each other, so all applications are able to access the same data.

Figure 5.1 illustrates a university database. Note that university applications from the registrar's office, the accounting department, and the athletics department access data through the database management system. Google's Knowledge Graph is an interesting example of a database, as you see in IT's About Business 5.1.

 **IT's [about business]**

### **5.1** Google's Knowledge Graph

When a person conducts a Google search, the conventional results are based on algorithms that look for matches with the search terms, rather than the actual meaning of the information entered into the search box. Google's algorithms first refer to data from past searches to determine which words in the query are most likely to be important, based on how often they have been used by previous searchers. Next, the software accesses a list of Web pages known to contain information related to these search terms. Finally, another calculation ranks the results displayed to the searcher.

Google's Knowledge Graph can be considered as a vast database that enables Google software to connect facts on people, places, and things to one another. The purpose of the Knowledge Graph is to enable Google's future products to truly understand the people who use them and the things they care about. The Knowledge Graph will enable searchers to use information to resolve their queries without having to navigate to other sites and assemble information themselves.

Google began the Knowledge Graph project when it bought a startup called Metaweb in 2010. At that time, Metaweb contained only 12 million entries. Today, the Knowledge Graph has more than 600 million entries containing more than 18 billion links.

Google designed the Knowledge Graph to interpret a searcher's query in a much more sophisticated way and directly retrieve relevant information. The Knowledge Graph adds useful context and detail to the list of links that Google provides. Searching for certain people, places, or things produces a box of facts alongside the regular search results. However, the Knowledge Graph still uses data from past searches to determine what information is most relevant.

The Knowledge Graph has uses beyond simply helping people who are searching for facts online. For example, Google has integrated Knowledge Graph into YouTube, where it is being used to organize videos by topic and to suggest new videos to users, based on the videos they just watched. The Knowledge Graph can also be used to connect and recommend news articles based on specific facts mentioned in stories.

The Knowledge Graph is a database that represents what Google knows about the world. A good analogy for the Knowledge Graph is maps. For a maps product, you have to build a database of the real world and you know that, in the physical world, there are entities called streets, rivers, and countries, among many others. Therefore, a map is a structure for the physical world.

The Knowledge Graph provides such a structure for the world of ideas and common sense. For example, Google has entities in the Knowledge Graph for foods, recipes, products, ideas in philosophy and history, famous people, and a myriad of others. The relationships among entities enable the Knowledge Graph to determine, for example, that these two people are married, that this place is located in this country, or that this person appears in this movie.

As Google crawls and indexes documents, it can now understand what each document is about. For example, if the document is about famous tennis players, the Knowledge Graph knows it is about sports and tennis. Every piece of information that Google crawls, indexes, or researches is analyzed in the context of the Knowledge Graph.

*Sources:* J. DeMers, "What Google's Knowledge Graph Means for the Future of Search," *Forbes*, October 28, 2014; J. Kahn, "Google Adds Video Game Data to Knowledge Graph in Search Results," *Techspot*, October 24, 2014; T. Simonite, "How a Database of the World's Knowledge Shapes Google's Future," *MIT Technology Review*, January 27, 2014; S. Perez, "Google's Knowledge Graph Now Being Used to Enhance Search Results," *TechCrunch*, January 22, 2014; A. Orlowski, "Google Stabs Wikipedia in the Front," *The Register*, January 13, 2014; G. Kohs, "Google's Knowledge Graph Boxes: Killing Wikipedia?" *Wikipediocracy*, January 6, 2014; J. Lee, "OK Google: 'The End of Search as We Know It'," *Search Engine Watch*, May 16, 2013; A. Isidoro, "Google's Knowledge Graph: One Step Closer to the Semantic Web?" *eConsultancy*, February 28, 2013; C. Newton, "How Google Is Taking the Knowledge Graph Global," *CNET*, December 14, 2012; T. Simonite, "Google's New Brain Could Have a Big Impact," *MIT Technology Review*, June 14, 2012.

**Questions**

1. Refer to the definition of a relational database. In what way can the Knowledge Graph be considered a database? Provide specific examples to support your answer.
2. Refer to the definition of an expert system in Technology Guide 4. Could the Knowledge Graph be considered an expert system? If so, provide a specific example to support your answer.
3. What are the advantages of the Knowledge Graph over traditional Google searches?

---

A database can contain vast amounts of data. To make these data more understandable and useful, they are arranged in a hierarchy. We take a closer look at this hierarchy in the next section.

## The Data Hierarchy

Data are organized in a hierarchy that begins with bits and proceeds all the way to databases (see Figure 5.2). A **bit** (*binary digit*) represents the smallest unit of data a computer can process. The term *binary* means that a bit can consist only of a 0 or a 1. A group of eight bits, called a **byte**, represents a single character. A byte can be a letter, a number, or a symbol. A logical grouping of characters into a word, a small group of words, or an identification number is called a **field**. For example, a student's name in a university's computer files would appear in the "name" field, and her or his Social Security number would appear in the "Social Security number" field. Fields can also contain data other than text and numbers. They can contain an image, or any other type of multimedia. Examples are a motor vehicle department's licensing database that contains a driver's photograph and a field that contains a voice sample to authorize access to a secure facility.

A logical grouping of related fields, such as the student's name, the courses taken, the date, and the grade, comprises a **record**. In the Apple iTunes Store, a song is a field in a record, with other fields containing the song's title, its price, and the album on which it appears. A logical grouping of related records is called a **data file** or a **table**. For example, a grouping of the records from a particular course, consisting of course number, professor, and students' grades, would constitute a data file for that course. Continuing up the hierarchy, a logical grouping of related files constitutes a *database*. Using the same example, the student course file could be grouped with files on students' personal histories and financial backgrounds to create a student database. In the next section, you will learn about relational database model.

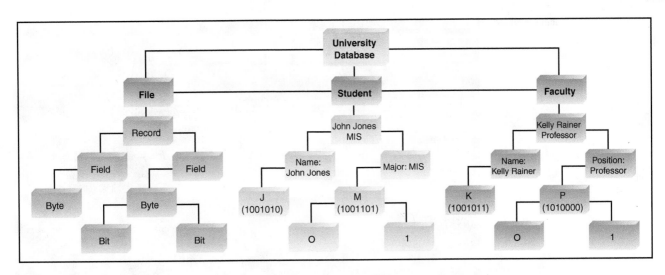

FIGURE 5.2 Hierarchy of data for a computer-based file.

## Database Management Systems

A **database management system (DBMS)** is a set of programs that provide users with tools to create and manage a database. Managing a database refers to the processes of adding, deleting, accessing, modifying, and analyzing data stored in a database. An organization can access the data by using query and reporting tools that are part of the DBMS or by using application programs specifically written to perform this function. DBMSs also provide the mechanisms for maintaining the integrity of stored data, managing security and user access, and recovering information if the system fails. Because databases and DBMSs are essential to all areas of business, they must be carefully managed.

There are a number of different database architectures, but we focus on the relational database model because it is popular and easy to use. Other database models (for example, the hierarchical and network models) are the responsibility of the MIS function and are not used by organizational employees. Popular examples of relational databases are Microsoft Access and Oracle.

Most business data—especially accounting and financial data—traditionally were organized into simple tables consisting of columns and rows. Tables allow people to compare information quickly by row or column. In addition, users can retrieve items rather easily by locating the point of intersection of a particular row and column.

The **relational database model** is based on the concept of two-dimensional tables. A relational database generally is not one big table—usually called a *flat file*—that contains all of the records and attributes. Such a design would entail far too much data redundancy. Instead, a relational database is usually designed with a number of related tables. Each of these tables contains records (listed in rows) and attributes (listed in columns).

To be valuable, a relational database must be organized so that users can retrieve, analyze, and understand the data they need. A key to designing an effective database is the data model. A **data model** is a diagram that represents entities in the database and their relationships. An **entity** is a person, place, thing, or event—such as a customer, an employee, or a product—about which information is maintained. Entities can typically be identified in the user's work environment. A record generally describes an entity. An **instance** of an entity refers to each row in a relational table, which is a specific, unique representation of the entity. For example, your university's student database contains an entity called STUDENT. An instance of the STUDENT entity would be a particular student. For instance, you are an instance of the STUDENT entity in your university's student database.

Each characteristic or quality of a particular entity is called an **attribute**. For example, if our entities were a customer, an employee, and a product, entity attributes would include customer name, employee number, and product color.

**FIGURE 5.3** Student database example.

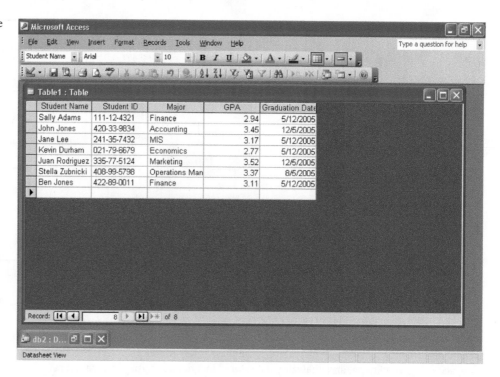

Consider the relational database example about students diagrammed in Figure 5.3. The table contains data about the entity called students. As you can see, each row of the table corresponds to one student record. (You have your own row in your university's student database.) Attributes of the entity are student name, undergraduate major, grade point average, and graduation date. The rows are the records on Sally Adams, John Jones, Jane Lee, Kevin Durham, Juan Rodriguez, Stella Zubnicki, and Ben Jones. Of course, your university keeps much more data on you than our example shows. In fact, your university's student database probably keeps hundreds of attributes on each student.

Every record in the database must contain at least one field that uniquely identifies that record so that it can be retrieved, updated, and sorted. This identifier field (or attribute) is called the **primary key**. For example, a student record in a U.S. university would use a unique student number as its primary key. (Note: In the past, your Social Security number served as the primary key for your student record. However, for security reasons, this practice has been discontinued.) You see that Sally Adams is uniquely identified by her student ID of 012345.

In some cases, locating a particular record requires the use of secondary keys. A **secondary key** is another field that has some identifying information, but typically does not identify the record with complete accuracy. For example, the student's major might be a secondary key if a user wanted to identify all of the students majoring in a particular field of study. It should not be the primary key, however, because many students can have the same major. Therefore, it cannot uniquely identify an individual student.

A **foreign key** is a field (or group of fields) in one table that uniquely identifies a row of another table. A foreign key is used to establish and enforce a link between two tables. We discuss foreign keys in more detail in Appendix to this chapter.

Organizations implement databases to efficiently and effectively manage their data. There are a variety of operations that can be performed on databases. We look at three of these operations in detail in Appendix to this chapter: query languages, normalization, and joins.

As we noted earlier in this chapter, organizations must manage huge quantities of data. Such data consist of structured and unstructured data and are called Big Data (discussed in Section 5.3). To manage Big Data, many organizations are using special types of databases, which we also discuss in Section 5.3.

Because databases typically process data in real time (or near real time), it is not practical to allow users access to the databases. After all, the data will change while the user is looking at them! As a result, data warehouses have been developed to allow users to access data for decision making. You will learn about data warehouses in Section 5.4.

# before you go on...

1. What is a data model?
2. What is a primary key? A secondary key?
3. What is an entity? An attribute? An instance?
4. What are the advantages and disadvantages of relational databases?

# Big Data

5.3

We are accumulating data and information at an increasingly rapid pace from many diverse sources. In fact, organizations are capturing data about almost all events—including events that, in the past, firms never used to think of as data at all, such as a person's location, the vibrations and temperature of an engine, and the stress at numerous points on a bridge—and then analyzing those data.

Organizations and individuals must process a vast amount of data that continues to rapidly increase. According to IDC (a technology research firm; *www.idc.com*), the world generates exabytes of data each year (an exabyte is 1 trillion terabytes). Furthermore, the amount of data produced worldwide is increasing by 50 percent each year. As we discussed at the beginning of the chapter, we refer to the superabundance of data available today as Big Data. That is, **Big Data** is a collection of data so large and complex that it is difficult to manage using traditional database management systems. (We capitalize *Big Data* to distinguish the term from large amounts of traditional data.)

Essentially, Big Data is about predictions. Predictions do not come from "teaching" computers to "think" like humans. Instead, predictions come from applying mathematics to huge quantities of data to infer probabilities. Consider the following examples:

- The likelihood that an e-mail message is spam.
- The likelihood that the typed letters "teh" are supposed to be "the."
- The likelihood that the trajectory and velocity of a person jaywalking indicate that he will make it across the street in time, meaning that a self-driving car need only slow down slightly.

Big Data systems perform well because they contain huge amounts of data on which to base their predictions. Moreover, these systems are configured to improve themselves over time by searching for the most valuable signals and patterns as more data are input.

## Defining Big Data

It is difficult to define Big Data. Here we present two descriptions of the phenomenon. First, the technology research firm Gartner (*www.gartner.com*) defines Big Data as diverse, high-volume, high-velocity information assets that require new forms of processing to enable enhanced decision making, insight discovery, and process optimization. Second, the Big Data Institute (TBDI; *www.the-bigdatainstitute.com*) defines Big Data as vast data sets that perform the following:

- Exhibit variety.
- Include structured, unstructured, and semistructured data.

     As recently as the year 2000, only 25 percent of the stored information in the world was digital. The other 75 percent was analog; that is, it was stored on paper, film, vinyl records, and the like. By 2015, the amount of stored information in the world was over 98 percent digital and less than 2 percent nondigital.

- Are generated at high velocity with an uncertain pattern.
- Do not fit neatly into traditional, structured, relational databases.
- Can be captured, processed, transformed, and analyzed in a reasonable amount of time only by sophisticated information systems.

Big Data generally consists of the following:

- *Traditional enterprise data*: Examples are customer information from customer relationship management systems, transactional enterprise resource planning data, Web store transactions, operations data, and general ledger data.
- *Machine-generated/sensor data*: Examples are smart meters; manufacturing sensors; sensors integrated into smartphones, automobiles, airplane engines, and industrial machines; equipment logs; and trading systems data.
- *Social data*: Examples are customer feedback comments; microblogging sites such as Twitter; and social media sites such as Facebook, YouTube, and LinkedIn.
- Images captured by billions of devices located throughout the world, from digital cameras and camera phones to medical scanners and security cameras.

Let's take a look at a few specific examples of Big Data:

- In 2015 Google was processing more than 27 petabytes of data every day.
- Facebook members upload more than 10 million new photos every hour. In addition, they click a "like" button or leave a comment nearly 3 billion times every day.
- The 800 million monthly users of Google's YouTube service upload more than an hour of video every second.
- The number of messages on Twitter is growing at 200 percent every year. By early 2015, the volume exceeded 550 million tweets per day.

## Characteristics of Big Data

Big Data has three distinct characteristics: volume, velocity, and variety. These characteristics distinguish Big Data from traditional data.

- *Volume*: We have noted the huge volume of Big Data. Consider machine-generated data, which are generated in much larger quantities than nontraditional data. For instance, sensors in a single jet engine can generate 10 terabytes of data in 30 minutes. (See our discussion of the Internet of Things in Chapter 8.) With more than 25,000 airline flights per day, the daily volume of data from just this single source is incredible. Smart electrical meters, sensors in heavy industrial equipment, and telemetry from automobiles compound the volume problem.
- *Velocity*: The rate at which data flow into an organization is rapidly increasing. Velocity is critical because it increases the speed of the feedback loop between a company, its customers, its suppliers, and its business partners. For example, the Internet and mobile technology enable online retailers to compile histories not only on final sales but also on their customers' every click and interaction. Companies that can quickly utilize that information—for example, by recommending additional purchases—gain competitive advantage.
- *Variety*: Traditional data formats tend to be structured and relatively well described, and they change slowly. Traditional data include financial market data, point-of-sale transactions, and much more. In contrast, Big Data formats change rapidly. They include satellite imagery, broadcast audio streams, digital music files, Web page content, scans of government documents, and comments posted on social networks.

Irrespective of their source, structure, format, and frequency, Big Data are valuable. If certain types of data appear to have no value today, it is because we have not yet been able to analyze them effectively. For example, several years ago when Google began harnessing satellite imagery, capturing street views, and then sharing these geographical data for free, few people understood its value. Today, we recognize that such data are incredibly valuable because analyses of Big Data yield deep insights. We discuss analytics in detail in Chapter 12.

## Issues with Big Data

Despite its extreme value, Big Data does have issues. In this section, we take a look at data integrity, data quality, and the nuances of analysis that are worth noting.

- *Big Data can come from untrusted sources:* As we discussed above, one of the characteristics of Big Data is variety, meaning that Big Data can come from numerous, widely varied sources. These sources may be internal or external to the organization. For instance, a company might want to integrate data from unstructured sources such as e-mails, call center notes, and social media posts with structured data about its customers from its data warehouse. The question is: How trustworthy are those external sources of data? For example, how trustworthy is a tweet? The data may come from an unverified source. Further, the data itself, reported by the source, can be false or misleading.

- *Big Data is dirty:* Dirty data refers to inaccurate, incomplete, incorrect, duplicate, or erroneous data. Examples of such problems are misspelling of words and duplicate data such as retweets or company press releases that appear numerous times in social media.

    Suppose a company is interested in performing a competitive analysis using social media data. The company wants to see how often a competitor's product appears in social media outlets as well as the sentiments associated with those posts. The company notices that the number of positive posts about the competitor is twice as large the number of positive posts about itself. This finding could simply be a case where the competitor is pushing out its press releases to multiple sources, in essence "blowing its own horn." Alternatively, the competitor could be getting many people to retweet an announcement.

- *Big Data changes, especially in data streams:* Organizations must be aware that data quality in an analysis can change, or the data itself can change, because the conditions under which the data are captured can change. For instance, imagine a utility company that analyzes weather data and smart-meter data to predict customer power usage. What happens when the utility is analyzing these data in real time and it discovers data missing from some of its smart meters?

## Managing Big Data

Big Data makes it possible to do many things that were previously impossible; for example, to spot business trends more rapidly and accurately, prevent disease, track crime, and so on. When properly analyzed, Big Data can reveal valuable patterns and information that were previously hidden because of the amount of work required to discover them. Leading corporations, such as Walmart and Google, have been able to process Big Data for years, but only at great expense. Today's hardware, cloud computing (see Technology Guide 3), and open-source software make processing Big Data affordable for most organizations.

The first step for many organizations toward managing data was to integrate information silos into a database environment and then to develop data warehouses for decision making. (An information silo is an information system that does not communicate with other, related information systems in an organization.) After completing this step, many organizations turned their attention to the business of information management—making sense of their proliferating data. In recent years, Oracle, IBM, Microsoft, and SAP have spent billions of dollars purchasing software firms that specialize in data management and business intelligence. (You will learn about business intelligence in Chapter 12.)

In addition to existing data management systems, today many organizations employ NoSQL databases to process Big Data. Think of them as "not only SQL" (structured query language) databases. (We discuss SQL in Section 5.6).

As you have seen in this chapter, traditional relational databases such as Oracle and MySQL store data in tables organized into rows and columns. Recall that each row is associated with a unique record and each column is associated with a field that defines an attribute of that account.

In contrast, NoSQL databases can manipulate structured as well as unstructured data and inconsistent or missing data. For this reason, NoSQL databases are particularly useful when working with Big Data. Many products utilize NoSQL databases, including Cassandra *(http://cassandra.apache.org)*, CouchDB *(http://couchdb.apache.org)*, MongoDB *(www.mongodb.org)*, and Hadoop *(http://hadoop.apache.org)*. IT's About Business 5.2 focuses on MongoDB, a leading NoSQL database vendor.

### Putting Big Data to Use

Organizations must manage Big Data and gain value from it. There are several ways to do this.

**Making Big Data Available.** Making Big Data available for relevant stakeholders can help organizations gain value. For example, consider open data in the public sector. Open data is accessible public data that individuals and organizations can use to create new businesses and solve complex problems. In particular, government agencies gather very large amounts of data, some of which is Big Data. Making that data available can provide economic benefits. The Open Data 500 study at the GovLab at New York University found some 500 examples of U.S.-based companies whose business models depend on analyzing open government data.

 # IT's [about business]

## 5.2 The MetLife Wall

Founded in 1868, the Metropolitan Life Insurance Company (MetLife) (*www.metlife.com*) is among the largest global providers of insurance, annuities, and employee benefit programs, with 90 million customers located in more than 60 countries. As a result of acquisitions, new products, and various software deployments over the years, MetLife had grown into a $68 billion company with 70 software systems that could not communicate with one another. To make matters worse, each system had its own database. These problems made it difficult for MetLife to communicate with its policyholders. For example, customer service representatives could not always tell if a client with an automobile insurance policy also had a disability plan with the company.

MetLife had to rely heavily on humans to integrate its separate systems and databases. Customer service representatives and claims researchers had to access multiple applications and utilize as many as 40 screens just to gather all of the data and documents required to answer customer questions. That process decreased both worker productivity and customer satisfaction. Because MetLife offers multiple lines of insurance as well as annuities and other lines of business, it was critical that the company develop a unified, consolidated view of its customers.

To accomplish this task, in 2013, MetLife turned to MongoDB, a document-oriented NoSQL database, to integrate all relevant customer data on a single screen. MetLife called the project, which was inspired by the Facebook Wall, the MetLife Wall. With the deployment of the Wall, MetLife representatives no longer view policyholders merely as ID numbers scattered among different insurance products. The MetLife Wall integrates different sources of customer data to let representatives review customers' histories, their conversations with the company, any claims filed and paid, and their various policies—all on a simple timeline. Representatives can access these data with one click, and they can settle issues more efficiently and quickly assess how a customer feels

about the company. The MetLife Wall has significantly increased customer satisfaction. Since the company implemented a limited launch in April 2013, more than 1,000 customer service representatives and claims researchers in the United States and Europe have been using MetLife's Wall successfully.

In addition to the MetLife Wall, MetLife is using MongoDB for two other applications. The first is a recruiting site to store résumés, which makes the résumés easier to analyze than would be the case if they were stored in Word files or PDFs. Next, MetLife deployed a customer-facing mobile app that allows its customers to upload documents, videos, photos, and other content that they can designate to be shared only with selected individuals at some future date. For example, access to a life insurance policy can be made available to the beneficiaries after the policyholder has passed away.

Celent, a research and consulting firm, awarded MetLife its 2014 Model Insurer of the Year. The award recognized MetLife's effective use of technology in the form of the company's MetLife Wall.

*Sources:* Compiled from "MetLife Honored as Celent 2014 Model Insurer of the Year," *MetLife Global Technology & Operations*, April 14, 2014; "5 Lessons Learned from the MetLife Wall," *inetpost.mobi*, May 1, 2014; J. Alserver, "Technology Is the Best Policy," *Fortune*, November 18, 2013; J. Alsever, "At MetLife, Technology Is the Best Policy," *CNN Money*, October 31, 2013; "Build in Record Time, the MetLife Wall Knocks Down Barriers to Great Customer Service," *MetLife Global Technology & Operations*, October 23, 2013; K. Nicole, "MetLife's Big Data Revolution," *Forbes*, October 11, 2013; D. Henschen, "When NoSQL Makes Sense," *InformationWeek*, October 7, 2013; D. Harris, "The Promise of Better Data Has MetLife Investing $300 M in New Tech," *GigaOM*, May 7, 2013; *www.metlife.com*, accessed February 27, 2015.

**Questions**

1. Describe the problems that MetLife was experiencing with customer data before it implemented the MetLife Wall.
2. Describe how these problems originated.

**Enabling Organizations to Conduct Experiments.**   Big Data allows organizations to improve performance by conducting controlled experiments. For example, Amazon (and many other companies such as Google and LinkedIn) constantly experiments by offering slight different "looks" on its Web site. These experiments are called A/B experiments, because each experiment has only two possible outcomes. Here is an example of an A/B experiment at Etsy. com, an online marketplace for vintage and handmade products.

When Etsy analysts noticed that one of its Web pages attracted customer attention but failed to keep it, they looked more closely at the page. They found that the page had few "calls to action." (A call to action is an item, such as a button, on a Web page that enables a customer to do something.) On this particular Etsy page, customers could leave, buy, search, or click on two additional product images. The analysts decided to show more product images on the page.

Consequently, one group of visitors to the page saw a strip across the top of the page that displayed additional product images. Another group of page visitors saw only the two original product images. On the page with additional images, customers viewed more products and bought more products. The results of this experiment revealed valuable information to Etsy.

**Microsegmentation of Customers.**   Segmentation of a company's customers means dividing them into groups that share one or more characteristics. Microsegmentation simply means dividing customers into very small groups, or even down to the individual level.

For example, Paytronix Systems (*www.paytronix.com*) provides loyalty and rewards program software to thousands of different restaurants. Paytronix gathers restaurant guest data from a variety of sources beyond loyalty and gift programs, including social media. Paytronix analyzes this Big Data to help its restaurant clients microsegment their guests. Restaurant managers are now able to more precisely customize their loyalty and gift programs. In doing so, the managers are noting improved performance in their restaurants in terms of profitability and customer satisfaction.

**Creating New Business Models.**   Companies are able to use Big Data to create new business models. For example, a commercial transportation company operated a large fleet of large, long-haul trucks. The company recently placed sensors on all its trucks. These sensors wirelessly communicate large amounts of information to the company, a process called telematics. The sensors collect data on vehicle usage (including acceleration, braking, cornering, etc.), driver performance, and vehicle maintenance.

By analyzing this Big Data, the transportation company was able to improve the condition of its trucks through near-real-time analysis that proactively suggested preventive maintenance. In addition, the company was able to improve the driving skills of its operators by analyzing their driving styles.

The transportation company then made its Big Data available to its insurance carrier. Using this data, the insurance carrier performed risk analysis on driver behavior and the condition of the trucks, resulting in a more precise assessment. The insurance carrier offered the transportation company a new pricing model that lowered the transportation company's premiums by 10 percent.

**Organizations Can Analyze More Data.**   In some cases, organizations can even process all the data relating to a particular phenomenon, meaning that they do not have to rely as much on sampling. Random sampling works well, but it is not as effective as analyzing an entire dataset. In addition, random sampling has some basic weaknesses. To begin with, its accuracy depends on ensuring randomness when collecting the sample data. However, achieving such randomness is problematic. Systematic biases in the process of data collection can cause the results to be highly inaccurate. For example, consider political polling using landline phones. This sample tends to exclude people who use only cell phones. This bias can seriously skew the results, because cell phone users are typically younger and more liberal than people who rely primarily on landline phones.

## Big Data Used in the Functional Areas of the Organization

In this section, we provide examples of how Big Data is valuable to various functional areas in the firm.

**Human Resources.** Employee benefits, particularly healthcare, represent a major business expense. Consequently, some companies have turned to Big Data to better manage these benefits. Caesars Entertainment (*www.caesars.com*), for example, analyzes health-insurance claim data for its 65,000 employees and their covered family members. Managers can track thousands of variables that indicate how employees use medical services, such as the number of emergency room visits and whether employees choose a generic or brand name drug.

Consider the following scenario: Data revealed that too many employees with medical emergencies were being treated at hospital emergency rooms rather than at less-expensive urgent-care facilities. The company launched a campaign to remind employees of the high cost of emergency room visits, and they provided a list of alternative facilities. Subsequently, 10,000 emergencies shifted to less-expensive alternatives, for a total savings of $4.5 million.

Big Data is also having an impact on *hiring*. An example is Catalyst IT Services (*www.catalystitservices.com*), a technology outsourcing company that hires teams for programming jobs. Traditional recruiting is typically too slow, and hiring managers often subjectively choose candidates who are not the best fit for the job. Catalyst addresses this problem by requiring candidates to fill out an online assessment. It then uses the assessment to collect thousands of data points about each candidate. In fact, the company collects more data based on *how* candidates answer than on *what* they answer.

For example, the assessment might give a problem requiring calculus to an applicant who is not expected to know the subject. How the candidate responds—laboring over an answer, answering quickly and then returning later, or skipping the problem entirely—provides insight into how that candidate might deal with challenges that he or she will encounter on the job. That is, someone who labors over a difficult question might be effective in an assignment that requires a methodical approach to problem solving, whereas an applicant who takes a more aggressive approach might perform better in a different job setting.

The benefit of this big-data approach is that it recognizes that people bring different skills to the table and that there is no one-size-fits-all person for any job. Analyzing millions of data points can reveal which attributes candidates bring to specific situations.

As one measure of success, employee turnover at Catalyst averages about 15 percent per year, compared with more than 30 percent for its U.S. competitors and more than 20 percent for similar companies overseas.

**Product Development.** Big Data can help capture customer preferences and put that information to work in designing new products. For example, Ford Motor Company (*www.ford.com*) was considering a "three blink" turn indicator that had been available on its European cars for years. Unlike the turn signals on its U.S. vehicles, this indicator flashes three times at the driver's touch and then automatically shuts off.

Ford decided that conducting a full-scale market research test on this blinker would be too costly and time consuming. Instead, it examined auto-enthusiast Web sites and owner forums to discover what drivers were saying about turn indicators. Using text-mining algorithms, researchers culled more than 10,000 mentions and then summarized the most relevant comments.

The results? Ford introduced the three-blink indicator on the new Ford Fiesta in 2010, and by 2013 it was available on most Ford products. Although some Ford owners complained online that they have had trouble getting used to the new turn indicator, many others defended it. Ford managers note that the use of text-mining algorithms was critical in this effort because they provided the company with a complete picture that would not have been available using traditional market research.

**Operations.** For years, companies have been using information technology to make their operations more efficient. Consider United Parcel Service (UPS). The company has long relied on data to improve its operations. Specifically, it uses sensors in its delivery vehicles that can, among other things, capture the truck's speed and location, the number of times it is placed in reverse, and whether the driver's seat belt is buckled. These data are uploaded at the end of each day to a UPS data center, where they are analyzed overnight. By combining GPS information and data from sensors installed on more than 46,000 vehicles, UPS reduced fuel consumption by 8.4 million gallons, and it cut 85 million miles off its routes.

**Marketing.** Marketing managers have long used data to better understand their customers and to target their marketing efforts more directly. Today, Big Data enables marketers to craft much more personalized messages.

The UK's InterContinental Hotels Group (IHG) (*www.ihg.com*) has gathered details about the members of its Priority Club rewards program, such as income levels and whether members prefer family-style or business-traveler accommodations. The company then consolidated all such information with information obtained from social media into a single data warehouse. Using its data warehouse and analytics software, the hotelier launched a new marketing campaign. Where previous marketing campaigns generated, on average, between 7 and 15 customized marketing messages, the new campaign generated more than 1,500. IHG rolled out these messages in stages to an initial core of 12 customer groups, each of which is defined by 4,000 attributes. One group, for instance, tends to stay on weekends, redeem reward points for gift cards, and register through IHG marketing partners. Utilizing this information, IHG sent these customers a marketing message that alerted them to local weekend events.

The campaign proved to be highly successful. It generated a 35 percent higher rate of customer conversions, or acceptances, than previous, similar campaigns.

**Government Operations.** With 55 percent of the population of the Netherlands living under the threat of flooding, water management is critically important to the Dutch government. The government operates a sophisticated water management system, managing a network of dykes or levees, canals, locks, harbors, dams, rivers, storm-surge barriers, sluices, and pumping stations.

In its water management efforts, the government makes use of a vast number of sensors embedded in every physical structure used for water control. The sensors generate at least 2 petabytes of data annually. As the sensors are becoming cheaper, the government is deploying more of them, increasing the amount of data generated.

In just one example of the use of sensor data, sensors in dykes can provide information on the structure of the dyke, how well it is able to handle the stress of the water it controls, and whether it is likely to fail. Further, the sensor data are providing valuable insights for new designs for Dutch dykes. The result is that Dutch authorities have reduced the costs of managing water by 15 percent.

# before you go on...

1. Define Big Data.
2. Describe the characteristics of Big Data.
3. Describe how companies can use Big Data to gain competitive advantage.

# Data Warehouses and Data Marts

# 5.4

Today, the most successful companies are those that can respond quickly and flexibly to market changes and opportunities. A key to this response is the effective and efficient use of data and information by analysts and managers. The challenge is providing users with access to corporate data so that they can analyze the data to make better decisions. Let's look at an example. If the manager of a local bookstore wanted to know the profit margin on used books at her store, she could obtain that information from her database, using SQL or QBE. However, if she needed to know the trend in the profit margins on used books over the past 10 years, she would have to construct a very complicated SQL or QBE query.

This example illustrates several reasons why organizations are building data warehouses and/or data marts. First, the bookstore's databases contain the necessary information to answer the manager's query, but this information is not organized in a way that makes it easy for her to find what she needs. Second, the organization's databases are designed to process millions of transactions every day. Therefore, complicated queries might take a long time to answer, and they also might degrade the performance of the databases. Third, transactional databases are designed to be updated. This update process requires extra processing. Data warehouses and data marts are read-only, and the extra processing is eliminated because data already contained in the data warehouse are not updated. Fourth, transactional databases are designed to access a single record at a time. Data warehouses are designed to access large groups of related records.

As a result of these problems, companies are using a variety of tools with data warehouses and data marts to make it easier and faster for users to access, analyze, and query data. You will learn about these tools in Chapter 12 on Business Analytics.

## Describing Data Warehouses and Data Marts

In general, data warehouses and data marts support business intelligence (BI) applications. As you will see in Chapter 12, business intelligence encompasses a broad category of applications, technologies, and processes for gathering, storing, accessing, and analyzing data to help business users make better decisions. A **data warehouse** is a repository of historical data that are organized by subject to support decision makers in the organization.

Because data warehouses are so expensive, they are used primarily by large companies. A **data mart** is a low-cost, scaled-down version of a data warehouse that is designed for the end-user needs in a strategic business unit (SBU) or an individual department. Data marts can be implemented more quickly than data warehouses, often in less than 90 days. Further, they support local rather than central control by conferring power on the user group. Typically, groups that need a single or a few BI applications require only a data mart, rather than a data warehouse.

The basic characteristics of data warehouses and data marts include the following:

- *Organized by business dimension or subject*: Data are organized by subject—for example, by customer, vendor, product, price level, and region. This arrangement differs from transactional systems, where data are organized by business process, such as order entry, inventory control, and accounts receivable.

- *Use online analytical processing*: Typically, organizational databases are oriented toward handling transactions. That is, databases use *online transaction processing* (OLTP), where business transactions are processed online as soon as they occur. The objectives are speed and efficiency, which are critical to a successful Internet-based business operation. Data warehouses and data marts, which are designed to support decision makers but not OLTP, use online analytical processing. *Online analytical processing* (OLAP) involves the analysis of accumulated data by end users. We consider OLAP in greater detail in Chapter 12.

- *Integrated*: Data are collected from multiple systems and then integrated around subjects. For example, customer data may be extracted from internal (and external) systems and then integrated around a customer identifier, thereby creating a comprehensive view of the customer.

- *Time variant*: Data warehouses and data marts maintain historical data (i.e., data that include time as a variable). Unlike transactional systems, which maintain only recent data (such as for the last day, week, or month), a warehouse or mart may store years of data. Organizations utilize historical data to detect deviations, trends, and long-term relationships.

- *Nonvolatile*: Data warehouses and data marts are nonvolatile—that is, users cannot change or update the data. Therefore, the warehouse or mart reflects history, which, as we just saw, is critical for identifying and analyzing trends. Warehouses and marts are updated, but through IT-controlled load processes rather than by users.

- *Multidimensional*: Typically, the data warehouse or mart uses a multidimensional data structure. Recall that relational databases store data in two-dimensional tables. In contrast, data warehouses and marts store data in more than two dimensions. For this reason, the data are said to be stored in a **multidimensional structure**. A common representation for this multidimensional structure is the *data cube*.

The data in data warehouses and marts are organized by *business dimensions*, which are subjects such as product, geographic area, and time period that represent the edges of the data cube. If you look ahead briefly to Figure 5.6 for an example of a data cube, you see that the product dimension is comprised of nuts, screws, bolts, and washers; the geographic area dimension is comprised of East, West, and Central; and the time period dimension is comprised of 2012, 2013, and 2014. Users can view and analyze data from the perspective of these business dimensions. This analysis is intuitive because the dimensions are presented in business terms that users can easily understand.

## A Generic Data Warehouse Environment

The environment for data warehouses and marts includes the following:

- Source systems that provide data to the warehouse or mart
- Data-integration technology and processes that prepare the data for use
- Different architectures for storing data in an organization's data warehouse or data marts
- Different tools and applications for the variety of users. (You will learn about these tools and applications in Chapter 12.)
- Metadata, data-quality, and governance processes that ensure that the warehouse or mart meets its purposes

Figure 5.4 depicts a generic data warehouse/data mart environment. Let's drill-down into the component parts.

*Source Systems.* There is typically some "organizational pain" (i.e., business need) that motivates a firm to develop its BI capabilities. Working backward, this pain leads to information requirements, BI applications, and source system data requirements. The data requirements can range from a single source system, as in the case of a data mart, to hundreds of source systems, as in the case of an enterprisewide data warehouse.

Modern organizations can select from a variety of source systems: operational/transactional systems, enterprise resource planning (ERP) systems, Web site data, third-party data (e.g., customer demographic data), and more. The trend is to include more types of data (e.g., sensing

**FIGURE 5.4** Data warehouse framework.

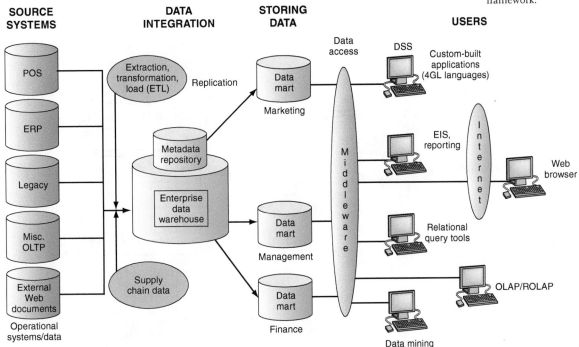

data from RFID tags). These source systems often use different software packages (e.g., IBM, Oracle) and store data in different formats (e.g., relational, hierarchical).

A common source for the data in data warehouses is the company's operational databases, which can be relational databases. To differentiate between relational databases and multidimensional data warehouses and marts, imagine your company manufactures four products— nuts, screws, bolts, and washers—and has sold them in three territories—East, West, and Central—for the previous three years—2012, 2013, and 2014. In a relational database, these sales data would resemble Figure 5.5a–c. In a multidimensional database, in contrast, these data would be represented by a three-dimensional matrix (or data cube), as depicted in Figure 5.6. This matrix represents sales *dimensioned by* products and regions and year. Notice that Figure 5.5a presents only sales for 2012. Sales for 2013 and 2014 are presented in Figure 5.5b and c, respectively. Figure 5.7a–c illustrates the equivalence between these relational and multidimensional databases.

**(a) 2011**

| Product | Region | Sales |
|---|---|---|
| Nuts | East | 50 |
| Nuts | West | 60 |
| Nuts | Central | 100 |
| Screws | East | 40 |
| Screws | West | 70 |
| Screws | Central | 80 |
| Bolts | East | 90 |
| Bolts | West | 120 |
| Bolts | Central | 140 |
| Washers | East | 20 |
| Washers | West | 10 |
| Washers | Central | 30 |

**(b) 2012**

| Product | Region | Sales |
|---|---|---|
| Nuts | East | 60 |
| Nuts | West | 70 |
| Nuts | Central | 110 |
| Screws | East | 50 |
| Screws | West | 80 |
| Screws | Central | 90 |
| Bolts | East | 100 |
| Bolts | West | 130 |
| Bolts | Central | 150 |
| Washers | East | 30 |
| Washers | West | 20 |
| Washers | Central | 40 |

**(c) 2013**

| Product | Region | Sales |
|---|---|---|
| Nuts | East | 70 |
| Nuts | West | 80 |
| Nuts | Central | 120 |
| Screws | East | 60 |
| Screws | West | 90 |
| Screws | Central | 100 |
| Bolts | East | 110 |
| Bolts | West | 140 |
| Bolts | Central | 160 |
| Washers | East | 40 |
| Washers | West | 30 |
| Washers | Central | 50 |

**FIGURE 5.5** Relational databases.

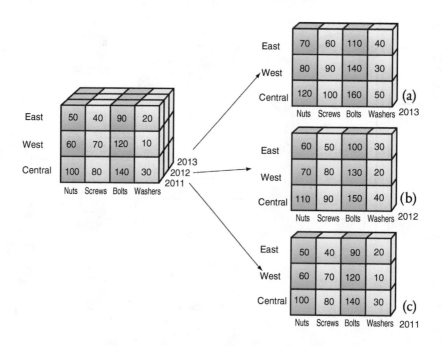

**FIGURE 5.6** Data cube.

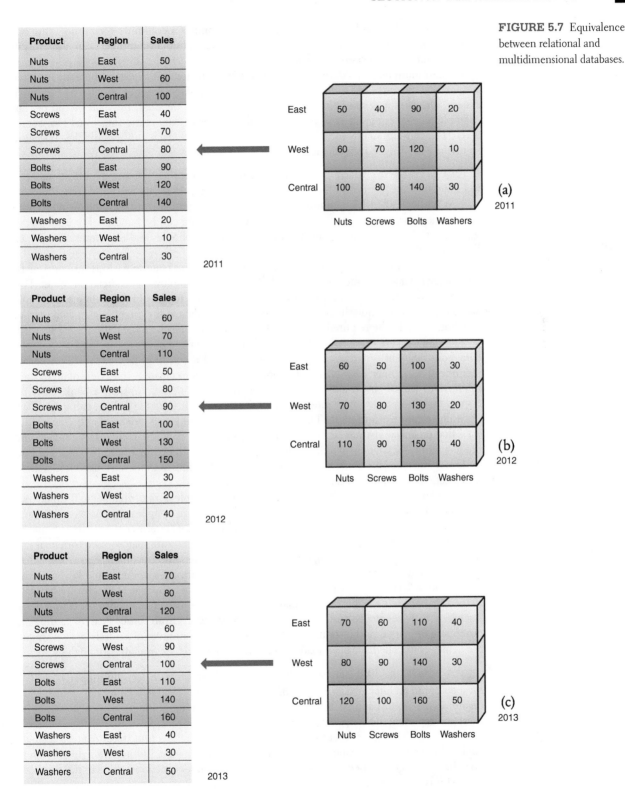

**FIGURE 5.7** Equivalence between relational and multidimensional databases.

Unfortunately, many source systems that have been in use for years contain "bad data" (e.g., missing or incorrect data) and are poorly documented. As a result, data-profiling software should be used at the beginning of a warehousing project to better understand the data. For example, this software can provide statistics on missing data, identify possible primary and foreign keys, and reveal how derived values (e.g., column 3 = column 1 + column 2) are calculated. Subject area database specialists (e.g., marketing, human resources) can also assist in understanding and accessing the data in source systems.

Organizations need to address other source systems issues as well. Often there are multiple systems that contain some of the same data and the best system must be selected as the source system. Organizations must also decide how granular (i.e., detailed) the data should be. For example, does the organization need daily sales figures or data at the individual transaction level? The conventional wisdom is that it is best to store data at a highly granular level because someone will likely request the data at some point.

**Data Integration.** In addition to storing data in their source systems, organizations need to *extract* the data, *transform* them, and then *load* them into a data mart or warehouse. This process is often called ETL, although the term *data integration* is increasingly being used to reflect the growing number of ways that source system data can be handled. For example, in some cases, data are extracted, loaded into a mart or warehouse, and then transformed (i.e., ELT rather than ETL).

Data extraction can be performed either by handwritten code (e.g., SQL queries) or by commercial data-integration software. Most companies employ commercial software. This software makes it relatively easy to specify the tables and attributes in the source systems that are to be used, map and schedule the movement of the data to the target (e.g., a data mart or warehouse), make the required transformations, and ultimately load the data.

After the data are extracted they are transformed to make them more useful. For example, data from different systems may be integrated around a common key, such as a customer identification number. Organizations adopt this approach to create a 360° view of all of their interactions with their customers. As an example of this process, consider a bank. Customers can engage in a variety of interactions: visiting a branch, banking online, using an ATM, obtaining a car loan, and more. The systems for these touch points—defined as the numerous ways that organizations interact with customers, such as e-mail, the Web, direct contact, and the telephone—are typically independent of one another. To obtain a holistic picture of how customers are using the bank, the bank must integrate the data from the various source systems into a data mart or warehouse.

Other kinds of transformations also take place. For example, format changes to the data may be required, such as using *male* and *female* to denote gender, as opposed to 0 and 1 or M and F. Aggregations may be performed, say on sales figures, so that queries can use the summaries rather than recalculating them each time. Data-cleansing software may be used to "clean up" the data; for example, eliminating duplicate records for the same customer.

Finally, data are loaded into the warehouse or mart during a specific period known as the "load window." This window is becoming smaller as companies seek to store ever-fresher data in their warehouses. For this reason, many companies have moved to real-time data warehousing where data are moved (using data-integration processes) from source systems to the data warehouse or mart almost instantly. For example, within 15 minutes of a purchase at Walmart, the details of the sale have been loaded into a warehouse and are available for analysis.

**Storing the Data.** A variety of architectures can be used to store decision-support data. The most common architecture is *one central enterprise data warehouse*, without data marts. Most organizations use this approach, because the data stored in the warehouse are accessed by all users and represent the *single version of the truth*.

Another architecture is *independent data marts*. This architecture stores data for a single application or a few applications, such as marketing and finance. Limited thought is given to how the data might be used for other applications or by other functional areas in the organization. This is a very application-centric approach to storing data.

The independent data mart architecture is not particularly effective. Although it may meet a specific organizational need, it does not reflect an enterprise-wide approach to data management. Instead, the various organizational units create independent data marts. Not only are these marts expensive to build and maintain, but they often contain inconsistent data. For example, they may have inconsistent data definitions such as: What is a customer? Is a particular individual a potential or current customer? They might also use different source systems (which may have different data for the same item, such as a customer address). Although independent data marts are an organizational reality, larger companies have increasingly moved to data warehouses.

Still another data warehouse architecture is the *hub and spoke*. This architecture contains a central data warehouse that stores the data plus multiple dependent data marts that source their data from the central repository. Because the marts obtain their data from the central repository, the data in these marts still comprise the *single version of the truth* for decision-support purposes.

The dependent data marts store the data in a format that is appropriate for how the data will be used and for providing faster response times to queries and applications. As you have learned, users can view and analyze data from the perspective of business dimensions and measures. This analysis is intuitive because the dimensions are in business terms, easily understood by users.

Metadata. It is important to maintain data about the data, known as *metadata*, in the data warehouse. Both the IT personnel who operate and manage the data warehouse and the users who access the data need metadata. IT personnel need information about data sources; database, table, and column names; refresh schedules; and data-usage measures. Users' needs include data definitions, report/query tools, report distribution information, and contact information for the help desk.

Data Quality. The quality of the data in the warehouse must meet users' needs. If it does not, users will not trust the data and ultimately will not use it. Most organizations find that the quality of the data in source systems is poor and must be improved before the data can be used in the data warehouse. Some of the data can be improved with data-cleansing software, but the better, long-term solution is to improve the quality at the source system level. This approach requires the business owners of the data to assume responsibility for making any necessary changes to implement this solution.

To illustrate this point, consider the case of a large hotel chain that wanted to conduct targeted marketing promotions using zip code data it collected from its guests when they checked in. When the company analyzed the zip code data, they discovered that many of the zip codes were 99999. How did this error occur? The answer is that the clerks were not asking customers for their zip codes, but they needed to enter something to complete the registration process. A short-term solution to this problem was to conduct the marketing campaign using city and state data instead of zip codes. The long-term solution was to make certain the clerks entered the actual zip codes. The latter solution required the hotel managers to take the responsibility for making certain their clerks enter the correct data.

Governance. To ensure that BI is meeting their needs, organizations must implement *governance* to plan and control their BI activities. Governance requires that people, committees, and processes be in place. Companies that are effective in BI governance often create a senior-level committee comprised of vice presidents and directors who (1) ensure that the business strategies and BI strategies are in alignment, (2) prioritize projects, and (3) allocate resources. These companies also establish a middle management–level committee that oversees the various projects in the BI portfolio to ensure that these projects are being completed in accordance with the company's objectives. Finally, lower-level operational committees perform tasks such as creating data definitions and identifying and solving data problems. All of these committees rely on the collaboration and contributions of business users and IT personnel.

Users. Once the data are loaded in a data mart or warehouse, they can be accessed. At this point the organization begins to obtain business value from BI; all of the prior stages constitute creating BI infrastructure.

There are many potential BI users, including IT developers; frontline workers; analysts; information workers; managers and executives; and suppliers, customers, and regulators. Some of these users are *information producers* whose primary role is to create information for other users. IT developers and analysts typically fall into this category. Other users—including managers and executives—are *information consumers*, because they utilize information created by others.

Companies have reported hundreds of successful data-warehousing applications. You can read client success stories and case studies at the Web sites of vendors such as NCR Corp. (*www.ncr.com*) and Oracle (*www.oracle.com*). For a more detailed discussion, visit the Data Warehouse Institute (*http://tdwi.org*). The benefits of data warehousing include the following:

- End users can access needed data quickly and easily via Web browsers because these data are located in one place.
- End users can conduct extensive analysis with data in ways that were not previously possible.
- End users can obtain a consolidated view of organizational data.

These benefits can improve business knowledge, provide competitive advantage, enhance customer service and satisfaction, facilitate decision making, and streamline business processes. IT's About Business 5.3 demonstrates the benefits of data warehousing to the Nordea Bank in Scandinavia.

Despite their many benefits, data warehouses have some limitations. First, they can be very expensive to build and to maintain. Second, incorporating data from obsolete mainframe systems can be difficult and expensive. Finally, people in one department might be reluctant to share data with other departments.

 **IT's [about business]**

### **5.3** Data Warehouse Gives Nordea Bank a Single Version of the Truth

Financial institutions across Europe must improve their data-management practices if they are to comply with the demanding legislation that arose in response to the global financial crisis of 2008. Banks must comply with numerous regulations developed by various authorities around the globe. These regulations require banks to report how much capital they hold and to document how they report risk.

In Europe, these regulations include Basel III affecting capital ratios, the European Central Bank demanding faster and more detailed reporting with MFI 3, and the European Banking Authority developing new financial reporting with Finrep. Meanwhile, in 2010 the United States passed the Foreign Account Tax Compliance Act (FATCA), which also places greater reporting requirements on banks operating in this country.

The new regulations, together with ongoing business challenges, made data vitally important at Nordea Bank AB (*www.nordea.com*). As a result, the bank implemented a data warehouse.

Nordea, which is headquartered in Stockholm, Sweden, advertises itself as "the largest financial services group in Northern Europe." Although the institution has a long history, the modern organization was formed in 2001 when major banks in Norway, Sweden, Denmark, and Finland merged their resources and operations. Today Nordea has more than 1,400 branches that conduct business in 19 countries. Its clientele includes 10 million private customers and 600,000 corporate clients. The group also operates an Internet bank, which services 6 million online customers.

Nordea's finance group agreed to lead a data warehouse project with a budget of €100 million. The project was managed by the finance group because that group "owned" the data and the data-management processes. The project had two overriding objectives: to improve customer service and to comply with all relevant regulations.

As noted, Nordea was created from the merger of four separate financial institutions, each with its own legacy information systems. (A legacy system refers to outdated information systems or application software that is used instead of available upgraded versions.) Data at Nordea were governed by manual processes, stored on spreadsheets, and managed locally. This arrangement was inadequate to meet the demands of a modern global banking system.

As a result of these data management problems, the most important principle for the data warehouse was to create a single version of the truth. Consequently, the finance team built common data definitions and master data necessary to compare variables across geographies and business functions. Based in Stockholm, the data warehouse stores 11 terabytes of data, including more than 7 billion records.

Nordea deployed the data warehouse with impressive results. Reporting lead times decreased from eight to four days. This process enabled the bank to conduct analyses more quickly and accurately at lower costs. All managers and financial controllers now receive the branch results in the same format, at the same time. They can drill down to the customer, account, and product data, all from the same coherent, consistent source.

The data warehouse enabled Nordea to introduce a customer profitability application for customer relationship managers. These managers can more easily prepare for meetings with customers because they do not have to obtain customer data from different databases.

The current financial climate requires banks to focus more carefully on compliance. The data warehouse enabled Nordea to meet relevant regulatory requirements more quickly and accurately. Further, the reduced costs of compliance enabled the bank to reallocate capital to address needs in other areas of the business.

Nordea continues to thrive. In the third quarter of 2014, the bank added new customers and reported more than €250 billion in total assets under management. Finally, the bank's loan loss level is below its 10-year average.

*Sources:* Compiled from "EBA Stress Test Confirms Nordea's Strong Position," *Nordea Press Release*, October 26, 2014; "Nordea Builds on a Financial Data Warehouse," *TechandFinance.com*, October 27, 2013;

R. Nielsen, "Nordea's 'One Platform:' Business Value with a Financial Data Warehouse," *Teradata Conference and Expo*, October, 2013; L. Clark, "European Banks Pull Data Together for Business and Legal Compliance," *Computer Weekly Europe*, September, 2013; L. Clark, "European Banks Raise Data Management Game in Response to New Regulations," *Computer Weekly Europe*, September, 2013; P. Swabey, "Nordea Prepares for Wave of Regulation with New Data Warehouse," *Information Age*, April 15, 2013; www.nordea.com, accessed February 27, 2015.

### Questions

1. What are other advantages (not mentioned in the case) that Nordea Bank might realize from its data warehouse?
2. What recommendations would you give to Nordea Bank about incorporating Big Data into its data management? Provide specific examples of what types of Big Data you think Nordea should consider.

## before you go on...

1. Differentiate between data warehouses and data marts.
2. Describe the characteristics of a data warehouse.
3. What are three possible architectures for data warehouses and data marts in an organization?

# Knowledge Management

5.5

As we have noted throughout this text, data and information are critically important organizational assets. Knowledge is a vital asset as well. Successful managers have always valued and utilized intellectual assets. These efforts were not systematic, however, and they did not ensure that knowledge was shared and dispersed in a way that benefited the overall organization. Moreover, industry analysts estimate that most of a company's knowledge assets are not housed in relational databases. Instead, they are dispersed in e-mail, word processing documents, spreadsheets, presentations on individual computers, and in people's heads. This arrangement makes it extremely difficult for companies to access and integrate this knowledge. The result frequently is less-effective decision making.

## Concepts and Definitions

**Knowledge management** is a process that helps organizations manipulate important knowledge that comprises part of the organization's memory, usually in an unstructured format. For an organization to be successful, knowledge, as a form of capital, must exist in a format that can be exchanged among persons. In addition, it must be able to grow.

Knowledge.   In the information technology context, knowledge is distinct from data and information. As you learned in Chapter 1, data are a collection of facts, measurements, and statistics; information is organized or processed data that are timely and accurate. Knowledge is information that is *contextual*, *relevant*, and *useful*. Simply put, knowledge is information in action. **Intellectual capital** (or **intellectual assets**) is another term for knowledge.

To illustrate, a bulletin listing all of the courses offered by your university during one semester would be considered data. When you register, you process the data from the bulletin to create your schedule for the semester. Your schedule would be considered information. Awareness of your work schedule, your major, your desired social schedule, and characteristics of different faculty members could be construed as knowledge, because it can affect the way you build your schedule. You see that this awareness is contextual and relevant (to developing an optimal schedule of classes) as well as useful (it can lead to changes in your schedule). The implication is that knowledge has strong experiential and reflective elements that distinguish it from information in a given context. Unlike information, knowledge can be utilized to solve a problem.

Numerous theories and models classify different types of knowledge. Here you will focus on the distinction between explicit knowledge and tacit knowledge.

**Explicit and Tacit Knowledge.** **Explicit knowledge** deals with more objective, rational, and technical knowledge. In an organization, explicit knowledge consists of the policies, procedural guides, reports, products, strategies, goals, core competencies, and IT infrastructure of the enterprise. In other words, explicit knowledge is the knowledge that has been codified (documented) in a form that can be distributed to others or transformed into a process or a strategy. A description of how to process a job application that is documented in a firm's human resources policy manual is an example of explicit knowledge.

In contrast, **tacit knowledge** is the cumulative store of subjective or experiential learning. In an organization, tacit knowledge consists of an organization's experiences, insights, expertise, know-how, trade secrets, skill sets, understanding, and learning. It also includes the organizational culture, which reflects the past and present experiences of the organization's people and processes, as well as the organization's prevailing values. Tacit knowledge is generally imprecise and costly to transfer. It is also highly personal. Finally, because it is unstructured, it is difficult to formalize or codify, in contrast to explicit knowledge. A salesperson who has worked with particular customers over time and has come to know their needs quite well would possess extensive tacit knowledge. This knowledge is typically not recorded. In fact, it might be difficult for the salesperson to put into writing, even if he or she were willing to share it.

## Knowledge Management Systems

The goal of knowledge management is to help an organization make the most productive use of the knowledge it has accumulated. Historically, management information systems have focused on capturing, storing, managing, and reporting explicit knowledge. Organizations now realize they need to integrate explicit and tacit knowledge into formal information systems. **Knowledge management systems (KMSs)** refer to the use of modern information technologies—the Internet, intranets, extranets, databases—to systematize, enhance, and expedite intrafirm and interfirm knowledge management. KMSs are intended to help an organization cope with turnover, rapid change, and downsizing by making the expertise of the organization's human capital widely accessible.

Organizations can realize many benefits with KMSs. Most importantly, they make **best practices**—the most effective and efficient ways of doing things—readily available to a wide range of employees. Enhanced access to best-practice knowledge improves overall organizational performance. For example, account managers can now make available their tacit knowledge about how best to manage large accounts. The organization can then utilize this knowledge when it trains new account managers. Other benefits include improved customer service, more efficient product development, and improved employee morale and retention.

At the same time, however, implementing effective KMSs presents several challenges. First, employees must be willing to share their personal tacit knowledge. To encourage this behavior, organizations must create a knowledge management culture that rewards employees who add their expertise to the knowledge base. Second, the organization must continually maintain and upgrade its knowledge base. Specifically, it must incorporate new knowledge and delete old, outdated knowledge. Finally, companies must be willing to invest in the resources needed to carry out these operations.

## The KMS Cycle

A functioning KMS follows a cycle that consists of six steps (see Figure 5.8). The reason the system is cyclical is that knowledge is dynamically refined over time. The knowledge in an effective KMS is never finalized because the environment changes over time and knowledge must be updated to reflect these changes. The cycle works as follows:

1. *Create knowledge:* Knowledge is created as people determine new ways of doing things or develop know-how. Sometimes external knowledge is brought in.

2. *Capture knowledge:* New knowledge must be identified as valuable and be represented in a reasonable way.

3. *Refine knowledge:* New knowledge must be placed in context so that it is actionable. This is where tacit qualities (human insights) must be captured along with explicit facts.

4. *Store knowledge:* Useful knowledge must then be stored in a reasonable format in a knowledge repository so that other people in the organization can access it.

5. *Manage knowledge:* Like a library, the knowledge must be kept current. It must be reviewed regularly to verify that it is relevant and accurate.

6. *Disseminate knowledge:* Knowledge must be made available in a useful format to anyone in the organization who needs it, anywhere and anytime.

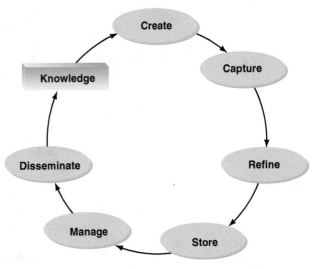

**FIGURE 5.8** The knowledge management system cycle.

## before you go on...

1. What is knowledge management?
2. What is the difference between tacit knowledge and explicit knowledge?
3. Describe the knowledge management system cycle.

# Appendix: Fundamentals of Relational Database Operations

## 5.6

There are many operations possible with relational databases. In this Technology Guide, we discuss three of these operations: query languages, normalization, and joins.

As you saw in this chapter, a relational database is a collection of interrelated two-dimensional tables, consisting of rows and columns. Each row represents a record, and each column (or field) represents an attribute (or characteristic) of that record. Every record in the database must contain at least one field that uniquely identifies that record so that it can be retrieved, updated, and sorted. This identifier field, or group of fields, is called the *primary key*. In some cases, locating a particular record requires the use of secondary keys. A *secondary key* is another field that has some identifying information, but typically does not uniquely identify the record. A *foreign key* is a field (or group of fields) in one table that matches the primary key value in a row of another table. A foreign key is used to establish and enforce a link between two tables.

These related tables can be joined when they contain common columns. The uniqueness of the primary key tells the DBMS which records are joined with others in related tables. This feature allows users great flexibility in the variety of queries they can make. Despite these features, however, the relational database model has some disadvantages. Because large-scale databases can be composed of many interrelated tables, the overall design can be complex, leading to slow search and access times.

### Query Languages

The most commonly performed database operation is searching for information. **Structured query language (SQL)** is the most popular query language used for interacting with a database. SQL allows people to perform complicated searches by using relatively simple statements or key words. Typical key words are SELECT (to choose a desired attribute), FROM (to specify the table or tables to be used), and WHERE (to specify conditions to apply in the query).

To understand how SQL works, imagine that a university wants to know the names of students who will graduate cum laude (but not magna or summa cum laude) in May 2014. (Refer to Figure 5.3.) The university IT staff would query the student relational database with an SQL statement such as

> SELECT Student_Name
> FROM Student_Database
> WHERE Grade_Point_Average>= 3.40 and
> Grade_Point_Average< 3.60;

The SQL query would return John Jones and Juan Rodriguez.

Another way to find information in a database is to use *query by example* (QBE). In QBE, the user fills out a grid or template—also known as a *form*—to construct a sample or a description of the data desired. Users can construct a query quickly and easily by using drag-and-drop features in a DBMS such as Microsoft Access. Conducting queries in this manner is simpler than keying in SQL commands.

## Entity-Relationship Modeling

Designers plan and create databases through the process of **entity–relationship (ER) modeling**, using an **entity–relationship** diagram. There are many approaches to ER diagramming. You will see one particular approach here, but there are others. The good news is that if you are familiar with one version of ER diagramming, then you will be able to easily adapt to any other version.

ER diagrams consist of entities, attributes, and relationships. To properly identify entities, attributes, and relationships, database designers first identify the business rules for the particular data model. **Business rules** are precise descriptions of policies, procedures, or principles in any organization that stores and uses data to generate information. Business rules are derived from a description of an organization's operations, and help create and enforce business processes in that organization. Keep in mind that *you* determine these business rules, not the MIS department.

Entities are pictured in rectangles, and relationships are described on the line between two entities. The attributes for each entity are listed, and the primary key is underlined. The **data dictionary** provides information on each attribute, such as its name, if it is a key, part of a key, or a non-key attribute, the type of data expected (alphanumeric, numeric, dates, etc.), and valid values. Data dictionaries can also provide information on why the attribute is needed in the database; which business functions, applications, forms, and reports use the attribute; and how often the attribute should be updated.

ER modeling is valuable because it allows database designers to communicate with users throughout the organization to ensure that all entities and the relationships among the entities are represented. This process underscores the importance of taking all users into account when designing organizational databases. Notice that all entities and relationships in our example are labeled in terms that users can understand.

**Relationships** illustrate an association between entities. The *degree of a relationship* indicates the number of entities associated with a relationship. A **unary relationship** exists when an association is maintained within a single entity. A **binary relationship** exists when two entities are associated. A **ternary relationship** exists when three entities are associated. In this Technology Guide, we discuss only binary relationships because they are the most common. Entity relationships may be classified as one-to-one, one-to-many, or many-to-many. The term, **connectivity**, describes the relationship classification.

Connectivity and cardinality are established by the business rules of a relationship. **Cardinality** refers to the maximum number of times an instance of one entity can be associated with an instance in the related entity. Cardinality can be mandatory single, optional single, mandatory many, or optional many. Figure 5A.1 displays the cardinality symbols. Note that we have four possible cardinality symbols: mandatory single, optional single, mandatory many, and optional many.

Let's look at an example from a university. An *entity* is a person, place, or thing that can be identified in the users' work environment. For example, consider student registration at a university. Students register for courses, and they also register their cars for parking permits. In this example, STUDENT, PARKING PERMIT, CLASS, and PROFESSOR are entities. Recall that an instance of an entity represents a particular student, parking permit, class, or professor. Therefore, a particular STUDENT (James Smythe, 8023445) is an instance of the STUDENT entity; a particular parking permit (91778) is an instance of the PARKING PERMIT entity; a particular class (76890) is an instance of the CLASS entity; and a particular professor (Margaret Wilson, 390567) is an instance of the PROFESSOR entity.

Entity instances have *identifiers*, or *primary keys*, which are attributes (attributes and identifiers are synonymous) that are unique to that entity instance. For example, STUDENT instances can be identified with Student Identification Number; PARKING PERMIT instances can be identified with Permit Number; CLASS instances can be identified with Class Number; and PROFESSOR instances can be identified with Professor Identification Number.

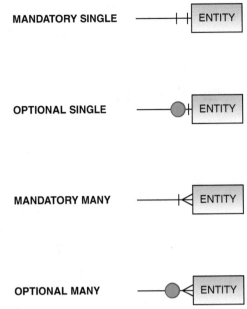

**FIGURE 5A.1** Cardinality symbols.

Entities have **attributes**, or properties, that describe the entity's characteristics. In our example, examples of attributes for STUDENT are Student Name and Student Address. Examples of attributes for PARKING PERMIT are Student Identification Number and Car Type. Examples of attributes for CLASS are Class Name, Class Time, and Class Place. Examples of attributes for PROFESSOR are Professor Name and Professor Department. (Note that each course at this university has one professor—no team teaching.)

Why is Student Identification Number an attribute of both the STUDENT and PARKING PERMIT entity classes? That is, why do we need the PARKING PERMIT entity class? If you consider all of the interlinked university systems, the PARKING PERMIT entity class is needed for other applications, such as fee payments, parking tickets, and external links to the state Department of Motor Vehicles.

Let's consider the three types of binary relationships in our example.

In a *one-to-one (1:1)* relationship, a single-entity instance of one type is related to a single-entity instance of another type. In our university example, STUDENT–PARKING PERMIT is a 1:1 relationship. The business rule at this university represented by this relationship is: Students may register only one car at this university. Of course, students do not have to register a car at all. That is, a student can have only one parking permit but does not need to have one.

Note that the relationship line on the PARKING PERMIT side shows a cardinality of optional single. A student can have, but does not have to have, a parking permit. On the STUDENT side of the relationship, only one parking permit can be assigned to one student, resulting in a cardinality of mandatory single. See Figure 5A.2.

The second type of relationship, *one-to-many (1:M)*, is represented by the CLASS–PROFESSOR relationship in Figure 5A.3. The business rule at this university represented by this relationship is: At this university, there is no team teaching. Therefore, each class must have only one professor. On the other hand, professors may teach more than one class. Note that the relationship line on the PROFESSOR side shows a cardinality of mandatory single. In contrast, the relationship line on the CLASS side shows a cardinality of optional many.

**FIGURE 5A.2** One-to-one relationship.

The third type of relationship, *many-to-many (M:M)*, is represented by the STUDENT–CLASS relationship. Most database management systems do not support many-to-many relationships. Therefore, we use *junction* (or *bridge*) *tables*, so that we have two one-to-many relationships. The business rule at this university represented by this relationship is: Students can register for one or more classes, and each class can have one or more students (see Figure 5A.4).

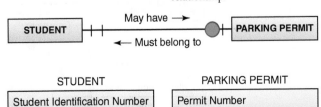

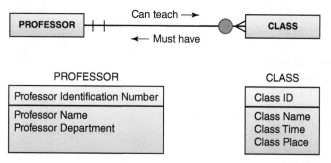

**FIGURE 5A.3** One-to-many relationship.

In this example, we create the REGISTRATION table as our junction table. Note that Student ID and Class ID are foreign keys in the REGISTRATION table.

Let's examine the relationships:

- The relationship line on the STUDENT side of the STUDENT–REGISTRATION relationship shows a cardinality of optional single.
- The relationship line on the REGISTRATION side of the STUDENT–REGISTRATION relationship shows a cardinality of optional many.
- The relationship line on the CLASS side of the CLASS–REGISTRATION relationship shows a cardinality of optional single.
- The relationship line on the REGISTRATION side of the CLASS–REGISTRATION relationship shows a cardinality of optional many.

## Normalization and Joins

To use a relational database management system efficiently and effectively, the data must be analyzed to eliminate redundant data elements. **Normalization** is a method for analyzing and reducing a relational database to its most streamlined form to ensure minimum redundancy, maximum data integrity, and optimal processing performance. Data normalization is a methodology for organizing attributes into tables so that redundancy among the non-key attributes is eliminated. The result of the data normalization process is a properly structured relational database.

Data normalization requires a list of all the attributes that must be incorporated into the database and a list of all of the defining associations, or functional dependencies, among the attributes. **Functional dependencies** are a means of expressing that the value of one particular attribute is associated with a specific single value of another attribute. For example, for a Student Number 05345 at a university, there is exactly one Student Name, John C. Jones, associated with it. That is, Student Number is referred to as the determinant because its value *determines* the value of the other attribute. We can also say that Student Name is functionally dependent on Student Number.

As an example of normalization, consider a pizza shop. This shop takes orders from customers on a form. Figure 5A.5 shows nonnormalized data gathered by the pizza shop. This table has two records, one for each order being placed. Because there are several pizzas on each order, the order number and customer information appear in multiple rows. Several attributes of each record have null values. A null value is an attribute with no data in it. For example, Order Number has four null values. Therefore, this table is not in first normal form. The data drawn from that form is shown in Figure 5A.5.

In our example, ORDER, CUSTOMER, and PIZZA are entities. The first step in normalization is to determine the functional dependencies among the attributes. The functional dependencies in our example are shown in Figure 5A.6.

**FIGURE 5A.4** Many-to-many relationship.

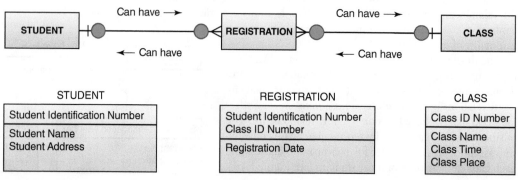

| Order Number | Order Date | Customer ID | Customer F Name | Customer L Name | Customer Address | Zip Code | Pizza Code | Pizza Name | Quantity | Price | Total Price |
|---|---|---|---|---|---|---|---|---|---|---|---|
| 1116 | 9/1/14 | 16421 | Rob | Penny | 123 Main St. | 37411 | P | Pepperoni | 1 | $11.00 | $41.00 |
|  |  |  |  |  |  |  | MF | Meat Feast | 1 | $12.00 |  |
|  |  |  |  |  |  |  | V | Vegetarian | 2 | $9.00 |  |
| 1117 | 9/2/14 | 17221 | Beth | Jones | 41 Oak St. | 29416 | HM | Ham and Mushroom | 3 | $10.00 | $56.00 |
|  |  |  |  |  |  |  | MF | Meat Feast | 1 | $12.00 |  |
|  |  |  |  |  |  |  | TH | The Hawaiian | 1 | $14.00 |  |

**FIGURE 5A.5** Raw Data Gathered from Orders at the Pizza Shop

In the normalization process, we will proceed from nonnormalized data, to first normal form, to second normal form, and then to third normal form. (There are additional normal forms, but they are beyond the scope of this book.)

Figure 5A.7 demonstrates the data in *first normal form*. The attributes under consideration are listed in one table and primary keys have been established. Our primary keys are Order Number, Customer ID, and Pizza Code. In first normal form, each ORDER has to repeat the order number, order date, customer first name, customer last name, customer address, and customer zip code. This data file contains repeating groups and describes multiple entities. That is, this relation has data redundancy, a lack of data integrity, and the flat file would be difficult to use in various applications that the pizza shop might need.

Consider Figure 5A.7, and notice the very first column (labeled Order Number). This column contains multiple entries for each order—three rows for Order Number 1116 and three rows for Order Number 1117. These multiple rows for an order are called *repeating groups*. Figure 5A.6 also contains multiple entities: ORDER, CUSTOMER, and PIZZA. Therefore, we move on to second normal form.

To produce second normal form, we break Figure 5A.5 into smaller tables to eliminate some of its data redundancy. Second normal form does not allow partial functional dependencies. That is, in a table in second normal form, every non-key attribute must be functionally dependent on the entire primary key of that table. Figure 5A.8 shows the data from the pizza shop in second normal form.

If you examine Figure 5A.8, you will see that second normal form has not eliminated all the data redundancy. For example, each Order Number is duplicated three times, as are all customer data. In *third normal form*, non-key attributes are not allowed to define other non-key attributes. That is, third normal form does not allow transitive dependencies in which one non-key attribute is functionally dependent on another. In our example, customer information depends both on Customer ID and Order Number. Figure 5A.9 shows the data from the pizza shop in third normal form. Third normal form structure has these important points:

- It is completely free of data redundancy.
- All foreign keys appear where needed to link related tables.

Let's look at the primary and foreign keys for the tables in third normal form:

- The ORDER relation: The primary key is Order Number and the foreign key is Customer ID.
- The CUSTOMER relation: The primary key is Customer ID.
- The PIZZA relation: The primary key is Pizza Code.
- The ORDER–PIZZA relation: The primary key is a composite key, consisting of two foreign keys, Order Number and Pizza Code.

**FIGURE 5A.6** Functional Dependencies in Pizza Shop Example

| Order Number | → | Order Date |
|---|---|---|
| Order Number | → | Quantity |
| Order Number | → | Total Price |
| Customer ID | → | Customer F Name |
| Customer ID | → | Customer L Name |
| Customer ID | → | Customer Address |
| Customer ID | → | Zip Code |
| Customer ID | → | Total Price |
| Pizza Code | → | Pizza Name |
| Pizza Code | → | Price |

| Order Number | Order Date | Customer ID | Customer F Name | Customer L Name | Customer Address | Zip Code | Pizza Code | Pizza Name | Quantity | Price | Total Price |
|---|---|---|---|---|---|---|---|---|---|---|---|
| 1116 | 9/1/14 | 16421 | Rob | Penny | 123 Main St. | 37411 | P | Pepperoni | 1 | $11.00 | $41.00 |
| 1116 | 9/1/14 | 16421 | Rob | Penny | 123 Main St. | 37411 | MF | Meat Feast | 1 | $12.00 | $41.00 |
| 1116 | 9/1/14 | 16421 | Rob | Penny | 123 Main St. | 37411 | V | Vegetarian | 2 | $9.00 | $41.00 |
| 1117 | 9/2/14 | 17221 | Beth | Jones | 41 Oak St. | 29416 | HM | Ham and Mushroom | 3 | $10.00 | $56.00 |
| 1117 | 9/2/14 | 17221 | Beth | Jones | 41 Oak St. | 29416 | MF | Meat Feast | 1 | $12.00 | $56.00 |
| 1117 | 9/2/14 | 17221 | Beth | Jones | 41 Oak St. | 29416 | TH | The Hawaiian | 1 | $14.00 | $56.00 |

**FIGURE 5A.7**  First Normal Form for Data from Pizza Shop

| Order Number | Order Date | Customer ID | Customer F Name | Customer L Name | Customer Address | Zip Code | Total Price |
|---|---|---|---|---|---|---|---|
| 1116 | 9/1/14 | 16421 | Rob | Penny | 123 Main St. | 37411 | $41.00 |
| 1116 | 9/1/14 | 16421 | Rob | Penny | 123 Main St. | 37411 | $41.00 |
| 1116 | 9/1/14 | 16421 | Rob | Penny | 123 Main St. | 37411 | $41.00 |
| 1117 | 9/2/14 | 17221 | Beth | Jones | 41 Oak St. | 29416 | $56.00 |
| 1117 | 9/2/14 | 17221 | Beth | Jones | 41 Oak St. | 29416 | $56.00 |
| 1117 | 9/2/14 | 17221 | Beth | Jones | 41 Oak St. | 29416 | $56.00 |

| Order Number | Pizza Code | Quantity |
|---|---|---|
| 1116 | P | 1 |
| 1116 | MF | 1 |
| 1116 | V | 2 |
| 1117 | HM | 3 |
| 1117 | MF | 1 |
| 1117 | TH | 1 |

| Pizza Code | Pizza Name | Price |
|---|---|---|
| P | Pepperoni | $11.00 |
| MF | Meat Feast | $12.00 |
| V | Vegetarian | $9.00 |
| HM | Ham and Mushroom | $10.00 |
| TH | The Hawaiian | $14.00 |

**FIGURE 5A.8**  Second Normal Form for Data from Pizza

ORDER

| Order Number | Order Date | Customer ID | Total Price |
|---|---|---|---|
| 1116 | 9/1/14 | 16421 | $41.00 |
| 1117 | 9/2/14 | 17221 | $56.00 |

CUSTOMER

| Customer ID | Customer F Name | Customer L Name | Customer Address | Zip Code |
|---|---|---|---|---|
| 16421 | Rob | Penny | 123 Main St. | 37411 |
| 17221 | Beth | Jones | 41 Oak St. | 29416 |

ORDER-PIZZA

| Order Number | Pizza Code | Quantity |
|---|---|---|
| 1116 | P | 1 |
| 1116 | MF | 1 |
| 1116 | V | 2 |
| 1117 | HM | 3 |
| 1117 | MF | 1 |
| 1117 | TH | 1 |

PIZZA

| Pizza Code | Pizza Name | Price |
|---|---|---|
| P | Pepperoni | $11.00 |
| MF | Meat Feast | $12.00 |
| V | Vegetarian | $9.00 |
| HM | Ham and Mushroom | $10.00 |
| TH | The Hawaiian | $14.00 |

**FIGURE 5A.9** Third Normal Form for Data from Pizza Shop

Now consider an order at the pizza shop. The tables in third normal form can produce the order in the following manner by using the join operation (see Figure 5A.10). The **join operation** combines records from two or more tables in a database to obtain information that is located in different tables. In our example, the join operation combines records from the four normalized tables to produce an ORDER. Here is how the join operation works:

- The ORDER relation provides the Order Number (the primary key), Order Date, and Total Price.
- The primary key of the ORDER relation (Order Number) provides a link to the ORDER–PIZZA relation (the link numbered 1 in Figure 5A.5).
- The ORDER–PIZZA relation supplies the Quantity to ORDER.
- The primary key of the ORDER–PIZZA relation is a composite key that consists of Order Number and Pizza Code. Therefore, the Pizza Code component of the primary key provides a link to the PIZZA relation (the link numbered 2 in Figure 5A.10).
- The PIZZA relation supplies the Pizza Name and Price to ORDER.
- The Customer ID in ORDER (a foreign key) provides a link to the CUSTOMER relation (the link numbered 3 in Figure 5A.10).
- The CUSTOMER relation supplies the Customer FName, Customer LName, Customer Address, and Zip Code to ORDER.

At the end of this join process, we have a complete ORDER. Normalization is beneficial when maintaining databases over a period of time. One example is the likelihood of having to change the price of each pizza. If the pizza shop increases the price of the Meat Feast from $12.00 to $12.50, this process is one easy step in Figure 5A.10. The price field is changed to $12.50 and the ORDER is automatically updated with the current value of the price.

**FIGURE 5A.10** The join process with the tables of third normal form to produce an order.

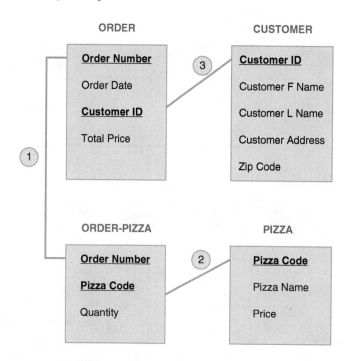

before you go on...

1. What is structured query language?
2. What is query by example?
3. What is an entity? An attribute? A relationship?
4. Describe one-to-one, one-to-many, and many-to-many relationships.
5. What is the purpose of normalization?
6. Why do we need the join operation?

# What's In IT For Me?

### For the Accounting Major

**ACCT**

The accounting function is intimately concerned with keeping track of the transactions and internal controls of an organization. Modern databases enable accountants to perform these functions more effectively. Databases help accountants manage the flood of data in today's organizations so that they can keep their firms in compliance with the standards imposed by Sarbanes–Oxley.

Accountants also play a role in cost justifying the creation of a knowledge base and then auditing its cost-effectiveness. In addition, if you work for a large CPA company that provides management services or sells knowledge, you will most likely use some of your company's best practices that are stored in a knowledge base.

### For the Finance Major

**FIN**

Financial managers make extensive use of computerized databases that are external to the organization, such as CompuStat or Dow Jones, to obtain financial data on organizations in their industry. They can use these data to determine if their organization meets industry benchmarks in return on investment, cash management, and other financial ratios.

Financial managers, who produce the organization's financial status reports, are also closely involved with Sarbanes–Oxley. Databases help these managers comply with the law's standards.

### For the Marketing Major

Databases help marketing managers access data from the organization's marketing transactions, such as customer purchases, to plan targeted marketing campaigns and to evaluate the success of previous campaigns. Knowledge about customers can make the difference between success and failure. In many databases and knowledge bases, the vast majority of information and knowledge concerns customers, products, sales, and marketing. Marketing managers regularly use an organization's knowledge base, and they often participate in its creation.

### For the Production/Operations Management Major

Production/operations personnel access organizational data to determine optimum inventory levels for parts in a production process. Past production data enable production/operations management (POM) personnel to determine the optimum configuration for assembly lines. Firms also collect quality data that inform them not only about the quality of finished products but also about quality issues with incoming raw materials, production irregularities, shipping and logistics, and after-sale use and maintenance of the product.

Knowledge management is extremely important for running complex operations. The accumulated knowledge regarding scheduling, logistics, maintenance, and other functions is very valuable. Innovative ideas are necessary for improving operations and can be supported by knowledge management.

### For the Human Resource Management Major

Organizations keep extensive data on employees, including gender, age, race, current and past job descriptions, and performance evaluations. HR personnel access these data to provide reports to government agencies regarding compliance with federal equal opportunity guidelines. HR managers also use these data to evaluate hiring practices, evaluate salary structures, and manage any discrimination grievances or lawsuits brought against the firm.

Databases help HR managers provide assistance to all employees as companies turn over more and more decisions about healthcare and retirement planning to the employees themselves. The employees can use the databases for help in selecting the optimal mix among these critical choices.

HR managers also need to use a knowledge base frequently to find out how past cases were handled. Consistency in how employees are treated not only is important, but it also protects the company against legal actions. In addition, training for building, maintaining, and using the knowledge system sometimes is the responsibility of the HR department. Finally, the HR department might be responsible for compensating employees who contribute their knowledge to the knowledge base.

### For the MIS Major

The MIS function manages the organization's data as well as the databases. MIS database administrators standardize data names by using the data dictionary. This process ensures that all users understand which data are in the database. Database personnel also help users access needed data and generate reports with query tools.

#### For All Business Majors

All business majors will have to manage data in their professional work. One way to manage data is through the use of databases and database management systems.

First, it is likely that you will need to obtain information from your organization's databases. You will probably use structured query language to obtain this information. Second, as your organization plans and designs its databases, it will most likely use entity–relationship diagrams. You will provide much of the input to these ER diagrams. For example, you will describe the entities that you use in your work, the attributes of those entities, and the relationships among them. You will also help database designers as they normalize database tables, by describing how the normalized tables relate to each other (e.g., through the use of primary and foreign keys). Finally, you will help database designers as they plan their join operations to give you the information that you need when that information is stored in multiple tables.

## [ Summary ]

1. **Discuss ways that common challenges in managing data can be addressed using data governance.**

   The following are three common challenges in managing data:

   - Data are scattered throughout organizations and are collected by many individuals using various methods and devices. These data are frequently stored in numerous servers and locations and in different computing systems, databases, formats, and human and computer languages.
   - Data come from multiple sources.
   - Information systems that support particular business processes impose unique requirements on data, which results in repetition and conflicts across an organization.

   One strategy for implementing data governance is master data management. Master data management provides companies with the ability to store, maintain, exchange, and synchronize a consistent, accurate, and timely "single version of the truth" for the company's core master data. Master data management manages data gathered from across an organization, manages data from multiple sources, and manages data across business processes in an organization.

2. **Discuss the advantages and disadvantages of relational databases.**

   Relational databases allow people to compare information quickly by row or column. In addition, items are easy to retrieve by finding the point of intersection of a particular row and column. On the other hand, large-scale relational databases can be composed of many interrelated tables, making the overall design complex with slow search and access times.

3. **Define Big Data, and discuss its basic characteristics.**

   Big Data is composed of high volume, high velocity, and high variety information assets that require new forms of processing to enable enhanced decision making, insight discovery, and process optimization. Big Data has three distinct characteristics: volume, velocity, and variety. These characteristics distinguish Big Data from traditional data:

   - *Volume:* Big Data consists of vast quantities of data.
   - *Velocity:* Big Data flows into an organization at incredible speeds.
   - *Variety:* Big Data includes a huge variety of different data in differing data formats.

4. **Explain the elements necessary to successfully implement and maintain data warehouses.**

   To successfully implement and maintain a data warehouse, an organization must

   - link source systems that provide data to the warehouse or mart,

- prepare the necessary data for the data warehouse using data integration technology and processes,
- decide on an appropriate architecture for storing data in the data warehouse or data mart,
- select the tools and applications for the variety of organizational users, and
- ensure that metadata, data quality, and governance processes are in place to ensure that the data warehouse or mart meets its purposes.

5. **Describe the benefits and challenges of implementing knowledge management systems in organizations.**

Organizations can realize many benefits with KMSs:

- Best practices are readily available to a wide range of employees.
- Improved customer service.
- More efficient product development.
- Improved employee morale and retention.

Challenges to implementing KMSs include the following:

- Employees must be willing to share their personal tacit knowledge.
- Organizations must create a knowledge management culture that rewards employees who add their expertise to the knowledge base.
- The knowledge base must be continually maintained and updated.
- Companies must be willing to invest in the resources needed to carry out these operations.

6. **Understand the processes of querying a relational database, entity–relationship modeling, and normalization and joins.**

The most commonly performed database operation is requesting information. *Structured query language* is the most popular query language used for this operation. SQL allows people to perform complicated searches by using relatively simple statements or key words. Typical key words are SELECT (to specify a desired attribute), FROM (to specify the table to be used), and WHERE (to specify conditions to apply in the query).

Another way to find information in a database is to use *query by example*. In QBE, the user fills out a grid or template—also known as a *form*—to construct a sample or a description of the data desired. Users can construct a query quickly and easily by using drag-and-drop features in a DBMS such as Microsoft Access. Conducting queries in this manner is simpler than keying in SQL commands.

Designers plan and create databases through the process of **entity–relationship modeling**, using an **entity–relationship diagram**. ER diagrams consist of entities, attributes, and relationships. Entities are pictured in boxes, and relationships are represented as diamonds. The attributes for each entity are listed, and the primary key is underlined.

ER modeling is valuable because it allows database designers to communicate with users throughout the organization to ensure that all entities and the relationships among the entities are represented. This process underscores the importance of taking all users into account when designing organizational databases. Notice that all entities and relationships in our example are labeled in terms that users can understand.

*Normalization* is a method for analyzing and reducing a relational database to its most streamlined form to ensure minimum redundancy, maximum data integrity, and optimal processing performance. When data are *normalized*, attributes in each table depend only on the primary key.

The *join operation* combines records from two or more tables in a database to produce information that is located in different tables.

# [ Chapter Glossary ]

**attribute** Each characteristic or quality of a particular entity.

**best practices** The most effective and efficient ways to do things.

**Big Data** A collection of data so large and complex that it is difficult to manage using traditional database management systems.

**binary relationship A relationship that exists when two entities are associated.**

**bit** A binary digit—that is, a 0 or a 1.

**business rules** Precise descriptions of policies, procedures, or principles in any organization that stores and uses data to generate information.

**byte** A group of eight bits that represents a single character.

**clickstream data** Data collected about user behavior and browsing patterns by monitoring users' activities when they visit a Web site.

**connectivity** Describes the classification of a relationship: one-to-one, one-to-many, or many-to-many.

**data dictionary** A collection of definitions of data elements; data characteristics that use the data elements; and the individuals, business functions, applications, and reports that use these data elements.

**data file (also table)** A collection of logically related records.

**data governance** An approach to managing information across an entire organization.

**data mart** A low-cost, scaled-down version of a data warehouse that is designed for the end-user needs in a strategic business unit (SBU) or a department.

**data model** A diagram that represents entities in the database and their relationships.

**data warehouse** A repository of historical data that are organized by subject to support decision makers in the organization.

**database management system (DBMS)** The software program (or group of programs) that provides access to a database.

**entity** Any person, place, thing, or event of interest to a user.

**entity–relationship (ER) diagram** Document that shows data entities and attributes and relationships among them.

**entity–relationship (ER) modeling** The process of designing a database by organizing data entities to be used and identifying the relationships among them.

**explicit knowledge** The more objective, rational, and technical types of knowledge.

**field** A characteristic of interest that describes an entity.

**foreign key** A field (or group of fields) in one table that uniquely identifies a row (or record) of another table.

**functional dependency** A means of expressing that the value of one particular attribute is associated with, or determines, a specific single value of another attribute.

**instance** Each row in a relational table, which is a specific, unique representation of the entity.

**intellectual capital (or intellectual assets)** Other terms for knowledge.

**join operation** A database operation that combines records from two or more tables in a database.

**knowledge management (KM)** A process that helps organizations identify, select, organize, disseminate, transfer, and apply information and expertise that are part of the organization's memory and that typically reside within the organization in an unstructured manner.

**knowledge management systems (KMSs)** Information technologies used to systematize, enhance, and expedite intra- and interfirm knowledge management.

**master data** A set of core data, such as customer, product, employee, vendor, geographic location, and so on, that span an enterprise's information systems.

**master data management** A process that provides companies with the ability to store, maintain, exchange, and synchronize a consistent, accurate, and timely "single version of the truth" for the company's core master data.

**multidimensional structure** Storage of data in more than two dimensions; a common representation is the *data cube*.

**normalization** A method for analyzing and reducing a relational database to its most streamlined form to ensure minimum redundancy, maximum data integrity, and optimal processing performance.

**primary key** A field (or attribute) of a record that uniquely identifies that record so that it can be retrieved, updated, and sorted.

**query by example** To obtain information from a relational database, a user fills out a grid or template—also known as a *form*—to construct a sample or a description of the data desired.

**record** A grouping of logically related fields.

**relational database model** Data model based on the simple concept of tables in order to capitalize on characteristics of rows and columns of data.

**relationships** Operators that illustrate an association between two entities.

**secondary key** A field that has some identifying information, but typically does not uniquely identify a record with complete accuracy.

**structured query language** The most popular query language for requesting information from a relational database.

**table** A grouping of logically related records.

**tacit knowledge** The cumulative store of subjective or experiential learning, which is highly personal and hard to formalize.

**ternary relationship** A relationship that exists when three entities are associated.

**unary relationship** A relationship that exists when an association is maintained within a single entity.

# [ Discussion Questions ]

1. Is Big Data really a problem on its own, or are the use, control, and security of the data the true problems? Provide specific examples to support your answer.

2. What are the implications of having incorrect data points in your Big Data? What are the implications of incorrect or duplicated customer data? How valuable are decisions that are based on faulty information derived from incorrect data?

3. Explain the difficulties involved in managing data.

4. What are the problems associated with poor-quality data?

5. What is master data management? What does it have to do with high-quality data?

6. Explain why master data management is so important in companies that have multiple data sources.

7. Describe the advantages and disadvantages of relational databases.

8. Explain why it is important to capture and manage knowledge.

9. Compare and contrast tacit knowledge and explicit knowledge.

10. Draw the entity–relationship diagram for a company that has departments and employees. In this company, a department must have at least one employee, and company employees may work in only one department.

11. Draw the entity–relationship diagram for library patrons and the process of checking out books.

12. You are working at a doctor's office. You gather data on the following entities: PATIENT, PHYSICIAN, PATIENT DIAGNOSIS, and TREATMENT. Develop a table for the entity, PATIENT VISIT. Decide on the primary keys and/or foreign keys that you want to use for each entity.

# [ Problem-Solving Activities ]

1. Access various employment Web sites (e.g., *www.monster.com* and *www.dice.com*) and find several job descriptions for a database administrator. Are the job descriptions similar? What are the salaries offered in these positions?

2. Access the Web sites of several real estate companies. Find the sites that take you through a step-by-step process for buying a home, that provide virtual reality tours of homes in your price range (say, $200,000–$250,000) and location, that provide mortgage and interest rate calculators, and that offer financing for your home. Do the sites require that you register to access their services? Can you request that an e-mail be sent to you when properties in which you might be interested become available? How does the process outlined influence your likelihood of selecting this company for your real estate purchase?

3. It is possible to find many Web sites that provide demographic information. Access several of these sites and see what they offer. Do the sites differ in the types of demographic information they offer? If so, how? Do the sites require a fee for the information they offer? Would demographic information be useful to you if you wanted to start a new business? If so, how and why?

4. Search the Web for uses of Big Data in homeland security. Specifically, read about the spying by the U.S. National Security Agency (NSA). What role did technology and Big Data play in this questionable practice?

5. Visit the website for HowStuffWorks (*www.howstuffworks.com*), and search for "Big Data: Friend or Foe?" What points does this article present concerning the delicate balance between shared data and customer privacy?

6. Access the Web sites of IBM (*www.ibm.com*), Sybase (*www.sybase.com*), and Oracle (*www.oracle.com*), and trace the capabilities of their latest data management products, including Web connections.

7. Enter the Web site of the Gartner Group (*www.gartner.com*). Examine the company's research studies pertaining to data management. Prepare a report on the state of the art.

8. Calculate your personal digital footprint at *http://www.emc.com/digital_universe/downloads/web/personal-ticker.htm*.

9. Diagram a knowledge management system cycle for a fictional company that sells customized T-shirts to students.

# [ Closing Case **Flurry Gathers Data from Smartphone Users** ] MKT MIS

A woman waits in an airline lounge. She scrolls through her iPhone and launches a free mobile game. An instant before the app loads, a company called Flurry (*www.flurry.com*) runs an auction targeted specifically for her. Flurry presents the woman to dozens of advertisers in multiple capacities: a new mother, a business traveler, a fashion follower, a woman in her late twenties, and someone located near the Atlanta airport. In a fraction of a second, the Flurry auction picks the highest bidder, an advertiser who is also most likely to be offering goods or services that the woman might want. The woman then views an ad for designer sunglasses. Significantly, she is completely unaware that any of this background activity has occurred.

Flurry (purchased by Yahoo! in 2014) is in the business of mobile, *real-time bidding* (RTB). RTB refers to the process whereby advertising inventory is bought and sold on a per-impression basis, via instantaneous auction. With real-time bidding, advertising buyers bid on an impression, and the winner's ad is instantly displayed. (An impression is a measure of the number of times an ad is seen. Each time an ad displays is counted as one impression.) A typical transaction begins with a user visiting a mobile website. This visit triggers a bid request that can include various pieces of data such as the user's demographic information, browsing history, location, and the page being loaded. The request is forwarded to an ad exchange, which submits it and the accompanying data to multiple advertisers. In turn these advertisers submit bids in real time to place their ads. The impression goes to the highest bidder, and their ad is served on the mobile page. In essence, Flurry provides a high-speed auction system for targeting ads to individuals.

Mobile RTB permits advertisers to bid for each impression. This system is in sharp contrast to a static auction, in which the advertisers typically bundle impressions in groups of 1,000.

Flurry recently launched a pair of real-time mobile ad exchanges that uniquely handle both demand and supply in the ad marketplace. Flurry maintains it has sufficient data to link the two exchanges together.

Flurry's other major selling point is the massive amount of data that it collects on mobile app users. The reason that you have never heard of Flurry is that *you never put it on your smartphone*. App makers did. In fact, in a typical device the software is contained in 7–10 apps. Why? The answer is that Flurry gives away an analytics tool that informs app makers as to how people are using their apps. More than 400,000 apps now use the Flurry tool. In return, they send much of that user data back to Flurry. Flurry, therefore, has a pipeline to more than 1.2 billion devices globally. The company collects, on average, 3 terabytes of data *every day*.

Flurry solves a huge problem for apps that are designed to sell ads. On a desktop computer, advertisers can target consumers by using cookies, which are tiny data files attached with your browser. (We discuss cookies in Chapter 4.) In contrast, mobile phones do not have cookies in their browser, so advertisers don't know who you are. Flurry's software assists advertisers by encrypting and combining identifying bits of data about each user to create an anonymous ID for each device. Specifically, it classifies each user into one of roughly 100 "personas"; that is, psychographic profiles such as "business traveler" and "sports fanatic." Note that each persona has multiple characteristics. Advertisers use the characteristics of these personas to target ads.

While providing a major benefit to advertisers, Flurry's policy of encrypting personal information into an anonymous ID has raised serious concerns among privacy advocates. For example, one legal researcher in Europe charges that Flurry is already in breach of the European Union's (EU) E-Privacy Directive, which applies to mobile devices. The directive states that end users should be notified of cookies or tracking programs above and beyond the opt-out option that Flurry offers. The researcher maintains that to satisfy these requirements Flurry should be required to obtain consent from each user. Specifically, each time an EU resident opens an app that uses Flurry, a pop-up must inform this individual that the tool is tracking him or her. Flurry counters by reassuring users that the company does not collect personally identifiable information.

*Sources:* Compiled from B. Shaul, "Flurry: Lifestyle and Shopping Apps Experience Huge Growth in 2014," *InsideMobileApps*, January 6, 2015; I. Lunden, "Yahoo Buys Mobile Analytics Firm Flurry for North of $200M," *TechCrunch*, July 21, 2014; K. Andrew, "Is Christmas Losing Its Sparkle? Flurry Points to Drop Off in Yuletide Download Growth," *PocketGamer.biz*, February 13, 2014; J. Aquino, "Why App Re-Engagement Ads Are the Next Big Thing in Mobile Advertising," *AdExchanger*, January 7, 2014; P. Olson, "We Know Everything," *Forbes*, November 18, 2013; C. Gibbs, "Real-Time Bidding for Mobile Ads: Promising in the Short Term, Questionable in the Long Term," *GigaOM*, May 8, 2013; P. Elmer-Dewitt, "Report: Americans Spend 2:38 Hours a Day Glued to Their Tablets and Smartphones," *CNN Money*, April 3, 2013; *www.flurry.com*, accessed February 22, 2015.

**Questions**

1. Do you feel that Flurry should be installed on your smartphone by various app makers without your consent? Why or why not? Support your answer.

2. What problems would Flurry encounter if someone other than the smartphone's owner uses the device? (Hint: Note how Flurry gathers data.)

3. Can Flurry survive the privacy concerns that are being raised about its business model?

# 6 Telecommunications and Networking

## [ LEARNING OBJECTIVES ]

1. Compare and contrast the major types of networks.

2. Describe the wireline communications media and transmission technologies.

3. Describe the most common methods for accessing the Internet.

4. Explain the impact that discovery network applications have had on business and everyday life.

5. Explain the impact that communication network applications have had on business and everyday life.

6. Explain the impact that collaboration network applications have had on business and everyday life.

7. Explain the impact that educational network applications have had on business and everyday life.

## [ CHAPTER OUTLINE ]

## [ WEB RESOURCES ]

- Student PowerPoints for note taking

**WileyPLUS Learning Space**

- E-book

- Author video lecture for each chapter section

- Practice quizzes

- Flash Cards for vocabulary review

- Additional "IT's About Business" cases

- Video interviews with managers

- Lab Manuals for Microsoft Office 2010 and 2013

## What's In IT For Me?

### This Chapter Will Help Prepare You To...

| ACCT | FIN | MKT | POM | HRM | MIS |
|------|-----|-----|-----|-----|-----|
| ACCOUNTING | FINANCE | MARKETING | PRODUCTION OPERATIONS MANAGEMENT | HUMAN RESOURCES MANAGEMENT | MIS |
| Collaborate with external auditors | Integrate internal and industry financial data | Coordinate activities of sales force | Collaborate project team | Deliver online training to employees | Implement and manage firm's networks |

# [ What to Do About Landline Tele- phones? ]

## The Problem

Large telecommunications companies such as AT&T (*www.att.com*) and Verizon Communications (*www.verizon.com*) want to get rid of their twisted-pair copper wire networks (discussed later in this chapter), called plain old telephone system (POTS). These companies want to replace their existing POTS networks with Internet Protocol (IP) systems that will use the same wired and wireless broadband networks that provide Internet access, cable television, and telephone service to your home. There are several reasons why these large carriers find this transition desirable.

First, the U.S. government has a universal service guarantee, established by the Communications Act of 1934, that mandates that every resident has a baseline level of telecommunications services. The Federal Communications Commission (FCC) recognizes that telephone services provide a vital link to emergency services, government services, and surrounding communities. Because of the universal service guarantee, carriers must frequently operate expensive copper twisted-pair phone lines in rural areas to support small populations when it would be less expensive to provide cellular coverage. The carriers are compensated for these costs through a tax on customers' phone bills called the Universal Service Fund.

Second, many Americans have either gotten rid of their landline telephones or are preparing to do so. In fact, only 8 percent of U.S. households rely exclusively on a landline telephone. As the carriers' revenues decrease due to the falling number of POTS subscribers, the costs of maintaining the old and obsolete POTS network are increasing. Put simply, landlines are becoming much less profitable.

Third, carriers want to increase their stock prices. The stock market favors companies with high revenue growth and punishes those that exhibit no growth or declining revenues. Because POTS networks inhibit revenue growth and profitability, they tend to hold down the stock prices of companies like AT&T and Verizon.

For example, in Mantoloking, New Jersey, Verizon wants to replace its POTS network, which Hurricane Sandy destroyed in 2012, with the company's wireless Voice Link. This operation would make Mantoloking the first community to be completely without POTS. However, not all residents favor this scenario. In addition, New Jersey's state legislature has concerns over losing credit card processing applications and building alarm systems because wireless systems cannot manage these applications and systems. Verizon tried to implement the same process on Fire Island, New York, when its POTS was destroyed. Public opposition, however, forced the company to install fiber-optic cable.

On the other hand, residents in metropolitan areas do not really have to worry about the end of POTS. High-speed wireline and wireless services are readily available replacements. In contrast, for people living in rural areas where cell towers are few and wireless capabilities are limited, eliminating POTS could create serious problems.

There are several arguments in favor of keeping POTS networks. First, consider safety. When you call 911 from a landline telephone, the emergency operator knows your exact address. In contrast, wireless phones do not have such specific location data available, even if they contain GPS systems. Consequently, operators can handle emergency calls from POTS networks more easily than class from IP networks.

Second, POTS does not require power for your landline phone to work. In a natural disaster, this advantage is critical. In contrast, in a natural disaster, cell towers are quickly jammed or become inoperable.

These issues concern the FCC. Because universal access to U.S. citizens is a key principle, the FCC is unwilling to let telecommunications companies drop geographically undesirable customers. Telecommunication companies must obtain FCC approval to completely eliminate services, the agency will not do so unless there is a viable competitor to provide communications to people who have none.

That is the crux of the problem: The carriers want to eliminate their existing POTS networks, but the universal service guarantee makes that process extremely difficult.

# Proposed Solutions

Although the FCC frequently denies permission to companies to eliminate POTS, it does allow carriers to experiment with the removal of landline telephones. To protect the universal service guarantee, however, carriers must meet certain FCC standards during these trials:

- Public safety communications must be available regardless of which technology is being used.
- All Americans must have access to affordable communications services.
- Competition in the marketplace must provide choice for consumers and businesses.
- Consumer protection must be paramount.

On February 28, 2014, AT&T announced a trial program to eliminate landline telephones in Carbon Hill, Alabama (population 2,071). AT&T plans to offer broadband and Voice-over-Internet-Protocol (VoIP) services in place of POTS. The company and the FCC want to know how households will reach 911, how small businesses will connect to customers, how people with medical-monitoring devices or home alarms will know that they are connected to a reliable network, and what the costs of converting from POTS to IP networks will be.

An additional challenge for AT&T in the Carbon Hill trial is that 4 percent of the residential customers are located too far away from AT&T facilities to receive broadband service. The carrier is investigating strategies to provide telephone service for these residents.

In addition to these trials, in early 2015 approximately 30 states had passed or were considering laws that restrict state government oversight of POTS networks. These laws eliminate the "carrier of last resort" rules. (A *carrier of last resort* is a telecommunications provider that is required by law to provide service to any customer in a service area who requests it, even if serving that customer is not economically viable at existing rates.) This move would abolish the universal service guarantee that gives every U.S. resident access to affordable telephone service. These states feel that telecommunications resources should be directed to modern telephone technologies, rather than supporting POTS networks.

# The Results

In early 2015, the outcome of the carriers' experiments and the state legislation remained largely unknown. However, it appears that the move away from POTS networks toward IP networks will continue.

*Sources*: "Carbon Hill, Alabama – 'The City with a Future' (Without Landlines)," *nojitter.com*, November 28, 2014; "Local Woman Fights Statewide Plan to Eliminate Landline Phones," *myFOXDetroit*, October 17, 2014; K. Vlahos, "FCC Tests Ways to Kill the Telephone Wire," *Digital Trends*, June 15, 2014; J. Waters, "Prepare to Hang Up the Phone, Forever," *Wall Street Journal*, March 29, 2014; B. Dyas, "11 Reasons to Bring Back Landlines in 2014 (Seriously)," *The Huffington Post*, January 23, 2014; "Opponents Say Bill to Eliminate Landline Service Threatens Public Safety," *ABC News*, December 9, 2013; M. Anders, "Controversial Landline Phone Legislation Passes Michigan Senate Committee," *mLive.com*, December 3, 2013; B. Fung, "We Spend Billions a Year Maintaining Phone Lines (Almost) Nobody Depends On. Should We Get Rid of Them?" *The Washington Post*, October 8, 2013; M. Cherney, "When Will the Old Phone Networks Die? Not Soon," *InformationWeek*, April 8, 2013; *www.fcc.gov*, accessed January 14, 2015.

## Questions

1. Should the large carriers be able to eliminate their POTS networks?
   a. Debate this argument from the viewpoint of the large telecommunications carriers.
   b. Debate this argument from the viewpoint of rural customers.
2. Why are wireless networks not able to take over all of the functions of POTS networks at this time (early 2015)?

# What We Learned from This Case

In addition to networks being fundamentally important in your personal lives (see chapter opening case), there are three fundamental points about network computing you need to know. First, in modern organizations computers do not work in isolation. Rather, they constantly exchange data with one another. Second, this exchange of data—facilitated by telecommunications technologies—provides companies with a number of very significant advantages. Third, this exchange can take place over any distance and over networks of any size.

Without networks, the computer on your desk would be merely another productivity-enhancement tool, just as the typewriter once was. The power of networks, however, turns your computer into an amazingly effective tool for accessing information from thousands of sources, thereby making both you and your organization more productive. Regardless of the type of organization (profit/not-for-profit, large/small, global/local) or industry (manufacturing, financial services, healthcare), networks in general, and the Internet in particular, have transformed—and will continue to transform—the way we do business.

Networks support new and innovative ways of doing business, from marketing to supply chain management to customer service to human resources management. In particular, the Internet and private intranets—a network located within a single organization that uses Internet software and TCP/IP protocols—have an enormous impact on our lives, both professionally and personally.

For all organizations regardless of their size, having a telecommunications and networking system is no longer just a source of competitive advantage. Rather, it is necessary for survival.

Computer networks are essential to modern organizations, for many reasons. First, networked computer systems enable organizations to become more flexible so that they can adapt to rapidly changing business conditions. Second, networks allow companies to share hardware, computer applications, and data across the organization and among different organizations. Third, networks make it possible for geographically dispersed employees and workgroups to share documents, ideas, and creative insights. This sharing encourages teamwork, innovation, and more efficient and effective interactions. In addition, networks are a critical link between businesses, their business partners, and their customers.

Clearly, networks are essential tools for modern businesses. But, why do *you* need to be familiar with networks? The simple fact is that if you operate your own business or work in a business, you cannot function without networks. You will need to communicate rapidly with your customers, business partners, suppliers, employees, and colleagues. Until about 1990, you would have used the postal service or the telephone system with voice or fax capabilities for business communication. Today, however, the pace of business is much faster—almost real time. To keep up with this incredibly fast pace, you will need to use computers, e-mail, the Internet, cell phones, and mobile devices. Furthermore, all of these technologies will be connected via networks to enable you to communicate, collaborate, and compete on a global scale.

Networking and the Internet are the foundations for commerce in the twenty-first century. Recall that one important objective of this book is to help you become an informed user of information systems. A knowledge of networking is an essential component of modern business literacy.

You begin this chapter by learning what a computer network is and identifying the various types of networks. You then study network fundamentals and follow by turning your attention to the basics of the Internet and the World Wide Web. You conclude the chapter by seeing the many network applications available to individuals and organizations—that is, what networks help you do.

## 6.1 What Is a Computer Network?

A computer network is a system that connects computers and other devices (e.g., printers) via communications media so that data and information can be transmitted among them. Voice and data communication networks are continually becoming faster—that is, their bandwidth is increasing—and cheaper. **Bandwidth** refers to the transmission capacity of a network; it is stated in bits per second. Bandwidth ranges from narrowband (relatively low transmission capacity) to broadband (relatively high network capacity).

The telecommunications industry itself has difficulty defining the term broadband. In February 2015, the Federal Communications Commission (FCC) proposed new rules defining **broadband** as the transmission capacity of a communications medium (discussed later in this chapter) faster than 25 megabits per second (Mbps) for download (transmission speed for material coming to you from an Internet server, such as a movie streamed from Netflix) and 4 Mbps for upload (transmission speed for material that you upload to an Internet server such as a Facebook post). The definition of broadband remains fluid, however, and it will undoubtedly continue to change to reflect greater transmission capacities in the future.

You are likely familiar with certain types of broadband connections, such as *digital subscriber line (DSL)* and cable to your homes and dorms. DSL and cable fall within the range of transmission capacity mentioned here and are thus defined as broadband connections.

The various types of computer networks range from small to worldwide. They include (from smallest to largest) personal area networks (PANs), local area networks (LANs), metropolitan area networks (MANs), wide area networks (WANs), and the ultimate WAN, the Internet. PANs are short-range networks—typically a few meters—that are used for communication among devices close to one person. They can be wired or wireless. (You will learn about wireless PANs in Chapter 8.) MANs are relatively large computer networks that cover a metropolitan area. MANs fall between LANs and WANs in size. WANs typically cover large geographical areas; in some cases they can span the entire planet.

## Local Area Networks

Regardless of their size, networks represent a compromise among three objectives: speed, distance, and cost. Organizations typically must select two of the three. To cover long distances, organizations can have fast communication if they are willing to pay for it, or cheap communication if they are willing to accept slower speeds. A third possible combination of the three trade-offs is fast, cheap communication with distance limitations. This is the idea behind local area networks.

A **local area network (LAN)** connects two or more devices in a limited geographical region, usually within the same building, so that every device on the network can communicate with every other device. Most LANs today use Ethernet (discussed later in this chapter). Figure 6.1 illustrates an Ethernet LAN that consists of four computers, a server, and a printer, all of which connect via a shared cable. Every device in the LAN has a *network interface card* (NIC) that allows the device to physically connect to the LAN's communications medium. This medium is typically unshielded twisted-pair wire (UTP).

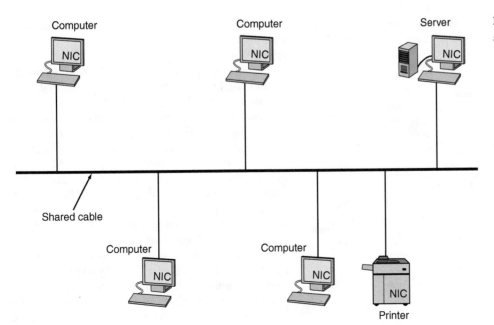

**FIGURE 6.1** Ethernet local area network.

Although it is not required, many LANs have a file server or network server. The server typically contains various software and data for the network. It also houses the LAN's network operating system, which manages the server and routes and manages communications on the network.

### Wide Area Networks

When businesses have to transmit and receive data beyond the confines of the LAN, they use wide area networks. Interestingly, the term *wide area network* did not even exist until local area networks appeared. Before that time, what we call a wide area network today was simply called a "network."

A **wide area network (WAN)** is a network that covers a large geographical area. WANs typically connect multiple LANs. They are generally provided by common carriers such as telephone companies and the international networks of global communications services providers. Examples of these providers include AT&T (*www.att.com*) in the United States, Deutsche Telekom in Germany (*www.telekom.com*), and NTT Communications (*www.ntt.com*) in Japan.

WANs have large capacity, and they typically combine multiple channels (e.g., fiber-optic cables, microwave, and satellite). The Internet is an example of a WAN.

WANs also contain routers. A **router** is a communications processor that routes messages from a LAN to the Internet, across several connected LANs, or across a wide area network such as the Internet.

### Enterprise Networks

Organizations today have multiple LANs and may have multiple WANs. All of these networks are interconnected to form an enterprise network. Figure 6.2 displays a model of enterprise computing. Note that the enterprise network in the figure has a backbone network. Corporate **backbone networks** are high-speed central networks to which multiple smaller networks (such as LANs and smaller WANs) connect. The LANs are called *embedded LANs* because they connect to the backbone WAN.

Unfortunately, traditional networks are rigid and lack the flexibility to keep pace with increasing business networking requirements. The reason for this problem is that the functions of traditional networks are distributed across physical routers and devices (i.e., hardware). This process means that to implement changes, each network device must be configured individually. In some cases, devices must be configured manually. *Software-defined networks* (SDN) are an emerging technology that is becoming increasingly important to help organizations manage their data flows across their enterprise networks.

With SDN, decisions controlling how network traffic flows across network devices are managed centrally by software. The software dynamically adjusts data flows to meet business and application needs.

Think of traditional networks as the road system of a city in 1920. Data packets are the cars that travel through the city. A traffic officer (physical network devices) controls each intersection and directs traffic by recognizing the turn signals, and size and shape of the vehicles passing through the intersection. The officers can direct only the traffic at their intersection. They do not know the overall traffic volume in the city nor do they know traffic movement across the city. Therefore, it is difficult to control the city's traffic patterns as a whole and to manage peak-hour traffic. When problems occur, the city must communicate with each individual officer via radio.

Now think of SDN as the road system of a modern city. Each traffic officer is replaced by a traffic light and a set of electronic vehicle counters, which are connected to central monitoring and control software. As such, the city's traffic can be instantly and centrally controlled.

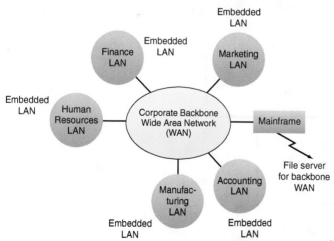

**FIGURE 6.2** Enterprise network.

The control software can direct traffic differently at various times of the day (say, rush hours). The software monitors traffic flow and automatically changes the traffic lights to help traffic flow through the city with minimal disruption.

# before you go on...

1. What are the primary business reasons for using networks?
2. What are the differences between LANs and WANs?
3. Describe an enterprise network.

# Network Fundamentals

## 6.2

In this section, you will learn the basics of how networks actually operate. You begin by studying wireline communications media, which enable computers in a network to transmit and receive data. You conclude this section by looking at network protocols and types of network processing.

Today, computer networks communicate via **digital signals**, which are discrete pulses that are either on or off, representing a series of *bits* (0's and 1's). This quality allows digital signals to convey information in a binary form that can be interpreted by computers.

The U.S. public telephone system (called the plain old telephone system) was originally designed as an analog network to carry voice signals or sounds in an *analog wave format* (see the chapter opening case). In order for this type of circuit to carry digital information, that information must be converted from an analog wave pattern by a *dial-up modem*. Dial-up modems are almost extinct in most parts of the developed world.

*Cable modems* are modems that operate over coaxial cable—for example, cable TV. They offer broadband access to the Internet or corporate intranets. Cable modem speeds vary widely. Most providers offer bandwidth between 1 and 6 million bits per second (Mbps) for downloads (from the Internet to a computer) and between 128 and 768 thousand bits per second (Kbps) for uploads. Cable modem services share bandwidth among subscribers in a locality. That is, the same cable line connects to many households. Therefore, when large numbers of neighbors access the Internet at the same time, cable speeds can decrease significantly.

*DSL modems* operate on the same lines as voice telephones and dial-up modems. DSL modems always maintain a connection, so an Internet connection is immediately available.

## Communications Media and Channels

Communicating data from one location to another requires some form of pathway or medium. A **communications channel** is such a pathway. It is comprised of two types of media: cable (twisted-pair wire, coaxial cable, or fiber-optic cable) and broadcast (microwave, satellite, radio, or infrared).

**Wireline media** or **cable media** use physical wires or cables to transmit data and information. Twisted-pair wire and coaxial cables are made of copper, and fiber-optic cable is made of glass. The alternative is communication over **broadcast media** or **wireless media**. The key to mobile communications in today's rapidly moving society is data transmissions over electromagnetic media—the "airwaves." In this section you will study the three wireline channels. Table 6.1 summarizes the advantages and disadvantages of each of these channels. You will become familiar with wireless media in Chapter 8.

**Twisted-Pair Wire.** **Twisted-pair wire** is the most prevalent form of communications wiring and is used for almost all business telephone wiring. As the name suggests, it consists of strands of copper wire twisted in pairs (see Figure 6.3). Twisted-pair wire is relatively inexpensive to purchase, widely available, and easy to work with. However, it also has some significant disadvantages. Specifically, it is relatively slow for transmitting data, it is subject to interference from other electrical sources, and it can be easily tapped by unintended receivers to gain unauthorized access to data.

**Table**

# 6.1

**Advantages and Disadvantages of Wireline Communications Channels**

| Channel | Advantages | Disadvantages |
|---|---|---|
| Twisted-pair wire | Inexpensive<br>Widely available<br>Easy to work with | Slow (low bandwidth)<br>Subject to interference<br>Easily tapped (low security) |
| Coaxial cable | Higher bandwidth than twisted-pair<br>Less susceptible to electromagnetic interference | Relatively expensive and inflexible<br>Easily tapped (low to medium security)<br>Somewhat difficult to work with |
| Fiber-optic cable | Very high bandwidth<br>Relatively inexpensive<br>Difficult to tap (good security) | Difficult to work with (difficult to splice) |

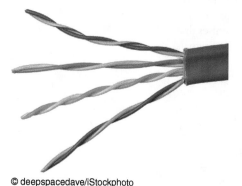

© deepspacedave/iStockphoto

**FIGURE 6.3** Twisted-pair wire.

**Coaxial Cable.** **Coaxial cable** (Figure 6.4) consists of insulated copper wire. Compared with twisted-pair wire, it is much less susceptible to electrical interference, and it can carry much more data. For these reasons, it is commonly used to carry high-speed data traffic as well as television signals (thus the term *cable TV*). However, coaxial cable is more expensive and more difficult to work with than twisted-pair wire. It is also somewhat inflexible.

**Fiber Optics.** **Fiber-optic cable** (Figure 6.5) consists of thousands of very thin filaments of glass fibers that transmit information via light pulses generated by lasers. The fiber-optic cable is surrounded by cladding, a coating that prevents the light from leaking out of the fiber.

Fiber-optic cables are significantly smaller and lighter than traditional cable media. They also can transmit far more data, and they provide greater security from interference and tapping. As of early-2015, optical fiber had reached data transmission rates of more than 50 trillion bits (terabits) per second in laboratory experiments. Fiber-optic cable is typically used as the backbone for a network, whereas twisted-pair wire and coaxial cable connect the backbone to individual devices on the network.

## Network Protocols

Computing devices that are connected to the network must access and share the network to transmit and receive data. These devices are often referred to as *nodes* of the network. They work together by adhering to a common set of rules and procedures—known as a **protocol**—that

**FIGURE 6.4** Two views of coaxial cable.

GIPhotoStock/Science Source

Cross-section view

©Piotr Malczyk/iStockphoto

How coaxial cable looks to us

**FIGURE 6.5** Two views of fiber-optic cable.

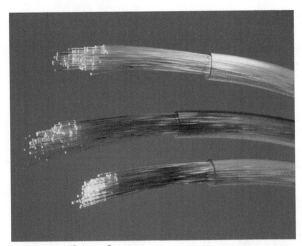

Phillip Hayson/Science Source

Cross-section view

Chris Knapton/Science Source

How fiber-optic cable looks to us

enable them to communicate with one another. The two major protocols are the Ethernet and Transmission Control Protocol/Internet Protocol.

**Ethernet.** A common LAN protocol is Ethernet. Many organizations use 100-gigabit Ethernet, where the network provides data transmission speeds of 100 gigabits (100 billion bits) per second. The 400-gigabit Ethernet is projected to be in service in 2017.

**Transmission Control Protocol/Internet Protocol.** The **Transmission Control Protocol/Internet Protocol (TCP/IP)** is the protocol of the Internet. TCP/IP uses a suite of protocols, the main ones being the Transmission Control Protocol (TCP) and the Internet Protocol (IP). The TCP performs three basic functions: (1) It manages the movement of data packets (see below) between computers by establishing a connection between the computers, (2) it sequences the transfer of packets, and (3) it acknowledges the packets that have been transmitted. The **Internet Protocol (IP)** is responsible for disassembling, delivering, and reassembling the data during transmission.

Before data are transmitted over the Internet, they are divided into small, fixed bundles called *packets*. The transmission technology that breaks up blocks of text into packets is called *packet switching*. Each packet carries the information that will help it reach its destination—the sender's IP address, the intended receiver's IP address, the number of packets in the message, and the sequence number of the particular packet within the message. Each packet travels independently across the network and can be routed through different paths in the network. When the packets reach their destination, they are reassembled into the original message.

It is important to note that packet-switching networks are reliable and fault tolerant. For example, if a path in the network is very busy or is broken, packets can be dynamically ("on the fly") rerouted around that path. Also, if one or more packets do not get to the receiving computer, then only those packets need to be resent.

Why do organizations use packet switching? The main reason is to achieve reliable end-to-end message transmission over sometimes unreliable networks that may have short-acting or long-acting problems.

The packets use the TCP/IP protocol to carry their data. TCP/IP functions in four layers (see Figure 6.6). The *application layer* enables client application programs to access the other layers, and it defines the protocols that applications use to exchange data. One of these application protocols is the Hypertext Transfer Protocol (HTTP), which defines how messages are formulated and how they are interpreted by their receivers. (We discuss hypertext in Section 6.3.) The *transport layer* provides the application layer with communication and packet services. This layer includes TCP and other protocols. The *Internet layer* is responsible for addressing, routing, and packaging data packets. The IP is one of the protocols in this layer. Finally, the

**FIGURE 6.6** The four layers of the TCP/IP reference model.

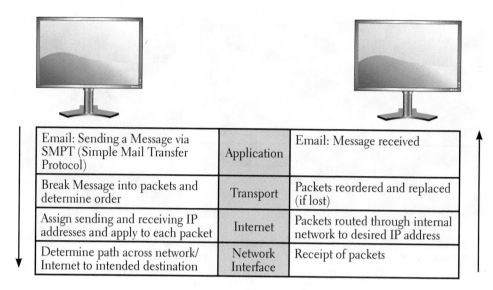

| Email: Sending a Message via SMPT (Simple Mail Transfer Protocol) | Application | Email: Message received |
| --- | --- | --- |
| Break Message into packets and determine order | Transport | Packets reordered and replaced (if lost) |
| Assign sending and receiving IP addresses and apply to each packet | Internet | Packets routed through internal network to desired IP address |
| Determine path across network/ Internet to intended destination | Network Interface | Receipt of packets |

*network interface layer* places packets on, and receives them from, the network medium, which can be any networking technology.

Two computers using TCP/IP can communicate even if they use different hardware and software. Data sent from one computer to another proceed downward through all four layers, beginning with the sending computer's application layer and going through its network interface layer. After the data reach the receiving computer, they travel up the layers.

TCP/IP enables users to send data across sometimes unreliable networks with the assurance that the data will arrive in uncorrupted form. TCP/IP is very popular with business organizations because of its reliability and the ease with which it can support intranets and related functions.

Let's look at an example of packet switching across the Internet. Figure 6.7 illustrates a message being sent from New York City to Los Angeles over a packet-switching network. Note that the different colored packets travel by different routes to reach their destination in Los Angeles, where they are reassembled into the complete message.

## Types of Network Processing

Organizations typically use multiple computer systems across the firm. Distributed processing divides processing work among two or more computers. This process enables computers in different locations to communicate with one another via telecommunications links. A common

**FIGURE 6.7** Packet switching.

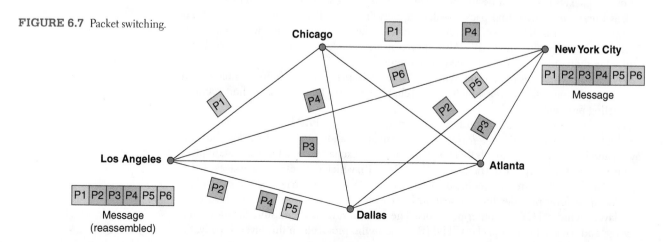

type of distributed processing is client/server processing. A special type of client/server processing is peer-to-peer processing.

**Client/Server Computing.** **Client/server computing** links two or more computers in an arrangement in which some machines, called *servers*, provide computing services for user PCs, called *clients*. Usually, an organization performs the bulk of its processing or application/data storage on suitably powerful servers that can be accessed by less powerful client machines. The client requests applications, data, or processing from the server, which acts on these requests by "serving" the desired commodity.

Client/server computing leads to the ideas of "fat" clients and "thin" clients. As discussed in Technology Guide 1, *fat clients* have large storage and processing power and therefore can run local programs (such as Microsoft Office) if the network goes down. In contrast, *thin clients* may have no local storage and only limited processing power. Thus, they must depend on the network to run applications. For this reason, they are of little value when the network is not functioning.

**Peer-to-Peer Processing.** **Peer-to-peer (P2P) processing** is a type of client/server distributed processing where each computer acts as *both* a client and a server. Each computer can access (as assigned for security or integrity purposes) all files on all other computers.

There are three basic types of peer-to-peer processing. The first type accesses unused CPU power among networked computers. An application of this type is SETI@home (*http://setiathome.ssl.berkeley.edu*). These applications are from open-source projects, and they can be downloaded at no cost.

The second form of peer-to-peer is real-time, person-to-person collaboration, such as Microsoft SharePoint Workspace (*http://office.microsoft.com/en-us/sharepoint-workspace*). This product provides P2P collaborative applications that use buddy lists to establish a connection and allow real-time collaboration within the application.

The third peer-to-peer category is advanced search and file sharing. This category is characterized by natural language searches of millions of peer systems. It enables users to discover other users, not just data and Web pages. One example of this category is BitTorrent.

BitTorrent (*www.bittorrent.com*) is an open-source, free, peer-to-peer file-sharing application that simplifies the problem of sharing large files by dividing them into tiny pieces, or "torrents." BitTorrent addresses two of the biggest problems of file sharing: (1) downloading bogs down when many people access a file at once, and (2) some people leech, meaning they download content but refuse to share it. BitTorrent eliminates the bottleneck by enabling all users to share little pieces of a file at the same time—a process called *swarming*. The program prevents leeching because users must upload a file while they download it. Thus, the more popular the content, the more efficiently it travels over a network.

## before you go on...

1. Compare and contrast the three wireline communications channels.
2. Describe the various technologies that enable users to send high-volume data over any network.
3. Describe the Ethernet and TCP/IP protocols.
4. Differentiate between client/server computing and peer-to-peer processing.

## The Internet and the World Wide Web 6.3

The **Internet** ("the Net") is a global WAN that connects approximately 1 million organizational computer networks in more than 200 countries on all continents, including Antarctica. It has become so widespread that it features in the daily routine of some 3 billion people. Participating computer systems include smartphones, PCs, LANs, databases, and mainframes.

The computers and organizational nodes on the Internet can be of different types and makes. They are connected to one another by data communications lines of different speeds. The primary network connections and telecommunications lines that link the nodes are referred to as the **Internet backbone**. For the Internet, the backbone is a fiber-optic network that is operated primarily by large telecommunications companies.

As a network of networks, the Internet enables people to access data in other organizations and to communicate, collaborate, and exchange information seamlessly around the world, quickly and inexpensively. Thus, the Internet has become a necessity for modern businesses.

The Internet grew out of an experimental project of the Advanced Research Project Agency (ARPA) of the U.S. Department of Defense. The project began in 1969 as the *ARPAnet*. Its purpose was to test the feasibility of a WAN over which researchers, educators, military personnel, and government agencies could share data, exchange messages, and transfer files.

Today, Internet technologies are being used both within and among organizations. An **intranet** is a network that uses Internet protocols so that users can take advantage of familiar applications and work habits. Intranets support discovery (easy and inexpensive browsing and search), communication, and collaboration inside an organization.

In contrast, an **extranet** connects parts of the intranets of different organizations. In addition, it enables business partners to communicate securely over the Internet using virtual private networks (VPNs) (explained in Chapter 4). Extranets offer limited accessibility to the intranets of participating companies, as well as necessary interorganizational communications. They are widely used in the areas of business-to-business (B2B) electronic commerce (see Chapter 7) and supply chain management (SCM) (see Chapter 11).

No central agency manages the Internet. Instead, the costs of its operation are shared among hundreds of thousands of nodes. Thus, the cost for any one organization is small. Organizations must pay a small fee if they wish to register their names, and they need to install their own hardware and software to operate their internal networks. The organizations are obliged to move any data or information that enter their organizational network, regardless of the source, to their destination, at no charge to the senders. The senders, of course, pay the telephone bills for using either the backbone or regular telephone lines.

Companies from every country conduct business on the Internet. China has the largest number of people accessing the Internet—some 618 million people. Let's take a look at its leading Internet firms.

- *Qihoo 360 (http://corp.360.cn)* is best known for its online security software, which has more than 600 million users. In addition, in 2012 it launched a search engine that now claims almost 25 percent of the Chinese market.

- *JD.com (www.jd.com)* is an online retailer with 140 million users that operates in a similar way to Amazon.com. JD.com has an English-language Web site that offers free global shipping for purchases over $49.

- *Jiayuan.com (www.jiayuan.com)* is one of China's oldest and best-known dating sites, with more than 100 million users. China's one child policy has created a gender gap in the population that is skewed toward males. At the same time, the media refer to women in their late 20s as "leftover women." Jiaynan, which means "beautiful destiny," is tailored to users looking to get married.

- *Netease (www.netease.com)* is a major news portal for China, with more than 590 million users. The site offers an e-mail service, search, online video, social networking, and online games.

- *58.com (www.58.com)*, China's version of Craigslist, covers 380 cities and 130 million monthly users who post jobs, special offers, and personal ads.

## Accessing the Internet

You can access the Internet in several ways. From your place of work or your university, you can utilize your organization's LAN. A campus or company backbone connects all of the various LANs and servers in the organization to the Internet. You can also log onto the Internet from your home or on the road, using either wireline or wireless connections.

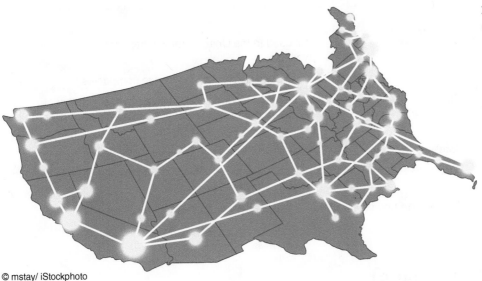

**FIGURE 6.8** Internet (backbone in white).

© mstay/ iStockphoto

**Connecting via an Online Service.** You can also access the Internet by opening an account with an Internet service provider. An **Internet service provider (ISP)** is a company that provides Internet connections for a fee. Large ISPs include Comcast (*www.comcast.com*), AT&T (*www.att.com*), Time Warner Cable (*www.timewarnercable.com*), and Verizon (*www.verizon.com*).

ISPs connect to one another through **network access points (NAPs)**. NAPs are exchange points for Internet traffic. They determine how traffic is routed. NAPs are key components of the Internet backbone. Figure 6.8 displays a schematic of the Internet. The white links at the top of the figure represent the Internet backbone; the brown dots where the white links meet are the NAPs.

**Connecting via Other Means.** There have been several attempts to make access to the Internet cheaper, faster, and easier. For example, terminals known as Internet kiosks have been located in such public places as libraries and airports (and even in convenience stores in some countries) for use by people who do not have their own computers. Accessing the Internet from smartphones and tablets is common, and fiber-to-the-home (FTTH) is growing rapidly. FTTH involves connecting fiber-optic cable directly to individual homes. This system initially was restricted to new residential developments, but it is rapidly spreading as you see in IT's About Business 6.1. Table 6.2 summarizes the various means of connecting to the Internet.

In addition, two companies are planning to deliver Internet access via low-earth orbit satellites. In January 2015, OneWeb (www.oneweb.world) announced that it will build a microsatellite network to bring Internet access to all corners of the globe. OneWeb aims to target rural markets, emerging markets, and in-flight Internet services on airlines. The company plans to create a network of 648 small satellites, each weighing some 285 pounds and orbiting 750 miles above the Earth. OneWeb plans to launch its Internet over satellite service in 2018.

On the other hand, Elon Musk (the founder of Tesla Motorcars and SpaceX) announced his plans to launch 700 satellites weighing less than 250 pounds each by November 2015. His satellites would also orbit the Earth at 750 miles. Musk said his Internet-over-satellite service was intended to be the primary means of long-distance Internet traffic for people in sparsely populated areas.

Another interesting idea is Google's Project Loon, which is a plan to provide Internet access via high-altitude balloons.

**Table 6.2**

**Internet Connection Methods**

| Service | Description |
|---|---|
| Dial-up | Still used in the United States where broadband is not available |
| DSL | Broadband access via telephone companies |
| Cable modem | Access over your cable TV coaxial cable. Can have degraded performance if many of your neighbors are accessing the Internet at once |
| Satellite | Access where cable and DSL are not available |
| Wireless | Very convenient, and WiMAX will increase the use of broadband wireless |
| Fiber-to-the-home (FTTH) | Expensive and usually placed only in new housing developments |

# IT's [about business]

## 6.1 Google Fiber

Cable distribution giants such as Verizon (*www.verizon.com*), Time Warner Cable (*www.timewarnercable.com*), and Comcast (*www.comcast.com*) enjoy healthy profit margins on their Internet services. Verizon's (*www.verizon.com*) fiber-optic network, called FiOS, serves home subscribers in 16 states. FiOS offers a variety of plans ranging from 25 megabits per second (Mbps) upload and download (in all FiOS areas) to 500 Mbps upload and download (only in limited FiOS areas).

None of these companies, however, appears to have plans to extend these services to additional geographical areas. Rather, their business goal is to sign up more people in their existing service areas. Why have they adopted this strategy? The answer is that focusing on existing service areas adds the most revenue without increasing the companies' capital costs. Essentially, there are no compelling business incentives for the established cable companies to expand their service offerings. This policy is unfortunate because most Americans have no choice but to do business with their local cable company. To compound this problem, few outside companies have the money to compete with the existing, cash-heavy telecommunications companies who control existing cable networks. Given these realities, what would it take to implement ultrafast fiber service throughout the United States?

One possible solution involves Google (*www.google.com*), which is installing and operating ultrafast fiber-optic cable service, known as Google Fiber, in several U.S. cities. Google has invited 34 cities in 9 metropolitan areas to collaborate with the company to explore strategies to bring gigabit-speed Google Fiber to their cities.

Google Fiber was first deployed to homes in Kansas City (Kansas and Missouri). Google secured guarantees from the Kansas City government that the company would receive rapid responses on matters such as city inspections, access to rights-of-way, and permission to place fiber in sewers.

Google's fiber and connections are off-the-shelf technologies, and Google's Fiber service is priced at just $70 per month, or $120 with bundled television. For the television service, Google made content deals that include some sports channels, although HBO is not yet part of Google's service content. Google Fiber comes with 2 terabytes of DVR storage, 1 additional terabyte of cloud storage, and an Android tablet for use as a remote control.

How can Google offer this level of service for such a low price? The answer is that Google appears to be willing to accept lower operating margins and profits for compelling business reasons. The company's long-term corporate fortunes are closely linked to heavy Web usage. Therefore, more Web traffic, and more people watching that traffic, translate to greater ad revenues for Google.

Kansas City families are pleased with Google Fiber. For instance, they are able to simultaneously stream four high-definition television shows, recording three of them on their DVR. That is two more shows than they could previously watch at once, with plenty of capacity to spare.

At one level, this project reflects Google's policy of developing new businesses by providing customers with ultrafast speeds and then offering them experimental services such as Google TV. However, if Google's business model for deploying fiber services works, then it may create a new era for privately built broadband.

By early 2015, Google's fiber service was operating in Kansas City; Austin, Texas; and Provo, Utah. In addition, the company is planning to expand this service to nine new markets: Atlanta, Georgia; Charlotte, North Carolina; Nashville, Tennessee; Phoenix, Arizona; Portland, Oregon; Raleigh-Durham, North Carolina; San Antonio, Texas; Salt Lake City, Utah; and San Jose, California.

Google's fundamental strategy is to identify profitable areas within a city, called "fiberhoods," in which to deploy its Fiber service. Google agrees to provide free (but lower performing) broadband services to low-income areas within its selected cities. Significantly, other ISPs are adopting Google's selective approach. For example, about seven months after Google announced its intentions to bring Fiber to Austin, AT&T announced it was introducing 1-Gbps service in the same city.

Interestingly, Los Angeles rejected Google's approach. Instead, it is soliciting contracts for citywide gigabit services. In addition, several municipal projects across the country are providing gigabit Internet access; for example, Chanute, Kansas; Chattanooga, Tennessee; and Santa Monica, California.

There are many cities where it may not be feasible to deploy fiber; for example, cities that have areas that are not densely populated or where construction costs are too high. Furthermore, in California, the provisions for securing environmental permits might make such a project cost-prohibitive.

Google is not the only organization that is bringing ultrafast fiber services to underserved areas. Some cities are taking matters into their own hands. For example, in 2010 the local power utility in Chattanooga, Tennessee, received $111 million in federal stimulus money to accelerate the build-out of a 1-gigabit per second (Gbps) network for a smart electric grid. In 2013, the utility began offering 1-Gbps Internet access for about $300 per month, depending on the television service the customer chooses.

*Sources*: Compiled from S. Mlot, "Salt Lake City Nabs Super-Fast Google Fiber," *PC Magazine*, March 24, 2015; "How Google Fiber Is Disrupting the Broadband Deployment Model," *Network World*, August 26, 2014; A. Barr, "Google Fiber Is Fast, But Is It Fair?" *The Wall Street Journal*, August 22, 2014; J. Gold, "Where's My Gigabit Internet, Anyway?" *Network World*, April 17, 2014; C. Neagle, "10 Cities That Provide 1-Gig Internet Services," *Network World*, February 26, 2014; "Gigabit Internet May Be Coming to 35 U.S. Cities," *KurzweilAI.net*, February 20, 2014; J. Sartain, "Google's Gigabit Internet: Not Coming to a Neighborhood Near You," *Network World*, November 19, 2013; D. Talbot, "Not So Fast: A Google Fiber One-Gigabit Mystery," *MIT Technology Review*, September 20, 2013; P. Olson, "The Google Effect," *Forbes*, May 27, 2013; D. Talbot, "Google Fiber's Ripple Effect," *MIT Technology Review*, April 26, 2013; J. Calacanis, "Google's Fiber Takeover Plan Expands, Will Kill Cable and Carriers," *Pandodaily.com*, April 19, 2013; http://fiber.google.com/about/, accessed March 25, 2015.

### Questions

1. Why would a "search company" such as Google decided to enter the fiber services business? Describe the benefits that Google expects to obtain from this venture.

2. Describe the various outcomes that might occur in an area that receives ultrafast fiber, regardless of the provider.

---

Other countries use cybercafes, which are places that provide Internet access to the public, usually for a time-based fee. These businesses often provide snacks and drinks, hence the café in the name. IT's About Business 6.2 illustrates how Cuba approaches Internet access.

# IT's [about business]

## 6.2 Internet Access in Cuba

The Internet in Cuba is among the most tightly controlled in the world. It is characterized by a low number of connections, limited bandwidth, extensive censorship, and high costs. Beginning in 2007, however, the situation seemed to display signs of improving. By early 2015, slightly more than 25 percent of the Cuban population had some type of Internet access. Although this statistic indicated some progress, Cuba still has the lowest Internet penetration rate in the Western Hemisphere. In fact, only 5 percent of Cubans can actually access the open Internet. Home Internet access is practically nonexistent, and only government officials, academicians, doctors, engineers, and government-approved journalists have Internet access at work.

Cuban citizens do have access, however, to a national intranet. The Cuban intranet provides a government-operated e-mail service and "government-friendly" Web sites hosted in the .cu domain. All of these services are subject to review by Cuba's Department of Revolutionary Orientation.

In spring 2013, Cuba linked up with two undersea fiber-optic Internet cables, and the country's state telecommunications company, ETECSA, opened 118 cybercafes with access to the wider Internet. Cuba's focus is on "collective points of access," as Cuba's deputy communications minister stated in the Communist Party daily newspaper, *Granma*.

In addition, at the cybercafes, connecting to the closed Cuban intranet costs only 70 cents per hour. In contrast, connecting to the Internet costs $5 per hour. Making matters worse, Cubans must show their national ID when signing up for Internet time. Some users have even been required to sign agreements not to do "anything online that might jeopardize 'public security.'"

With such limited access, Cubans have become creative in accessing the Internet. One of the most popular methods of access is to download online articles onto flash drives and then pass them around to friends and family. Also, some Cubans with Internet access either sell this access to other users or share accounts. Others build their own antennas or use illegal dial-up connections. However, the Cuban government electronically "sniffs" (scans) neighborhoods for ham radios and satellite dishes. Some Cubans call a phone number in the United States and record an anonymous message that is automatically converted to text and shared via Twitter or Facebook. Still other Cubans circumvent government restrictions by using satellite smartphones, many of which are paid for by friends and relatives living abroad.

Despite limiting access, Cuba does have a strong presence on the Internet. The country's cyber militia, made up of students from the University of Computer Sciences in Havana, constitute one element of a propaganda initiative called Operation Truth. Their mission is to discredit government critics and promote the government's agenda. The situation in Cuba demonstrates that when the government controls online communications, it is possible to allow "expanded" Internet access without providing much, if any, digital freedom.

*Sources*: Compiled from J. Tamayo, "Google Exec Says Cuban Internet Is Old and Censored," *The Miami Herald*, July 1, 2014; L. Franceschi-Bicchierai, "The Internet in Cuba: 5 Things You Need to Know," *Mashable*, April 3, 2014; S. Willis, "Cuba's Internet: It's Bad but It Might Get Better," *Fusion.net*, October 25, 2013; "A Cyber Café in Cuba? No Chance," *Translating Cuba*, October 20, 2013; "Cuba Plans Internet in Homes by Late 2014," *Fox News Latino*, June 22, 2013; D. Talbot, "Cuba's New Internet Service Is Also No

Bed of Roses," *MIT Technology Review*, July 16, 2013; F. Revsberg, "Cuba's New Cybercafes: A Piecemeal Strategy," *Havana Times*, May 30, 2013; R. Schoon, "Cuba to Offer Public Internet at Cyber Cafes, but Access Comes with Hefty Price Tag," *Latinos Post*, May 28, 2013; M. Frank, "Cuba's Mystery Fiber-Optic Internet Cable Stirs to Life," *Reuters*, January 22, 2013; *www.cuba.cu*, accessed March 1, 2015.

### Questions

1. Describe the advantages and disadvantages of the global Internet to Cuban citizens.
2. Describe the advantages and disadvantages of the global Internet to the Cuban government.

---

**Addresses on the Internet.** Each computer on the Internet has an assigned address, called the **Internet Protocol (IP) address**, that distinguishes it from all other computers. The IP address consists of sets of numbers, in four parts, separated by dots. For example, the IP address of one computer might be 135.62.128.91. You can access a Web site by typing this number in the address bar of your browser.

Currently, there are two IP addressing schemes. The first scheme, IPv4, is the most widely used. IP addresses using IPv4 consist of 32 bits, meaning that there are $2^{32}$ possibilities for IP addresses, or 4,294,967,295 distinct addresses. Note that the IP address in the preceding paragraph (135.62.128.91) is an IPv4 address. At the time that IPv4 was developed, there were not as many computers that need addresses as there are today. Therefore, a new IP addressing scheme has been developed, IPv6.

IP addresses using IPv6 consist of 128 bits, meaning that there are $2^{128}$ possibilities for distinct IP addresses, which is an unimaginably large number. IPv6, which is replacing IPv4, will accommodate the rapidly increasing number of devices that need IP addresses, such as smartphones.

IP addresses must be unique so that computers on the Internet know where to find one another. The Internet Corporation for Assigned Names (ICANN) (*www.icann.org*) coordinates these unique addresses throughout the world. Without that coordination, we would not have one global Internet.

ICANN planned to transition its functions to a "global multistakeholder community" in 2015. In early 2015, that community had yet to be identified.

Because the numeric IP addresses are difficult to remember, most computers have names as well. ICANN accredits certain companies called *registrars* to register these names, which are derived from a system called the domain name system (DNS). Domain names consist of multiple parts, separated by dots, that are read from right to left. For example, consider the domain name *business.auburn.edu*. The rightmost part (or zone) of an Internet name is its top-level domain (TLD). The letters *edu* in business.auburn.edu indicate that this is an educational site. The following are popular U.S. TLDs:

com     commercial sites
edu     educational sites
mil     military government sites
gov     civilian government sites
org     organizations

To conclude our domain name example, *auburn* is the name of the organization (Auburn University), and *business* is the name of the particular machine (server) within the organization to which the message is being sent.

A top-level domain (TLD) is the domain at the highest level in the hierarchical Domain Name System of the Internet. The top-level domain names are located in the root zone (rightmost zone) of the name. Management of most TLDs is delegated to responsible organizations by ICANN. ICANN operates the Internet Assigned Numbers Authority (IANA), which is in charge of maintaining the DNS root zone. Today, IANA distinguishes the following groups of TLDs:

- *Country-code top-level domains (ccTLD)*: Two letter domains established for countries or territories. For example, *de* stands for Germany, *it* for Italy, and *ru* for Russia.
- *Internationalized country code top-level domains (IDN ccTLD)*: These are ccTLDs in non-Latin character sets (e.g., Arabic or Chinese).
- *Generic top-level domains (gTLD)*: Top-level domains with three or more characters. gTLDs initially consisted of .gov, .edu, .com, .mil, .org, and .net. In late 2000, ICANN introduced .aero, .biz, .coop, .info, .museum, .name, and .pro. In June 2012, ICANN revealed nearly 2,000 applications for new top-level domains.

## The Future of the Internet

Researchers assert that if Internet bandwidth is not improved rapidly, then within a few years the Internet will be able to function only at a much reduced speed. The Internet sometimes is too slow for data-intensive applications such as full-motion video files (movies) and large medical files (X-rays). In addition, the Internet is unreliable and is not secure. As a result, Internet2 has been developed by many U.S. universities collaborating with industry and government. **Internet2** develops and deploys advanced network applications such as remote medical diagnosis, digital libraries, distance education, online simulation, and virtual laboratories. It is designed to be fast, always on, everywhere, natural, intelligent, easy, and trusted. Note that Internet2 is not a separate physical network from the Internet. At the end of 2014, Internet2 had over 500 members, including 252 institutions of higher education and 82 members from industry. For more details, see *www.internet2.edu*.

## The World Wide Web

Many people equate the Internet with the World Wide Web. However, they are not the same thing. The Internet functions as a transport mechanism, whereas the World Wide Web is an application that uses those transport functions. Other applications, such as e-mail, also run on the Internet.

The **World Wide Web (The Web, WWW, or W3)** is a system of universally accepted standards for storing, retrieving, formatting, and displaying information via a client/server architecture. The Web handles all types of digital information, including text, hypermedia, graphics, and sound. It uses graphical user interfaces (GUIs) (explained in Technology Guide 2), so it is very easy to navigate.

**Hypertext** is the underlying concept defining the structure of the World Wide Web. Hypertext is the text displayed on a computer display or other electronic device with references, called hyperlinks, to other text that the reader can immediately access, or where text can be revealed progressively at additional levels of details. A hyperlink is a connection from a hypertext file or document to another location or file, typically activated by clicking on a highlighted word or image on the screen, or by touching the screen.

Organizations that wish to offer information through the Web must establish a *home page*, which is a text and graphical screen display that usually welcomes the user and provides basic information on the organization that has established the page. In most cases, the home page will lead users to other pages. All the pages of a particular company or individual are collectively known as a **Web site**. Most Web pages provide a way to contact the organization or the individual. The person in charge of an organization's Web site is its *Webmaster*. (Note: *Webmaster* is a gender-neutral title.)

To access a Web site, the user must specify a **uniform resource locator (URL)**, which points to the address of a specific resource on the Web. For instance, the URL for Microsoft is *http://www.microsoft.com*. Recall that HTTP stands for hypertext transport protocol. The remaining letters in this URL—*www.microsoft.com*—indicate the domain name that identifies the Web server that stores the Web site.

Users access the Web primarily through software applications called browsers. Browsers provide a graphical front end that enables users to point-and-click their way across the Web, a process called *surfing*. Web browsers became a means of universal access because they deliver the same interface on any operating system on which they run.

# before you go on... 𝕏𝕏𝕏𝕏

1. Describe the various ways that you can connect to the Internet.
2. Identify each part of an Internet address.
3. Describe the difference between the Internet and the World Wide Web.
4. What are the functions of browsers?

## 6.4 Network Applications: Discovery

Now that you have a working knowledge of what networks are and how you can access them, the key question is: How do businesses use networks to improve their operations? In the next four sections of this chapter, we explore four network applications: discovery, communication, collaboration, and education. These applications, however, are merely a sampling of the many network applications currently available to users. Even if these applications formed an exhaustive list today, they would not do so tomorrow when something new will be developed. Furthermore, placing network applications in categories is difficult because there will always be borderline cases. For example, telecommuting really combines communication and collaboration.

The Internet enables users to access or *discover information* located in databases all over the world. By browsing and searching data sources on the Web, users can apply the Internet's discovery capability to areas ranging from education to government services to entertainment to commerce. Although having access to all this information is a great benefit, it is critically important to realize that there is no quality assurance for information on the Web. The Web is truly democratic in that *anyone* can post information to it. Therefore, the fundamental rule about information on the Web is "User beware!"

In addition, the Web's major strength—the vast stores of information it contains—also presents a major challenge. The amount of information on the Web can be overwhelming, and it doubles approximately each year. As a result, navigating through the Web and gaining access to necessary information are becoming more and more difficult. To accomplish these tasks, people increasingly are using search engines, directories, and portals.

### Search Engines and Metasearch Engines

A **search engine** is a computer program that searches for specific information by keywords and then reports the results. A search engine maintains an index of billions of Web pages. It uses that index to find pages that match a set of user-specified keywords. Such indexes are created and updated by *webcrawlers*, which are computer programs that browse the Web and create a copy of all visited pages. Search engines then index these pages to provide fast searches.

In mid-2015, four search engines accounted for almost all searches in the United States. They are, in order, Google (*www.google.com*), Bing (*www.bing.com*), Yahoo! (*www.yahoo.com*), and Ask (*www.ask.com*). The leading search engine in China is Baidu (*www.baidu.com*), which claimed approximately three-fourths of the Chinese market in mid-2015.

There are an incredible number of other search engines that are quite useful, many of which perform very specific searches. Examples include: Boardreader (*www.boardreader.com*), BuzzSumo (*www.buzzsumo.com*), CrunchBase (*www.crunchbase.com*), DuckDuckGo (*https://duckduckgo.com*), and Topsy (*www.topsy.com*).

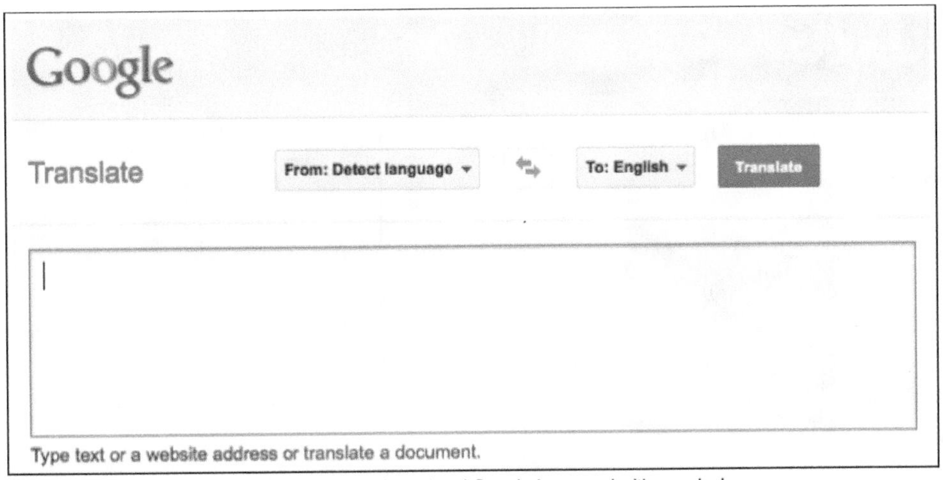

**FIGURE 6.9** Google Translate.

Google and the Google logo are registered trademarks of Google Inc., used with permission

For an even more thorough search, you can use a metasearch engine. **Metasearch engines** search several engines at once and then integrate the findings to answer users' queries. Examples are Surf-wax (*www.surfwax.com*), Metacrawler (*www.metacrawler.com*), Mamma (*www.mamma.com*), KartOO (*www.kartoo.com*), and Dogpile (*www.dogpile.com*).

## Publication of Material in Foreign Languages

Not only is there a huge amount of information on the Internet, but it is also written in many different languages. How, then, do you access this information? The answer is that you use an *automatic translation* of Web pages. Such translation is available to and from all major languages, and its quality is improving with time. Some major translation products are Microsoft's Bing translator (*http://www.microsofttranslator.com*) and Google (*www.google.com/language_tools*) (see Figure 6.9), as well as products and services available at Trados (*www.trados.com*).

Companies invest resources to make their Web sites accessible in multiple languages as a result of the global nature of the business environment. That is, multilingual Web sites are now a competitive necessity. When companies are disseminating information around the world, getting that information correct is essential. It is not enough for companies to translate Web content. They must also localize that content and be sensitive to the needs of the people in local markets.

To reach 80 percent of the world's Internet users, a Web site needs to support a minimum of 10 languages: English, Chinese, Spanish, Japanese, German, Korean, French, Italian, Russian, and Portuguese. At 20 cents and more per word, translation services are expensive. Companies supporting 10 languages can spend $200,000 annually to localize information and another $50,000 to maintain the Web sites. Translation budgets for major multinational companies can run in millions of dollars. Many large companies use Systran S.A. (*www.systransoft.com*) for high-quality machine translation services.

## Portals

Most organizations and their managers encounter information overload. Information is scattered across numerous documents, e-mail messages, and databases at different locations and systems. Finding relevant and accurate information is often time-consuming and may require users to access multiple systems.

One solution to this problem is to use portals. A **portal** is a Web-based, personalized gateway to information and knowledge that provides relevant information from different IT systems and the Internet using advanced search and indexing techniques. After reading the next section, you will be able to distinguish among four types of portals: commercial, affinity, corporate, and industrywide. The four types of portals are differentiated by the audiences they serve.

A **commercial (public) portal** is the most popular type of portal on the Internet. It is intended for broad and diverse audiences, and it offers routine content, some of it in real time (e.g., a stock ticker). Examples are Lycos (*www.lycos.com*) and Microsoft Network (*www.msn.com*).

**Welcome to myUWG**

Welcome to the University of West Georgia's myUWG website.
Please login to the right.

**Pay Fees By Credit Card**
Click here to pay fees by credit card.

**What's Inside?**

**E-mail:** Send and receive e-mail, and create your own personal address book.

**Calendar:** Access and manage your personal, course and school calendars.

**Groups:** Create, manage and join group homepages for clubs, affiliations and interests.

**and much more...**

**Secure Access Login**

User Name:

Password:

Login     Cancel

Having problems logging in?
Click here for new Password Change Rules and supported browsers.

Lost your password?

Lookup your Username

Copyright © SunGard Higher Education 1998 - 2009.

Courtesy of the University of West Georgia.

Top   UNIVERSITY of West Georgia

**FIGURE 6.10** University of West Georgia affinity portal.

In contrast, an **affinity portal** offers a single point of entry to an entire community of affiliated interests, such as a hobby group or a political party. Your university most likely has an affinity portal for its alumni. Figure 6.10 displays the affinity portal for the University of West Georgia. Other examples of affinity portals are *www.techweb.com* and *www.zdnet.com*.

As the name suggests, a **corporate portal** offers a personalized, single point of access through a Web browser to critical business information located inside and outside an organization. These portals are also known as *enterprise portals, information portals*, and *enterprise information portals*. In addition to making it easier to find needed information, corporate portals offer customers and employees self-service opportunities.

Whereas corporate portals are associated with a single company, an **industrywide** portal serves entire industries. An example is TruckNet (*www.truck.net*), a portal for the trucking industry and the trucking community, including professional drivers, owner/operators, and trucking companies.

# before you go on...

1. Differentiate between search engines and metasearch engines.
2. What are some reasons why publication of material in a number of languages is so important?
3. Describe the various reasons that portals are useful to us.

# 6.5 Network Applications: Communication

The second major category of network applications is communication. There are many types of communication technologies, including e-mail, call centers, chat rooms, and voice. Further, we discuss an interesting application of communication: telecommuting. (Note: You will read about other types of communication, blogging, and microblogging, in Chapter 9.)

## Electronic Mail

Electronic mail (e-mail) is the largest-volume application running over the Internet. Studies have found that almost all companies conduct business transactions via e-mail, and the vast majority confirm that e-mail is tied to their means of generating revenue. On the other hand, the amount of e-mail that managers receive has become overwhelming. In fact, too much e-mail can lead to a loss of productivity. In IT's About Business 6.3, you see how Atos SE is trying to eliminate e-mail entirely.

# IT's [about business]

## 6.3 Get Rid of E-Mail? Seriously?

The first e-mail message was sent in 1971. Since then, e-mail has become the dominant means of communication and collaboration in business. (In fact, e-mail is probably the dominant means of communication between faculty and students at your university.)

Over time, however, organizations have begun to associate e-mail with information overload and stress. Time-pressed managers are finding it more difficult to get work done than they did five years ago as their workloads increase and organizational resources become scarcer.

Adding to their workloads, managers are spending much of their time sifting through a seemingly endless barrage of e-mail messages. By compulsively checking e-mail, managers become distracted and are unable to devote sufficient time to other, more productive work. In addition, managers frequently assert that many of the e-mails they have to read and respond to add little or no value to their organization.

Even managers who are disciplined enough to check their e-mails only at certain times can become frustrated. At the end of the day, they may have an inbox full of messages that need to be addressed before the next morning. This process can be exhausting, particularly if e-mail is the only means of communication between managers and their teams. The bottom line is that e-mail's usefulness in a fast-paced and collaboration-based business environment is diminishing.

How are organizations responding to these problems? One organization, Atos SE (*http://atos.net*), took a rather drastic step: They banned e-mail.

Atos SE is a French multinational IT services corporation headquartered in Bezons, France. The firm provides IT consulting, systems integration, and managed IT services. Atos also receives contracts for outsourced public IT services from several governments, including the United Kingdom.

In 2011, Atos introduced a Zero Email initiative that banned e-mail as a form of internal communications, except for use with customers and prospects. The company instituted the ban after it conducted an internal research study that revealed that a sample of 300 employees collectively sent or received roughly 85,000 e-mails in one week.

As part of its Zero Email initiative, Atos acquired the French software company blueKiwi (*www.bluekiwi-software.com*) in 2012 and deployed its ZEN enterprise social networking software across the organization. This software enables employees to selectively subscribe to relevant subject and networking groups—called communities—that are composed of employees with common business interests and activities. Atos discovered that its 76,000 employees are able to reduce or even eliminate e-mails by participating (or posting, as on Facebook) in relevant groups.

Group communities are the central information and communication hub for different work topics (e.g., a project). Employees use blogs, wikis, instant messaging, and social media tools in place of e-mail.

And the results? By the end of 2013, Atos had drastically reduced e-mail by some 60 percent. At the same time, more than 74,000 employees were utilizing blueKiwi to participate in 7,500 communities.

By early 2015, the Zero Email initiative had made great strides in reducing (but still not eliminating) internal e-mail at Atos. Additionally, Atos's initiative has attracted interest from other businesses. Although not as drastic as the Atos approach, Volkswagen, for example, now prevents its BlackBerry servers from sending e-mail messages to employees outside work hours. Other companies are encouraging their employees to take "e-mail breaks"; that is, devoting a defined time period for e-mails, much like a coffee break.

*Sources:* Compiled from R. Greenfield, "Inside the Company that Got Rid of Email," *Fast Company*, September 25, 2014; N. Burg, "Is It Possible to Get Rid of Business Email Altogether?" *Forbes*, April 4, 2014; P. Karcher, "What You Can Learn from Atos's Zero Email Initiative," *Forrester*, December 11, 2013; P. Karcher, "Enterprise Social Does Not Stem Email Overload," *Forrester*, October 31, 2013; J. Morgan, "How to Get Rid of Email in Your Company," *Forbes*, October 23, 2013; B. Profitt, "30 Days with Inbox Zero: Cleaning Out Messages – And Stress," *ReadWrite*, April 15, 2013; L. Timmins, "Why Atos Is Eliminating Email," *Computer Weekly*, March 22, 2013; P. Taylor, "Atos' 'Zero Email Initiative' Succeeding," *Financial Times*, March 7, 2013; D. du Preez, "Atos Drives for Zero Email with blueKiwi Roll Out," *ComputerWorldUK*, November 7, 2012; *http://atos.net*, accessed March 4, 2015.

### Questions

1. Is it feasible for your university to eliminate e-mail? Why or why not? Would you support such a policy at your school? Why or why not?

2. Describe the advantages and disadvantages of eliminating e-mail from an organization. Provide specific examples to support your answers.

## Web-Based Call Centers

Effective personalized customer contact is becoming an important aspect of Web-based customer support. Such service is provided through *Web-based call centers*, also known as *customer care centers*. For example, if you need to contact a software vendor for technical support, you will usually be communicating with the vendor's Web-based call center, using e-mail, a telephone conversation, or a simultaneous voice/Web session. Web-based call centers are sometimes located in foreign countries such as India. Such *offshoring* is an important issue for the U.S. companies. (We will discuss offshoring in detail in Chapter 13.)

Significantly, some of the U.S. companies are moving their call center operations back to the United States, for several reasons. First, they believe they have less control of their operations when the centers are located overseas. They must depend on the vendor company to uphold their standards, such as quality of service. A second difficulty is language differences, which can create serious communication problems. Third, companies that manage sensitive information risk breaching customer confidentiality and security. Finally, the call center representatives typically work with many companies. As a result, they may not deliver the same level of customer services that each company requires.

## Electronic Chat Rooms

*Electronic chat* refers to an arrangement whereby participants exchange conversational messages in real time in a chat room. Chat programs allow you to send messages to people who are connected to the same channel of communication at the same time. Anyone can join in the conversation. Messages are displayed on your screen as they arrive.

There are two major types of chat programs. The first type is Web based, which allows you to send messages to Internet users by using a Web browser and visiting a Web chat site (e.g., *http://messenger.yahoo.com*). The second type is e-mail based (text only); it is called *Internet Relay Chat* (IRC). A business can use IRC to interact with customers, provide online experts for answers to questions, and so on.

## Voice Communication

The plain old telephone system has been largely replaced by Internet telephony. With **Internet telephony**, also known as **Voice-over-Internet Protocol** or **VoIP**, phone calls are treated as just another kind of data. That is, your analog voice signals are digitized, sectioned into packets, and then sent over the Internet.

Consider Skype (*www.skype.com*), which provides several VoIP services for free: voice and video calls to users who also have Skype, instant messaging, short message service, voice mail, one-to-one and group chats, and conference calls with up to nine people. As of early 2015, the most current version of Skype offered full-screen, high-definition video calling, Skype Access (to access WiFi hotspots), call transfer to a Skype contact on either a mobile or a landline phone, improved quality of calls, and ease of use. It also provided additional functions for which users pay. For example, SkypeOut allows you to make calls to landline phones and mobile phones. SkypeIn provides a number that your friends can call from any phone, and you pick up the call in Skype.

Vonage (*www.vonage.com*) also provides VoIP services, but for a fee ($9.99 per month for the first six months and then $28 per month). With Vonage you make and receive calls with your existing home phone through your broadband Internet connection. Your phone actually connects to Vonage instead of an actual phone company. The person whom you are calling does not need to have Vonage or even an Internet connection.

## Unified Communications

In the past, organizational networks for wired and wireless data, voice communications, and videoconferencing operated independently, and the IT department managed each network separately. This arrangement increased costs and reduced productivity.

**Unified communications** (UC) simplifies and integrates all forms of communications—voice, voice mail, fax, chat, e-mail, instant messaging, short message service, presence (location) services, and videoconferencing—on a common hardware and software platform. *Presence services* enable users to know where their intended recipients are and if they are available, in real time.

UC unifies all forms of human and computer communications into a common user experience. For example, UC allows an individual to receive a voice mail message and then read it in his or her e-mail inbox. In another example, UC enables users to seamlessly collaborate with another person on a project, regardless of where the users are located. One user could quickly locate the other user by accessing an interactive directory, determining whether that user is available, engaging in a text messaging session, and then escalating the session to a voice call or even a video call, all in real time.

## Telecommuting

Knowledge workers are being called the distributed workforce, or "digital nomads." This group of highly prized workers is now able to work anywhere and anytime, a process called **telecommuting**. Distributed workers are those who have no permanent office at their companies, preferring to work at home offices, in airport lounges, or client conference rooms, or on a high school stadium bleacher. The growth of the distributed workforce is driven by globalization, extremely long commutes to work, rising gasoline prices, ubiquitous broadband communications links (wireline and wireless), and powerful laptop computers and computing devices.

Telecommuting offers a number of potential advantages for employees, employers, and society. For employees, the benefits include reduced stress and improved family life. In addition, telecommuting offers employment opportunities for housebound people such as single parents and persons with disabilities. Benefits for employers include increased productivity, the ability to retain skilled employees, and the ability to attract employees who do not live within commuting distance.

However, telecommuting also has some potential disadvantages. For employees, the major disadvantages are increased feelings of isolation, possible loss of fringe benefits, lower pay (in some cases), no workplace visibility, the potential for slower promotions, and lack of socialization. In a 2013 study, researchers at Stanford University found that telecommuting employees are 50 percent less likely to receive a promotion than onsite workers. The researchers concluded that a lack of "face time" with bosses caused careers to stall.

In addition, telecommuting employees often have difficulties "training" their families to understand that they are at work even though they are physically at home. Families have to understand that they should not disturb the telecommuter for anything that they would not have disturbed him or her about in a "real" office. The major disadvantages to employers are difficulties in supervising work and potential data security problems.

Yahoo! CEO Marissa Mayer banned telecommuting in her company in February 2013. Best Buy and HP followed suit that same year. Despite being banned at these three large companies, telecommuting continues to grow.

# before you go on...

1. Discuss the advantages and disadvantages of electronic mail.
2. Why are many companies bringing their call centers back to the U.S.?
3. Describe voice-over-Internet Protocol.
4. What are the advantages and disadvantages of telecommuting to you as an individual?

# 6.6 Network Applications: Collaboration

The third major category of network applications is collaboration. **Collaboration** refers to efforts by two or more entities—that is, individuals, teams, groups, or organizations—who work together to accomplish certain tasks. The term **workgroup** refers specifically to two or more individuals who act together to perform some task.

**Workflow** is the movement of information as it progresses through the sequence of steps that make up an organization's work procedures. Workflow management makes it possible to pass documents, information, and tasks from one participant to another in a way that is governed by the organization's rules or procedures. Workflow systems are tools for automating business processes.

If group members are working in different locations, they constitute a **virtual group (team)**. Virtual groups conduct *virtual meetings*—that is, they "meet" electronically. **Virtual collaboration** (or *e-collaboration*) refers to the use of digital technologies that enable organizations or individuals who are geographically dispersed to collaboratively plan, design, develop, manage, and research products, services, and innovative applications. Organizational employees frequently collaborate virtually with one another. In addition, organizations collaborate virtually with customers, suppliers, and other business partners to become more productive and competitive.

Collaboration can be *synchronous*, meaning that all team members meet at the same time. Teams may also collaborate *asynchronously* when team members cannot meet at the same time. Virtual teams, whose members are located throughout the world, typically must collaborate asynchronously.

A variety of software products are available to support all types of collaboration. Among the most prominent are Google Drive (*http://drive.google.com*), Microsoft SharePoint Workspace (*www.microsoft.com/ Sharepoint/default.mspx*), Jive (*www.jivesoftware.com*), and IBM Lotus Quickr (*www.ibm.com/lotus/quickr*). In general, these products provide online collaboration capabilities, workgroup e-mail, distributed databases, bulletin whiteboards, electronic text editing, document management, workflow capabilities, instant virtual meetings, application sharing, instant messaging, consensus building, voting, ranking, and various application development tools.

These products also provide varying degrees of content control. Google Drive, Microsoft SharePoint Workspace, and Jive provide for shared content with *version management*, whereas Microsoft SharePoint Workspace and IBM Lotus Quickr offer *version control*. Products that provide version management track changes to documents and provide features to accommodate multiple people working on the same document at the same time. In contrast, version-control systems provide each team member with an account that includes a set of permissions. Document directories are often set up so that users must check out documents before they can edit them. When one team member checks out a document, no other member can access it. Once the document has been checked in, it becomes available to other members.

## Crowdsourcing

One type of collaboration is **crowdsourcing**, in which an organization outsources a task to an undefined, generally large group of people in the form of an open call. Crowdsourcing provides many potential benefits to organizations. First, crowds can explore problems—and often resolve them—at relatively low cost, and often very quickly. Second, the organization can tap a wider range of talent than might be present among its employees. Third, by listening to the crowd, organizations gain firsthand insight into their customers' desires. Finally, crowdsourcing taps into the global world of ideas, helping companies work through a rapid design process. Let's look at some examples of crowdsourcing.

MIS

- *Crowdsourcing help desks:* IT help desks are a necessary service on college campuses because students depend on their computers and Internet access to complete their schoolwork and attend class online. At Indiana University at Bloomington, new IT help desks use crowdsourcing to alleviate the cost and pressure of having to answer so many calls. Students and professors post their IT problems on an online forum, where other students and amateur IT experts answer them.

- *Recruitment:* Champlain College in Vermont developed a Champlain For Reel program, inviting students to share via YouTube videos recounting their experiences at the school and the ways they benefited from their time there. The YouTube channel serves to recruit prospective students and updates alumni on campus and community events.

- Scitable (*www.nature.com/scitable*) combines social networking and academic collaboration. Through crowdsourcing, students, professors, and scientists discuss problems, find solutions, and swap resources and journals. Scitable is a free site that lets each individual user turn to crowdsourcing for answers even while helping others.

- Procter & Gamble (P&G) uses InnoCentive (*www.innocentive.com*), where company researchers post their problems. P&G offers cash rewards to problem solvers.

- SAP's Idea Place (*https://ideas.sap.com*) generates ideas for not-yet- developed software improvements and innovation. Any person can view the content in the Idea Place. The Idea Place is organized into numerous sessions, or categories, under which the ideas are organized. Once you have posted your idea, other users can vote on it and add comments. Status updates on your idea allow you to follow it as it progresses through the Idea Place. Every idea is reviewed by a team of experts made up of engineers, product managers, and community managers who evaluate the potential for implementation. The ideas with the most votes will receive a higher level of attention from SAP.

Although crowdsourcing has numerous success stories, there are many questions and concerns about this system, including the following:

- Should the crowd be limited to experts? If so, then how would a company go about implementing this policy?

- How accurate is the content created by the nonexperts in the crowd? How is accuracy maintained?

- How is crowd-created content being updated? How can companies be certain the content is relevant?

- The crowd may submit too many ideas, with most of them being worthless. In this scenario, evaluating all of these ideas can be prohibitively expensive. For example, during the BP oil spill in 2010, crowds submitted more than 20,000 suggestions on how to stem the flow of oil. The problem was very technical, so there were many poor suggestions. Nevertheless, despite the fact that BP was under severe time constraints, the company had to evaluate all of the ideas.

- Content contributors may violate copyrights, either intentionally or unintentionally.

- The quality of content (and therefore subsequent decisions) depends on the composition of the crowd. The best decisions may come if the crowd is made up of people with diverse opinions and ideas. In many cases, however, companies do not know the makeup of the crowd in advance.

## Electronic Teleconferencing and Video Conferencing

**Teleconferencing** is the use of electronic communication technology that enables two or more people at different locations to hold a conference. There are several types of teleconferencing. The oldest and simplest is a telephone conference call, where several people talk to one another from multiple locations. The biggest disadvantage of conference calls is that they do not allow the participants to communicate face to face nor can they see graphs, charts, and pictures at other locations.

To overcome these shortcomings, organizations are increasingly turning to video teleconferencing or videoconferencing. In a **videoconference**, participants in one location can view participants, documents, and presentations at other locations. The latest version of videoconferencing, called *telepresence*, enables participants to seamlessly share data, voice, pictures, graphics, and animation by electronic means. Conferees can also transmit data along

**FIGURE 6.11** Telepresence system.

HO Marketwire Photos/NewsCom

with voice and video, which allows them to work together on documents and to exchange computer files.

Telepresence systems range from on-premise, high-end systems to cloud-based systems. (We discuss on-premise computing and cloud computing in Technology Guide 3). On-premise, high-end systems are expensive and require dedicated rooms with large high-definition screens to show people sitting around conference tables (see Figure 6.11). These systems have advanced audio capabilities that let everyone talk at once without canceling out any voices. These systems also require technical staff to operate and maintain. Examples of high-end systems include Cisco's TelePresence system (*www.cisco.com*) and Polycom's RealPresence Immersive system (*www.polycom.com*).

Interestingly, in 2006, Cisco's telepresence system cost approximately $300,000 per installation, but in early 2015 the company offered its system for approximately $20,000. This steep decline in pricing is a good example of Moore's Law in action. (See Technology Guide 1.)

However, having dedicated rooms where telepresence meetings take place is not particularly useful when so many employees work remotely. As a result, companies such as Fuze (*www.fuze.com*) and BlueJeans Nework (*www.bluejeans.com*) offer telepresence systems that utilize cloud computing. The cloud delivery model means that Fuze and BlueJeans provide systems that are cheaper, more flexible, and require fewer in-house technical staff to operate and maintain. In addition, Fuze and BlueJeans can deliver their telepresence systems to any device, including smartphones, tablets, and laptop and desktop computers.

Monthly telepresence subscription fees for Fuze and BlueJeans cost $10–15 per user per month. In response, Cisco is now offering cloud-based telepresence systems at monthly rates of $25 per user and high-end, conference room telepresence systems at monthly rates of $5,100 per user.

# before you go on...

1. Describe virtual collaboration and why it is important to you.

2. Define crowdsourcing and provide two examples of crowdsourcing not mentioned in this section.

3. Identify the business conditions that have made videoconferencing more important.

# Network Applications: Educational

The fourth major category of network applications consists of education applications. In this section, we discuss e-learning, distance learning, and virtual universities.

## E-Learning and Distance Learning

E-learning and distance learning are not the same thing, but they do overlap. **E-learning** refers to learning supported by the Web. It can take place inside classrooms as a support to conventional teaching, such as when students work on the Web during class. It also can take place in virtual classrooms, in which all coursework is completed online and classes do not meet face-to-face. In these cases, e-learning is a part of distance learning. **Distance learning** (DL) refers to any learning situation in which teachers and students do not meet face-to-face.

Today, the Web provides a multimedia interactive environment for self-study. Web-enabled systems make knowledge accessible to those who need it, when they need it, anytime, anywhere. For this reason, e-learning and DL can be useful for both formal education and corporate training.

There are many benefits of e-learning. For example, online materials can deliver very current content that is of high quality (created by content experts) and consistent (presented the same way every time). It also gives students the flexibility to learn at any place, at any time, and at their own pace. In corporate training centers that use e-learning, learning time generally is shorter, which means that more people can be trained within a given time frame. This system reduces training costs and eliminates the expense of renting facility space.

Despite these benefits, e-learning has some drawbacks. For one, students must be computer literate. Also, they may miss the face-to-face interaction with instructors and fellow students. In addition, accurately assessing students' work can be problematic because instructors really do not know who completed the assignments.

E-learning does not usually replace the classroom setting. Rather, it enhances it by taking advantage of new content and delivery technologies. Advanced e-learning support environments, such as Blackboard (*www.blackboard.com*), add value to traditional learning in higher education.

A new form of distance learning has recently appeared, called *massive open online courses* or *MOOCs*. MOOCs are a tool for democratizing higher education. Hundreds of thousands of students around the world who lack access to universities are using MOOCs to acquire sophisticated skills and high-paying jobs without having to pay tuition or obtain a college degree. IT's About Business 6.4 takes a closer look at MOOCs.

# IT's [about business]

## 6.4 Massive Open Online Courses

Massive open online courses—known as MOOCs—are designed to democratize education. Hundreds of thousands of students around the world who lack access to education have enrolled in MOOCs as a way to acquire sophisticated skills and high-paying jobs without having to pay tuition fees or obtain a college degree.

Consider Stanford University's experience. In fall 2011, roughly 160,000 students in 190 countries enrolled in a single Artificial Intelligence course. An additional 200 students registered for the course on campus. A few weeks into the semester, attendance for the on-campus course decreased to about 30, as students decided to watch online videos instead of physically attending the class. The course gave rise to its own community, including a Facebook group, online discussions among participants, and volunteer translators who made the course available in 44 languages. The 23,000 students who completed the course received a PDF file (suitable for framing) by e-mail that indicated their percentile score. However, the file did not contain the name "Stanford University."

### The Positive

Several factors have contributed to the growth of MOOCs, including improved technology and the rapidly increasing costs of traditional universities. MOOCs are highly automated, complete with computer-graded assignments and exams. Nonetheless, they provide many opportunities for social interaction. The Stanford MOOCs, for example, offered virtual office hours and online discussion forums where students could ask and answer questions—and vote on which questions were important enough to filter up to the professors.

Many universities are offering MOOCs. For example, in 2013, the Georgia Institute of Technology (*www.gatech.edu*) enrolled several hundred computer science students in an online master's degree program offered by Udacity (*www.udacity.com*). The program costs $6,600 for the equivalent of a three-semester course of study. However, this cost is less than one-third what an in-state student would pay at Georgia Tech and less than one-seventh what an out-of-state student would pay.

The Georgia Tech program is the first accredited degree to be offered by a provider of MOOCs. Georgia Tech professors will teach the courses and manage student admissions and program accreditation, and students will receive a Georgia Tech diploma when they complete the program. Interestingly, AT&T (*www.att.com*) is covering the costs of the program by contributing $2 million in seed capital in the hope of gaining access to well-educated computer science graduates.

## The Negative

Despite early enthusiasm for MOOCs, the entire concept is being called into question. Consider the experiment to use MOOCs at San Jose State University (SJSU) in California. The professor credited with originating the MOOC, Sebastian Thrun, collaborated with California governor Jerry Brown, who was trying to address problems such as rising tuition costs, poor student performance, and overcrowding in California universities. SJSU offered MOOCs in three subjects—remedial math, college algebra, and elementary statistics—that would count toward credit at the university.

The results were not encouraging. Only 25 percent of the students taking the remedial math course passed. Further, a student enrolled in an algebra classroom course was 52 percent more likely to pass than one taking algebra in a MOOC.

MOOCs have not yet proved that they can effectively teach the thousands of students who enroll in them. In addition, they do not provide revenues for universities. Further, MOOCs can register a mixture of high school students, retirees, faculty, enrolled students, and working professionals. Designing a course that adequately meets the needs of such a diverse student population is difficult. Finally, although initial registrations for a MOOC might exceed 100,000 students, completion rates in any one MOOC tend to be less than 10 percent.

*Sources*: Compiled from J. Haber, "Solutions to the High 'Freaking' Cost of College," *The Huffington Post*, April 15, 2015; M. Jawaharial, "The MOOC Experiment," *The Huffington Post*, March 18, 2015; J. Pope, "What Are MOOCs Good For?" *MIT Technology Review*, December 15, 2014; "A MOOC Sees Its Greatest Impact in the Classroom at MIT," *MIT News*, November 14, 2014; J. Selingo, "Demystifying the MOOC," *The New York Times*, October 29, 2014; M. Chafkin, "Uphill Climb," *Fast Company*, December 2013/January 2014; "Data Mining Exposes Embarrassing Problems for Massive Open Online Courses," *MIT Technology Review*, December 18, 2013; E. Booker, "Will MOOCs Matter?" *InformationWeek*, October, 2013; "Online Learning at Stanford Goes Open Source with OpenEdX," *KurzweilAI.net*, June 13, 2013; "Stanford Software Engineering MOOC Aims at Future Startup CEOs," *KurzweilAI.net*, June 6, 2013; www.udacity.com, www.mit.edu, www.stanford.edu, accessed March 4, 2015.

### Questions

1. Discuss possible quality control issues with MOOCs. For each issue that you list, describe how you would solve the problem.
2. What are some specific examples of the impact that MOOCs could have on traditional higher education? Explain your answer.
3. Would you be willing to enroll in a MOOC as a full-time student at your university? Why or why not?
4. Would you be willing to enroll in a MOOC after you graduate? Why or why not?

## Virtual Universities

**Virtual universities** are online universities in which students take classes via the Internet either at home or in an off-site location. A large number of existing universities offer online education of some form. Some universities, such as the University of Phoenix (*www.phoenix.edu*), California Virtual Campus (*www.cvc.edu*), and the University of Maryland (*www.umuc.edu*), offer thousands of courses and dozens of degrees to students worldwide, all of them online. Other universities offer limited online courses and degrees, but they employ innovative teaching methods and multimedia support in the traditional classroom.

# before you go on... 

1. Describe the differences between e-learning and distance learning.
2. What are virtual universities? Would you be willing to attend a virtual university? Why or why not?

### For the Accounting Major

Accounting personnel use corporate intranets and portals to consolidate transaction data from legacy systems to provide an overall view of internal projects. This view contains the current costs charged to each project, the number of hours spent on each project by individual employees, and an analysis of how actual costs compare with projected costs. Finally, accounting personnel use Internet access to government and professional Web sites to stay informed on legal and other changes affecting their profession.

### For the Finance Major

Corporate intranets and portals can provide a model to evaluate the risks of a project or an investment. Financial analysts use two types of data in the model: historical transaction data from corporate databases via the intranet and industry data obtained via the Internet. In addition, financial services firms can use the Web for marketing and to provide services.

### For the Marketing Major

Marketing managers use corporate intranets and portals to coordinate the activities of the sales force. Sales personnel access corporate portals via the intranet to discover updates on pricing, promotion, rebates, customer information, and information about competitors. Sales staff can also download and customize presentations for their customers. The Internet, particularly the Web, opens a completely new marketing channel for many industries. Just how advertising, purchasing, and information dispensation should occur appears to vary from industry to industry, product to product, and service to service.

### For the Production/Operations Management Major

Companies are using intranets and portals to speed product development by providing the development team with three-dimensional models and animation. All team members can access the models for faster exploration of ideas and enhanced feedback. Corporate portals, accessed via intranets, enable managers to carefully supervise their inventories as well as real-time production on assembly lines. Extranets are also proving valuable as communication formats for joint research and design efforts among companies. The Internet is also a great source of cutting-edge information for POM managers.

### For the Human Resources Management Major

Human resources personnel use portals and intranets to publish corporate policy manuals, job postings, company telephone directories, and training classes. Many companies deliver online training obtained from the Internet to employees through their intranets. Human resources departments use intranets to offer employees healthcare, savings, and benefit plans, as well as the opportunity to take competency tests online. The Internet supports worldwide recruiting efforts; it can also be the communications platform for supporting geographically dispersed work teams.

### For the MIS Major

As important as the networking technology infrastructure is, it is invisible to users (unless something goes wrong). The MIS function is responsible for keeping all organizational networks up and running all the time. MIS personnel, therefore, provide all users with an "eye to the world" and the ability to compute, communicate, and collaborate anytime, anywhere. For example, organizations have access to experts at remote locations without having to duplicate that expertise in multiple areas of the firm. Virtual teaming allows experts physically located in different cities to work on projects as though they were in the same office.

# [ Summary ]

**1. Compare and contrast the two major types of networks.**

The two major types of networks are local area networks (LANs) and wide area networks (WANs). LANs encompass a limited geographical area and are usually composed of one communications medium. In contrast, WANs encompass a broad geographical area and are usually composed of multiple communications media.

**2. Describe the wireline communications media and channels.**

*Twisted-pair wire*, the most prevalent form of communications wiring, consists of strands of copper wire twisted in pairs. It is relatively inexpensive to purchase, widely available, and easy to work with. However, it is relatively slow for transmitting data, it is subject to interference from other electrical sources, and it can be easily tapped by unintended receivers.

*Coaxial cable* consists of insulated copper wire. It is much less susceptible to electrical interference than is twisted-pair wire and it can carry much more data. However, coaxial cable is more expensive and more difficult to work with than twisted-pair wire. It is also somewhat inflexible.

*Fiber-optic cables* consist of thousands of very thin filaments of glass fibers that transmit information via light pulses generated by lasers. Fiber-optic cables are significantly smaller and lighter than traditional cable media. They can also transmit far more data, and they provide greater security from interference and tapping. Fiber-optic cable is often used as the backbone for a network, whereas twisted-pair wire and coaxial cable connect the backbone to individual devices on the network.

**3. Describe the most common methods for accessing the Internet.**

Common methods for connecting to the Internet include dial-up, DSL, cable modem, satellite, wireless, and fiber to the home.

**4. Explain the impact that discovery network applications have had on business and everyday life.**

*Discovery* involves browsing and information retrieval, and provides users the ability to view information in databases, download it, and/or process it. Discovery tools include search engines, directories, and portals. Discovery tools enable business users to efficiently find needed information.

**5. Explain the impact that communication network applications have had on business and everyday life.**

Networks provide fast, inexpensive *communications*, via e-mail, call centers, chat rooms, voice communications, and blogs. Communications tools provide business users with a seamless interface among team members, colleagues, business partners, and customers.

*Telecommuting* is the process whereby knowledge workers are able to work anywhere and anytime. Telecommuting provides flexibility for employees, with many benefits and some drawbacks.

**6. Explain the impact that collaboration network applications have had on business and everyday life.**

*Collaboration* refers to mutual efforts by two or more entities (individuals, groups, or companies) who work together to accomplish tasks. Collaboration is enabled by workflow systems. Collaboration tools enable business users to collaborate with colleagues, business partners, and customers.

7. **Explain the impact that educational network applications have had on business and everyday life.**

> *E-learning* refers to learning supported by the Web. Distance learning refers to any learning situation in which teachers and students do not meet face-to-face. E-learning provides tools for business users to enable their lifelong learning.

> *Virtual universities* are online universities in which students take classes via the Internet at home or an off-site location. Virtual universities make it possible for students to obtain degrees while working full time, thus increasing their value to their firms.

## [ Chapter Glossary ]

**affinity portal** A Web site that offers a single point of entry to an entire community of affiliated interests.

**backbone networks** High-speed central networks to which multiple smaller networks (e.g., LANs and smaller WANs) connect.

**bandwidth** The transmission capacity of a network, stated in bits per second.

**broadband** The transmission capacity of a communications medium faster than 4 Mbps.

**broadcast media** (also called **wireless media**) Communications channels that use electromagnetic media (the "airwaves") to transmit data.

**browsers** Software applications through which users primarily access the Web.

**cable media** (also called **wireline media**) Communications channels that use physical wires or cables to transmit data and information.

**chat room** A virtual meeting place where groups of regulars come to "gab" electronically.

**client/server computing** Form of distributed processing in which some machines (servers) perform computing functions for end-user PCs (clients).

**clients** Computers, such as users' personal computers, that use any of the services provided by servers.

**coaxial cable** Insulated copper wire; used to carry high-speed data traffic and television signals.

**collaboration** Mutual efforts by two or more individuals who perform activities in order to accomplish certain tasks.

**commercial (public) portal** A Web site that offers fairly routine content for diverse audiences; offers customization only at the user interface.

**communications channel** Pathway for communicating data from one location to another.

**computer network** A system that connects computers and other devices via communications media so that data and information can be transmitted among them.

**corporate portal** A Web site that provides a single point of access to critical business information located inside and outside of an organization.

**crowdsourcing** A process in which an organization outsources a task to an undefined, generally large group of people in the form of an open call.

**digital signals** A discrete pulse, either on or off, that conveys information in a binary form.

**distance learning** (DL) Learning situations in which teachers and students do not meet face-to-face.

**distributed processing** Network architecture that divides processing work between two or more computers, linked together in a network.

**domain name system** (DNS) The system administered by the Internet Corporation for Assigned Names (ICANN) that assigns names to each site on the Internet.

**domain names** The name assigned to an Internet site, consisting of multiple parts, separated by dots, which are translated from right to left.

**e-learning** Learning supported by the Web; can be done inside traditional classrooms or in virtual classrooms.

**enterprise network** An organization's network composed of interconnected multiple LANs and WANs.

**Ethernet** A common local area network protocol.

**extranet** A network that connects parts of the intranets of different organizations.

**fiber-optic cable** A communications medium consisting of thousands of very thin filaments of glass fibers, surrounded by cladding, that transmit information via light pulses generated by lasers.

**file server** (also called **network server**) A computer that contains various software and data files for a local area network and contains the network operating system.

**hyperlink** A connection from a hypertext file or document to another location or file, typically activated by clicking on a highlighted word or image on the screen, or by touching the screen.

**hypertext** Text displayed on a computer display with references, called hyperlinks, to other text that the reader can immediately access.

**Hypertext Transport Protocol** (HTTP) The communications standard used to transfer pages across the WWW portion of the Internet; defines how messages are formulated and transmitted.

**industrywide portal** A Web-based gateway to information and knowledge for an entire industry.

**Internet (the Net)** A massive global WAN that connects approximately 1 million organizational computer networks in more than 200 countries on all continents.

**Internet backbone** The primary network connections and telecommunications lines that link the computers and organizational nodes of the Internet.

**Internet Protocol (IP)** A set of rules responsible for disassembling, delivering, and reassembling packets over the Internet.

**Internet Protocol (IP) address** An assigned address that uniquely identifies a computer on the Internet.

**Internet service provider (ISP)** A company that provides Internet connections for a fee.

**Internet telephony (Voice-over-Internet Protocol or VoIP)** The use of the Internet as the transmission medium for telephone calls.

**Internet2** A new, faster telecommunications network that deploys advanced network applications such as remote medical diagnosis, digital libraries, distance education, online simulation, and virtual laboratories.

**intranet** A private network that uses Internet software and TCP/IP protocols.

**local area network (LAN)** A network that connects communications devices in a limited geographic region, such as a building, so that every user device on the network can communicate with every other device.

**metasearch engine** A computer program that searches several engines at once and integrates the findings of the various search engines to answer queries posted by users.

**modem** Device that converts signals from analog to digital and vice versa.

**network access points (NAPs)** Computers that act as exchange points for Internet traffic and determine how traffic is routed.

**network server** See file server.

**packet switching** The transmission technology that divides blocks of text into packets.

**peer-to-peer (P2P) processing** A type of client/server distributed processing that allows two or more computers to pool their resources, making each computer both a client and a server.

**portal** A Web-based personalized gateway to information and knowledge that provides information from disparate information systems and the Internet, using advanced search and indexing techniques.

**protocol** The set of rules and procedures governing transmission across a network.

**router** A communications processor that routes messages from a LAN to the Internet, across several connected LANs, or across a wide area network such as the Internet.

**search engine** A computer program that searches for specific information by keywords and reports the results.

**servers** Computers that provide access to various network services, such as printing, data, and communications.

**telecommuting** A work arrangement whereby employees work at home, at the customer's premises, in special workplaces, or while traveling, usually using a computer linked to their place of employment.

**teleconferencing** The use of electronic communication that allows two or more people at different locations to have a simultaneous conference.

**Transmission Control Protocol/Internet Protocol (TCP/IP)** A file transfer protocol that can send large files of information across sometimes unreliable networks with assurance that the data will arrive uncorrupted.

**twisted-pair wire** A communications medium consisting of strands of copper wire twisted together in pairs.

**unified communications** Common hardware and software platform that simplifies and integrates all forms of communications—voice, e-mail, instant messaging, location, and video-conferencing—across an organization.

**uniform resource locator (URL)** The set of letters that identifies the address of a specific resource on the Web.

**videoconference** A virtual meeting in which participants in one location can see and hear participants at other locations and can share data and graphics by electronic means.

**virtual collaboration** The use of digital technologies that enable organizations or individuals to collaboratively plan, design, develop, manage, and research products, services, and innovative information systems and electronic commerce applications.

**virtual group (team)** A workgroup whose members are in different locations and who meet electronically.

**virtual universities** Online universities in which students take classes via the Internet at home or at an off-site location.

**Voice-over-Internet Protocol (VoIP)** See **Internet telephony**.

**Web site** Collectively, all of the Web pages of a particular company or individual.

**wide area network (WAN)** A network, generally provided by common carriers, that covers a wide geographical area.

**wireless media** See **broadcast media**.

**wireline media** See **cable media**.

**workflow** The movement of information as it flows through the sequence of steps that make up an organization's work procedures.

**workgroup** Two or more individuals who act together to perform some task, on either a permanent or on a temporary basis.

**World Wide Web** (the Web, WWW, or W3) A system of universally accepted standards for storing, retrieving, formatting, and displaying information via a client/server architecture; it uses the transport functions of the Internet.

# [ Discussion Questions ]

1. What are the implications of having fiber-optic cable to everyone's home?

2. What are the implications of BitTorrent for the music industry? For the motion picture industry?

3. Discuss the pros and cons of P2P networks.

4. Should the Internet be regulated? If so, by whom?

5. Discuss the pros and cons of delivering this book over the Internet.

6. Explain how the Internet works. Assume you are talking with someone who has no knowledge of information technology (in other words, keep it very simple).

7. How are the network applications of communication and collaboration related? Do communication tools also support collaboration? Give examples.

8. Search online for the article from *The Atlantic*: "Is Google Making Us Stupid?" *Is* Google making us stupid? Support your answer.

9. Refer to the chapter closing case:
   a. How do you feel about the net neutrality issue?
   b. Do you believe heavier bandwidth users should pay for more bandwidth?
   c. Do you believe wireless carriers should operate under different rules than wireline carriers?
   d. Evaluate your own bandwidth usage. (For example: Do you upload and download large files, such as movies?) If network neutrality were to be eliminated, what would the impact be for you?

10. Should businesses monitor network usage? Do you see a problem with employees using company-purchased bandwidth for personal use? Please explain your answer.

# [ Problem-Solving Activities ]

1. Calculate how much bandwidth you consume when using the Internet every day. How many e-mails do you send daily and what is the size of each? (Your e-mail program may have e-mail file size information.) How many music and video clips do you download (or upload) daily and what is the size of each? If you view YouTube often, surf the Web to find out the size of a typical YouTube file. Add up the number of e-mail, audio, and video files you transmit or receive on a typical day. When you have calculated your daily Internet usage, determine if you are a "normal" Internet user or a "power" Internet user. What impact does network neutrality have on you as a "normal" user? As a "power" user?

2. Access several P2P applications, such as SETI@home. Describe the purpose of each application, and indicate which ones you would like to join.

3. Access *http://ipv6.com* and *www.ipv6news.info* and learn about more advantages of IPv6.

4. Access *www.icann.org* and learn more about this important organization.

5. Set up your own Web site using your name for the domain name (e.g., KellyRainer).
   a. Explain the process for registering a domain.
   b. Which top-level domain will you use and why?

6. Access *www.icann.org* and obtain the name of an agency or company that can register a domain for the TLD that you selected. What is the name of that agency or company?

7. Access the Web site for that agency or company (in question 6) to learn the process that you must use. How much will it initially cost to register your domain name? How much will it cost to maintain that name in the future?

8. You plan to take a two-week vacation in Australia this year. Using the Internet, find information that will help you plan the trip. Such information includes, *but is not limited to*, the following:
   a. Geographical location and weather conditions at the time of your trip
   b. Major tourist attractions and recreational facilities
   c. Travel arrangements (airlines, approximate fares)
   d. Car rental; local tours
   e. Alternatives for accommodation (within a moderate budget) and food
   f. Estimated cost of the vacation (travel, lodging, food, recreation, shopping, etc.)
   g. Country regulations regarding the entrance of your dog
   h. Shopping
   i. Passport information (either to obtain one or to renew one)
   j. Information on the country's language and culture
   k. What else do you think you should research before going to Australia?

9. From your own experience or from the vendor's information, list the major capabilities of Lotus Notes/Domino. Do the same for Microsoft Exchange. Compare and contrast the products. Explain how the products can be used to support knowledge workers and managers.

10. Visit Web sites of companies that manufacture telepresence products for the Internet. Prepare a report. Differentiate between telepresence products and videoconferencing products.

11. Access Google (or YouTube) videos and search for "Cisco Magic." This video shows Cisco's telepresence system. Compare and contrast it with current telepresence systems.

12. Access the Web site of your university. Does the Web site provide high-quality information (right amount, clear, accurate, etc.)? Do you think a high-school student who is thinking of attending your university would feel the same way?

13. Compare and contrast Google Sites (*www.google.com/sites*) and Microsoft Office Live (*www.liveoffice.com*). Which site would you use to create your own Web site? Explain your choice.

14. Access the Web site of the Recording Industry Association of America (*www.riaa.com*). Discuss what you find there regarding copyright infringement (i.e., downloading music files). How do you feel about the RIAA's efforts to stop music downloads? Debate this issue from your point of view and from the RIAA's point of view.

15. Research the companies involved in Internet telephony (Voice-over IP). Compare their offerings as to price, necessary technologies, ease of installation, and so on. Which company is the most attractive to you? Which company might be the most attractive for a large company?

16. Access various search engines other than Google. Search for the same terms on several of the alternative search engines and on Google. Compare the results on breadth (number of results found) and precision (results are what you were looking for).

17. Second Life (*www.secondlife.com*) is a three-dimensional, online world built and owned by its residents. Residents of Second Life are avatars who have been created by real people. Access Second Life, learn about it, and create your own avatar to explore this world. Learn about the thousands of people who are making "real-world" money from operations in Second Life.

18. Access Microsoft's Bing translator (*http://www.microsoft-translator.com*) or Google (*www.google.com/language_tools*) translation pages. Type in a paragraph in English and select, for example, English-to-French. When you see the translated paragraph in French, copy it into the text box, and select French-to-English. Is the paragraph that you first entered the same as the one you are looking at now? Why or why not? Support your answer.

# [ Closing Case **Network Neutrality Wars** ]

## The Problem

The explosive growth of streaming video and mobile technologies is creating bandwidth problems over the Internet. The Internet was designed to transmit content such as e-mails and Web pages. However, media items being transmitted across the Internet today, such as high-definition movies, are vastly larger in size. To compound this problem, there are (in early 2015) over 180 million smartphone users in the United States, many of whom use the Internet to stream video content to their phones.

The Internet bandwidth issue is as much about economics as it is about technology. Currently, consumers can send 1-kilobyte e-mails or watch the latest 30-gigabyte movie on their large-screen televisions for the same monthly broadband fee. Unlike the system used for power and water bills where higher usage results in higher fees, monthly broadband fees are not tied to consumer usage.

A study from Juniper Networks (*www.juniper.net*) highlights this "revenue-per-bit" problem. The report predicts that Internet revenue for carriers such as AT&T (*www.att.com*) and Comcast (*www.comcast.com*) will grow by 5 percent per year through 2020. At the same time, Internet traffic will increase by 27 percent annually, meaning that carriers will have to increase their bandwidth investment by 20 percent per year just to keep up with demand. Under this model, the carriers'

business models will face pressures, because their total necessary investment will exceed revenue growth.

Few industry analysts expect carriers to stop investing in new capacity. Nevertheless, analysts agree that a financial crunch is coming. As Internet traffic soars, analysts expect revenue per megabit to decrease. These figures translate into a far lower return on investment (ROI). Although carriers can find ways to increase their capacity, it will be difficult for them to reap any revenue benefits from doing so.

The heart of the problem is that, even if the technology is equal to the task of transmitting huge amounts of data, no one is sure how to pay for these technologies. One proposed solution is to eliminate network neutrality.

## A Possible Solution

*Network neutrality* is an operating model under which Internet service providers (ISPs) must allow customers equal access to content and applications, regardless of the source or nature of the content. That is, Internet backbone carriers must treat all Web traffic equally, not charging different rates by user, content, site, platform, or application.

Telecommunications and cable companies want to replace network neutrality with an arrangement in which they can charge differentiated prices based on the amount of bandwidth consumed by the content that is being delivered over the Internet. These companies believe that differentiated pricing is the most equitable method by which they can finance the necessary investments in their network infrastructures.

To bolster their argument, ISPs point to the enormous amount of bandwidth required to transmit pirated versions of copyrighted materials over the Internet. In fact, Comcast reported in 2010 that illegal file sharing of copyrighted material was consuming 50 percent of its network capacity. ISPs further contend that net neutrality hinders U.S. international competitiveness by decreasing innovation and discouraging capital investments in new network technologies. Without such investments and innovations, ISPs will be unable to handle the exploding demand for Internet and wireless data transmission.

From the opposite perspective, proponents of network neutrality are petitioning Congress to regulate the industry to prevent network providers from adopting strategies similar to Comcast. They argue that the risk of censorship increases when network providers can selectively block or slow access to certain content, such as access to competing low-cost services such as Skype and Vonage. They also assert that a neutral Internet encourages innovation. Finally, they contend that the neutral Internet has helped to create many new businesses.

For example, one venture capital firm said that it would avoid funding startups in the video and media arenas. The firm further stated it would not invest in payment systems or mobile wallets, which require rapid transaction times to be successful.

In another example, the U.S. Federal Trade Commission (FTC) is suing AT&T after the carrier allegedly "misled" millions of its smartphone customers regarding its unlimited data plans. The FTC claimed that AT&T charged its customers for "unlimited data," but still reduced browsing speeds for as many as 3.5 million users.

Most analysts expect that users who consume the most data eventually will have to pay more, most likely in the form of tiered pricing plans. Americans, however, have never had to contend with limits on the amount of data they upload and download. So, there may be pushback from users.

In 2008, Comcast openly challenged net neutrality when it slowed down the transmission of BitTorrent (*www.bittorrent.com*) files, a form of peer-to-peer transmission that is frequently used for piracy and illegal sharing of copyrighted materials. The Federal Communications Commission (FCC) responded by ordering Comcast to restore its previous service. Comcast then filed a lawsuit challenging the FCC's authority to enforce network neutrality. In April 2010, the Washington D.C. Circuit Court of Appeals ruled in favor of Comcast, declaring that the FCC did not have the authority to regulate how an ISP manages its network. By endorsing differentiated pricing, the court struck a major blow against network neutrality.

Despite this ruling, on December 21, 2010, the FCC approved network neutrality rules that prohibited wireline-based broadband providers —but not mobile broadband providers—from engaging in "unreasonable discrimination"

against Web traffic. These rules are known as the Open Internet Order.

## The Results

In 2012, Verizon initiated a legal action against the Open Internet Order, claiming the FCC had overstepped its authority and arguing that its network neutrality rules are unconstitutional. Verizon may have a valid point. The FCC can regulate the physical infrastructure over which packets travel on the network. It is less clear, however, whether it can also regulate the actual service or content those packets deliver.

In January 2014 Verizon won a partial victory. The U.S. Court of Appeals for the Washington, D.C. Circuit rejected Verizon's claim that the FCC lacks jurisdiction over broadband providers. However, it also ruled that the FCC cannot regulate broadband service providers the same way it regulates telephone companies. This ruling suggests that network neutrality cannot be enforced without further legislative intervention.

On February 23, 2014, Netflix agreed to a deal with Comcast to ensure that its movies and TV shows stream more quickly. This agreement demonstrates a shift in the balance of power in favor of ISPs. It also suggests that prices for consumers will increase.

On May 15, 2014, the FCC decided to consider two options regarding the network neutrality issue: (1) permit fast and slow broadband lanes, which would compromise network neutrality; or (2) reclassify broadband as a telecommunications service rather than an information service, which would preserve network neutrality. The FCC accepted a first round of public comments through July 15, 2014, and a second round through September 15, 2014.

On November 10, 2014, President Obama asked the FCC "to implement the strongest possible rules to protect net neutrality," and to extend those rules to cover mobile broadband. The president's plan would prevent ISPs from blocking legal content; prevent ISPs from slowing data flows; and ban paid prioritization of Internet traffic. (Paid prioritization means that users will have to pay more for faster service.)

In early 2015, FCC Chairman Tom Wheeler indicated that the agency will classify ISPs as telecommunications services under the Communications Act of 1934. This vote will provide the FCC with the legal authority to prevent ISPs from lowering transmission speeds or prioritizing speeds for certain content providers in exchange for payment. In essence, the vote will favor network neutrality.

*Sources*: S. Lohr, "Utility-Type Oversight for Web Is FCC Aim," *The New York Times*, February 3, 2015; J. Sanders, "The FCC's Possible Reclassification of ISPs Signals Hope for Net Neutrality," *TechRepublic*, January 20, 2015; T. Claburn, "Net Neutrality: Let There Be Laws," *InformationWeek*, November 12, 2014; Z. Whittaker, "FTC Says AT&T 'Misled Millions', Charging for Unlimited Data but Throttling Speeds," *ZDNet*, October 28, 2014; T. Claburn, "Net Neutrality: 5 Things to Know," *InformationWeek*, September 17, 2014; "Internet: Net Neutrality Fight Heats Back Up," *The Week*, August 1, 2014; "Searching for Fairness on the Internet," *The New York Times*, May 15, 2014; Carr, D. "Warnings Along F.C.C.'s Fast Lane," *The New York Times*, May 11, 2014; D. Talbot, "Talk of an Internet Fast Lane Is Hurting

Some Entrepreneurs," *MIT Technology Review*, May 7, 2014; R. Yu, "Netflix Deal Has Its Catches," *USA Today*, February, 24, 2014; D. Talbot, "Is Netflix Slowing Down? Good Luck Finding Out Why," *MIT Technology Review*, February 21, 2014; E. Malykhina, "FCC: We're Not Done with Net Neutrality," *InformationWeek*, February 20, 2014; J. Feldman, "Why Carriers Won't Win War on Netflix," *Information-Week*, February 6, 2014; B. Butler, "Verizon Denies Throttling Amazon's Cloud, Netflix Services," *Network World*, February 5, 2014; D. Talbot, "Around the World, Net Neutrality Is Not a Reality," *MIT Technology Review*, January 20, 2014; J. Feldman, "Net Neutrality: Regulation Makes Evil Empire Giggle," *InformationWeek*, January 17, 2014; J. Feldman, "Net Neutrality Court Ruling Won't Ruin the Internet," *InformationWeek*, January 15, 2014; G. Gross, "Appeals Court Strikes Down FCC Net Neutrality Rule," *Network World*, January 14, 2014; T. Claburn, "FCC Net Neutrality Rules Rejected," *InformationWeek*, January 14, 2014; S. Higginbotham, "Analyst: Verizon's Network Neutrality Challenge May Have to Wait Until Fall," *GigaOM*, March 25, 2013; J. Brodkin, "Time Warner, Net Neutrality Foes Cry Foul over Netflix Super HD Demands," *Ars Technica*, January 17, 2013; M. Reardon, "Verizon to FCC: Free Speech Trumps Net Neutrality Rules," *CNET News*, July 3, 2012; www.fcc.gov, accessed March 17, 2015.

## Questions

1. Are the ISPs correct in claiming that network neutrality will limit their development of new technologies? Support your answer.

2. Are the content providers (e.g., Netflix) correct in claiming that eliminating network neutrality will encourage censorship by the ISPs? Support your answer.

3. Are the content providers correct in claiming that eliminating network neutrality will result in consumers paying higher prices for the content they watch over the Internet? Support your answer.

4. Why is the debate over network neutrality so important to you? Support your answer.

**7**

# E-Business and E-Commerce

| [ LEARNING OBJECTIVES ] | [ CHAPTER OUTLINE ] | [ WEB RESOURCES ] |
|---|---|---|
| 1. Describe the six common types of electronic commerce. | 7.1 Overview of E-Business and E-Commerce | • Student PowerPoints for note taking |
| 2. Describe the various online services of business-to-consumer (B2C) commerce, providing specific examples of each. | 7.2 Business-to-Consumer (B2C) Electronic Commerce | **WileyPLUS Learning Space**<br>• E-book<br>• Author video lecture for each chapter section |
| 3. Describe the three business models for business-to-business electronic commerce. | 7.3 Business-to-Business (B2B) Electronic Commerce | • Practice quizzes<br>• Flash Cards for vocabulary review |
| 4. Identify the ethical and legal issues related to electronic commerce, providing examples. | 7.4 Ethical and Legal Issues in E-Business | • Additional "IT's About Business" cases<br>• Video interviews with managers<br>• Lab Manuals for Microsoft Office 2010 and 2013 |

## What's In IT For Me?

### This Chapter Will Help Prepare You To...

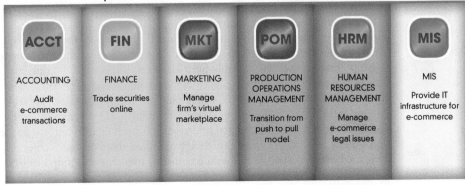

| ACCT | FIN | MKT | POM | HRM | MIS |
|---|---|---|---|---|---|
| ACCOUNTING | FINANCE | MARKETING | PRODUCTION OPERATIONS MANAGEMENT | HUMAN RESOURCES MANAGEMENT | MIS |
| Audit e-commerce transactions | Trade securities online | Manage firm's virtual marketplace | Transition from push to pull model | Manage e-commerce legal issues | Provide IT infrastructure for e-commerce |

# [ The Omni-Channel Strategy to Compete with Amazon ]

## The Business Problem

In recent years, the traditional bricks-and-mortar strategy for large retailers, with its accompanying high overhead costs, has become a liability rather than an asset. Amazon (*www.amazon.com*), which has no stores, has achieved major market share—and grown into the world's largest Internet retailer—through a combination of lower prices and huge selection. The third battleground is location, and retailers are not conceding that field to Amazon.

Regarding location, Amazon poses additional problems to traditional retailers. For same-day delivery, Amazon customer pay an extra $8.99 or more at checkout. For $99 per year, the company offers its Prime service, which includes free two-day shipping for most items as well as same-day service starting at $3.99.

Going further, Amazon's same-day delivery system works only if (a) Amazon has the item in stock at a nearby warehouse or (b) a third-party seller can immediately ship the order. To improve its delivery times, Amazon is adding robots, storage space, and refrigerators at more than 90 of its warehouses, which function as the company's fulfillment centers.

Amazon routes deliveries via carriers such as FedEx and UPS, and now on Sundays using the U.S. Postal Service. To reach more U.S. customers more quickly, the company has spent about $14 billion since 2011 on new warehouses. It is adding some 5,000 full-time warehouse jobs.

As of early 2015, Amazon could reach about 15 percent of the U.S. population with same-day delivery. The company is building another five warehouses, and it hopes to eventually reach 50 percent of Americans if it can secure storage space near the top 20 metropolitan areas.

## The Solution

To compete with Amazon, some of the world's largest retailers are adopting an omni-channel strategy. In this strategy, customers seamlessly combine their experience of online shopping on any device with in-store shopping. This strategy is becoming increasingly important as Amazon builds its own fulfillment centers closer to customers.

To compete more effectively online against Amazon, major retailers are turning their stores into mini-distribution hubs. Instead of fulfilling Web orders from warehouses located hundreds of miles from shoppers' homes, retailers such as Walmart (*www.walmart.com*), Best Buy (*www.bestbuy.com*), Target (*www.target.com*), Nordstrom (*www.nordstrom.com*), Macy's (*www.macys.com*), Lowe's (*www.lowes.com*), and Gap (*www.gap.com*) are routing orders to nearby stores. Store employees pick products from shelves, pack them into boxes, and drop them into FedEx and UPS trucks that take the items to customers.

This trend, known as *ship-from-store*, saves money by utilizing shorter delivery routes. More importantly, it speeds up deliveries, avoids expensive markdowns on unsold products, and recoups sales that have been lost to Amazon. Let's take a closer look at Gap's omni-channel strategy.

As the largest specialty apparel chain in the United States, Gap (*www.gap.com*) must keep its shelves well stocked at its approximately 3,000 worldwide stores. This process requires Gap to maintain an extensive in-store inventory. At the same time, Gap needs sufficient inventory in its e-commerce fulfillment channel to meet the growing customer demand. One element of Gap's mission is to make shopping seamless to its customers through its digital strategy.

To integrate its in-store and e-commerce inventories, Gap developed an algorithm, known as Ship From Store, which it implemented in its Web site e-commerce system. Ship From Store allows online shoppers to purchase Gap products directly from the store inventory. The system is integrated seamlessly into Gap's e-commerce system, so that customers are not aware of it.

Ship From Store is not available from all stores, a factor that is critical to making the new feature profitable. The challenge was that the e-commerce system would bog down if it had to check the inventory of every store, which changes hour by hour. So, knowing which stores to include in the system is "the secret sauce," according to Gap's senior vice president of information technology. Claiming that the information is proprietary, Gap will not reveal how many stores the system taps, or what percentage of online shoppers receive items from warehouses compared with the situation before the company implemented Ship From Store.

There is another reason why not all Gap locations are included: The staff in participating stores must be trained and equipped to receive an order and ship the goods, just as they would in a fulfillment and distribution center. When the Web site informs a customer that a purchase will be delivered the next day, then it is up to Gap staffers to make that happen.

The blurring lines between the physical channel (stores) and the online channel help explain why Gap's IT and product management teams are located next to each other in the retailer's headquarters. They also explain why both groups are located within the company's growth, innovation, and digital business unit.

Most customers engage in preshopping, meaning they go to the company's Web site and browse the merchandise. For customers who want to see an item, feel its fabric, or try it on, Gap added a Find In Store function, which advises shoppers where to find the nearest store that stocks that item. Find In Store led to Reserve In Store, where a shopper can place a hold on an item for 24 hours.

The progression demonstrates that Ship From Store was not a single project that the IT group launched into production and then moved on to the next project. With the added functionalities, IT must constantly review how the system as a whole is functioning and make any necessary revisions. The algorithm is not static.

## Results

Let's take a closer look at three retailers: Walmart, Best Buy, and Gap. In early 2015, Walmart was shipping online orders from 35 stores. This ship-from-store strategy has exceeded expectations, and Walmart is planning to expand the service to hundreds of its stores.

Nearly 70 percent of the U.S. population live within five miles of a Walmart, so the company is using store locations as nodes in a broader distribution network that includes storage warehouses and specific fulfillment centers for online orders. In early 2015, roughly 10 percent of the items ordered on Walmart.com were shipped from stores, and the majority of those packages were delivered within two days or less. Walmart charges a $10 fee for same-day delivery service. In some cases, the company uses third-party carriers to ship items from its stores. In addition, Walmart employees sometimes deliver products by car.

Best Buy, the largest U.S. consumer electronics retailer, was labeled a "Big Box Zombie" on the cover of *Bloomberg BusinessWeek* in October 2012. However, the company is experiencing a rebound. A crucial part of this turnaround is the ship-from-store process, which Best Buy has deployed in about 50 stores.

Best Buy receives about 1 billion online visits per year. In 2–4 percent of those cases, shoppers cannot buy products because the products are out of stock in the company's e-commerce warehouses. However, in 80 percent of those cases, Best Buy has the products in one of its physical stores.

Ship From Store was first implemented at Gap stores, and the retailer has added this service to the e-commerce systems of two Gap-owned chains, Banana Republic and Athleta. Not coincidentally, Gap's annual revenue increased by $500 million in 2013.

*Sources:* Compiled from "The Omni-Channel Opportunity for Retailers: What's the Story?" *The Guardian*, January 14, 2015; J. Popovec, "Nordstrom, Walgreens Praised for Omni-Channel Strategies," *National Real Estate Investor*, October 9, 2014; D. Newman, "The Omni-Channel Experience: Marketing Meets Ubiquity," *Forbes*, July 22, 2014; J. Green, "Why and How Brands Must Go Omni-Channel in 2014, *Marketing Land*, January 27, 2014; R. Borison, "Gap Expands Omnichannel Inventory Program for Added Convenience," *Mobile Commerce Daily*, November 22, 2013; "Gap and Banana Republic Make Shopping Easier for Customers This Holiday Season," *MarketWatch*, November 20, 2013; "Get Online Orders in a Matter of Hours," *Bloomberg BusinessWeek*, November 14, 2013; A. Barr, "'Ship From Store' Strategy Saves Money Through Shorter Delivery Routes," *USA Today*, October 6, 2013; T. Stapleton, "Retail Innovation Shout Out: Gap Blurs Channel Lines with 'Ship From Store' Service," *Kalypso Viewpoints*, September 17, 2013; C. Babcock, "Gap Connects Store and Web," *InformationWeek*, September 9, 2013; C. Babcock, "How Gap Connects Store and Online Channels," *InformationWeek*, September 5, 2013; A. Blair, "Gap Pilots Reserve-In-Store Capability for Online Shoppers," *Retail Information System News*, June 3, 2013; A. Barr, "E-Tailers Embrace Same-Day Delivery, but U.S. Shoppers Shrug: Survey," *Reuters*, March 5, 2013; www.gap.com, accessed January 29, 2015.

### Questions

1. Why is an "omni-channel" strategy such an important component of retailers' missions today?

2. Describe the problems retailers face in implementing a ship-from-store strategy.

3. Identify some strategies that Amazon could employ to counter the ship-from-store strategy from traditional bricks-and-mortar retailers.

# Introduction

One of the most profound changes in the modern world of business is the emergence of electronic commerce. Electronic commerce (EC or e-commerce) describes the process of buying, selling, transferring, or exchanging products, services, or information via computer networks, including the Internet. E-commerce is transforming all of the business functional areas we discussed in Chapter 1 as well as their fundamental tasks, from advertising to paying bills. Its impact is so pervasive that it is affecting almost every modern organization. Regardless of where you land a job, your organization likely will be practicing electronic commerce.

Electronic commerce influences organizations in many significant ways. First, it increases an organization's *reach*, defined as the number of potential customers to whom the company can market its products. In fact, e-commerce provides unparalleled opportunities for companies to expand worldwide at a small cost, to increase market share, and to reduce costs. By utilizing electronic commerce, many small businesses can now operate and compete in market spaces that formerly were dominated by larger companies.

Another major impact of electronic commerce has been to remove many of the barriers that previously impeded entrepreneurs seeking to start their own businesses. E-commerce offers amazing opportunities for you to open your own business by developing an e-commerce Web site.

Electronic commerce is also fundamentally transforming the nature of competition through the development of new online companies, new business models, and the diversity of EC-related products and services. Recall your study of competitive strategies in Chapter 2, particularly the impact of the Internet on Porter's five forces. You learned that the Internet can both endanger and enhance a company's position in a given industry. In fact, this chapter's opening case illustrates how Amazon's electronic commerce operations have created a lasting competitive advantage for the company.

It is important for you to have a working knowledge of electronic commerce because your organization almost certainly will be employing e-commerce applications that will affect its strategy and business model. This knowledge will make you more valuable to your organization, and it will enable you to quickly contribute to the e-commerce applications employed in your functional area. As you read What's in IT for Me? at the end of the chapter, envision yourself performing the activities discussed in your functional area.

Going further, you may decide to become an entrepreneur and start your own business, as illustrated in IT's About Business 7.1. It is interesting that the two founders of FlightCar were 17 years old. If you start your own business, it is even more essential for you to understand electronic commerce, because e-commerce, with its broad reach, will probably be critical for your business to survive and thrive.

In this chapter, you will discover the major applications of e-business, and you will be able to identify the services necessary for its support. You will then study the major types of electronic commerce: business-to-consumer (B2C), business-to-business (B2B), consumer-to-consumer (C2C), business-to employee (B2E), and government-to-citizen (G2C). You conclude by examining several legal and ethical issues that have arisen as a result of the rapid growth of e-commerce.

## IT's [about business]

### 7.1 FlightCar POM

Airport parking in most major cities represents a major challenge. Parking places can be difficult to locate and expensive as well. In addition, your car just sits there until you return. Now, FlightCar (*www.flightcar.com*) wants to transform your car into a revenue generator while you are away.

FlightCar lets its customers park their cars for free in the FlightCar parking lot at the airport. Then, FlightCar rents out the cars while its customers are traveling. Airports are fighting the startup, but FlightCar is moving ahead.

FlightCar insures all rentals up to $1 million, and it prescreens all renters to root out poor drivers. If you put your car up for rent, then you park for free at the FlightCar location. After the team checks you in on an iPad, they drive you to the airport and drop you off. If your car is rented while you are gone, they pay you 20 cents per mile.

When you return, you either call 1-866-FLIGHTCAR for a pickup or use FlightCar's Web app. The company then sends a town car to pick you up from curbside. If you do not want to wait for a town car, then you can take a cab to the FlightCar lot, and the company will reimburse you for your cab fare. When you arrive at FlightCar's parking lot, your car will have been washed and vacuumed. You later receive a check in the mail if your car was rented.

Thus far FlightCar has not experienced any major accidents. If a car is involved in an accident, then FlightCar will contact the owner's insurance provider. If the owner approves, then the company will attempt to have the car fixed by the time the owner returns. If the car is not repaired by that time, then FlightCar provides loaner cars.

As of early 2015, FlightCar had facilitated about 6,000 rentals to 13,000 customers in Boston, Los Angeles, and San Francisco. One user has used the company about 10 times over the course of one year to rent out his 2011 Hyundai Accent. His car was rented half of those times, and he has made about $100 on those rentals. He has also saved more than that amount in airport parking fees. He identifies FlightCar's value as a combination of convenience and customer service.

FlightCar does have problems. The city of San Francisco, for example, refuses to acknowledge a difference between peer-to-peer car sharing and car rentals. As a result, it is suing FlightCar over lost fees and taxes. (The city collects fees and taxes from car rental companies.) Another problem is the competition. Relay-Rides (*https://relayrides.com*) and Hubber (*www.drivehubber.com*) provide similar services at airports.

Despite these problems, by early 2015, FlightCar appeared to be experiencing success. In fact, the company raised $20 million for expansion to different airports. Furthermore, by November 2014, FlightCar was operating in the San Francisco, Los Angeles, Boston, and Seattle airports. The company has planned to expand its service to three new airports: Dallas Love Field, Philadelphia International, and Washington Dulles.

*Sources:* Compiled from "FlightCar: Airbnb for Cars," *Associated Press*, February 22, 2015; H. Baskas, "FlightCar Launches Service at Three More Airports," *CNBC*, November 18, 2014; "FlightCar Raises $20M in Total Funding to Focus on Expansion," *PRWeb*, September 10, 2014; R. Lawler, "Peer-to-Peer Car Rental Startup FlightCar Lands Some Senior Execs," *TechCrunch*, March 19, 2014; C. Forrest, "How Two 17-Year-Olds Disrupted the Transportation Industry, Got Sued, Got Funded," *TechRepublic*, February 21, 2014; J. Leo, "For Inexpensive Car Rental, Consider FllightCar. com," *The Los Angeles Times*, February 16, 2014; "FlightCar Launches New Service for Frequent Business Travelers to Participate in Peer-to-Peer Car Sharing," *PR Web*, February 4, 2014; "Travelport Teams Up with Flight-Car," *Auto Rental News*, December 18, 2013; R. Lawler, "Airport Car Rental Startup FlightCar Launches at LAX, Unveils Mobile Web App," *TechCrunch*, November 13, 2013; C. Deamicis, "Let the Fight to the Car Sharing Death Begin: FlightCar Moves into Hubber's Territory," *Pando Daily*, November 13, 2013; J. Melvin, "Flightcar: San Francisco Sues Unruly SFO Car Rental Startup from Santa Clara," *San Jose Mercury News*, June 4, 2013; *www. flightcar.com*, *www.drivehubber.com*, *https://relayrides.com*, accessed March 20, 2015.

**Questions**

1. What are possible disadvantages of FlightCar's business model for its customers? Provide specific examples to support your answer.
2. Can FlightCar survive in its marketplace? Why or why not? Support your answer.
3. Would you allow FlightCar to rent your car while you were traveling? Why or why not? Support your answer. Does your answer to this question have any bearing on your answer to Question 2?

---

# Overview of E-Business and E-Commerce    7.1

Any entrepreneur or company that decides to practice **electronic commerce** must develop a strategy to do so effectively. The first step is to determine exactly *why* you want to do business over the Internet using a Web site. There are several reasons for employing Web sites:

- To sell goods and services
- To induce people to visit a physical location
- To reduce operational and transaction costs
- To enhance your reputation

A Web site can accomplish any of these goals. Unless a company (or you) has substantial resources, it is difficult to accomplish all of them at the same time. The appropriate Web site for achieving each goal will be somewhat different. As you set up your Web site, you must consider how the site will generate and retain traffic, as well as a host of other issues. The point here is that when you are studying the various aspects of electronic commerce, you should keep in mind the strategy of the organization or entrepreneur. This will help you determine the type of Web site to use.

This section examines the basics of e-business and e-commerce. First, we define these two concepts. You then become familiar with pure and partial electronic commerce. You then examine the various types of electronic commerce. Next, you focus on e-commerce mechanisms, which are the ways that businesses and people buy and sell over the Internet. You conclude this section by considering the benefits and limitations of e-commerce.

## Definitions and Concepts

Recall that electronic commerce describes the process of buying, selling, transferring, or exchanging products, services, or information via computer networks, including the Internet. **Electronic business** (e-business) is a somewhat broader concept. In addition to the buying and selling of goods and services, **e-business** refers to servicing customers, collaborating with business partners, and performing electronic transactions within an organization.

Electronic commerce can take several forms depending on the degree of digitization involved. The *degree of digitization* is the extent to which the commerce has been transformed from physical to digital. This concept can relate to both the product or service being sold and the delivery agent or intermediary. In other words, the product can be either physical or digital, and the delivery agent can also be either physical or digital.

In traditional commerce, both dimensions are physical. Purely physical organizations are referred to as **brick-and-mortar organizations**. (You may also see the term *bricks-and-mortar*.) In contrast, in *pure EC* all dimensions are digital. Companies engaged only in EC are considered **virtual** (or **pure-play**) **organizations**. All other combinations that include a mix of digital and physical dimensions are considered *partial* EC (but not pure EC). **Clicks-and-mortar organizations** conduct some e-commerce activities, yet their primary business is carried out in the physical world. A common alternative to the term *clicks-and-mortar* is *clicks-and-bricks*. You will encounter both terms. Therefore, clicks- and-mortar organizations are examples of partial EC. E-commerce is now so well established that people generally expect companies to offer this service in some form.

Purchasing a shirt at Walmart Online or a book from Amazon.com is an example of partial EC because the merchandise, although bought and paid for digitally, is physically delivered by FedEx or UPS. In contrast, buying an e-book from Amazon.com or a software product from Buy.com constitutes pure EC because the product itself as well as its delivery, payment, and transfer are entirely digital. To avoid confusion, we use the term *electronic commerce* to denote both pure and partial EC.

## Types of E-Commerce

E-commerce can be conducted between and among various parties. In this section, you will identify the six common types of e-commerce, and you will learn about three of them—C2C, B2E, and e-government—in detail. You then consider B2C and B2B in separate sections because they are very complex. We discuss mobile commerce in detail in Chapter 8.

- *Business-to-consumer electronic commerce (B2C):* In B2C, the sellers are organizations, and the buyers are individuals. You learn about B2C electronic commerce in Section 7.2.

- *Business-to-business electronic commerce (B2B):* In B2B transactions, both the sellers and the buyers are business organizations. B2B comprises the vast majority of EC volume. You will learn more about B2B electronic commerce in Section 7.3. Figure 1.5 also illustrates B2B electronic commerce.

- *Consumer-to-consumer electronic commerce (C2C):* In C2C (also called customer-to-customer), an individual sells products or services to other individuals. The major strategies for conducting C2C on the Internet are auctions and classified ads.

In dozens of countries, the volume of C2C selling and buying on auction sites is exploding. Most auctions are conducted by intermediaries such as eBay (*www.ebay.com*). Consumers can also select general sites such as *www.auctionanything.com*, a company that sells software and services that help individuals and organizations conduct their own auctions. In addition, many individuals are conducting their own auctions.

The major categories of online classified ads are similar to those found in print ads: vehicles, real estate, employment, pets, tickets, and travel. Classified ads are available through most Internet service providers (AOL, MSN, etc.), at some portals (Yahoo!, etc.), and from Internet directories and online newspapers. Many of these sites contain search engines that help shoppers narrow their searches. Craigslist (*www.craigslist.org*) is the largest online classified ad provider.

Internet-based classified ads have one major advantage over traditional types of classified ads: They provide access to an international, rather than a local, audience. This wider audience greatly increases both the supply of goods and services and the number of potential buyers. It is important to note that the value of expanded geographical reach depends greatly on what is being bought or sold. For example, you might buy software from a company located 1,000 miles from you, but you would not buy firewood from someone at such a distance.

- *Business-to-employee (B2E)*: In B2E, an organization uses EC internally to provide information and services to its employees. For example, companies allow employees to manage their benefits and to take training classes electronically. In addition, employees can buy discounted insurance, travel packages, and tickets to events on the corporate intranet. They can also order supplies and materials electronically. Finally, many companies have electronic corporate stores that sell the company's products to its employees, usually at a discount.

- *E-government*: E-government is the use of Internet technology in general and e-commerce in particular to deliver information and public services to citizens (called government-to-citizen or G2C EC) and to business partners and suppliers (called government-to-business or G2B EC). G2B EC is much like B2B EC, usually with an overlay of government procurement regulations. That is, G2B EC and B2B EC are similar conceptually. However, the functions of G2C EC are conceptually different from anything that exists in the private sector (e.g., B2C EC).

  E-government is also an efficient way of conducting business transactions with citizens and businesses and within the governments themselves. E-government makes government more efficient and effective, especially in the delivery of public services. An example of G2C electronic commerce is electronic benefits transfer, in which governments transfer benefits, such as Social Security and pension payments, directly to recipients' bank accounts.

- *Mobile commerce (m-commerce)*: The term *m-commerce* refers to e-commerce that is conducted entirely in a wireless environment. An example is using cell phones to shop over the Internet. You will learn about m-commerce in Chapter 8.

Each type of EC is executed in one or more business models. A **business model** is the method by which a company generates revenue to sustain itself. Table 7.1 summarizes the major EC business models.

| | | Table |
|---|---|---|
| Online direct marketing | Manufacturers or retailers sell directly to customers. Very efficient for digital products and services. Can allow for product or service customization (*www.dell.com*) | **7.1** E-Commerce Business Models |
| Electronic tendering system | Businesses request quotes from suppliers. Uses B2B with a reverse auction mechanism | |
| Name-your-own-price | Customers decide how much they are willing to pay. An intermediary tries to match a provider (*www.priceline.com*) | |

**Table 7.1** (continued)

| | |
|---|---|
| Find-the-best-price | Customers specify a need; an intermediary compares providers and shows the lowest price. Customers must accept the offer in a short time, or they may lose the deal (*www.hotwire.com*) |
| Affiliate marketing | Vendors ask partners to place logos (or banners) on partner's site. If customers click on logo, go to vendor's site, and make a purchase, then the vendor pays commissions to the partners |
| Viral marketing | Recipients of your marketing notices send information about your product to their friends |
| Group purchasing (e-coops) | Small buyers aggregate demand to create a large volume; the group then conducts tendering or negotiates a low price |
| Online auctions | Companies run auctions of various types on the Internet. Very popular in C2C, but gaining ground in other types of EC as well (*www.ebay.com*) |
| Product customization | Customers use the Internet to self-configure products or services. Sellers then price them and fulfill them quickly (*build-to-order*) (*www.jaguar.com*) |
| Electronic marketplaces and exchanges | Transactions are conducted efficiently (more information to buyers and sellers, lower transaction costs) in electronic marketplaces (private or public) |
| Bartering online | Intermediary administers online exchange of surplus products and/or company receives "points" for its contribution, which it can use to purchase other needed items (*www.bbu.com*) |
| Deep discounters | Company offers deep price discounts. Appeals to customers who consider only price in their purchasing decisions (*www.half.com*) |
| Membership | Only members can use the services provided, including access to certain information, conducting trades, etc. (*www.egreetings.com*) |

## Major E-Commerce Mechanisms

Businesses and customers can buy and sell on the Internet through a number of mechanisms. The most widely used mechanisms are as follows:

- Electronic catalogs
- Electronic auctions
- E-storefronts

- E-malls
- E-marketplaces

Let's look at each one more closely.

Catalogs have been printed on paper for generations. Today, however, they are available over the Internet. Electronic catalogs consist of a product database, a directory and search capabilities, and a presentation function. They are the backbone of most e-commerce sites.

An **auction** is a competitive buying and selling process in which prices are determined dynamically by competitive bidding. Electronic auctions (e-auctions) generally increase revenues for sellers by broadening the customer base and shortening the cycle time of the auction. Buyers generally benefit from e-auctions because they can bargain for lower prices. In addition, they do not have to travel to an auction at a physical location.

The Internet provides an efficient infrastructure for conducting auctions at lower administrative costs and with a greater number of involved sellers and buyers. Both individual consumers and corporations can participate in auctions.

There are two major types of auctions: forward and reverse. In **forward auctions**, sellers solicit bids from many potential buyers. Usually, sellers place items at sites for auction, and buyers bid continuously for them. The highest bidder wins the items. Both sellers and buyers can be either individuals or businesses. The popular auction site eBay.com is a forward auction.

In **reverse auctions**, one buyer, usually an organization, wants to purchase a product or a service. The buyer posts a request for quotation (RFQ) on its Web site or on a third-party site. The RFQ provides detailed information on the desired purchase. Interested suppliers study the RFQ and then submit bids electronically. Everything else being equal, the lowest-price bidder wins the auction. The reverse auction is the most common auction model for large purchases (in terms of either quantities or price). Governments and large corporations frequently use this approach, which may provide considerable savings for the buyer.

Auctions can be conducted from the seller's site, the buyer's site, or a third party's site. For example, eBay, the best-known third-party site, offers hundreds of thousands of different items in several types of auctions. Overall, more than 300 major companies, including Amazon.com and Dellauction.com, sponsor online auctions.

An *electronic storefront* is a Web site that represents a single store. An *electronic mall*, also known as a *cybermall* or an *e-mall*, is a collection of individual shops consolidated under one Internet address. Electronic storefronts and electronic malls are closely associated with B2C electronic commerce. You will study each one in more detail in Section 7.2.

An *electronic marketplace* (*e-marketplace*) is a central, virtual market space on the Web where many buyers and many sellers can conduct e-commerce and e-business activities. Electronic marketplaces are associated with B2B electronic commerce. You will learn about electronic marketplaces in Section 7.3.

## Electronic Payment Mechanisms

Implementing EC typically requires electronic payments. **Electronic payment mechanisms** enable buyers to pay for goods and services electronically, rather than writing a check or using cash. Payments are an integral part of doing business, whether in the traditional manner or online. Traditional payment systems have typically involved cash and/or checks.

In most cases, traditional payment systems are not effective for EC, especially for B2B. Cash cannot be used because there is no face-to-face contact between buyer and seller. Not everyone accepts credit cards or checks, and some buyers do not have credit cards or checking accounts. Finally, contrary to what many people believe, it may be *less* secure for the buyer to use the telephone or mail to arrange or send payments, especially from another country, than to complete a secured transaction on a computer. For all of these reasons, a better method is needed to pay for goods and services in cyberspace. This method is electronic payment systems. Let's take a closer look at three types of electronic payment: electronic checks, electronic cards, and digital wallets.

Electronic Checks.    *Electronic checks* (*e-checks*), which are used primarily in B2B, are similar to regular paper checks. A customer who wishes to use e-checks must first establish a checking account with a bank. Then, when the customer buys a product or a service, he or she e-mails an encrypted electronic check to the seller. The seller deposits the check in a bank account, and the funds are transferred from the buyer's account into the seller's account.

Like regular checks, e-checks carry a signature (in digital form) that can be verified (see *www.authorize.net*). Properly signed and endorsed e-checks are exchanged between financial institutions through electronic clearinghouses. (For example, see *www.eccho.org for details.*)

**Electronic Cards.** There are a variety of electronic cards, and they are used for different purposes. The most common types are electronic credit cards, purchasing cards, stored-value money cards, and smart cards.

*Electronic credit cards* allow customers to charge online payments to their credit card account. These cards are used primarily in B2C and in shopping by small-to-medium enterprises (SMEs). Here is how e-credit cards work (see Figure 7.1).

- Step 1: When you purchase a book from Amazon, for example, your credit card information and purchase amount are encrypted in your browser. This procedure ensures the information is safe while it is "traveling" on the Internet to Amazon.
- Step 2: When your information arrives at Amazon, it is not opened. Rather, it is transferred automatically (in encrypted form) to a *clearinghouse*, where it is decrypted for verification and authorization.
- Step 3: The clearinghouse asks the bank that issued you your credit card (the card issuer bank) to verify your credit card information.
- Step 4: Your card issuer bank verifies your credit card information and reports this to the clearinghouse.
- Step 5: The clearinghouse reports the result of the verification of your credit card to Amazon.
- Step 6: Amazon reports a successful purchase and amount to you.
- Step 7: Your card issuer bank sends funds in the amount of the purchase to Amazon's bank.
- Step 8: Your card issuer bank notifies you (either electronically or in your monthly statement) of the debit on your credit card.
- Step 9: Amazon's bank notifies Amazon of the funds credited to its account.

*Purchasing cards* are the B2B equivalent of electronic credit cards (see Figure 7.2). In some countries, purchasing cards are the primary form of payment between companies. Unlike credit cards, where credit is provided for 30–60 days (for free) before payment is made to the merchant, payments made with purchasing cards are settled within a week.

**Stored-value money cards** allow you to store a fixed amount of prepaid money and then spend it as necessary. These cards are used to pay for photocopies in your library, for

**FIGURE 7.1** How e-credit cards work. (The numbers 1–9 indicate the sequence of activities.)

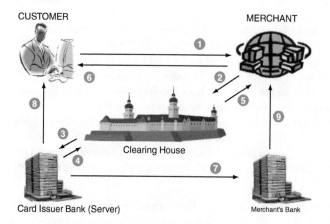

transportation, and for telephone calls. Each time you use the card, the amount is reduced by the amount you spent. Figure 7.3 illustrates a New York City Metro (subway and bus) card.

Finally, **smart cards** contain a chip that can store a large amount of information (see Figure 7.4). Smart cards are frequently multipurpose—that is, you can use them as a credit card, a debit card, a stored-value money card, or a loyalty card. Smart cards are ideal for *micropayments*, which are small payments of a few dollars or less.

Digital Wallets. A **digital wallet** is an application used for making financial transactions. These apps can be on users' desktops or on their smartphones. When the app is on a smartphone, it becomes a mobile payment system. Digital wallets replace the need to carry physical credit and debit cards, gift cards, and loyalty cards, as well as boarding passes and other forms of identification. Digital wallets may also store insurance and loyalty cards, drivers' licenses, ID cards, Web site passwords, and login information. Furthermore, digital wallets eliminate having to enter shipping, billing, and credit card data each time you make a purchase at a Web site. The data are encrypted in the user's machine, and the wallet contains a digital certificate that identifies the authorized cardholder. Because smartphones know their current location, nearby stores can send offers to users, and the wallet ensures the appropriate discounts are taken if a purchase is made.

A digital wallet allows the user to pay for merchandise in a store by tapping the phone on the merchant's terminal or by scanning a QR code. Security is provided by the phone's fingerprint reader or by entering a PIN. The wallet transmits user data to the terminal using Bluetooth or near field communication (NFC).

Examples of digital wallets include PayPal (*www.paypal.com*), Google Wallet (*https://www.google.com/wallet*), and Apple Pay (*www.apple.com*). The competition in this field is intense.

For example, the adoption of Apple Pay has been slowed by the Merchant Customer Exchange (MCX) (*www.mcx.com*). MCX is a company created by a consortium of U.S. retail companies to develop a merchant-owned mobile payment system, which will be called "CurrentC." The company is led by merchants such as 7-Eleven, Alon Brands, Best Buy, CVS Health, Darden Restaurants, HMSHost, Hy-Vee, Lowe's, Michaels, Publix, Sears Holdings, Shell Oil Products US, Sunoco, Target Corporation, and Walmart. MCX's flagship product is CurrentC, a digital wallet. CurrentC is designed primarily to prevent merchants from paying credit card transaction fees. Shortly after CurrentC was launched in early 2015, Best Buy and Walmart explicitly stated that they would not accept Apple Pay, while in October 2014, CVS Pharmacy and Rite-Aid disabled all NFC payment systems. On the other hand, Walt Disney World began accepting Apple Pay beginning December 24, 2014.

On February 23, 2015, Google acquired the Softcard digital wallet's intellectual property and integrated it into Google Wallet. The Softcard digital wallet was a joint venture between AT&T (*www.att.com*), T-Mobile (*www.t-mobile.com*), and Verizon (*www.verizon.com*). On February 23, 2015, Google acquired Softcard's intellectual property and integrated it into its Google Wallet.

Mike Clarke/AFP/Getty Images/NewsCom

**FIGURE 7.2** Example of purchasing card.

© Clarence Holmes Photography/Alamy Limited

**FIGURE 7.3** The New York City Metro Card.

© MARKA/Alamy Limited

**FIGURE 7.4** Smart cards are frequently multipurpose.

## Benefits and Limitations of E-Commerce

Few innovations in human history have provided as many benefits to organizations, individuals, and society as e-commerce has. E-commerce benefits organizations by making national and international markets more accessible and by lowering the costs of processing, distributing, and retrieving information. Customers benefit by being able to access a vast number of products and services, around the clock. The major benefit to society is the ability to easily and conveniently deliver information, services, and products to people in cities, rural areas, and developing countries.

Despite all these benefits, EC has some limitations, both technological and nontechnological, that have restricted its growth and acceptance. One major technological limitation is the lack of universally accepted security standards. Also, in less-developed countries, telecommunications bandwidth often is insufficient, and accessing the Web is expensive. Nontechnological limitations include the perceptions that EC is insecure, has unresolved legal issues, and lacks a critical mass of sellers and buyers. As time passes, these limitations, especially the technological ones, will diminish or be overcome. In fact, IT's About Business 7.2 describes two instances of how these limitations are being overcome in the developing world.

# IT's [about business]

## 7.2 Overcoming the Limitations of Electronic Commerce in the Developing World

### China

A series of food safety scandals has created a demand in China's big cities for natural or traditionally grown food. Two beneficiaries of this new market are Li Chengcai (83 years old) and Cheng You-fang (76 years old), who grow radishes on their tiny farm. Although the couple are illiterate and speak only their local dialect, they sell their produce via electronic commerce to urban customers who are willing to pay extra for flavorful, safe food. Here is how they became engaged in e-commerce.

Zhang Yu, a 26-year-old "young village official"—that is her actual title—and other young village officials launched an account on Sina Weibo (http://english.sina.com/weibo), a Chinese microblogging Web site, to post items about the fresh, traditionally grown produce of their region. Soon afterward, they opened an online store through Alibaba Group's Taobao (www.engtaobao.com) Web site to connect local farmers with urban buyers. The online grocery, officially known as the Young Village Officials' Farm, has customers in Beijing, Shanghai, and elsewhere, and about 10,000 followers on Weibo. Customers place orders online, and Zhang visits farmers to verbally inform them of the order. Zhang handles the logistics, shipping, and quality control of the produce.

Zhang maintains the reason for the success of the grocery is a renewed interest in local farming traditions—which she documents in photographs on social media—and strict quality control. In an area where the average monthly household income is only about 600 yuan ($99), farmers selling produce through the online grocery store can increase their income by one-third.

### Nigeria

There is an old saying in Nigeria that "You can outfit your entire home in a single drive across Lagos (Nigeria's largest city)." Today,

you can buy everything from cutlery and furniture to food and décor from the thousands of hawkers who aggressively sell their goods along, and in the middle of, the congested city's potholed streets. Unfortunately, shopping locally historically has meant higher prices, less selection, and often sitting in traffic for hours to get to stores, which rely on generators to cope with almost daily power outages.

Today, however, Nigerians have another option for comprehensive shopping: the online marketplace Jumia (www.jumia.com.ng). For example, when Gbemiga Omotoso bought a Samsung tablet in 2014, he handed over his cash to a man in a van. The transaction was part of online retailer Jumia's attempt to adapt its operation to the unique challenges of selling in Nigeria. With many of the country's 160 million residents suspicious of paying online, the Lagos-based retailer wins over skeptical shoppers by accepting payment on delivery and offering free returns.

Jumia and local rival Konga (www.konga.com) are delivering electronics, clothes, and even refrigerators to Nigerians' front doors. To combat fears of online fraud and to educate Nigerians about shopping online securely, the company employs a direct sales team of about 200 who travel around major cities such as Lagos and Port Harcourt carrying tablet computers. They wear outfits displaying Jumia's logo, and they hold impromptu shopping sessions in businesses, churches, and homes, showing consumers how to order and answering questions.

Jumia is building its own fleet of about 200 vehicles. Almost 70 percent are motorbikes that are easier to navigate through the country's traffic jams. To keep robberies at a minimum, the last deliveries take place at 7 PM. The company promises to deliver any item in its 90,000 square foot central warehouse in Lagos to any location in the city within a single day, and anywhere in the entire country within five days.

In early 2015, Jumia had 1,500 employees. In addition to Nigeria, the company operates in Kenya, Morocco, Ivory Coast, Egypt, Uganda, and South Africa. Although not yet profitable, Jumia claims monthly revenues of "a couple of million" dollars as well as rapidly increasing sales. Significantly, in 2014 Jumia secured additional funding totaling €120 million.

*Sources:* Compiled from "How Jumia Redefined Nigerian E-Commerce in 2014," *Tech Moran*, January 5, 2015; "E-Commerce Makes Strong Resurgence in Nigeria," *African Business Magazine*, December 24, 2014; A. Lee, "How Did Alabara Capture 80% of Chinese E-Commerce?" *Forbes*, May 8, 2014; H. Rauf, "Trends in China's E-Commerce Market," *China Briefing*, June 4, 2014; "'Taobao Village' Phenomenon Boosts E-Commerce in Rural China," *Fashionbi 247*, March 5, 2014; C. Larson, "In Rural China, You Don't Have to Read to Buy and Sell Online," *Bloomberg BusinessWeek*, February 17–23, 2014; "Ecommerce Transforms Rural Chinese Villages," *Financial Times*, February 16, 2014; B. Marino, "Alibaba Opens Ecommerce Door for Chinese Villagers," *Financial Times*, February 16, 2014; J. Erickson, "Viral Villages: E-Commerce Is Spreading in China's Agrarian Hinterlands," *Alizila*, February 11, 2014; K. Mbote, "Uganda: Jumia Extends Services to Uganda," *CIO East Africa*, February 8, 2014; P. Adepoju, "Jumia Nigeria Wins Best Online Retail Brand of the Year Award," *Biz Community*, January 31, 2014; B. Tan, "The Social Side of E-Commerce: Lessons from Rural China," *The Conversation*, January 6, 2014; "E-Commerce Booming in Africa," *IT Web Retail Technology*, December 10, 2013; C. Kay, C. Spillane, and J. Kew, "Trying to Build the Next Amazon – In Nigeria," *Bloomberg BusinessWeek*, November 25–December 1, 2013; C. Sheets, "Nigeria's Jumia: The Company Behind the 'Amazonification' of Africa," *International Business Times*, September 18, 2013; http://english.sina.com/weibo, www.jumia.com.ng, accessed March 21, 2015.

## Questions

1. Describe how the Young Village Officials' Farm and Jumia are trying to overcome the limitations of electronic commerce. Provide specific examples to support your answer.
2. What are the advantages of electronic commerce to rural farmers in China (above and beyond increased income)?
3. What are the advantages of electronic commerce to the people of Nigeria?

# before you go on...

1. Define e-commerce, and distinguish it from e-business.
2. Differentiate among B2C, B2B, C2C, and B2E electronic commerce.
3. Define e-government.
4. Discuss forward and reverse auctions.
5. Discuss the various online payment mechanisms.
6. Identify some benefits and limitations of e-commerce.

# Business-to-Consumer (B2C) Electronic Commerce

7.2

B2B EC is much larger than B2C EC by volume, but B2C EC is more complex. The reason is that B2C involves a large number of buyers making millions of diverse transactions per day from a relatively small number of sellers. As an illustration, consider Amazon, an online retailer that offers thousands of products to its customers. Each customer purchase is relatively small, but Amazon must manage every transaction as if that customer were its most important one. The company needs to process each order quickly and efficiently, and ship the products to the customer in a timely manner. In addition, it has to manage returns. Multiply this simple example by millions, and you get an idea of how complex B2C EC can be. Overall, B2B complexities tend to be more business related, whereas B2C complexities tend to be more technical and volume related. IT's About Business 7.3 illustrates how Swipely helps businesses better understand their customers. That is, Swipely is an example of B2C commerce.

# IT's [about business]

### 7.3 Swipely

Founded in 2009, Swipely (*www.swipely.com*) is a service that processes credit card transactions for merchants. The online software works with point-of-sale systems and terminals used by independent businesses, including restaurants, salons, boutiques, grocers, and other retailers without requiring these businesses to implement additional hardware. Merchants in the Swipely network use the product to integrate customer spending, social media, and other data to obtain valuable insights into customer behavior.

Swipely's competitive advantage lies in helping merchants to better understand their customers. Its cloud servers (we describe cloud computing in detail in Technology Guide 3) analyze the data left by card swipes, delete personally identifying factors for security, and then present the data to merchants in the form of customer dashboards that reveal which goods each card number purchased and when. The dashboards are capable of performing very finely tuned analyses, such as how a rainy Tuesday affects profits. Swipely integrates with a merchant's social accounts so that owners can see how campaigns on Facebook or reviews on Yelp affect business in their restaurants or stores.

Swipely becomes even more effective if customers provide merchants with their name and e-mail address, which 20 percent are willing to do. These additional data enable the dashboards to incorporate marketing histories such as responses to e-mail or coupon offers. This type of customer management software can cost hundreds of dollars per month, but Swipely adds it free.

Swipely competes with numerous payment processing services, including Square (*www.squareup.com*), Heartland Payment Systems (*www.heartlandpaymentsystems.com*), and Chase Paymentech (*www.chasepaymentech.com*). Many companies are competing in this arena because information about customers' spending habits is extremely valuable. Square (*www.squareup.com*), for example, is competing for the same customers as Swipely. One of these customers—the Blue Bottle Coffee Company

(*www.bluebottlecoffee.com*), which has more than a dozen locations in Oakland, San Francisco, and New York—recently switched its registers to Square. It would be a small step for Square to offer its clients analytics on customer behaviors.

Swipely's competitive advantage over Square, for now, is price. Swipely takes an average of 2.65 percent of its merchants' customer transactions. Swipely's average charge is 10 basis points less per swipe than Square. (A basis point is 1/100 of 1 percent.) Furthermore, because Swipely is a cloud-based service that can communicate with more than 50 register systems, merchants do not have to purchase equipment to train on and then discard.

So, how is Swipely doing? In May 2015, Swipely was processing more than $4 billion of customer transactions (annualized) with its participating merchants.

*Sources:* Compiled from M. Seekamp, "A Better Way to Approach Brand-Level Sales Reporting," *Swipely Press Release*, January 6, 2015; "Swipely Announces Managing $4B in Annual Sales," *QSR Magazine*, November 21, 2014; E. Ducoff, "Swipely Reveals How Menu and Server Performance Impact Sales," *Swipely Press Release*, February 11, 2014; "Swipely Release Helps Operators Track Behavior," *QSR Magazine*, January 24, 2014; A. Wilhelm, "Now Processing $1B Annually, Swipely Announces a Partner Network to Support Growth," *TechCrunch*, September 24, 2013; E. Carlyle, "Plastic Insights," *Forbes*, May 27, 2013; O. Thomas, "When Hurricane Sandy Struck, This Company Changed Its Entire Sales Plan – In Minutes," *Business Insider*, January 19, 2013; L. Baverman, "Swipely Brings Big Data to Small Biz," *Upstart Business Journal*, November 8, 2012; T. Geron, "Swipely Expands Credit Card-Based Loyalty Service," *Forbes*, December 15, 2011; L. Gannes, "Swipely Aims to (Politely) Turn Purchases into Conversations," *GigaOM*, May 10, 2010; *www.swipely.com*, accessed February 4, 2015.

**Questions**

1. Describe the advantages that Swipely offers merchants that help it maintain a competitive advantage in the marketplace.
2. Refer back to Chapter 2. Does Swipely function as a strategic information system for a merchant? Why or why not?

---

This section addresses the primary issues in B2C EC. We begin by studying the two basic mechanisms that customers utilize to access companies on the Web: electronic storefronts and electronic malls. In addition to purchasing products over the Web, customers also access online services. Therefore, the next section covers several online services, such as banking, securities trading, job searching, and travel. The complexity of B2C EC creates two major challenges for sellers: channel conflict and order fulfillment. We examine these two topics in detail. Finally, companies engaged in B2C EC must "get the word out" to prospective customers. Therefore, this section concludes with a look at online advertising.

## Electronic Storefronts and Malls

For several generations, home shopping from catalogs, and later from television shopping channels, has attracted millions of customers. Today, shopping online offers an alternative to catalog and television shopping. **Electronic retailing (e-tailing)** is the direct sale of products and services through electronic storefronts or electronic malls, usually designed around an electronic catalog format and/or auctions.

Like any mail-order shopping experience, e-commerce enables you to buy from home and to do so 24 hours a day, 7 days a week. Compared with mail order, however, EC offers a wider variety of products and services, including the most unique items, often at lower prices. Furthermore, within seconds, shoppers can access very detailed supplementary product information. In addition, they can easily locate and compare competitors' products and prices. Finally, buyers can find hundreds of thousands of sellers. Two popular online shopping mechanisms are electronic storefronts and electronic malls.

**Electronic Storefronts.** As we saw earlier in the chapter, an **electronic storefront** is a Web site that represents a single store. Today, Internet shoppers can access hundreds of thousands of electronic storefronts. Each storefront has a unique uniform resource locator (URL), or Internet address, at which buyers can place orders. Some electronic storefronts are extensions of physical stores such as Hermes, The Sharper Image, and Walmart. Others are new businesses started by entrepreneurs who discovered a niche on the Web (e.g., Restaurant.com and Alloy.com). Manufacturers (e.g., *www.dell.com*) and retailers (e.g., *www.officedepot.com*) also use storefronts.

**Electronic Malls.** Whereas an electronic storefront represents a single store, an **electronic mall**, also known as a *cybermall* or an *e-mall*, is a collection of individual shops grouped under a single Internet address. The basic idea of an electronic mall is the same as that of a regular shopping mall: to provide a one-stop shopping place that offers a wide range of products and services. A cybermall may include thousands of vendors. For example, Microsoft Shopping (now Bing shopping, *www.bing.com/shopping*) includes tens of thousands of products from thousands of vendors.

There are two types of cybermalls. In the first type, known as *referral malls* (e.g., *www.hawaii.com*), you cannot buy anything. Instead, you are transferred from the mall to a participating storefront. In the second type of mall (e.g., *http://shopping.google.com*), you can actually make a purchase. At this type of mall, you might shop from several stores, but you make only one purchase transaction at the end. You use an *electronic shopping cart* to gather items from various vendors and then pay for all of them in a single transaction. The mall organizer, such as Google, takes a commission from the sellers for this service.

## Online Service Industries

In addition to purchasing products, customers can also access needed services via the Web. Selling books, toys, computers, and most other products on the Internet can reduce vendors' selling costs by 20–40 percent. Further reduction is difficult to achieve because the products must be delivered physically. Only a few products, such as software and music, can be digitized and then delivered online for additional savings. In contrast, services, such as buying an airline ticket and purchasing stocks or insurance, can be delivered entirely through e-commerce, often with considerable cost reduction. Not surprisingly, then, online delivery of services is growing very rapidly, with millions of new customers being added each year.

One of the most pressing EC issues relating to online services (as well as in marketing tangible products) is **disintermediation**. Intermediaries, also known as middlemen, have two functions: (1) they provide information, and (2) they perform value-added services such as consulting. The first function can be fully automated and most likely will be assumed by e-marketplaces and portals that provide information for free. When this development occurs, the intermediaries who perform only (or primarily) this function are likely to be eliminated. The process whereby intermediaries are eliminated is called disintermediation. IT's About Business 7.4 provides an example of disintermediation.

# IT's [about business]

## 7.4 Penske Used Trucks

Throughout 2009 and 2010, used trucks grew more appealing to businesses because the economy was in poor shape. Penske Truck Leasing (*www.pensketruckleasing.com*), which has a steady supply of used trucks coming off leases, realized that it was missing out on revenue by selling those trucks at reduced prices to wholesalers rather than directly to would-be buyers.

To sell its used trucks, Penske had relied on a bare-bones Web site used primarily by wholesale buyers, as well as by local Penske used-truck coordinators who visited the site for reference material when assisting wholesalers. Penske needed a high-quality Web site that would generate sales to wholesalers as well as directly to the end customers, such as the owner of a flower store or hardware store who needed a cargo van or box truck.

The result, PenskeUsedTrucks (*www.penskeusedtrucks.com*), illustrates how various business units must work together to implement a major electronic commerce project. Penske's vehicle remarketing group recognized the value of used trucks, and they realized that the company was losing money with its current business model. To remedy this problem, they brought in the company's marketing staff to evaluate how Penske could employ a new Web site to attract more buyers. The two groups then collaborated with the information technology group to build the Web site.

Penske faced several challenges in creating the site. To begin with, the site had to incorporate the correct terminology and keywords to attract the attention of shoppers and search engines. To address this challenge, IT and marketing interviewed customers to obtain feedback concerning effective keywords. They discovered, for example, that Penske calls one type of truck a "cargo van," whereas some potential customers refer to it as a "high cube" or a "box truck." Ultimately, the additional keywords and cross-referencing dramatically expanded Penske's keyword base from roughly 100 vehicle names to more than 2,000.

Another problem was collecting and organizing photos. In most cases obtaining images for a Web site is a fairly straightforward process. Unfortunately, in Penske's case this task was more complicated because the company does not have a centralized truck lot. Rather, its fleet operates out of 2,500 locations nationwide. The solution required Penske to reengineer its fleet management system. In addition, Penske implemented a policy mandating that whenever the company lists a new vehicle for sale on its Web site, five images must come with the vehicle.

The resulting Web site resembles CarMax (*www.carmax.com*) more than it does Penske's previous site: a Web-based catalog. Every type of Penske vehicle, from a standard cargo van to a refrigerated 18-wheel trailer truck, is searchable on the site, and Penske updates the inventory every day. The number of vehicles for sale can vary from 3,500 to 5,000 units. A vehicle-comparison tool enables a buyer to compare up to five trucks side-by-side in terms of price, mileage, weight, horsepower, and other specifications. Maintenance reports display a vehicle's repair and maintenance history for the previous three years. Finally, buyers can close the sale on a single truck or a fleet of trucks by phone via Penske's call center.

Offering a good product and building a useful Web site are basic strategic necessities in the digital era. Successful companies must do better than this. Attracting customers requires an aggressive search engine optimization (SEO) and social media strategy as well. *Search engine optimization* is the process of maximizing the number of visitors to a particular Web site by ensuring that the site appears high on the list of results returned by a search engine.

The Penske marketing team followed Google's SEO advice to incorporate keywords that customers use when searching across the Web site. Penske uses Adobe Analytics (*www.adobe.com*) software to obtain information such as which keywords drive visitors to the Web site, where buyers are coming from, how long they stay on the site, and which pages they visit.

Google search results also include rich details such as the price and availability of a vehicle. The SEO helped increase Google search traffic for the Penske site by 37 percent.

Penske also extended its marketing strategy to include social media and blogging. The marketing team uses a company blog called Move Ahead (blog.gopenske.com) as a content hub where the team posts daily truck specials and directs traffic to the PenskeUsedTrucks.com Web site. The team also tweets about daily truck specials in both the morning and the evening. Furthermore, Penske has active company pages on Facebook, YouTube, Pinterest, and Google+. In October 2013, Penske added a mobile version of PenskeUsedTrucks.com.

Penske's Used Trucks has become so successful that in 2014 the operation doubled its commercial truck dealership in North America. The company opened centers in the Dallas, Atlanta, and Toronto areas.

*Sources:* Compiled from "Penske Used Trucks Doubling Dealerships," *Reading Eagle*, January 29, 2015; M. Hernandez, "Dominate SEO with Long Tail Keywords," *Huffington Post*, March 17, 2014; J. Martin, "20 SEO Tips, Trends and Predictions for 2014," *CIO*, January 16, 2014; "Penske Ranked Fourth on InformationWeek 500 List for Used Truck Website," *PR Newswire*, September 10, 2013; S. O'Neill, "Website Drives Used Truck Sales," *InformationWeek*, September 9, 2013; S. O'Neill, "What Penske Learned from Rebuilding Its E-Commerce Site," *Information Week*, September 5, 2013; *www.pensketruckleasing.com*, *www.penskeusedtrucks.com*, accessed January 29, 2015.

**Questions**

1. Describe how disintermediation works in this case. Provide an example to support your answer.
2. Why is it so important for different functional areas in an organization to work together in designing an organizational Web site?
3. Referencing Question 2, discuss the implications of this statement: "Regardless of your major, an understanding of information technology will be of value to you."

In contrast to simply providing information, performing value-added services requires expertise. Unlike the information function, then, this function can be only partially automated. Thus, intermediaries who provide value-added services not only are likely to survive but they may also actually prosper. The Web helps these employees in two situations: (1) when the number of participants is enormous, as with job searches, and (2) when the information that must be exchanged is complex.

In this section, you will examine some leading online service industries: banking, trading of securities (stocks, bonds), job matching, travel services, and advertising.

**Cyberbanking.** *Electronic banking*, also known as **cyberbanking**, involves conducting various banking activities from home, at a place of business, or on the road instead of at a physical bank location. Electronic banking has capabilities ranging from paying bills to applying for a loan. For customers, it saves time and it is convenient. For banks, it offers an inexpensive alternative to branch banking—for example, about 2 cents cost per transaction versus $1.07 at a physical branch. Cyberbanking also enables banks to attract remote customers. In addition to regular banks with added online services, *Internet-only banks*, which are dedicated solely to Internet transactions, are emerging, as you see in IT's About Business 7.5. Another example of an Internet-only bank is First Internet Bank of Indiana (*www.firstib.com*).

## IT's [about business]

### 7.5 Can Simple Disrupt Traditional Banking?

Consumer banking is an industry that is ready to be disrupted. Banks are known for hidden fees, confusing language, and customer frustration. Online-only banks may provide the business model that can help solve these problems and enhance customer satisfaction.

One such bank, Simple (*www.simple.com*), was founded in 2009 and launched commercially in July 2012. Instead of seeking a new bank charter, Simple chose to partner with Bancorp to sponsor them in the payment networks and to ensure that all of their banking services are FDIC insured. Simple was founded on the idea that traditional banks do not provide adequate online and mobile tools to properly service their customers.

Think of Simple as an online-only bank with a heavy focus on customer service that incorporates financial tracking and budgeting tools similar to those offered by Mint (*www.mint.com*). Mint is a free, Web-based personal financial management service for the United States and Canada. Mint's primary service allows users to track bank, credit card, investment, and loan transactions and balances, as well as to make budgets. Intuit (*www.intuit.com*) acquired Mint in 2009.

Simple's plan is to provide easy-to-use, cloud-based apps and outstanding customer service. The company's Web site and apps are attractive and uncluttered, with a minimalist design that is easy to navigate. They focus on Simple's financial management tools like Goals, which allows customers to establish financial goals to save toward, for example, a vacation or a down payment on a car. Goals then regularly updates customers as to how much progress they are making toward achieving that goal. Another innovative tool is Safe to Spend, which displays the amount in the checking account that will be available after customers pay their scheduled bills and set aside money toward their goals.

Simple also offers a unique feature called "push notification" that it sends to customers' smartphones after they make a purchase. With push notification, customers can take a picture of a purchase, which is automatically *geotagged*—meaning location data are added to the image. They can then add notes about the purchase for their records. This information can help customers to better understand their spending habits and to track specific types of purchases they have made in the past.

Simple makes money from interest margins and interchange revenue from payment networks, which is the fee that companies pay to be able to accept card-based transactions. Simple has no IT infrastructure and no physical branches to support, so they are able to operate on a lower profit margin than traditional banks.

Simple's market is paradoxical, in that banking customers desire the convenience of Internet banking, but they remain wary of the Internet itself. (For example, see the case about the Target breach in Chapter 4.) Despite these concerns, however, Pew research (*www.pewresearch.org*) reported in 2013 that 51 percent of all U.S. adults conduct some banking online.

Simple experienced rapid growth, attracting roughly 100,000 customers across the United States by the end of 2013. That year the bank completed $1.6 billion in transactions. Then, in February 2014, Simple was purchased by BBVA Compass Bank (*www.bbvacompass.com*) for $117 million. Simple promised that it would continue to operate as it always had and that nothing would change for its existing customers.

Despite these assurances, however, the purchase raised several serious questions:

- How can Simple, which built a loyal following by criticizing annoying banking practices, keep its business model intact as a subsidiary of a huge traditional bank?
- Can Simple retain its current customer base?
- What does BBVA intend to do with Simple? Will it allow Simple to maintain its traditional business practices? How much independence will it allow the bank?

- Given that Internet-only banks are typically small startups, what does this purchase mean for the future of such banks?

- What are the implications of this purchase for the disruption of the banking industry as a whole?

Pointing out a problem with Internet-only banking, in August 2014 approximately 10 percent of Simple's 120,000 customers lost access to their money for an entire day. The problem resulted when the company moved to a new information system for processing financial transactions. Simple's CEO apologized, and the bank awarded every customer who experienced the outage a $50 credit.

*Sources:* Compiled from P. Crosman, "Technical Glitches at Simple Show Digital Banks'Weakness," *American Banker*, September 15, 2014; J. Reich, "Simple's CEO Says He's 'Deeply Sorry' for Outage That Kept Thousands from Their Bank Accounts," *Oregon Live*, August 21, 2014; D. Wolman, "The Bank and the Anti-Bank," *The New Yorker*, February 26, 2014; D.

Etherington, "Banking Startup Simple Acquired for $117M, Will Continue to Operate," *TechCrunch*, February 20, 2014; "BBVA Acquires Digital Banking Service Pioneer Simple," *BBVA Press Release*, February 20, 2014; C. Forrest, "Appetite for Disruption: Can Simple and the Web Reinvent Banking?" *TechRepublic*, January 17, 2014; A. Jeffries, "Simple's Online-Only Banking App Launches on Android," *The Verge*, January 15, 2013; A. Robertson, "Banking Substitute Simple Releases iPhone App," *The Verge*, May 9, 2012; *www.simple.com*, accessed March 20, 2015.

**Questions**

1. Would you be willing to bank with an Internet bank? Why or why not?

2. What are the disadvantages of Simple's banking model? Provide examples to support your answer.

3. Check on the status of Simple today. Now, answer the "five serious questions" listed in the case regarding BBVA Compass Bank's purchase of Simple in 2014.

International banking and the ability to handle trading in multiple currencies are critical for international trade. Transfers of electronic funds and electronic letters of credit are vital services in international banking. An example of support for EC global trade is provided by TradeCard, in conjunction with MasterCard. TradeCard is an international company that provides a secure method for buyers and sellers to make digital payments anywhere on the globe (see the demo at *www.tradecard.com*). In another example, banks and companies such as Oanda (*www.oanda.com*) provide conversions of more than 160 currencies.

**Online Securities Trading.** Millions of Americans use computers to trade stocks, bonds, and other financial instruments. In fact, several well-known securities companies, including E*Trade, Ameritrade, and Charles Schwab, offer only online trading. In Korea, more than half of stock traders are already using the Internet for that purpose. Why? Because it is cheaper than a full-service or discount broker. On the Web, investors can find a considerable amount of information regarding specific companies or mutual funds in which to invest (e.g., *http://money.cnn.com* and *www.bloomberg.com*).

**FIN**

Let's say, for example, that you have an account with Scottrade. You access Scottrade's Web site (*www.scottrade.com*) from your personal computer or your Internet-enabled mobile device, enter your account number and password to access your personalized Web page, and then click on "stock trading." Using a menu, you enter the details of your order—buy or sell, margin or cash, price limit, market order, and so on. The computer informs you of the current "ask" and "bid" prices, much as a broker would do over the telephone. You can then approve or reject the transaction.

**HRM**

**The Online Job Market.** The Internet offers a promising new environment for job seekers and for companies searching for hard-to-find employees. Thousands of companies and government agencies advertise available positions, accept resumes, and take applications via the Internet.

Job seekers use the online job market to reply online to employment ads, to place resumes on various sites, and to use recruiting firms (e.g., *www.monster.com*, *www.simplyhired.com*, *www.linkedin.com*, and *www.truecareers.com*). Companies that have jobs to offer advertise these openings on their Web sites, and they search the bulletin boards of recruiting firms. In many countries (including the United States), governments must advertise job openings on the Internet.

**Travel Services.** The Internet is an ideal place to plan, explore, and arrange almost any trip economically. Online travel services allow you to purchase airline tickets, reserve hotel rooms, and rent cars. Most sites also offer a fare-tracker feature that sends you e-mail messages about low-cost flights. Examples of comprehensive online travel services are Expedia.com, Travelocity.com, and Orbitz.com. Online services are also provided by all major airline vacation services, large conventional travel agencies, car rental agencies, hotels (e.g., *www.hotels.com*), and tour companies. In a variation of this process, Priceline.com allows you to set a price you are willing to pay for an airline ticket or hotel accommodations. It then attempts to find a vendor that will match your price.

One costly problem that e-commerce can cause is "mistake fares" in the airline industry. For example, on August 6, 2012, El Al (*www.elal.com*), Israel's national airline, offered flights to Israel worth up to $1,600 for as little as some $300. This price was incorrect; the actual price was higher. By the time El Al noticed the mistake and pulled the fare, however, several tickets had been sold, thanks in part to online travel discussion groups.

**Online Advertising.**   *Advertising* is the practice of disseminating information in an attempt to influence a buyer–seller transaction. Traditional advertising on TV or in newspapers involves impersonal, one-way mass communication. In contrast, direct response marketing, or telemarketing, contacts individuals by direct mail or telephone and requires them to respond in order to make a purchase. The direct response approach personalizes advertising and marketing. At the same time, however, it can be expensive, slow, and ineffective. It can also be extremely annoying to the consumer.

Internet advertising redefines the advertising process, making it media rich, dynamic, and interactive. It improves on traditional forms of advertising in a number of ways. First, Internet ads can be updated any time at minimal cost and therefore can be kept current. In addition, these ads can reach very large numbers of potential buyers all over the world. Furthermore, they are generally cheaper than radio, television, and print ads. Finally, Internet ads can be interactive and targeted to specific interest groups and/or individuals.

**Advertising Methods.**   The most common online advertising methods are banners, pop-ups, and e-mail. Banners are simply electronic billboards. Typically, a banner contains a short text or a graphical message to promote a product or a vendor. It may even contain video clips and sound. When customers click on a banner, they are transferred to the advertiser's home page. Banner advertising is the most commonly used form of advertising on the Internet.

A major advantage of banners is that they can be customized to the target audience. If the computer system knows who you are or what your profile is, it might send you a banner that is specifically intended to match your interests. A major disadvantage of banners is that they can convey only limited information because of their small size. Another drawback is that many viewers simply ignore them.

Pop-up and pop-under ads are contained in a new browser window that is automatically launched when you enter or exit a Web site. A **pop-up ad** appears in front of the current browser window. A **pop-under ad** appears underneath the active window; when users close the active window, they see the ad. Many users strongly object to these ads, which they consider intrusive. Modern browsers let users block pop-up ads, but this feature must be used with caution because some Web sites depend on pop-up capabilities to present content other than advertising.

E-mail is another Internet advertising and marketing channel. It is generally cost-effective to implement, and it provides a better and quicker response rate than other advertising channels. Marketers develop or purchase a list of e-mail addresses, place them in a customer database, and then send advertisements via e-mail. A list of e-mail addresses can be a very powerful tool because the marketer can target a group of people or even individuals.

As you have probably concluded by now, there is a potential for misuse of e-mail advertising. In fact, some consumers receive a flood of unsolicited e-mail, or *spam*. **Spamming** is the indiscriminate distribution of electronic ads without the permission of the receiver. Unfortunately, spamming is becoming worse over time.

Two important responses to spamming are permission marketing and viral marketing. **Permission marketing** asks consumers to give their permission to voluntarily accept online advertising and e-mail. Typically, consumers are asked to complete an electronic form that asks what they are interested in and requests permission to send related marketing information. Sometimes, consumers are offered incentives to receive advertising.

Permission marketing is the basis of many Internet marketing strategies. For example, millions of users periodically receive e-mails from airlines such as American and Southwest. Users of this marketing service can ask to be notified of low fares from their hometown or to their favorite destinations. Significantly, they can easily unsubscribe at any time. Permission marketing is also extremely important for market research (e.g., search for "Media Metrix" at *www.comscore.com*).

In one particularly interesting form of permission marketing, companies such as Click-dough.com, ExpressPaidSurveys.com, and CashSurfers.com have built customer lists of millions of people who are happy to receive advertising messages whenever they are on the Web. These customers are paid $0.25–0.50 an hour to view messages while they do their normal surfing.

**Viral marketing** refers to online word-of-mouth marketing. The strategy behind viral marketing is to have people forward messages to friends, family members, and other acquaintances suggesting they "check this out." For example, a marketer can distribute a small game program embedded with a sponsor's e-mail that is easy to forward. The marketer releases only a few thousand copies, with the expectation that the recipients in turn will forward the program to many more thousands of potential customers. In this way, viral marketing enables companies to build brand awareness at a minimal cost without having to spam millions of uninterested users.

## Issues in E-Tailing

Despite e-tailing's increasing popularity, many e-tailers continue to face serious issues that can restrict their growth. Perhaps the two most significant issues are channel conflict and order fulfillment.

Clicks-and-mortar companies may face a conflict with their regular distributors when they sell directly to customers online. This situation, known as **channel conflict**, can alienate the distributors. Channel conflict has forced some companies to avoid direct online sales. For example, Walmart, Lowe's, and Home Depot would rather have customers come to their stores. Therefore, although all three companies maintain e-commerce Web sites, their sites place more emphasis on providing information—products, prices, specials, and store locations—than on online sales.

Channel conflict can arise in areas such as pricing and resource allocation—for example, how much money to spend on advertising. Another potential source of conflict involves the logistics services provided by the offline activities to the online activities. For example, how should a company handle returns of items purchased online? Some companies have completely separated the "clicks" (the online portion of the organization) from the "mortar" or "bricks" (the traditional bricks-and-mortar part of the organization). However, this approach can increase expenses, reduce the synergy between the two organizational channels, and alienate customers. As a result, many companies are integrating their online and offline channels, a process known as **multichanneling**. In fact, many companies are calling this process omni-channeling, as you see in this chapter's opening case.

Multichanneling has created the opportunity for showrooming. *Showrooming* occurs when shoppers visit a brick-and-mortar store to examine a product in person. They then conduct research about the product on their smartphones. Often, they purchase the product from the Web site of a competitor of the store they are visiting. Showrooming is causing problems for brick-and-mortar retailers, such as Target, Best Buy, and others. At the same time, showrooming benefits Amazon, eBay, and other online retailers.

The second major issue confronting e-commerce is order fulfillment, which can create problems for e-tailers as well. Any time a company sells directly to customers, it is involved in various order-fulfillment activities. It must perform the following activities: quickly find the products to be shipped; pack them; arrange for the packages to be delivered speedily to the customer's door; collect the money from every customer, either in advance, by COD, or by individual bill; and handle the return of unwanted or defective products.

It is very difficult to accomplish these activities both effectively and efficiently in B2C, because a company has to ship small packages to many customers and do it quickly. For this reason, companies involved in B2C activities often experience difficulties in their supply chains.

In addition to providing customers with the products they ordered and doing it on time, order fulfillment provides all related customer services. For example, the customer must receive assembly and operation instructions for a new appliance. In addition, if the customer is unhappy with a product, the company must arrange an exchange or a return.

In the late 1990s, e-tailers faced continuous problems in order fulfillment, especially during the holiday season. These problems included late deliveries, delivering wrong items, high delivery costs, and compensation to unsatisfied customers. For e-tailers, taking orders over the Internet is the easy part of B2C e-commerce. Delivering orders to customers' doors is the hard part. In contrast, order fulfillment is less complicated in B2B. These transactions are much larger, but they are fewer in number. In addition, these companies have had order fulfillment mechanisms in place for many years.

## before you go on...

1. Describe electronic storefronts and malls.
2. Discuss various types of online services, such as cyberbanking, securities trading, job searches, travel services, and so on.
3. Discuss online advertising, its methods, and its benefits.
4. Identify the major issues related to e-tailing.
5. What are spamming, permission marketing, and viral marketing?

# Business-to-Business (B2B) Electronic Commerce

**7.3**

In *business to business (B2B)* e-commerce, the buyers and sellers are business organizations. B2B comprises about 85 percent of EC volume. It covers a broad spectrum of applications that enable an enterprise to form electronic relationships with its distributors, resellers, suppliers, customers, and other partners. Organizations can use B2B to restructure their supply chains and their partner relationships.

B2B applications utilize any of several business models. The major models are sell-side marketplaces, buy-side marketplaces, and electronic exchanges.

## Sell-Side Marketplaces

In the **sell-side marketplace** model, organizations attempt to sell their products or services to other organizations electronically from their own private e-marketplace Web site and/or from a third-party Web site. This model is similar to the B2C model in which the buyer is expected to come to the seller's site, view catalogs, and place an order. In the B2B sell-side marketplace, however, the buyer is an organization.

The key mechanisms in the sell-side model are forward auctions and electronic catalogs that can be customized for each large buyer. Sellers such as Dell Computer (*www.dellauction.com*) use auctions extensively. In addition to conducting auctions from their own Web sites, organizations can use third-party auction sites, such as eBay, to liquidate items. Companies such as Ariba (*www.ariba.com*) are helping organizations to auction old assets and inventories.

The sell-side model is used by hundreds of thousands of companies. It is especially powerful for companies with superb reputations. The seller can be either a manufacturer (e.g., Dell or IBM), a distributor (e.g., *www.avnet.com*), or a retailer (e.g., *www.bigboxx.com*). The seller uses EC to increase sales, reduce selling and advertising expenditures, increase delivery speed, and lower administrative costs. The sell-side model is especially suitable to customization. Many companies allow their customers to configure their orders online. For example, at Dell (*www.dell.com*), you can determine the exact type of computer that you want. You can choose the type of chip, the size of the hard drive, the type of monitor, and so on. Similarly, the Jaguar Web site (*www.jaguar.com*) allows you to customize the Jaguar you want. Self-customization greatly reduces any misunderstandings concerning what customers want, and it encourages businesses to fill orders more quickly.

### Buy-Side Marketplaces

*Procurement* is the overarching function that describes the activities and processes to acquire goods and services. Distinct from purchasing, procurement involves the activities necessary to establish requirements, sourcing activities such as market research and vendor evaluation, and negotiation of contracts. *Purchasing* refers to the process of ordering and receiving goods and services. It is a subset of the procurement process.

The **buy-side** marketplace is a model in which organizations attempt to procure needed products or services from other organizations electronically. A major method of procuring goods and services in the buy-side model is the reverse auction.

The buy-side model uses EC technology to streamline the procurement process. The goal is to reduce both the costs of items procured and the administrative expenses involved in procuring them. In addition, EC technology can shorten the procurement cycle time.

Procurement by using electronic support is referred to as e-procurement. **E-procurement** uses reverse auctions, particularly group purchasing. In **group purchasing**, multiple buyers combine their orders so that they constitute a large volume and therefore attract more seller attention. In addition, when buyers place their combined orders on a reverse auction, they can negotiate a volume discount. Typically, the orders of small buyers are aggregated by a third-party vendor, such as the United Sourcing Alliance (*www.usa-llc.com*).

### Electronic Exchanges

Private exchanges have one buyer and many sellers. Electronic marketplaces (e-marketplaces), called **public exchanges** or just **exchanges**, are independently owned by a third party, and they connect many sellers with many buyers. Public exchanges are open to all business organizations. They are frequently owned and operated by a third party. Public exchange managers provide all of the necessary information systems to the participants. Thus, buyers and sellers merely have to "plug in" in order to trade. B2B public exchanges are often the initial point of contacts between business partners. Once the partners make contact, they may move to a private exchange or to private trading rooms provided by many public exchanges to conduct their subsequent trading activities.

Electronic exchanges deal in both direct and indirect materials. *Direct materials* are inputs to the manufacturing process, such as safety glass used in automobile windshields and windows. *Indirect materials* are those items, such as office supplies, that are needed for maintenance, operations, and repairs (MRO).

There are three basic types of public exchanges: vertical, horizontal, and functional. All three types offer diversified support services, ranging from payments to logistics.

*Vertical exchanges* connect buyers and sellers in a given industry. Examples of vertical exchanges are *www.plasticsnet.com* in the plastics industry and *www.papersite.com* in the paper industry. The vertical e-marketplaces offer services that are particularly suited to the community they serve. Vertical exchanges are frequently owned and managed by a *consortium*, a term for a group of major players in an industry. For example, Marriott and Hyatt own a procurement consortium for the hotel industry, and Chevron owns an energy e-marketplace.

*Horizontal exchanges* connect buyers and sellers across many industries. They are used primarily for MRO materials. Examples of horizontal exchanges are TradersCity (*www.traderscity.com*), Globalsources (*www.globalsources.com*), and Alibaba (*www.alibaba.com*).

Finally, in *functional exchanges*, needed services such as temporary help or extra office space are traded on an "as-needed" basis. For example, Employease (*www.employease.com*) can find temporary labor by searching employers in its Employease Network.

# before you go on...

1. Briefly differentiate between the sell-side marketplace and the buy-side marketplace.

2. Briefly differentiate among vertical exchanges, horizontal exchanges, and functional exchanges.

# Ethical and Legal Issues in E-Business

7.4

Technological innovation often forces a society to reexamine and modify its ethical standards. In many cases, the new standards are incorporated into law. In this section, you will learn about two important ethical considerations—privacy and job loss—as well as various legal issues arising from the practice of e-business.

## Ethical Issues

Many of the ethical and global issues related to IT also apply to e-business. Here you will learn about two basic issues: privacy and job loss.

By making it easier to store and transfer personal information, e-business presents some threats to privacy. To begin with, most electronic payment systems know who the buyers are. It may be necessary, then, to protect the buyers' identities. Businesses frequently use encryption to provide this protection.

Another major privacy issue is tracking. For example, individuals' activities on the Internet can be tracked by cookies (discussed in Chapter 4). Cookies store your tracking history on your personal computer's hard drive, and any time you revisit a certain Web site, the server recognizes the cookie. In response, antivirus software packages routinely search for potentially harmful cookies.

In addition to compromising individual privacy, the use of EC may eliminate the need for some of a company's employees, as well as brokers and agents. The manner in which these unneeded workers, especially employees, are treated can raise ethical issues: How should the company handle the layoffs? Should companies be required to retrain employees for new positions? If not, how should the company compensate or otherwise assist the displaced workers?

## Legal and Ethical Issues Specific to E-Commerce

Many legal issues are related specifically to e-commerce. A business environment in which buyers and sellers do not know one another and cannot even see one another creates opportunities for dishonest people to commit fraud and other crimes. During the first few years of EC, the public witnessed many such crimes. These illegal actions ranged from creating a virtual bank that disappeared along with the investors' deposits to manipulating stock prices on the Internet. Unfortunately, fraudulent activities on the Internet are increasing. In the following section, you will explore some of the major legal issues that are specific to e-commerce.

**Fraud on the Internet.** Internet fraud has grown even faster than Internet use itself. In one case, stock promoters falsely spread positive rumors about the prospects of the companies they touted in order to boost the stock price. In other cases, the information provided might have been true, but the promoters did not disclose that they were paid to talk up the companies. Stock promoters specifically target small investors who are lured by the promise of fast profits. Stocks are only one of many areas where swindlers are active. Auctions are especially conducive to fraud, by both sellers and buyers. Other types of fraud include selling bogus investments and setting up phantom business opportunities. Because of the growing use of e-mail, financial criminals now have access to many more potential victims. The U.S. Federal Trade Commission (FTC) (*www.ftc.gov*) regularly publishes examples of scams that are most likely to be spread via e-mail or to be found on the Web. Later in this section, you will see some ways in which consumers and sellers can protect themselves from online fraud.

**Domain Names.** Another legal issue is competition over domain names. Domain names are assigned by central nonprofit organizations that check for conflicts and possible infringement of trademarks. Obviously, companies that sell goods and services over the Internet want customers to be able to find them easily. In general, the closer the domain name matches the company's name, the easier the company is to locate.

A domain name is considered legal when the person or business who owns the name has operated a legitimate business under that name for some time. Companies such as Christian Dior, Nike, Deutsche Bank, and even Microsoft have had to fight or pay to acquire the domain name that corresponds to their company's name. Consider the case of Delta Air Lines. Delta originally could not obtain the Internet domain name delta.com because Delta Faucet had already purchased it. Delta Faucet had been in business under that name since 1954, so it had a legitimate business interest in using the domain name. Delta Air Lines had to settle for delta-airlines.com until it bought the domain name from Delta Faucet. Delta Faucet is now at deltafaucet.com. Several cases of disputed domain names are currently in court.

**Cybersquatting.** **Cybersquatting** refers to the practice of registering or using domain names for the purpose of profiting from the goodwill or the trademark that belongs to someone else. The Anti-Cybersquatting Consumer Protection Act (1999) permits trademark owners in the United States to sue for damages in such cases.

However, some practices that could be considered cybersquatting are not illegal, although they may well be unethical. Perhaps the more common of these practices is "domain tasting." Domain tasting lets registrars profit from the complex money trail of pay-per-click advertising. The practice can be traced back to the policies of the organization responsible for regulating Web names, the Internet Corporation for Assigned Names and Numbers (ICANN) (*www.icann.org*). In 2000, ICANN established the "create grace period," a five-day period during which a company or person can claim a domain name and then return it for a full refund of the $6 registry fee. ICANN implemented this policy to allow someone who mistyped a domain to return it without cost. In some cases, companies engage in cybersquatting by registering domain names that are very similar to their competitors' domain names in order to generate traffic from people who misspell Web addresses.

Domain tasters exploit this policy by claiming Internet domains for five days at no cost. These domain names frequently resemble those of prominent companies and organizations. The tasters then jam these domains full of advertisements that come from Yahoo! and Google. Because this process involves zero risk and 100 percent profit margins, domain tasters register millions of domain names every day—some of them over and over again. Experts estimate that registrants ultimately purchase less than 2 percent of the sites they sample. In the vast majority of cases, they use the domain names for only a few days to generate quick profits.

**Taxes and Other Fees.** In offline sales, most states and localities tax business transactions that are conducted within their jurisdiction. The most obvious example is sales taxes. Federal, state, and local authorities are now scrambling to create some type of taxation policy for e-business. This problem is particularly complex for interstate and international e-commerce. For example, some people claim that the state in which the *seller* is located deserves the entire sales tax (in some countries, it is a value-added tax (VAT)). Others contend that the state in which the *server* is located should also receive some of the tax revenues.

In addition to the sales tax, there is a question about where—and in some cases, whether—electronic sellers should pay business license taxes, franchise fees, gross receipts taxes, excise taxes, privilege taxes, and utility taxes. Furthermore, how should tax collection be controlled? Legislative efforts to impose taxes on e-commerce are opposed by an organization named the Internet Freedom Fighters.

In December 2013, the U.S. Supreme Court declined to get involved in state efforts to force Web retailers such as Amazon to collect sales tax from customers even in places where the companies do not have a physical presence. The court's decision to stay out of the issue may put pressure on Congress to come up with a national solution, as both online and traditional retailers complain about a patchwork of state laws and conflicting lower court decisions. As of early 2015, all but five states impose sales taxes on online purchases, and an increasing number have passed legislation to force online retailers to begin collecting those taxes from customers.

Even before electronic commerce over the Internet emerged, the basic law was that as long as a retailer did not have a physical presence in the state where the consumer was shopping, that retailer did not have to collect a sales tax. Shoppers are supposed to track such purchases and then pay the taxes owed in their annual tax filings. Few people, however, do this or are even aware of it.

The result is that online retailers have been able to undercut the prices of their non-Internet (e.g., brick-and-mortar stores) competitors for years. As state and local governments have increasingly experienced large cash shortcomings since the recession, they have fought back. As of early 2015, some 23 states required Amazon to collect sales taxes.

**Copyright.**   Recall from Chapter 3 that intellectual property is protected by copyright laws and cannot be used freely. This point is significant because many people mistakenly believe that once they purchase a piece of software, they have the right to share it with others. In fact, what they have bought is the right to *use* the software, not the right to *distribute* it. That right remains with the copyright holder. Similarly, copying material from Web sites without permission is a violation of copyright laws. Protecting intellectual property rights in e-commerce is extremely difficult, however, because it involves hundreds of millions of people in 200 countries with differing copyright laws who have access to billions of Web pages.

## before you go on...

1. List and explain some ethical issues in EC.
2. Discuss the major legal issues associated with EC.
3. Describe buyer protection and seller protection in EC.

**What's In IT For Me?**

### For the Accounting Major

Accounting personnel are involved in several EC activities. Designing the ordering system and its relationship with inventory management requires accounting attention. Billing and payments are also accounting activities, as are determining cost and profit allocation. Replacing paper documents with electronic means will affect many of the accountant's tasks, especially the auditing of EC activities and systems. Finally, building a cost-benefit and cost-justification system to determine which products/services to take online and creating a chargeback system are critical to the success of EC.

### For the Finance Major

The worlds of banking, securities and commodities markets, and other financial services are being reengineered because of EC. Online securities trading and its supporting infrastructure are growing more rapidly than any other EC activity. Many innovations already in place are changing the rules of economic and financial incentives for financial analysts and managers. Online banking, for example, does not recognize state boundaries, and it may create a new framework for financing global trades. Public financial information is now accessible in seconds. These innovations will dramatically change the manner in which finance personnel operate.

### For the Marketing Major

A major revolution in marketing and sales is taking place because of EC. Perhaps its most obvious feature is the transition from a physical to a virtual marketplace. Equally important, however, is the radical transformation to one-on-one advertising and sales and to customized and interactive marketing. Marketing channels are being combined, eliminated, or recreated. The EC revolution is creating new products and markets and significantly altering existing ones. Digitization of products and services also has implications for marketing and sales. The direct producer-to-consumer channel is expanding rapidly and is fundamentally changing the nature of customer service. As the battle for customers intensifies, marketing and sales personnel are becoming the most critical success factor in many organizations. Online marketing can be a blessing to one company and a curse to another.

### For the Production/Operations Management Major

EC is changing the manufacturing system from product-push mass production to order-pull mass customization. This change requires a robust supply chain, information support, and reengineering of processes that involve suppliers and other business partners. Suppliers can use extranets to monitor and replenish inventories without the need for constant reorders. In addition, the Internet and intranets help reduce cycle times. Many production/operations problems that have persisted for years, such as complex scheduling and excess inventories, are being solved rapidly with the use of Web technologies. Companies can now use external and internal networks to find and manage manufacturing operations in other countries much more easily. Also, the Web is reengineering procurement by helping companies conduct electronic bids for parts and subassemblies, thus reducing cost. All in all, the job of the progressive production/operations manager is closely tied in with e-commerce.

### For the Human Resource Management Major

HR majors need to understand the new labor markets and the impacts of EC on old labor markets. Also, the HR department may use EC tools for such functions as procuring office supplies. Moreover, becoming knowledgeable about new government online initiatives and online training is critical. In addition, HR personnel must be familiar with the major legal issues related to EC and employment.

### For the MIS Major

The MIS function is responsible for providing the information technology infrastructure necessary for electronic commerce to function. In particular, this infrastructure includes the company's networks, intranets, and extranets. The MIS function is also responsible for ensuring that electronic commerce transactions are secure.

## [ Summary ]

**1. Describe the six common types of electronic commerce.**

In *business-to-consumer* (B2C) electronic commerce, the sellers are organizations and the buyers are individuals. In *business-to-business* (B2B) electronic commerce, the sellers and the buyers are businesses. In *consumer-to-consumer* (C2C) electronic commerce, an individual sells products or services to other individuals. In *business-to-employee*

(B2E) electronic commerce, an organization uses EC internally to provide information and services to its employees. *E-government* is the use of Internet technology in general and e-commerce in particular to deliver information and public services to citizens (called government-to-citizen or G2C EC) and business partners and suppliers (called government-to-business or G2B EC). *Mobile commerce* refers to e-commerce that is conducted entirely in a wireless environment. We leave the examples of each type to you.

2. **Describe the various online services of business-to-consumer (B2C) commerce, providing specific examples of each.**

   *Electronic banking*, also known as cyberbanking, involves conducting various banking activities from home, at a place of business, or on the road instead of at a physical bank location.

   *Online securities trading* involves buying and selling securities over the Web.

   *Online job matching* over the Web offers a promising environment for job seekers and for companies searching for hard-to-find employees. Thousands of companies and government agencies advertise available positions, accept resumes, and take applications via the Internet.

   *Online travel services* allow you to purchase airline tickets, reserve hotel rooms, and rent cars. Most sites also offer a fare-tracker feature that sends you e-mail messages about low-cost flights. The Internet is an ideal place to plan, explore, and arrange almost any trip economically.

   *Online advertising* over the Web makes the advertising process media-rich, dynamic, and interactive.

   We leave the examples to you.

3. **Describe the three business models for business-to-business electronic commerce.**

   In the *sell-side marketplace* model, organizations attempt to sell their products or services to other organizations electronically from their own private e-marketplace Web site and/or from a third-party Web site. Sellers such as Dell Computer (*www.dellauction.com*) use sell-side auctions extensively. In addition to auctions from their own Web sites, organizations can use third-party auction sites, such as eBay, to liquidate items.

   The *buy-side marketplace* is a model in which organizations attempt to buy needed products or services from other organizations electronically.

   E-marketplaces, in which there are many sellers and many buyers, are called *public exchanges*, or just exchanges. Public exchanges are open to all business organizations. They are frequently owned and operated by a third party. There are three basic types of public exchanges: vertical, horizontal, and functional. *Vertical exchanges* connect buyers and sellers in a given industry. *Horizontal exchanges* connect buyers and sellers across many industries. In *functional exchanges*, needed services such as temporary help or extra office space are traded on an "as-needed" basis.

4. **Identify the ethical and legal issues related to electronic commerce, providing examples.**

   E-business presents some threats to privacy. First, most electronic payment systems know who the buyers are. It may be necessary, then, to protect the buyers' identities with encryption. Another major privacy issue is tracking, where individuals' activities on the Internet can be tracked by cookies.

   The use of EC may eliminate the need for some of a company's employees, as well as brokers and agents. The manner in which these unneeded workers, especially employees, are treated can raise ethical issues: How should the company handle the layoffs? Should companies be required to retrain employees for new positions? If not, how should the company compensate or otherwise assist the displaced workers?

   We leave the examples to you.

# [ Chapter Glossary ]

**auction** A competitive process in which either a seller solicits consecutive bids from buyers or a buyer solicits bids from sellers, and prices are determined dynamically by competitive bidding.

**banner** Electronic billboards, which typically contain a short text or graphical message to promote a product or a vendor.

**brick-and-mortar organizations** Organizations in which the product, the process, and the delivery agent are all physical.

**business model** The method by which a company generates revenue to sustain itself.

**business-to-business electronic commerce (B2B)** Electronic commerce in which both the sellers and the buyers are business organizations.

**business-to-consumer electronic commerce (B2C)** Electronic commerce in which the sellers are organizations and the buyers are individuals; also known as e-tailing.

**business-to-employee electronic commerce (B2E)** An organization using electronic commerce internally to provide information and services to its employees.

**buy-side marketplace** B2B model in which organizations buy needed products or services from other organizations electronically, often through a reverse auction.

**channel conflict** The alienation of existing distributors when a company decides to sell to customers directly online.

**clicks-and-mortar organizations** Organizations that do business in both the physical and digital dimensions.

**consumer-to-consumer electronic commerce (C2C)** Electronic commerce in which both the buyer and the seller are individuals (not businesses).

**cyberbanking** Various banking activities conducted electronically from home, a business, or on the road instead of at a physical bank location; also known as *electronic banking*.

**cybersquatting** Registering domain names in the hope of selling them later at a higher price.

**disintermediation** Elimination of intermediaries in electronic commerce.

**e-government** The use of electronic commerce to deliver information and public services to citizens, business partners, and suppliers of government entities, and those working in the public sector.

**electronic business (e-business)** A broader definition of electronic commerce, including buying and selling of goods and services, and servicing customers, collaborating with business partners, conducting e-learning, and conducting electronic transactions within an organization.

**electronic commerce (EC or e-commerce)** The process of buying, selling, transferring, or exchanging products, services, or information via computer networks, including the Internet.

**electronic mall** A collection of individual shops under one Internet address; also known as a *cybermall* or an *e-mall*.

**electronic marketplace** A virtual market space on the Web where many buyers and many sellers conduct electronic business activities.

**electronic payment mechanisms** Computer-based systems that allow customers to pay for goods and services electronically, rather than writing a check or using cash.

**electronic retailing (e-tailing)** The direct sale of products and services through storefronts or electronic malls, usually designed around an electronic catalog format and/or auctions.

**electronic storefront** The Web site of a single company, with its own Internet address, at which orders can be placed.

**e-procurement** Purchasing by using electronic support.

**exchanges** (see **public exchanges**)

**forward auctions** Auctions that sellers use as a selling channel to many potential buyers; the highest bidder wins the items.

**group purchasing** The aggregation of purchasing orders from many buyers so that a volume discount can be obtained.

**mobile commerce (m-commerce)** Electronic commerce conducted in a wireless environment.

**multichanneling** A process in which a company integrates its online and offline channels.

**permission marketing** Method of marketing that asks consumers to give their permission to voluntarily accept online advertising and e-mail.

**person-to-person payments** A form of electronic cash that enables the transfer of funds between two individuals, or between an individual and a business, without the use of a credit card.

**pop-under ad** An advertisement that is automatically launched by some trigger and appears underneath the active window.

**pop-up ad** An advertisement that is automatically launched by some trigger and appears in front of the active window.

**public exchanges (or exchanges)** Electronic marketplaces in which there are many sellers and many buyers, and entry is open to all; frequently owned and operated by a third party.

**reverse auctions** Auctions in which one buyer, usually an organization, seeks to buy a product or a service, and suppliers submit bids; the lowest bidder wins.

**sell-side marketplace** B2B model in which organizations sell to other organizations from their own private e-marketplace and/or from a third-party site.

**smart cards** Cards that contain a microprocessor (chip) that enables the card to store a considerable amount of information (including stored funds) and to conduct processing.

**spamming** Indiscriminate distribution of e-mail without the receiver's permission.

**stored-value money cards** A form of electronic cash on which a fixed amount of prepaid money is stored; the amount is reduced each time the card is used.

**viral marketing** Online word-of-mouth marketing.

**virtual (or pure play) organizations** Organizations in which the product, the process, and the delivery agent are all digital.

# [ Discussion Questions ]

1. Discuss the major limitations of e-commerce. Which of these limitations are likely to disappear? Why?

2. Discuss the reasons for having multiple EC business models.

3. Distinguish between business-to-business forward auctions and buyers' bids for RFQs.

4. Discuss the benefits to sellers and buyers of a B2B exchange.

5. What are the major benefits of G2C electronic commerce?

6. Discuss the various ways to pay online in B2C. Which method(s) would you prefer and why?

7. Why is order fulfillment in B2C considered difficult?

8. Discuss the reasons for EC failures.

9. Should Mr. Coffee sell coffeemakers online? (Hint: Take a look at the discussion of channel conflict in this chapter.)

10. In some cases, individuals engage in cybersquatting so that they can sell the domain names to companies expensively. In other cases, companies engage in cybersquatting by registering domain names that are very similar to their competitors' domain names in order to generate traffic from people who misspell Web addresses. Discuss each practice in terms of its ethical nature and legality. Is there a difference between the two practices? Support your answer.

11. Do you think information technology has made it easier to do business? Or has it only raised the bar on what is required to be able to do business in the 21st century? Support your answer with specific examples.

12. With the rise of electronic commerce, what do you think will happen to those without computer skills, Internet access, computers, smartphones, and so on? Will they be able to survive and advance by hard work?

# [ Problem-Solving Activities ]

1. Assume you are interested in buying a car. You can find information about cars at numerous Web sites. Access five Web sites for information about new and used cars, financing, and insurance. Decide which car you want to buy. Configure your car by going to the car manufacturer's Web site. Finally, try to find the car from *www.autobytel.com*. What information is most supportive of your decision-making process? Write a report about your experience.

2. Compare the various electronic payment methods. Specifically, collect information from the vendors cited in this chapter and find additional vendors using Google.com. Pay attention to security level, speed, cost, and convenience.

3. Conduct a study on selling diamonds and gems online. Access such sites as *www.bluenile.com*, *www.diamond.com*, *www.thaigem.com*, *www.tiffany.com*, and *www.jewelryexchange.com*.

   a. What features do these sites use to educate buyers about gemstones?

   b. How do these sites attract buyers?

   c. How do these sites increase customers' trust in online purchasing?

   d. What customer service features do these sites provide?

4. Access *www.nacha.org*. What is NACHA? What is its role? What is the ACH? Who are the key participants in an ACH e-payment? Describe the "pilot" projects currently underway at ACH.

5. Access *www.espn.com*. Identify at least five different ways the site generates revenue.

6. Access *www.queendom.com*. Examine its offerings and try some of them. What type of electronic commerce is this? How does this Web site generate revenue?

7. Access *www.ediets.com*. Prepare a list of all the services the company provides. Identify its revenue model.

8. Access *www.theknot.com*. Identify the site's revenue sources.

9. Access *www.mint.com*. Identify the site's revenue model. What are the risks of giving this Web site your credit and debit card numbers, as well as your bank account number?

10. Research the case of *www.nissan.com*. Is Uzi Nissan cybersquatting? Why or why not? Support your answer. How is Nissan (the car company) reacting to the *www.nissan.com* Web site?

11. Enter *www.alibaba.com*. Identify the site's capabilities. Look at the site's private trading room. Write a report. How can such a site help a person who is making a purchase?

12. Enter *www.grubhub.com*. Explore the site. Why is the site so successful? Could you start a competing site? Why or why not?

13. Enter *www.dell.com*, go to "Desktops," and configure a system. Register to "My Cart" (no obligation). What calculators are used there? What are the advantages of this process as compared with buying a computer in a physical store? What are the disadvantages?

14. Enter *www.checkfree.com* and *www.lmlpayment.com* to identify their services. Prepare a report.

15. Access various travel sites such as *www.travelocity.com,* *www.orbitz.com, www.expedia.com, www.kayak.com,* and *www.pinpoint.com.* Compare these Web sites for ease of use and usefulness. Note differences among the sites. If you ask each site for the itinerary, which one gives you the best information and the best deals?

16. Access *www.outofservice.com,* and answer the musical taste and personality survey. When you have finished, click on "Results" and see what your musical tastes say about your personality. How accurate are the findings about you?

### Tips for Safe Electronic Shopping

- Look for reliable brand names at sites such as Walmart Online, Disney Online, and Amazon. Before purchasing, ensure that the site is authentic by entering the site directly and not from an unverified link.
- Search any unfamiliar selling site for the company's address and phone and fax numbers. Call up and quiz the employees about the seller.
- Check out the vendor with the local Chamber of Commerce or Better Business Bureau (*www.bbbonline.org*). Look for seals of authenticity such as TRUSTe.
- Investigate how secure the seller's site is by examining the security procedures and by reading the posted privacy policy.
- Examine the money-back guarantees, warranties, and service agreements.
- Compare prices with those in regular stores. Too low prices are too good to be true and some catch is probably involved.
- Ask friends what they know. Find testimonials and endorsements on community Web sites and well-known bulletin boards.
- Find out what your rights are in case of a dispute. Consult consumer protection agencies and the National Consumer League's Fraud Center (*www.fraud.org*).
- Check Consumerworld (*www.consumerworld.org*) for a collection of useful resources.
- For many types of products, *www.resellerratings.com* is a useful resource.

## [ Closing Case **Uber: Disrupting the Taxi Industry** ]

### The Business Problem

The problem is universal: As a passenger, what is the best way to find a cab when you need one?

The taxi industry has problems. Take San Francisco, for example. The city, like other major urban centers, has a long-standing policy of limiting the number of operating licenses for taxis, despite the fact that its population has increased. In addition, dispatchers at the major cab companies do not seem to care about prompt customer service because they make their money primarily by leasing their cars to drivers. As one Massachusetts Institute of Technology (MIT) professor observed, "The taxi industry is characterized by high prices, poor service, and no accountability."

Another problem is that taxis tend to be scarce when passengers need them the most. For example, a Princeton University economist found that New York City taxi drivers tend to go home after they reach their target income for the day. Common sense would dictate that on days when demand is high—such as when it is raining—drivers would keep driving to maximize their income. It turns out, however, that cabbies prefer to stabilize their income from day to day. Therefore, when the weather is bad and the demand for taxis is greater than normal, taxis are actually more difficult to find. The reason is not simply that more people are hailing cabs. Rather, the supply is constricted, by cabbies who have made their daily quota more rapidly and have turned on the off-duty sign. In short, the taxi industry has long been ripe for disruption. Today, information technology is enabling that disruption.

### A Possible Solution

Uber (*www.uber.com*), founded in 2010, allows passengers to directly book the nearest cab or limousine by smartphone and then track the vehicle on a map as it approaches their location. After the ride, Uber automatically compensates the driver from the customer's credit card—no tipping required. It is a simple experience and a much less frustrating way to get a ride than stepping onto a busy street and waving vigorously at oncoming traffic.

### How Uber Works.

Uber recruits partners—either limousine companies or individual drivers, all of whom own their own cars and assume responsibility for licensing, vehicle maintenance, gas, and auto insurance. The company then trains them to use its software. Uber also performs background checks on its drivers. Drivers normally keep 80% of the fare. Drivers like the work and assignment flexibility that Uber offers.

Uber drivers can choose which hours they work. Some drivers have credited Uber for increasing their potential earnings by 30 percent. Their cars are held to high standards and are rigorously inspected. Drivers and riders rate each other after each trip. This arrangement improves the experience for both the driver and the rider.

The one complaint by Uber drivers involves the company's tipping policies. Uber informs potential customers that the ride might cost slightly more than a cab ride, but they do not have to tip. Uber's pricing is similar to metered taxis, although all hiring and payment are handled exclusively through Uber and not with the driver personally.

To fulfill its promise of a ride within five minutes of the touch of a smartphone button, Uber must constantly optimize the algorithms that govern, among other things, how many of its cars are on the road, where they go, and how much a ride costs. In the company's San Francisco headquarters, a software tool called God View displays all of the vehicles on the Uber system moving at once. Tiny eyeballs on the same map indicate the location of every customer who is currently accessing the Uber app on his or her smartphone. Uber's job is to bring together those cars and eyeballs as seamlessly as possible.

Uber offers standard local rates for its various options. However, the company also engages in *dynamic pricing*; that is, it increases these rates at times of peak demand. Uber refers to this policy as "surge pricing." Some critics (and customers) call it "price gouging." Uber denies these accusations. The company maintains that to meet increased demand, drivers need an extra incentive to get out on the road. Uber also notes that many goods are dynamically priced; for example, airline tickets and happy hour cocktails.

## Battles with the Establishment.

Uber has a significant problem with the "establishment," including the taxi industry and local authorities. Regulators and politicians claim that Uber cars are breaking the law by not following the same regulatory rules as taxi and limousine companies. Uber contends that because it is a software provider and not a taxi or limousine operator, it should not be subject to the same regulatory oversight. Rather, the responsibility to observe the rules falls on its drivers.

Local governments in several of Uber's markets have taken legal actions to shut down Uber. Meanwhile, the $6 billion taxi industry has declared an unofficial war on the company. And, numerous professional limo services have attacked the company over its business tactics.

For example, in 2010 San Francisco's transportation agency issued Uber a cease-and-desist letter, classifying the company as an unlicensed taxi service. Again, Uber argued that it merely provided the software that connected drivers and riders. The company continued to offer rides, building its stature among its customers, a constituency that city politicians are reluctant to alienate.

Uber has also encountered government and industry hostility in other cities, notably New York, Chicago, Boston, and Washington, DC. The Washington city council ultimately passed a legal framework in favor of Uber that the company called "an innovative model for city transportation legislation across the country." The city law includes the following:

- It explicitly defines a separate class of for-hire vehicles that operate through digital dispatch and charge by time and distance.

- It creates a single operator license for taxis, sedans, and limousines, and it requires the Washington, DC Taxi Commission to actually issue licenses.

- It sets standards for price transparency that will benefit consumers.

- It brings regulatory certainty to the vehicle-for-hire marketplace, making it clear that Uber and its partners, the licensed/regulated sedan companies and drivers, cannot be regulated out of existence.

Uber drivers can also get caught between local government regulations and Uber's rules. For example, several Uber drivers were ticketed for dropping off passengers at San Francisco International Airport after the airport began enforcing a policy that requires these drivers to be regulated as a taxi service. The drivers had to decide whether to continue their airport service and run the risk of being ticketed. Significantly, most drivers, who had grown accustomed to the flexible schedule and decent income, concluded it was worth the risk.

Uber has won enough of these fights to threaten the market share of the entrenched players. The company not only offers a more efficient way to hail a ride but also provides drivers with an entirely new method to identify the areas with the greatest demand. In the process, Uber is opening up sections of cities that taxis and car services previously had ignored.

In addition to its battles with the establishment, Uber faces competition from lower cost, real-time ridesharing startups such as Lyft (*www.lyft.me*) and SideCar (*https://www.side.cr*). To compete at lower price levels, Uber has introduced Uber-Taxi, in which the company partners with local taxi commissions. This strategy has led to dissatisfaction among existing Uber limo drivers whose earnings have decreased.

## Results

In the last quarter of 2014, Uber drivers earned more than $650 million, according to an analysis of Uber data by Princeton economist Alan Kreuger. At the end of 2014, Uber had more than 160,000 active drivers offering at least four drives per month. Kreuger's analysis also indicated that Uber drivers make at least as much money as regular taxi drivers and chauffeurs, while enjoying flexible hours. Uber is leveraging its exponential success to expand its operations.

For example, on Valentine's Day 2013, Uber offered flowers to customers in 15 cities. On that day, customers could select the "Rose button" on the Uber app, and an Uber driver would deliver a dozen long-stemmed red roses to a sweetheart. A few months later, Uber launched another one-day special, offering to send an ice cream truck to any customer who hit a special button. These specials represent more than simple brand-building efforts. They are tests to see whether Uber can become not just a car service but also a delivery service; that is, an on-the-ground logistics network with the capability to move many types of products and experiences on the fly.

With its efficient algorithms and on-the-ground reach—all of those vehicles roaming around picking up and dropping off people on any given day—Uber may become a local logistics network that can transport anything anywhere on a moment's notice, challenging firms such as FedEx and UPS.

If Uber were to expand into delivery, its competition—for now other ridesharing startups such as Lyft and Sidecar—could grow to include Amazon, eBay, and Walmart. One strategy for Uber to navigate its rivalry with such giants is to offer itself as the technology that can power same-day online retail. Consider the following scenario. In the fall of 2013, Google launched its shopping express service in San Francisco. The program allows customers to shop online at local stores through a Google-powered app. Google then delivers their purchases the same day via courier. That courier could be an Uber driver.

A final note: By early 2015, Uber had expanded to some 200 cities in 53 countries, and the company was valued at approximately $40 billion.

*Sources:* Compiled from E. Porter, "Job Licenses in Spotlight as Uber Rises," *The New York Times*, January 28, 2015; M. Carney, "Uber's Current Legal Battles Could Lock It Out of Nearly Half the World's GDP," *Pando Daily*, January 12, 2015; A. Taylor, "How the Anti-Uber Backlash Is Spreading Around the World," *The Washington Post*, December 9, 2014; H. Blodget, "I Just Heard Some Startling Things About Uber...." *Business Insider*, June 11, 2014; B. Stone, "Invasion of the Taxi Snatchers: Uber Leads an Industry's Disruption," *Bloomberg BusinessWeek*, February 20, 2014; R. Dillet, "Protesting Taxi Drivers Attack Uber Car Near Paris," *Tech Crunch*, January 13, 2014; M. Wohlsen, "Uber in Overdrive," *Wired*, January, 2014; J. Hempel, "Why the Surge-Pricing Fiasco Is Great for Uber," *Fortune*, December 30, 2013; B. Fung, "How Uber Could Reinforce Car Culture," *The Washington Post*, December 24, 2013; J. Roberts, "Uber CEO Taunts Price Critics, Points to Airline 'Surge Pricing'," *GigaOM*, December 24, 2013; M. Wolff, "Wolff: The Tech Company of the Year Is Uber," *USA Today*, December 22, 2013; N. Bolton, "Customers Out in the Cold Balk at Uber's Surge Pricing," *The New York Times*, December 16, 2013; J. Hempel, "Hey Taxi Company, You Talkin' to Me?" *Fortune*, October 7, 2013; K. Yeung, "California Becomes First State to Regulate Ridesharing Services Benefiting Uber, Lyft, Sidecar, and InstantCab," *TheNextWeb*, September 19, 2013; T. Knowlton, "Uber Toronto Activates Surge Pricing During Storm, Triggering a Bad PR Storm of Its Own, " *Techvibes.com*, July 9, 2013; N. Jackson, "Hailing a Cab with Your Phone," *The Atlantic*, November 16, 2010; www.uber.com, www.lyft.me, www.side.cr, accessed January 21, 2015.

**Questions**

1. Discuss how taxi companies could combat Uber, Lyft, and SideCar. (Hint: Why couldn't taxi companies deploy similar types of information technology?)

2. Describe the disadvantages of Uber's business model. Provide specific examples to support your answer.

# Chapter

**8**

# Wireless, Mobile Computing, and Mobile Commerce

| [ LEARNING OBJECTIVES ] | [ CHAPTER OUTLINE ] | [ WEB RESOURCES ] |
|---|---|---|

**[ LEARNING OBJECTIVES ]**

1. Identify advantages and disadvantages of each of the four main types of wireless transmission media.

2. Explain how businesses can use short-range, medium-range, and long-range wireless networks.

3. Provide a specific example of how each of the five major m-commerce applications can benefit a business.

4. Describe the Internet of Things, and provide examples of how organizations can utilize the Internet of Things.

5. Explain how the four major threats to wireless networks can damage a business.

**[ CHAPTER OUTLINE ]**

8.1 Wireless Technologies

8.2 Wireless Computer Networks and Internet Access

8.3 Mobile Computing and Mobile Commerce

8.4 The Internet of Things

8.5 Wireless Security

**[ WEB RESOURCES ]**

- Student PowerPoints for note taking

**WileyPLUS Learning Space**

- E-book
- Author video lecture for each chapter section
- Practice quizzes
- Flash Cards for vocabulary review
- Additional "IT's About Business" cases
- Video interviews with managers
- Lab Manuals for Microsoft Office 2010 and 2013

## What's In IT For Me?

**This Chapter Will Help Prepare You To...**

| ACCT | FIN | MKT | POM | HRM | MIS |
|---|---|---|---|---|---|
| ACCOUNTING | FINANCE | MARKETING | PRODUCTION OPERATIONS MANAGEMENT | HUMAN RESOURCES MANAGEMENT | MIS |
| Count and audit inventory | Manage wireless payment systems | Manage locationbased advertising | Increase productivity in warehouses | Improved employee communications | Provide firm's wireless infrastructure |

# [ Republic Wireless and Freedom-Pop Could Disrupt the Wireless Industry ]

# The Business Problem

In 2012, more than 30 percent of all data traffic from smartphones passed through a Wi-Fi router, according to Cisco Systems (*www.cisco.com*). Cisco expects that figure to rise to almost 50 percent by 2017. This trend is even more pronounced with tablets, nearly 70 percent of which connect to the Internet exclusively through Wi-Fi. This trend represents a problem for large U.S. carriers, who have purchased land on which to place their transmitter towers as well as exclusive rights to a part of the electromagnetic spectrum. Their strategy is to sell faster, more expensive data plans as their revenue from voice plans decreases.

In contrast, Wi-Fi networks were substantially less expensive to build. The transmitter is the router in the corner of your living room. You do not pay for the spectrum, because Wi-Fi does not require a license from the Federal Communications Commission, and you are already paying for access to the Internet with your home Internet service.

After a decade in which the big four U.S. wireless carriers—AT&T (*www.att.com*); Verizon (*www.verizon.com*), T-Mobile (*www.t-mobile.com*), and Sprint (*www.sprint.com*)—spent tens of billions of dollars to upgrade their networks, arguably the fastest and largest network is the one we have all been building together, namely, Wireless Fidelity.

Cisco's report indicated that traffic over cellular networks did not grow as much as expected in 2012, partly because mobile device users adjusted their settings to automatically jump to their home and office Wi-Fi networks whenever possible. This strategy enabled the users to avoid the fees for exceeding carriers' new limits on data.

Industry analysts note that the rule of thumb in the wireless industry is that a smartphone uses 4 gigabytes of data per month. One gigabyte travels over a cellular network, and the remaining 3 gigabytes travel through Wi-Fi, usually at home. The question for the carrier is: "How can I make money from the 3 gigabytes?" The question for the consumer is: "How can I minimize the cost of the 1 gigabyte?"

Large carriers typically are too focused on their 4G cellular networks to pay attention to Wi-Fi. In the United States, AT&T is the only major carrier that currently offers what the industry calls "seamless offloading." Seamless offloading works like this. AT&T has agreements with about 32,000 Wi-Fi hotspots at businesses and other public places. A customer walks into range, the hotspot recognizes his or her smartphone, and it immediately logs him or her onto the Wi-Fi network. Once on Wi-Fi, the customer no longer pays for data. Several foreign companies, such as China Mobile (*www.chinamobileltd.com*), TIM Participacoes (*www.tim .com.br*) in Brazil, and O₂ (*www.o2.co.uk*) in the United Kingdom provide seamless offloading as well.

As AT&T implemented its seamless offloading, it realized that in some areas Wi-Fi is more economical not only for the smartphone user but also for the carrier. One efficient method to improve a wireless network is to densely pack the transmitters that send and receive data. For a crowded area such as a mall, the carrier receives greater benefits from working with the property owner to build a number of shorter range Wi-Fi cells than from building a massive tower somewhere nearby. For big carriers, this process could lead to billions in savings over time. Elsewhere in the world, the shift to Wi-Fi has prompted wireline Internet service providers such as British Telecom (*http://home.bt.com*), France's Free Mobile (*http://mobile.free.fr*), and Japan's KDDI (*www.kddi.com*) to realize that they actually own an extra wireless network because they power the Wi-Fi of every customer.

Because only one major carrier in the United States offers seamless offloading and Wi-Fi networks are so prevalent and essentially free to use, the wireless industry appears to be ripe for disruption. One potential disruption is called "inverting" the network. A network is "inverted" when Wi-Fi is a carrier's primary service and cellular network functions as its backup service. Two providers that have adopted this model are Republic Wireless and FreedomPop.

# Two Disruptive Solutions

Republic Wireless (*https://republicwireless.com*) is a wireless communications service provider that offers unlimited calls and texts for $5 per month and unlimited data for an additional $20 per month. Republic can offer such low prices because it has not built a cellular network.

Instead, for its customers who travel, the company rents network capacity from Sprint. All other Republic calls, texts, and data use Wi-Fi. Wi-Fi constitutes 50 percent of Republic's calls and texts and 90 percent of its data.

Republic launched its wireless service in November 2013. The carrier requires each customer to purchase an Android smartphone that is modified to use the customer's home or business Wi-Fi network to make phone calls. The company offers three smartphones: the Motorola Moto G, Moto E, and Moto X.

Republic relies on a proprietary Voice-over-Internet Protocol (VoIP) for the Android operating system, which can seamlessly switch between Sprint's mobile network and Wi-Fi (assuming Wi-Fi service is available). Republic users can transfer between service plans directly from their devices so that they can take advantage of Wi-Fi, 3G, and 4G cellular signals based on their individual needs. Further, members can change their plans up to twice per month. Republic users can place calls and send texts over available wireless networks, and they can access Sprint's cellular network when no wireless network is available.

FreedomPop (*www.freedompop.com*) sells refurbished Android phones for $99 to $199, with no contract. In addition, it gives away 500 megabytes of 4G data per month, plus unlimited texting and 200 anytime call minutes, as well as unlimited calls to other FreedomPop phones. FreedomPop sells 2 or more gigabytes of data starting at $18 per month. Compare these figures with a "Share Everything" plan from Verizon iPhone plan, which costs $40 per month for unlimited voice and text plus $60 for 2 gigabytes of data. In essence, FreedomPop charges $18 for what Verizon offers for $100.

FreedomPop uses VoIP to transmit voice and data over bandwidth purchased from Sprint. The startup entices new customers with its free plan. However, after customers have signed on, the company offers them many $3.99 services such as faster download speeds, monthly rollover of unused data, and device insurance. More than 50 percent of FreedomPop customers now pay something, either via monthly plans (25 percent of customers) or added features (28 percent). These add-on services have gross margins of 90 percent. (The gross margin is the difference between revenue and cost before accounting for certain other costs.)

FreedomPop uses proven social marketing tactics. Anyone with a FreedomPop device can share minutes with another user, which increases customer loyalty and boosts usage. Customers also receive free data rewards when they sign up friends. How attractive is this feature? Consider that the company generates 17 invites on its site from each subscriber.

In January 2015 FreedomPop began selling Wi-Fi service on a Wi-Fi network comprised of 10 million hotspots. The company offers users an unlimited voice, short message service (SMS), and Wi-Fi data plan for $5 per month. The Wi-Fi network is actually owned and operated by many different Internet service providers (ISPs) and hotspot aggregators, such as Google, AT&T, and cable operators (e.g., Comcast). FreedomPop's Wi-Fi service is available at Starbucks, Burger King, McDonalds, Panera Bread, Walmart, Home Depot, malls, and outdoor hotspots in major metropolitan areas. FreedomPop also plans to ask its users to bring their own personal Wi-Fi routers into the network, creating an even more powerful crowdsourced network.

## The Results

As of early 2015, both Republic Wireless and FreedomPop were essentially startups. As such, it is unclear whether either company will achieve success. It is also unclear how they will impact the major carriers. It does appear, however, that whatever the outcomes, the ultimate winners will be the consumers.

*Sources:* Compiled from J. Donovan, "Paying Too Much? 5 Unknown Wireless Carriers That Could Cut Your Bill in Half," *Digital Trends*, January 30, 2015; M. Gokey, "Unlimited Wi-Fi Service for $5 a Month Comes to FreedomPop," *Digital Trends*, January 21, 2015; K. Fitchard, "FreedomPop Cobbles Together a Wi-Fi Network of 10M Hotspots," *Gigaom*, January 21, 2015; R. Broida, "The One Real Problem with Republic Wireless," *CNET*, March 10, 2014; B. Greeley, "The Biggest, Cheapest Network of All," *Bloomberg BusinessWeek*, January 6–12, 2014; M. Reardon, "Is Republic Wireless Too Good to Be True?" *CNET*, January 4, 2014; D. McNay, "Republic Wireless: Game Changer in Revolution Against AT&T, Verizon," *The Huffington Post*, November 26, 2013; " W. Mossberg, "Smartphone with Wi-Fi Smarts," *The Wall Street Journal*, November 26, 2013; A. Atkins, "Wi-Fi vs. Cellular Networks: Why Wi-Fi Wins Every Time," *Scratch Wireless*, November 25, 2013; M. Miller, "Republic Wireless Moto X Review: Top Consumer Smartphone and Low Cost Service Are a Killer Combo," *ZD Net*, November 25, 2013;

"Republic Wireless Offers Moto X for $299 and Four New Plans Starting at $5 Per Month," *Republic Wireless Press Release*, November 13, 2013; T. Geron, "Data for Nothing, Calls for Free," *Forbes*, June 24, 2013; S. Vaughan-Nichols, "The Merger of Cellular and Wi-Fi: The Wireless Network's Future," *ZD Net*, January 9, 2013; S. Segan, "Republic Wireless: It's All About Wi-Fi," *PC Magazine*, November 8, 2011; *https://republicwireless.com, www.freedompop.com*, accessed March 11, 2015.

### Questions

1. Describe how Republic Wireless and FreedomPop can be disruptive to the major U.S. cellular service providers.

2. What actions should the major cellular service providers take to combat Republic and FreedomPop's business models?

# Introduction

The traditional working environment that required users to come to a wired computer is ineffective and inefficient. The solution was to build computers that are small enough to carry or wear and that can communicate via wireless networks. The ability to communicate anytime and anywhere provides organizations with a strategic advantage by increasing productivity and speed and improving customer service. The term **wireless** is used to describe telecommunications in which electromagnetic waves, rather than some form of wire or cable, carry the signal between communicating devices such as computers, smartphones, and iPads.

Before you continue, it is important to distinguish between the terms *wireless* and *mobile*, because they can mean different things. The term *wireless* means exactly what it says: without wires. In contrast, *mobile* refers to something that changes its location over time. Some wireless networks, such as MiFi (discussed later in this chapter), are also mobile. Others, however, are fixed. For example, microwave towers form fixed wireless networks.

Wireless technologies enable individuals and organizations to conduct mobile computing, mobile commerce, and the Internet of Things. We define these terms here, and then we discuss each one in detail later in the chapter.

*Mobile computing* refers to a real-time, wireless connection between a mobile device and other computing environments, such as the Internet or an intranet. *Mobile commerce*—also known as *m-commerce*—refers to e-commerce (EC) transactions (see Chapter 7) conducted with a mobile device. The Internet of Things means that virtually every object has processing power with either wireless or wired connections to a global network.

Wireless technologies and mobile commerce are spreading rapidly, replacing or supplementing wired computing. In fact, Cisco (*www.cisco.com*) predicts that the volume of mobile Web traffic will continue to increase rapidly over the next decade.

Almost all (if not all) organizations utilize wireless computing. Therefore, when you begin your career, you likely will be assigned a company smartphone and a wirelessly enabled computer. Clearly, then, it is important for you to learn about wireless computing not only because you will be using wireless applications but also because wireless computing will be so important to your organization. In your job, you will be involved with customers who conduct wireless transactions, with analyzing and developing mobile commerce applications, and with wireless security. And the list goes on.

Simply put, an understanding of wireless technology and mobile commerce applications will make you more valuable to your organization. When you look at "What's in IT for Me?" at the end of the chapter, envision yourself performing the activities discussed in your functional area. In addition, for those of you who are so inclined, an understanding of wireless technology can help you start and grow your own business.

The wireless infrastructure upon which mobile computing is built may reshape the entire IT field. The technologies, applications, and limitations of mobile computing and mobile commerce are the focus of this chapter. You begin the chapter by learning about wireless devices and wireless transmission media. You continue by examining wireless computer networks and wireless Internet access. You then look at mobile computing and mobile commerce, which are made possible by wireless technologies. Next, you turn your attention to the Internet of Things. You conclude by familiarizing yourself with a critical component of the wireless environment—namely, wireless security.

# Wireless Technologies 8.1

Wireless technologies include both wireless devices, such as smartphones, and wireless transmission media, such as microwave, satellite, and radio. These technologies are fundamentally changing the ways organizations operate.

Individuals are finding wireless devices convenient and productive to use, for several reasons. First, people can make productive use of time that was formerly wasted—for example, while commuting to work on public transportation. Second, because people can take these devices with them, their work locations are becoming much more flexible. Third, wireless technology enables them to schedule their working time around personal and professional obligations.

## Wireless Devices

Wireless devices provide three major advantages to users:

- They are small enough to easily carry or wear.
- They have sufficient computing power to perform productive tasks.
- They can communicate wirelessly with the Internet and other devices.

Modern smartphones exhibit a process called *dematerialization*. Essentially, dematerialization occurs when the functions of many physical devices are included in one other physical device. Consider that your smartphone includes the functions of digital cameras for images and video, radios, televisions, Internet access via Web browsers, recording studios, editing suites, movie theaters, GPS navigators, word processors, spreadsheets, stereos, flashlights, board games, card games, video games, an entire range of medical devices, maps, atlases, encyclopedias, dictionaries, translators, textbooks, watches, alarm clocks, books, calculators, address books, credit card swipers, magnifying glasses, money and credit cards, car keys, hotel keys, cellular telephony, Wi-Fi, e-mail access, text messaging, a full QWERTY keyboard, and many, many others. Figure 8.1 illustrates the process of dematerialization with smartphones.

One downside of smartphones is that people can use them to copy and pass on confidential information. For example, if you were an executive at Intel, would you want workers snapping pictures of their colleagues with your secret new technology in the background? After all, one of the functions of a smartphone is that of a digital camera that can transmit wirelessly. New jamming devices are being developed to counter the threat. Some companies, such as Samsung (*www.samsung.com*), have recognized the danger and have banned these devices from their premises altogether. Regardless of any disadvantages, however, cell phones, and particularly smartphones, have had a far greater impact on human society than most of us realize.

Consider Africa, for example. One in six of Africa's 1 billion inhabitants now use a cell phone. These phones are transforming healthcare across the continent in many ways:

- For the first time, medical personnel are obtaining high-quality data that can inform them of who is dying and from what causes, who is sick, and where clusters of disease are occurring.
- Cell phones are now making it possible for parents to register the birth of a child very easily and for governments to more accurately plan healthcare interventions, such as vaccination schedules.
- Cell phones are improving vaccine supply chains, preventing unnecessary stockouts, and ensuring that vaccines are available when children are brought into clinics to be immunized.
- Healthcare workers in the field can access health records and schedule appointments with patients.

**FIGURE 8.1** Dematerialization with smartphones.

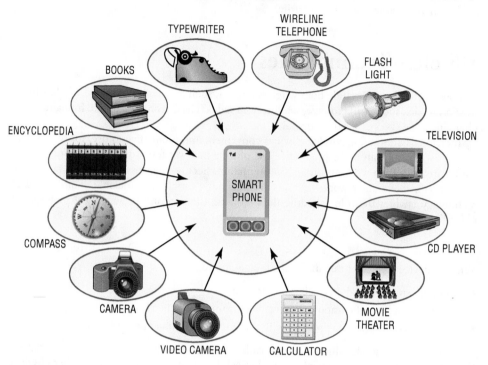

**DEMATERIALIZATION**

## Wireless Transmission Media

Wireless media, or broadcast media, transmit signals without wires. The major types of wireless media are microwave, satellite, and radio. Table 8.1 lists the advantages and disadvantages of each type.

**Microwave.** **Microwave transmission systems** transmit data via electromagnetic waves. These systems are used for high-volume, long-distance, line-of-sight communication. *Line-of-sight* means that the transmitter and receiver are in view of each other. This requirement creates problems because the Earth's surface is curved rather than flat. For this reason, microwave towers usually cannot be spaced more than 30 miles apart.

**Table 8.1**

**Advantages and Disadvantages of Wireless Media**

| Channel | Advantages | Disadvantages |
|---|---|---|
| Microwave | High bandwidth<br>Relatively inexpensive | Must have unobstructed line of sight<br>Susceptible to environmental interference |
| Satellite | High bandwidth<br>Large coverage area | Expensive<br>Must have unobstructed line of sight<br>Signals experience propagation delay<br>Must use encryption for security |
| Radio | High bandwidth<br>Signals pass through walls<br>Inexpensive and easy to install | Creates electrical interference problems<br>Susceptible to snooping unless encrypted |

Table **8.2**
**Three Basic Types of Telecommunications Satellites**

| Type | Characteristics | Orbit | Number | Use |
|------|-----------------|-------|--------|-----|
| GEO | • Satellites stationary relative to point on Earth<br>• Few satellites needed for global coverage<br>• Transmission delay (approximately 0.25 second)<br>• Most expensive to build and launch<br>• Longest orbital life (many years) | 22, 300 miles | 8 | TV signal |
| MEO | • Satellites move relative to point on Earth<br>• Moderate number needed for global coverage<br>• Requires medium-powered transmitters<br>• Negligible transmission delay<br>• Less expensive to build and launch<br>• Moderate orbital life (6–12 years) | 6,434 miles | 10–12 | GPS |
| LEO | • Satellites move rapidly relative to point on Earth<br>• Large number needed for global coverage<br>• Requires only low-power transmitters<br>• Negligible transmission delay<br>• Least expensive to build and launch<br>• Shortest orbital life (as low as 5 years) | 400–700 miles | Many | Telephone |

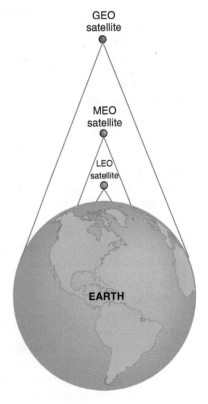

Clearly, then, microwave transmissions offer only a limited solution to data communications needs, especially over very long distances. In addition, microwave transmissions are susceptible to environmental interference during severe weather such as heavy rain and snowstorms. Although long-distance microwave data communications systems are still widely used, they are being replaced by satellite communications systems.

Satellite. **Satellite transmission systems** make use of communication satellites. Currently, there are three types of satellites circling Earth: geostationary-earth-orbit (GEO), medium-earth-orbit (MEO), and low-earth-orbit (LEO). Each type has a different orbit, with the GEO being farthest from Earth and the LEO the closest. In this section, you examine the three types of satellites and then discuss two major satellite applications: global positioning systems and Internet transmission via satellites. Table 8.2 compares and contrasts the three types of satellites.

As with microwave transmission, satellites must receive and transmit data via line-of-sight. However, the enormous *footprint*—the area of Earth's surface reached by a satellite's transmission—overcomes the limitations of microwave data relay stations. The most basic rule governing footprint size is simple: The higher a satellite orbits, the larger its footprint. Thus, medium-earth-orbit satellites have a smaller footprint than geostationary satellites, and low-earth-orbit satellites have the smallest footprint of all. Figure 8.2 compares the footprints of the three types of satellites.

There are an incredible number of applications of satellites, one of which is commercial images from orbit. IT's About Business 8.1 illustrates how Skybox is providing users with high-quality images.

**FIGURE 8.2** Comparison of satellite footprints.

# IT's [about business]

### 8.1 Skybox Imaging Provides Commercial Images from Earth's Orbit

Of the 1,000 or more satellites orbiting the Earth at any given time, only about 100 transmit visual data. Of those 100, only 12 send back high-resolution pictures, which are defined as an image in which each pixel represents a square meter or less of ground. Further, only 9 of these 12 sell to the commercial space-based imaging market. Roughly 80 percent of that market is controlled by the U.S. government, which has priority over all other buyers. Basically, if government agencies decide that they want satellite time for themselves, they can simply demand it.

In January 2013, after the government reduced its imaging budget, the market's two largest companies—DigitalGlobe (*www.digitalglobe.com*) and GeoEye, which between them operated five of the nine commercial geoimaging satellites—were forced to merge under the name DigitalGlobe. Due to the small number of satellites and the government's claim on their operations, ordering and obtaining an image of a specific place can take days, weeks, or even months.

With the image resolutions—*resolution* means sharpness or clarity—allowed by the government for commercial purposes, an orbiting satellite can clearly show individual cars and other objects that are just a few feet across. As a result, an almost entirely untapped source of data—information that companies and governments sometimes try to keep secret—is orbiting in space right above us.

A startup called Skybox Imaging (Skybox; *www.skyboximaging.com*) has designed and built something unprecedented. Using inexpensive consumer hardware, the company plans to ring the Earth with constellations of imaging satellites that are dramatically less expensive to build and maintain than existing satellites. By blanketing the Earth's orbit with its cameras, Skybox will quickly disrupt the commercial space-imaging industry. Even with only six small satellites orbiting Earth, Skybox can provide practically real-time images of the same spot twice a day at a fraction of the current cost.

Over the long term, Skybox's real payoff will not be in the images that the company sells. Instead, it will derive from the massive collection of unsold images its satellites capture every day—images that, when analyzed either by computer vision or by humans, can be translated into extremely useful, desirable, and valuable data. Let's consider some examples:

- The number of cars in the parking lot of every Walmart in America.

- The number of fuel tankers on the roads of the three fastest-growing economic zones in China.

- The size of the pits and slag heaps outside the largest gold mines in southern Africa. These images would allow analysts to estimate a mine's productivity.

- The rate at which the electrical wattage along key stretches of the Ganges River in India is growing brighter as a result of population growth and industrialization.

These images contain clues about the economic health of countries, industries, and individual businesses. Skybox has already brainstormed entirely practical ways to estimate major economic indicators for any country, based entirely on satellite images. The same analysis process will yield even more direct insight into the revenues of a retail chain, a mining company, or an electronics company, once the company analysts determine which of the trucks leaving their factories are shipping out goods or key components.

Many people want real-time access to these data— investors, environmentalists, activists, journalists—and no one currently has it, with the exception of certain government agencies. Skybox can dramatically alter this situation by putting enough satellites into orbit, transmitting the image streams back to Earth, and then analyzing them. This is exactly what the company has done.

Significantly, Skybox has made only incremental changes to existing inexpensive off-the-shelf technologies, which anyone can purchase. The company started with CubeSat (*www.cubesat.org*), a type of low-cost satellite built entirely from inexpensive components or prepackaged kits. The result was a cube, 4 inches on each side, containing a basic sensor and communications payload, solar panels, and a battery, that could be built and launched for less than $60,000.

Skybox launched the first CubeSats in 2003. Since that time there have been astounding advances in computer processing power and speed, and similar advances in telecommunications technologies. Consequently, Skybox engineers were able to build a 220-pound satellite about 3 feet tall, with a payload of optics equipment designed to capture commercial-grade images. Also, Skybox uses a 6-foot antenna to communicate with a dish the size of a dinner plate instead of the much more expensive 30-foot antenna that commercial satellite-imaging companies typically require.

Unlike the other satellite companies, which concentrated on hardware, Skybox focused on software. Consider the cameras that Skybox uses. Compared with most satellites, they are cheap, low resolution, and unsophisticated. But, by writing custom-built software algorithms to integrate dozens of images, Skybox creates one super-high-quality image that enables users to distinguish things they cannot see in any of the individual images. The company focuses on *off-board processing*; that is, processing that is handled by computers on the ground rather than on the satellite itself. As a result, less processing has to be performed on the satellite. Therefore, the satellite can be lighter and less expensive.

As an analogy to what Skybox has accomplished, consider your smartphone. There was a time when you had a phone, a pocket organizer (such as the Palm), a personal computer, and a camera. Now, information and communications technologies have improved to such an extent that all of these functions are integrated into a much smaller physical package (today's smartphones) at a much lower cost.

Skybox launched its first satellite, SkySat-1, on November 21, 2013, from Yasny, Russia, aboard a Dnepr rocket. The satellite began capturing its first images just hours after the payload door opened. The image quality exceeded Skybox's expectations. Even in the photos' uncalibrated state, it is possible to make out details such as car windshields, varying car colors, and road markings. Because these satellites are so cost-effective, Skybox intends to launch 24 of them to provide comprehensive coverage of Earth, beaming back images in near real-time.

Despite these successes, Skybox faces certain problems. The disruptive threat that the company poses to the space-based commercial imaging market could present a threat to U.S. national security. As a result, the government could deny the company licenses, seize its technology or bandwidth, and place restrictions on the frequency and users of its service. In the end, the government will likely commandeer some of Skybox's imaging capabilities under similar terms to those imposed on other vendors. However, Skybox feels confident that its network will be so wide and so nimble that there will be plenty of images and data left over for everyone else.

In June 2014, Google purchased Skybox for $500 million. Google noted that Skybox imagery will help keep Google Maps up-to-date.

At least two other startups are building a business around satellite imagery. One, Urthecast (*www.urthecast.com*), has the rights to images collected by two powerful telescopes attached to the International Space Station (ISS). The company broadcasts the images in near-real time at Ustream (*www.ustream.tv*). Urthecast is planning on offering its satellite imagery on smartphones, tablets, and online. If you are in the path of the two telescopes, Urthecast will inform you when the ISS will next be overhead. So, if your timing is correct, a few hours later you will have a video of your event from orbit.

Urthecast images are also used in the fight against deforestation. Urthecast has joined forces with DeforestACTION's Earthwatchers program to assign participants a 10-square-kilometer area of rainforest to monitor. You track any changes you see and inform local authorities of deforestation.

The other startup, Planet Labs (*www.planet-labs.com*), plans to launch a network of ultralow-cost (though also less powerful) satellites. In March 2014 the company announced it would launch more than 100 satellites over the next year. At the end of 2014, the company had launched 67 of those satellites. This satellite constellation enables Planet Labs to image the entire earth every 24 hours. The company states that it wants to help with deforestation and overfishing while improving agricultural yields.

*Sources:* Compiled from M. Weinberger, "It's a Bird, It's the Rebirth of Satellite Internet," *Network World*, February 5, 2015; R. Trenholm, "How Urthecast Lets You Film Your Party from Space – and Save the Rainforests Too," *CNET*, January 21, 2015; "Google Buys Satellite Firm Skybox Imaging for $500M," *BBC News*, June 10, 2014; D. Messier, "Planet Labs to Launch 100 Satellite Constellation," *Parabolic Arc*, March 17, 2014; M. Kelley, "HD Video from Space Is Going to Change the World," *Business Insider*, March 7, 2014; B. Mason, "Incredible HD Video of Earth from Space Brings Maps to Life," *Wired*, March 4, 2014; R. Sharma, "All Set for Take-Off: Silicon Valley Startups Redefine Space Imaging Market," *Forbes*, February 26, 2014; "Satellite Images of the Protests in Kiev," *The New York Times*, February 18, 2014; "Emirates Space Imaging Ties Up with Skybox Imaging for Meena," *Skybox Imaging Press Release*, February 13, 2014; D. Werner, "Planet Labs CubeSats Deployed from ISS with Many More to Follow," *Space News*, February 11, 2014; D. Butler, "Many Eyes on Earth," *Nature*, January 8, 2014; R. Meyer, "Silicon Valley's New Spy Satellites," *The Atlantic*, January 7, 2014; R. Meyer, "For the First Time Ever, You Can Buy HD Video of Earth from Space," *The Atlantic*, December 27, 2013; "Exelis to Help Advance Near Real-Time Global Observation," *The Wall Street Journal*, December 17, 2013; A. Truong, "Proof That Cheaper Satellites Can Take Incredibly Detailed Photos of Earth," *Fast Company*, December 11, 2013; "Skybox Unveils First Images from Newly Launched Earth-Observation Satellite," *Space News*, December 11, 2013; "Skybox Launch Successful," *Directions Magazine*, November 22, 2014; D. Samuels, "The Watchers," *Wired*, July 2013; J. Dorrier, "Tiny CubeSat Satellites Spur Revolution in Space," *Singularity Hub*, June 23, 2013; www.skyboximaging.com, www.urthecast.com, www.planet-labs.com, accessed March 13, 2015.

## Questions

1. Describe other possible applications of Skybox Imaging (not mentioned in the case).
2. Why might the U.S. government object to Skybox Imaging's business? Provide specific examples in your answer.
3. Might other nations object to Skybox Imaging's business? If so, which ones, and why?
4. Describe other applications for Urthecast satellites.

In contrast to line-of-sight transmission with microwave, satellites use *broadcast* transmission, which sends signals to many receivers at one time. So, even though satellites are line-of-sight like microwave, they are high enough for broadcast transmission, thus overcoming the limitations of microwave.

**Types of Orbits.** *Geostationary-earth-orbit satellites* orbit 22,300 miles directly above the Equator. These satellites maintain a fixed position above Earth's surface because, at their altitude, their orbital period matches the 24-hour rotational period of Earth. For this reason, receivers on Earth do not have to track GEO satellites. GEO satellites are excellent for sending television programs to cable operators and for broadcasting directly to homes.

One major limitation of GEO satellites is that their transmissions take a quarter of a second to send and return. This brief pause, one kind of **propagation delay**, makes two-way telephone conversations difficult. Also, GEO satellites are large and expensive, and they require substantial amounts of power to launch.

*Medium-earth-orbit satellites* are located about 6,000 miles above Earth's surface. MEO orbits require more satellites to cover Earth than GEO orbits because MEO footprints are smaller. MEO satellites have two advantages over GEO satellites: They are less expensive, and they do not have an appreciable propagation delay. However, because MEO satellites move with respect to a point on Earth's surface, receivers must track these satellites. (Think of a satellite dish slowly turning to remain oriented to a MEO satellite.)

*Low-earth-orbit satellites* are located 400–700 miles above Earth's surface. Because LEO satellites are much closer to Earth, they have little, if any, propagation delay. Like MEO satellites, however, LEO satellites move with respect to a point on Earth's surface and therefore must be tracked by receivers. Tracking LEO satellites is more difficult than tracking MEO satellites because LEO satellites move much more quickly relative to a point on Earth.

Unlike GEO and MEO satellites, LEO satellites can pick up signals from weak transmitters. This feature makes it possible for satellite telephones to operate via LEO satellites, because they can operate with less power using smaller batteries. Another advantage of LEO satellites is that they consume less power and cost less to launch.

At the same time, however, the footprints of LEO satellites are small, which means that many satellites are needed to cover the planet. For this reason, a single organization often produces multiple LEO satellites, known as *LEO constellations*. Two examples are Iridium and Globalstar.

Iridium (*www.iridium.com*) has placed a LEO constellation in orbit that consists of 66 satellites and 12 in-orbit spare satellites. The company claims it provides complete satellite communications coverage of Earth's surface, including the polar regions. Globalstar (*www.globalstar. com*) also has a LEO constellation in orbit.

**Global Positioning Systems.** The **global positioning system (GPS)** is a wireless system that utilizes satellites to enable users to determine their position anywhere on Earth. GPS is supported by 24 MEO satellites that are shared worldwide. The exact position of each satellite is always known because the satellite continuously broadcasts its position along with a time signal. By using the known speed of the signals and the distance from three satellites (for two-dimensional location) or four satellites (for three-dimensional location), it is possible to find the location of any receiving station or user within a range of 10 feet. GPS software can also convert the user's latitude and longitude to an electronic map.

Most of you are probably familiar with GPS in automobiles, which "talks" to drivers when giving directions. Figure 8.3 illustrates two ways for drivers to obtain GPS information in a car: a dashboard navigation system and a GPS app (in this case, TomTom; *www.tomtom.com*) on an iPhone.

Commercial use of GPS for activities such as navigating, mapping, and surveying has become widespread, particularly in remote areas. Cell phones in the United States now must have a GPS embedded in them so that the location of a person making an emergency call—for example, 911, known as wireless 911—can be detected immediately.

Three other global positioning systems are either planned or operational. The Russian GPS, *GLONASS*, was completed in 1995. However, the system fell into disrepair with the collapse of the Russian economy. In 2010, however, GLONASS achieved 100 percent coverage of Russian territory. The European Union GPS is called *Galileo*. The first determination of a position relying on Galileo satellites occurred in March 2013. The entire Galileo system is expected to be completed by 2019. China expects to complete its GPS, *Beidou*, by 2020.

**Internet over Satellite.** In many regions of the world, Internet over Satellite (IoS) is the only option available for Internet connections because installing cables is either too expensive or physically impossible. IoS enables users to access the Internet via GEO satellites from a dish mounted on the side of their homes. Although IoS makes the Internet available to many people who otherwise could

Jeff Chiu/ASSOCIATED PRESS

**FIGURE 8.3** Obtaining GPS information in an automobile.

not access it, it has its drawbacks. Not only do GEO satellite transmissions involve a propagation delay, but they also can be disrupted by environmental influences such as thunderstorms.

Radio. **Radio transmission** uses radio-wave frequencies to send data directly between transmitters and receivers. Radio transmission has several advantages. First, radio waves travel easily through normal office walls. Second, radio devices are fairly inexpensive and easy to install. Third, radio waves can transmit data at high speeds. For these reasons, radio increasingly is being used to connect computers to both peripheral equipment and local area networks (LANs; discussed in Chapter 6). (Note: Wi-Fi and cellular also use radio wave frequencies.)

As with other technologies, however, radio transmission has its drawbacks. First, radio media can create electrical interference problems. Also, radio transmissions are susceptible to snooping by anyone who has similar equipment that operates on the same frequency.

Another problem with radio transmission is that when you travel too far away from the source station, the signal breaks up and fades into static. Most radio signals can travel only 30 to 40 miles from their source. However, satellite radio overcomes this problem. **Satellite radio** (or *digital radio*) offers uninterrupted, near CD-quality transmission that is beamed to your radio, either at home or in your car, from space. In addition, satellite radio offers a broad spectrum of stations, including many types of music, news, and talk.

XM Satellite Radio and Sirius Satellite Radio were competitors that launched satellite radio services. XM broadcast its signals from GEO satellites, while Sirius used MEO satellites. In July 2008, the two companies merged to form Sirius XM (*www.siriusxm.com*). Listeners subscribe to the service for a monthly fee.

Au: Please check if the intended meaning of the sentence "Note: Wi-Fi and cellular also use radio wave frequencies." is retained after the edits.

## before you go on...

1. Describe the most common types of wireless devices.
2. Describe the various types of transmission media.

# Wireless Computer Networks and Internet Access

8.2

You have learned about various wireless devices and how these devices transmit wireless signals. These devices typically form wireless computer networks, and they provide wireless Internet access. In this section, you will study wireless networks, which we organize by their effective distance: short range, medium range, and wide area.

## Short-Range Wireless Networks

Short-range wireless networks simplify the task of connecting one device to another. In addition, they eliminate wires, and they enable users to move around while they use the devices. In general, short-range wireless networks have a range of 100 feet or less. In this section, you consider three basic short-range networks: Bluetooth, ultra-wideband (UWB), and near-field communications (NFC).

Bluetooth. **Bluetooth** (*www.bluetooth.com*) is an industry specification used to create small personal area networks. A personal area network is a computer network used for communication among computer devices—for example, telephones, personal digital assistants, and smartphones—located close to one person. Bluetooth 1.0 can link up to eight devices within a 10-meter area (about 30 feet) with a bandwidth of 700 kilobits per second (Kbps) using low-power, radio-based communication. Bluetooth 4.0 can transmit up to approximately 25 megabits per second (Mbps) up to 100 meters (roughly 300 feet). Ericsson, the Scandinavian mobile handset company that developed this standard, called it Bluetooth after the tenth-century Danish King Harald Blatan (*Blatan* means "Bluetooth"). Ericsson selected this name because Blatan unified previously separate islands into the nation of Denmark.

Common applications for Bluetooth are wireless handsets for cell phones and portable music players. Advantages of Bluetooth include low power consumption and the fact that it uses omnidirectional radio waves—that is, waves that are emitted in all directions from a transmitter. For this reason, you do not have to point one Bluetooth device at another to create a connection.

Bluetooth low energy, marketed as *Bluetooth Smart*, enables applications in the healthcare, fitness, security, and home entertainment industries. Compared to "classic" Bluetooth, Bluetooth Smart is less expensive and consumes less power, although it has a similar communication range. Bluetooth Smart is fueling the "wearables" (wearable computer) development and adoption.

**Ultra-Wideband.** **Ultra-wideband** is a high-bandwidth wireless technology with transmission speeds in excess of 100 Mbps. This very high speed makes UWB a good choice for applications such as streaming multimedia from, say, a personal computer to a television.

Time Domain (*www.timedomain.com*), a pioneer in UWB technology, has developed many UWB applications. One interesting application is the PLUS Real-Time Location System (RTLS). An organization can utilize PLUS to locate multiple people and assets simultaneously. Employees, customers, and/or visitors wear the PLUS Badge Tag. PLUS Asset Tags are placed on equipment and products. PLUS is extremely valuable for healthcare environments, where knowing the real-time location of caregivers (e.g., doctors, nurses, technicians) and mobile equipment (e.g., laptops, monitors) is critical.

**Near-Field Communications.** Near-field communications has the smallest range of any short-range wireless networks. It is designed to be embedded in mobile devices such as cell phones and credit cards. For example, using NFC, you can place (or wave) your device or card within a few centimeters of POS terminals to pay for items.

## Medium-Range Wireless Networks

Medium-range wireless networks are the familiar **wireless local area networks (WLANs)**. The most common type of medium-range wireless network is Wireless Fidelity, or Wi-Fi. WLANs are useful in a variety of settings, some of which may be challenging.

**Wireless Fidelity** is a medium-range WLAN, which is a wired LAN but without the cables. In a typical configuration, a transmitter with an antenna, called a wireless access point (see Figure 8.4), connects to a wired LAN or to satellite dishes that provide an Internet connection. A wireless access point provides service to a number of users within a small geographical perimeter (up to approximately 300 feet), known as a **hotspot**. Multiple wireless access points are needed to support a larger number of users across a larger geographical area. To communicate wirelessly, mobile devices, such as laptop PCs, typically have a built-in wireless network interface capability.

Wi-Fi provides fast and easy Internet or intranet broadband access from public hotspots located at airports, hotels, Internet cafés, universities, conference centers, offices, and homes. Users can access the Internet while walking across a campus, to their office, or through their homes. In addition, users can access Wi-Fi with their laptops, desktops, or PDAs by adding a wireless network card. Most PC and laptop manufacturers incorporate these cards in their products.

The Institute of Electrical and Electronics Engineers (IEEE) has established a set of standards for wireless computer networks. The IEEE standard for Wi-Fi is the 802.11 family. As of mid-2014, there were several standards in this family:

© Roman Samokhin/Shutterstock

**FIGURE 8.4** Wireless access point.

- 802.11a: supports wireless bandwidth up to 54 Mbps; high cost; short range; difficulty penetrating walls.
- 802.11b: supports wireless bandwidth up to 11 Mbps; low cost; longer range.
- 802.11g: supports wireless bandwidth up to 54 Mbps; high cost; longer range.
- 802.11n: supports wireless bandwidth exceeding 600 Mbps; higher cost than 802.11g; longer range than 802.11g.

- 802.11ac: will support wireless bandwidth of 1.3 Gbps (1.3 billion bits per second); will provide the ability to fully support a "multimedia home" in which high-definition video can be streamed simultaneously to multiple devices. Essentially, you will be able to wirelessly network your TV, DVR, smartphone, and sound system for complete on-demand access through any Internet-enabled device.
- 802.11 ad: supports wireless bandwidth up to 7 Gbps; targeted to the "wireless office" as opposed to the "wireless home."

The major benefits of Wi-Fi are its low cost and its ability to provide simple Internet access. It is the greatest facilitator of the wireless Internet—that is, the ability to connect to the Internet wirelessly.

Corporations are integrating Wi-Fi into their strategies. For example, Starbucks, McDonald's, Panera, and Barnes & Noble offer customers Wi-Fi in many of their stores, primarily for Internet access. The Winter Olympic Games in Sochi, Russia utilized Wi-Fi extensively, as you see in IT's About Business 8.2.

 **IT's [about business]**

**8.2** A Wi-Fi Network Provides Communications at the 2014 Winter Olympic Games

Sochi, a Russian city of 350,000 people located on the Black Sea, hosted the 2014 Winter Olympic Games. There were actually two Olympic venues—the Olympic village in Sochi and a group of Alpine venues in the nearby Krasnaya Polyana Mountains. In addition to investing in a telecommunications infrastructure, Russia spent billions of dollars to upgrade Sochi's electric power grid, its transportation system, and its sewage treatment facilities. Unfortunately, Russia had to start from zero to build the IT infrastructure for the games.

One essential component of Sochi's IT infrastructure was communications. To create a modern, large-scale communications network, the International Olympic Committee (IOC) selected Avaya (www.avaya.com), a California-based business solutions company. Avaya built a Wi-Fi network for the Winter Games that was designed to handle 54 terabits (trillions of bits or Tbps) per second when the games opened on February 7, 2014.

One reason the IOC chose Avaya was that the company had built the Wi-Fi network for the 2010 Winter Olympic Games in Vancouver, Canada. However, the Sochi games were a stark contrast from the 2010 Games, where the wireless network was capable of handling only 4 Tbps. In Vancouver, Avaya installed an Internet Protocol (IP) voice, data, and video network. This project gave the company invaluable experience, which enabled it to deploy the same type of IP network at Sochi. Interestingly, in Vancouver, Avaya allowed only one mobile device per user. At that time, wired traffic at the Games outnumbered wireless traffic by 4:1. In Sochi, this scenario was reversed: Wireless traffic outnumbered wired traffic by the same ratio.

Building the Wi-Fi network in Sochi presented numerous challenges for Avaya. Let's consider some of them.

- The network had to serve 40,000 athletes and their families, administrators and staff, media, IOC officials, and volunteers with data, voice, video, and full Internet access across 11 competition venues and 3 Olympic villages in addition to multiple media centers, celebration centers, and data centers.
- Avaya realized that the athletes, journalists, and roughly 75,000 daily visitors at the Games would have an unprecedented number of smartphones, tablets, and other mobile devices. To meet this challenge, Avaya actually installed the capacity to support up to 120,000 devices on the Sochi Wi-Fi network, without issues or interruptions. To maintain this system, the company also installed 2,500 wireless access points.
- Avaya had to deliver 30 Internet Protocol high-definition Olympic television channels, all of which had to be available to Olympic family users over the network. Support from Internet Protocol Television (IPTV) eliminated the need for a separate cable television (CATV) network.
- Still another challenge was moving goods into Russia, a process that can be time consuming in the best of situations. To expedite this process, Avaya placed employees in Sochi 18 months before the opening ceremony, coordinating the logistics and ensuring that supplies arrived where and when they were needed. This was a nervous experience for Avaya. As one example, one of its equipment trucks lost radio contact for days while traveling through rural Kazakhstan. Another truck arrived in Sochi with unprotected/uncushioned computer hardware after driving over hundreds of miles of bumpy roads. Fortunately, in both cases the equipment arrived in usable shape.
- Another challenge was training. In line with their agreement with Avaya's Russian partners, the company trained 170 Russian technicians to provide network support during the Games.
- Avaya had to design its network equipment to operate in extreme weather, in case such weather occurred.

- Despite these many challenges, Avaya successfully deployed its Wi-Fi network in time for the opening ceremonies. The network consisted of five subnetworks: one for the athletes, two for media (one free, one paid), one for the Olympics staff, and one for dignitaries. Avaya provided each group with its own access password, and it added extra layers of password protection where needed. The company distributed the Wi-Fi traffic with approximately 2,500 802.11n wireless access points across the Olympics Games sites, including, for the first time, inside the stands. It also provided voice services and more than 6,500 voicemail inboxes at the Games.

- The Avaya network was headquartered in a primary Technical Operations Center (TOC) in the coastal city of Adler. The secondary TOC was located at the Sochi Olympic Park, 10 miles northeast of Adler at the Games site. While one TOC was in use, the other was kept in standby mode by a skeleton crew. Each TOC was connected to the outside world by 10 gigabit-per-second wireline cables provided by Rostelecom (*www.rostelecom.ru*), Russia's national telecommunications operator. The TOCs were placed in separate locations to ensure redundancy in the case of a natural disaster or a manmade incident.

- What type of traffic did Avaya's Wi-Fi network have to handle? According to the company's network analytics, during *just a four-hour period* within the first week of the Games, the network managed 5,130 megabytes of data from Twitter, 2,222 megabytes from Facebook, 1,475 megabytes from Skype, and 746 megabytes from Instagram.

- After the Games concluded on February 23, much of Avaya's infrastructure was removed. However, the telecommunications facilities it built for the Games—including the telephone and IP networking for the Olympics skiing venue in the Caucasus, where a new resort town is being built—will remain.

*Sources:* Compiled from N. Cochrane, "The Most Data-Intensive Games Ever, Sochi Takes Mobile Gold," *The Sydney Morning Herald*, February 24, 2014; K. Bent, "Game Time: How Avaya's Technology Fueled the 2014 Winter Olympics," *CRN*, February 21, 2014; N. Shchelko, "Forget Its Hotels, Sochi's Tech Has Been Up for the Olympic Challenge, " *Ars Technica*, February 20, 2014; L. Leavitt, "Sochi Is the First Truly Connected Olympics," *Forbes*, February 18, 2014; "Avaya Technology Firsts Keep the Sochi 2014 Olympic Winter Games Connected," *Evoke Telecom*, February 13, 2014; S. Leaks, "How Avaya Will Keep Sochi Connected for the 2014 Winter Olympics," *Sport Techie*, February 7, 2014; D. Poeter, "Mid Olympic Hacking Fears, Avaya Offers Safer Surfing in Sochi," *PC Magazine*, February 6, 2014; J. Careless, "Avaya Builds Massive Wi-Fi Net for 2014 Winter Olympics," *Network World*, December 16, 2013; E. Lai, "Going for Gold," *Avaya Innovations Magazine*, Quarter 3, 2013; *www.avaya.com*, accessed January 28, 2015.

**Questions**

1. Describe why wireless communications were critical to the success of the 2014 Winter Olympic Games. Provide specific examples to support your answer.
2. What other potential problems did Avaya have to consider that were not mentioned in this case? Provide specific examples to support your answer.

---

Although Wi-Fi has become extremely popular, it is not without problems. Three factors are preventing the commercial Wi-Fi market from expanding even further: roaming, security, and cost.

- At this time, users cannot roam from hotspot to hotspot if the hotspots use different Wi-Fi network services. Unless the service is free, users have to log on to separate accounts and, where required, pay a separate fee for each service. (Some Wi-Fi hotspots offer free service, while others charge a fee.)

- Security is the second barrier to greater acceptance of Wi-Fi. Because Wi-Fi uses radio waves, it is difficult to shield from intruders.

- The final limitation to greater Wi-Fi expansion is cost. Even though Wi-Fi services are relatively inexpensive, many experts question whether commercial Wi-Fi services can survive when so many free hotspots are available to users.

Wi-Fi Direct.   Until late 2010, Wi-Fi could operate only if the hotspot contained a wireless antenna. Because of this limitation, organizations have typically used Wi-Fi for communications of up to about 800 feet. For shorter, peer-to-peer connections they have used Bluetooth.

This situation changed following the introduction of a new iteration of Wi-Fi known as Wi-Fi Direct. Wi-Fi Direct enables peer-to-peer communications, so devices can connect directly. It allows users to transfer content among devices without having to rely on a wireless antenna. It can connect pairs or groups of devices at Wi-Fi speeds of up to 250 Mbps and at distances of up to 800 feet. Further, devices with Wi-Fi Direct can broadcast their availability to other devices just as Bluetooth devices can. Finally, Wi-Fi Direct is compatible with the more than 1 billion Wi-Fi devices currently in use.

Wi-Fi Direct will probably challenge the dominance of Bluetooth in the area of device-to-device networking. It offers a similar type of connectivity but with greater range and much faster data transfer.

**MiFi.** **MiFi** is a small, portable wireless device that provides users with a permanent Wi-Fi hotspot wherever they go. Thus, users are always connected to the Internet. The range of the MiFi device is about 10 meters (roughly 30 feet). Developed by Novatel, the MiFi device is also called an intelligent mobile hotspot. Accessing Wi-Fi through the MiFi device allows up to five persons to be connected at the same time, sharing the same connection. MiFi also allows users to use voice-over-IP technology (discussed in Chapter 6) to make free (or cheap) calls, both locally and internationally.

MiFi provides broadband Internet connectivity at any location that offers 3G cellular network coverage. One drawback is that MiFi is expensive both to acquire and to use.

**Super Wi-Fi.** The term *Super Wi-Fi* was coined by the U.S. Federal Communications Commission (FCC) to describe a wireless network proposal that creates long-distance wireless Internet connections. (Despite the name, Super Wi-Fi is *not* based on Wi-Fi technology.) Super Wi-Fi uses the lower-frequency "white spaces" between broadcast TV channels. These frequencies enable the signal to travel further and penetrate walls better than normal Wi-Fi frequencies.

Super Wi-Fi is already in use in Houston, Texas, Wilmington, North Carolina, and the University of West Virginia. The technology threatens cell phone carriers' 3G technology, and it could eventually bring broadband wireless Internet access to rural areas.

## Wide-Area Wireless Networks

Wide-area wireless networks connect users to the Internet over a geographically dispersed territory. These networks typically operate over the licensed spectrum—that is, they use portions of the wireless spectrum that are regulated by the government. In contrast, Bluetooth, Wi-Fi, and Super Wi-Fi operate over the unlicensed spectrum and are therefore more prone to interference and security problems. In general, wide-area wireless network technologies fall into two categories: cellular radio and wireless broadband.

**Cellular Radio.** **Cellular telephones (cell phones)** provide two-way radio communications over a cellular network of base stations with seamless handoffs. Cellular telephones differ from cordless telephones, which offer telephone service only within a limited range through a single base station attached to a fixed landline—for example, within a home or an office.

The cell phone communicates with radio antennas, or towers, placed within adjacent geographic areas called *cells* (see Figure 8.5). A telephone message is transmitted to the local cell—that is, the antenna—by the cell phone and then is passed from cell to cell until it reaches the cell of its destination. At this final cell, the message either is transmitted to the receiving cell phone or it is transferred to the public switched telephone system to be transmitted to a wireline telephone. This is why you can use a cell phone to call other cell phones as well as standard wireline phones.

Cellular technology is quickly evolving, moving toward higher transmission speeds and richer features. The technology has progressed through several stages:

- *First generation* (*1G*) cellular networks used analog signals and had low bandwidth (capacity).
- *Second generation* (*2G*) uses digital signals primarily for voice communication; it provides data communication up to 10 Kbps.
- *2.5G* uses digital signals and provides voice and data communication up to 144 Kbps.

**FIGURE 8.5** Smartphone and GPS system.

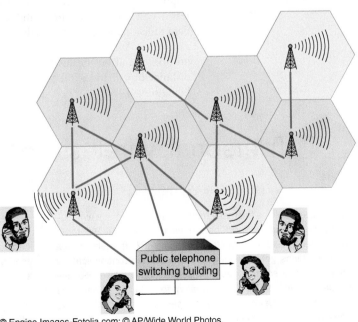

Public telephone switching building

© Engine Images-Fotolia.com; © AP/Wide World Photos.

- *Third generation* (3G) uses digital signals and can transmit voice and data up to 384 Kbps when the device is moving at a walking pace, 128 Kbps when it is moving in a car, and up to 2 Mbps when it is in a fixed location. 3G supports video, Web browsing, and instant messaging.

    3G does have disadvantages. Perhaps the most fundamental problem is that cellular companies in North America use two separate technologies: Verizon and Sprint use Code Division Multiple Access (CDMA), while AT&T and T-Mobile use Global System for Mobile Communications (GSM). CDMA companies are currently using *Evolution-Data Optimized (EV-DO)* technology, which is a wireless broadband cellular radio standard.

    In addition, 3G is relatively expensive. In fact, most carriers limit how much information you can download and what you can use the service for. For instance, some carriers prohibit you from downloading or streaming audio or video. If you exceed the carriers' limits, they reserve the right to cut off your service.

- *Fourth generation* (4G) is not one defined technology or standard. The International Telecommunications Union (ITU) has specified speed requirements for 4G: 100 Mbps (million bits per second) for high-mobility communications such as cars and trains, and 1 Gbps (billion bits per second) for low-mobility communications such as pedestrians. A 4G system is expected to provide a secure all-IP-based mobile broadband system to all types of mobile devices. Many of the current "4G" offerings do not meet the ITU specified speeds, but they call their service 4G nonetheless. See "IT's Personal" for more information.

- Long-term evolution (LTE) is a wireless broadband technology designed to support roaming Internet access via smartphones and handheld devices. LTE is approximately 10 times faster than 3G networks.

- XLTE (advanced LTE) is designed to handle network congestion when too many people in one area try to access an LTE network. XLTE is designed to provide all users with no decrease in bandwidth.

- *Fifth generation* (5G) is expected to be deployed by 2020. 5G networks are predicted to be faster and more intelligent than previous generations of cellular networks. With 5G, wearable computers (e.g., Fitbit), smartphones, tablets, and other devices with sensors that are location- and context-aware will work together with apps and services that you use.

**Wireless Broadband or WiMAX.**   Worldwide Interoperability for Microwave Access, popularly known as WiMAX, is the name for IEEE Standard 802.16. WiMAX has a wireless access range of up to 31 miles, compared to 300 feet for Wi-Fi. WiMAX also has a data transfer rate of up to 75 Mbps. It is a secure system, and it offers features such as voice and video. WiMAX antennas can transmit broadband Internet connections to antennas on homes and businesses located miles away. For this reason, WiMAX can provide long-distance broadband wireless access to rural areas and other locations that are not currently being served.

 **IT's [personal: wireless and mobile]**

### What the GSM3GHSDPA+4GLTE???

This chapter explains the many mobile platforms that are available to you as a consumer. Specifically, it discusses cellular, Bluetooth, Wi-Fi, satellite, and other wireless options. Within the cellular area, however, things get confusing because the telecommunications companies use so many acronyms these days. Have you ever wondered if Verizon 3G was equivalent to AT&T 3G? What about 4G and 4G LTE? Of course, most people assume that 4G is faster than 3G, but by how much?

To appreciate this confusion, consider that when Apple released one update to its mobile operating system (iOS), AT&T suddenly began to display 4G rather than 3G on the iPhone—despite the fact that the phone had not been upgraded! Pretty nice, right? Wrong. In this instance, the "upgrade" simply consisted of a new terminology for the existing technology. The speed of the 3G/4G network had *not* changed. (Note: AT&T "4G LTE" is a different technology that does offer significantly higher speeds than AT&T 3G or 4G.)

Actual connection speeds are described in bit rates, meaning how many bits (1s or 0s) a device can transmit in 1 second. For example, a speed listed as 1.5 Mbps translates to 1.5 million bits per second. That sounds like a tremendous rate. Knowing the bits per second, however, is only part of understanding the actual speed. In reality, connection speed is not the same as *throughput*, which is the amount of bandwidth actually available for you to use. Throughput will always be less than the connection speed.

To understand this point, consider how your car operates. It is probably capable of driving more than 100 mph. However, you are "throttled down" by various speed limits, so you never reach this potential speed. Your actual speed varies depending on the route you take, the speed limits imposed along that route, the weather, the amount of traffic, and many other factors. In the same way, even though AT&T, Verizon, Sprint, and other companies boast incredible wireless speeds ("Up to 20 Mbps!"), they will always say "up to" because they know that you will never actually download a file at that rate.

The best method for determining the actual speeds of the various networks is to go to your local wireless store and run a speed test using the demo model they have on display. This test will give you first-hand experience of the actual throughput speed you can expect from their network. The result is much more realistic than terms such as 3G, 4G, and 4G LTE.

Here is how to perform the test: First, make certain the unit is connected only to a cellular network (not Wi-Fi). Then go to *http://speedtest.net*, and click "Begin Test." I just ran this test from my iPhone 4S on AT&T's 4G (not 4G LTE) network. My download speed was 3.80 Mbps, and my upload speed was 1.71 Mbps. These numbers are more informative than any name they are given (3G, 4G, etc.) because they indicate exactly what I can expect from my wireless connection. Run this test at competing stores (AT&T, Verizon, Sprint, T-Mobile, etc.), and you will have real data to compare. As names change, you can always run a test to find the facts.

## before you go on...

**1.** What is Bluetooth? What is a WLAN?

**2.** Describe Wi-Fi, cellular service, and WiMAX.

# Mobile Computing and Mobile Commerce 8.3

In the traditional computing environment, users come to a computer, which is connected with wires to other computers and to networks. Because these networks need to be linked by wires, it is difficult or even impossible for people on the move to use them. In particular, salespeople, repair people, service employees, law enforcement agents, and utility workers can be more effective if they can use IT while in the field or in transit. Mobile computing was designed for workers who travel outside the boundaries of their organizations as well as for anyone traveling outside his or her home.

**Mobile computing** refers to a real-time connection between a mobile device and other computing environments, such as the Internet or an intranet. This innovation is revolutionizing how people use computers. It is spreading at work and at home; in education, healthcare, and entertainment; and in many other areas.

Mobile computing has two major characteristics that differentiate it from other forms of computing: mobility and broad reach. *Mobility* means that users carry a device with them and can initiate a real-time contact with other systems from wherever they happen to be. *Broad reach* refers to the fact that when users carry an open mobile device, they can be reached instantly, even across great distances.

Mobility and broad reach create five value-added attributes that break the barriers of geography and time: ubiquity, convenience, instant connectivity, personalization, and localization of products and services. A mobile device can provide information and communication regardless of the user's location (*ubiquity*). With an Internet-enabled mobile device, users can access the Web, intranets, and other mobile devices quickly and easily, without booting up a PC or placing a call via a modem (*convenience* and *instant connectivity*). A company can customize information and send it to individual consumers as a short message service (SMS) (*customization*). And, knowing a user's physical location helps a company advertise its products and services (*localization*). Mobile computing provides the foundation for mobile commerce (m-commerce).

## Mobile Commerce

In addition to affecting our everyday lives, mobile computing is also transforming the way organizations conduct business by allowing businesses and individuals to engage in mobile commerce. As you saw at the beginning of this chapter, **mobile commerce** (or *m-commerce*) refers to electronic commerce (EC) transactions that are conducted in a wireless environment, especially via the Internet. Like regular EC applications, m-commerce can be transacted via the Internet, private communication lines, smart cards, and other infrastructures. M-commerce creates opportunities for businesses to deliver new services to existing customers and to attract new customers. To see how m-commerce applications are classified by industry, visit *www.wirelessresearch.eu*.

The development of m-commerce is driven by the following factors:

- *Widespread availability of mobile devices.* By mid-2014, some 6 billion cell phones were in use throughout the world. Cell phones are spreading more quickly in the developing world than the developed world. Experts estimate that within a few years about 70 percent of cell phones in developed countries will have Internet access. Mobile Internet access in developing countries will increase rapidly as well. Thus, a mass market has developed for mobile computing and m-commerce.
- *Declining prices.* The price of wireless devices is declining and will continue to decline.
- *Bandwidth improvement.* To properly conduct m-commerce, you need sufficient bandwidth for transmitting text, voice, video, and multimedia. Wi-Fi, 4G cellular technology, and WiMAX all provide the necessary bandwidth.

Mobile computing and m-commerce include many applications, which result from the capabilities of various technologies. You will examine these applications and their impact on business activities in the next section.

## Mobile Commerce Applications

Mobile commerce applications are many and varied. The most popular applications include location-based applications, financial services, intrabusiness applications, accessing information, and telemetry. The rest of this section examines these various applications and their effects on the ways people live and do business.

**Location-Based Applications and Services.** M-commerce B2C applications include location-based services and location-based applications. Location-based mobile commerce is called location-based commerce (or L-commerce).

Location-based services provide information that is specific to a given location. For example, a mobile user can (1) request the nearest business or service, such as an ATM or a restaurant; (2) receive alerts, such as a warning of a traffic jam or an accident; and (3) find a friend. Wireless carriers can provide location-based services such as locating taxis, service personnel, doctors, and rental equipment; scheduling fleets; tracking objects such as packages and train boxcars; finding information such as navigation, weather, traffic, and room schedules; targeting advertising; and automating airport check-ins.

Consider, for example, how location-based advertising can make the marketing process more productive. Marketers can use this technology to integrate the current locations and preferences of mobile users. They can then send user-specific advertising messages concerning nearby shops, malls, and restaurants to consumers' wireless devices. Apple's iBeacon app is an interesting location-based service, which is illustrated in IT's About Business 8.3.

 **IT's [about business]**

**8.3** Apple's iBeacon

Apple's (*www.apple.com*) iBeacon, a new feature found in iOS 7, is a location-based iPhone app that provides location-aware, contextual information to users. iBeacon uses a collection of beacons, which are Bluetooth low-energy (also called Bluetooth

Smart; see Section 8.2) transmitters. The beacons, which can be placed anywhere that contextual information would be valuable, are tiny discs a little wider and thicker than a quarter. They locate a smartphone's location by broadcasting Bluetooth signals.

The purpose of iBeacon is to allow advertisers and business partners to deliver information, coupons, and other media relevant to a person's location. Reported uses for iBeacon span a wide range of interactive applications for museums, city tours, and shopping experiences. Users can view location-relevant information on exhibits, be guided around on a city tour, and receive notifications for deals while walking past or into stores, without relying on GPS technology. iBeacons also enable shoppers to make purchases at point-of-sale terminals without having to remove their wallet or credit card.

As an example of the use of iBeacons, let's look at Major League Baseball (MLB) (*www.mlb.com*). At Citi Field, home of the New York Mets, iBeacons provide messages such as a simple greeting or a discount at the stadium store. For example, as a fan nears the threshold of the gates from the walkway to the ballpark, a message appears on his iPhone 5S, "Welcome to Citi Field." When he is within a few feet of the stadium turnstiles, the app opens on his smartphone. A prompt asks him if he would like to view his ticket for that day's game. (With this app, fans would not create logjams at the turnstiles looking for their tickets on their e-mail.) When he encounters the Mets Home Run Apple in front of the stadium, he holds his iPhone near a sign by the landmark, and a video appears on his smartphone detailing the landmark's history.

When the fan enters the stadium, another message pops up, this time greeting him as a first-time visitor to Citi Field. The stadium "knows" how many times he has been there. It can utilize this knowledge to send special coupons and discounts to fans who, for instance, are attending their 10th game.

Major League Baseball is also collaborating with Apple to integrate the iBeacon app with MLB's At the Ballpark app. MLB prefers Bluetooth Smart over other technologies because it is more flexible. The iBeacon app can be tuned for a wide variety of distances, depending on the application. Only fans who walk through the door of the Mets store, for instance, will be sent a coupon. Other fans who walk past the store will not be sent anything.

The iBeacon app became commercially available in ballparks in 2014, with individual stadiums offering different features depending on the preferences of the ball club. MLB is also investigating mobile payments powered by iBeacon and Bluetooth Smart at the ballparks.

Location-based services such as iBeacon are challenging to implement. Although retailers love the idea of targeting customers who walk by their stores, there is an inherent unease associated with knowing too much about individuals. Some customers may appreciate offers, whereas others might be nervous or irritated by the idea that stores are tracking their movements. To avoid alienating potential customers, most retailers use an "opt-in" feature. For instance, MLB purposely designed its At the Ballpark app so that only users who are running it (even in the background) will receive offers. MLB maintains that it does not want to surprise any fans.

Privacy concerns have not stopped other businesses from employing technologies that can track a person's location. Significantly, each of these technologies has its own drawbacks. GPS is not particularly accurate indoors, and its use quickly drains a device's battery. Quick response (QR) codes require users to open a specific app and take a clear photo of the code. NFC requires users to tap a specific spot on their devices. Even when they do, it does not always function correctly.

Consider a shoe store, for example. When a customer visits the store, an iBeacon mounted under a shelf will alert her smartphone that she (Jane, loyalty card number 12345) is in a particular physical location in front of the Nike shoe section. The storeowner can monitor her behavior: How long is she looking at Nike shoes? In addition, the store can send her a discount coupon for Nike shoes.

Other interesting applications of iBeacon:

- An indoor location app for a museum that (1) provides a map for you to use in navigating the museum, (2) knows which gallery you are visiting, and (3) offers information about the exhibits in that gallery as you move around.

- A conference management system that tracks which sessions you attend as you enter each session and automatically downloads the session videos to your smartphone after they are published.

- Imagine approaching your front door and having it automatically unlock as you are a step away. When you enter your living room, the television automatically turns on—to your favorite channel.

- For gas stations, customers become more valuable when they do more than buy gas. Thanks to an iBeacon, the station could know when a customer is pumping gas. That is the perfect chance to offer a discount on a sandwich or a drink.

*Sources:* Compiled from R. Bodan, "Brooklyn Museum Reports on BLE Issues," *NFC World*, February 18, 2015; "Cleveland Cavaliers Now Using iBeacons at Quicken Loans Arena," *iBeacon Insider*, February 6, 2015; A. Bohna, "iBeacons: An Overview," *YMC*, February 6, 2014; M. McFarland, "How iBeacons Could Change the World Forever," *The Washington Post*, January 7, 2014; M. Panzarino, "inMarket Rolls Out iBeacons to 200 Safeway, Giant Eagle Grocery Stores to Reach Shoppers When It Matters," *Tech Crunch*, January 6, 2014; K. Vanhemert, "4 Reasons Why Apple's iBeacon Is About to Disrupt Interaction Design," *Wired*, December 11, 2013; "iBeacon – The Game Changer in InStore Navigation," *Technopark Living*, December 8, 2013; L. Tung, "Apple Launches iBeacon in 254 Stores to Streamline Shopping Experience," *ZD Net*, December 6, 2013; E. Anderson, "Shelfbucks Shares Use Cases for Apple's iBeacon for Retailers," *Bestfit Mobile*, November 20, 2013; "Apple iBeacons Explained – Smart Home Occupancy Sensing Explained?" *Automated Home*, October 3, 2013; J. O'Grady, "iBeacons: Coming Soon to a Baseball Stadium Near You," *ZD Net*, October 1, 2013; R. Cheng, "Baseball's Beacon Trials Hint at Apple's Location Revolution," *CNET*, September 28, 2013; *www.apple.com*, accessed March 18, 2015.

### Questions

1. What other uses for iBeacon can you think of?
2. Other than privacy concerns, what are other possible disadvantages of the iBeacon app? Provide specific examples to support your answer.

**Financial Services.** Mobile financial applications include banking, wireless payments and micropayments, money transfers, wireless wallets, and bill payment services. The bottom line for mobile financial applications is to make it more convenient for customers to transact business regardless of where they are or what time it is. Harried customers are demanding such convenience.

In many countries, banks increasingly offer mobile access to financial and account information. For example, Citibank (*www.citibank.com*) alerts customers on their digital cell phones about changes to their account information.

If you took a taxi ride in Frankfurt, Germany, you could use your cell phone to pay the taxi driver. Such very small purchase amounts (generally less than $10) are called *micropayments*.

Web shoppers historically have preferred to pay with credit cards. Because credit card companies sometimes charge fees on transactions, however, credit cards are an inefficient way to make very small purchases. The growth of relatively inexpensive digital content, such as music (e.g., iTunes), ring tones, and downloadable games, is driving the growth of micropayments, as merchants seek to avoid paying credit card fees on small transactions.

Ultimately, however, the success of micropayment applications will depend on the costs of the transactions. Transaction costs will be small only when the volume of transactions is large. One technology that can increase the volume of transactions is wireless **mobile wallets** (m-wallets). Various companies offer m-wallet technologies that enable cardholders to make purchases with a single click from their mobile devices.

In China, SmartPay allows people to use their mobile phones to pay their phone bills and utility bills, buy lottery tickets and airline tickets, and make other purchases. SmartPay launched 172.com (see *www.172.com*), a portal that centralizes the company's mobile, telephone, and Internet-based payment services for consumers. The company designed the portal to provide a convenient, centralized source of information for all of these transactions.

**Intrabusiness Applications.** Although business-to-consumer (B2C) m-commerce receives considerable publicity, most of today's m-commerce applications actually are used *within* organizations. In this section, you will see how companies use mobile computing to support their employees.

Mobile devices increasingly are becoming an integral part of workflow applications. For example, companies can use non-voice mobile services to assist in dispatch functions—that is, to assign jobs to mobile employees, along with detailed information about the job. Target areas for mobile delivery and dispatch services include transportation (delivery of food, oil, newspapers, cargo; courier services; tow trucks; taxis), utilities (gas, electricity, phone, water); field service (computers, office equipment, home repair); healthcare (visiting nurses, doctors, social services); and security (patrols, alarm installation).

**Accessing Information.** Another vital function of mobile technology is to help users obtain and utilize information. Two types of technologies—mobile portals and voice portals—are designed to aggregate and deliver content in a form that will work within the limited space available on mobile devices. These portals provide information to users anywhere and at any time.

A **mobile portal** is a lean, or stripped down, version of a Web site that is optimized for viewing on a mobile device. Mobile portals try to match the functionality of a Web site while keeping data transfers to a minimum. An excellent example of a mobile portal is i-mode from NTT DoCoMo (*www.nttdocomo.com*), which was developed in Japan. Major players in Europe are Vodafone, O2, and T-Mobile. Some traditional portals—for example, Yahoo!, AOL, and MSN—have mobile portals as well.

A **voice portal** is the voice equivalent of a Web portal, providing access to information through spoken commands and voice responses. (Recall our discussion of Web portals in Chapter 6.) For example, most airlines utilize voice portals to provide real-time information on flight status.

Another example of a voice portal is the voice-activated 511 travel-information line developed by Tellme.com. This technology enables callers to inquire about weather, local restaurants, current traffic, and other valuable information.

In addition to retrieving information, some sites provide true interaction. For example, iPing (*www.iping.com*) is a reminder and notification service that allows users to enter information via the Web and receive reminder calls. This service can even call a group of people to notify them of a meeting or conference call.

**Telemetry Applications.** **Telemetry** is the wireless transmission and receipt of data gathered from remote sensors. Telemetry has numerous mobile computing applications. For example, technicians can use telemetry to identify maintenance problems in equipment. As another example, doctors can monitor patients and control medical equipment from a distance. IT's About Business 8.4 shows how the Miami Children's Hospital (MCH) employs telemedicine.

# IT's [about business]

## 8.4 Telemedicine at the Miami Children's Hospital

The Miami Children's Hospital (*www.mch.com*) deployed its telehealth command center to expand the reach of pediatric care while creating new sources of revenue for the hospital. The $2 million command center provides high-definition cameras and large monitors to enable physician-to-patient and physician-to-physician communications as well as remote reading of diagnostic tests. MCH used the command center to develop three telemedicine models—mobile, semistatic, and extremely static—through which patients from as far away as Ecuador and Ukraine can connect with MCH specialists.

### Mobile Model

In the mobile model, MCH IT developers created an iPad app that acts as a virtual examination room. Families download the app, log in from home, and request an appointment with a general physician ($30 out-of-pocket per consultation) or a specialist ($50). MCH views this app as a cash business that sidesteps the usual billing process that inevitably involves an insurance company. The cloud-based app provides an interface for clinical care and patient billing. (We discuss cloud computing in Technology Guide 3).

A separate physician app allows doctors to log in from the MCH command center or from their own devices and choose patients who are online in the virtual waiting room. They then select a patient and engage in an encrypted video consult. This app is most appropriate for consultative services because the physician is limited to a visual examination. It is intended for patients with nonemergency symptoms such as a cold or sinus infection.

MCH is also integrating at-home diagnostic medical tools into the mobile app. These tools include Bluetooth-enabled medical devices—such as blood pressure cuffs and stethoscopes—that families use to provide data to physicians. MCH plans to broaden the geographic reach of the mobile app, with physicians staffed at the command center around the clock.

The app also integrates with MCH's electronic health record (EHR) by Cerner (*www.cerner.com*). MCH executives are confident that patients and family members will find the experience similar to consumer services such as Apple's FaceTime.

In addition to using the iPad for telehealth, the tablet platform has been integrated into MCH's administrative infrastructure. Patients register using an app that allows them to input initial medical, billing, and demographic information through the tablet. MCH collects payment when patients swipe a credit card through a device attached to the iPad. Patients can also read and sign consent forms on the iPad.

MCH has focused its technology strategy on reducing the time it takes for patients to register. The iPad-enabled registration process is part of the improvement. It is a transition from a paper system to an electronic system that uses Bluetooth-enabled medical devices to transmit patient data directly into the EHR. Previously, a nurse would take a patient's vital signs, write down the data on paper, and then manually input those data into the EHR. Now, the data are transmitted from the blood pressure cuff or stethoscope directly to the EHR. These technology-enabled process changes will help healthcare providers make more effective use of IT.

### Semistatic Model

In the semistatic model, MCH has deployed a number of medical carts equipped with videoconferencing technology and clinical tools (such as a stethoscope, blood pressure cuff, and examination camera) to hospitals in the United States and abroad. For $100 per hour, patients can receive a live consultation with an MCH specialist working out of the Miami command center. A local hospital physician is present with the patient to operate the clinical tools and conduct a physician-to-physician conversation with the patient in the room. Clinicians can move the cart around the hospital as needed. MCH has placed carts in hospitals in Ecuador, the Cayman Islands, the Vatican, Ukraine, and other locations.

MCH leases the carts to hospitals for about $1,000 per year. The carts are leased rather than sold so that MCH can ensure that the technology remains up-to-date.

### Extremely Static Model

In the extremely static model, MCH is partnering with HealthSpot (*www.healthspot.net*), a medical kiosk producer, to bring medical care to retail environments such as malls and shopping centers. The kiosk has videoconferencing equipment and clinical tools such as thermometer, stethoscope, blood pressure cuff, and otoscope (for checking ears), but a physician is not physically present. Instead, a nurse or other practitioner assists with the consult as an MCH physician conducts a virtual examination via videoconference. All the consultations are recorded and can be referenced by both the physician and the patient.

The kiosks create new market opportunities for MCH. For example, there is a global shortage of pediatric subspecialists. With the kiosks, these providers can be present in rural counties and areas where the demand is greatest. The kiosks are intended for nonurgent care patients. Beyond shopping malls, MCH envisions kiosks at places such as airports and even cruise ship ports.

*Sources:* Compiled from G. Iversen, "Ready to Consult with Your Physician via Internet? Most Americans Are," *DotMed*, January 26, 2015; B. Guarino, "Telemedicine Shows Satisfaction and Safety, but Obstacles Remain,"

*Pharmacy Practice News*, February 28, 2014; D. Alexander, "Kiosk Company Wants to Bring the Doctor's Office to Workplaces, Pharmacies, and Impoverished Villages," *Forbes*, February 17, 2014; A. Rudansky, "Telemedicine Creates Opportunity," *InformationWeek*, September 9, 2013; D. Brazell, "Telemedicine to Help Save More Lives," *Medical University of South Carolina*, August 2, 2013; S. Wunker, "A New Age for Healthcare Kiosks – Five Ways Next Generation Kiosks Disrupt Medicine and Healthcare Marketing," *Forbes*, July 16, 2013; E. Huizenga, "Pediatric Care Benefiting from the Advantages of Telemedicine," *SearchHealthIT*, May 3, 2013; "HealthSpot and Miami Children's Hospital Pursue a Superior Healthcare Experience," *EMRandEHRNews*, January 8, 2013; *www.mch.com*, accessed March 1, 2015.

**Questions**

1. Describe the advantages and the disadvantages of the iPad mobile app for patients. Do the same for medical carts and medical kiosks.

2. Describe the advantages and the disadvantages of the iPad mobile app for Miami Children's Hospital. Do the same for medical carts and medical kiosks.

Car manufacturers use telemetry applications for remote vehicle diagnosis and preventive maintenance. For instance, drivers of many General Motors cars use its OnStar system (*www.onstar.com*) in numerous ways.

An interesting telemetry application for individuals is an iPhone app called Find My iPhone. Find My iPhone is a part of the Apple iCloud (*www.apple.com/icloud*). This app provides several very helpful telemetry functions. If you lose your iPhone, for example, it offers two ways to find its approximate location on a map. First, you can sign into the Apple iCloud from any computer. Second, you can use the Find My iPhone app on another iPhone, iPad, or iPod touch.

If you remember where you left your iPhone, you can write a message and display it on your iPhone's screen. The message might say, "Left my iPhone. Please call me at 301-555-1211." Your message appears on your iPhone, even if the screen is locked. And, if the map indicates that your iPhone is nearby—perhaps in your office under a pile of papers—you can tell Find My iPhone to play a sound that overrides the volume or silent setting.

If you left your iPhone in a public place, you may want to protect its contents. You can remotely set a four-digit passcode lock to prevent people from using your iPhone, accessing your personal information, or tampering with your settings. Going further, you can initiate a remote wipe (erase all contents) to restore your iPhone to its factory settings. If you eventually find your phone, then you can connect it to your computer and use iTunes to restore the data from your most recent backup.

If you have lost your iPhone and you do not have access to a computer, you can download the Find My iPhone app to a friend's iPhone, iPad, or iPod touch and then sign in to access all the Find My iPhone features.

# before you go on...

1. What are the major drivers of mobile computing?
2. Describe mobile portals and voice portals.
3. Describe wireless financial services.
4. Discuss some of the major intrabusiness wireless applications.

# The Internet of Things

8.4

The **Internet of Things (IoT)**, also called the *Internet of Everything*, the *Internet of Anything*, the *Industrial Internet*, and *machine-to-machine (M2M) communication*, is a system in which any object, natural or manmade, has a unique identity (i.e., its own IP address) and is able to send and receive information over a network (i.e., the Internet) without human interaction. The adoption of IPv6 (discussed in Chapter 6), which created a vast number of IP addresses, has been an important factor in the development of the IoT. In fact, there are enough IP addresses to uniquely identify every object on the earth.

The IoT can be considered as invisible "everywhere computing" that is embedded in the objects around us. Examples of objects are your clock radio, your kitchen appliances, your thermostat, your clothing, your smartphone, a cardiac patient's heart monitor, a chip in a farm animal, and automobile sensors that alert a driver when tire pressure is low or the gas tank needs to be refilled.

Wireless sensors are an underlying technology of the Internet of Things. A **wireless sensor** is an autonomous device that monitors its own condition, as well as physical and environmental conditions around it, such as temperature, sound, pressure, vibration, and movement. Sensors can also control physical systems; for example, opening and closing a valve and controlling the fuel mixture in your car.

Wireless sensors collect data from many points over an extended space. A sensor contains processing, storage, and radio-frequency antennas for sending and receiving messages. Each sensor "wakes up" or activates for a fraction of a second when it has data to transmit. It then relays those data to its nearest neighbor. So, rather than every sensor transmitting its data to a remote computer, the data travel from sensor to sensor until they reach a central computer where they are stored and analyzed. An advantage of this process is that if one sensor fails, then another one can pick up the data. This process is efficient, reliable, and extends battery life of the sensor. Also, if the network requires additional bandwidth, then operators can boost performance by placing new sensors when and where they are required.

Wireless sensors provide information that enables a central computer to integrate reports of the same activity from different angles within the network. This system enables the network to determine with much greater accuracy myriad types of information such as the direction in which a person is moving, the weight of a vehicle, and the amount of rainfall over a field of crops.

One type of sensor uses radio-frequency identification (RFID) technology, which we discuss next.

© Oehoeboeroe/iStockphoto — QR code

## Radio-Frequency Identification

**Radio-frequency identification** technology allows manufacturers to attach tags with antennas and computer chips on goods and then track their movement via radio signals. RFID was developed to replace bar codes.

A typical bar code, known as the *Universal Product Code (UPC)*, is made up of 12 digits that are batched in various groups. Bar codes have worked well, but they have limitations. First, they require a line-of-sight to the scanning device. This system works well in a store, but it can pose substantial problems in a manufacturing plant or a warehouse or on a shipping/receiving dock. Second, because bar codes are printed on paper, they can be ripped, soiled, or lost. Third, the bar code identifies the manufacturer and product but not the actual item.

QR codes are also used in place of bar codes. A *QR code* is a two-dimensional code, readable by dedicated QR readers and camera phones. Figure 8.6 illustrates bar codes, QR codes, and an RFID tag. QR codes have several advantages over bar codes:

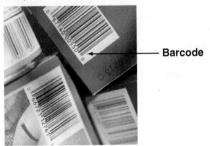
© ra-photos/iStockphoto — RFID tag

Barcode

Media Bakery

**FIGURE 8.6** Bar codes, RFID tags, and QR codes.

- QR codes can store much more information.
- Data types stored in QR codes include numbers, text, URLs, and even Japanese characters.

© Ecken, Dominique/
Keystone Pressedienst/Zuma
Press

**FIGURE 8.7** Small RFID reader and RFID tag.

- QR codes are smaller because they store information both horizontally and vertically.
- QR codes can be read from any direction or angle, so they are less likely to be misread.
- QR codes are more resistant to damage.

RFID systems use tags with embedded microchips, which contain data, and antennas to transmit radio signals over a short distance to RFID readers. The readers pass the data over a network to a computer for processing. The chip in the RFID tag is programmed with information that uniquely identifies an item. It also contains information about the item such as its location and where and when it was made. Figure 8.7 shows a small RFID reader and RFID tag.

There are two basic types of RFID tags: active and passive. *Active RFID tags* use internal batteries for power, and they broadcast radio waves to a reader. Because active tags contain batteries, they are more expensive than passive RFID tags, and they can be read over greater distances. Therefore, they are used primarily for more expensive items. In contrast, *passive RFID tags* rely entirely on readers for their power. They are less expensive than active tags, but they can be read only up to 20 feet. For these reasons, they are generally applied to less expensive merchandise. Problems with RFID include expense and the comparatively large size of the tags. There are many uses for RFID technology, as you see in IT's About Business 8.5.

 **IT's [about business]**

## 8.5 Marks & Spencer Embraces RFID

Marks & Spencer (M&S) (*www.marksandspencer.com*) is one of the United Kingdom's leading retailers, selling high-quality clothing, home products, and innovative food items. Traditionally, M&S relied on optical scanners and bar codes to track its inventory. However, the process was too slow and error prone. As a result, M&S decided to implement RFID technology. The company has since become a pioneer in RFID use.

In 2001, M&S began attaching reusable RFID tags to food trays to track deliveries of fresh food between its suppliers and distribution centers and to determine how well the RFID technology functioned. M&S suppliers place information on the tags indicating the content and expiration dates of the items on the trays. RFID readers scan the tags upon entry to the receiving depots, and they are then used to ensure that fresh merchandise is shipped rapidly to M&S stores. Empty trays are returned to suppliers to be washed, after which they are refilled and recoded. The RFID deployment worked so well that M&S now tracks approximately 10 million RFID-tagged food trays, as well as trays containing fresh flowers and plants, as they move along its supply chain.

Based on the success of its initial efforts, in 2004 M&S deployed RFID to tag and track 10,000 items of men's suits, shirts, and ties. This effort increased inventory accuracy so impressively that M&S expanded the deployment to additional types of clothing, such as men's formal and casual trousers, jackets, and shirts, as well as ladies' knitwear, coats, formal and casual trousers, and suits.

M&S identified the clothing items with RFID tags from Avery Dennison Corporation, which had supplied M&S with 1 billion tags as of early 2015. Avery Dennison is a global manufacturer of pressure-sensitive adhesive materials, apparel labels and tags, and RFID tags.

Initially, M&S used fixed RFID readers that were built into carts equipped with lead acid batteries as a power source. In 2006 and 2007, the company replaced these readers with two-piece readers that consisted of a reader linked to a handheld scanner via Bluetooth. The readers are stored in the back office and are deployed on the sales floor either in the early morning or in the evening.

Sales assistants select a store department from a drop-down menu on the handheld device and then read each item located on the sales floor and within the store's stockroom. The RFID system enables M&S to accurately read merchandise at a rate of up to 15,000 items per hour. It also removes duplicate reads. After the scanning is completed, the mobile device transmits the data to a central RFID database via the store's wireless network. The company then uses this information to automatically update the store's database.

The item-level tagging of clothing provided M&S with a number of benefits. Perhaps most importantly, the retailer knows the exact amount of each particular item at each of its stores. Thanks to the new technology, M&S can ensure that the correct products are shipped to the right stores at the proper time. Inventory turnover has increased by 50 percent, and out-of-stock products have been reduced by 40 percent.

Essentially, RFID creates a "single version of the truth" for the inventory levels in a particular store. These inventory levels are then used by all other M&S systems to calculate the correct allocation of stock for each store. Missing items in each store are replenished by the distribution system as part of the normal daily store deliveries.

Also, the company's ability to keep the right number of clothes for each clothing size in its stores has improved customer satisfaction.

Another benefit of the RFID system is the time savings generated by the reduced number of calls that individual stores make to the head office or distribution center to order missing stock. The stores are confident that if stock is available, it will be sent to them. This process has enabled store teams to focus on customer service rather than on stock inventories and adjustments.

In 2012, M&S began deploying Generation 2 RFID technology on home goods such as bedding, accessories, and kitchenware. This technology enables users to manage multiple RFID readers and multiple RFID applications in close proximity. That is, it can manage interference between RFID readers. Generation 2 technology is also faster and more accurate than Generation 1.

M&S will use some tags for various apparel goods, others for beauty products, and still others for items containing metal. M&S is also working with Avery Dennison to develop a tag for liquid products. Metals and thick liquids can interfere with RFID signals, so they typically require more powerful RFID tags.

RFID also enables M&S offer its customers more complete product descriptions, including size, color, style, manufacturer, destination, and many other features. Further, it provides M&S with greater visibility into its supply chain in addition to more accurate item-level inventory. The retailer has reduced the costs associated with taking inventory annually, with excessive markdowns, and with theft and fraud. RFID also offers M&S the opportunity to implement an entire range of customer information services that help to seamlessly integrate the multiple channels through which customers interact with the retailer.

In 2014, M&S achieved a landmark when it became the first retailer to have 100 percent of its merchandise tagged with RFID technology.

*Sources:* Compiled from "Avery Dennison Expands Line of RFID-Enabled Solutions for Retailers," *Avery Dennison Press Release*, April 8, 2014; "Marks & Spencer Expands RFID Rollout," *RFID24-7*, February 27, 2014; "Marks & Spencer Introduce RFID Enabled Footwear Inspiration Station," *Retail Innovation*, February 23, 2014; "Accurate Inventory Tracking Benefits M&S," *Retail Technology*, February 18, 2014; "RFID Leader Marks & Spencer Drives Apparel Sales with Accurate Inventory Tracking," *Avery Dennison Press Release,* 2013; B. Violino, "Marks & Spencer Rolls Out RFID to All Its Stores," *RFID Journal*, March 25, 2013; "M&S Extends RFID Across Departments," *Logistics Manager*, January 17, 2013; T. Sharma, "Marks & Spencer Extends Its Use of RFID Technology," *RFID Ready*, January 17, 2013; L. Barrie, "Marks & Spencer Expands RFID to All Clothing," *Just-Style*, January 15, 2013; L. Bateman, "M&S Sets Its Sights on Becoming Closed Loop," *Greenwise Business*, June 19, 2012; C. Swedberg, "Marks & Spencer to Tag Items at 120 Stores," *RFID Journal*, November 16, 2006; J. Collins, "Marks & Spencer to Extend Trial to 53 Stores," *RFID Journal*, February 18, 2005; B. Violino, "EPC in Fashion at Marks & Spencer," *RFID Journal*, April 10, 2003; *www.marksandspencer.com*, accessed March 12, 2015.

**Questions**

1. Describe how RFID technology can generate increased customer satisfaction.
2. What are potential disadvantages to implementing RFID technology in a retailer such as Marks & Spencer?
3. Why did Marks & Spencer initially deploy RFID technology on a limited basis? In your opinion, was this the correct strategy? Why or why not? Be specific.

## Examples of the Internet of Things in Use

There are numerous examples of how the Internet of Things is being deployed. We discuss just a few of them here.

- *The Smart Home*: In a *smart home*, your home computer, television, lighting and heating controls, home security system (including smart window and door locks), thermostats, and appliances have embedded sensors and can communicate with one another via a home network. You control these networked objects through various devices, including your pager, smartphone, television, home computer, and even your automobile. Appropriate service providers and homeowners can access the devices for which they are authorized. Smart home technology can be applied to any building, turning it into a smart building.

  Consider Nest Labs (*www.nest.com*; now owned by Google), which produces a digital thermostat that combines sensors and Web technology. The thermostat senses not only air temperature but also the movements of people in a house. It then adjusts room temperatures accordingly to save energy.

- *Healthcare*: Patients with non-life-threatening conditions can wear sensors, or have them implanted—for example, to monitor blood pressure or glucose levels—that are monitored by medical staff. In many cases, the patients can be shown how to interpret the sensor data themselves. Also, consumer-oriented sensors such as the Fitbit can encourage people to adopt healthier lifestyles.

- *Automotive*: Modern cars have many sensors that monitor functions such as engine operation, tire pressure, fluid levels, and many others. Cars can warn drivers of impending mechanical or other problems and automatically summon roadside assistance or emergency services when necessary. Further, cars can detect vehicles in other lanes to help eliminate blindspots.

- *Supply Chain Management*: The IoT can make a company's supply chain much more transparent. A company can now track, in real time, the movement of raw materials and parts through the manufacturing process to finished products delivered to the customer. Sensors in fleet vehicles (e.g., trucks) can monitor the condition of sensitive consignments (e.g., the temperature of perishable food). In addition, they can trigger automatic security alerts if a container is opened unexpectedly.

- *Environmental monitoring*: Sensors monitor air and water quality, atmospheric and soil conditions, and the movements of wildlife.

- *Infrastructure management*: Sensors monitor infrastructures such as bridges, railway tracks, and roads. They can identify and report changes in structural conditions that can compromise safety.

- *Energy management*: Sensors will be integrated into all forms of energy-consuming devices; for example, switches, power outlets, light bulbs, and televisions. They will be able to communicate directly with utility companies via smart meters to balance power generation and energy usage. Another valuable application of sensors is to use them in smart electrical meters, thereby forming a *smart grid*. Smart meters monitor electricity usage, and they transmit those data in real time to the utility companies. In turn, the utilities can utilize these data to match power demand with production. This process can lead to fewer brownouts and blackouts during periods of peak usage, such as air-conditioning during hot summer days.

- *Agriculture*: Sensors monitor, in real time, air temperature, humidity, soil temperature, soil moisture, leaf wetness, atmospheric pressure, solar radiation, trunk/stem/fruit diameter, wind speed and direction, and rainfall. The data from these sensors are used in precision agriculture. (Precision agriculture is a farming technique based on observing, measuring, and responding to inter- and intrafield variability in crops.)

- *Transportation*: Sensors placed on complex transportation machines such as jet engines and locomotives can provide critical information on their operations. Consider General Electric (GE) (*www.ge.com*), which embeds "intelligence" in the form of 250 sensors in each of its giant locomotives. The sensors produce 9 million data points every hour. How can these sensors improve the performance of such a huge machine?

One of the biggest problems of locomotives is faulty bearings. If a bearing fails, then an axle might freeze, leaving a train marooned on the tracks. In remote areas, this situation could be disastrous, not to mention expensive, because other trains would back up for miles behind the stalled one. In this situation the company would have to send a crane to lift the locomotive off the track and transport it back to a shop.

To avoid this type of scenario, GE embeds one sensor inside each locomotive's gear case that transmits data on oil levels and contaminants. By examining these data, GE can predict the conditions that cause bearings to fail and axles to freeze. GE data analysts claim that sensors that predict part failures before they occur will translate into billions of dollars of savings for GE's rail customers.

GE also uses locomotive sensors to optimize the entire network of U.S. trains. Today, the average velocity of a freight train operating between U.S. cities ranges from 20 to 25 miles per hour. Why is this number so low? The reason is a combination of factors: congestion in the train yards, breakdowns (see above), and the frequent necessity of letting other trains pass. GE has developed a software tool called Movement Planner that gathers and integrates sensor data on velocity, traffic, and location from many locomotives. This analysis increases the average speed of its customers' trains. One of GE's customers, Norfolk Southern, states that an average speed increase of 1 mile per hour for its trains would be worth $200 million. GE's goal is to increase average train speeds by 4 miles per hour.

## before you go on...

1. Define the Internet of Things and RFID.
2. Provide two examples (other than those mentioned in this section) of how the Internet of Things benefits organizations (public sector, private sector, for-profit, or not-for-profit).
3. Provide two specific business uses of RFID technology.

# Wireless Security

8.5

Clearly, wireless networks provide numerous benefits for businesses. However, they also present a huge challenge to management—namely, their inherent lack of security. Wireless is a broadcast medium, and transmissions can be intercepted by anyone who is close enough and has access to the appropriate equipment. There are four major threats to wireless networks: rogue access points, war driving, eavesdropping, and radio-frequency jamming.

A *rogue access point* is an unauthorized access point to a wireless network. The rogue could be someone in your organization who sets up an access point meaning no harm but fails to inform the IT department. In more serious cases, the rogue is an "evil twin"—someone who wishes to access a wireless network for malicious purposes.

In an *evil twin attack*, the attacker is in the vicinity with a Wi-Fi-enabled computer and a separate connection to the Internet. Using a *hotspotter*—a device that detects wireless networks and provides information on them (see *www.canarywireless.com*)—the attacker simulates a wireless access point with the same wireless network name, or SSID, as the one that authorized users expect. If the signal is strong enough, users will connect to the attacker's system instead of the real access point. The attacker can then serve them a Web page asking for them to provide confidential information such as usernames, passwords, and account numbers. In other cases, the attacker simply captures wireless transmissions. These attacks are more effective with public hotspots (e.g., McDonald's and Starbucks) than with corporate networks.

*War driving* is the act of locating WLANs while driving (or walking) around a city or elsewhere. To war drive or walk, you simply need a Wi-Fi detector and a wirelessly enabled computer. If a WLAN has a range that extends beyond the building in which it is located, then an unauthorized user might be able to intrude into the network. The intruder can then obtain a free Internet connection and possibly gain access to important data and other resources.

*Eavesdropping* refers to efforts by unauthorized users to access data that are traveling over wireless networks. Finally, in *radio-frequency (RF) jamming*, a person or a device intentionally or unintentionally interferes with your wireless network transmissions.

## before you go on...

1. Describe the four major threats to the security of wireless networks.
2. Which of the four threats is the most dangerous for a business? Which is the most dangerous for an individual? Support your answers.

# What's In IT For Me?

### For the Accounting Major

Wireless applications help accountants to count and audit inventory. They also expedite the flow of information for cost control. Price management, inventory control, and other accounting-related activities can be improved with the use of wireless technologies.

### For the Finance Major

Wireless services can provide banks and other financial institutions with a competitive advantage. For example, wireless electronic payments, including micropayments, are more convenient (anywhere, anytime) than traditional means of payment, and they are less expensive. Electronic bill payment from mobile devices is becoming more popular, increasing security and accuracy, expediting cycle time, and reducing processing costs.

### For the Marketing Major

Imagine a whole new world of marketing, advertising, and selling, with the potential to increase sales dramatically. Such is the promise of mobile computing. Of special interest for marketing are location-based advertising as well as the new opportunities resulting from the Internet of Things and RFID. Finally, wireless technology also provides new opportunities in sales force automation (SFA), enabling faster and better communications with both customers (CRM) and corporate services.

### For the Production/Operations Management Major

Wireless technologies offer many opportunities to support mobile employees of all kinds. Wearable computers enable off-site employees and repair personnel working in the field to service customers faster, better, and less expensively. Wireless devices can also increase productivity within factories by enhancing communication and collaboration as well as managerial planning and control. In addition, mobile computing technologies can improve safety by providing quicker warning signs and instant messaging to isolated employees.

### For the Human Resource Management Major

Mobile computing can improve HR training and extend it to any place at any time. Payroll notices can be delivered as SMSs. In addition, wireless devices can make it even more convenient for employees to select their own benefits and update their personal data.

### For the MIS Major

MIS personnel provide the wireless infrastructure that enables all organizational employees to compute and communicate anytime, anywhere. This convenience provides exciting, creative, new applications for organizations to reduce expenses and improve the efficiency and effectiveness of operations (e.g., to achieve transparency in supply chains). Unfortunately, as you saw earlier, wireless applications are inherently insecure. This lack of security is a serious problem with which MIS personnel must contend.

## [ Summary ]

1. **Identify advantages and disadvantages of each of the three main types of wireless transmission media.**

   *Microwave transmission* systems are used for high-volume, long-distance, line-of-sight communication. One advantage is the high volume. A disadvantage is that microwave transmissions are susceptible to environmental interference during severe weather such as heavy rain and snowstorms.

*Satellite transmission* systems make use of communication satellites, and they receive and transmit data via line-of-sight. One advantage is that the enormous footprint—the area of Earth's surface reached by a satellite's transmission—overcomes the limitations of micro-wave data relay stations. Like microwaves, satellite transmissions are susceptible to environmental interference during severe weather.

*Radio transmission* systems use radio-wave frequencies to send data directly between transmitters and receivers. An advantage is that radio waves travel easily through normal office walls. A disadvantage is that radio transmissions are susceptible to snooping by anyone who has similar equipment that operates on the same frequency.

2. **Explain how businesses can use short-range, medium-range, and long-range wireless networks, respectively.**

*Short-range wireless networks* simplify the task of connecting one device to another, eliminating wires, and enabling people to move around while they use the devices. In general, short-range wireless networks have a range of 100 feet or less. Short-range wireless networks include Bluetooth, ultra-wideband, and near-field communications. A business application of ultra-wideband is the PLUS Real-Time Location System from Time Domain. Using PLUS, an organization can locate multiple people and assets simultaneously.

*Medium-range wireless networks* include Wi-Fi networks. *Wi-Fi* provides fast and easy Internet or intranet broadband access from public hotspots located at airports, hotels, Internet cafés, universities, conference centers, offices, and homes.

*Wide-area wireless networks* connect users to the Internet over geographically dispersed territory. They include cellular telephones and wireless broadband. *Cellular telephones* provide two-way radio communications over a cellular network of base stations with seamless handoffs. *Wireless broadband* has a wireless access range of up to 31 miles and a data transfer rate of up to 75 Mbps. WiMAX can provide long-distance broadband wireless access to rural areas and remote business locations.

3. **Provide a specific example of how each of the five major m-commerce applications can benefit a business.**

*Location-based services* provide information specific to a location. For example, a mobile user can (1) request the nearest business or service, such as an ATM or restaurant; (2) receive alerts, such as a warning of a traffic jam or an accident; and (3) find a friend. With *location-based advertising*, marketers can integrate the current locations and preferences of mobile users. They can then send user-specific advertising messages about nearby shops, malls, and restaurants to wireless devices.

*Mobile financial applications* include banking, wireless payments and micropayments, money transfers, wireless wallets, and bill payment services. The bottom line for mobile financial applications is to make it more convenient for customers to transact business regardless of where they are or what time it is.

*Intrabusiness applications* consist of m-commerce applications that are used *within* organizations. Companies can use non-voice mobile services to assist in dispatch functions—that is, to assign jobs to mobile employees, along with detailed information about the job.

When it comes to *accessing information*, mobile portals and voice portals are designed to aggregate and deliver content in a form that will work within the limited space available on mobile devices. These portals provide information anywhere and anytime to users.

*Telemetry* is the wireless transmission and receipt of data gathered from remote sensors. Company technicians can use telemetry to identify maintenance problems in equipment. Car manufacturers use telemetry applications for remote vehicle diagnosis and preventive maintenance.

4. **Describe the Internet of Things and provide examples of how various organizations can utilize the Internet of Things.**

   The **Internet of Things (IoT)** is a system where any object, natural or manmade, has a unique identity (using IPv6) and the ability to send and receive information over a network (i.e., the Internet) without human interaction.

   We leave the examples of various uses of the IoT to the student.

5. **Explain how the four major threats to wireless networks can damage a business.**

   The four major threats to wireless networks are rogue access points, war driving, eavesdropping, and radio-frequency jamming. A *rogue access point* is an unauthorized access point to a wireless network. *War driving* is the act of locating WLANs while driving around a city or elsewhere. *Eavesdropping* refers to efforts by unauthorized users to access data that are traveling over wireless networks. *Radio-frequency jamming* occurs when a person or a device intentionally or unintentionally interferes with wireless network transmissions.

# [ Chapter Glossary ]

**Bluetooth** Chip technology that enables short-range connection (data and voice) between wireless devices.

**cellular telephones (cell phones)** Phones that provide two-way radio communications over a cellular network of base stations with seamless handoffs.

**global positioning system (GPS)** A wireless system that uses satellites to enable users to determine their position anywhere on Earth.

**hotspot** A small geographical perimeter within which a wireless access point provides service to a number of users.

**Internet of Things (IoT)** A scenario in which objects, animals, and people are provided with unique identifiers and the ability to automatically transfer data over a network without requiring human-to-human or human-to-computer interaction.

**location-based commerce (L-commerce)** Mobile commerce transactions targeted to individuals in specific locations, at specific times.

**microwave transmission** A wireless system that uses microwaves for high-volume, long-distance, point-to-point communication.

**mobile commerce (or m-commerce)** Electronic commerce transactions that are conducted with a mobile device.

**mobile computing** A real-time connection between a mobile device and other computing environments, such as the Internet or an intranet.

**mobile portal** A portal that aggregates and provides content and services for mobile users.

**mobile wallet (m-wallet)** A technology that allows users to make purchases with a single click from their mobile devices.

**near-field communications (NFC)** The smallest of the short-range wireless networks that is designed to be embedded in mobile devices such as cell phones and credit cards.

**personal area network** A computer network used for communication among computer devices close to one person.

**propagation delay** Any delay in communications from signal transmission time through a physical medium.

**radio-frequency identification (RFID) technology** A wireless technology that allows manufacturers to attach tags with antennas and computer chips on goods and then track their movement through radio signals.

**radio transmission** Uses radio-wave frequencies to send data directly between transmitters and receivers.

**satellite radio (or digital radio)** A wireless system that offers uninterrupted, near CD-quality music that is beamed to your radio from satellites.

**satellite transmission** A wireless transmission system that uses satellites for broadcast communications.

**telemetry** The wireless transmission and receipt of data gathered from remote sensors.

**ultra-wideband (UWB)** A high-bandwidth wireless technology with transmission speeds in excess of 100 Mbps that can be used for applications such as streaming multimedia from, say, a personal computer to a television.

**voice portal** The voice equivalent of a Web portal, providing access to information through spoken commands and voice responses.

**wireless** Telecommunications in which electromagnetic waves carry the signal between communicating devices.

**wireless access point** An antenna connecting a mobile device to a wired local area network.

**Wireless Fidelity (Wi-Fi)** A set of standards for wireless local area networks based on the IEEE 802.11 standard.

**wireless local area network (WLAN)** A computer network in a limited geographical area that uses wireless transmission for communication.

# [ Discussion Questions ]

1. Given that you can lose a cell phone as easily as a wallet, which do you feel is a more secure way of carrying your personal data? Support your answer.

2. If mobile computing is the next wave of technology, would you ever feel comfortable with handing a waiter or waitress your cell phone to make a payment at a restaurant the way you currently hand over your credit or debit card? Why or why not?

3. What happens if you lose your NFC-enabled smartphone or it is stolen? How do you protect your personal information?

4. In your opinion, is the mobile (or digital) wallet a good idea? Why or why not?

5. Discuss how m-commerce can expand the reach of e-business.

6. Discuss how mobile computing can solve some of the problems of the digital divide.

7. List three to four major advantages of wireless commerce to consumers and explain what benefits they provide to consumers.

8. Discuss the ways in which Wi-Fi is being used to support mobile computing and m-commerce. Describe the ways in which Wi-Fi is affecting the use of cellular phones for m-commerce.

9. You can use location-based tools to help you find your car or the closest gas station. However, some people see location-based tools as an invasion of privacy. Discuss the pros and cons of location-based tools.

10. Discuss the benefits of telemetry in healthcare for the elderly.

11. Discuss how wireless devices can help people with disabilities.

12. Some experts say that Wi-Fi is winning the battle with 3G cellular service. Others disagree. Discuss both sides of the argument and support each one.

13. Which of the applications of the Internet of Things do you think are likely to gain the greatest market acceptance over the next few years? Why?

# [ Problem-Solving Activities ]

1. Investigate commercial applications of voice portals. Visit several vendors, for example, Microsoft and Nuance. What capabilities and applications do these vendors offer?

2. Using a search engine, try to determine whether there are any commercial Wi-Fi hotspots in your area.

3. Examine how new data-capture devices such as RFID tags help organizations accurately identify and segment their customers for activities such as targeted marketing. Browse the Web, and develop five potential new applications not listed in this chapter for RFID technology. What issues would arise if a country's laws mandated that such devices be embedded in everyone's body as a national identification system?

4. Investigate commercial uses of GPS. Start with *www.neigps.com*. Can some of the consumer-oriented products be used in industry? Prepare a report on your findings.

5. Access *www.bluetooth.com*. Examine the types of products being enhanced with Bluetooth technology. Present two of these products to the class and explain how they are enhanced by Bluetooth technology.

6. Explore *www.nokia.com*. Prepare a summary of the types of mobile services and applications Nokia currently supports and plans to support in the future.

7. Enter *www.ibm.com*. Search for "wireless e-business." Research the resulting stories to determine the types of wireless capabilities and applications IBM's software and hardware support. Describe some of the ways these applications have helped specific businesses and industries.

8. Research the status of 3G and 4G cellular service by visiting various links. Prepare a report on the status of 3G and 4G based on your findings.

9. Enter Pitney Bowes Business Insight (*www.pbinsight.com*). Click on "MapInfo Professional," then click on the "Resources" tab, then on the "Demos" tab. Look for the location-based services demos. Try all the demos. Summarize your findings.

10. Enter *www.packetvideo.com*. Examine the demos and products and list their capabilities.

11. Enter *www.onstar.com*. What types of *fleet* services does OnStar provide? Are these any different from the services OnStar provides to individual car owners? (Play the movie.)

12. Access various search engines to find articles about the "Internet of Things." What is the "Internet of Things?" What types of technologies are necessary to support it? Why is it important?

# [ Closing Case Has Facebook Solved the Mobile Ad Problem? ]

## The Business Problem

In 2012, Facebook (*www.facebook.com*) was unsuccessfully managing the shift of online activities from computers to smartphones and tablets. Immediately before its initial public offering (IPO) in May 2012, the company revealed that it was not earning "any significant revenue" from either its mobile Web site or its mobile app, despite the fact that more than half of its members used its service on their mobile devices.

Facebook had to deal with the two most common problems associated with mobile devices: small screens and gaps in marketers' ability to measure the impact of mobile ads. These factors made ads look far less effective on mobile devices. Consequently, marketers were less willing to pay for them.

Compounding these issues, Facebook's advertising team was too preoccupied with pushing a new kind of desktop Web ad, called Sponsored Stories, to pay much attention to mobile. Sponsored Stories are actions by a Facebook member, such as "liking" a page or checking in at a store, that marketers can then promote, for a fee, to the member's friends. CEO Mark Zuckerberg viewed these ads as the future of Facebook advertising because users were more likely to respond to real posts from friends.

By August 2013, the widening gap between mobile usage and revenue caused Facebook shares to drop by 50 percent of their offering price. Zuckerberg admitted in September 2013 that the company had made a "bunch of missteps" in mobile.

## The IT Solution

Facebook discovered that integrating ads directly into a user's flow of natural activities—in Facebook's case, the main feed where people view updates from friends—is far more effective than banners and pop-up ads. Although these "native ads" might be controversial, they appear to be advertising's most successful adaptation yet to mobile computing.

Facebook began running its ads not just in the right-hand section reserved for ads but also on its prime real estate: the news feed, where people spend most of their time on the social network. Facebook executives realized this was a risky step—particularly when they extended the same type of ads to mobile as well. What if the ads in the news feed really annoyed people?

Fortunately for Facebook, that fear did not materialize. Sponsored Stories still got more clicks than it had previously. However, the mobile ads got twice as many clicks as Sponsored Stories and commanded nearly three times as much revenue from advertisers as ads on the desktop, according to a study by advertising agency TBG Digital. Within a short time, the mobile ads were grossing $500,000 per day.

Facebook then launched other mobile ads, including one that allowed makers of mobile apps to encourage users to install their games or programs. This step was an even bigger leap. It was the first ad in the mobile news feed that did not require advertisers to wait for a "Like" or some other social action to create it. Advertisers instead could use Facebook's huge quantity of biographical data from user profiles to target likely prospects, as they already were doing with traditional ads.

This process worked as well. For instance, Cie Games used app installation ads to draw players for its first iPhone game, Car Town Streets. The cost of acquiring the ads was 40 percent lower using Facebook's ads than using ads from other mobile ad networks. In addition, Walmart purchases 50 million mobile ads from Facebook annually.

## The Results

Consider this trend for Facebook mobile ads:

- Revenue from mobile apps totaled $305 million for the fourth quarter of 2012, a figure that amounted to 23 percent of overall Facebook ad sales.

- For the fourth quarter of 2013, Facebook reported that mobile ads accounted for 53 percent of the company's total ad revenue, for a total of $1.24 billion.

- Facebook's ad revenue in the fourth quarter, 2014, totaled $3.6 billion, with mobile ads comprising nearly 70 percent of this total, or $2.5 billion.

Facebook's success has exploded several myths concerning mobile marketing. Advertisers often complain that they cannot run big, flashy ads on tiny screens. However, Facebook's mobile ads take up a larger part of the screen than desktop ads do, which is one reason why they attract so many clicks. In fact, an increasing number of mobile ads now contain photographs, and Facebook is actively looking to incorporate video into mobile ads.

Industry analysts worried that users might balk at ads that are mixed with posts from friends. So far, that has not happened. Research revealed that the ads reduced comments, likes, and other interaction with posts by only 2 percent, a decline that Facebook considers acceptable However, Facebook will have to be careful not to overdo mobile ads to the point of overloading its users' feeds.

*Sources:* Compiled from C. Farivar, "Those Mobile Ads Work: Facebook Gobbles Up $701M Profit in Q4 2014," *Ars Technica*, January 28, 2015; D. Goldman, "Facebook Is Growing – So Are Its Costs," *CNN Money*, January 28, 2015; T. Huddleston, "Mobile Ads Fuel Facebook's Growth, Again," *Time*, January 28, 2015; A. Campos, "Why Facebook Is Releasing News Feed Video Ads," *The Motley Fool*, March 17, 2014; Z. Terrelonge, "Facebook Officially Launches 15-Second 'Premium Video Ads'," *Mobile Entertainment*, March 14, 2014; S. Parkerson, "New Premium Video Ads Are Facebook's Latest Move to Dominate Ad Dollars," *App Developer Magazine*, March 14, 2014; E. Price, "Prepare Yourself: Facebook Video Ads Are Headed Your Way Soon," *Engadget*, March 13, 2014; J. Edwards, "Facebook Is Powering Millions of App Downloads a Year," *Slate*, March 13, 2014; H. Weber, "Facebook Finally Launches

Autoplaying Video Ads on Desktop and Mobile," *VentureBeat*, March 13, 2014; R. Tate, "Facebook Lures Developers with Mobile Ads and a Promise of Riches," *Wired*, March 12, 2014; D. Serfaty, "Why CMOs Must Change Their Plans for Facebook," *Forbes*, March 11, 2014; L. White, "Digital Ad Spend Quickly Shifting to Mobile: Are You Ready?" *Marketing Land*, February 27, 2014; M. Mawad, "Facebook Mobile Strength Breeds Apps in Hunt for Ad Dollars," *Bloomberg*, February 24, 2014; M. Charski, "Facebook, Twitter Retargeting Tools Appeal to Creators of Mobile Ads," *Data Informed*, February 18, 2014; *www.facebook.com*, accessed March 18, 2015.

## Questions

1. Explain why mobile ads are so effective on Facebook. Provide specific examples to support your answer.

2. You are accessing Facebook on your smartphone or tablet. Would ads placed directly into your news feed bother you? Why or why not?

3. You are accessing Facebook from your desktop computer. Would ads placed directly into your news feed bother you? Why or why not?

4. If there is a difference between your answers to questions 2 and 3 above, explain why.

## What's In IT For Me?

### This Chapter Will Help Prepare You To...

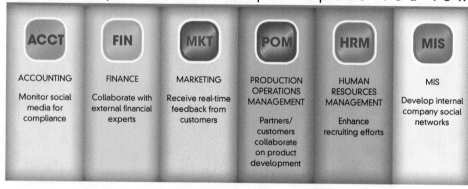

| ACCT | FIN | MKT | POM | HRM | MIS |
|---|---|---|---|---|---|
| ACCOUNTING | FINANCE | MARKETING | PRODUCTION OPERATIONS MANAGEMENT | HUMAN RESOURCES MANAGEMENT | MIS |
| Monitor social media for compliance | Collaborate with external financial experts | Receive real-time feedback from customers | Partners/customers collaborate on product development | Enhance recruiting efforts | Develop internal company social networks |

A generation of young people has started recognizing the potential dangers associated with social media. The Web is a scary place, where every mistake becomes permanent. For instance, college administrators review prospective students' social media profiles before admitting them. Similarly, potential employers view the tangible evidence of youthful indiscretions committed by recent graduates.

The disappearing photo-sending service Snapchat (*www.snapchat.com*) wants to tap into these fears. Snapchat's signature feature allows users to take photos, record videos, add text and drawings, and then send these files to a controlled list of recipients. These photos and videos are known as "Snaps." Users set a time limit for how long recipients can view their Snaps. (As of early 2015, the range was 1–10 seconds.) After the time limit expires, the Snaps are hidden from the recipient's device and deleted from Snapchat's servers. Just as e-mail revolutionized the way people "talk" to one another at work and Twitter is transforming the way people broadcast information, Snapchat has become the "language" of a younger generation.

Snapchat began to catch on in 2011. The first users were Orange County (Los Angeles area) high school students who had learned about the app from one of the founder's cousins. From those humble beginnings, Snapchat has mushroomed into a giant service with tens of millions of users, who send as many as 400 million Snaps per day. And, it continues to grow.

Early on, Snapchat caught the attention of Mark Zuckerberg, CEO of Facebook. Facebook initially responded by experimenting with a copycat feature called "Poke," but the effort failed. Subsequently, in the fall of 2013, Zuckerberg tried to purchase Snapchat for $3 billion. Snapchat's founders, however, refused to sell. Shortly thereafter, Google offered $4 billion. Again, the founders declined the offer.

In October 2013, Snapchat introduced a new feature called "Snapchat Stories" in which photos do not immediately disappear. Users and their friends can use Stories to build "chains" of photos, which are basically a digital photo album that is available to all of their contacts for 24 hours. Stories represent an evolution for Snapchat. It offers users slightly less privacy and urgency, while moving toward the kind of product that marketers would find appealing. As of early 2015, however, the response to Stories had been tepid.

Thus far, only a few marketers are running tests on Snapchat. One company, Taco Bell (*www.tacobell.com*), used Snapchat in May 2013 to distribute photos of its new Beefy Crunch Burrito, and it publicized its photo campaign on Twitter. Other companies that are experimenting with Snapchat include Web retailer Kamaloop (*www.kamaloop.com*) and 16 Handles (*http://16handles.com*), a New York-based frozen yogurt chain.

The "disappearing" nature of transactions on Snapchat, which is the essence of its service, is a huge negative to marketers, who want to monitor and track customers' every move. To survive, Snapchat must persuade marketers that the benefits of reaching its coveted youth audience outweigh the relative anonymity of that audience. The question is: How does Snapchat, which collects no data on its users, make money?

Of course, there are other strategies Snapchat can employ to make money. As one example, game publishers have used messaging platforms in Asia, including Chinese online giant Tencent's WeChat (*www.wechat.com*), to publicize their games and to allow users to share their experiences. Snapchat could perform a similar function. After building a larger user base, Snapchat could also experiment with premium services, such as storing photos.

Snapchat suffered a setback of sorts when it was hacked on December 31, 2013. The breach revealed parts of approximately 4.6 million user names and phone numbers. In January 2014, Snapchat responded by releasing an updated version of its application that would let users opt out of the "Find Friends" feature, which required users to store their phone numbers so that other users could easily locate them.

In January 2015, Great Britain's Prime Minister David Cameron stated that he would stop the use of communications methods that cannot be read by security services even if they had a warrant. Cameron could block WhatsApp and Snapchat if he wins the next election. Cameron's statement was part of his revival of the "snoopers' charter" designed to help security services spy on Internet communications.

*Sources:* Compiled from A. Griffin, "WhatsApp and IMessage Could Be Banned under New Surveillance Plans," *The Independent*, January 14, 2015; R. Murray, "What Really Happens to Your Deleted Internet Messages and Photos," *ABC News*, May 9, 2014; R. Bushey, "Snapchat Finally Apologizes after 4.6 Million User Phone Numbers Leak—Here's How to Make Sure It Doesn't Happen Again," *Business Insider*, January 9, 2014; R. Lawler, "Snapchat Acknowledges Hack, Updated App Coming That Lets Users Opt-Out of Find Friends," *Engadget*, January 2, 2014; M. Peckham, "How to Survive the Snapchat Hack (and Others)," *Time*, January 2, 2014; J. Leyden, "Snapchat: In 'Theory' You Could Hack…. Oh CRAP Is That 4.6 MILLION Users' Details?" *The Register*, January 2, 2014; J. Hempel and A. Lashinsky, "Countdown to the Snapchat Revolution," *Fortune*, December 18, 2013; J. Kleinman, "Snapchat Allegedly Rejected $4B Buyout Offer from Google," *TechnoBuffalo*, November 15, 2013; E. Rusli and D. MacMillan, "Snapchat Spurned $3B Acquisition Offer from Facebook," *The Wall Street Journal*, November 13, 2013; A. Holpuch, "Snapchat Admits to Handing Unopened 'Snaps' to U.S. Law Enforcement," *The Guardian*, October 15, 2013; D. Etherington, "Snapchat Gets Its Own Timeline with Snapchat Stories, 24-Hour Photo & Video Tales," *TechCrunch*, October 3, 2013; N. Kemp, "What Marketers Should Know About Snapchat," *Brand Republic*, June 13, 2013; *www.snapchat.com*, accessed March 23, 2015.

### Questions

1. Describe the advantages and disadvantages of Snapchat to its users. Provide specific examples of both to support your answer.

2. Do you think that Snapchat can become profitable (i.e., survive) in the marketplace? Why or why not? Support your answer with specific examples.

3. How will the Snapchat breach affect marketers who are considering using the app in their campaigns?

4. Should Snapchat's founders have sold the service to Facebook or Google? Why or why not? If you were the founder of Snapchat, would you have accepted either of these offers? Why or why not?

# Introduction

Humans are social individuals. Therefore, human behavior is innately social. Humans typically orient their behavior around other members of their community. As a result, people are sensitive to the behavior of people around them, and their decisions are generally influenced by their social context.

Traditional information systems support organizational activities and business processes, and they concentrate on cost reductions and productivity increases. A variation of this traditional model, social computing, is a type of IT that combines social behavior and information systems to create value. Social computing is focused on improving collaboration and interaction among people and on encouraging user-generated content. Significantly, in social computing, social information is not anonymous. Rather, it is important precisely because it is linked to particular individuals, who in turn are linked to their own networks of individuals.

Social computing makes socially produced information available to everyone. This information may be provided directly, as when users rate a movie (e.g., at Rotten Tomatoes), or indirectly, as with Google's PageRank algorithm, which sequences search results. However, many people do not want their social information available to everyone, as you see in this chapter's opening case.

In social computing, users, rather than organizations, produce, control, use, and manage content via interactive communications and collaboration. As a result, social computing is transforming power relationships within organizations. Employees and customers are empowered by their ability to use social computing to organize themselves. Thus, social computing can influence people in positions of power to listen to the concerns and issues of "ordinary people." Organizational customers and employees are joining this social computing phenomenon, with serious consequences for most organizations.

Significantly, most governments and companies in modern developed societies are not prepared for the new social power of ordinary people. Today, managers, executives, and government officials can no longer control the conversation around policies, products, and other issues.

In the new world of business and government, organizational leaders will have to demonstrate authenticity, even-handedness, transparency, good faith, and humility. If they do not, then customers and employees may distrust them, to potentially disastrous effects. For example, customers who do not like a product or service can quickly broadcast their disapproval. Another example is that prospective employees do not have to take their employers at their word for what life is like at their companies—they can find out from people who already work there. A final example is that employees now have many more options to start their own companies, which could compete with their former employers.

As you see from these examples, the world is becoming more democratic and reflective of the will of ordinary people, enabled by the power of social computing. On the one hand, social power can help keep a company vital and can enable customers and employee activists to become a source of creativity, innovation, and new ideas that will move a company forward. On the other hand, companies that show insensitivity toward customers or employees quickly find themselves on a downward slide.

For instance, Kenneth Cole came under fire for suggesting on Twitter that news of its spring collection led to riots in Egypt, and American Apparel was blasted online for offering a Hurricane Sandy sale. Lesson to be learned: If companies want to win the favor and loyalty of customers, they should refrain from making comments that may suggest that they were trying to profit from other people's misery.

Another example is CVS Pharmacy. CVS asked its customers to sign up for the company's Twitter account, become followers, and offer feedback. However, CVS's account was locked, so customers could not follow it or view tweets without asking for permission. Lesson to be learned: Make certain you understand the mechanics of how a social media platform works before you try to use it.

Social computing is exploding worldwide, with China having the world's most active social media population. In one McKinsey survey, 91 percent of Chinese respondents reported that they had visited a social media site in the previous six months, compared with 70 percent in South Korea, 67 percent in the United States, and 30 percent in Japan. Interestingly, the survey found that social media has a greater influence on purchasing decisions for Chinese consumers than for consumers anywhere else in the world.

Social computing is also increasing dramatically in Africa. Facebook in particular is growing rapidly in African countries, and it is the dominant social network in most of them. However, Facebook does have rivals in Africa, including the following:

- In South Africa, Mxit (*www.mxit.com*) has 10 million active users, more than double Facebook's number.
- In Ghana, a mobile social network called Saya.im (*www.saya.im*) gained more than 50,000 members in six weeks after the site launched.
- In Kenya, a mobile social network called iCow (*www.icow.co.ke*) provides farmers and other members with livestock management and other agricultural information.

Businesses today are using social computing in a variety of innovative ways, including marketing, customer relationship management, and human resource management. In fact, so many organizations are competing to use social computing in as many new ways as possible that an inclusive term for the use of social computing in business has emerged: *social commerce*. Because social computing is facilitated by Web 2.0 tools and sites, you begin this chapter by examining these technologies. You then turn your attention to a diverse number of social commerce activities, including shopping, advertising, market research, customer relationship management, and human resource management. You conclude by studying the risks and concerns associated with social computing.

When you complete this chapter, you will have a thorough understanding of social computing and the ways in which modern organizations use this technology. You will be familiar with the advantages and disadvantages of social computing as well as the risks and rewards it can bring to your organization. For example, most of you already have pages on social networking sites, so you are familiar with the positive and negative features of these sites. This chapter will enable you to apply this knowledge to your organization's efforts in the social computing arena. You will be in a position to contribute to your organization's policies on social computing. You will also be able to help your organization create a strategy to utilize social computing. Finally, social computing offers incredible opportunities for entrepreneurs who want to start their own businesses.

# 9.1 Web 2.0

The World Wide Web, which you learned about in Chapter 6, first appeared in 1990. Web 1.0 was the first generation of the Web. We did not use this term in Chapter 6 because there was no need to say "Web 1.0" until Web 2.0 emerged.

The key developments of Web 1.0 were the creation of Web sites and the commercialization of the Web. Users typically had minimal interaction with Web 1.0 sites. Rather, they passively received information from those sites.

Web 2.0 is a popular term that has proved difficult to define. According to Tim O'Reilly, a noted blogger, **Web 2.0** is a loose collection of information technologies and applications, plus the Web sites that use them. These Web sites enrich the user experience by encouraging user participation, social interaction, and collaboration. Unlike Web 1.0 sites, Web 2.0 sites are not so much online places to visit as Web locations that facilitate information sharing, user-centered design, and collaboration. Web 2.0 sites often harness collective intelligence (e.g., wikis); deliver functionality as services, rather than packaged software (e.g., Web services); and feature remixable applications and data (e.g., mashups).

In the following sections, we discuss five Web 2.0 information technology tools: tagging, Really Simple Syndication (RSS), blogs, microblogs, and wikis. We then turn our attention to the two major types of Web 2.0 sites: social networking sites and mashups.

## Tagging

A **tag** is a keyword or term that describes a piece of information—for example, a blog, a picture, an article, or a video clip. Users typically choose tags that are meaningful to them. Tagging allows users to place information in multiple, overlapping associations rather than in rigid categories. For example, a photo of a car might be tagged with "Corvette," "sports car," and "Chevrolet." Tagging is the basis of *folksonomies*, which are user-generated classifications that use tags to categorize and retrieve Web pages, photos, videos, and other Web content.

One specific form of tagging, known as *geotagging*, refers to tagging information on maps. For example, Google Maps allows users to add pictures and information, such as restaurant or hotel ratings, to maps. Therefore, when you access Google Maps, your experience is enriched because you can see pictures of attractions, reviews, and things to do, posted by everyone, and all related to the map location you are viewing.

## Really Simple Syndication

**Really Simple Syndication** is a Web 2.0 feature that allows you to receive the information you want (customized information), when you want it, without having to surf thousands of Web sites. RSS allows anyone to syndicate (publish) his or her blog, or any other content, to anyone who has an interest in subscribing to it. When changes to the content are made, subscribers receive a notification of the changes and an idea of what the new content contains. Subscribers can then click on a link that will take them to the full text of the new content.

For example, CNN.com provides RSS feeds for each of its main topic areas, such as world news, sports news, technology news, and entertainment news. NBC uses RSS feeds to allow viewers to download the most current version of shows such as *Meet the Press* and *NBC Nightly News*.

You can find thousands of Web sites that offer RSS feeds at Syndic8 (*www.syndic8.com*) and NewsIsFree (*www.newsisfree.com*). Figure 9.1 illustrates how to search an RSS and locate RSS feeds.

To use RSS, you can utilize a special newsreader that displays RSS content feeds from the Web sites you select. Many such readers are available, several of them for free. Examples

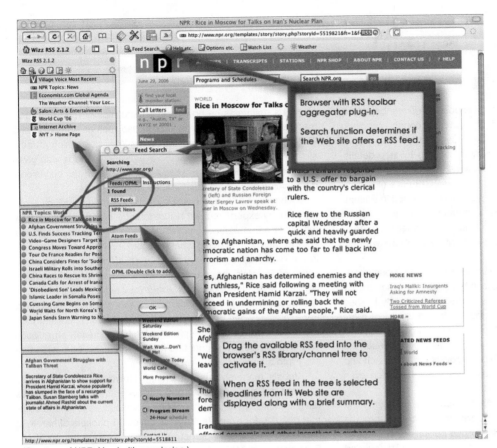

**FIGURE 9.1** The Web site of National Public Radio (NPR) with RSS toolbar aggregator and search function.

are AmphetaDesk (*www.disobey.com/amphetadesk*) and Pluck (*www.pluck.com*). In addition, most browsers have built-in RSS readers. For an excellent RSS tutorial, visit *www.mnot.net/rss/tutorial*.

## Blogs

A **weblog** (**blog** for short) is a personal Web site, open to the public, in which the site creator expresses his or her feelings or opinions via a series of chronological entries. *Bloggers*—people who create and maintain blogs—write stories, convey news, and provide links to other articles and Web sites that are of interest to them. The simplest method of creating a blog is to sign up with a blogging service provider, such as *www.blogger.com* (now owned by Google), *www.xanga.com*, and *www.sixapart.com*. The **blogosphere** is the term for the millions of blogs on the Web.

Many companies listen to consumers in the blogosphere who express their views on the companies' products. Marketers refer to these views as *consumer-generated media*. For example, Nielsen (*www.nielsen-online.com*) "mines" the blogosphere to provide information for its clients in several areas. Nielsen helps clients find ways to serve potential markets, ranging from broad-based to niche markets. The company also helps clients detect false rumors before these rumors appear in the mainstream media, and it gauges the potency of a marketing push or the popularity of a new product.

Blogs often provide incredibly useful information, often before the information becomes available in traditional media outlets (e.g., television, newspapers). IT's About Business 9.1 describes Brian Krebs's blog on information security.

# IT's [about business]

## 9.1 Brian Krebs Blogs on Information Security

Brian Krebs has built a business by exposing security breaches. He has an outstanding record of security scoops, exposing organizational weaknesses in online security in his blog (*http://krebsonsecurity.com*). Krebs typically posts step-by-step details, without revealing his sources, of how he has uncovered which hackers breached whose corporate defenses. Krebs's blog covers profit-seeking cybercriminals, many of them based in Eastern Europe, who make billions of dollars off fraudulent pharmaceutical sales, malware, spam, frauds, and heists like the recent ones at Adobe, Target, and Neiman Marcus, all of which Krebs was the first to uncover.

Krebs's blog performs a valuable service for consumers. Unlike physical crime—for example, a bank robbery—that quickly becomes public knowledge, online thefts are frequently hushed up by companies that worry that the disclosure will inflict more damage than the theft by frightening away customers. For this reason, hackers can raid multiple companies before consumers hear about it. Therefore, when Krebs uncovers a data breach and quickly publicizes it, the public gains valuable information even though the company might try to keep it quiet.

In 2005, Krebs started the *Washington Post's* Security Fix blog, and he began to infiltrate the online forums and chat rooms where criminals often operate. He learned hacker slang, listened to hundreds of hours of Russian language lessons, and persuaded industry sources to share their security knowledge and techniques.

Krebs was the first person to report the existence of the Stuxnet virus. He also broke the news of a hack at Adobe Systems, and he uncovered how the credit bureau Experian was tricked into selling consumer data to identity thieves.

In mid-December 2013, Krebs began to hear of a major data breach. A source at a large bank directed him to Web sites that were selling stolen information from credit cards it had issued, all of which had recently been used at various Target stores. Krebs checked with a source at a second bank that also had witnessed a spike in fraud. Together, they visited one Web site and bought a number of stolen cards. Again, the cards appeared to have one thing in common: They had been used at Target from late November to mid-December 2013.

Krebs had corroborated the information he had received in mid-December. Then, on December 18, 2013, he posted that hackers had stolen the financial data of tens of millions of Target customers (see closing case in Chapter 4). Krebs then identified a Ukrainian man he had concluded was selling the stolen data. In an online chat that Krebs later posted, the man offered him $10,000 to back off. Krebs declined, and he ran the story. In the following weeks, Krebs discovered breaches at Neiman Marcus and White Lodging, which manages franchises for major hotel chains like Hilton, Marriott, and Starwood hotels. The total number of victims from the breaches at these stores exceeds one-third of the U.S. population.

Krebs maintains he now makes more money than he did at the *Washington Post*. Security businesses such as Authentify and IBM's Trusteer division advertise on his Web site, which attracts almost one million unique visitors every month. Krebs also gives a dozen paid speeches per year, and he takes on the occasional data-mining project, usually for financial companies.

Krebs also has become well known internationally. Many security industry experts request his assistance in understanding how the Eastern European criminals operate, how they work with one another, and who is doing what to whom. Krebs is so entrenched in the digital underground that he is on a first-name basis with some of Russia's major cybercriminals. Many of them call him regularly, leak him documents about their rivals, and try to bribe and threaten him to keep their names and dealings off his blog. For example, when two Russian spammers who processed payments for fraudulent online pharmacies hacked each other, each one sent the other's accounting files to Krebs. Krebs turned that story into a book called *Spam Nation*.

Krebs's readership is expanding. However, there are risks involved in functioning as a one-man operation. Cybercriminals have exhibited their loathing of him in various ways. In the summer of 2013, for example, Krebs received 13 packets of heroin at his home. (The alleged perpetrator was arrested in Italy in 2014.) Even worse, in March 2013 a SWAT team arrived at his home, lured by a fake report of a hostage situation. At precisely the same time, Krebs's computer system was experiencing a distributed denial-of-service (DDoS) attack. (We discuss DDoS attacks in Chapter 7).

*Sources:* Compiled from E. Johnson, "Don't Ignore the Simple Cyber Attacks, Says Security Blogger Brian Krebs (Q&A)," *recode.net*, January 12, 2015; L. Vaas, "Hacker Who Plotted to Send Heroin to Brian Krebs Arrested in Italy," *nakedsecurity.sophos.com*, June 29, 2014; N. Perlroth, "Reporting from the Web's Underbelly," *The New York Times*, February 17, 2014; K. Weise, "The Blogger Hackers Love to Hate," *Bloomberg BusinessWeek*, January 20–26, 2014; M. Stencel, "Tech Reporter Brian Krebs Hacks It on His Own, One Scoop at a Time," *Poynter*, January 16, 2014; N. Perlroth, "Who Is Selling Target's Data?" *The New York Times*, December 24, 2013; J. Bort, "Security Blogger Brian Krebs Is Trying to Track Down the Target Hacker by Talking to Suspected Credit Card Thieves," *SFGate*, December 24, 2013; C. Franzen, "Security Blogger Brian Krebs Suffers Simultaneous Cyber Attack, Police Raid," *The Verge*, March 15, 2013; J. Waters, "What to Do If You Fear Your Credit Card's Hacked," *MarketWatch*, March 30, 2012; M. Gross, "A Declaration of Cyber-War," *Vanity Fair*, April, 2011; krebsonsecurity.com, accessed January 21, 2015.

### Questions

1. List various ways in which Krebs can make money from his blog.

2. You are the chief security officer for a company. How would you incorporate Krebs's blog into your security efforts?

Although blogs can be very useful, they also have shortcomings. Perhaps the primary value of blogs is their ability to bring current, breaking news to the public in the fastest time possible. Unfortunately, in doing so, bloggers sometimes cut corners, and their blogs can be inaccurate. Regardless of their various problems, however, blogs have transformed the ways in which people gather and consume information.

## Microblogging

**Microblogging** is a form of blogging that allows users to write short messages (or capture an image or embedded video) and publish them. These messages can be submitted via text messaging from mobile phones, instant messaging, e-mail, or simply over the Web. The content of a microblog differs from that of a blog because of the limited space per message (usually up to 140 characters). A popular microblogging service is Twitter.

**Twitter** is a free microblogging service that allows its users to send messages and read other users' messages and updates, known as **tweets**. Tweets are displayed on the user's profile page and delivered to other users who have signed up to receive them.

Twitter is becoming a very useful business tool. It allows companies to quickly share information with people interested in their products, thereby creating deeper relationships with their customers. Businesses also use Twitter to gather real-time market intelligence and customer feedback. As an individual user, you can use Twitter to inform companies about your experiences with their business, offer product ideas, and learn about great offers.

Sina Weibo (*http://english.sina.com/weibo/*) is the most popular microblogging service in China. This chapter's closing case discusses how many multinational companies are using this service in their marketing efforts in China.

## Wikis

A **wiki** is a Web site made up entirely of content posted by users. Wikis have an "edit" link on each page that allows any user to add, change, or delete material, thus fostering easy collaboration.

Wikis take advantage of the combined input of many individuals. Consider Wikipedia (*www.wikipedia.org*), an online encyclopedia that is the largest existing wiki. Wikipedia contains more than 4.5 million articles in English (as of early 2015), which attract some 500 million views every day. Wikipedia relies on volunteer administrators who enforce a neutral point of view, and it encourages users to delete copy that displays a clear bias. Nevertheless, there are still major debates over the reliability of Wikipedia articles. Many educators will not allow students to cite references from Wikipedia because Wikipedia content is of uncertain origin. Moreover, Wikipedia does not provide any quality assessment or fact checking by experts. Therefore, academics and other professionals have major concerns about the accuracy of user-provided content.

Organizations use wikis in several ways. In project management, for example, wikis provide a central repository for capturing constantly updated product features and specifications, tracking issues, resolving problems, and maintaining project histories. In addition, wikis enable companies to collaborate with customers, suppliers, and other business partners on projects. Wikis are also valuable in knowledge management. For example, companies use wikis to keep enterprisewide documents, such as guidelines and frequently asked questions, accurate and current.

## Social Networking Web Sites

A **social network** is a social structure composed of individuals, groups, or organizations linked by values, visions, ideas, financial exchange, friendship, kinship, conflict, or trade. **Social networking** refers to activities performed using social software tools (e.g., blogging) or social networking features (e.g., media sharing). Social networking allows convenient connections to those of similar interest.

A social network can be described as a map of all relevant links or connections among the network's members. For each individual member that map is his or her **social graph**.

Mark Zuckerberg of Facebook originally coined this term to refer to the social network of relationships among Facebook users. The idea was that Facebook would take advantage of relationships among individuals to offer a richer online experience.

Social networks can also be used to determine the social capital of individual participants. **Social capital** refers to the number of connections a person has within and between social networks.

Participants congregate on *social networking Web sites* where they can create their own profile page for free and on which they can write blogs and wikis; post pictures, videos, or music; share ideas; and link to other Web locations they find interesting. Social networkers chat using instant messaging and Twitter, and they tag posted content with their own keywords, making content searchable and facilitating interactions and transactions. Social networkers converse, collaborate, and share opinions, experiences, knowledge, insights, and perceptions with one another. They also use these Web sites to find like-minded people online, either to pursue an interest or a goal or just to establish a sense of community among people who may never meet in the real world.

Participants who post on social networking sites tend to reveal a great deal of personal information. As a result, if they are not careful, bad things can happen. IT's About Business 9.2 illustrates a negative outcome that resulted from a Facebook post.

Table 9.1 displays the variety of online social networking platforms. Social networking Web sites allow users to upload their content to the Web in the form of text, voice, images, and videos.

# IT's [about business]

## 9.2 Trip to Europe: Cancelled

Patrick Snay was the headmaster at Gulliver Preparatory School in Miami for several years. In 2010, the school did not renew his contract. Snay sued his former employer for age discrimination and for retaliation that involved his daughter, Dana, who was a student at the school.

Gulliver settled the case in November 2011, agreeing to pay Snay $10,000 in back wages and an $80,000 settlement, as well as $60,000 to Snay's attorneys. The settlement depended on a confidentiality agreement that required Snay and his wife to keep the "terms and existence" of the agreement private. Snay immediately informed his daughter, that he had settled with Gulliver and was happy with the results.

Rather than keeping this news private, Dana bragged about the case on Facebook. Her post read: "Mama and Papa Snay won the case against Gulliver. Gulliver is now officially paying for my vacation to Europe this summer."

Dana had 1,200 Facebook friends, many of whom were current and former Gulliver students. News of the post made its way back to the school's lawyers, who appealed the verdict in the Snay case to a circuit court. Snay won this round when the court upheld the settlement. The school then appealed to the Third District Court of Appeals, which threw out the settlement. This court ruled that Snay and his daughter had breached the terms of a confidentiality agreement when she posted about it on Facebook.

Snay is now headmaster at Riviera Preparatory Academy in Coral Gables, Florida. He is allowed to file a motion for rehearing and also to appeal to the Florida Supreme Court. However, attorneys maintain that the odds of his winning an appeal are slim. They note that Facebook is a public forum and that is where the mistake was made.

And the irony of it all? It seems that Dana was just kidding about the European vacation.

*Sources:* Compiled from J. Allen, "Dana Snay's Facebook Post Costs Father $80K," *WebProNews*, March 6, 2014; P. Caufield, "Daughter's Facebook Post Botches Dad's $80,000 Settlement," *New York Daily News*, March 3, 2014; T. Greene, "Who Is Dana Snay? College Student's Facebook Bragging Costs Father $80,000 Lawsuit Settlement," *International Business Times*, February 28, 2014; E. Sole, "Daughter's Facebook Brag Costs Her Family $80,000," *Yahoo! Shine*, February 28, 2014; K. Waldman, "Teen's Facebook Post Costs Her Dad $80,000. Oops," *Slate*, February 28, 2014; "80,000 Mistake: Who Is to Blame?" *Babysitter Community*, February 28, 2014; D. Smiley, "Daughter's Facebook Boast Costs Former Gulliver Prep Headmaster $80,000 Discrimination Settlement," *Miami Herald*, February 26, 2014.

### Questions

1. Clearly you should be careful of what you should post on Facebook. However, based on this case, how do you know what is appropriate and what is not appropriate to post? Can you suggest some guidelines on what to post on social media?
2. What mistake, if any, did the parents make when they informed Dana about the settlement? Telling her at all? Not telling her about the dangers of posting details on social media?

Table

# 9.1

**Categories of Social
Networking Web Sites**

**Socially oriented:** Socially focused public sites, open to anyone
- Facebook (*www.facebook.com*)
- Google Orkut (*www.orkut.com*)
- Google+ (*https://plus.google.com*)
- Hi5 (*www.hi5.com*)

**Professional networking:** Focused on networking for business professionals
- LinkedIn (*www.linkedin.com*)

**Media sharing**
- *Netcasting* includes podcasting (audio) and videocasting (audio and video). For example, educational institutions use netcasts to provide students with access to lectures, lab demonstrations, and sports events. In 2007, Apple launched iTunes U, which offers free content provided by major U.S. universities such as Stanford and MIT.
- **Web 2.0 media** sites allow people to come together and share user-generated digital media, such as pictures, audio, and video.
  - *Video (Amazon Video on Demand, YouTube, Hulu, Facebook)*
  - *Music (Amazon MP3, Last.fm, Rhapsody, Pandora, Facebook, iTunes)*
  - *Photographs (Photobucket, Flickr, Shutterfly, Picasa, Facebook)*

**Communication**
- *Blogs*: Blogger, LiveJournal, Open Diary, TypePad, WordPress, Vox, Expression Engine, Xanga
- *Microblogging/Presence applications*: Twitter, Plurk, Tumblr, Yammer, Qaiku

**Collaboration:** Wikis (Wikimedia, PBworks, Wetpaint)

**Social bookmarking** (or *social tagging*): Focused on helping users store, organize, search, and manage bookmarks of Web pages on the Internet
- Delicious (*www.delicious.com*)
- StumbleUpon (*www.stumbleupon.com*)
- Google Reader (*http://reader.google.com*)
- CiteULike (*www.citeulike.com*)

**Social news:** Focused on user-posted news stories that are ranked by popularity based on user voting
- Digg (*www.digg.com*)
- Chime.in (*http://chime.in*)
- Reddit (*www.reddit.com*)

**Events:** Focused on alerts for relevant events, people you know nearby, etc.
- Eventful (*www.eventful.com*)
- Meetup (*www.meetup.com*)
- Foursquare (*www.foursquare.com*)

**Virtual meeting place:** Sites that are essentially three-dimensional worlds, built and owned by the residents (the users)
- Second Life (*www.secondlife.com*)

**Interesting new social networks**
- Empire Avenue (*www.empireavenue.com*) is a social exchange network where members invest virtual currency in people and brands that interest them.
- Color (*www.color.com*) is a free mobile app that creates an instant social network based on users' locations and proximity to others. Users can instantly share images, videos, and text conversations with other nearby users.

<table>
<tr><td>**Table**<br>**9.1** (continued)</td><td>
<ul>
<li>Foursquare (*http://foursquare.com*) is a location-based mobile service that enables participants to share their location with friends by checking in via a smartphone app.</li>
<li>Hunch (*www.hunch.com*) maps people's interests by asking them a series of questions. The site creates a "taste graph,"  which tracks everything that a user likes and dislikes.</li>
</ul>

**Online marketplaces for microjobs**
<ul>
<li>For example, TaskRabbit (*www.taskrabbit.com*) and Zaarly (*www.zaarly.com*) enable people to farm out chores to a growing number of temporary personal assistants. Thousands of unemployed and underemployed workers use these sites. The part-time or full-time tasks are especially popular with stay-at-home moms, retirees, and students. Workers choose their jobs and negotiate their rates.</li>
</ul>
</td></tr>
</table>

### Enterprise Social Networks

**MIS**

Business-oriented social networks can be public, such as LinkedIn.com. As such, they are owned and managed by an independent company.

However, an increasing number of companies have created in-house, private social networks for their employees, former employees, business partners, and/or customers. Such networks are "behind the firewall" and are often referred to as *corporate social networks*. Employees utilize these networks to create connections that allow them to establish virtual teams, bring new employees up to speed, improve collaboration, and increase employee retention by creating a sense of community. Employees are able to interact with their coworkers on a level that is typically absent in large organizations or in situations where people work remotely.

Corporate social networks are used for many processes, including

- Networking and community building, both inside and outside an organization
- *Social collaboration*: collaborative work and problem solving using wikis, blogs, instant messaging, collaborative office, and other special-purpose Web-based collaboration platforms; for example, see Laboranova (*www.laboranova.com*)
- *Social publishing*: employees and others creating, either individually or collaboratively, and posting contents—photos, videos, presentation slides, and documents—into a member's or a community's accessible-content repository such as YouTube, Flickr, SlideShare, and DocStoc
- Social views and feedback
- *Social intelligence and social analytics*: monitoring, analyzing, and interpreting conversations, interactions, and associations among people, topics, and ideas to gain insights. Social intelligence is useful for examining relationships and work patterns of individuals and groups and for discovering people and expertise. IT's About Business 9.3 illustrates how the Chicago Police Department uses social analytics to gather social intelligence about gang members.

# IT's [about business]

## 9.3 Social Network Analysis Applied to Gangs

Gang violence typically is not random. Rather, it involves territorial disputes or personal disagreements. That is, gang violence is related to geographical, cultural, and social connections. Some police departments have enjoyed limited success monitoring social networks such as Facebook for clues about where violence might occur next. However, a new kind of software being implemented in Chicago can turn an entire database of arrest records into visual portrayals of real-life social networks. This technology might enable police officers to quickly identify a person's friends and enemies and hopefully pinpoint locations where violence could erupt.

Major Paulo Shakarian, an assistant professor at the U.S. Military Academy at West Point, had been developing software to better understand networks of insurgents abroad. The software had been tested in Afghanistan, but it was not widely deployed. In 2012, Chicago police officer John Bertetto came across one of Shakarian's papers and asked him a question: "Could social network analysis help Chicago?"

Shakarian and Bertetto created the Organizational, Relationship, and Contact Analyzer (ORCA), a software program that in seconds generates networks that would take people with whiteboards and unstructured databases hours or even days to produce. In the summer of 2013, they put ORCA to the test. The software analyzed three years of anonymized arrests (5,418 total) from one district, turning the arrests into social connection visualizations and reports on individuals. (Anonymized arrests are those where personally identifiable information has been removed.)

ORCA begins by linking people who had been arrested together, which is the most objective evidence that, at the very least, people have been at the same place at the same time. From there, ORCA categorizes individuals who had admitted a gang affiliation. Then, based on social links, the software assigns other persons a numerical probability of having a particular affiliation. ORCA further analyzes clusters of people within the network to identify groups and subgroups. A subgroup occupying a street corner, for example, could be one of a gang's "crews." By zeroing in on people who are connected across many groups and subgroups, ORCA singles out the most influential individuals.

The analysis revealed more than 11,000 relationships among the arrested individuals. From these data, ORCA created a social network consisting of nearly 1,500 individuals who are members of 18 gangs. ORCA identified "seed sets," which are small groups within a gang who are highly connected and therefore highly influential. ORCA also discovered individuals known as "connectors"

who link one gang with another; for example, by selling drugs from one gang to another. Interestingly, ORCA performed all of these analyses on a standard laptop in just over 30 seconds.

In early 2015, ORCA remains under development. Future iterations may integrate geolocation data, time-based data, and intelligence from informants. The time element is particularly important because gang members switch allegiances and regularly start new gangs.

*Sources:* Compiled from M. Mruk, "Building a Social Network of Crime," *Popular Science*, January 14, 2014; C. Wood, "Counter-Insurgency Software Goes Stateside," *Government Technology*, July 24, 2013; P. Ball, "Unmasking Organised Crime Networks with Data," *BBC News*, July 9, 2013; D. Coldewey, "Gangs' Pecking Order Revealed by Army Software," *NBC News*, July 8, 2013; K. Campbell-Dollaghan, "The Army's Insurgent Tracking Software Is Now Being Used to Track Gangs," *Gizmodo*, July 7, 2013; "How Military Counterinsurgency Software Is Being Adapted to Tackle Gang Violence in Mainland USA," *MIT Technology Review*, July 4, 2013.

### Questions

1. What other data could the Chicago Police Department add to ORCA?
2. What are the potential disadvantages of ORCA? Provide specific examples to support your answer.

## Mashups

A **mashup** is a Web site that takes different content from a number of other Web sites and mixes them together to create a new kind of content. The launch of Google Maps is credited with providing the start for mashups. A user can take a map from Google, add his or her data, and then display a map mashup on his or her Web site that plots crime scenes, cars for sale, or anything else (see Figure 9.2). There are many examples of mashups (for a complete list of mashups, see *www.programmableweb.com*):

- Craigslist developed a dynamic map of all available apartments in the United States that are listed on their Web site (*www.housingmaps.com*).

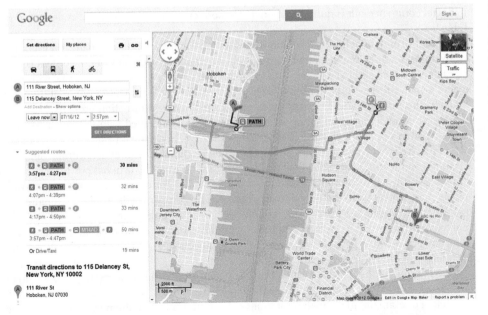

**FIGURE 9.2** Google Maps (*www.googlemaps.com*) is a classic example of a mashup. In this case, Google Maps is pulling in information from public transportation Web sites to provide the customer with transit directions.

- Everyblock.com is a mashup of Web services that integrates content from newspapers, blogs, and government databases to inform citizens of cities such as Chicago, New York, and Seattle about what is happening in their neighborhoods. This information includes criminal activities, restaurant inspections, and local photos posted on Flickr.

## before you go on...

**1.** Differentiate between blogs and wikis.

**2.** Differentiate between social networking Web sites and corporate social networks.

## 9.2 Fundamentals of Social Computing in Business

**Social computing** in business, or **social commerce**, refers to the delivery of electronic commerce activities and transactions through social computing. Social commerce also supports social interactions and user contributions, allowing customers to participate actively in the marketing and selling of products and services in online marketplaces and communities. With social commerce, individuals can collaborate online, obtain advice from trusted individuals, and find and purchase goods and services. Below we list a few examples of social commerce:

- Disney allows people to book tickets on Facebook without leaving the social network.
- PepsiCo provides a live notification when its customers are close to physical stores (grocery, restaurants, and gas stations) that sell Pepsi products. The company then uses Foursquare to send them coupons and discount information.
- Mountain Dew attracts video game lovers and sports enthusiasts via Dewmocracy contests. The company also encourages the most dedicated community members to contribute ideas on company products.
- Levi's advertises on Facebook by enabling consumers to populate a "shopping cart" based on what their friends think they would like.
- Wendy's uses Facebook and Twitter to award $50 gift cards to people who submit the funniest and quirkiest responses to various challenges.

Social commerce offers numerous benefits to both customers and vendors, as described in Table 9.2.

Despite all of its benefits, social computing does involve risks. It is problematic, for example, to advertise a product, brand, or company on social computing Web sites where content is user generated and is not edited or filtered. Companies that employ this strategy must be willing to accept negative reviews and feedback. Of course, negative feedback can be some of the most valuable information that a company receives, if it utilizes this information properly.

Companies that engage in social computing are always concerned with negative posts. For example, when a company creates a Facebook business page, by default the site allows other members of the Web site—potentially including disgruntled customers or unethical competitors—to post notes on the firm's Facebook Wall and to comment on what the firm has posted.

Going further, if the company turns off the feature that lets other users write on its Wall, people may wonder what the company is afraid of. The company will also be eliminating its opportunity to engage in great customer conversations, particularly conversations that could market the firm's products and services better than the company could do itself. Similarly, the company could delete posts. However, that policy only encourages the post author to scream even louder about being censored.

Another risk is the 20–80 rule of thumb, which posits that a minority of individuals (20 percent) contribute most of the content (80 percent) to blogs, wikis, social computing Web sites, etc. For example, in an analysis of thousands of submissions to the news voting site Digg

Table
# 9.2
**Potential Benefits of Social Commerce**

**Benefits to Customers**
- Better and faster vendor responses to complaints, because customers can air their complaints in public (on Twitter, Facebook, and YouTube)
- Customers can assist other customers (e.g., in online forums)
- Customers' expectations can be met more fully and quickly
- Customers can easily search, link, chat, and buy while staying on a social network's page

**Benefits to Businesses**
- Can test new products and ideas quickly and inexpensively
- Learn a lot about their customers
- Identify problems quickly and alleviate customer anger
- Learn about customers' experiences via rapid feedback
- Increase sales when customers discuss products positively on social networking site
- Create more effective marketing campaigns and brand awareness
- Use low-cost user-generated content, for example, in marketing campaigns
- Obtain free advertising through viral marketing
- Identify and reward influential brand advocates

over a three-week time frame, the *Wall Street Journal* reported that roughly 33 percent of the stories that made it to Digg's homepage were submitted by 30 contributors (out of 900,000 registered members).

Other risks of social computing include the following:

- Information security concerns
- Invasion of privacy
- Violation of intellectual property and copyright
- Employees' reluctance to participate
- Data leakage of personal information or corporate strategic information
- Poor or biased quality of users' generated content
- Cyberbullying/cyberstalking and employee harassment

Consider Rosetta Stone (*www.rosettastone.com*), which produces software for language translation. To obtain the maximum possible mileage out of social computing and limit the firm's risks on social media, Rosetta Stone implemented a strategy to control its customer interaction on Facebook. The strategy involves both human intervention and software to help monitor the firm's Facebook presence. Specifically, the software helps to monitor Wall posts and respond to them constructively.

Fans of facebook.com/RosettaStone who post questions on its Wall are likely to receive a prompt answer because the Facebook page is integrated with customer service software from Parature (*www.parature.com*). The software scans Wall posts and flags those posts that require a company response, as opposed to those in which fans of the company are talking among themselves. Rosetta Stone customer service representatives are also able to post responses to the Wall that are logged in the Parature issue tracking database.

Companies are engaged in many types of social commerce activities, including shopping, advertising, market research, customer relationship management, and human resource management. In the next sections of this chapter, you will learn about each social commerce activity.

# before you go on...

1. Briefly describe the benefits of social commerce to customers.
2. Briefly describe the risks of social commerce to businesses.

# 9.3  Social Computing in Business: Shopping

**Social shopping** is a method of electronic commerce that takes all of the key aspects of social networks—friends, groups, voting, comments, discussions, reviews, etc.—and focuses them on shopping. Social shopping helps shoppers connect with one another based on tastes, location, age, gender, and other selected attributes.

The nature of shopping is changing, especially shopping for brand-name clothes and related items. For example, popular brands such as Gap, Shopbop, InStyle, and Lisa Klein are joining communities on Stylehive (*www.stylehive.com*) to help promote the season's latest fashion collections. Shoppers are using sites like ThisNext (*www.thisnext.com*) to create profiles and blogs about their favorite products in social communities. Shoppers can tag each item, so that all items become searchable. Moreover, searching within these Web sites can yield results targeted specifically to individual customers.

There are several methods to shop socially. You will learn about each of them in the next section.

## Ratings, Reviews, and Recommendations

Prior to making a purchase, customers typically collect information such as what brand to buy, from which vendor, and at what price. Online customers obtain this information via shopping aids such as comparison agents and Web sites such as Epinions (*www.epinions.com*). Today, customers also use social networking to guide their purchase decisions. They are increasingly utilizing ratings, reviews, and recommendations from friends, fans, followers, and experienced customers.

*Ratings, reviews,* and *recommendations* are usually available in social shopping. In addition to seeing what is already posted, shoppers have an opportunity to contribute their own ratings and reviews and to discuss ratings and reviews posted by other shoppers (see Figure 9.3). The ratings and reviews come from the following sources:

- *Customer ratings and reviews*: integrated into the vendor's Web page, a social network page, a customer review site, or in customer feeds (e.g., Amazon, iTunes, Buzzillions, Epinions).

**FIGURE 9.3** Epinions (*www.epinions.com*) is a Web site that allows customers to rate anything from cars to music. In this screenshot, customers review a popular children's film.

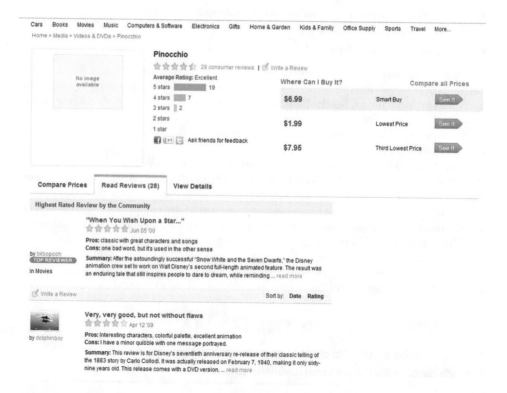

- *Expert ratings and reviews*: views from an independent authority (e.g., Metacritic).
- *Sponsored reviews*: paid-for reviews (e.g., SponsoredReviews, PayPerPost).
- *Conversational marketing*: individuals converse via e-mail, blog, live chat, discussion groups, and tweets. Monitoring these conversations yields rich data for market research and customer service.

As one example, Maui Jim (*www.mauijim.com*), the sunglass company, employed favorable word-of-mouth marketing as a key sales driver. The company uses Bazaarvoice's Ratings & Reviews to allow customers to contribute 5-point ratings and authentic product reviews on the company's entire line of sunglasses and accessories. In effect, Maui Jim extended customers' word-of-mouth reviews across the Web.

Maui Jim encourages its customers to share their candid opinions on the style, fit, and performance of all of its sunglass models. To accomplish this goal, the company integrates customer reviews into its Web site search function to ensure that shoppers who are interested in a particular product will see that product's rating in the search results. Customer response to this rating system has been overwhelmingly positive.

Social recommendation Web sites such as ShopSocially (*www.shopsocially.com*), Blippy (*www.blippy.com*), and Swipely (*www.swipely.com*) encourage conversations about purchases. The product recommendations are submitted by users' friends and acquaintances and arguably are more trustworthy than reviews posted by strangers.

This Next (*www.thisnext.com*) is a Web site where people recommend their favorite products to others. The site blends two powerful elements of real-world shopping: word-of-mouth recommendations from trusted sources and the ability to browse products in a way that naturally leads to discovery.

## Group Shopping

Group shopping Web sites such as Groupon (*www.groupon.com*) and LivingSocial (*www.livingsocial.com*, see Figure 9.4) offer major discounts or special deals during a short time frame. Group buying is closely associated with special deals (flash sales).

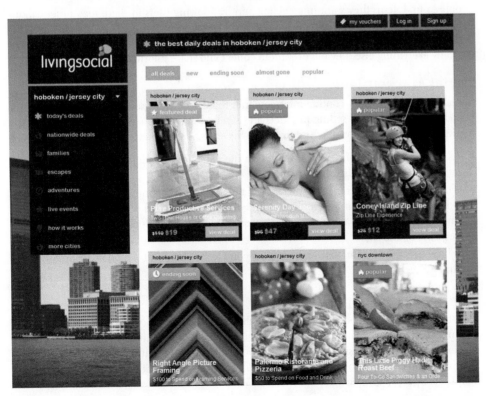

**FIGURE 9.4** LivingSocial (*www.livingsocial.com*) is a popular example of a group shopping Web site.

People who sign up with LivingSocial receive e-mails that offer deals at, for example, a restaurant, a spa, or an event in a given city. They can click on either "Today's Deal" or "Past Deal" (some past deals can still be active). They can also click on an icon and receive the deal the next day. Customers who purchase a deal receive a unique link to share with their friends. If a customer convinces three or more people to buy that specific deal using his or her link, then the customer's deal is free.

Vinobest is a French wine merchant that uses Facebook for group buying and flash deals. The company offers opinions by oenologists (wine experts) and selections by sommeliers (wine stewards) for group-buying deals. Vinobest offers active pricing—the more the people who buy, the cheaper the wine.

Individuals can also shop together virtually in real time. In this process, shoppers log on to a Web site and then contact their friends and family. Everyone then shops online at the same time. Some real-time shopping providers, such as DoTogether (*www.dotogether.com*) and Wet Seal (*www.wetseal.com*), have integrated their shopping service directly into Facebook. Customers log in to Facebook, install the firm's app, and then invite their friends to join them on a virtual retail shopping experience.

## Shopping Communities and Clubs

Shopping clubs host sales for their members that last just a few days and usually feature luxury brands at heavily discounted prices. Club organizers host three to seven sales per day, usually via e-mail messages that entice club members to shop at more than 70 percent off retail—but quickly, before supplies run out.

Luxury brands effectively partner with online shopping clubs to dispose of special-run, sample, overstock, or liquidation goods. These clubs are rather exclusive, which prevents the brands' images from being diminished. Examples are Beyond the Rack (*www.beyondtherack .com*), Gilt Groupe (*www.gilt.com*), Rue La La (*www.ruelala.com*), and One King's Lane (*www .onekingslane.com*).

Kaboodle (*www.kaboodle.com*) is another example of a shopping community. Kaboodle is a free service that lets users collect information from the Web and store it on a Kaboodle list that they can share with other shoppers. Kaboodle simplifies shopping by making it easier for people to find items they want in a catalog and by allowing users to share recommendations with one another using Kaboodle lists and groups. People can also use Kaboodle lists for planning vacations, sharing research for work and school, sharing favorite bands with friends, and basically everything else they might want to collect and share information about.

## Social Marketplaces and Direct Sales

**Social marketplaces** act as online intermediaries that harness the power of social networks for introducing, buying, and selling products and services. A social marketplace helps members market their own creations (see Etsy in Figure 9.5). Other examples are as follows:

- Craigslist (*www.craigslist.com*) provides online classifieds in addition to supporting social activities such as meetings and events.
- Fotolia (*www.fotolia.com*) is a social marketplace for the community of creative people who enjoy sharing, learning, and expressing themselves through images, forums, and blogs; members provide royalty-free stock images that other individuals and professionals can legally buy and share.
- Flipsy (*www.flipsy.com*) can be used by anyone to list, buy, and sell books, music, movies, and games.

## Peer-to-Peer Shopping Models

Peer-to-peer shopping models are the high-tech version of old-fashioned bazaars and bartering systems. Individuals use these models to sell, buy, rent, or barter online with other individuals. For example, many Web sites have emerged to facilitate online sharing. SnapGoods created a community of people who rent goods to people in need, usually for the short term. SnapGoods helps these people connect over the Internet.

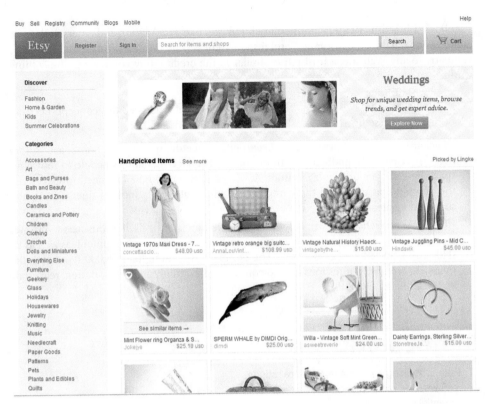

**FIGURE 9.5** Etsy (*www.etsy .com*) is a social marketplace for all handmade or vintage items.

All of these peer-to-peer sites encourage **collaborative consumption**—that is, an economic model based on sharing, swapping, trading, or renting products and services, enabling access over ownership. Collaborative consumption is also called *the sharing economy*.

This trend accelerated as the result of the recession, because people had less money to spend and turned to sharing and renting. In addition, collaborative consumption has an environmentally "green" aspect. Producing a product has significant environmental impacts when the natural resources (e.g., water, lumber, minerals, and electricity) needed to product it are taken into account. Sharing goods among people is much more resource efficient than everyone buying the same goods.

Collaborative consumption includes person-to-person sharing and business-to-business sharing. There are many exciting developments in each of these areas.

**Person-to-Person Sharing.**   The main sectors of the person-to-person sharing marketplace include the following:

- *Peer-to-peer lending*: for example, Lending Club (*www.lendingclub.com*) and Prosper (*www .prosper.com*)
- *Peer-to-peer accommodations*: for example, Airbnb (*www.airbnb.com*)
- *Car sharing*: for example, Zipcar (*www.zipcar.com*), RelayRides (*http://relayrides.com*), and Car2Go (*www.car2go.com*)

Perhaps the greatest concern associated with person-to-person sharing is trust. Sharing works well only when the participants' reputations are involved. Most sharing platforms try to address this issue by creating a self-policing community. Almost all platforms require profiles of both parties, and they feature community rating systems.

Startups like TrustCloud (*http://trustcloud.com*) are endeavoring to become the portable reputation system for the Web. The company has built an algorithm that collects (if you choose to opt in) your online "data exhaust"—the trail you leave as you engage with others on

Facebook, LinkedIn, Twitter, commentary-filled sites like TripAdvisor, and others. It then calculates your reliability, consistency, and responsiveness. The result is a contextual badge that you carry to any Web site, a trust rating similar to the credit rating you have in the "offline" world.

**Business-to-Business Sharing.** Many companies have embraced this concept. Let's take a look at two of these firms.

- Marriott International (*www.marriott.com*) offers meeting spaces on LiquidSpace (*https:// liquidspace.com*). LiquidSpace is an online marketplace that allows people to rent office space by the hour or the day. Hundreds of Marriott hotels now list meeting spaces, and the program has expanded the company's reach by attracting local businesspeople from surrounding areas.

- FLOOW2 (*www.floow2.com*), based in the Netherlands, calls itself a "business-to-business sharing marketplace where companies and institutions can share equipment, as well as the skills and knowledge of personnel." The company lists more than 25,000 types of equipment and services in industries such as construction, agriculture, transportation, real estate, and healthcare.

## before you go on...

1. Prior to making a purchase, why are ratings, reviews, and recommendations so important to potential customers?

2. Define collaborative consumption, and describe how collaborative consumption is a "green" phenomenon.

# 9.4 Social Computing in Business: Marketing

**MKT**

*Marketing* can be defined as the process of building profitable customer relationships by creating value for customers and capturing value in return. There are many components to a marketing campaign, including (1) define your target audience; (2) develop your message (i.e., how you will solve their problem); (3) decide on how you will deliver your message (e.g., e-mail, snail mail, Web advertising, and/or social networks); and (4) follow up. Social computing is particularly useful for two marketing processes: advertising and market research.

## Advertising

**Social advertising** refers to advertising formats that make use of the social context of the user viewing the ad. Social advertising is the first form of advertising to leverage forms of social influence such as peer pressure and friend recommendations and likes.

Many experts believe advertising is the solution to the challenge of making money from social networking sites and social commerce sites. Advertisers have long noted the large number of visitors on social networks and the amount of time they spend there. As a result, they are willing to pay to place ads and run promotions on social networks. Advertisers now post ads on all major social networking Web sites.

Most ads in social commerce consist of branded content paid for by advertisers. These ads belong to two major categories: *social advertisements* (or *social ads*) and *social apps*. Social advertisements are ads placed in paid-for media space on social media networks. Social apps are branded online applications that support social interactions and user contributions (e.g., Nike+).

*Viral marketing*—that is, word-of-mouth advertising—lends itself especially well to social networking. For example, Stormhoek Vineyards (*www.stormhoek.com*) initiated a marketing campaign by offering bloggers a free bottle of wine. Within six months, roughly 100 of these bloggers had posted voluntary comments—the majority of them positive—about the winery on their blogs. In turn, these comments were read by other bloggers.

There are other innovative methods to advertise in social media. Consider the following:

- Use a company Facebook page, including a store that attracts fans and lets them "meet" other customers. Then, advertise in your Facebook store.
- Tweet business success stories to your customers.
- Integrate ads into YouTube videos.
- Mercedes-Benz launched a "Tweet Race," which challenged four teams to drive across the country in Mercedes automobiles to Dallas, Texas, where the 2011 Super Bowl was being played. Each team collected Twitter followers with the help of a celebrity coach. Each tweet or retweet earned the team points, as did other activities, such as photographing other Mercedes cars during the road trip. The team that accumulated the most points by the end of the trip was declared the winner.

For an interesting example of social advertising, you need look no further than YouTube. IT's About Business 9.4 illustrates how YouTube is battling traditional television to provide online content and in the process is increasing its ad revenue.

## Market Research

Traditionally, marketing professionals used demographics compiled by market research firms as one of their primary tools to identify and target potential customers. Obtaining this information was time-consuming and costly, because marketing professionals had to ask potential customers to provide it. Today, however, members of social networks provide this information voluntarily on their pages! (Think about all the information that you provide on your favorite social networking Web sites.) Because of the open nature of social networking, merchants can easily find their customers, see what they do online, and learn who their friends are.

This information provides a new opportunity to assess markets in near real time. Word of mouth has always been one of the most powerful marketing methods—more often than not, people use products that their friends like and recommend. Social media sites can provide this type of data for numerous products and services.

Companies are utilizing social computing tools to obtain feedback from customers. This trend is referred to as *conversational marketing*. These tools enable customers to supply feedback via blogs, wikis, online forums, and social networking sites. Again, customers are providing much of this feedback to companies voluntarily and for free.

Social computing not only generates faster and cheaper results than traditional focus groups but also fosters closer customer relationships. For example, Dell Computer operates a feedback Web site called IdeaStorm that allows customers to suggest and vote on improvements in its offerings (see Figure 9.6).

Retailers are aware that customers, especially younger ones, not only want to be heard but also want to know whether other customers agree with them. Consequently, retailers are increasingly opening up their Web sites to customers, allowing them to post product reviews, ratings, and, in some cases, photos and videos.

As a result of this strategy, customer reviews are emerging as prime locations for online shoppers to visit. Approximately one-half of consumers consult reviews before making an online purchase, and almost two-thirds are more likely to purchase from a site that offers ratings and reviews.

Using social computing for market research is not restricted to businesses. Customers also enjoy the capabilities that social computing offers when they are shopping.

# IT's [about business]

## 9.4 YouTube versus Television

YouTube (*www.youtube.com*) is growing rapidly. Viewership increased by about 50 percent in 2013, an astonishing growth rate for a Web site that already attracts 1 billion users each month from around the world. Its viewers consume 6 billion hours of YouTube videos per month, and many devoted fans enjoy their favorite shows day after day. With traditional television audiences stagnating, YouTube has emerged as a leading platform for professional artists and producers who want to connect directly to audiences.

YouTube and its content partners are transforming the site from a chaotic collection of cat videos and viral hits like "Gangnam Style" into a legitimate destination for a new generation of professional videos. The viral hits and zany clips are still there, of course, and they continue to draw the largest and most global entertainment audience anywhere.

YouTube is not going to kill television. However, it is definitely starting to disrupt mainstream entertainment. Americans have their TV sets on for 34 hours per week, according to Nielsen. In contrast, they watch only 1 hour of video on the Internet per week. However, viewing habits among young people point to a dramatic shift: 18- to 24-year-olds watch just 23 hours of TV and 2.5 hours of online video.

The first era of video entertainment was network television with a few channels, and the second era was cable with hundreds of channels. Today, the third era is the Web with tens of thousands of channels increasingly tailored to niche audiences. In this era, YouTube is not only the largest distribution platform but also the era's organizing force. Essentially, YouTube is an open platform where anyone can upload content. In turn, YouTube collects nearly half of the revenue from all of the ads that run on the site.

More searches are conducted on YouTube than on any other search engine other than Google. The video-sharing site helps Google deliver the right audiences for advertisers, particularly on mobile devices, where video consumption is growing most rapidly.

YouTube also provides a wealth of data about consumer behavior that helps Google fine-tune its services. Going further, YouTube has fortified the advertising industry by empowering brands to become content creators and publishers that increasingly plan to create their own viral hits.

Other technology companies are developing Web video platforms. Amazon, Hulu, Yahoo!, and Microsoft are all competing in the online entertainment marketplace. Furthermore, Netflix has commissioned high-quality original programming such as *House of Cards*. However, none of these companies rivals YouTube for producing made-for-Web content that is quickly becoming a mainstay for a new generation of viewers.

YouTube executives describe traditional television as a wholesale business, with producers selling their programs to a broadcast or cable network that acts as a content gatekeeper. YouTube, in contrast, is all about retailing. Creators develop shows designed to appeal to their audiences rather than the middlemen who have traditionally purchased distribution rights to the content. YouTube performers and producers receive instant feedback from their viewers, and they make programming decisions based on this feedback. The YouTube medium is truly interactive, with the audience responding to content with comments, shares, and sometimes their own videos. In fact, Google executives note that traditional television is one-way, whereas YouTube "talks back."

Consider AwesomenessTV, an American sketch-comedy reality series targeted to young teens, that launched as a YouTube channel in July 2013. Awesomeness's marketing team hoped to attract 100,000 subscribers in its first year. In fact, the channel reached that mark in *one month*. In mid-2014, DreamWorks Animation purchased Awesomeness for $33 million.

Google now collects $3.6 billion in annual revenue on YouTube, almost all of it from advertising. Keep in mind, however, that traditional network television remains a cash cow, thanks to continued strong advertising fees for sporting events as well as the high fees paid by cable operators and telecommunications companies.

*Sources:* Compiled from A. Taube, "If YouTube Were a TV Channel, Its Revenues Would Terrify Its Broadcast Network Rivals," *Business Insider*, December 13, 2013; M. Helft, "How YouTube Changes Everything," *Fortune*, August 12, 2013; A. Penny, "Why the Battle between YouTube and TV Matters to Brands," *The Guardian*, June 28, 2013; "YouTube: Battle with TV Is Already Over," *Associated Press*, May 2, 2013; A. Knapp, "Indie Hip-Hop Star Destorm Power on YouTube and the Future of Music," *Forbes*, March 1, 2012; H. Shaughnessy, "YouTube Creators and the Rise of Social Entertainment," *Forbes*, February 21, 2012; A. Knapp, "Meredith Valiando Is Bringing YouTube to Concert Halls," *Forbes*, February 18, 2012; H. Shaughnessy, "Where Is the Big Time Headed? RockStar, Comic, Actor, and the Story of the Social Brand," *Forbes*, February 1, 2012; J. Perez, "YouTube to Boost Original, Professional Programming," *CIO*, October 29, 2011; *www.youtube.com*, accessed March 22, 2015.

## Questions

1. Describe the differences in how traditional television and YouTube provide online content to audiences.
2. If you were the CEO of a traditional television network, how would you combat YouTube?

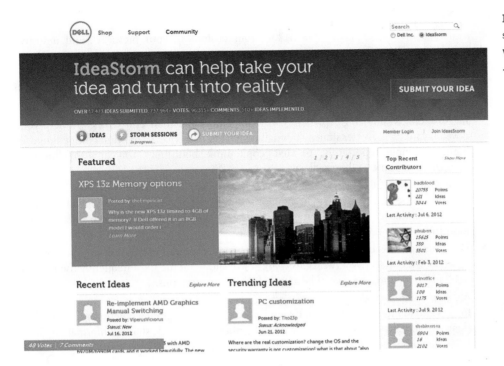

## Conducting Market Research Using Social Networks

Customer sentiment expressed on Twitter, Facebook, and similar sites represents an incredibly valuable source of information for companies. Customer activities on social networking sites generate huge amounts of data that must be analyzed, so that management can conduct better marketing campaigns and improve their product design and their service offerings. The monitoring, collection, and analysis of socially generated data, and the resultant strategic decisions are combined in a process known as **social intelligence**.

An example of social intelligence is Wendy's International (*www.wendys.com*), which uses software to sift through the more than 500,000 customer messages the fast-food chain collects each year. Using Clarabridge (*www.clarabridge.com*) text analytics software, Wendy's analyzes comments from its online notes, e-mails, receipt-based surveys, and social media. Prior to adopting this software, the company used a combination of spreadsheets and keyword searches to review comments in what it describes as a slow and expensive manual approach. In contrast, the new software enables Wendy's to track customer experiences at the store level within minutes.

Social networks provide excellent sources of valuable information for market research. In this section you will see illustrative examples of how to use Facebook, Twitter, and LinkedIn for market research.

**Using Facebook for Market Research.**   There are several ways to use Facebook for market research. Consider the following examples:

- Obtain feedback from your Facebook fans (and their friends if possible) on advertising campaigns, market research, etc. It is equivalent to holding a free focus group.
- Test-market your messages. Provide two or three options, and ask fans which one they prefer and why.
- Use Facebook for survey invitations (i.e., to recruit participants). Essentially, turn Facebook into a giant panel, and ask users to participate in a survey. Facebook offers a self-service model for displaying ads, which can function as invitations to take a survey. Facebook also allows you to target your audience very specifically based on traditional demographic criteria such as age and gender.

**Using Twitter for Market Research.** Your customers, your prospects, and industry thought leaders all use Twitter, making it a rich source of instantly updated information. Consider the following examples:

- Visit Twitter Search (*www.twitter.com/search*). Enter a company's Twitter name. Not only can you follow what the company is saying, you can also follow what everyone is saying to them. Monitoring replies to your competitors and their employees will help you develop your own Twitter strategy by enabling you to observe (a) what your competitors are doing and, more importantly, (b) what people think about them. You can also follow the company's response to this feedback.

- Take advantage of the tools that enable you to find people in the industries in which they operate. Use search.twitter.com to monitor industry-specific keywords. Check out Twellow (*www.twellow.com*). This site automatically categorizes a Twitter user into one to three industries based on that person's bio and tweets.

- Do you want to know what topic is on most people's minds today? If so, then review the chart on TweetStats (*www.tweetstats.com*). It will show you the most frequently used words in all of Tweetdom, so you can be a part of those conversations.

- An increasing number of companies are utilizing Twitter to solicit information from customers and to interact with them. Examples are Dell (connecting with customers), JetBlue (learning about customers), Teusner Wines (gathering feedback, sharing information), and Pepsi (rapid response time in dealing with complaints).

**Using LinkedIn for Market Research.** Post a question (e.g., solicit advice) regarding the topic or issue you are interested in. You may obtain a better result if you go to a specific LinkedIn group.

## before you go on... 

1. Is social advertising more effective than advertising without a social component? Why or why not?
2. Describe how marketing professionals use social networks to perform marketing research.

## 9.5 Social Computing in Business: Customer Relationship Management

The customer service profession has undergone a significant transformation, both in the ways that customer service professionals conduct business and in the ways that customers adapt to interacting with companies in a newly connected environment. Social computing has vastly altered both the expectations of customers and the capabilities of corporations in the area of customer relationship management. (We discuss customer relationship management in detail in Chapter 11.)

Customers are now incredibly empowered. Companies are closely monitoring social computing not only because they are mindful of the negative comments posted by social network members but also because they perceive an opportunity to involve customers proactively to reduce problems through improved customer service.

Empowered customers know how to use the wisdom and power of crowds and communities to their benefit. These customers choose how they interact with companies and brands, and they have elevated expectations concerning their experiences with a company. They are actively involved with businesses, not just as purchasers but also as advocates and influencers. As a result, businesses must respond to customers quickly and appropriately.

Fortunately, social computing provides many opportunities for businesses to do just that, thereby offering businesses the opportunity to turn disgruntled customers into champions for the firm.

Consider this example: Papa John's Pizza fired a cashier at one of its New York restaurants and apologized to an Asian-American customer for a receipt that identified her as "lady chinky eyes." Minhee Cho, a communications manager at the nonprofit investigative journalism group ProPublica, posted a photo of the receipt on her Twitter account, and it was viewed almost 200,000 times in a single day. John Schnatter, chairman and CEO of Papa John's, immediately posted an apology on Facebook. In his apology, he asserted that he had apologized personally to Ms. Cho as well.

## before you go on...

1. Discuss why social computing is so important in customer relationship management.

2. Describe how social computing improves customer service.

# Social Computing in Business: Human Resource Management

**9.6**

Human resource (HR) departments in many organizations use social computing applications both outside their organizations (recruiting) and inside their organizations (employee development). For example, Deloite Touche Tohmatsu created a social network to assist its HR managers in downsizing and regrouping teams.

## Recruiting

Both recruiters and job seekers are moving to online social networks as recruiting platforms. Enterprise recruiters are scanning online social networks, blogs, and other social resources to identify and find information about potential employees. If job seekers are online and active, there is a good chance that they will be seen by recruiters. In addition, on social networks there are many passive job seekers—people who are employed but would take a better job if one appeared. So, it is important that both active and passive job seekers maintain online profiles that accurately reflect their background and skills. This chapter's closing case takes a look at the rewards and the difficulties inherent in the online recruiting process. It also provides some tips to assist you in a job search.

In another example, one HR director uses the HR social media management software Bullhorn Reach (*www.bullhornreach.com*), which allows her to post jobs to eight different social networks simultaneously. Bullhorn Reach also enables her to analyze metrics that measure the effectiveness of her social recruiting efforts.

## Finding a Job

The other side of organizational recruiting is those people looking for jobs. Let's say you want to find a job. Like the majority of job hunters, you will probably conduct at least part of your search online because the vast majority of entry-level positions in the United States are now listed only online. Job sites are the fastest, least expensive, and most efficient method to connect employers with potential employees.

Today, job searchers use traditional job sites and social networks such as LinkedIn. Applicants like you have helped LinkedIn raise its market share in job searches from 4.7 percent in 2010 to more than 12 percent by early 2015.

To find a job, your best bet is to begin with LinkedIn (*www.linkedin.com*), which has roughly 165 million members. You should definitely have a profile on LinkedIn, which, by the way, is free. (See the end of this case for mistakes to avoid on your LinkedIn profile.)

LinkedIn's success comes from its ability to accurately identify its market segment. The company's automated approach does not lend itself well to the upper tier of the job market—for example, CEO searches—where traditional face-to-face searches continue to be the preferred strategy. At the other end of the spectrum—that is, low-paying, low-skill jobs such as cashiers and truck drivers—job boards provide faster results. LinkedIn targets the vast sweet spot between these two extremes, helping to fill high-skill jobs that pay anywhere from $50,000 to $250,000 or more per year. This is the spot you will likely occupy when you graduate.

A number of job-search companies are competing with LinkedIn. These companies are trying to create better-targeted matching systems that leverage social networking functionality. These companies include Monster (*www.monster.com*), Simply Hired (*www.simplyhired.com*), Career Builder (*www.careerbuilder.com*), Indeed (*www.indeed.com*), Jobvite (*http://recruiting.jobvite.com*), Dice Open Web (*www.dice.com/openweb*), and many others.

The most important secret to making online job-search sites work for you is to use them carefully. Job coaches advise you to spend 80 percent of your day networking and directly contacting the people in charge of jobs you want. Devote another 10 percent to headhunters. Spend only the remaining 10 percent of your time online.

Here is how to make your time online count. To start with, as you saw above, you should have a profile on LinkedIn. The following list shows you the mistakes NOT to make on your LinkedIn profile.

- Do have a current, professional picture. (No dogs, no spouses, no babies, etc.)
- Do make certain your LinkedIn Status is correct and current.
- Do join groups related to your field of study or even to your personal interests.
- Do list an accurate skill set. Do not embellish.
- Do not use the standard connection request. Do some research on that person, and tailor your connection request to that person.
- Do not neglect LinkedIn's privacy settings. When you have a job and are looking for another one, you will want to be discreet. You can set your privacy settings so that your boss does not see that you are looking for opportunities.
- Do not skip the Summary. The Summary is a concise way of selling yourself. Write it in the first person.
- Do not eliminate past jobs or volunteer work.
- Do not say you have worked with someone when you have not.

Next, access the job sites such as those listed above. These sites list millions of jobs and they make it easy to narrow your search using filters. These filters include title, company name, location, and many others. Indeed allows you to search within a specific salary range. Simply-Hired lets you sort for friendly, socially responsible, and even dog-friendly workplaces.

These sites have advanced search options. Try plugging in the name of a company you might want to work for or an advanced degree that qualifies you for specialized work. For example, you could enter "CFA" if you are a certified financial analyst or "LEED" if you are a building engineer with expertise in environmental efficiency.

SimplyHired has a useful tool called "Who do I know." If you have a LinkedIn profile, then this tool will instantly display your LinkedIn contacts with connections to various job listings. "Who do I know" also syncs with Facebook.

One more trick to using the aggregators: Configure them to deliver listings to your inbox. Set up an e-mail alert that delivers new job postings to you every day.

You should also search for niche sites that are specific to your field. For technology-related jobs, for instance, Dice (*www.dice.com*) has a strong reputation. For nonprofit jobs, try Idealist (*www.idealist.org*). For government jobs, the U.S. government's site is an excellent resource: *www.usajobs.gov*.

One more great online resource is Craigslist (*www.craigslist.com*). It is one site the aggregators do not tap. Craigslist focuses on local listings, and it is especially useful for entry-level jobs and internships.

Beyond locating listings for specific jobs, career coaches contend that job sites can be a resource for keywords and phrases that you can pull from job descriptions and include in your resume, cover letters, and e-mails. Use the language from a job description in your cover letter.

Web sites like Vault (*www.vault.com*), Monster, and CareerBuilder provide some helpful career tips. Vault, in particular, offers very useful career guides.

The bottom line: It is critical to extend most of your efforts *beyond* an online search.

### Employee Development

Human resource managers know that the best strategy to enable, encourage, and promote employee development is to build relationships with employees. To this end, a number of HR professionals are using enterprise social tools such as Chatter (*www.salesforce.com/chatter*), Yammer (*www.yammer.com*), and Tibbr (*www.tibbr.com*) to tap into the wisdom of every employee. These tools help connect employees to work efficiently across organizations and to collaborate on sales opportunities, campaigns, and projects. They help companies simplify workflows and capture new ideas. They enable HR managers to find subject matter experts within the organization, recommending relevant people for every project team, sales team, and other functions.

As HR managers learn more about employees' skills, expertise, and passions through such tools, they can better motivate them, thereby helping them become more engaged and excited about their work. Employees can then be better rewarded for their expertise.

Another area of employee development is training. A large percentage of the time and expense of employee education and learning management can be minimized by utilizing e-learning and interactive social learning tools. These tools help create connections among learners, instructors, and information. Companies find that these tools facilitate knowledge transfer within departments and across teams. Examples of these tools are Moodle (*http://moodle.com*), Joomia (*www.joomia.org*), and Bloomfire (*www.bloomfire.com*).

## before you go on...

1. Explain why LinkedIn has become so important in the recruiting process.
2. If you are looking for a job, what is the major problem with restricting your search to social networks?

---

### For the Accounting Major

Audit teams use social networking technologies internally to stay in touch with team members who are working on multiple projects. These technologies serve as a common channel of communications. For example, an audit team manager can create a group, include his or her team members as subscribers, and then push information regarding projects to all members at once. Externally, these technologies are useful in interfacing with clients and other third parties for whom the firm and its staff provide services.

### For the Finance Major

Many of the popular social networking sites have users who subscribe to finance-oriented subgroups. Among these groups are finance professionals who collaborate and share knowledge as well as nonfinancial professionals who are potential clients.

### For the Marketing Major

Social computing tools and applications enable marketing professionals to become closer to their customers in a variety of ways, including blogs, wikis, ratings, and recommendations. Marketing professionals now receive almost real-time feedback on products.

What's In IT For Me?

**For the** Production/Operations Management Major

Social computing tools and applications allow production personnel to "enlist" business partners and customers in product development activities.

**For the** Human Resource Management Major

Social networks offer tremendous benefits to human resource professionals. HR personnel can perform a great deal of their recruiting activities by accessing such sites as LinkedIn. They can also check out potential new hires by accessing a large number of social networking sites. Internally, HR personnel can utilize private, internal social networks for employee expertise and experience in order to find the best person for a position or project team.

**For the** MIS Major

The MIS department is responsible for two aspects of social computing usage: (1) monitoring employee usage of social computing applications while at work, both time and content, and (2) developing private, internal social networks for company employees and then monitoring the content of these networks.

# [ Summary ]

**1. Describe five Web 2.0 tools and two major types of Web 2.0 sites.**

A *tag* is a keyword or term that describes a piece of information (e.g., a blog, a picture, an article, or a video clip).

*Really Simple Syndication* allows you to receive the information you want (customized information), when you want it, without having to surf thousands of Web sites.

A *weblog* (*blog* for short) is a personal Web site, open to the public, in which the site creator expresses his or her feelings or opinions with a series of chronological entries.

*Microblogging* is a form of blogging that allows users to write short messages (or capture an image or embedded video) and publish them.

A *wiki* is a Web site on which anyone can post material and make changes to already posted material. Wikis foster easy collaboration and they harness the collective intelligence of Internet users.

*Social networking* Web sites allow users to upload their content to the Web in the form of text (e.g., blogs), voice (e.g., podcasts), images, and videos (e.g., videocasts).

A *mashup* is a Web site that takes different content from a number of other Web sites and mixes them together to create a new kind of content.

**2. Describe the benefits and risks of social commerce to companies.**

*Social commerce* refers to the delivery of electronic commerce activities and transactions through social computing.

*Benefits of social commerce to customers* include the following: better and faster vendors' response to complaints; customers can assist other customers; customers' expectations can be met more fully and quickly; customers can easily search, link, chat, and buy while staying in the social network's page.

*Benefits of social commerce to vendors* include the following: can test new products and ideas quickly and inexpensively; learn much about their customers; identify problems quickly and alleviate anger; learn from customers' experiences with rapid feedback; increase sales when customers discuss products positively on social networking site; create better marketing campaigns and brand awareness; use low-cost user-generated content, for example, in marketing campaigns; get free advertising through viral marketing; identify influential brand advocates and reward them.

*Risks of social computing* include information security concerns; invasion of privacy; violation of intellectual property and copyright; employees' reluctance to participate; data leakage of personal information or corporate strategic information; poor or biased quality of users' generated content; cyberbullying/cyberstalking and employee harassment.

3. **Identify the methods used for shopping socially.**

   *Social shopping* is a method of electronic commerce that takes all of the key aspects of social networks—friends, groups, voting, comments, discussions, reviews, etc.—and focuses them on shopping.

   Methods for shopping socially include what other shoppers say; group shopping; shopping communities and clubs; social marketplaces and direct sales; and peer-to-peer shopping.

4. **Discuss innovative ways to use social networking sites for advertising and market research.**

   *Social advertising* represents advertising formats that employ the social context of the user viewing the ad.

   Innovative ways to advertise in social media include the following: create a company Facebook page; tweet business success stories to your customers; integrate ads into You-Tube videos; add a Facebook "Like" button with its sponsored story to your product.

   *Using Facebook for market research*: get feedback from your Facebook fans (and their friends if possible) on advertising campaigns, market research, etc.; test-market your messages; use Facebook for survey invitations.

   *Using Twitter for market research*: use Twitter Search; use Twellow; look at the chart on TweetStats.

   *Using LinkedIn for market research*: post a question (e.g., solicit advice) regarding the topic or issue you are interested in.

5. **Describe how social computing improves customer service.**

   Customers are now incredibly empowered. Companies are closely monitoring social computing not only because they are mindful of the negative comments posted by social network members but also because they see an opportunity to involve customers proactively to reduce problems by improved customer service.

   Empowered customers know how to use the wisdom and power of crowds and communities to their benefit. These customers choose how they interact with companies and brands, and they have elevated expectations. They are actively involved with businesses, not just as purchasers but also as advocates and influencers. As a result, businesses must respond to customers quickly and accurately. Fortunately, social computing provides many opportunities for businesses to do just that, thereby giving businesses the opportunity to turn disgruntled customers into champions for the firm.

6. **Discuss different ways in which human resource managers make use of social computing.**

   *Recruiting*: Both recruiters and job seekers are moving to online social networks as new recruiting platforms. Enterprise recruiters are scanning online social networks, blogs, and other social resources to identify and find information about potential employees. If job seekers are online and active, there is a good chance that they will be seen by recruiters. In addition, on social networks there are many passive job seekers—people who are employed but would take a better job if it appeared. So, it is important that both active and passive job seekers maintain profiles online that truly reflect them.

   *Employee development*: HR managers are using social tools to build relationships with employees. As HR managers learn more about employees, they can help them become more engaged and excited about their work.

# [ Chapter Glossary ]

**blog (weblog)** A personal Web site, open to the public, in which the site creator expresses his or her feelings or opinions with a series of chronological entries.

**blogosphere** The term for the millions of blogs on the Web.

**collaborative consumption** Peer-to-peer sharing or renting mashup Web site that takes different content from a number of other Web sites and mixes them together to create a new kind of content.

**microblogging** A form of blogging that allows users to write short messages (or capture an image or embedded video) and publish them.

**Really Simple Syndication** A technology that allows users to receive the information they want, when they want it, without having to surf thousands of Web sites.

**social advertising** Advertising formats that make use of the social context of the user viewing the ad.

**social capital** The number of connections a person has within and between social networks.

**social commerce** The delivery of electronic commerce activities and transactions through social computing.

**social computing** A type of information technology that combines social behavior and information systems to create value.

**social graph** A map of all relevant links or connections for one member of a social network.

**social intelligence** The monitoring, collection, and analysis of socially generated data and the resultant strategic decisions.

**social marketplaces** These act as online intermediaries that harness the power of social networks for introducing, buying, and selling products and services.

**social network** A social structure composed of individuals, groups, or organizations linked by values, visions, ideas, financial exchange, friendship, kinship, conflict, or trade.

**social networking** Activities performed using social software tools (e.g., blogging) or social networking features (e.g., media sharing).

**social shopping** A method of electronic commerce that takes all of the key aspects of social networks—friends, groups, voting, comments, discussions, reviews, etc.—and focuses them on shopping.

**tag** A keyword or term that describes a piece of information.

**tweet** Messages and updates posted by users on Twitter.

**Twitter** A free microblogging service that allows its users to send messages and read other users' messages and updates.

**Web 2.0** A loose collection of information technologies and applications, plus the Web sites that use them.

**Web 2.0 media** Any Web site that provides user-generated media content and promotes tagging, rating, commenting, and other interactions among users and their media contributions.

**weblog** (see blog)

**wiki** A Web site on which anyone can post material and make changes to other material.

# [ Discussion Questions ]

1. How would you describe Web 2.0 to someone who has not taken a course in information systems?

2. If you were the CEO of a company, would you pay attention to blogs about your company? Why or why not? If yes, would you consider some blogs to be more important or more reliable than are others? If so, which ones? How would you find blogs relating to your company?

3. Do you have a page on a social networking Web site? If yes, why? If no, what is keeping you from creating one? Is there any content that you definitely would *not* post on such a page?

4. How can an organization best employ social computing technologies and applications to benefit its business processes?

5. What factors might cause an individual, an employee, or a company to be cautious in the use of social networks?

6. Why are advertisers so interested in social networks?

7. What sorts of restrictions or guidelines should firms place on the use of social networks by employees? Are social computing sites a threat to security? Can they tarnish a firm's reputation? If so, how? Can they enhance a firm's reputation? If so, how?

8. Why are marketers so interested in social networks?

9. Why are human resource managers so interested in social networks?

# [ Problem-Solving Activities ]

1. Enter *www.programmableweb.com* and study the various services that the Web site offers. Learn how to create mashups and then propose a mashup of your own. Present your mashup to the class.

2. Go to Amazon's Mechanical Turk Web site (*www.mturk.com*). View the available Human Intelligence Tasks (HITs). Are there any HITs that you would be interested in to make some extra money? Why or why not?

3. Access Pandora (*www.pandora.com*). Why is Pandora a social networking site?

4. Access ChatRoulette (*www.chatroulette.com*). What is interesting about this social networking site?

5. Using a search engine, look up the following:
   - *Most popular or most visited blogs*. Pick two and follow some of the posts. Why do you think these blogs are popular?

- *Best blogs* (try *www.bloggerschoiceawards.com*). Pick two and consider why they might be the "best blogs."

6. Research how to be a successful blogger. What does it take to be a successful blogger? What time commitment might be needed? How frequently do successful bloggers post?

# [ Closing Case Establishing a Presence in China via Microblogging ]

## The Business Problem

Multinational companies are looking for cost-effective methods to market their products to the vast, rapidly growing market of China. Many of these companies believe they have found a strategy to establish, consolidate, or increase their market presence in China: microblogging. They are using microblogging to enhance communications with consumers, launch business campaigns, deliver positive information about their products, and build their brands.

## The IT Solution

Mercedes-Benz, Starbucks, and Nokia have widely different lines of business. Nevertheless, in China they share the same marketing platform: They are participants in the "virtual town square." In China, the virtual town square is a microblog, a platform that is now an integral component of global companies' strategies to expand their operations in that country.

The leading microblogging Web site in China is Sina Weibo (called Weibo; *http://english.sina.com/weibo/*). In 2013 this site attracted an estimated 500 million users, according to the China Internet Network Information Center. The Center further reported that there were more than 260,000 active company accounts on microblogs in 2013, of which more than 1,000 belonged to multinational companies. These companies span 22 different industries.

Since their Chinese debut in August 2009, microblogs have developed into a huge online society where people from all walks of life share personal experiences, participate in social activities, and voice opinions on diverse topics. From a commercial perspective, the power to influence opinion and ultimately increase purchases makes microblogs appealing to multinational companies. In addition, microblogs have become an effective means for companies to reduce spending on conventional advertising. In contrast, for example, television advertising in China is prohibitively expensive.

Chinese microblogs differ from their Western counterparts such as Twitter in terms of the added features they offer. The fundamental difference between Chinese and Western microblogs lies in Twitter's relatively low penetration rate in the U.S. market. Of the 74 percent of U.S. adults who use the Internet, only 8 percent use Twitter, according to a recent study by Pew Research Center (*www.pewresearch.org*). In contrast, by the end of 2012, 55 percent Chinese adults who use the Internet were microbloggers.

Another key difference is that Weibo enables users to watch videos and view pictures seamlessly. In contrast, Twitter typically presents video and pictures in the form of a hyperlink that users have to click on to access the content. Going further, Twitter limits users to 140 characters for each post. Weibo, by contrast, allows 140 characters in addition to various other features such as pictures, videos, and hyperlinks. These additional features enable companies to create more vivid marketing campaigns.

## The Results

Let's review some examples of how multinational companies have fared using microblogs in China.

- **Mercedes-Benz** (*www.mercedes-benz.com*). The German luxury brand Mercedes-Benz appreciates the power of microblogging in China. In January 2013, the company initiated a campaign to sell a limited edition of its Smart cars in China, and it decided to conduct this campaign via a microblog. The result? Mercedes-Benz sold all 666 units of the Smart 2013 New Year Edition offered via Weibo in *eight hours*!

- **Starbucks** (*www.starbucks.com*). Starbucks opened its Weibo account in May 2012. Today the coffee giant has more than 700,000 followers in China. The company's initiative started with routine marketing campaigns. Starbucks quickly discovered, however, that targeted marketing campaigns can be converted into real-time store purchases.

In 2013, Starbucks introduced a campaign to increase Frappuccino sales on its microblog. During the two-month warm-up campaign, Starbucks put up more than 60 posts on its microblog, which generated 234,541 reposts and comments, according to JWT Shanghai, the advertising company that conducted the campaign.

In terms of quantifiable returns, the company's 500,000 yuan ($80,600) microblog campaign resulted in more than 95 million friend-to-friend recommendations and helped generate a 14 percent growth in Frappuccino sales in China.

- **Ikea** (*www.ikea.com*). The Swedish furniture retailer set up its Weibo account in October 2010. Its microblog performs a dual role: listening to consumer feedback and suggestions and providing positive, timely feedback on their concerns and needs. Ikea's daily schedule includes answering consumers' questions, forwarding complaints to relevant after-sales departments, supervising keywords, and overseeing comments relating to sensitive topics on other microblogs that could affect the company.

- **McDonald's** (*www.mcdonalds.com*). In March 2012, China Central Television reported that McDonald's was selling expired food at its branch in the upmarket Sanlitun area in eastern Beijing. Within one hour of that report, the U.S. fast food giant announced it was suspending business at that branch. It also apologized on its microblog, triggering nearly 389,000 posts, the vast majority of which were positive. This strategy enabled the company to quickly and successfully resolve the crisis.

All of these examples convey good news. Now, what is the bad news? Approximately 28 million people abandoned Weibo in 2013, according to a Chinese government report. Why? The answer is that the Chinese government has blocked Twitter since 2009, so many Chinese were using Weibo as a source of unfiltered information. Weibo attracted the attention of Chinese authorities, who moved to silence dissenting voices online. The government passed a law that empowered the authorities to jail microbloggers, and dozens were arrested.

These developments have put a damper on multinational companies' marketing efforts. However, citizens have turned to instant mobile messaging services, such as WeChat (*www.wechat.com*), whose user base has expanded dramatically. Therefore, multinationals might utilize WeChat for future marketing efforts.

*Sources:* Compiled from "China Has 649 Million People Online, But Fewer Are Microblogging After Crackdown on Speech," *Associated Press*, February 3, 2015; C. Bailey, "Weibo Wants You to Ride China's Micro-Blogging Explosion," *The Street*, March 20, 2014; "Chinese Microblogging Site Weibo Files $500M IPO," *Reuters*, March 14, 2014; "A Record of Over 800K Weibo Posts Published in the First Minute of Year of the Horse," *China Internet Watch*, February 19, 2014; "China Microblogging Site Weibo Sees Decline in Users," *BBC News Asia*, January 17, 2014; "9 Facts About Microblog Marketing in China," *Advangent*, October 29, 2013; K. Tang, "Why Starbucks Is Suddenly Becoming Rebel Chic in China," *BuzzFeed*, October 22, 2013; H. Shao, "Updated: Criticism of Starbucks by China's State Broadcaster Backfires," *Forbes*, October 22, 2013; "China Employs Two Million Microblog Monitors State Media Say," *BBC News China*, October 4, 2013; G. Hamblin, "Social Media Marketing: Microblogging," *TruCounsel Marketing*, August 14, 2013; V. Chu, A. Girdhar, and R. Sood, "Couching Tiger Tames the Dragon," *Business Today*, July 21, 2013; L. Jing and C. Yingqun, "Talking It Up Online," *China Daily*, April 22, 2013; "Mercedes-Benz Becomes First Brand to Sell Cars Via Weibo," *Tech & Science*, January 24, 2013; "Mercedes-Benz Experiments with Selling Smart Cars on China's Sina Weibo Microblog," *TheNextWeb*, January 21, 2013; N. Madden, "Marketers Like Starbucks Are Learning to Use Microblog Sina Weibo in China," *Advertising Age*, September 28, 2011; *http://english.sina.com/weibo/*, accessed March 22, 2015.

**Questions**

1. Describe the various advantages and benefits that multinational companies hope to attain from their marketing efforts on Weibo.

2. Describe the disadvantages that multinational companies might encounter from their marketing efforts on Weibo.

3. Should companies use a social media outlet that is monitored, censored, or otherwise controlled by a government? Why or why not? Support your answer.

# 10 Information Systems within the Organization

| [ LEARNING OBJECTIVES ] | [ CHAPTER OUTLINE ] | [ WEB RESOURCES ] |
|---|---|---|
| 1. Explain the purpose of transaction processing systems. | 10.1 Transaction Processing Systems | • Student PowerPoints for note taking |
| 2. Explain the types of support that information systems can provide for each functional area of the organization. | 10.2 Functional Area Information Systems | **WileyPLUS Learning Space** |
| 3. Identify advantages and drawbacks to businesses implementing an enterprise resource planning system. | 10.3 Enterprise Resource Planning (ERP) Systems | • E-book<br>• Author video lecture for each chapter section |
| 4. Describe the three main business processes supported by ERP systems. | 10.4 ERP Support for Business Processes | • Practice quizzes<br>• Flash Cards for vocabulary review<br>• Additional "IT's About Business" cases<br>• Video interviews with managers<br>• Lab Manuals for Microsoft Office 2010 and 2013 |

## What's In IT For Me?

### This Chapter Will Help Prepare You To...

| ACCT | FIN | MKT | POM | HRM | MIS |
|---|---|---|---|---|---|
| ACCOUNTING | FINANCE | MARKETING | PRODUCTION OPERATIONS MANAGEMENT | HUMAN RESOURCES MANAGEMENT | MIS |
| Annual budget | Analyze cash flows | Understand customers' needs, wants | Manage materials handling | Manage recruiting | Responsible for firm's information systems |

# [ General Motors Transforms Its Information Technology Strategy ]

## The Problem

General Motors (GM) (*www.gm.com*) is in the middle of transforming its information technology (IT) operations and strategy away from outsourcing and toward hiring thousands of U.S. technology professionals. This process is called *insourcing*.

Currently, however, GM's most pressing issue arises from allegations that the carmaker was far too slow to recall its Chevy Cobalt and other vehicles with faulty ignition switches. These failures are linked to 13 deaths, and they have sparked a series of lawsuits as well as a congressional investigation. The recall covers 1.6 million vehicles built between 2003 and 2007. This crisis makes improving the company's IT infrastructure all the more critical.

GM's ability to discover vehicle quality problems early on was hindered by the company's failure to consolidate its manufacturing data for analysis. Instead, the data were divided by brands and then subdivided by vehicle models inside those brands. Reporters asked, "Would the current enterprise data warehouse (EDW) have helped GM identify a problem like the faulty ignition switches and deal with it sooner?" GM's CIO Randy Mott responded, "Had we had an easy-to-use, broad way to analyze data, would we have come to different conclusions in the past? I'm sure we would." (We discussed enterprise data warehouses in detail in Chapter 5.)

## The IT Solution

Creating a single EDW for quality analysis and other purposes was always part of the IT transformation plan at GM. By mid-2014, GM had moved more than 1 petabyte of data relating to product development, procurement, logistics, quality, manufacturing, customer care, sales, marketing, finance, and other functions into its new warehouse, and it plans to incorporate even more. The EDW's primary function is to help GM plan for the future. In fact, GM has started using the data to improve vehicle quality. The EDW enables GM to segment and analyze the data down to the vehicle identification number (VIN), to improve safety and quality, and to assess profitability.

GM has collapsed 55 of the 200 data marts scattered across its operations and regions worldwide into its EDW. The company is inputting both structured and unstructured data from its 170 factories worldwide. GM is also incorporating data from new applications that its IT team is building, such as an app that helps GM dealers manage their service operations. The company predicts that by the end of 2015 it will have transferred 100 percent of IT operations data, 90 percent of quality data, and 50 percent of logistics and procurement data into the EDW.

Beyond its EDW efforts, GM is moving forward with other elements of its IT transformation. Mott believes that employees are more cost-effective, drive more innovation, and obtain results faster than outsourced IT teams. Accordingly, the carmaker, which performed 10 percent of its IT work in-house as of January 2013, plans to increase that share to 90 percent by the end of 2015. As a result of this transformation, GM expects to employ about 12,000 in-house IT professionals by 2018, with 2,000 of them performing "run the business" IT functions and the rest focusing on new application development.

Mott is skeptical of classical IT outsourcing for operations such as application development and data center operations. He is examining GM's logistics contracts, requesting that their IT component be moved in-house. Why does Mott believe that GM could perform logistics-related IT better than a company that specializes in this field? He asserts that at GM's scale, the carmaker can usually deliver technology that is cheaper and better aligned to its unique needs. He further contends that GM is already "moving" $142 billion worth of components around the world. So, why shouldn't the firm provide the IT to support its logistics function?

GM transitioned more than 340 mainframe applications from the data centers of outsourcing vendors to GM's new data center over two weekends in October 2013. Mott points to that successful process as proof that his in-house IT team is a professional operation.

The real test will be whether GM's IT team delivers innovation that is better than its competitors who still outsource some of their IT functions. Let's consider several examples of the company's IT transformation. One innovation is a tablet app that GM will distribute to its dealers free of charge. The app will enable salespeople to look up the inventory, products in the supply chain, and incentives for a vehicle on a mobile device without having to go back to their desktops. GM is also deploying a new service lane automation application aimed at helping dealers better manage their vehicle service operations, in hopes of providing a better customer experience.

GM is also focused on simplifying its engineers' systems so they spend less time moving and managing data and more time developing vehicles. In addition, GM is increasing its high-performance computing initiatives to provide more accurate simulations for crash tests and to speed up new vehicle development. In the manufacturing sector, the automaker is applying monitoring and analytics to processes such as understanding the quality of a plant's paint jobs in real time, so that its employees can spot problems before the vehicles reach final inspection or even the dealer's lot.

## The Results

Mary Barra, GM's CEO since January 2014, has apologized for the company's mismanagement of the recall. She also initiated an investigation into what went wrong. In addition, she created the new position of vice president for global vehicle safety, whose mandate is to utilize data to prevent safety problems. This individual will scan the entire organization, identify and analyze safety data, and provide GM with an accurate, real-time safety performance picture of all of its vehicles around the globe.

It is too early to report on the results of the numerous initiatives discussed above. However, GM reported a revenue increase of 1% in 2014. However, the costs of the recall are estimated to be approximately $1.7 billion.

*Sources:* Compiled from S. Kim, "Deaths from GM Ignition Switch Defect Exceed Initial Estimate," *ABC News*, September 15, 2014; B. Snavely, "GM Victims' Fund Receives 63 Death Claims in First Week," *USA Today*, August 10, 2014; P. Lebeau, "Many GM Cars Unlikely to Get Faults Fixed, Despite Major Recall," *NBC News*, April 8, 2014; S. Glinton, "Just How New Is the 'New' GM?" *NPR*, April 8, 2014; G. Wallace, "General Motors Owners Still Waiting for Recall Repairs," *CNN Money*, April 7, 2014; J. Nocera, "GM's Cobalt Crisis," *New York Times*, April 7, 2014; C. Murphy, "GM's Data Strategy Pushed to Center Stage," *InformationWeek*, March 27, 2014; S. Frizell, "General Motors Hit with Class Action Lawsuit over Recall," *Time*, March 15, 2014; S. Gallagher, "General Motors Is Literally Tearing Its Competition to Bits," *Ars Technica*, September 26, 2013; A. Luft, "Why Did GM Choose Arizona, Texas, Georgia, and Michigan for Its 4 IT Innovation Centers?" *GM Authority*, March 12, 2013; M. Wayland, "GM Announces $21 Million Innovation Center, Final in 'IT Transformation'," *MLive*, March 6, 2013; "GM Hiring 1 000 Information Technology Workers in Arizona," *Automotive News*, March 6, 2013; P. Lucas, "GM: Information Technology Center in Roswell, Ga., Will Create 1,000 Jobs," *The Augusta Chronicle*, January 10, 2013; "GM Now Hiring – 10,000 Information Technology Workers," *NBC News*, October 8, 2012; www.gm.com, accessed April 8, 2015.

### Questions

1. Take the "pros" side, and discuss GM's insourcing strategy.
2. Take the "cons" side, and discuss GM's insourcing strategy.
3. Discuss the ways in which information technology can help GM prevent safety problems such as the 2014 recall.
4. Explain how GM's insourcing strategy relates to the topic of this chapter.

# Introduction

The opening case illustrates the integral part that information systems (IS) play in an organization's success. In fact, General Motors is insourcing most of its information systems to better meet the business needs of the organization. In addition, the company is using information systems to more effectively monitor quality control in manufacturing operations. IS are everywhere, and they affect organizations in countless ways. Although IS are frequently discussed within the context of large organizational settings, they also play a critical role in small organizations.

It is important to note that "systems within organizations" do not have to be owned by the organization itself. Instead, organizations can deploy very productive IS that are owned by an external vendor. The key point here is that "systems within an organization" are intended to support internal processes, regardless of who actually owns the systems.

It is important for you to have a working knowledge of IS within your organization, for a variety of reasons. First, your job will require you to access corporate data that are supplied primarily by your firm's transaction processing systems and enterprise resource planning systems. Second, you will have a great deal of input into the format and content of the reports that you receive from these systems. Third, you will utilize the information contained in these reports to perform your job more productively.

This chapter will teach you about the various information systems that modern organizations utilize. You begin by considering transaction processing systems, the most fundamental organizational information systems. You continue with the functional area management information systems, and you conclude with enterprise resource planning systems.

## 10.1 Transaction Processing Systems

Millions (sometimes billions) of transactions occur in large organizations every day. A **transaction** is any business event that generates data worthy of being captured and stored in a database. Examples of transactions are a product manufactured, a service sold, a person hired, and a payroll check generated. In another example, when you are checking out of Walmart, each time the cashier swipes an item across the bar code reader is one transaction.

A **transaction processing system (TPS)** supports the monitoring, collection, storage, and processing of data from the organization's basic business transactions, each of which generates data. The TPS collects data continuously, typically in *real time*—that is, as soon as the data are generated—and it provides the input data for the corporate databases. The TPSs are critical to the success of any enterprise because they support core operations.

In the modern business world, TPSs are inputs for the functional area information systems and business intelligence systems, as well as business operations such as customer relationship management, knowledge management, and e-commerce. TPSs have to efficiently handle both high volumes of data and large variations in those volumes (e.g., during periods of peak processing). In addition, they must avoid errors and downtime, record results accurately and securely, and maintain privacy and security. Figure 10.1 illustrates how TPSs manage data. Consider these examples of how TPSs handle the complexities of transactional data:

- When more than one person or application program can access the database at the same time, the database has to be protected from errors resulting from overlapping updates. The most common error is losing the results of one of the updates.

- When processing a transaction involves more than one computer, the database and all users must be protected against inconsistencies arising from a failure of any component at any time. For example, an error that occurs at some point in an ATM withdrawal can enable a customer to receive cash, although the bank's computer indicates that he or she did not. (Conversely, a customer might not receive cash, although the bank's computer indicates that he or she did.)

- It must be possible to reverse a transaction in its entirety if it turns out to have been entered in error. It is also necessary to reverse a transaction when a customer returns a purchased

**FIGURE 10.1** How transaction processing systems manage data.

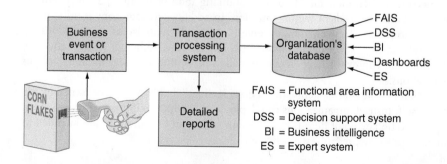

item. For example, if you return a sweater that you have purchased, then the store must credit your credit card for the amount of the purchase, refund your cash, or offer you an in-store credit to purchase another item. In addition, the store must update its inventory.

- It is frequently important to preserve an audit trail. In fact, for certain transactions an audit trail may be legally required.

These and similar issues explain why organizations spend millions of dollars on expensive mainframe computers. In today's business environment, firms must have the dependability, reliability, and processing capacity of these computers to handle their transaction processing loads.

Regardless of the specific data processed by a TPS, the actual process tends to be standard, whether it occurs in a manufacturing firm, a service firm, or a government organization. As the first step in this procedure, people or sensors collect data, which are entered into the computer via any input device. Generally speaking, organizations try to automate the TPS data entry as much as possible because of the large volume involved, a process called *source data automation* (discussed in Technology Guide 1).

Next, the system processes data in one of two basic ways: batch processing and online processing. In **batch processing**, the firm collects data from transactions as they occur, placing them in groups or *batches*. The system then prepares and processes the batches periodically (say, every night).

In **online transaction processing (OLTP)**, business transactions are processed online as soon as they occur. For example, when you pay for an item at a store, the system records the sale by reducing the inventory on hand by one unit, increasing sales figures for the item by one unit, and increasing the store's cash position by the amount you paid. The system performs these tasks in real time by means of online technologies.

# before you go on...

1. Define TPS.
2. List the key functions of a TPS.

# Functional Area Information Systems

10.2

Each department or functional area within an organization has its own collection of application programs, or information systems. Each of these **functional area information systems (FAISs)** supports a particular functional area in the organization by increasing each area's internal efficiency and effectiveness. FAISs often convey information in a variety of reports, which you will see later in this chapter. Examples of FAISs are accounting IS, finance IS, production/ operations management (POM) IS, marketing IS, and human resources IS.

As illustrated in Figure 10.1, the FAIS access data from the corporate databases. The following sections discuss the support that FAISs provide for these functional areas.

## Information Systems for Accounting and Finance

A primary mission of the accounting and finance functional areas is to manage money flows into, within, and out of organizations. This mission is very broad because money is involved in all organizational functions. Therefore, accounting and finance information systems are very diverse and comprehensive. In this section, you focus on certain selected activities of the accounting/finance functional area.

**Financial Planning and Budgeting.** Appropriate management of financial assets is a major task in financial planning and budgeting. Managers must plan for both acquiring and utilizing resources.

- *Financial and economic forecasting:* Knowledge about the availability and cost of money is a key ingredient for successful financial planning. Cash flow projections are particularly important because they inform organizations what funds they need, when they need them, and how they will acquire them.

  Funds for operating organizations come from multiple sources, including stockholders' investments, bond sales, bank loans, sales of products and services, and income from investments. Decisions concerning funding for ongoing operations and for capital investment can be supported by decision support systems and business intelligence applications (discussed in Chapter 12), as well as expert systems (discussed in Technology Guide 4). In addition, numerous software packages for conducting economic and financial forecasting are available. Many of these packages can be downloaded from the Internet, some of them for free.

- *Budgeting:* An essential component of the accounting/finance function is the annual budget, which allocates the organization's financial resources among participants and activities. The budget allows management to distribute resources in the way that best supports the organization's mission and goals.

Several software packages are available to support budget preparation and control and to facilitate communication among participants in the budget process. These packages can reduce the time involved in the budget process. Furthermore, they can automatically monitor exceptions for patterns and trends.

**Managing Financial Transactions.**   Many accounting/finance software packages are integrated with other functional areas. For example, Peachtree by Sage (*www.peachtree.com*) offers a sales ledger, a purchase ledger, a cash book, sales order processing, invoicing, stock control, a fixed assets register, and more.

Companies involved in electronic commerce need to access customers' financial data (e.g., credit line), inventory levels, and manufacturing databases (to determine available capacity and place orders). For example, Microsoft Dynamics GP (formerly Great Plains Software) offers 50 modules that meet the most common financial, project, distribution, manufacturing, and e-business needs.

Organizations, business processes, and business activities operate with, and manage, financial transactions. Consider these examples:

- *Global stock exchanges:* Financial markets operate in global, 24/7/365, distributed electronic stock exchanges that use the Internet both to buy and sell stocks and to broadcast real-time stock prices.

- *Managing multiple currencies:* Global trade involves financial transactions that are carried out in different currencies. The conversion ratios of these currencies are constantly in flux. Financial and accounting systems utilize financial data from different countries, and they convert the currencies from and to any other currency in seconds. Reports based on these data, which formerly required several days to generate, can now be produced in only seconds. In addition to currency conversions, these systems manage multiple languages as well.

- *Virtual close:* Companies traditionally closed their books (accounting records) quarterly, usually to meet regulatory requirements. Today, many companies want to be able to close their books at any time, on very short notice. Information systems make it possible to close the books quickly in what is called a *virtual close*. This process provides almost real-time information on the organization's financial health.

- *Expense management automation: Expense management automation* (EMA) refers to systems that automate the data entry and processing of travel and entertainment expenses. EMA systems are Web-based applications that enable companies to quickly and consistently collect expense information, enforce company policies and contracts, and reduce unplanned purchases as well as airline and hotel expenses. They also allow companies to reimburse their employees more quickly because expense approvals are not delayed by poor documentation.

**Investment Management.**    Organizations invest large amounts of money in stocks, bonds, real estate, and other assets. Managing these investments is a complex task, for several reasons. First, organizations have literally thousands of investment alternatives dispersed throughout the world to choose from. In addition, these investments are subject to complex regulations and tax laws, which vary from one location to another.

Investment decisions require managers to evaluate financial and economic reports provided by diverse institutions, including federal and state agencies, universities, research institutions, and financial services firms. In addition, thousands of Web sites provide financial data, many of them for free.

To monitor, interpret, and analyze the huge amounts of online financial data, financial analysts employ two major types of IT tools: (1) Internet search engines and (2) business intelligence and decision support software.

**Control and Auditing.**    One major reason why organizations go out of business is their inability to forecast and/or secure a sufficient cash flow. Underestimating expenses, overspending, engaging in fraud, and mismanaging financial statements can lead to disaster. Consequently, it is essential that organizations effectively control their finances and financial statements. Let's examine some of the most common forms of financial control.

- *Budgetary control:* After an organization has finalized its annual budget, it divides those monies into monthly allocations. Managers at various levels monitor departmental expenditures and compare them against the budget and the operational progress of corporate plans.
- *Auditing:* Auditing has two basic purposes: (1) to monitor how the organization's monies are being spent and (2) to assess the organization's financial health. Internal auditing is performed by the organization's accounting/finance personnel. These employees also prepare for periodic external audits by outside CPA firms.
- *Financial ratio analysis:* Another major accounting/finance function is to monitor the company's financial health by assessing a set of financial ratios. Included here are liquidity ratios (the availability of cash to pay debt), activity ratios (how quickly a firm converts noncash assets to cash assets), debt ratios (measure the firm's ability to repay long-term debt), and profitability ratios (measure the firm's use of its assets and control of its expenses to generate an acceptable rate of return).

## Information Systems for Marketing

It is impossible to overestimate the importance of customers to any organization. Therefore, any successful organization must understand its customers' needs and wants and then develop its marketing and advertising strategies around them. Information systems provide numerous types of support to the marketing function. In fact, customer-centric organizations are so important that we devote the first half of Chapter 11 to this topic.

## Information Systems for Production/Operations Management

The POM function in an organization is responsible for the processes that transform inputs into useful outputs as well as for the overall operation of the business. Because of the breadth and variety of POM functions, you see only four here: in-house logistics and materials management, planning production and operation, computer-integrated manufacturing (CIM), and product lifecycle management (PLM).

The POM function is also responsible for managing the organization's supply chain. Because supply chain management is vital to the success of modern organizations, we address this topic in detail in Chapter 11.

**In-House Logistics and Materials Management.**    Logistics management deals with ordering, purchasing, inbound logistics (receiving), and outbound logistics (shipping) activities. Related activities include inventory management and quality control.

Inventory Management. As the name suggests, inventory management determines how much inventory an organization should maintain. Both excessive inventory and insufficient inventory create problems. Overstocking can be expensive, because of storage costs and the costs of spoilage and obsolescence. However, keeping insufficient inventory is also expensive, because of last-minute orders and lost sales. As you see in IT's About Business 10.1, yield management systems in the case of theater, are inventory management systems, with the inventory being theater seats.

# IT's [about business]

## 10.1 The Lion King Roars Back

*The Lion King* opened on Broadway in 1997 to critical acclaim. The play went on to win six Tony Awards, including best musical. Like many Broadway hit shows, *The Lion King* enjoyed increasing ticket sales early on, often grossing $1 million per week. Earnings eventually leveled off, however, as newer musicals such as *The Producers* (2001) became hot attractions. To reverse this trend, Disney actually discounted tickets to *The Lion King* for a period of time.

In 2006, Disney moved *The Lion King* from the New Amsterdam Theater to the slightly smaller Minskoff Theater to make way for its *Mary Poppins* musical. At this time, Disney executives were occupied with opening new musicals such as *The Little Mermaid*. The entertainment giant made the mistake of bundling those shows with *The Lion King* in their ads, even though the target audiences for the two shows were different. Ticket sales for *The Lion King* remained uneven, both before and after the 2008 recession. By March 2009 weekly gross revenues had declined to $813,000.

To reinvigorate ticket sales, in 2011 the show's producers, Disney Theatrical Productions, implemented a proprietary yield management system (YMS)—also known as dynamic pricing—to recommend the highest ticket prices that audiences would be likely to pay for each of the 1,700 seats at every performance at the Minskoff. Although other shows employ YMSs to increase seat prices during tourist-heavy holiday weeks, only Disney has reached the level of yield management sophistication achieved by the airline and hotel industries. Disney uses its system to analyze and set prices based on demand and ticket purchasing patterns.

Yield management systems enable businesses to implement a variable pricing strategy, based on understanding, anticipating, and influencing consumer behavior to maximize revenue from a fixed, perishable resource (e.g., airline seats, hotel rooms, and theater seats). YMSs are designed to sell inventory to the right customer at the right time for the right price.

In the case of *The Lion King*, Disney's YMS analyzes historical data for 11.5 million audience members. It then recommends prices for different types of performances—for example, peak dates such as Christmas, off-peak dates such as a weeknight in February, and periods in between. Historical ticket demand for a particular week, for instance, will influence price recommendations for that week in subsequent years.

To help keep audience demand strong, Disney has made a highly unusual choice among Broadway hit shows. The company has factored in an upper ticket price limit of $227 in its YMS. This price is well below the top prices for blockbuster shows such as *The Book of Mormon* ($477), *Kinky Boots* ($349), and *Wicked* ($300). This pricing strategy provides at least three benefits: (1) It makes *The Lion King* relatively affordable for large groups and families; (2) it reduces the chance of buyer's remorse (the sense of regret after having made a purchase), which can generate negative word-of-mouth feedback; and (3) it offers Disney the flexibility to raise prices over the long term.

Based on the results Disney obtained from its YMS, the company abandoned the traditional strategy of charging one price for entire sections of seats. Instead, the producers raise prices for busy weeks by making predictions based on the show's historical data. An interactive seating map accompanies the YMS that allows customers to visually pick their seats. Disney has discovered that customers often choose better, pricier seats 0hen they examine the seating chart.

How successful was Disney's yield management system? In 2013 *The Lion King* stunned Broadway by replacing *Wicked* as the Number 1 earner, a position it had not enjoyed for 10 years. By March 2014 the play was grossing $1.5 million per week. Additionally, consumer demand has grown. In 2013 the show attracted 700,000 theater goers, which was 50,000 more than in 2008. By early 2015, *The Lion King* had become the highest-grossing Broadway play of all time.

*Sources:* Compiled from A. Phadnis, "SpiceJet Revenue Management GM Quits Two Days After Discount Sale," *Business Standard*, April 3, 2014; J. Gereben, "Dynamic Ticket Pricing," *San Francisco Classical Voice*, March 18, 2014; S. Sluis, "Dynamic Pricing Finds a Seat on Broadway," *Destination CRM*, March 17, 2014; P. Healy, "Ticket Pricing Puts 'Lion King' Atop Broadway's Circle of Life," *New York Times*, March 17, 2014; L. Homer, "3 Rules for Pricing Right," *TRG Arts*, October 16, 2013; C. Jones, "How Theater Ticket Prices Are Changing Like Airline Fares," *Chicago Tribune*, October 22, 2012; "Marriott Takes Revenue Management to the Next Level," *Marriott Press Release*, June 4, 2012; P. Healy, "Broadway Hits Make Most of Premium Pricing," *New York Times*, November 24, 2011; www.lionking.com, accessed April 8, 2015.

### Questions

1. Why are yield management systems so important to the producers of Broadway shows? Hint: What is the value of an unsold seat once the curtain goes up?
2. Describe potential disadvantages of Disney's yield management system.

Operations personnel make two basic decisions: when to order and how much to order. Inventory models, such as the economic order quantity (EOQ) model, support these decisions. A large number of commercial inventory software packages are available that automate the application of these models.

Many large companies allow their suppliers to monitor their inventory levels and ship products as they are needed. This strategy, called *vendor-managed inventory* (VMI), eliminates the need for the company to submit purchasing orders. We discuss VMI in Chapter 13.

**Quality Control.** Quality control systems used by manufacturing units provide information about the quality of incoming material and parts, as well as the quality of in-process semifinished and finished products. These systems record the results of all inspections and then compare these results with established metrics. They also generate periodic reports that contain information about quality—for example, the percentage of products that contain defects or that need to be reworked. Quality control data, collected by Web-based sensors, can be interpreted in real time. Alternatively, they can be stored in a database for future analysis.

**Planning Production and Operations.** In many firms, POM planning is supported by IT. POM planning has evolved from material requirements planning (MRP) to manufacturing resource planning (MRP II), to enterprise resource planning (ERP). We briefly discuss MRP and MRP II here, and we examine ERP in detail later in this chapter.

Inventory systems that use an EOQ approach are designed for items for which demand is completely independent—for example, the number of identical personal computers a computer manufacturer will sell. In manufacturing operations, however, the demand for some items is interdependent. Consider, for example, a company that makes three types of chairs, all of which use the same screws and bolts. In this case, the demand for screws and bolts depends on the total demand for all three types of chairs and their shipment schedules. The planning process that integrates production, purchasing, and inventory management of interdependent items is called *material requirements planning* (MRP).

MRP deals only with production scheduling and inventories. More complex planning also involves allocating related resources, such as money and labor. For these cases, more complex, integrated software, called *manufacturing resource planning* (MRP II), is available. MRP II integrates a firm's production, inventory management, purchasing, financing, and labor activities. Thus, MRP II adds functions to a regular MRP system. In fact, MRP II has evolved into enterprise resource planning.

**Computer-Integrated Manufacturing.** **Computer-integrated manufacturing** (CIM) (also called *digital manufacturing*) is an approach that integrates various automated factory systems. CIM has three basic goals: (1) to simplify all manufacturing technologies and techniques, (2) to automate as many of the manufacturing processes as possible, and (3) to integrate and coordinate all aspects of design, manufacturing, and related functions via computer systems.

**Product Lifecycle Management.** Even within a single organization, designing and developing new products can be expensive and time consuming. When multiple organizations are involved, the process can become very complex. *Product lifecycle management* (PLM) is a business strategy that enables manufacturers to share product-related data that support product design and development and supply chain operations. PLM applies Web-based collaborative technologies to product development. By integrating formerly disparate functions, such as a manufacturing process and the logistics that support it, PLM enables these functions to collaborate, essentially forming a single team that manages the product from its inception through its completion, as shown in Figure 10.2.

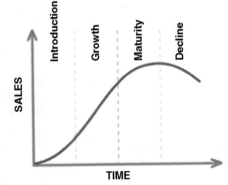

**FIGURE 10.2** Product lifecycle.

## Information Systems for Human Resource Management

Initial human resource information system (HRIS) applications dealt primarily with transaction processing systems, such as managing benefits and keeping records of vacation days. As organizational systems have moved to intranets and the Web, so have HRIS applications.

Many HRIS applications are delivered via an HR portal. (See our discussion of LinkedIn in Chapter 9.) For example, numerous organizations use their Web portals to advertise job openings and to conduct online hiring and training. In this section, you consider how organizations are using IT to perform some key HR functions: recruitment, HR maintenance and development, and HR planning and management.

**Recruitment.**   Recruitment involves finding potential employees, evaluating them, and deciding which ones to hire. Some companies are flooded with viable applicants; others have difficulty finding the right people. IT can be helpful in both cases. In addition, IT can assist in related activities such as testing and screening job applicants.

With millions of resumes available online (in particular, LinkedIn), it is not surprising that companies are trying to find appropriate candidates on the Web, usually with the help of specialized search engines. Companies also advertise hundreds of thousands of jobs on the Web. Online recruiting can reach more candidates, which may bring in better applicants. In addition, the costs of online recruitment are usually lower than traditional recruiting methods such as advertising in newspapers or in trade journals.

**Human Resources Development.**   After employees are recruited, they become part of the corporate human resources pool, which means they must be evaluated and developed. IT provides support for these activities.

Most employees are periodically evaluated by their immediate supervisors. In addition, in some organizations, peers or subordinates also evaluate other employees. Evaluations are typically digitized, and they are used to support many decisions, ranging from rewards to transfers to layoffs.

IT also plays an important role in training and retraining. Some of the most innovative developments are taking place in the areas of intelligent computer-aided instruction and the application of multimedia support for instructional activities. For example, companies conduct much of their corporate training over their intranet or via the Web.

**Human Resources Planning and Management.**   Managing human resources in large organizations requires extensive planning and detailed strategy. IT support is particularly valuable in the following three areas:

- *Payroll and employees' records*: The HR department is responsible for payroll preparation. This process is typically automated, meaning that paychecks are printed or money is transferred electronically into employees' bank accounts.

- *Benefits administration*: In return for their work contributions to their organizations, employees receive wages, bonuses, and various benefits. These benefits include healthcare and dental care, pension contributions (in a decreasing number of organizations), 401K contributions, wellness centers, and child care centers.

   Managing benefits is a complex task because multiple options are available and organizations typically allow employees to choose and trade off their benefits. In many organizations, employees can access the company portal to self-register for specific benefits.

- *Employee relationship management*: In their efforts to better manage employees, companies are developing *employee relationship management* (ERM) applications. A typical ERM application is a call center for employees' problems.

Table 10.1 provides an overview of the activities that the FAIS support. Figure 10.3 shows many of the information systems that support these five functional areas.

## Reports

All information systems produce reports: transaction processing systems, functional area information systems, ERP systems, customer relationship management systems, business

Table
# 10.1
**Activities Supported
by Functional Area
Information Systems**

**Accounting and Finance**

Financial planning—and cost of money

Budgeting—allocates financial resources among participants and activities

Capital budgeting—financing of asset acquisitions

Managing financial transactions

Handling multiple currencies

Virtual close—the ability to close the books at any time on short notice

Investment management—managing organizational investments in stocks, bonds, real estate, and other investment vehicles

Budgetary control—monitoring expenditures and comparing them against the budget

Auditing—ensuring the accuracy of the organization's financial transactions and assessing the condition of the organization's financial health

Payroll

**Marketing and Sales**

Customer relations—know who customers are and treat them like royalty

Customer profiles and preferences

Sales force automation—using software to automate the business tasks of sales, thereby improving the productivity of salespeople

**Production/Operations and Logistics**

Inventory management—when to order new inventory, how much inventory to order, and how much inventory to keep in stock

Quality control—controlling for defects in incoming material and defects in goods produced

Materials requirements planning—planning process that integrates production, purchasing, and inventory management of interdependent items (MRP)

Manufacturing resource planning—planning process that integrates an enterprise's production, inventory management, purchasing, financing, and labor activities (MRP II)

Just-in-time systems—a principle of production and inventory control in which materials and parts arrive precisely when and where needed for production (JIT)

Computer-integrated manufacturing—a manufacturing approach that integrates several computerized systems, such as computer-assisted design (CAD), computer-assisted manufacturing (CAM), MRP, and JIT

Product lifecycle management—business strategy that enables manufacturers to collaborate on product design and development efforts, using the Web

**Human Resource Management**

Recruitment—finding employees, testing them, and deciding which ones to hire

Performance evaluation—periodic evaluation by superiors

Training

Employee records

Benefits administration—retirement, disability, unemployment, and so on

intelligence systems, and so on. We discuss reports here because they are so closely associated with FAIS and ERP systems. These reports generally fall into three categories: routine, ad hoc (on-demand), and exception.

| | | | | |
|---|---|---|---|---|
| Profitability Planning | Financial Planning | Employment Planning, Outsourcing | Product Life Cycle Management | Sales Forecasting, Advertising Planning |
| Auditing, Budgeting | Investment Management | Benefits Administration, Performance Evaluation | Quality Control, Inventory Management | Customer Relations, Sales Force Automation |
| Payroll, Accounts Payable, Accounts Receivable | Manage Cash, Manage Financial Transactions | Maintain Employee Records | Order Fulfillment, Order Processing | Set Pricing, Profile Customers |
| **ACCOUNTING** | **FINANCE** | **HUMAN RESOURCES** | **PRODUCTION/ OPERATIONS** | **MARKETING** |

Strategic / Tactical / Operational labels appear to the right of each row (STRATEGIC, TACTICAL, OPERATIONAL).

**FIGURE 10.3** Examples of information systems supporting the functional areas.

**Routine reports** are produced at scheduled intervals. They range from hourly quality control reports to daily reports on absenteeism rates. Although routine reports are extremely valuable to an organization, managers frequently need special information that is not included in these reports. At other times, they need the information that is normally included in routine reports, but at different times ("I need the report today, for the last three days, not for one week").

Such out-of-the routine reports are called **ad hoc (on-demand) reports**. Ad hoc reports can also include requests for the following types of information:

- **Drill-down reports** display a greater level of detail. For example, a manager might examine sales by region and decide to "drill down" by focusing specifically on sales by store and then by salesperson.
- **Key indicator reports** summarize the performance of critical activities. For example, a chief financial officer might want to monitor cash flow and cash on hand.
- **Comparative reports** compare, for example, the performances of different business units or of a single unit during different times.

Some managers prefer exception reports. **Exception reports** include only information that falls outside certain threshold standards. To implement *management by exception*, management first establishes performance standards. The company then creates systems to monitor performance (via the incoming data about business transactions such as expenditures), to compare actual performance to the standards, and to identify exceptions to the standards. The system alerts managers to the exceptions via exception reports.

Let's use sales as an example. First, management establishes sales quotas. The company then implements an FAIS that collects and analyzes all of the sales data. An exception report would identify only those cases where sales fell outside an established threshold—for example, more than 20 percent short of the quota. It would *not* report expenditures that fell *within* the accepted range of standards. By leaving out all "acceptable" performances, exception reports save managers time, thus helping them focus on problem areas.

## before you go on...

1. Define a functional area information system and list its major characteristics.
2. How do information systems benefit the finance and accounting functional area?
3. Explain how POM personnel use information systems to perform their jobs more effectively and efficiently.
4. What are the most important HRIS applications?
5. Compare and contrast the three basic types of reports.

# Enterprise Resource Planning (ERP) Systems  10.3

Historically, the functional area information systems were developed independent of one another, resulting in *information silos*. These silos did not communicate well with one another, and this lack of communication and integration made organizations less efficient. This inefficiency was particularly evident in business processes that involve more than one functional area, such as procurement and fulfillment.

Enterprise resource planning (ERP) systems are designed to correct a lack of communication among the functional area IS. ERP systems resolve this problem by tightly integrating the functional area IS via a common database. For this reason, experts credit ERP systems with greatly increasing organizational productivity. **ERP systems** adopt a business process view of the overall organization to integrate the planning, management, and use of all of an organization's resources, employing a common software platform and database.

The major objectives of ERP systems are to tightly integrate the functional areas of the organization and to enable information to flow seamlessly across them. Tight integration means that changes in one functional area are immediately reflected in all other pertinent functional areas. In essence, ERP systems provide the information necessary to control the business processes of the organization.

It is important to understand here that ERP systems are an evolution of FAIS. That is, ERP systems have much the same functionality as FAIS, and they produce the same reports. ERP systems simply integrate the functions of the individual FAIS.

Although some companies have developed their own ERP systems, most organizations use commercially available ERP software. The leading ERP software vendor is SAP (*www.sap.com*). Other major vendors include Oracle (*www.oracle.com*) and PeopleSoft (*www.peoplesoft.com*), now an Oracle company. (With more than 700 customers, PeopleSoft is the market leader in higher education). For up-to-date information on ERP software, visit *http://erp.ittoolbox.com*.

Although implementing ERP systems can be difficult because they are large and complicated, many companies have done so successfully. IT's About Business 10.2 recounts a successful ERP deployment at a large German engineering company.

## IT's [about business]

### 10.2 GEA Group Uses SAP for Financial Reporting

With 25,000 employees worldwide, GEA Group (GEA) (*www.gea. com*) develops, produces, and sells innovative and energy-efficient systems in the food and energy industries. The company's goals are to help its customers process food using highly efficient methods and to conserve scarce energy resources. Sales in these two industries account for 70 percent of the company's revenue, which totaled approximately $8 billion in 2014.

As a public corporation whose stock is listed on the MDAX index (a stock index that lists German companies), GEA is required to publish its quarterly, midyear, and year-end financial statements by specific deadlines. GEA provides the consolidated balance sheet, profit and loss (P&L) statement, cash flow statement, statement of stockholders' equity, notes concerning these statements, as well as management reporting, the firm's business outlook, and other stock-related information.

Creating these financial statements was a time-consuming process. At GEA, the responsibility for this task lies with a relatively small team within the accounting department, which is based in the company's headquarters located in *Düsseldorf*, Germany. The team begins by gathering the required financial data from the business divisions, which it then consolidates to create a draft report. As new and more current data and financial figures are added on an ongoing basis, the team constantly has to modify and update the content and the graphics of its reports.

This process was extremely time consuming, because most of the processes for creating the reports were performed manually and were not standardized. Furthermore, manual data manipulation carries with it a high risk of introducing errors and of circulating different versions of the same report. In short, GEA did not have a satisfactory solution for the inherent weaknesses in the processes it used to generate its financial statements.

To resolve these problems, GEA implemented the SAP (*www.sap.com*) Disclosure Management application, one of the SAP solutions for enterprise performance management. This software delivers all of the financial data and information necessary for preparing financial statements. It provides GEA with a consistent data repository, which enables the firm to set up end-to-end workflows (business processes) in accounting. In addition, it enables multiple users to process a single report simultaneously, in parallel.

In collaboration with SAP partner cundus AG, the accounting department at GEA successfully implemented the new solution in only eight weeks. The approximately 20 users required only minimal training because the application is user-friendly and straightforward. Many of the functions are self-explanatory. The implementation took place in parallel with the generation of the firm's quarterly financial statements.

GEA now gathers all of the data and information necessary for creating financial statements, and it manages those data in the accounting department. For the team members, many processes have become simpler. All of the data required to produce the financial reports—the balance sheet figures, notes, text, graphics, and tables from the business divisions—now flow seamlessly into the SAP solution.

At the same time, all of the steps of the process are documented in an audit-compliant manner, while built-in authorization requirements precisely govern access rights. Therefore, both the company's management and external auditors can use the audit trail created by the solution to track the source of the financial figures and to determine who changed them and when.

Furthermore, GEA can now produce reports in all of the desired and required formats—including Microsoft Word, Microsoft Excel, Microsoft PowerPoint, and Adobe PDF files. The simplification of the process extends to the external graphic design agency, which can now create the print version of the financial statements more quickly.

The GEA accounting department now has a clear view of the current status of a report at any time. The result has been a tangible improvement in the flow of information to GEA's management. The new solution also offers integrated version control, a feature that prevents multiple versions of the same report from being circulated.

Thanks to the SAP solution, GEA can create their financial reports 20 percent faster than previously. As a result, the company is better able to meet the increasingly tough legal requirements within Germany and abroad regarding timely external reporting.

*Sources:* Compiled from "GEA Raises Revenue Expectations for Fiscal 2014," *GEA Press Release*, January 12, 2015; "GEA Revenue and Profit Hit New Record High in 2013," *GEA Press Release*, 2014; "Innovating for Sustainable Business Practices," *SAP Customer Success Story*, 2014; *www .gea.com*, accessed April 9, 2015.

**Questions**
1. Discuss the reasons why financial reports must be timely.
2. Explain how the SAP solution enabled the GEA Group to produce their financial reports in an efficient, timely manner.
3. What are the advantages of the SAP solution to the GEA Group?

## ERP II Systems

ERP systems were originally deployed to facilitate business processes associated with manufacturing, such as raw materials management, inventory control, order entry, and distribution. However, these early ERP systems did not extend to other functional areas, such as sales and marketing. They also did not include any customer relationship management (CRM) capabilities that enable organizations to capture customer-specific information. Finally, they did not provide Web-enabled customer service or order fulfillment.

Over time, ERP systems evolved to include administrative, sales, marketing, and human resources processes. Companies now employ an enterprisewide approach to ERP that utilizes the Web and connects all facets of the value chain. (You might want to review our discussion of value chains in Chapter 2.) These systems are called ERP II.

**ERP II systems** are interorganizational ERP systems that provide Web-enabled links among a company's key business systems—such as inventory and production—and its customers, suppliers, distributors, and other relevant parties. These links integrate internal-facing ERP applications with the external-focused applications of supply chain management and customer

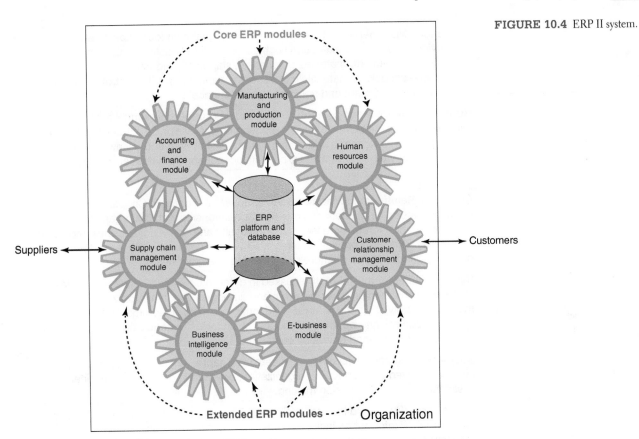

**FIGURE 10.4** ERP II system.

relationship management. Figure 10.4 illustrates the organization and functions of an ERP II system.

The various functions of ERP II systems are now delivered as e-business suites. The major ERP vendors have developed modular, Web-enabled software suites that integrate ERP, customer relationship management, supply chain management, procurement, decision support, enterprise portals, and other business applications and functions. Examples are Oracle's e-Business Suite and SAP's mySAP. The goal of these systems is to enable companies to execute most of their business processes using a single Web-enabled system of integrated software rather than a variety of separate e-business applications.

ERP II systems include a variety of modules that are divided into core ERP modules—financial management, operations management, and human resource management—and extended ERP modules—customer relationship management, supply chain management, business intelligence, and e-business. If a system does not have the core ERP modules, then it is not a legitimate ERP system. The extended ERP modules, in contrast, are optional. Table 10.2 describes each of these modules.

---

| **CORE ERP MODULES** | **Table** |
|---|---|
| **Financial Management.** These modules support accounting, financial reporting, performance management, and corporate governance. They manage accounting data and financial processes such as general ledger, accounts payable, accounts receivable, fixed assets, cash management and forecasting, product-cost accounting, cost-center accounting, asset accounting, tax accounting, credit management, budgeting, and asset management. | **10.2**<br>**ERP Modules** |

| | |
|---|---|
| **Table**<br>**10.2**<br>**(continued)** | **Operations Management.** These modules manage the various aspects of production planning and execution such as demand forecasting, procurement, inventory management, materials purchasing, shipping, production planning, production scheduling, materials requirements planning, quality control, distribution, transportation, and plant and equipment maintenance. |
| | **Human Resource Management.** These modules support personnel administration (including workforce planning, employee recruitment, assignment tracking, personnel planning and development, and performance management and reviews), time accounting, payroll, compensation, benefits accounting, and regulatory requirements. |
| | **EXTENDED ERP MODULES** |
| | **Customer Relationship Management.** (Discussed in detail in Chapter 11.) These modules support all aspects of a customer's relationship with the organization. They help the organization to increase customer loyalty and retention, and thus improve its profitability. They also provide an integrated view of customer data and interactions, helping organizations to be more responsive to customer needs. |
| | **Supply Chain Management.** (Discussed in detail in Chapter 11.) These modules manage the information flows between and among stages in a supply chain to maximize supply chain efficiency and effectiveness. They help organizations plan, schedule, control, and optimize the supply chain from the acquisition of raw materials to the receipt of finished goods by customers. |
| | **Business Intelligence.** (Discussed in detail in Chapter 12.) These modules collect information used throughout the organization, organize it, and apply analytical tools to assist managers with decision making. |
| | **E-Business.** (Discussed in detail in Chapter 7.) Customers and suppliers demand access to ERP information including order status, inventory levels, and invoice reconciliation. Furthermore, they want this information in a simplified format that can be accessed via the Web. As a result, these modules provide two channels of access into ERP system information—one channel for customers (B2C) and one for suppliers and partners (B2B). |

## Benefits and Limitations of ERP Systems

ERP systems can generate significant business benefits for an organization. The major benefits fall into the following categories:

- *Organizational flexibility and agility:* As you have seen, ERP systems break down many former departmental and functional silos of business processes, information systems, and information resources. In this way, they make organizations more flexible, agile, and adaptive. The organizations can therefore respond quickly to changing business conditions and capitalize on new business opportunities.

- *Decision support:* ERP systems provide essential information on business performance across functional areas. This information significantly improves managers' ability to make better, more timely decisions.

- *Quality and efficiency:* ERP systems integrate and improve an organization's business processes, generating significant improvements in the quality of production, distribution, and customer service.

Despite all of their benefits, however, ERP systems do have drawbacks. The major limitations of ERP implementations include the following:

The business processes in ERP software are often predefined by the best practices that the ERP vendor has developed. *Best practices* are the most successful solutions or problem-solving methods for achieving a business objective. As a result, companies may need to change their existing business processes to fit the predefined business processes incorporated into the ERP software. For companies with well-established procedures, this requirement can create serious problems, especially if employees do not want to abandon their old ways of working and therefore resist the changes.

At the same time, however, an ERP implementation can provide an opportunity to improve and in some cases completely redesign inefficient, ineffective, or outdated procedures. In fact, many companies benefit from implementing best practices for their accounting, finance, and human resource processes, as well as other support activities that companies do not consider a source of competitive advantage.

Recall from Chapter 2, however, that different companies organize their value chains in different configurations to transform inputs into valuable outputs and achieve competitive advantage. Therefore, although the vendor's best practices, by definition, are appropriate for most organizations, they might not be the "best" one for your company if they change those processes that give you competitive advantage.

ERP systems can be extremely complex, expensive, and time consuming to implement. (We discuss the implementation of ERP systems in detail in the next section.) In fact, the costs and risks of failure in implementing a new ERP system are substantial. Quite a few companies have experienced costly ERP implementation failures. Specifically, they have suffered losses in revenue, profits, and market share when core business processes and information systems failed or did not work properly. In many cases, orders and shipments were lost, inventory changes were not recorded correctly, and unreliable inventory levels caused major stock outs. Companies such as Hershey Foods, Nike, A-DEC, and Connecticut General sustained losses in amounts up to hundreds of millions of dollars. In the case of FoxMeyer Drugs, a $5 billion pharmaceutical wholesaler, the ERP implementation was so poorly executed that the company had to file for bankruptcy protection.

In almost every ERP implementation failure, the company's business managers and IT professionals underestimated the complexity of the planning, development, and training that were required to prepare for a new ERP system that would fundamentally transform their business processes and information systems. The following are the major causes of ERP implementation failure:

- Failure to involve affected employees in the planning and development phases and in change management processes
- Trying to accomplish too much too fast in the conversion process
- Insufficient training in the new work tasks required by the ERP system
- The failure to perform proper data conversion and testing for the new system

## Implementing ERP Systems

Companies can implement ERP systems by using either on-premise software or software-as-a-service (SaaS). We differentiate between these two methods in detail in Technology Guide 3.

On-Premise ERP Implementation.  Depending on the types of value chain processes managed by the ERP system and a company's specific value chain, there are three strategic approaches to implementing an on-premise ERP system:

- *The vanilla approach:* In this approach, a company implements a standard ERP package, using the package's built-in configuration options. When the system is implemented in this way, it will deviate only minimally from the package's standardized settings. The vanilla approach can enable the company to perform the implementation more quickly. However, the extent to which the software is adapted to the organization's specific processes is limited. Fortunately, a vanilla implementation provides general functions that can support the firm's common business processes with relative ease, even if they are not a perfect fit for those processes.
- *The custom approach:* In this approach, a company implements a more customized ERP system by developing new ERP functions designed specifically for that firm. Decisions concerning the ERP's degree of customization are specific to each organization. To utilize the custom approach, the organization must carefully analyze its existing business processes

to develop a system that conforms to the organization's particular characteristics and processes. In addition, customization is expensive and risky because computer code must be written and updated every time a new version of the ERP software is released. Going further, if the customization does not perfectly match the organization's needs, then the system can be very difficult to use.

- *The best of breed approach:* This approach combines the benefits of the vanilla and customized systems while avoiding the extensive costs and risks associated with complete customization. Companies that adopt this approach mix and match core ERP modules as well as other extended ERP modules from different software providers to best fit their unique internal processes and value chains. Thus, a company may choose several core ERP modules from an established vendor to take advantage of industry best practices—for example, for financial management and human resource management. At the same time, it may also choose specialized software to support its unique business processes—for example, for manufacturing, warehousing, and distribution. Sometimes companies arrive at the best of breed approach the hard way. For example, Dell wasted millions of dollars trying to customize an integrated ERP system from a major vendor to match its unique processes before it realized that a smaller, more flexible system that integrated well with other corporate applications was the answer.

**Software-as-a-Service ERP Implementation.** Companies can acquire ERP systems without having to buy a complete software solution (i.e., on-premise ERP implementation). Many organizations are utilizing software-as-a-service (SaaS) (discussed in Chapter 13 and Technology Guide 3) to acquire cloud-based ERP systems. (We discuss cloud computing in Technology Guide 3).

In this business model, the company rents the software from an ERP vendor who offers its products over the Internet using the SaaS model. The ERP cloud vendor manages software updates and is responsible for the system's security and availability.

Cloud-based ERP systems can be a perfect fit for some companies. For instance, companies that cannot afford to make large investments in IT, yet already have relatively structured business processes that need to be tightly integrated, might benefit from cloud computing.

The relationship between the company and the cloud vendor is regulated by contracts and by service level agreements (SLAs). The SLAs define the characteristics and quality of service; for instance, a guaranteed uptime, or the percentage of time that the system is available. Cloud vendors that fail to meet these conditions can face penalties.

The decision about whether to use on-premise ERP or SaaS ERP is specific to each organization, and it depends on how the organization evaluates a series of advantages and disadvantages. The following are the three major advantages of using a cloud-based ERP system:

- The system can be used from any location that provides Internet access. Consequently, users can work from any location using online shared and centralized resources (data and databases). Users access the ERP system via a secure virtual private network (VPN) connection (discussed in Chapter 4) with the provider.

- Companies using cloud-based ERP avoid the initial hardware and software expenses that are typical of on-premise implementations. For instance, to run SAP on-premise, a company must purchase SAP software as well as a license to use SAP. The magnitude of this investment can hinder small- to medium-sized enterprises (SMEs) from adopting ERP.

- Cloud-based ERP solutions are scalable, meaning it is possible to extend ERP support to new business processes and new business partners (e.g., suppliers) by purchasing new ERP modules.

There are also disadvantages of adopting cloud-based ERP systems that a company must carefully evaluate. The following are the three major disadvantages of using a cloud-based ERP system:

- It is not clear whether cloud-based ERP systems are more secure than on-premise systems. In fact, a survey conducted by North Bridge Venture Partners indicated that security was the primary reason why organizations did not adopt cloud-based ERP.

- Companies that adopt cloud-based ERP systems sacrifice their control over a strategic IT resource. For this reason, some companies prefer to implement an on-premise ERP system, utilizing a strong in-house IT department that can directly manage the system.

- A third disadvantage is a direct consequence of the lack of control over IT resources. This disadvantage occurs when the ERP system experiences problems; for example, some ERP functions are temporarily slow or are not available. In such cases, having an internal IT department that can solve problems immediately rather than dealing with the cloud vendor's system support can speed up the system recovery process.

This situation is particularly important for technology-intensive companies. In such companies, IT is crucial to conduct any kind of business with customers. Examples are e-commerce companies, banks, and government organizations that manage emergencies or situations that might involve individual and national security (e.g., healthcare organizations, police, homeland security department, antiterrorism units, and others).

Finally, slow or unavailable software from a cloud-based ERP vendor creates business continuity problems for the client. (We discuss business continuity in Chapter 4.) That is, a sudden system problem or failure makes it impossible for the firm to operate. Companies lose money when they lose business continuity because customers cannot be serviced and employees cannot do their jobs. A loss of business continuity also damages the company's reputation because customers lose trust in the firm.

### Enterprise Application Integration

For some organizations, integrated ERP systems are not appropriate. This situation is particularly true for companies that find the process of converting from their existing system too difficult or time consuming.

Such companies, however, may still have isolated information systems that need to be connected with one another. To accomplish this task, these companies can use enterprise application integration. An **enterprise application integration (EAI) system** integrates existing systems by providing software, called *middleware*, that connects multiple applications. In essence, the EAI system allows existing applications to communicate and share data, thereby enabling organizations to utilize existing applications while eliminating many of the problems caused by isolated information systems. EAI systems also support implementation of "best of breed" ERP solutions by connecting software modules from different vendors.

## before you go on...

1. Define ERP, and describe its functions.
2. What are ERP II systems?
3. Differentiate between core ERP modules and extended ERP modules.
4. List some drawbacks of ERP software.
5. Highlight the differences between ERP configuration, customization, and best of breed implementation strategies.

# ERP Support for Business Processes 10.4

ERP systems effectively support a number of standard business processes. In particular, ERP systems manage end-to-end, cross-departmental processes. A **cross-departmental process** is one that (1) originates in one department and ends in a different department or (2) originates and ends in the same department but involves other departments.

## The Procurement, Fulfillment, and Production Processes

The following are the three prominent examples of cross-departmental processes:

- The *procurement process*, which originates in the warehouse department (need to buy) and ends in the accounting department (send payment)
- The *fulfillment process*, which originates in the sales department (customer request to buy) and ends in the accounting department (receive payment)
- The *production process*, which originates and ends in the warehouse department (need to produce and reception of finished goods), but involves the production department as well.

These three processes are examined in more detail in the following sections, focusing on the steps that are specific to each one.

**The Procurement Process.** The **procurement process** originates when a company needs to acquire goods or services from external sources, and it concludes when the company receives and pays for them. Let's consider a procurement process where the company needs to acquire physical goods. This process involves three main departments—Warehouse, Purchasing, and Accounting—and it consists of the following steps:

- The process originates in the Warehouse department, which generates a purchase requisition to buy the needed products.
- The Warehouse forwards the requisition to the Purchasing department, which creates a purchase order (PO) and forwards it to a vendor. Generally, companies can choose from a number of vendors, and they select the one that best meets their requirements in terms of convenience, speed, reliability, and/or other characteristics.
- After the company places the order, it receives the goods in its Warehouse department, where someone physically checks the delivery to make certain that it corresponds to what the company ordered. He or she performs this task by comparing a packing list attached to the shipment against the PO.
- If the shipment matches the order, then the Warehouse issues a goods receipt document.
- At the same time or shortly thereafter, the Accounting department receives an invoice from the vendor. Accounting then checks that the PO, the goods receipt document, and the invoice match. This process is called the *three-way-match*.
- After Accounting verifies the match, it processes the payment and sends it to the vendor.

Figure 10.5 illustrates the procurement process.

**The Order Fulfillment Process.** In contrast to procurement, in which the company purchases goods from a vendor, in the **order fulfillment process**, also known as the *order-to-cash process*, the company sells goods to a customer. Fulfillment originates when the company receives a customer order, and it concludes when the company receives a payment from the customer.

The fulfillment process can follow two basic strategies: sell-from-stock and configure-to-order. *Sell-from-stock* involves fulfilling customer orders directly using goods that are in the warehouse (stock). These goods are standard, meaning that the company does not customize them for buyers. In contrast, in *configure-to-order*, the company customizes the product in response to a customer request.

**FIGURE 10.5** Departments and documents flow in the procurement process.

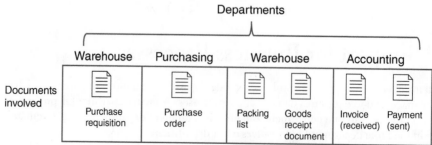

Departments

| Sales | | Sales | | Warehouse | | Accounting | |
|---|---|---|---|---|---|---|---|
| Customer inquiry | Quotation | Customer purchase order | Sales order | Picking document | Packing list | Invoice (sent) | Payment (received) |

Documents involved

FIGURE 10.6 Departments and documents flow in the fulfillment process.

A fulfillment process involves three main departments: Sales, Warehouse, and Accounting.  This process includes the following steps:

- The Sales department receives a customer inquiry, which essentially is a request for information concerning the availability and price of a specific good. (We restrict our discussion here to fulfilling a customer order for physical goods rather than services.)
- After Sales receives the inquiry, it issues a quotation that indicates availability and price.
- If the customer agrees to the price and terms, then Sales creates a customer purchase order (PO) and a sales order.
- Sales forwards the sales order to the Warehouse. The sales order is an interdepartmental document that helps the company keep track of the internal processes that are involved in fulfilling a specific customer order. In addition, it provides details of the quantity, price, and other characteristics of the product.
- The Warehouse prepares the shipment and produces two other internal documents: the picking document, which it uses to remove goods from the Warehouse, and the packing list, which accompanies the shipment and provides details about the delivery.
- At the same time, Accounting issues an invoice for the customer.
- The process concludes when Accounting receives a payment that is consistent with the invoice.

Figure 10.6 shows the fulfillment process. Note that it applies to both sell-from-stock and configure-to-order, because the basic steps are the same for both strategies.

**The Production Process.** The **production process** does not occur in all companies because not all companies produce physical goods. In fact, many businesses limit their activities to buying (procurement) and selling products (e.g., retailers).

The production process can follow two different strategies: make-to-stock and make-to-order. (See the discussion of the pull model and the push model in Chapter 11.) *Make-to-stock* occurs when the company produces goods to create or increase an *inventory*; that is, finished products that are stored in the warehouse and are available for sales. In contrast, *make-to-order* occurs when production is generated by a specific customer order.

Manufacturing companies that produce their own goods manage their interdepartmental production process across the Production and Warehouse departments. The production process involves the following steps:

- The Warehouse department issues a planned order when the company needs to produce a finished product, either because the Warehouse has insufficient inventory or because the customer placed a specific order for goods that are not currently in stock.
- Once the planned order reaches Production, the production controller authorizes the order and issues a production order, which is a written authorization to start the production of a certain amount of a specific product.
- To assemble a finished product, Production requires a number of materials (or parts). To acquire these materials, Production generates a material withdrawal slip, which lists all of the needed parts, and forwards it to the Warehouse.

**FIGURE 10.7** Departments and documents flow in the production process.

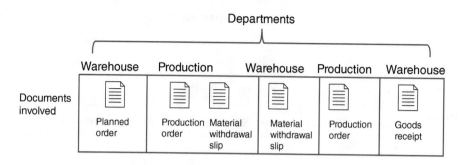

If the parts are available in the Warehouse, then the Warehouse delivers them to Production. If the parts are not available, then the company must purchase them via the procurement process.

- After Production has created the products, it updates the production order specifying that, as planned, a specific number of units of product can now be shipped to the Warehouse.
- As soon as the Warehouse receives the finished goods, it issues a goods receipt document that certifies how many units of a product it received that are available for sales.

This overview of the Production process is a highly simplified one. In reality, the process is very complex, and it frequently involves additional steps. In addition, ERP systems collect a number of other documents and pieces of information such as the bill of materials (a list of all materials needed to assemble a finished product), the list of work centers (locations where the production takes place), and the product routing (production steps). All of these topics require an in-depth analysis of the production process and are therefore beyond the scope of our discussion here. Figure 10.7 illustrates the production process.

A number of events can occur that create exceptions or deviations in the procurement, fulfillment, and production processes. Deviations may include the following:

- A delay in the receipt of products
- Issues related to an unsuccessful three-way-match regarding a shipment and its associated invoice (procurement)
- Rejection of a quotation
- A delay in a shipment
- A mistake in preparing the shipment or in invoicing the customer (fulfillment)
- Overproduction of a product
- Reception of parts that cannot be used in the production process
- Nonavailability of certain parts from a supplier

Companies use ERP systems to manage procurement, fulfillment, and production because these systems track all of the events that occur within each process. Furthermore, the system stores all of the documents created in each step of each process in a centralized database, where they are available as needed in real time. Therefore, any exceptions or mistakes made during one or more interdepartmental processes are handled right away by simply querying the ERP system and retrieving a specific document or piece of information that needs to be revised or examined more carefully. Therefore, it is important to follow each step in each process and to register the corresponding document into the ERP system.

Figure 10.8 portrays the three cross-functional business processes we just discussed. It specifically highlights the integration of the three processes, which is made possible by ERP systems.

## Interorganizational Processes: ERP with SCM and CRM

Although the procurement and the fulfillment processes involve suppliers and customers, they are considered (together with the production process) intraorganizational processes because they originate and conclude within the company. However, ERP systems can also manage processes that originate in one company and conclude in another company. These processes

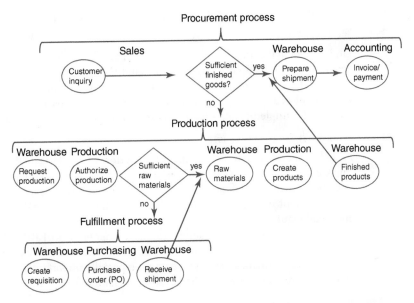

**FIGURE 10.8** Integrated processes with ERP systems.

are called *interorganizational processes*, and they typically involve supply chain management (SCM) and customer relationship management (CRM) systems. You can find a more detailed description of CRM and SCM in Chapter 11. Here, we focus on the integration of these processes within a firm's industry value chain.

SCM and CRM processes help multiple firms in an industry coordinate activities such as the production-to-sale of goods and services. Let's consider a chain of grocery stores whose supply chain must properly manage perishable goods. On the one hand, store managers need to stock only the amount of perishable products that they are reasonably sure they will sell before the products' expiration dates. On the other hand, they do not want to run out of stock of any products that customers need.

ERP SCM systems have the capability to place automatic requests to buy fresh perishable products from suppliers in real time. That is, as each perishable product is purchased, the system captures data on that purchase, adjusts store inventory levels, and transmits these data to the grocery chain's warehouse as well as the products' vendors. The system executes this process by connecting the point-of-sale barcode scanning system with the Warehouse and Accounting departments, as well as with the vendors' systems. In addition, SCM systems utilize historical data to predict when fresh products need to be ordered before the store's supply becomes too low.

ERP CRM systems also benefit businesses by generating forecasting analyses of product consumption based on critical variables such as geographical area, season, day of the week, and type of customer. These analyses help grocery stores coordinate their supply chains to meet customer needs for perishable products. Going further, CRM systems identify particular customer needs and then utilize this information to suggest specific product campaigns. These campaigns can transform a potential demand into sales opportunities, and convert sales opportunities into sales quotations and sales orders. This process is called the *demand-to-order* process.

# before you go on...

1. What are the three main intraorganizational processes that are typically supported by ERP systems?
2. Why is it important that all steps in each process generate a document that is stored in the ERP system?
3. What is the difference between intraorganizational and interorganizational processes?
4. What are the two main ES systems that support interorganizational processes?

# What's In IT For Me?

## For the Accounting Major

Understanding the functions and outputs of TPSs effectively is a major concern of any accountant. It is also necessary to understand the various activities of all functional areas and how they are interconnected. Accounting information systems are a central component in any ERP package. In fact, all large CPA firms actively consult with clients on ERP implementations, using thousands of specially trained accounting majors.

## For the Finance Major

IT helps financial analysts and managers perform their tasks better. Of particular importance is analyzing cash flows and securing the financing required for smooth operations. In addition, financial applications can support such activities as risk analysis, investment management, and global transactions involving different currencies and fiscal regulations.

Finance activities and modeling are key components of ERP systems. Flows of funds (payments), at the core of most supply chains, must be executed efficiently and effectively. Financial arrangements are especially important along global supply chains, where currency conventions and financial regulations must be considered.

## For the Marketing Major

Marketing and sales expenses are usually targets in a cost-reduction program. Also, sales force automation improves not only salespeoples' productivity (and thus reduces costs) but also customer service.

## For the Production/Operations Management Major

Managing production tasks, materials handling, and inventories in short time intervals, at a low cost, and with high quality is critical for competitiveness. These activities can be achieved only if they are properly supported by IT. In addition, IT can greatly enhance interaction with other functional areas, especially sales. Collaboration in design, manufacturing, and logistics requires knowledge of how modern information systems can be connected.

## For the Human Resource Management Major

Human resources managers can increase their efficiency and effectiveness by using IT for some of their routine functions. Human resources personnel need to understand how information flows between the HR department and the other functional areas. Finally, the integration of functional areas via ERP systems has a major impact on skill requirements and scarcity of employees, which are related to the tasks performed by the HRM department.

## For the MIS Major

The MIS function is responsible for the most fundamental information systems in organizations: the transaction processing systems. The TPSs provide the data for the databases. In turn, all other information systems use these data. MIS personnel develop applications that support all levels of the organization (from clerical to executive) and all functional areas. The applications also enable the firm to do business with its partners.

# [ Summary ]

**1. Explain the purpose of transaction processing systems.**

TPSs monitor, store, collect, and process data generated from all business transactions. These data provide the inputs into the organization's database.

**2. Explain the types of support that information systems can provide for each functional area of the organization.**

The major business functional areas are production/operations management, marketing, accounting/finance, and human resources management. Table 10.1 provides an overview of the many activities in each functional area supported by FAIS.

**3. Identify advantages and drawbacks to businesses of implementing an ERP system.**

Enterprise resource planning (ERP) systems integrate the planning, management, and use of all of the organization's resources. The major objective of ERP systems is to tightly integrate the functional areas of the organization. This integration enables information to flow seamlessly across the various functional areas.

The following are the major benefits of ERP systems:

- Because ERP systems integrate organizational resources, they make organizations more flexible, agile, and adaptive. The organizations can therefore react quickly to changing business conditions and capitalize on new business opportunities.
- ERP systems provide essential information on business performance across functional areas. This information significantly improves managers' ability to make better, more timely decisions.
- ERP systems integrate organizational resources, resulting in significant improvements in the quality of customer service, production, and distribution.

The following are the major drawbacks of ERP systems:

- The business processes in ERP software are often predefined by the best practices that the ERP vendor has developed. As a result, companies may need to change existing business processes to fit the predefined business processes of the software. For companies with well-established procedures, this requirement can be a huge problem.
- ERP systems can be extremely complex, expensive, and time consuming to implement. In fact, the costs and risks of failure in implementing a new ERP system are substantial.

**4. Describe the three main business processes supported by ERP systems.**

The *procurement process*, which originates in the warehouse department (need to buy) and ends in the accounting department (send payment).

The *fulfillment process* that originates in the sales department (customer request to buy) and ends in the accounting department (receive payment).

The *production process* that originates and ends in the warehouse department (need to produce and reception of finished goods), but involves the production department as well.

We leave the details of the steps in each of these processes to you.

# [ Chapter Glossary ]

**ad hoc (on-demand) reports** Nonroutine reports that often contain special information that is not included in routine reports.

**batch processing** Transaction processing system (TPS) that processes data in batches at fixed periodic intervals.

**comparative reports** Reports that compare performances of different business units or times.

**computer-integrated manufacturing (CIM)** An information system that integrates various automated factory systems; also called *digital manufacturing*.

**cross-departmental process** A business process that originates in one department and ends in another department, and/or originates and ends in the same department while involving other departments.

**drill-down reports** Reports that show a greater level of details than is included in routine reports.

**enterprise application integration (EAI) system** A system that integrates existing systems by providing layers of software that connect applications together.

**enterprise resource planning (ERP) systems** Information systems that take a business process view of the overall organization to integrate the planning, management, and use of all of an organization's resources, employing a common software platform and database.

**ERP II systems** Interorganizational ERP systems that provide Web-enabled links among key business systems (e.g., inventory and production) of a company and its customers, suppliers, distributors, and others.

**exception reports** Reports that include only information that exceeds certain threshold standards.

**functional area information systems (FAIS)** Systems that provide information to managers (usually midlevel) in the functional areas, in order to support managerial tasks of planning, organizing, and controlling operations.

**key indicator reports** Reports that summarize the performance of critical activities.

**online transaction processing (OLTP)** Transaction processing system (TPS) that processes data after transactions occur, frequently in real time.

**order fulfillment process** A cross-functional business process that originates when the company receives a customer order, and it concludes when it receives a payment from the customer.

**procurement process** A cross-functional business process that originates when a company needs to acquire goods or services from external sources, and it concludes when the company receives and pays for them.

**production process** A cross-functional business process in which a company produces physical goods.

**routine reports** Reports produced at scheduled intervals.

**transaction** Any business event that generates data worth capturing and storing in a database.

**transaction processing system (TPS)** Information system that supports the monitoring, collection, storage, and processing of data from the organization's basic business transactions, each of which generates data.

# [ Discussion Questions ]

1. Why is it logical to organize IT applications by functional areas?
2. Describe the role of a TPS in a service organization.
3. Describe the relationship between TPS and FAIS.
4. Discuss how IT facilitates the budgeting process.
5. How can the Internet support investment decisions?
6. Describe the benefits of integrated accounting software packages.
7. Discuss the role that IT plays in support of auditing.
8. Investigate the role of the Web in human resources management.
9. What is the relationship between information silos and enterprise resource planning?

# [ Problem-Solving Activities ]

1. Finding a job on the Internet is challenging as there are almost too many places to look. Visit the following sites: *www.careerbuilder.com*, *www.craigslist.org*, *www.linkedin.com*, *www.jobcentral.com*, and *www.monster.com*. What does each of these sites provide you as a job seeker?
2. Enter *www.sas.com* and access *revenue optimization* there. Explain how the software helps in optimizing prices.
3. Enter *www.eleapsoftware.com* and review the product that helps with online training (training systems). What are the most attractive features of this product?
4. Examine the capabilities of the following (and similar) financial software packages: Financial Analyzer (from

Oracle) and CFO Vision (from SAS Institute). Prepare a report comparing the capabilities of the software packages.
5. Surf the Net and find free accounting software. (Try *www.cnet.com*, *www.rkom.com*, *www.tucows.com*, *www.passtheshareware.com*, and *www.freeware-guide.com*.) Download the software and try it. Compare the ease of use and usefulness of each software package.
6. Examine the capabilities of the following financial software packages: TekPortal (from *www.tekknowledge.com*), Financial Analyzer (from *www.oracle.com*), and Financial Management (from *www.sas.com*). Prepare a report comparing the capabilities of the software packages.

7. Find Simply Accounting Basic from Sage Software (*http://us.simplyaccounting.com*). Why is this product recommended for small businesses?

8. Enter *www.halogensoftware.com* and *www.successfactors.com*. Examine their software products and compare them.

9. Enter *www.iemployee.com* and find the support it provides to human resources management activities. View the demos and prepare a report on the capabilities of the products.

# [ Closing Case Airlines Use Information Technology to Combat Flight Cancellations ]

## The Problem

A very difficult winter in 2013–2014 led to the cancellation of tens of thousands of airline flights, leaving airlines scrambling to find alternative ways to get travelers to their destinations. Once a flight is cancelled, it takes an estimated 18 hours for travelers to reach their destinations, according to masFlight (*www.masflight.com*), a data and software company that specializes in air travel. On February 14, 2014, masFlight reported that the airline industry had already experienced 76,400 cancellations that year, affecting 5.7 million passengers and making the winter of 2014 the worst for flight operations since 2010.

However, the weather is not the only problem associated with cancelled flights. Federal regulations that require pilots to get more rest time and threaten airlines with fines if they keep passengers on a plane that is sitting on the tarmac for longer than three hours are also increasing the number of flight cancellations.

## The IT Solution

Although the cancellation rate increased during the winters of 2013–2014, the ability of the airlines to utilize information technology to efficiently get passengers to their destinations has increased as well. Airlines are now taking proactive steps before a storm breaks out, and they have implemented software that automatically rebooks fliers when their flights are cancelled. Furthermore, passengers can use the airlines' Web sites and mobile applications to reroute their trips.

Consider Delta as an example. When the airline receives advance warning about a potentially disruptive weather event, it starts waiving ticket change fees 24–36 hours before the weather strikes. This policy affords passengers the opportunity to travel before, as well as after, the storm. Passengers who elect to cancel rather than reschedule their flights will receive a refund.

The major airlines have multiple hubs, which makes reworking an itinerary somewhat easier. For example, if Atlanta (a Delta hub) is experiencing bad weather, passengers can be rerouted through Detroit, Minneapolis, or Salt Lake City. Improved automated booking software has smoothed out the process of rebooking passengers. Previously, this was a manual, time-intensive process. The newer rebooking systems have automated this process, enabling the airlines to find accommodations on other flights, and other airlines, much more quickly.

## The Results

So, how are the airlines' systems working? To answer this question, let's consider the case of Fred Jones. In the middle of February's (2014) winter storm, which bombarded the South and Northeast with snow and ice, Jones was scheduled to fly from Atlanta to Houston. However, thanks to a call from his airline, he was able to get around the storm. The airline alerted him to potential cancellations and rerouted him successfully, enabling him to attend an important business meeting. Of course, Fred represents only a single, successful example. In fact, during that winter storm, many travelers had to sleep in airports around the country while the airlines were struggling to get them to their destinations.

*Sources:* Compiled from M. Schlangenstein, "American Airlines Says Winter Storms Cut $115 Million in Revenue, " *Bloomberg BusinessWeek*, April 8, 2014; A. Langfield, "Pent-Up Winter Demand to Boost Business Travel Spending, " *CNBC*, April 7, 2014; C. Jones, "Airlines, Airports Improve Technology for Passengers, " *USA Today*, April 7, 2014; C. Jones, "Airlines Better at Getting Stuck Fliers Up in Air, " *USA Today*, February 27, 2014; "Winter Storms Force Airlines to Scrap Most Flights in 25 Years," Associated Press, February 14, 2014; J. Glanz, "Is Big Data an Economic Big Dud?" *The New York Times*, August 17, 2013; *www.masflight.com*, accessed April 8, 2015.

### Questions

1. Describe why many passengers still experience long delays when the weather disrupts flight operations.

2. Refer to Chapter 2. Do you consider the airlines' automated booking software to be a strategic information system? Why or why not?

# 11 Customer Relationship Management and Supply Chain Management

# What's In IT For Me?

## This Chapter Will Help Prepare You To...

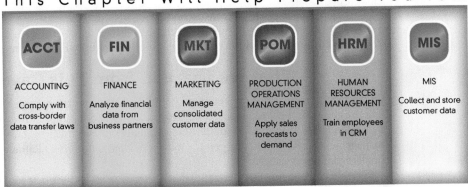

| ACCT | FIN | MKT | POM | HRM | MIS |
|------|-----|-----|-----|-----|-----|
| ACCOUNTING | FINANCE | MARKETING | PRODUCTION OPERATIONS MANAGEMENT | HUMAN RESOURCES MANAGEMENT | MIS |
| Comply with cross-border data transfer laws | Analyze financial data from business partners | Manage consolidated customer data | Apply sales forecasts to demand | Train employees in CRM | Collect and store customer data |

---

## [ Organic and Beyond Corporation Manages Its New B2C Channel ]

Over the past decade, food safety has drawn increasing attention from the Chinese government and the Chinese populace. This interest created an opportunity for the organic agriculture market in China. In 2013, total organic food sales in China approached US$2 billion, and this total was expected to increase by more than 30 percent every year.

Founded in 2007, Organic and Beyond Corporation (OABC) (*www.oabc.cc/en/*) cultivates, produces, distributes, and delivers organic food. Headquartered in Beijing, the company has six branches in China. OABC has established farms to grow organic vegetables, fruits, grains, Chinese lake crabs, and many other products.

As late as 2013, OABC operated a primarily business-to-business (B2B) model, selling produce to retail establishments such as restaurants. In contrast, the company's business-to-consumer (B2C) channel was relatively small. However, OABC wanted to expand its B2C operations to increase its revenues. To accomplish this task, the enterprise had to reconfigure its information systems—which were designed to manage bulk sales and deliveries—so that they could also handle potentially millions of small orders. To make this transition possible, OABC had to reinvent itself to find new ways to service the B2C marketplace.

OABC engaged IBM Global Business Services to implement customer-centric business processes and systems that would encompass the entire customer fulfillment business process. OABC and IBM selected Oracle's Siebel Customer Relationship Management (CRM) system to serve as the foundation for OABC's B2C operations.

By implementing Siebel CRM, OABC was able to upgrade its CRM operations, thereby enhancing sales management, optimizing distribution, decreasing order fulfillment time, and personalizing service. The company also implemented systems that enable managers to visualize the order process, the delivery process, and overall company performance.

The near-real-time information systems allow OABC to understand its customers in its new B2C market, adjust its production and delivery processes to match demand, and operate at very low costs with minimal waste. In addition, the company can now closely track sales performance and identify opportunities for improvement.

Today OABC is able to profitably provide home-delivery service to 200,000 families in six cities: Beijing, Shanghai, Guangzhou, Shenzhen, Hangzhou, and Tianjin. This innovation has helped OABC to capture a significant share of the B2C organic foods marketplace.

*Sources:* Compiled from "EnfoDesk: China B2C Market Hit 763.71 Billion Yuan in 2013," *China Internet Watch*, March 19, 2014; "China Online Shopping Maintains High Growth in Q3 2013," *iResearch China*, December 3, 2013; "China B2C Online Shopping Industry Report, 2013–2016," *PRNewswire*, October 17, 2013; "OABC Grows Organically to Reach More than 400,000 Consumers," *IBM Sales and Distribution Success Story*, September, 18, 2013; S. Millward, "China's E-Commerce to

Hit $71 Billion in Q2: These Are the Top 10 E-Stores," *Tech in Asia*, August 28, 2013; "Top 10 China B2C E-Commerce Websites," *Advangent*, August 20, 2013; M. Klein, "What B2B Can Learn from B2C," *Direct Marketing News*, August 2, 2013; *www.oabc.cc/en/*, accessed April 6, 2015.

### Questions

1. Why is B2C electronic commerce so important in China?
2. Why is customer relationship management so important to B2C electronic commerce?

## What We Learned from This Case

Organizations increasingly are emphasizing a customer-centric approach to their business practices because they realize that long-term customer relationships provide sustainable value that extends beyond an individual business transaction. Significantly, customer relationship management (CRM) is not important solely for large enterprises. Rather, it is essential for small organizations as well.

The chapter opening case points out that an organization's customers can be other organizations (e.g., B2B electronic commerce) as well as individuals (e.g., B2C electronic commerce). Emphasizing the importance of CRM for both types of customers, OABC had to implement information systems to manage individual customers in its new B2C channel.

In Chapter 10, you learned about information systems that supported organizational activities within the organization. In this chapter, you study information systems that support organizational activities that extend outside the organization to customers and suppliers. The first half of this chapter addresses customer relationship management (CRM) systems, and the second half addresses supply chain management (SCM) systems.

At this point, you might be asking yourself: Why should *I* learn about CRM and SCM? The answer, as you will see in this chapter, is that customers and suppliers are supremely important to *all* organizations. Regardless of your job, you will have an impact, whether direct or indirect, on managing your firm's customers and suppliers. When you read the What's in IT for Me? section at the end of the chapter, you will learn about opportunities to make immediate contributions on your first job. Therefore, it is essential that you acquire a working knowledge of CRM and CRM systems, as well as SCM and SCM systems.

## 11.1 Defining Customer Relationship Management

Before the supermarket, the mall, and the automobile, people purchased goods at their neighborhood store. The owners and employees recognized customers by name and knew their preferences and wants. For their part, customers remained loyal to the store and made repeated purchases. Over time, however, this personal customer relationship became impersonal as people moved from farms and small towns to cities, consumers became mobile, and supermarkets and department stores achieved economies of scale through mass marketing. Although prices were lower and products were more uniform in quality, the relationship with customers became nameless and impersonal.

The customer relationship has become even more impersonal with the rapid growth of the Internet and the World Wide Web. In today's hypercompetitive marketplace, customers are increasingly powerful; if they are dissatisfied with a product and/or a service from one organization, a competitor is often just one mouse click away. Furthermore, as more and more customers shop on the Web, an enterprise does not even have the opportunity to make a good first impression *in person*.

**Customer relationship management** returns to personal marketing. That is, rather than market to a mass of people or companies, businesses market to each customer individually. By employing this approach, businesses can use information about each customer—for example, previous purchases, needs, and wants—to create highly individualized offers that customers are more likely to accept. That is, the CRM approach is designed to achieve *customer intimacy*.

Customer relationship management is a customer-focused and customer-driven organizational strategy. That is, organizations concentrate on assessing customers' requirements for products and services and then providing a high-quality, responsive customer experience. CRM is not a process or a technology per se; rather, it is a customer-centric way of thinking and acting. The focus of modern organizations has shifted from conducting business transactions to managing customer relationships. In general, organizations recognize that customers are the core of a successful enterprise, and the success of the enterprise depends on effectively managing relationships with them.

The CRM approach is enabled by information technology in the form of various systems and applications. However, CRM is not only about the software. Sometimes the problem with managing relationships is simply time and information. Old systems may contain the needed information, but this information may take too long to access and may not be usable across a variety of applications. The result is that companies have less time to spend with their customers.

In contrast, modern CRM strategies and systems build sustainable long-term customer relationships that create value for the company as well as for the customer. That is, CRM helps companies acquire new customers and to retain and expand their relationships with profitable existing customers. Retaining customers is particularly important because repeat customers are the largest generator of revenue for an enterprise. Also, organizations have long understood that winning back a customer who has switched to a competitor is vastly more expensive than keeping that customer satisfied in the first place. One company that has become successful and famous for its customer-centric policies is Amazon, as you see in IT's About Business 11.1.

# IT's [about business]

## 11.1 Amazon: Truly Superb Customer Service

Customer experience is a top priority for 86 percent of executives, according to Gartner's "Amplifying the Enterprise: The CIO Agenda." Amazon (*www.amazon.com*) is amazingly effective at managing customer relationships. The company has achieved its phenomenal success by combining data efficiency and customer service in ways that no previous business has ever managed to do.

Amazon's basic CRM strategy has always focused on anticipation and prevention. Amazon realizes that after a customer orders a product, his or her next question is, "When will I receive it?" Therefore, the retailer proactively informs customers (either by e-mail or on the purchase page), "You will receive your order on Tuesday." This process eliminates phone calls and impresses customers with Amazon's level of service.

Consider Amazon's optimized product information pages, which include the following:

- Product details, including specifications, special features, and competitive advantages
- Real-time inventory and availability
- Price comparisons
- Shipping and payment options, special offers, and product promotions
- Cross-sold products frequently purchased along with the current product
- Predictable product delivery timing

By presenting such information in a single, user-friendly view, Amazon helps shoppers make informed and efficient buying decisions. When customers return to the site, Amazon analyzes their transaction histories, including products previously browsed, to present a personalized, sales-optimized page that encourages additional purchases. All of this information is accurate, real-time, and integrated. It includes product details, user reviews, product availability, fulfillment information, and payment options.

Essentially, Amazon has radically disrupted the business model of retailing: how customers interact with businesses, what customers expect of businesses, how products are handled, and how shipping and delivery are managed. Amazon has restored the customer experience into a highly personalized one. The company provides a vast but manageable set of services to customers on a platform that allows them to choose which products they want, when they want them.

To better understand Amazon's CRM philosophy, let's consider two innovative services: Amazon Prime and Mayday. Amazon Prime began as a service to provide customers with less expensive two-day shipping. Today, it offers not only free shipping but also thousands of free videos that customers can watch and download. Amazon has found that its Prime customers spend 40 percent more than they did before joining the service.

Mayday is another popular customer service. Amazon's tablet—the Amazon Kindle HDX series—contains a Mayday button. Click on that button, and within 15 seconds a live customer service representative appears in a small video window on the screen. The representative has the ability to take over your tablet (with your permission) to handle your customer service questions. Mayday is available 24/7/365.

In addition to these services, Amazon is planning a future innovation: Amazon Prime Air. In late 2013, Amazon founder Jeff Bezos announced that the company was exploring the use of unmanned, autonomous, flying drones to deliver packages. The packages will be lifted off the shipping lines by "octocopters" and then flown to the delivery address via GPS coordinates. Amazon acknowledges that there are many obstacles to implementing such a delivery system (think about the Federal Aviation Administration's regulations, for example). Nevertheless, the company is, once again, relentlessly focused on providing superb customer services.

And the results of this focus? Since Amazon introduced these innovations, a number of prominent retailers have struggled to keep pace. Consider, for example, the office supplies company, Staples (www.staples.com). In 2013, sales at Staples declined to about $6 billion. Moreover, nearly half of those sales were generated by the store's online channel. Responding to these developments, in March 2014 Staples closed 225 brick-and-mortar stores

in the United States and Canada. Interestingly however, on February 4, 2015 Staples announced that it was buying Office Depot.

As another example, RadioShack (www.radioshack.com) closed 1,100 stores after a huge decline in profits. On February 5, 2015, RadioShack filed for bankruptcy protection. BestBuy (www.bestbuy.com) is also continuing to suffer decreases in revenues. This trend has been called the "Amazon Effect."

*Sources:* Compiled from M. Wulfraat, "Logistics Comment: How the 'Amazon Effect' Is Changing the American Manufacturing Industry," *Supply Chain Digest*, March 26, 2014; I. Lunden, "The Amazon Effect: Staples to Close 225 Stores, Says It's Now Making Half of All Sales Online," *TechCrunch*, March 6, 2014; "How Technology Contributes to Customer Experience," *Baseline Magazine*, March 6, 2014; J. Bort, "Larry Ellison: Amazon, Salesforce.com Are Now Oracle's Biggest Competitors," *Business Insider*, January 2014; P. Greenberg, "Why Customer-Obsessed Amazon Is Our Most Important Business Force," *ZDNet*, January 22, 2014; S. Raisch, "Retailers Need to Adapt to the Amazon Effect," *Today's Garden Center*, January 6, 2014; D. Gross, "Amazon's Drone Delivery: How Would It Work?" *CNN Technology News*, December 2, 2013; J. Talton, "Digging into the 'Amazon Effect'," *The Seattle Times*, July 30, 2013; S. Duplessie, "IT Is About to Meet the Amazon Effect," *Computerworld*, June 5, 2013; K. Liyakasa, "Uncovering the 'Amazon Effect'," *Destination CRM*, August 16, 2012; www.amazon.com, accessed April 7, 2015.

### Questions

1. Describe the advantages that Amazon has over bricks-and-mortar retailers.
2. Describe the many facets of Amazon's relentless focus on customer relationship management.

---

Figure 11.1 depicts the CRM process. The process begins with marketing efforts, where the organization solicits prospects from a target population of potential customers. A certain number of these prospects will make a purchase and thus become customers. A certain number of these customers will become repeat customers. The organization then segments its repeat customers into low- and high-value repeat customers. An organization's overall goal is to maximize the *lifetime value* of a customer, which is that customer's potential revenue stream over a number of years.

Over time all organizations inevitably lose a certain percentage of customers, a process called *customer churn*. The optimal result of the organization's CRM efforts is to maximize the number of high-value repeat customers while minimizing customer churn.

CRM is a fundamentally simple concept: Treat different customers differently, because their needs differ, and their value to the company may also differ. A successful CRM strategy not only improves customer satisfaction but also makes the company's sales and service employees more productive, which in turn generates increased profits. In fact, researchers at the National Quality Research Center at the University of Michigan discovered that a 1 percent increase in customer satisfaction can lead to as much as a 300 percent increase in a company's *market capitalization*, defined as the number of shares of the company's stock outstanding multiplied by the price per share of the stock. Put simply, a minor increase in customer satisfaction can generate a major increase in a company's overall value.

Up to this point, you have been looking at an organization's CRM strategy. It is important to distinguish between a CRM *strategy* and CRM *systems*. Basically, CRM systems are information systems designed to support an organization's CRM strategy. For organizations to pursue excellent relationships with their customers, they need to employ CRM systems that provide the infrastructure needed to support those relationships. Because customer service and support

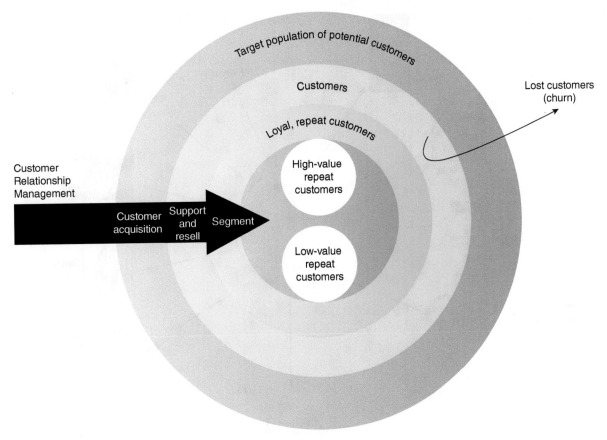

**Customer Relationship Management**

Customer acquisition → Support and resell → Segment

Target population of potential customers

Customers

Loyal, repeat customers

High-value repeat customers

Low-value repeat customers

Lost customers (churn)

**FIGURE 11.1** The customer relationship management process.

are essential to a successful business, organizations must place a great deal of emphasis on both their CRM strategy and their CRM systems.

Broadly speaking, CRM systems lie along a continuum, from *low-end CRM systems*—designed for enterprises with many small customers—to *high-end CRM systems*—for enterprises with a few large customers. An example of a low-end system is Amazon, which uses its CRM system to recommend products to returning customers. An example of a high-end system is Boeing, which uses its CRM system to coordinate staff activities in a campaign to sell its new 787 aircraft to Delta Airlines. As you study the cases and examples in this chapter, consider where on the continuum a particular CRM system would fall.

Although CRM varies according to circumstances, all successful CRM policies share two basic elements. First, the company must identify the many types of customer touch points. Second, it needs to consolidate data about each customer. Let's examine these two elements in more detail.

## Customer Touch Points

Organizations must recognize the numerous and diverse interactions they have with their customers. These interactions are referred to as customer touch points. Traditional customer touch points include telephone contact, direct mailings, and actual physical interactions with customers during their visits to a store. Organizational CRM systems, however, must manage many additional customer touch points that occur through the use of popular personal technologies. These touch points include e-mail, Web sites, and communications via smartphones (see Figure 11.2).

The business–customer relationship is constantly evolving. As personal technology usage changes, so too must the methods that businesses use to interface with their customers. As you

**FIGURE 11.2** Customer touch points.

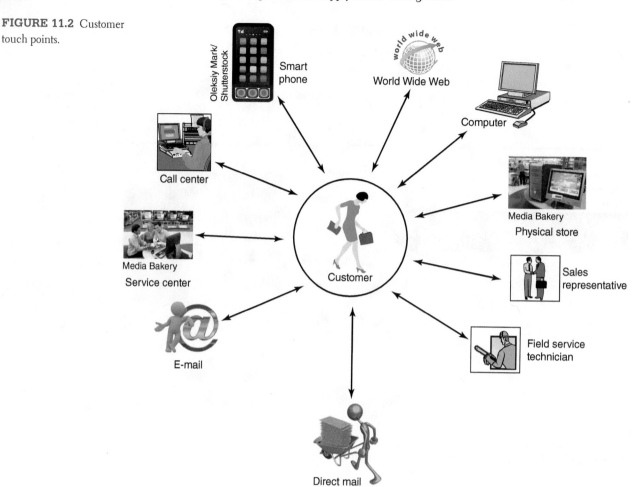

see with StellaService in IT's About Business 11.2, it is important to rate online customer service for two reasons. First, customers can see how well companies are performing in a variety of areas. Second, companies can see how well they and their competitors are performing. The StellaService rating is particularly important given the increase in online shopping, which is typically more impersonal than in-store shopping.

## Data Consolidation

Data consolidation is also critical to an organization's CRM efforts. The organization's CRM systems must manage customer data effectively. In the past, customer data were stored in isolated systems (or silos) located in different functional areas across the business—for example, in separate databases in the finance, sales, logistics, and marketing departments. Consequently, data for individual customers were difficult to share across the various functional areas.

As you saw in Chapter 5, modern interconnected systems built around a data warehouse now make all customer-related data available to every unit of the business. This complete data set on each customer is called a *360° view* of that customer. By accessing this view, a company can enhance its relationship with its customers and ultimately make more productive and profitable decisions.

Data consolidation and the 360° view of the customer enable the organization's functional areas to readily share information about customers. This information sharing leads to collaborative CRM. **Collaborative CRM systems** provide effective and efficient interactive communication with the customer throughout the entire organization. That is, they integrate communications between the organization and its customers in all aspects of marketing, sales,

# IT's [about business]

## 11.2 Rating Online Customer Service

In the past year, how many times have you interacted online with a retailer? Of those times, how often did you provide feedback? Chances are that you have done so very few times, if at all. In fact, consumers typically provide feedback only when their experience is either incredibly good or incredibly bad. Unfortunately for retailers, these instances fail to capture roughly 95 percent of customer interactions. However, these experiences are the sweet spot for StellaService.

StellaService (*www.stellaservice.com*) wants to rate online customer service just as J.D. Power & Associates (*www.jdpower.com*) rates new car quality and long-term dependability and Nielsen (*www.nielsen.com*) rates television viewers, radio listeners, and newspaper readers. That is, the enterprise measures and rates the customer service performance of online retailers via a process audited by the global accounting and auditing firm KPMG (*www.kpmg.com*). Their mission is to enhance transparency in online customer care.

To implement this policy, StellaService employees act as real-life customers at Sears and thousands of other retailers, ordering and returning $10 shirts, $1,000 bicycle parts, and almost every conceivable product in between. These anonymous shoppers stress-test and track 300 or so metrics in 20,000 Internet transactions each month. StellaService then sells these data back to companies such as Sears—and their competitors. In the case of Sears, for example, their "package fit and quality" and Twitter response time to shopper queries receive high marks, but their speed at refunding returns could use some improvement.

Retailers who use StellaService's service include Amazon and its shoe subsidiary Zappos, Diapers.com, 1-800-Flowers.com, and boutique sites such as GiltGroupe. Retailers who provide consistently high-quality customer service are awarded StellaService's seal of approval, a logo they can then display on their Web site and their advertising materials.

Companies can spend more than $100,000 per year for feedback on their online services. Only 50 percent of the businesses that pay StellaService for evaluations win a seal of approval. These businesses can also peruse their competitors' data to discover what they are doing wrong.

StellaService has also entered into a partnership with Google's Trusted Stores initiative. How does this arrangement work? As an example, a Google search for a pair of earrings will display StellaService data alongside Goggle's check mark of approval. These approvals will make shoppers more confident that they are buying from online merchants that consistently provide a superior experience.

Let's look at an example of StellaService in action. According to data provided by the company, wait times to contact Target spiked after its massive 2013 data breach. Following news of the breach, callers employed by StellaService were disconnected from the line during three separate calls they made on each of two days. In two other instances, the caller waited on hold for 20 minutes before terminating the call. StellaService also noted that Target experienced spikes in e-mail communications to its customer support center, particularly from December 18–25, with the longest response time being 2 days and 18 hours on December 23. By comparison, the retailer's average response time over the three months prior to the breach had been less than eight hours.

*Sources*: Compiled from "PriceGrabber Partners with StellaService to Bring More Transparency to Online Shopping," *PRNewswire*, April 16, 2014; K. Gustafson, "Target Shoppers Faced Long Waits Post-Security Breach," *CNBC*, January 8, 2014; G. Marvin, "Google Trusted Stores Now Integrates with AdWords, Shows StellaService Ratings in US," *Search Engine Land*, November 25, 2013; C. O'Connor, "Thinking Inside the Box," *Forbes*, September 23, 2013; L. Stangel, "Google Rolling Out E-Commerce Customer Service Ratings," *Silicon Valley Business Journal*, May 30, 2013; A. Barr, "Google to License Retailer Ratings from StellaService," *Reuters*, May 29, 2013; M. Creamer, "StellaService Strives to Give E-Tailers Credibility They Desire," *Advertising Age*, March 29, 2011; *www.stellaservice.com*, accessed April 1, 2015.

## Questions

1. Why is it so valuable for an online retailer to be able to post StellaService's seal of approval on its Web site and advertising materials?
2. Why doesn't StellaService provide the same service for bricks-and-mortar retailers?

---

and customer support. Collaborative CRM systems also enable customers to provide direct feedback to the organization. As you read in Chapter 9, Web 2.0 applications such as blogs and Wikis are very important to companies that value customer input into their product and service offerings, as well as into new product development.

An organization's CRM system contains two major components: operational CRM systems and analytical CRM systems. You will learn about these components in the next two sections.

# before you go on...

**1.** What is the definition of customer relationship management?

**2.** Why is CRM so important to any organization?

**3.** Define and provide examples of customer touch points.

## 11.2 Operational Customer Relationship Management Systems

Operational CRM systems support front-office business processes. Front-office processes are those that directly interact with customers; that is, sales, marketing, and service. The two major components of operational CRM systems are customer-facing applications and customer-touching applications (discussed below). Operational CRM systems provide the following benefits:

- Efficient, personalized marketing, sales, and service
- A 360° view of each customer
- The ability of sales and service employees to access a complete history of customer interaction with the organization, regardless of the touch point.

An example of an operational CRM system involves Caterpillar, Inc. (*www.cat.com*), an international manufacturer of industrial equipment. Caterpillar uses its CRM tools to accomplish the following objectives:

- Improve sales and account management by optimizing the information shared by multiple employees and by streamlining existing processes (e.g., taking orders using mobile devices)
- Form individualized relationships with customers, with the aim of improving customer satisfaction and maximizing profits
- Identify the most profitable customers, and provide them with the highest level of service
- Provide employees with the information and processes necessary to know their customers
- Understand and identify customer needs, and effectively build relationships among the company, its customer base, and its distribution partners

### Customer-Facing Applications

In **customer-facing CRM applications**, an organization's sales, field service, and customer interaction center representatives interact directly with customers. These applications include customer service and support, sales force automation, marketing, and campaign management.

**Customer Service and Support.** Customer service and support refers to systems that automate service requests, complaints, product returns, and requests for information. Today, organizations have implemented **customer interaction centers** (CIC), where organizational representatives use multiple channels such as the Web, telephone, fax, and face-to-face interactions to communicate with customers. The CIC manages several different types of customer interaction.

One of the most well-known customer interaction centers is the *call center*, a centralized office set up to receive and transmit a large volume of requests by telephone. Call centers enable companies to respond to a large variety of questions, including product support and complaints.

Organizations also use the CIC to create a call list for the sales team, whose members contact sales prospects. This type of interaction is called *outbound telesales*. In these interactions, the customer and the sales team collaborate in discussing products and services that can satisfy customers' needs and generate sales.

Customers can communicate directly with the CIC to initiate a sales order, inquire about products and services before placing an order, and obtain information about a transaction they have already made. These interactions are referred to as *inbound teleservice*. Teleservice representatives respond to requests either by utilizing service instructions stored in an organizational knowledge base or by noting incidents that can be addressed only by field service technicians.

The CIC also provides the Information Help Desk. The Help Desk assists customers with their questions concerning products or services, and it also processes customer complaints. Complaints generate follow-up activities such as quality control checks, delivery of replacement parts or products, service calls, generation of credit memos, and product returns. New technologies are extending the traditional CIC's functionality to include e-mail and Web interaction. For example, Epicor (*www.epicor.com*) provides software solutions that combine Web channels, such as automated e-mail reply, with Web knowledge bases. The information the software provides is available to CIC representatives and field service personnel. Another new technology, live chat, allows customers to connect to a company representative and conduct an instant messaging session. The advantage of live chat over a telephone conversation is that live chat enables the participants to share documents and photos (see *www.livechatinc.com* and *www.websitealive.com*). Some companies conduct the chat with a computer using natural language processing rather than with a real person.

**Sales Force Automation.**   **Sales force automation (SFA)** is the component of an operational CRM system that automatically records all of the components in a sales transaction process. SFA systems include a *contact management system*, which tracks all communications between the company and the customer, the purpose of each communication, and any necessary follow-up. This system eliminates duplicated contacts and redundancy, which in turn reduces the risk of irritating customers. SFA also includes a *sales lead tracking system*, which lists potential customers or customers who have purchased related products; that is, products similar to those that the salesperson is trying to sell to the customer.

Other elements of an SFA system can include a *sales forecasting system*, which is a mathematical technique for estimating future sales, and a *product knowledge system*, which is a comprehensive source of information regarding products and services. More-developed SFA systems also have online product-building features, called *configurators*, that enable customers to model the product to meet their specific needs. For example, you can customize your own running shoe at NikeID (*http://nikeid.nike.com*). Finally, many current SFA systems enable the salesperson in the field to connect remotely with customers and the home office via Web-based interfaces on their smartphones.

**Marketing.**   Thus far, you have focused primarily on how sales and customer service personnel can benefit from CRM systems. However, CRM systems have many important applications for an organization's marketing department as well. For example, they enable marketers to identify and target their best customers, to manage marketing campaigns, and to generate quality leads for the sales teams. Additionally, CRM marketing applications can sift through volumes of customer data—a process known as data mining (discussed in Chapter 12)—to develop a *purchasing profile*; that is, a snapshot of a consumer's buying habits that may lead to additional sales through cross-selling, upselling, and bundling.

**Cross-selling** is the marketing of additional related products to customers based on a previous purchase. This sales approach has been used very successfully by banks. For example, if you have a checking and savings account at your bank, then a bank officer will recommend other products for you, such as certificates of deposit (CDs) or other types of investments.

**Upselling** is a strategy in which the salesperson provides customers with the opportunity to purchase related products or services of greater value in place of, or along with, the consumer's initial product or service selection. For example, if a customer goes into an electronics store to buy a new television, a salesperson may show him a pricey 1080i HD LED television placed next to a less expensive LCD television in the hope of selling the more expensive set (assuming that the customer is willing to pay more for a sharper picture). Other common examples of upselling are warranties on electronics merchandise and the purchase of a carwash after buying gas at the gas station.

Finally, **bundling** is a form of cross-selling in which a business sells a group of products or services together at a lower price than their combined individual prices. For example, your cable company might bundle cable TV, broadband Internet access, and telephone service at a lower price than you would paid for each service separately.

Campaign Management. **Campaign management applications** help organizations plan campaigns that send the right messages to the right people through the right channels. Organizations manage their campaigns very carefully to avoid targeting people who have opted out of receiving marketing communications. Furthermore, companies use these applications to personalize individual messages for each particular customer.

## Customer-Touching Applications

Corporations have used manual CRM systems for many years. In the mid-1990s, for example, organizations began to utilize the Internet, the Web, and other electronic touch points (e.g., e-mail, point-of-sale terminals) to manage customer relationships. In contrast with customer-facing applications, where customers deal with a company representative, customers who utilize these technologies interact directly with the applications themselves. For this reason, these applications are called **customer-touching CRM applications** or **electronic CRM (e-CRM) applications**. Customers typically can use these applications to help themselves. There are many types of e-CRM applications. Let's examine some of the major ones.

Search and Comparison Capabilities. It is often difficult for customers to find what they want from the vast array of products and services available on the Web. To assist customers, many online stores and malls offer search and comparison capabilities, as do independent comparison Web sites (see *www.mysimon.com*).

Technical and Other Information and Services. Many organizations offer personalized experiences to induce customers to make purchases or to remain loyal. For example, Web sites often allow customers to download product manuals. One example is General Electric's Web site (*www.ge.com*), which provides detailed technical and maintenance information and sells replacement parts to customers who need to repair outdated home appliances. Another example is Goodyear's Web site (*www.goodyear.com*), which provides information about tires and their use.

Customized Products and Services. Another customer-touching service that many online vendors use is mass customization, a process in which customers can configure their own products. For example, Dell (*www.dell.com*) allows customers to configure their own computer systems. The Gap (*www.gap.com*) enables customers to "mix and match" an entire wardrobe. Web sites such as Hitsquad (*www.hitsquad.com*), MusicalGreeting (*www.musicalgreeting.com*), Apple iTunes (*www.apple.com/itunes*), and Surprise (*www.surprise.com*) allow customers to pick individual music titles from a library and customize a CD, a feature that traditional music stores do not offer.

In addition, customers can now view account balances or check the shipping status of orders at any time from their computers or smartphones. If you order books from Amazon, for example, you can look up the anticipated arrival date. Many other companies, including FedEx and UPS, provide similar services (see *www.fedex.com* and *www.ups.com*).

Personalized Web Pages. Many organizations permit their customers to create personalized Web pages. Customers use these pages to record purchases and preferences, as well as problems and requests. For example, American Airlines generates personalized Web pages for each of its registered travel-planning customers.

FAQs. Frequently asked questions (FAQs) are a simple tool for answering repetitive customer queries. Customers may find the information they need by using this tool, thereby eliminating the need to communicate with an actual person.

**E-mail and Automated Response.** The most popular tool for customer service is e-mail. Inexpensive and fast, companies use e-mail not only to answer customer inquiries but also to disseminate information, send alerts and product information, and conduct correspondence on any topic.

**Loyalty Programs.** **Loyalty programs** recognize customers who repeatedly use a vendor's products or services. Loyalty programs are appropriate when two conditions are met: a high frequency of repeat purchases, and limited product customization for each customer.

Although loyalty programs are frequently referred to as "rewards programs," their actual purpose is not to reward *past* behavior, but, rather, to influence *future* behavior. Significantly, the most profitable customers are not necessarily those whose behavior can be most easily influenced. As one example, most major U.S. airlines provide some "elite" benefits to anyone who flies 25,000 miles with them and their partners over the course of a year. Customers who fly first class pay much more for a given flight than those who fly in discount economy.

Nevertheless, these customers reach elite status only 1.5–2 times faster than economy-class passengers. Why is this true? The reason is that, although first-class passengers are far more profitable than discount seekers, they also are less influenced by loyalty programs. Discount flyers respond much more enthusiastically to the benefits of frequent flyer programs. Therefore, airlines award more benefits to discount flyers than to first-class flyers (relative to their spending).

The airlines' frequent flyer programs are probably the best-known loyalty programs. Other popular loyalty programs are casino players' clubs, which reward frequent players, and supermarkets, which reward frequent shoppers. Loyalty programs use a database or data warehouse to maintain a record of the points (or miles) a customer has accrued and the rewards to which he or she is entitled. The programs then use analytical tools to mine the data and learn about customer behavior.

# before you go on...

1. Differentiate between customer-facing applications and customer-touching applications.
2. Provide examples of cross-selling, upselling, and bundling (other than the examples presented in the text).

# Analytical Customer Relationship Management Systems

## 11.3

Whereas operational CRM systems support front-office business processes, **analytical CRM systems** provide business intelligence by analyzing customer behavior and perceptions. For example, analytical CRM systems typically provide information concerning customer requests and transactions, as well as customer responses to the organization's marketing, sales, and service initiatives. These systems also create statistical models of customer behavior and the value of customer relationships over time, as well as forecasts about acquiring, retaining, and losing customers. Figure 11.3 illustrates the relationship between operational CRM systems and analytical CRM systems.

Important technologies in analytical CRM systems include data warehouses, data mining, decision support, and other business intelligence technologies. After these systems have completed their various analyses, they supply information to the organization in the form of reports and digital dashboards. We discuss all of these topics in Chapter 12.

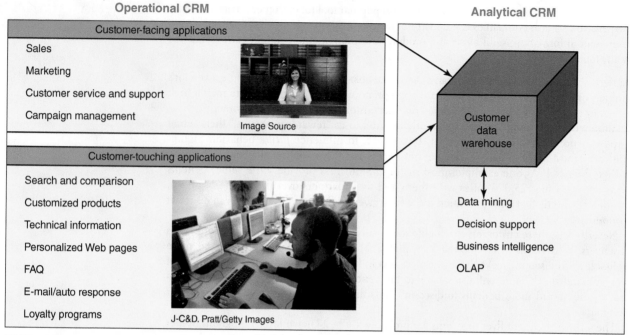

**FIGURE 11.3** The relationship between operational CRM and analytical CRM.

Analytical CRM systems analyze customer data for a variety of purposes:

- Designing and executing targeted marketing campaigns
- Increasing customer acquisition, cross-selling, and upselling
- Providing input into decisions relating to products and services (e.g., pricing and product development)
- Providing financial forecasting and customer profitability analysis

## before you go on...

**1.** What is the relationship between operational CRM systems and analytical CRM systems?

**2.** What are some of the functions of analytical CRM systems?

## 11.4 Other Types of Customer Relationship Management

Now that you have examined operational and analytical CRM systems, let's shift our focus to other types of CRM systems. Four exciting developments in this area are on-demand CRM systems, mobile CRM systems, open-source CRM systems, and social CRM.

### On-Demand CRM Systems

Customer relationship management systems may be implemented as either *on-premise* or *on-demand*. Traditionally, organizations utilized on-premise CRM systems, meaning that they purchased the systems from a vendor and then installed them on site. This arrangement was expensive, time consuming, and inflexible. Some organizations, particularly smaller ones, could not justify the costs of these systems.

On-demand CRM systems became a solution for the drawbacks of on-premise CRM systems. An **on-demand CRM system** is one that is hosted by an external vendor in the vendor's data center. This arrangement spares the organization the costs associated with purchasing the system. In addition, because the vendor creates and maintains the system, the organization's employees need to know only how to access and utilize it. The concept of on-demand is also known as *utility computing* or *software-as-a-service* (SaaS) (see Technology Guide 3).

Salesforce (*www.salesforce.com*) is the best-known on-demand CRM vendor. The company's goal is to provide a new business model that allows companies to rent the CRM software instead of buying it. The secret to their success appears to be that CRM has common requirements across many customers. Consequently, Salesforce's product meets the demands of its customers without a great deal of customization.

One Salesforce customer is Babson College (*www.babson.edu*) in Wellesley, Massachusetts. Babson's goal is to deliver the best applicant experience possible. To accomplish this mission, the school decided to use Salesforce to bring together all of the information on prospective students in a single location. All personnel who are involved with admissions have immediate access to candidate contact information, applications, and reports that indicate the status of each applicant within the enrollment process. This system makes it easy for administrators to deliver valuable information to applicants at the right time.

Using the Salesforce platform, Babson built an admissions portal with a fully personalized user experience for prospective students. The portal consolidates all of the information that potential students need. Furthermore, it displays different information to students at different points in the application process.

Despite their benefits, on-demand CRM systems have potential problems. First, the vendor could prove to be unreliable, in which case the client company would have no CRM functionality at all. Second, hosted software is difficult or impossible to modify, and only the vendor can upgrade it. Third, vendor-hosted CRM software may be difficult to integrate with the organization's existing software. Finally, giving strategic customer data to vendors always carries security and privacy risks.

## Mobile CRM Systems

A **mobile CRM** system is an interactive system that enables an organization to conduct communications related to sales, marketing, and customer service activities through a mobile medium for the purpose of building and maintaining relationships with its customers. Simply put, mobile CRM systems involve interacting directly with consumers through portable devices such as smartphones. Many forward-thinking companies believe that mobile CRM systems have tremendous potential to create personalized customer relationships that may be accessed anywhere and at any time. In fact, the opportunities offered by mobile marketing appear so rich that many companies have already identified mobile CRM systems as a cornerstone of their future marketing activities. IT's About Business 11.3 discusses a mobile CRM application at Disney World.

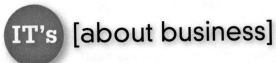 **IT's [about business]**

### 11.3 Mobile CRM at Disney World

In the past, guests at Disney World (*https://disneyworld.disney. go.com*) passed through entrance turnstiles, redeemed paper tickets, decided which rides to take, and bought food and merchandise with cash or credit cards. They could also use Disney hotel key cards to charge items. People would race to Fast-Pass kiosks, which dispensed a limited number of free line-skipping tickets. However, gridlock quickly set in, and people waited and waited.

To address these problems and enhance their customers' experiences, Disney introduced a mobile CRM system called

MyMagic+ that has drastically transformed the way Disney World guests—some 30 million people per year—do just about everything. The intent of MyMagic+ is to make the experience of visiting Disney parks less difficult and more reflective of modern customer behavior. Disney is betting that MyMagic+ will make guests happier and less stressed, so they will spend more money at the company's parks.

MyMagic+ allows users of a new Web site and app—called My Disney Experience—to preselect three FastPasses before they leave home. Customers can use these passes for rides or V.I.P. seating for parades, fireworks displays, and character meet-and-greets. Orlando-bound guests can also preregister for RFID bracelets, called MagicBands. These bands function as a room key, park ticket, FastPass, and credit card.

With MyMagic+, Disney World guests do not have to wait at turnstiles or use cash. Instead, to enter the park, they simply tap their MagicBands on a post. The MagicBands are encoded with credit card information, so guests can purchase corn dogs and Mickey Mouse ears with a tap of the wrist. Smartphone alerts signal when it is time to ride Space Mountain without standing in line.

MagicBands are also encoded with personal details, which allow customers to interact with Disney employees in a more personalized manner. Previously, the employee playing Cinderella could say hello only in a general way. Now—if parents opt in—hidden sensors will read MagicBand data, providing information needed for a personalized greeting: "Hi, Susan," the character might say without prompting. "I understand today is your birthday!"

Disney World also uses these data to make waiting areas for rides less boring. A new Magic Kingdom ride called Under the Sea, for instance, features a robotic version of Scuttle the seagull from *The Little Mermaid* that is able to chitchat with MagicBand wearers. Disney wants to take experiences that historically have been passive and make them as interactive as possible.

To alleviate privacy concerns, Disney will not require guests to use the MagicBand system. Moreover, customers who use it will decide how much information they want to share. An online options menu, for example, offers various controls: Do you want park employees to know your name? Do you want Disney to send you special offers when you get home? What about during your stay? However, even if a guest chooses the most restrictive settings, the MagicBand will still gather general information about how he or she uses the park.

Disney faced considerable logistical challenges in deploying MyMagic+ and MagicBand. Disney World has 60,000 employees, many of whom had to be retrained to use the new technology. Disney World had already installed Wi-Fi, so smartphone users can access the My Disney experience app more readily. In addition, all of the new technology and procedures must be communicated to Super Bowl-sized crowds every day.

What happens if your MagicBand is lost or stolen? You have two options. First, park employees are trained to deactivate them. Alternatively, you can use the My Disney Experience app in place of your band. As a safety precaution, Disney requires guests to enter a PIN when using the wristbands to make purchases of $50 or more. Disney notes that the bands themselves contain no personally identifiable information.

## The Good News

MyMagic+ helps Disney track its guests as they move about its parks, enabling the company to manage and allocate its workforce more efficiently. MyMagic+ allows guests to plan in advance how they will tour the parks. Hopefully, this capability will discourage them from, for example, making impromptu visits to Universal's Wizarding World of Harry Potter. This process will cut down on long lines and wait times.

## The Potentially Bad News

The new CRM system places Disney in the middle of the debate on privacy and personal data collection. Like most major companies, Disney wants to collect as much information about its customers' preferences as it can, so that it can market to them more efficiently.

Disney is aware of potential privacy concerns, especially regarding children. However, Disney has decided that MyMagic+ is essential to its marketing and CRM strategies. The company argues that it must aggressively integrate new technology into the customer experience at its parks—without damaging the sense of nostalgia on which the experience depends—or risk becoming irrelevant to future generations of guests.

When asked about privacy issues, one Disney guest replied: "As far as 'Big Brother' watching us as we wander the parks, anyone worried about 'real' privacy would not be wandering around a theme park already full of security cameras."

*Sources:* Compiled from B. Barnes, "Billion-Dollar Bracelet Is Key to Magical Kingdom," *New York Times*, April 2, 2014; D. Peterson, "Walt Disney World Offers MyMagic+, FastPass+, and MagicBands to Day Guests," *Examiner*, March 31, 2014; D. Bevil, "Disney World: MyMagic+, MagicBands Ready for Day Guests," *Orlando Sentinel*, March 31, 2014; K. Gambacorta, "Putting Disney MagicBands to the Test," *Fox News*, March 21, 2014; R. Brigante, "Walt Disney World Readies Full Rollout of MyMagic+ as MagicBands Become Available for Annual Passholders," *Inside the Magic*, March 7, 2014; W. Pramik, "New Disney MagicBands Make Touring – and Spending – Easy," *Cleveland Plain Dealer*, March 5, 2014; D. Lansky, "What Disney Got Wrong with Its Magic Bands," *The Huffington Post*, March 4, 2014; S. Sekula, "Disney Gets Personal with New MyMagic+ System," *USA Today*, February 25, 2014; E. Dockterman, "Now Disney Can Track Your Every Move with NSA-Style Wristbands," *Time*, January 2, 2014; L. Jenkins, "MyMagic+ Debuts at Disney," *Fodor's Travel*, December 13, 2013; J. Burstein, "Disney's Latest Experiment with Technology: MagicBands," *Miami Herald*, November 27, 2013; B. Barnes, "At Disney Parks, a Bracelet Meant to Build Loyalty (and Sales)," *New York Times*, January 7, 2013; https://disneyworld.disney.go.com, accessed April 1, 2015.

### Questions

1. How do MyMagic+ and MagicBands contribute positively to the customer experience at Disney parks? Provide specific examples to support your answer.

2. Other than privacy, what are other disadvantages of MyMagic+ and MagicBands to guests? To Disney? To Disney employees? Provide specific examples to support your answer.

## Open-Source CRM Systems

As explained in Technology Guide 2, the source code for open-source software is available at no cost. **Open-source CRM systems**, therefore, are CRM systems whose source code is available to developers and users.

Open-source CRM systems provide the same features or functions as other CRM software, and they may be implemented either on-premise or on-demand. Leading open-source CRM vendors include SugarCRM (*www.sugarcrm.com*), Concursive (*www.concursive.com*), and Vtiger (*www.vtiger.com*).

The benefits of open-source CRM systems include favorable pricing and a wide variety of applications. In addition, these systems are easy to customize. This is an attractive feature for organizations that need CRM software that is designed for their specific needs. Finally, updates and bug (software error) fixes for open-source CRM systems are rapidly distributed, and extensive support information is available free of charge. IT's About Business 11.4 explains how uShip obtained many benefits from implementing SugarCRM.

# IT's [about business]

## 11.4 uShip Benefits from SugarCRM

uShip (*www.uship.com*) is a global online marketplace for shipping services. Individuals and businesses post items they need shipped in a variety of categories, including automobile transport, boat shipping, home and office moving and removal services, and the transport of heavy industrial equipment.

Transportation service providers on uShip place competing bids for the right to haul a customer's shipment. For some categories, including boats, automobiles, and less-than-truckload (LTL) freight, customers can (1) select an upfront quote for transport services or (2) enter an acceptable price to be matched with a transporter. Customers can either book a shipment immediately from these quotes or opt to wait for auction bids, similar to eBay's "buy it now" feature. The site's reverse auction format reduces the cost of shipping by enabling service providers to find shipments along their routes and to fill empty cargo space.

uShip uses a feedback rating system for both service providers and customers. Transport companies maintain company profiles that feature past customer feedback in several service categories, equipment photos, videos, cargo insurance data, and information about U.S. Department of Transportation licensing, operating authority, and licensing verification.

Fans of A&E's reality TV show *Shipping Wars* are familiar with uShip. It is the shipping marketplace used by the show, where six independent shippers bid to transport items that traditional carriers will not transport.

At first, uShip focused primarily on the consumer market, building a partnership with eBay. Then, in late 2013 the company began to develop two segments of its commercial business: full truckload (FTL) and less-than-truckload (LTL). However, uShip's existing infrastructure was inadequate to support its rapid growth. The company needed a centralized point of access for customer contact information, such as notes and call data. Complicating the customer management issues, commercial accounts require longer term management than retail customers, so uShip required a system that accommodated both. In addition, uShip's LTL sales team is field based, whereas the retail and FTL sales teams are located in-house. uShip wanted all of its sales teams to utilize the same CRM platform.

uShip selected SugarCRM (*www.sugarcrm.com*) as its CRM platform. SugarCRM had the capability to integrate with uShip's telephony system, its databases, the uship.com Web site, and its help desk application. To help implement the SugarCRM solution, uShip chose the systems integration firm Epicom (*www.epicom.com*). Epicom employed a phased approach in the system's implementation. Phase 1 developed a solution for uShip's commercial accounts, Phase 2 developed a solution for its retail accounts, and Phase 3 developed a solution for its telephony system.

SugarCRM enables uShip to efficiently in-process new customers, manage hundreds of disparate accounts utilizing a single interface, provide a superior customer experience, and support the company's rapid growth. The new system has also enabled every area of uShip's business to enhance its speed and productivity. In fact, it has increased uShip's overall efficiency by 20 percent.

As one example, if a problem arises that needs to be handled by customer service, in the past it had taken uShip a minute or two to find the account. With SugarCRM, the account is displayed to the uShip customer representative instantly. Company reporting is also more efficient and effective, saving six to eight hours per week per employee. In addition, the workload of the analytics group has been substantially reduced. Without the SugarCRM package, uShip would have had to hire additional staff to manage this workload.

*Sources:* Compiled from "uShip, eBay Deal Puts Spotlight on Larger-Than-Parcel Shipping," *Business Wire*, March 10, 2014; "New Service for LTL Spot Rate Marketplace from uShip," *Fleet News Daily*, March, 2014; J. Berman, "uShip Introduces Online LTL Spot Rate Marketplace," Logistics Management, January 23, 2014; A. Heim, "Online Shipping Marketplace uShip Plans on Leveraging Brazil's Logistics Woes to Bolster Its Business," *TheNextWeb*, January 23, 2013; "uShip," *SugarCRM Case Study*, 2012; www.uship.com, www.sugarcrm.com, www.epicom.com, accessed April 2, 2015.

**Questions**

1. Describe the advantages provided to uShip by the SugarCRM system.
2. Describe the business needs of uShip that led to the company's decision to implement a CRM system.

---

Like all software, however, open-source CRM systems have certain risks. The most serious risk involves quality control. Because open-source CRM systems are created by a large community of unpaid developers, there sometimes is no central authority responsible for overseeing the quality of the product. (We discuss open-source software in Technology Guide 2). Furthermore, for best results, companies must have the same IT platform in place as the one on which the open-source CRM system was developed.

### Social CRM

**Social CRM** is the use of social media technology and services to enable organizations to engage their customers in a collaborative conversation in order to provide mutually beneficial value in a trusted and transparent manner. In fact, social CRM is the company's response to the customers' ownership of this two-way conversation. In social CRM, organizations monitor services such as Facebook, Twitter, and LinkedIn (among many others) for relevant mentions of their products, services, and brand, and they respond accordingly.

Social media are also providing methods that customers are using to obtain faster, better customer service. IT's About Business 11.5 recounts how one customer was pleasantly surprised when Morton's Steakhouse responded to his tweet.

## IT's [about business]

### **11.5** Morton's Steakhouse Surprises a Customer

Peter Shankman was tied up in meetings all day, and he had to take a later flight home that caused him to miss his dinner. So, he jokingly tweeted Morton's Steakhouse (*www.mortons.com*) and requested that the restaurant meet him at the airport with a porterhouse steak when he landed.

Morton's saw the Tweet, discovered that the tweeter was a frequent customer (and frequent tweeter—Shankman has 100,000 Twitter followers), pulled data on what he typically ordered, identified the flight he was on, and then sent a delivery person to Newark Airport (New Jersey) to serve him his dinner. When Shankman got to the reception lobby at the airport, he noticed a man in a tuxedo holding a card with Shankman's name. The man was also carrying a bag that contained a 24-ounce Porterhouse steak, an order of Colossal shrimp, a side order of potatoes, bread, two napkins, and silverware.

The closest Morton's restaurant was 24 miles from the airport, and Shankman's flight took only two hours. This scenario says a lot about both Morton's customer service and the speed of social media. Admittedly, the entire scenario was a publicity stunt that went explosively viral over the Internet. This is not the point, however. The questions that businesses should be asking themselves are: Would your company even consider doing something like this? If not, why not?

*Sources:* C. Chan, "Morton's Steakhouse Met a Man at the Airport with a Steak After He Asked for One on Twitter, " *Gizmodo*, August 19, 2011; M. Flacy, "After a Single Tweet, Air Traveler Gets a Morton's Surprise at Newark Airport, " *Digital Trends*, August 18, 2011; "Peter Shankman Tweet Joke Leads to Morton's Surprise Steak Dinner at Newark Airport, " *The Huffington Post*, August 11, 2013; www.mortons.com, accessed March 31, 2015.

**Questions**

1. Explain how Morton's monitoring of social media illustrates how CRM is reviving personal marketing.
2. Do you see any disadvantages in such close monitoring of social media? Provide specific examples to support your answer.

# before you go on...

1. Describe on-demand CRM.
2. Describe mobile CRM.
3. Describe open-source CRM.
4. Describe social CRM.

# Supply Chains

**11.5**

Modern organizations are increasingly concentrating on their core competencies and on becoming more flexible and agile. To accomplish these objectives, they rely on other companies, rather than on companies they themselves own, to supply the goods and services they need. Organizations recognize that these suppliers can perform these activities more efficiently and effectively than they themselves can. This trend toward relying on an increasing number of suppliers has led to the concept of supply chains. A **supply chain** is the flow of materials, information, money, and services from raw material suppliers, through factories and warehouses, to the end customers. A supply chain also includes the *organizations* and *processes* that create and deliver products, information, and services to the end customers.

Supply chains enhance trust and collaboration among supply chain partners, thus improving supply chain visibility and inventory velocity. **Supply chain visibility** refers to the ability of all organizations within a supply chain to access or view relevant data on purchased materials as these materials move through their suppliers' production processes and transportation networks to their receiving docks. In addition, organizations can access or view relevant data on outbound goods as they are manufactured, assembled, or stored in inventory and then shipped through their transportation networks to their customers' receiving docks. The more quickly a company can deliver products and services after receiving the materials required to make them—that is, the higher the *inventory velocity*—the more satisfied the company's customers will be.

Supply chain information that was previously obtained manually is increasingly being generated by sensors, RFID tags, meters, GPS, and other devices and systems. How does this transformation affect supply chain managers? For one thing, they now have real-time information on all products moving through their supply chains. Supply chains will therefore rely less on labor-based tracking and monitoring, because the new technology will allow shipping containers, trucks, products, and parts to report on their own status. The overall result is a vast improvement in supply chain visibility.

Supply chains are a vital component of the overall strategies of many modern organizations. To utilize supply chains efficiently, a business must be tightly integrated with its suppliers, business partners, distributors, and customers. A critical component of this integration is the use of information systems to facilitate the exchange of information among the participants in the supply chain.

## The Structure and Components of Supply Chains

The term *supply chain* comes from a picture of how the partnering organizations are linked together. Figure 11.4 illustrates a typical supply chain. (Recall that Figure 1.5 also illustrated a supply chain, in a slightly different way.) Note that the supply chain involves three segments:

1. *Upstream*, where sourcing or procurement from external suppliers occurs.

In this segment, supply chain managers select suppliers to deliver the goods and services the company needs to produce its product or service. Furthermore, SC managers develop the pricing, delivery, and payment processes between a company and its suppliers. Included here are processes for managing inventory, receiving and verifying shipments, transferring goods to manufacturing facilities, and authorizing payments to suppliers.

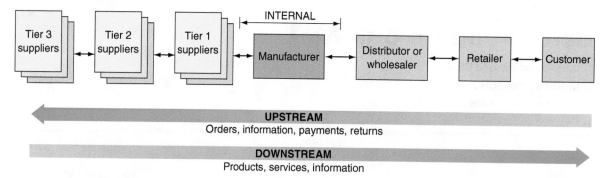

**FIGURE 11.4** Generic supply chain.

2. *Internal*, where packaging, assembly, or manufacturing takes place.

SC managers schedule the activities necessary for production, testing, packaging, and preparing goods for delivery. In addition, they monitor quality levels, production output, and worker productivity.

3. *Downstream*, where distribution takes place, frequently by external distributors.

In this segment, SC managers coordinate the receipt of orders from customers, develop a network of warehouses, select carriers to deliver products to customers, and implement invoicing systems to receive payments from customers.

The flow of information and goods can be bidirectional. For example, damaged or unwanted products can be returned, a process known as *reverse flows* or *reverse logistics*. In the retail clothing industry, for example, reverse logistics involves clothing that customers return, either because the item had defects or because the customer did not like the item.

**Tiers of Suppliers.** Figure 11.4 shows several tiers of suppliers. As the diagram indicates, a supplier may have one or more subsuppliers, a subsupplier may have its own subsupplier(s), and so on. For an automobile manufacturer, for example, Tier 3 suppliers produce basic products such as glass, plastic, and rubber; Tier 2 suppliers use these inputs to make windshields, tires, and plastic moldings; and Tier 1 suppliers produce integrated components such as dashboards and seat assemblies.

**The Flows in the Supply Chain.** There are typically three flows in the supply chain: material, information, and financial. *Material flows* are the physical products, raw materials, supplies, and so forth that flow along the chain. Material flows also include the reverse flows discussed above. A supply chain thus involves a *product life cycle* approach, from "dirt to dust."

*Information flows* consist of data related to demand, shipments, orders, returns, and schedules, as well as changes in any of these data. Finally, *financial flows* involve money transfers, payments, credit card information and authorization, payment schedules, e-payments, and credit-related data.

Significantly, different supply chains have different numbers and types of flows. For instance, in service industries there may be no physical flow of materials, but frequently there is a flow of information, often in the form of documents (physical or electronic copies). For example, the digitization of software, music, and other content can create a supply chain without any physical flow. Notice, however, that in such a case there are two types of information flows: one that replaces materials flow (digitized software), and another that provides the supporting information (orders, billing, and so on). To manage the supply chain, an organization must coordinate all three flows among all of the parties involved in the chain, a topic we turn to next.

# before you go on...

**1.** What is a supply chain?

**2.** Describe the three segments of a supply chain.

**3.** Describe the flows in a supply chain.

# Supply Chain Management

## 11.6

The function of **supply chain management (SCM)** is to improve the processes a company uses to acquire the raw materials it needs to produce a product or service and then deliver that product or service to its customers. That is, supply chain management is the process of planning, organizing, and optimizing the various activities performed along the supply chain. There are five basic components of SCM:

1. *Plan:* Planning is the strategic component of SCM. Organizations must have a strategy for managing all the resources that are involved in meeting customer demand for their product or service. Planning involves developing a set of metrics (measurable deliverables) to monitor the organization's supply chain to ensure that it is efficient and it delivers high quality and value to customers for the lowest cost.

2. *Source:* In the sourcing component, organizations choose suppliers to deliver the goods and services they need to create their product or service. Supply chain managers develop pricing, delivery, and payment processes with suppliers, and they create metrics to monitor and improve their relationships with their suppliers. They also develop processes for managing their goods and services inventory, including receiving and verifying shipments, transferring the shipped materials to manufacturing facilities, and authorizing supplier payments.

3. *Make:* This is the manufacturing component. Supply chain managers schedule the activities necessary for production, testing, packaging, and preparation for delivery. This component is the most metric-intensive part of the supply chain, where organizations measure quality levels, production output, and worker productivity.

4. *Deliver:* This component, often referred to as logistics, is where organizations coordinate the receipt of customer orders, develop a network of warehouses, select carriers to transport their products to their customers, and create an invoicing system to receive payments.

5. *Return:* Supply chain managers must create a responsive and flexible network for receiving defective, returned, or excess products back from their customers, as well as for supporting customers who have problems with delivered products.

Like other functional areas, SCM utilizes information systems. The goal of SCM systems is to reduce the problems, or friction, along the supply chain. Friction can increase time, costs, and inventories and decrease customer satisfaction. SCM systems, therefore, reduce uncertainty and risks by decreasing inventory levels and cycle time while improving business processes and customer service. These benefits make the organization more profitable and competitive.

Significantly, SCM systems are a type of interorganizational information system. In an **interorganizational information system (IOS)**, information flows among two or more organizations. By connecting the IS of business partners, IOSs enable the partners to perform a number of tasks:

- Reduce the costs of routine business transactions
- Improve the quality of the information flow by reducing or eliminating errors
- Compress the cycle time involved in fulfilling business transactions
- Eliminate paper processing and its associated inefficiencies and costs
- Make the transfer and processing of information easier for users

One of the most important goals of SCM systems is to give an organization visibility into its supply chain. *Supply chain visibility* is the ability of an organization to track products in transit from the manufacturer to their final destination. The goal of SCV is to improve the supply chain by making data readily available to all parties in the supply chain. Supply chain visibility promotes quick responses to problems or changes along the supply chain by enabling companies to shift products to where they are needed. IT's About Business 11.6 illustrates how Crate & Barrel improved its supply chain visibility.

## The Push Model Versus the Pull Model

Many SCM systems employ the **push model**. In this model, also known as *make-to-stock*, the production process begins with a forecast, which is simply an educated guess as to customer demand. The forecast must predict which products customers will want and in what quantities.

## IT's [about business]

### 11.6 Crate & Barrel Improves Its Supply Chain Visibility

Crate & Barrel (CB) (*www.crateandbarrel.com*), a leading retailer in the area of home furniture and furnishings, is finding that globalization brings many opportunities, but it also increases challenges and risk. The company has used an import model for much of its merchandise, meaning that when it sources (procures) goods from overseas, it ships those goods to the United States and then distributes them back to overseas markets. The retailer wants to improve its supply chain transparency significantly, so, for example, it can source goods from overseas and ship them directly to nearby overseas markets without going through the United States, an arrangement known as *international transfers*. That is, Crate & Barrel is working to evolve what had been a U.S.-centric supply chain into a truly global supply chain. The retailer's ultimate goal is to put any CB product anywhere in the world, quickly and cost-effectively.

CB sources from about three dozen different countries, and it was expanding its international store locations. As a result, the challenges of importing and exporting continue to increase. Adding to the complexity of its supply chain are myriad new regulations involving product quality, plant security, and other related areas. Furthermore, these regulations are increasing both within the United Sates and globally.

In addition to globalization, electronic commerce has also created a number of opportunities and challenges. The opportunity occurs because consumers across the globe can purchase CB products online. The challenges occur because e-commerce also increases customer expectations in terms of service and information. In fact, the price transparency that comes with e-commerce has made cost reduction a key supply chain imperative for CB.

To reduce both supply chain costs and risk, CB set out to increase its supply chain visibility. To accomplish these goals, the company needed data about the products in its supply chain such as what the products are, where they are, and when they will arrive at their destination. CB implemented a new supply chain visibility system from Amber Road (*www.amberroad.com*), a provider of software solutions for global trade management.

The new system provides detailed end-to-end views of orders, inventory, shipments, events, and many more variables across CB's entire global supply chain. The system includes inbound import visibility, outbound export visibility, and international transfers.

Supply chain visibility enhances supply chain flexibility. Supply chain flexibility is necessary because problems inevitably occur along the supply chain, forcing companies to make appropriate adjustments on the fly. Using Amber Road's system, Crate & Barrel can now identify where inventory is "stuck" in a location, and it can move this inventory to areas where it is needed. CB hopes that this process will enable it to make smaller, more frequent shipments that may actually cost more per unit shipped but will pay off in higher sales and reduced inventory costs. In essence, the costs that accompany inventory that a company owns too long, or that is in the wrong place in the company's supply chain, are higher than the costs of shipping less cost-effectively.

*Sources:* Compiled from A. Gonzalez, "Where Will You Find Supply Chain Innovation," *LinkedIn Pulse*, April 10, 2014; "Supply Chain News: eFulfillment Wars Continue On, with New Ordering Gizmo from Amazon, New Retail Partners for eBay Now," *Supply Chain Digest*, April 7, 2014; "Ultriva's New Strategic Insights Regarding End to End Supply Chain Visibility Featuring Research from Gartner," *PR.com*, April 6, 2014; S. Hickman, "Indonesian Teak Farmers Achieve Traceability to the Tree Stump," *The Guardian*, March 18, 2014; "Crate & Barrel's Vision for Global Supply Chain Visibility Is Crystal Clear," *Supply Chain Digest*, January 16, 2014; B. Heaney, "Supply Chain Visibility," *Aberdeen Group*, May, 2013; D. Kent, "Finding Profitable Proximity," *EBN*, December 24, 2012; www.crateandbarrel.com, www.amberroad.com, accessed April 11, 2015.

### Questions

1. Discuss the advantages of supply chain visibility for any organization.
2. Explain how an increase in shipping costs can actually generate higher revenues for Crate & Barrel.

The company then produces the amount of products in the forecast, typically by using mass production, and sells, or "pushes," those products to consumers.

Unfortunately, these forecasts are often incorrect. Consider, for example, an automobile manufacturer that wants to produce a new car. Marketing managers conduct extensive research, including customer surveys and analyses of competitors' cars, and then provide the results to forecasters. If the forecasters' predictions are too high—that is, if they predict that customers will purchase a certain number of these new cars but actual demand falls below this amount—then the automaker has excess cars in inventory and will incur large carrying costs (the costs of storing unsold inventory). Furthermore, the company will probably have to sell the excess cars at a discount.

From the opposite perspective, if the forecasters' predictions are too low—that is, actual customer demand exceeds expectations—then the automaker probably will have to run extra shifts to meet the demand, thereby incurring substantial overtime costs. Furthermore, the company risks losing business to its competitors if the car that customers want is not available. Thus, using the push model in supply chain management can cause problems, as you will see in the next section.

To avoid the uncertainties associated with the push model, many companies now employ the pull model of supply chain management, using Web-enabled information flows. In the **pull model**, also known as *make-to-order*, the production process begins with a customer order. Therefore, companies make only what customers want, a process closely aligned with mass customization (discussed in Chapter 1).

A prominent example of a company that uses the pull model is Dell Computer. Dell's production process begins with a customer order. This order not only specifies the type of computer the customer wants but also alerts each Dell supplier as to the parts of the order for which that supplier is responsible. That way, Dell's suppliers ship only the parts that Dell needs to produce the computer.

Not all companies can use the pull model. Automobiles, for example, are far more complicated and more expensive to manufacture than computers, so automobile companies require longer lead times to produce new models. Automobile companies do use the pull model, but only for specific automobiles that some customers order (e.g., Rolls-Royce, Bentley, and other extremely expensive cars).

## Problems Along the Supply Chain

As you saw earlier, friction can develop within a supply chain. One major consequence of friction is poor customer service. In some cases, supply chains do not deliver products or services when and where customers—either individuals or businesses—need them. In other cases, the supply chain provides poor-quality products. Other problems associated with supply chain friction are high inventory costs and revenue loss.

The problems along the supply chain arise primarily from two sources: (1) uncertainties, and (2) the need to coordinate multiple activities, internal units, and business partners. A major source of supply chain uncertainties is the *demand forecast*. Demand for a product can be influenced by numerous factors such as competition, price, weather conditions, technological developments, overall economic conditions, and customers' general confidence. Another uncertainty is delivery times, which can be affected by numerous factors ranging from production machine failures to road construction and traffic jams. In addition, quality problems in materials and parts can create production delays, which also generate supply chain problems.

One major challenge that managers face in setting accurate inventory levels throughout the supply chain is known as the bullwhip effect. The **bullwhip effect** refers to erratic shifts in orders up and down the supply chain (see Figure 11.5). Basically, the variables that affect customer demand can become magnified when they are viewed through the eyes of managers at each link in the supply chain. If each distinct entity that makes ordering and inventory decisions places its interests above those of the chain, then stockpiling can occur at as many as seven or eight locations along the chain. Research has shown that in some cases such hoarding has led to as much as a 100-day supply of inventory that is waiting "just in case" versus the 10–20-day supply manufacturers normally keep at hand.

**FIGURE 11.5** The bull-whip effect.

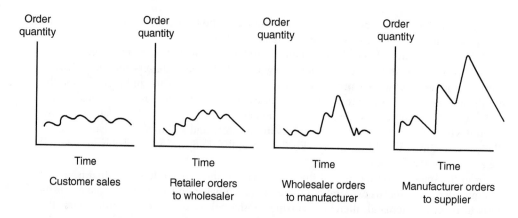

## Solutions to Supply Chain Problems

Supply chain problems can be very costly. Therefore, organizations are motivated to find innovative solutions. During the oil crises of the 1970s, for example, Ryder Systems, a large trucking company, purchased a refinery to control the upstream part of the supply chain and to ensure it had sufficient gasoline for its trucks. Ryder's decision to purchase a refinery is an example of vertical integration. **Vertical integration** is a business strategy in which a company purchases its upstream suppliers to ensure that its essential supplies are available as soon as the company needs them. Ryder later sold the refinery because it could not manage a business it did not understand and because oil became more plentiful.

Ryder's decision to vertically integrate was not the best method for managing its supply chain. In the remainder of this section, you will look at some other possible solutions to supply chain problems, many of which are supported by IT.

**Using Inventories to Solve Supply Chain Problems.** Undoubtedly, the most common solution to supply chain problems is *building inventories* as insurance against supply chain uncertainties. As you have learned, holding either too much or too little inventory can be very costly. Thus, companies make major attempts to optimize and control inventories.

One widely utilized strategy to minimize inventories is the **just-in-time (JIT) inventory system**. Essentially, JIT systems deliver the precise number of parts, called *work-in-process* inventory, to be assembled into a finished product at precisely the right time.

Although JIT offers many benefits, it has certain drawbacks as well. To begin with, suppliers are expected to respond instantaneously to requests. As a result, they have to carry more inventory than they otherwise would. In this sense, JIT does not *eliminate* excess inventory; rather it simply *shifts* it from the customer to the supplier. This process can still reduce the overall inventory size if the supplier can spread the increased inventory over several customers. However, that is not always possible.

In addition, JIT replaces a few large supply shipments with a large number of smaller ones. In terms of transportation, then, the process is less efficient.

**Information Sharing.** Another common approach to solving supply chain problems, and especially to improving demand forecasts, is *sharing information* along the supply chain. Information sharing can be facilitated by electronic data interchange and extranets, topics you will learn about in the next section.

One notable example of information sharing occurs between large manufacturers and retailers. For example, Walmart provides Procter & Gamble with access to daily sales information from every store for every item that P&G makes for Walmart. This access enables P&G to manage the *inventory replenishment* for Walmart's stores. By monitoring inventory levels, P&G knows when inventories fall below the threshold for each product at any Walmart store. These data trigger an immediate shipment.

Information sharing between Walmart and P&G is executed automatically. It is part of a vendor-managed inventory strategy. **Vendor-managed inventory (VMI)** occurs when the supplier, rather than the retailer, manages the entire inventory process for a particular product or group of products. Significantly, P&G has similar agreements with other major retailers. The benefit for P&G is accurate and timely information on consumer demand for its products. Thus, P&G can plan production more accurately, minimizing the bullwhip effect.

## before you go on...

1. Differentiate between the push model and the pull model.
2. Describe various problems that can occur along the supply chain.
3. Discuss possible solutions to problems along the supply chain.

# Information Technology Support for Supply Chain Management

# 11.7

Clearly, SCM systems are essential to the successful operation of many businesses. As you have seen, these systems—and IOSs in general—rely on various forms of IT to resolve problems. Three technologies, in particular, provide support for IOSs and SCM systems: electronic data interchange, extranets, and Web services. You will learn about Web services in Technology Guide 3. In this section, you examine the other two technologies.

## Electronic Data Interchange (EDI)

**Electronic data interchange (EDI)** is a communication standard that enables business partners to exchange routine documents, such as purchasing orders, electronically. EDI formats these documents according to agreed-upon standards (e.g., data formats). It then transmits messages over the Internet using a converter, called *translator*.

EDI provides many benefits that are not available with a manual delivery system. To begin with, it minimizes data entry errors, because each entry is checked by the computer. In addition, the length of the message can be shorter, and the messages are secured. EDI also reduces cycle time, increases productivity, enhances customer service, and minimizes paper usage and storage. Figure 11.6 contrasts the process of fulfilling a purchase order with and without EDI.

EDI does have some disadvantages. Business processes sometimes must be restructured to fit EDI requirements. Also, there are many EDI standards in use today, so one company might have to use several standards in order to communicate with multiple business partners.

In today's world, where every business has a broadband connection to the Internet and where multimegabyte design files, product photographs, and PDF sales brochures are routinely e-mailed, the value of reducing a structured e-commerce message from a few thousand XML bytes to a few hundred EDI bytes is negligible. As a result, EDI is being replaced by XML-based Web services. (You will learn about XML in Technology Guide 3.)

## Extranets

To implement IOSs and SCM systems, a company must connect the intranets of its various business partners to create extranets. **Extranets** link business partners over the Internet by providing them access to certain areas of each other's corporate intranets (see Figure 11.7).

The primary goal of extranets is to foster collaboration between and among business partners. A business provides extranet access to selected B2B suppliers, customers, and other partners. These individuals access the extranet through the Internet. Extranets enable people located outside a company to collaborate with the company's internal employees. They also allow external business partners to enter the corporate intranet, via the Internet, to access data,

**FIGURE 11.6** Comparing purchase order (PO) fulfillment with and without EDI.

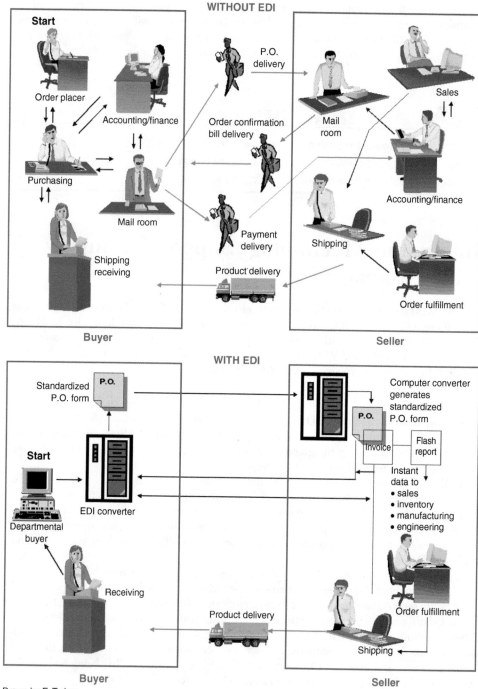

Drawn by E. Turban.

place orders, check the status of those orders, communicate, and collaborate. Finally, they make it possible for partners to perform self-service activities such as checking inventory levels.

Extranets use virtual private network (VPN) technology to make communication over the Internet more secure. The major benefits of extranets are faster processes and information flow, improved order entry and customer service, lower costs (e.g., for communications, travel, and administrative overhead), and overall improved business effectiveness.

There are three major types of extranets. The type that a company chooses depends on the business partners involved and the purpose of the supply chain. We present each type below, along with its major business applications.

**FIGURE 11.7** The structure of an extranet.

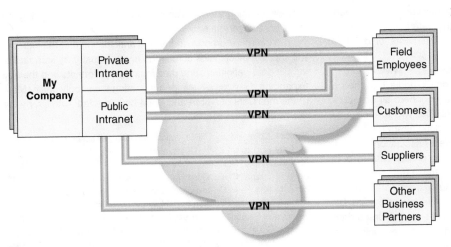

**FIGURE 11.7** The structure of an extranet.

**A Company and Its Dealers, Customers, or Suppliers.** This type of extranet centers on a single company. An example is the FedEx extranet, which allows customers to track the status of a delivery. Customers use the Internet to access a database on the FedEx intranet. Enabling customers to monitor deliveries saves FedEx the cost of hiring human operators to perform that task over the phone.

**An Industry's Extranet.** Just as a single company can set up an extranet, the major players in an industry can team up to create an extranet that will benefit all of them. For example, ANXeBusiness (*www.anx.com*) enables companies to collaborate effectively through a network that provides a secure global medium for B2B information exchange. This network is used for mission-critical business transactions by leading international organizations in aerospace, automotive, chemical, electronics, financial services, healthcare, logistics, manufacturing, transportation, and related industries. It offers customers a reliable extranet as well as VPN services. IT's About Business 11.7 provides another example of an industry extranet.

**Joint Ventures and Other Business Partnerships.** In this type of extranet, the partners in a joint venture use the extranet as a vehicle for communication and collaboration. An example is Bank of America's extranet for commercial loans. The partners involved in making these loans include a lender, a loan broker, an escrow company, and a title company. The extranet connects lenders, loan applicants, and the loan organizer, Bank of America. A similar case is Lending Tree (*www.lendingtree.com*), a company that provides mortgage quotes for homeowners and also sells mortgages online. Lending Tree uses an extranet for its business partners (e.g., the lenders).

 IT's [about business]

## **11.7** India's New Automotive Supply Chain Extranet

A major obstacle to implementing efficient and effective supply chain management is a lack of connectivity and integration among supply chain partners. Consider the automotive supply chain in India, for example. This supply chain includes more than 40 automotive original equipment manufacturers (OEMs) operating in India, as well as 700 suppliers.

India's automotive supply chain relies primarily on manual communications in areas such as purchase orders, invoices, and forecasts. Furthermore, the methods by which the transactional data are shared in India among suppliers, manufacturers, suppliers, and customers have been highly inconsistent. As a result, the supply chain regularly experiences processing delays, inaccurate transactions, and other inefficiencies. For instance, a given supplier may be required to send data in dozens of different formats to meet the specific requirements of different manufacturers.

In an attempt to address these issues, IBM (*www.ibm.com*) and two automotive industry associations in India launched a new SCM extranet that will electronically connect all of India's automobile manufacturers and suppliers. The two associations are the Society of Indian Automobile Manufacturers (SIAM) and the Automotive Components Manufacturers Association (ACMA).

In this extranet, suppliers will need to create data in only one standard format. They will then send those data to a cloud-based network, called Auto DX (*www.autodx.org*). Manufacturers can work directly with those data. Alternatively, Auto DX will translate the message into a particular manufacturer's data format. The extranet supports many different electronic data interchange (EDI) transactions and document types. In addition, it provides Web-based software tools for suppliers that are not EDI-enabled.

All participants in Auto DX, including the OEMs, will share in the network's cost of operations. India's manufacturers designed that cost structure from the beginning to avoid the impression that

they were forcing a system on the suppliers and then requiring the suppliers to bear the entire cost.

The Indian automotive industry is anticipating that the extranet will improve efficiencies across the entire industry by standardizing the data definitions and data interchange formats and thereby expanding the possibilities for automating the supply chain. Most of the members of ACMA and SIAM had adopted Auto DX by the end of 2014.

*Sources:* Compiled from "IBM, Indian Auto Groups Launch Ambitious Connectivity Hub to Integrate OEMs, Parts Suppliers," *Supply Chain Digest*, April 2, 2014; J. Brandon, "Automotive CIOs Say Cloud Exchange Could Reduce Supply Chain Costs 80%," *Business Cloud News*, March 10, 2014; N. Roy, "IBM Cloud-Based AutoDX Exchange for Indian Automotive Industry," *Rush Lane*, March 6, 2014; "Auto DX to Improve Supply Chain in Automotive Sector," *Support Biz*, February 26, 2014; R. Mani, "Auto CIOs-Industry Get Into Turbo Mode: Launch AutoDX," *Dynamic CIO*, February 5, 2014; "SIAM, ACMA Launch AutoDX," *Gaadi.com*, February 4, 2014; *www.autodx.org*, accessed April 10, 2015.

**Questions**

1. Discuss the difficulties involved in implementing Auto DX.
2. Describe the advantages of Auto DX to the Indian automotive supply chain.

## Portals and Exchanges

As you saw in Chapter 6, corporate portals offer a single point of access through a Web browser to critical business information in an organization. In the context of B2B supply chain management, these portals enable companies and their suppliers to collaborate very closely.

There are two basic types of corporate portals: procurement (sourcing) portals for a company's suppliers (upstream in the supply chain), and distribution portals for a company's customers (downstream in the supply chain). **Procurement portals** automate the business processes involved in purchasing or procuring products between a single buyer and multiple suppliers. For example, Boeing has deployed a procurement portal called the Boeing Supplier Portal through which it conducts business with its suppliers. **Distribution portals** automate the business processes involved in selling or distributing products from a single supplier to multiple buyers. For example, Dell services its business customers through its distribution portal at *http://premier.dell.com*.

# before you go on... 

1. Define EDI, and list its major benefits and limitations.
2. Define an extranet, and explain its infrastructure.
3. List and briefly define the major types of extranets.
4. Differentiate between procurement portals and distribution portals.

## For Accounting Majors

*Customer Relationship Management.* CRM systems can help companies establish controls for financial reporting related to interactions with customers in order to support compliance with legislation. For example, Sarbanes-Oxley requires companies to establish and maintain an adequate set of controls for accurate financial reporting that can be audited by a third party. Other sections [302 and 401(b)] have implications for customer activities, including the requirements that sales figures reported for the prior year be correct. Section 409 requires companies to report material changes to financial conditions, such as the loss of a strategic customer or significant customer claims about product quality.

CRM systems can track document flow from a sales opportunity to a sales order, to an invoice, to an accounting document, thus enabling finance and accounting managers to monitor the entire flow. CRM systems that track sales quotes and orders can be used to incorporate process controls that identify questionable sales transactions. CRM systems can provide exception-alert capabilities to identify instances outside defined parameters that put companies at risk.

*Supply Chain Management.* The cost accountant will play an important role in developing and monitoring the financial accounting information associated with inventory and cost of goods sold. In a supply chain, much of the data for these accounting requirements will flow into the organization from various partners within the chain. It is up to the chief accountant, the comptroller or CFO, to prepare and review these data.

Going further, accounting rules and regulations and the cross-border transfer of data are critical for global trade. IOSs can facilitate such trade. Other issues that are important for accountants are taxation and government reports. In addition, creating information systems that rely on EDI requires the attention of accountants. Finally, fraud detection in global settings (e.g., transfers of funds) can be facilitated by appropriate controls and auditing.

## For the Finance Major

*Customer Relationship Management.* CRM systems allow companies to track marketing expenses, collecting appropriate costs for each individual marketing campaign. These costs then can be matched to corporate initiatives and financial objectives, demonstrating the financial impact of the marketing campaign.

Pricing is another key area that impacts financial reporting. For example, what discounts are available? When can a price be overridden? Who approves discounts? CRM systems can put controls into place for these issues.

*Supply Chain Management.* In a supply chain, the finance major will be responsible for analyzing the data created and shared among supply chain partners. In many instances, the financial analyst will recommend actions to improve supply chain efficiencies and cash flow. This may benefit all the partners in the chain. These recommendations will be based on financial models that incorporate key assumptions such as supply chain partner agreements for pricing. Through the use of extensive financial modeling, the financial analyst helps to manage liquidity in the supply chain.

Many finance-related issues exist in implementing IOSs. For one thing, establishing EDI and extranet relationships involves structuring payment agreements. Global supply chains may involve complex financial arrangements, which may have legal implications.

## For the Marketing Major

*Customer Relationship Management.* CRM systems are an integral part of every marketing professional's work activities. CRM systems contain the consolidated customer data that provides the foundation for making informed marketing decisions. Using these data, marketers develop well- timed and targeted sales campaigns with

# What's In IT For Me?

customized product mixes and established price points that enhance potential sales opportunities and therefore increase revenue. CRM systems also support the development of forecasting models for future sales to existing clients through the use of historical data captured from previous transactions.

*Supply Chain Management.* A tremendous amount of useful sales information can be derived from supply chain partners through the supporting information systems. For example, many of the customer support activities take place in the downstream portion of the supply chain. For the marketing manager, an understanding of how the downstream activities of the supply chain relate to prior chain operations is critical.

Furthermore, a tremendous amount of data is fed from the supply chain supporting information systems into the CRM systems that are used by marketers. The information and a complete understanding of its genesis are vital for mixed-model marketing programs.

## For the Production/Operations Management Major

*Customer Relationship Management.* Production is heavily involved in the acquisition of raw materials, conversion, and distribution of finished goods. However, all of these activities are driven by sales. Increases or decreases in the demand for goods result in a corresponding increase or decrease in a company's need for raw materials. Integral to a company's demand is forecasting future sales, an important part of CRM systems. Sales forecasts are created from the historical data stored in CRM systems.

This information is critically important to a production manager who is placing orders for manufacturing processes. Without an accurate future sales forecast, production managers may face inventory problems (discussed in detail in this chapter). The use of CRM systems for production and operational support is critical to efficiently managing the resources of the company.

*Supply Chain Management.* The production/operations management major plays a major role in the supply chain development process. In many organizations, the production/operations management staff may even lead the supply chain integration process because of their extensive knowledge of the manufacturing components of the organization. Because they are in charge of procurement, production, materials control, and logistical handling, a comprehensive understanding of the techniques of SCM is vital for the production/operations staff.

The downstream segment of supply chains is where marketing, distribution channels, and customer service are conducted. An understanding of how downstream activities are related to the other segments is critical. Supply chain problems can reduce customer satisfaction and negate marketing efforts. It is essential, then, that marketing professionals understand the nature of such problems and their solutions. Also, learning about CRM, its options, and its implementation is important for designing effective customer services and advertising.

As competition intensifies globally, finding new global markets becomes critical. Use of IOSs provides an opportunity to improve marketing and sales. Understanding the capabilities of these technologies as well as their implementation issues will enable the marketing department to excel.

## For the Human Resources Major

*Customer Relationship Management.* Companies trying to enhance their customer relationships must recognize that employees who interact with customers are critical to the success of CRM strategies. Essentially, the success of CRM is based on the employees' desire and ability to promote the company and its CRM initiatives. In fact, research analysts have found that customer loyalty is based largely on employees' capabilities and their commitment to the company.

As a result, human resource managers know that a company that desires valued customer relationships needs valued relationships with its employees. Therefore, HR managers are implementing programs to increase employee satisfaction and are training employees to execute CRM strategies.

*Supply Chain Management.* Supply chains require interactions among the employees of partners in the chain. These interactions are the responsibility of the Human Resources Manager. The HR Manager must be able to address supply chain issues that relate to staffing, job descriptions, job rotations, and accountability. All of these areas are complex within a supply chain and require the HR function to understand the relationship among partners as well as the movement of resources.

Preparing and training employees to work with business partners (frequently in foreign countries) requires knowledge about how IOSs operate. Sensitivity to cultural differences and extensive communication and collaboration can be facilitated with IT.

### For the MIS Major

*Customer Relationship Management.* The IT function in the enterprise is responsible for the corporate databases and data warehouse, as well as the correctness and completeness of the data in them. That is, the IT department provides the data used in a 360° view of the customer. Furthermore, IT personnel provide the technologies underlying the customer interaction center.

*Supply Chain Management.* The MIS staff will be instrumental in the design and support of information systems—both internal organizational and interorganizational—that will underpin the business processes that are part of the supply chain. In this capacity, the MIS staff must have a concise knowledge of the business, the systems, and the points of intersection between the two.

## [ Summary ]

1. **Identify the primary functions of both customer relationship management (CRM) and collaborative CRM.**

*Customer relationship management* (CRM) is an organizational strategy that is customer focused and customer driven. That is, organizations concentrate on assessing customers' requirements for products and services and then on providing high-quality, responsive services. CRM functions include acquiring new customers, retaining existing customers, and growing relationships with existing customers.

*Collaborative CRM* is an organizational CRM strategy where data consolidation and the 360° view of the customer enable the organization's functional areas to readily share information about customers. The functions of collaborative CRM include integrating communications between the organization and its customers in all aspects of marketing, sales, and customer support processes, and enabling customers to provide direct feedback to the organization.

2. **Describe how businesses might use applications of each of the two major components of operational CRM systems.**

Operational CRM systems support the front-office business processes that interact directly with customers (i.e., sales, marketing, and service). The two major components of operational CRM systems are customer-facing applications and customer-touching applications.

*Customer-facing CRM applications* include customer service and support, sales force automation, marketing, and campaign management. *Customer-touching applications* include search and comparison capabilities, technical and other information and services, customized products and services, personalized Web pages, FAQs, e-mail and automated response, and loyalty programs.

### 3. Discuss the benefits of analytical CRM systems to businesses.

*Analytical CRM systems* analyze customer behavior and perceptions in order to provide business intelligence. Organizations use analytical systems for many purposes, including designing and executing targeted marketing campaigns; increasing customer acquisition, cross-selling, and upselling; providing input into decisions relating to products and services (e.g., pricing and product development); and providing financial forecasting and customer profitability analysis.

### 4. Explain the advantages and disadvantages of mobile CRM systems, on-demand CRM systems, and open-source CRM systems.

*On-demand CRM systems* are those hosted by an external vendor in the vendor's data center. Advantages of on-demand CRM systems include lower costs and a need for employees to know only how to access and utilize the software. Drawbacks include possibly unreliable vendors, difficulty in modifying the software, and difficulty in integrating vendor-hosted CRM software with the organization's existing software.

*Mobile CRM systems* are interactive systems where communications related to sales, marketing, and customer service activities are conducted through a mobile medium for the purpose of building and maintaining customer relationships between an organization and its customers. Advantages of mobile CRM systems include convenience for customers and the chance to build a truly personal relationship with customers. A drawback could be difficulty in maintaining customer expectations; that is, the company must be extremely responsive to customer needs in a mobile, near-real-time environment.

*Open-source CRM systems* are those whose source code is available to developers and users. The benefits of open-source CRM systems include favorable pricing, a wide variety of applications, easy customization, rapid updates and bug (software error) fixes, and extensive free support information. The major drawback of open-source CRM systems is quality control.

### 5. Describe the three components and the three flows of a supply chain.

A *supply chain* is the flow of materials, information, money, and services from raw material suppliers, through factories and warehouses, to the end customers. A supply chain involves three segments: upstream, where sourcing or procurement from external suppliers occurs; internal, where packaging, assembly, or manufacturing takes place; and downstream, where distribution takes place, frequently by external distributors.

There are three flows in the supply chain: *material flows*, which are the physical products, raw materials, supplies, and so forth; *information flows*, which consist of data related to demand, shipments, orders, returns, and schedules, as well as changes in any of these data; and *financial flows*, which involve money transfers, payments, credit card information and authorization, payment schedules, e-payments, and credit-related data.

### 6. Identify popular strategies to solving different challenges of supply chains.

Two major challenges in setting accurate inventory levels throughout a supply chain are the *demand forecast* and the bullwhip effect. Demand for a product can be influenced by numerous factors such as competition, prices, weather conditions, technological developments, economic conditions, and customers' general confidence. The *bullwhip effect* refers to erratic shifts in orders up and down the supply chain.

The most common solution to supply chain problems is *building inventories* as insurance against SC uncertainties. Another solution is the *just-in-time* (JIT) inventory system, which delivers the precise number of parts, called *work-in-process inventory*, to be assembled into a finished product at precisely the right time. The third possible solution is *vendor-managed inventory* (VMI), which occurs when the vendor, rather than the retailer, manages the entire inventory process for a particular product or group of products.

7. **Explain the utility of each of the three major technologies that support supply chain management.**

*Electronic data interchange* (EDI) is a communication standard that enables the electronic transfer of routine documents, such as purchasing orders, between business partners.

*Extranets* are networks that link business partners over the Internet by providing them access to certain areas of each other's corporate intranets. The main goal of extranets is to foster collaboration among business partners.

*Corporate portals* offer a single point of access through a Web browser to critical business information in an organization. In the context of business-to-business supply chain management, these portals enable companies and their suppliers to collaborate very closely.

## [ Chapter Glossary ]

**analytical CRM system** CRM system that analyzes customer behavior and perceptions in order to provide actionable business intelligence.

**bullwhip effect** Erratic shifts in orders up and down the supply chain.

**bundling** A form of cross-selling where an enterprise sells a group of products or services together at a lower price than the combined individual price of the products.

**campaign management applications** CRM applications that help organizations plan marketing campaigns that send the right messages to the right people through the right channels.

**collaborative CRM system** A CRM system where communications between the organization and its customers are integrated across all aspects of marketing, sales, and customer support processes.

**cross-selling** The practice of marketing additional related products to customers based on a previous purchase.

**customer-facing CRM applications** Areas where customers directly interact with the organization, including customer service and support, sales force automation, marketing, and campaign management.

**customer interaction center (CIC)** A CRM operation where organizational representatives use multiple communication channels to interact with customers in functions such as inbound teleservice and outbound telesales.

**customer relationship management (CRM)** A customer-focused and customer-driven organizational strategy that concentrates on addressing customers' requirements for products and services, and then providing high-quality, responsive services.

**customer-touching CRM applications** (also called **electronic CRM** or **e-CRM**) Applications and technologies with which customers interact and typically help themselves.

**customer touch point** Any interaction between a customer and an organization.

**distribution portals** Corporate portals that automate the business processes involved in selling or distributing products from a single supplier to multiple buyers.

**electronic CRM (e-CRM)** See **customer-touching CRM applications**.

**electronic data interchange (EDI)** A communication standard that enables the electronic transfer of routine documents between business partners.

**extranets** Networks that link business partners over the Internet by providing them access to certain areas of each other's corporate intranets.

**front-office processes** Those processes that directly interact with customers; that is, sales, marketing, and service.

**interorganizational information system (IOS)** An information system that supports information flow among two or more organizations.

**just-in-time (JIT)** inventory system A system in which a supplier delivers the precise number of parts to be assembled into a finished product at precisely the right time.

**loyalty program** Programs that offer rewards to customers to influence future behavior.

**mobile CRM system** An interactive CRM system where communications related to sales, marketing, and customer service activities are conducted through a mobile medium for the purpose of building and maintaining customer relationships between an organization and its customers.

**on-demand CRM system** A CRM system that is hosted by an external vendor in the vendor's data center.

**open-source CRM system** CRM software whose source code is available to developers and users.

**operational CRM system** The component of CRM that supports the front-office business processes that directly interact with customers (i.e., sales, marketing, and service).

**procurement portals** Corporate portals that automate the business processes involved in purchasing or procuring products between a single buyer and multiple suppliers.

**pull model** A business model in which the production process begins with a customer order and companies make only what customers want, a process closely aligned with mass customization.

**push model** A business model in which the production process begins with a forecast, which predicts the products that customers will want as well as the quantity of each product. The company then produces the amount of products in the forecast, typically by using mass production, and sells, or "pushes," those products to consumers.

**sales force automation (SFA)** The component of an operational CRM system that automatically records all the aspects in a sales transaction process.

**social CRM** The use of social media technology and services to enable organizations to engage their customers in a collaborative conversation in order to provide mutually beneficial value in a trusted and transparent manner.

**supply chain** The coordinated movement of *resources* from organizations through *conversion* to the end consumer.

**supply chain management (SCM)** An activity in which the leadership of an organization provides extensive oversight for the partnerships and processes that compose the supply chain and leverages these relationships to provide an operational advantage.

**supply chain visibility** The ability of all organizations in a supply chain to access or view relevant data on purchased materials as these materials move through their suppliers' production processes.

**upselling** A sales strategy where the organizational representative provides to customers the opportunity to purchase higher-value related products or services in place of, or along with, the consumer's initial product or service selection.

**vendor-managed inventory (VMI)** An inventory strategy where the supplier monitors a vendor's inventory for a product or group of products and replenishes products when needed.

**vertical integration** Strategy of integrating the upstream part of the supply chain with the internal part, typically by purchasing upstream suppliers, in order to ensure timely availability of supplies.

## [ Discussion Questions ]

1. How do customer relationship management systems help organizations achieve customer intimacy?
2. What is the relationship between data consolidation and CRM systems?
3. Discuss the relationship between CRM and customer privacy.
4. Distinguish between operational CRM systems and analytical CRM systems.
5. Differentiate between customer-facing CRM applications and customer-touching CRM applications.
6. Explain why Web-based customer interaction centers are critical for successful CRM systems.
7. Why are companies so interested in e-CRM applications?
8. Discuss why it is difficult to justify CRM applications.
9. You are the CIO of a small company with a rapidly growing customer base. Which CRM system would you use: an on-premise CRM system, an on-demand CRM system, or an open-source CRM system? Remember that open-source CRM systems may be implemented either on-premise or on-demand. Discuss the pros and cons of each type of CRM system for your business.
10. Refer to the example concerning the CRM efforts of Caterpillar. Where on the CRM continuum (low-end to high-end) does the company's CRM strategy fit? Explain your answer.
11. List and explain the important components of a supply chain.
12. Explain how a supply chain approach may be part of a company's overall strategy.
13. Explain the important role that information systems play in supporting a supply chain strategy.
14. Would Rolls-Royce Motorcars (*www.rolls-roycemotorcars.com*) use a push model or a pull model in its supply chain? Support your answer.
15. Why is planning so important in supply chain management?

## [ Problem-Solving Activities ]

1. Access *www.ups.com* and *www.fedex.com*. Examine some of the IT-supported customer services and tools provided by the two companies. Compare and contrast the customer support provided on the two companies' Web sites.

2. Enter *www.anntaylor.com*, *www.hermes.com*, and *www.tiffany.com*. Compare and contrast the customer service activities offered by these companies on their Web sites. Do you see marked similarities? Differences?

3. Access your university's Web site. Investigate how your university provides for customer relationship management. (Hint: First decide who your university's customers are.)

4. Access *www.sugarcrm.com*, and take the interactive tour. Prepare a report on SugarCRM's functionality to the class.

5. Access *www.ups.com* and *www.fedex.com*. Examine some of the IT-supported customer services and tools provided by the two companies. Write a report on how the two companies contribute to supply chain improvements.

6. Enter *www.supply-chain.org*, *www.cio.com*, *www.findarticles.com*, and *www.google.com*, and search for recent information on supply chain management.

7. Surf the Web to find a procurement (sourcing) portal, a distribution portal, and an exchange (other than the examples presented in this chapter). List the features they have in common and those features that are unique.

# [ Closing Case **Super Retail Group Consolidates Demand Forecasting and Replenishment** ]

## The **Problem**

Super Retail Group (Super) (*www.superretailgroup.com.au*) is one of the largest leisure retailers in Australia, with annual sales of more than AU$2 billion. Its seven retail brands focus on automotive products, cycling products, and sporting goods, which it sells through more than 600 stores in Australia and New Zealand.

Since 2005, Super has grown exponentially through a series of acquisitions. Although this growth has added sales volume and brand strength, it has also made the company's supply chain extremely complex. Historically, the company has operated each brand as a separate division. As a result, by 2011 it was managing seven distinct supply chains, which spanned from procurement in Asia to distribution in Australia and New Zealand. Adding to the complexity of managing Super's supply chains was the huge, yet sparsely populated geography of Australia.

Accordingly, Super's executives decided to invest more than AU$50 million in supply chain and inventory management improvements during 2012–2015. The initiative included centralizing a disparate set of distribution centers, consolidating procurement in Asia, developing online sales fulfillment for home delivery, and strengthening relationships with key trading partners.

In essence, the company's key strategic initiative was to consolidate demand forecasting and replenishment across its diverse brands. As the firm acquired other businesses and expanded its scale of private-label products, demand planning became increasingly important. The company needed to manage the lead times associated with procuring from Asia, as well as extreme seasonal and promotional volatility within its brands.

Super had also added more soft (digital) goods, which had different demand patterns than hard (physical) goods. In sum, the retailer needed a forecasting and replenishment model that could handle its geographical complexity, as well as the stock-keeping unit (SKU) complexity, and demand variation across its seven brands.

## The **IT Solution**

To integrate demand planning and fulfillment and to increase its customer focus across brands, Super implemented software from JDA (*www.jda.com*) into its Leisure Retailing division. Within 10 months, the system was operational, thanks to a rapid deployment in JDA's cloud. (We discuss cloud computing in Technology Guide 3.) The company elected to launch the software in a cloud environment to expedite the implementation and to minimize expenses.

Deploying the system in the cloud enabled Super Retail to contain its IT infrastructure costs. That is, the company was spared the expenses of purchasing hardware (servers and storage), software (the applications), and networking capabilities. The retailer understood that not all hardware and software expenses are obvious; rather, building an IT infrastructure frequently involves hidden costs. For example, Super estimated that hosting its own software solution would cost the firm AU$20,000 per month in electricity alone. Additionally, Super did not have the internal IT resources to implement the software, or the capacity to grow its IT team sufficiently to support the new software.

The pilot test in the Leisure Retailing division initially included 400,000 SKUs. It was then expanded to accommodate 1.4 million SKUs. Because there was so much product complexity in Leisure Retailing, the division served as an effective pilot test for the new system. Consider one example. Because Australia is home to 68 targeted fishing species—more than anywhere else in the world—Super sells many different fishing lures, and it has to manage many regionally specific product ranges.

## The **Results**

Not only has the cloud services model proved to be scalable across the division's enormous product diversity, but it has also proved to be very reliable. The system's availability has been nearly 100 percent—a critical factor given the enormous amounts of data the retailer needs to manage. After just six months of operation, Super realized tangible results from the pilot test. For instance, inventory had been reduced by 20 percent.

From a strategic perspective, Super's new system is helping to support the customer focus that the company needs to compete successfully in the marketplace. In fact, Super executives contend that the JDA software has made the firm's entire mindset more customer-centric.

Super completed its pilot test in the Leisure Retailing division, and it is now piloting the new system in its Auto Business division. The company's ultimate goal is to launch and manage all future JDA solutions in the cloud.

*Sources:* Compiled from S. Small, "Super Retail Group Posts Damp Profit Result after 'Internal' Issues," *Courier-Mail*, February 20, 2014; S. Davis, "Super Retail Group Ltd's 'Positive' Rating Reaffirmed at Deutsche Bank," *WKRB*, February 4, 2014; E. Knight, "Camping, Sporting Goods Company Super Retail Group Finds Life No Picnic of Late," *The Sydney Morning Herald*, January 18, 2014; M. King, "Why Super Retail Group Ltd Shares Sank," *The Motley Fool*, January 17, 2014; "Super Retail Group to Grow Store Footprint Following Solid Results," *Retail Biz*, October 24, 2013; L. Tay, "Super Retail Group Boosts IT Spend," *IT News*, February 20, 2013; "Catching Success via the Cloud," *JDA Case Study*, 2012; *www.superretailgroup.com.au*, accessed April 10, 2015.

### Questions

1. Explain why Super Retail Group decided to use JDA software along its supply chain.

2. Why did Super Retail Group pilot test in its Leisure Retailing division?

3. Why did Super Retail Group implement a cloud-based solution? Do you believe this was the correct decision? Why or why not?

# 12 Business Intelligence

| [ LEARNING OBJECTIVES ] | [ CHAPTER OUTLINE ] | [ WEB RESOURCES ] |
| --- | --- | --- |

**[ LEARNING OBJECTIVES ]**

1. Identify the phases in the decision-making process, and use a decision support framework to demonstrate how technology supports managerial decision making.

2. Describe and provide examples of different ways that organizations use business intelligence (BI).

3. Specify the BI application available to users for data analysis, and provide examples of how each application can be used to solve a business problem at your university.

4. Describe three BI applications that present the results of data analyses to users, and offer examples of how businesses and government agencies can use each of these applications.

**[ CHAPTER OUTLINE ]**

12.1 Managers and Decision Making

12.2 What Is Business Intelligence?

12.3 Business Intelligence Applications for Data Analysis

12.4 Business Intelligence Applications for Presenting Results

**[ WEB RESOURCES ]**

- Student PowerPoints for note taking

**WileyPLUS Learning Space**

- E-book
- Author video lecture for each chapter section
- Practice quizzes
- Flash Cards for vocabulary review
- Additional "IT's About Business" cases
- Video interviews with managers
- Lab Manuals for Microsoft Office 2010 and 2013

## What's In IT For Me?

**This Chapter Will Help Prepare You To...**

**ACCT**
ACCOUNTING
Uncover fraudulent transactions

**FIN**
FINANCE
Make stock market investment decisions

**MKT**
MARKETING
Allocate advertising budgets

**POM**
PRODUCTION OPERATIONS MANAGEMENT
Schedule production activities

**HRM**
HUMAN RESOURCES MANAGEMENT
Control job applicant process

**MIS**
MIS
Provide information in dashboards

# [ ConocoPhillips Uses Business Intelligence to Produce More Oil and Gas ]

## The Business Problem

ConocoPhillips (CP) (*www.conocophillips.com*) is a $9 billion U.S. multinational energy corporation. It is the world's largest independent energy exploration and production company. The company explores for, produces, transports, and markets crude oil and natural gas on a worldwide basis.

Finding oil and gas is a first step for CP. The next step is to invest millions of dollars to drill each well to extract those resources. The company must then spend additional money to manage the natural decline in production at each well. With returns and profitability directly linked to production, CP must try to extract every barrel of oil or cubit foot of gas it can from its wells.

## The IT Solution

There is nothing new about energy companies using analytics to find and produce more oil and gas. An excellent example of analytics at work in the energy industry is the custom-developed plunger lift surveillance and optimization software tool (PLOT) from CP. PLOT enables the company to optimize a well to its true capacity. The tool gathers data specifically related to CP's use of plunger lifts, which are installed inside a well to lift accumulated fluids that are stopping the flow of gas. PLOT enables the energy giant to maximize the lift's capabilities as well as to recognize sooner when the plunger lift will require maintenance.

Plunger lift technology has been around since the 1950s. This technology provided only basic gas pressure and flow rate data. CP stored and compiled data from these wells in spreadsheets, and any analyses they performed on the data were manual and labor intensive.

In the PLOT initiative, CP installed additional sensors to capture pressure and temperature readings. The company samples those readings every 30–60 seconds, as opposed to once per hour or per day. PLOT accumulates approximately 4.5 million daily data points from monitoring CP's wells.

PLOT calculates pressure and temperature at different parts of the well, enabling well operators to identify which wells are producing efficiently and which ones are not. Company managers claim that PLOT provides them with greater transparency into how the wells are functioning because they have access to higher frequency data. One manager stated that with CP's old technology, analyzing data was similar to looking at snapshots at certain points in time. In contrast, with PLOT, analyzing data resembles watching a movie because managers are analyzing nearly real-time data.

PLOT provides 43 performance dashboards for individual wells and gas fields. Simple threshold alerts alert operators when plunger lift operating cycles must be adjusted to eliminate fluid buildup that is restricting the flow of gas. The dashboards remotely monitor wells and notify well operators when problems are likely to occur, so that the operators can quickly recognize problems.

To continuously connect more of its far-flung wells, the company is building its own radio and Wi-Fi towers to cover remote energy fields in South Texas, where commercial carriers do not offer mobile coverage. This private communications network will transmit data from wells to company data centers in Houston, Texas, and Bartlesville, Oklahoma, where the information is stored and analyzed.

One challenge that ConocoPhillips encountered when it implemented PLOT was change management. Many well operators adopted the new dashboards quickly, adjusted plunger lift cycles, and tweaked well operations every day to increase output. Others, however, either did not understand what to change or they failed to follow through on recommended actions from PLOT. To resolve this problem, CP is moving to a centralized approach, where a dozen people in an operation center monitor all of the wells in a geographic area and direct optimization efforts rather than count on the hundreds of well operators—the people who travel from well to well to make adjustments and maintain equipment—to interpret the dashboards and determine which actions to take. The operations center staff will be able to identify which wells are operating within expected parameters and which ones are not. They will also be able to instruct the operators as to which wells to visit and what to do when they arrive on site.

# The Results

Significantly, CP did not spend large amounts of money on PLOT. Nevertheless, the system has generated major benefits for the company. PLOT has increased production from more than 4,500 natural gas wells by an average of 5 percent. In turn, this increased production has improved the company's revenue from its wells, reduced greenhouse gas emissions tied to inefficient wells, and eliminated unnecessary operator trips to each well by using remote monitoring. The project is also reducing U.S. dependence on imported oil by making maximum use of domestic energy sources.

CP has realized another advantage from PLOT—improved data quality. Data quality historically has been a major challenge for the company. CP has deployed different generations of computers and sensors stationed in and at the wells themselves, as well as different communications methods (over cellular, radio, and Wi-Fi), which have contributed to data complexity and variability.

These benefits are just a start. ConocoPhillips is now using PLOT in thousands of additional plunger-lift-style gas wells in the United States and Canada. In addition, the company is applying the techniques and lessons learned from PLOT to other types of gas wells. For example, CP is expanding PLOT to its gas fields in Canada and the North Slope of Alaska.

*Sources:* Compiled from G. Allouche, "Mining for Oil with Big Data," *Toad World*, February 10, 2014; "A PLOT to Increase Production," *ConocoPhillips Onshore*, 2014; "The Big Deal About Big Data in Upstream Oil and Gas," *Hitachi Data Systems White Paper*, 2014; C. Murphy, "ConocoPhillips CIO Talks Live on Big Data Analytics," *InformationWeek*, December 16, 2013; M. DiLallo, "How ConocoPhillips Plots to Use Technology to Improve Production," *The Motley Fool*, October 1, 2013; "Data Analysis Tool Helps ConocoPhillips Boost Natural Gas Production," *SmartBrief*, September 11, 2013; D. Henschen, "Drilling Down into Big Data," *InformationWeek*, September 9, 2013; D. Henschen, "ConocoPhillips Taps Big Data for Gas Well Gains," *InformationWeek*, September 5, 2013; D. McDonald, "Even Oil Companies Are Using the New Oil, Big Data Analytics," *Teradata*, December 11, 2012; "How Big Data Is Changing the Oil & Gas Industry," *Analytics Magazine*, November/December 2012; R. Thomas, "The Looming Global Analytics Talent Mismatch in Oil and Gas," *Accenture White Paper*, October 2012; *www.conocophillips.com*, accessed March 7, 2015.

## Questions

1. Describe the impact of the PLOT system on the quantity and quality of the data collected from ConocoPhillips's wells. Now, describe the impact of these data on the quality of the analyses from the PLOT system. What relationship you can infer between the quality and quantity of data and the quality of the analysis performed on that data?

2. If plunger lift technology had been in place for 50 years, why is ConocoPhillips just now developing its PLOT system?

3. Speculate how well operators will react to PLOT. Positively or negatively? Support your answer.

# Introduction

The chapter opening case illustrates the importance and far-reaching nature of business intelligence applications. **Business intelligence (BI)** is a broad category of applications, technologies, and processes for gathering, storing, accessing, and analyzing data to help business users make better decisions. BI applications enable decision makers to quickly ascertain the status of a business enterprise by examining key information. Large firms that want to invest in single-family homes to rent need current, timely, and accurate information to predict the rents they can charge to maximize their return on investment (ROI). Conoco's BI applications provided the information that the energy giant needed.

Before we proceed, we need to distinguish between the terms "business intelligence" and "business analytics." In his book *Analytics at Work: Smarter Decisions, Better Results*, Thomas Davenport argued that business intelligence should be divided into querying, reporting, online analytical processing, and business analytics. He defined business analytics as a subset of BI based on statistics, prediction, and optimization. Essentially, BI can answer questions such as: What happened, how many, how often, where the problem is, and what actions are needed? In contrast, business analytics can answer questions such as: Why is this happening, what will happen if these trends continue, what will happen next, and what is the best (or worst) that can happen?

Despite this distinction, however, both BI and business analytics rely on data (particularly Big Data) and statistical methods. In fact, many experts argue that the terms should be used interchangeably. In this chapter, we adopt this approach.

This chapter describes information systems that support *decision making*. It begins by reviewing the manager's job and the nature of modern managerial decisions. This discussion will help you to understand why managers need computerized support. It then considers how business intelligence can support individuals, groups, and entire organizations.

It is impossible to overstate the importance of business intelligence within modern organizations. Recall from Chapter 1 that the essential goal of information systems is to provide the right information to the right person, in the right amount, at the right time, in the right format. In essence, BI achieves this goal. BI systems provide business intelligence that you can act on in a timely fashion.

It is also impossible to overstate the importance of your input into the BI process within an organization, for several reasons. First, you (the user community) will decide what data should be stored in your organization's data warehouse. You will then work closely with the MIS department to obtain these data.

Further, you will use your organization's BI applications, probably from your first day on the job. With some BI applications such as data mining and decision support systems, you will decide how you want to analyze the data (user-driven analysis). With other BI applications such as dashboards, you will decide which data you need and in which format. Again, you will work closely with your MIS department to ensure that these applications meet your needs.

Much of this chapter is concerned with large-scale BI applications. You should keep in mind, however, that smaller organizations, and even individual users, can implement small-scale BI applications as well. For example, Excel spreadsheets provide some BI functions, as do SQL queries of a database. IT's About Business 12.1 illustrates how a small company uses analytics to predict how much rent investors can charge in the single-family-home market.

The most popular BI tool by far is Excel. For years, BI vendors "fought" against the use of Excel. Eventually, however, they decided to "join it" by designing their software so that it interfaces with Excel. How does this process work? Essentially, users download plug-ins that add functionality (e.g., the ability to list the top 10 percent of customers, based on purchases) to Excel. This process can be thought of as creating "Excel on steroids." Excel then connects to the vendor's application server—which provides additional data analysis capabilities—which in turn connects to a backend database, such as a data mart or warehouse. This arrangement gives Excel users the functionality and access to data typical of sophisticated BI products, while allowing them to work with a familiar client—Excel.

Microsoft has made similar changes to its product line. Specifically, Excel now can be used with MS SQL Server (a database product), and it can be utilized in advanced BI applications, such as dashboards and data mining/predictive analysis.

After you finish this chapter, you will have a basic understanding of decision making, the business intelligence process, and the incredibly broad range of BI applications employed in modern organizations. This knowledge will enable you to immediately and confidently provide input into your organization's BI processes and applications. Further, this chapter will help you use your organization's BI applications to effectively analyze data and thus make better decisions. Enjoy!

# 12.1 Managers and Decision Making

**Management** is a process by which an organization achieves its goals through the use of resources (people, money, materials, and information). These resources are considered to be *inputs*. Achieving the organization's goals is the *output* of the process. Managers oversee this process in an attempt to optimize it. A manager's success often is measured by the ratio between the inputs and outputs for which he or she is responsible. This ratio is an indication of the organization's **productivity**.

# IT's [about business]

## 12.1 How Much Rent Can You Charge?

Renting out single-family homes was largely a mom-and-pop business until the U.S. housing bust (roughly from 2006 until 2012). In the aftermath of the bust, large investment firms began investing substantial sums of money in this market. For example, Blackstone Group (*www.blackstone.com*), the largest investor, has spent $4 billion on 24,000 homes. The big investors initially focused on the most depressed markets, including Phoenix, Arizona, and Atlanta, Georgia. As competition from other bargain hunters grew and prices in those areas rose, Blackstone started looking across the country for other opportunities.

Enter RentRange (*www.rentrange.com*). RentRange provides analyses about purchasing foreclosed and low-priced single-family homes and then renting them out. Using data from 12 million properties around the United States, RentRange can estimate how much monthly rent a property is likely to generate. Such predictive analyses provide critical input into the financial models that investors use to determine where to buy homes to convert to rentals, as well as how much rent they can charge.

Wally Charnoff, who founded RentRange in 2008, used his own money to purchase data from property managers, rental listing Web sites, and landlords. To predict a likely rent, RentRange's predictive algorithms integrate those raw data with additional data, such as whether dogs or smoking have been, and are, allowed and whether the local area is already saturated with rental homes.

Customers pay $50,000 for five years of RentRange data at regional, county, city, and zip code levels to help identify potentially profitable markets. Once investors pick a market, they pay $2 to $12 for rental estimates for specific properties.

How accurate are RentRange's rent predictions? One large investment firm manager claims that RentRange's estimates have generally been within 1 to 3 percent of what the firm ultimately charged.

RentRange, which has a staff of 22, saw its revenue increase 1,900 percent between 2011 and 2014. The company became profitable in 2012. Company officials claim that almost 19,000 users, including 50 institutional clients, buy data directly from RentRange.

Renters now occupy 35 percent of all single-family homes in the United States, up from 30 percent in 2005, according to the Goldman Sachs Group (*www.goldmansachs.com*). As a result, it is not clear how long the buy-to-rent boom will last, as rising home prices make the process less profitable. In 2014, Clear Capital, a provider of real estate data and analysis, noted that home prices had increased about 10 percent over 2013.

If the buy-to-rent market does lose momentum, then Rent-Range has other customers to fall back on. For example, some credit card companies have begun using RentRange's predictions to evaluate applicants' creditworthiness.

*Sources:* Compiled from "Looking to Buy to Rent?" *The Melton Times*, March 8, 2014; J. Gittelsohn and H. Perlberg, "Goldman Sachs Said to Lead American Homes 4 Rent Bond Deal," *Bloomberg BusinessWeek*, January 29, 2014; "PRAXIS Launches Fourth Single Family Home 'Buy to Rent' Fund," *PR Web*, January 23, 2014; D. Bloomquist, "Foreclosure Auction Discounts Shrinking under Buy-to-Rent Spotlight," *Forbes*, December 20, 2013; "Blackstone Establishes Single-Family Buy-to-Rent Lending Platform," *Blackstone Group*, November 15, 2013; "Single Family Homes as Rentals Remains a Viable Investment," *National Mortgage Professional*, September 9, 2013; K. Weise and H. Perlberg, "The Data King of the Rental Market," *Bloomberg BusinessWeek*, May 6–12, 2013; T. Durden, "Is the 'Buy to Rent' Party Over?" *Zerohedge*, March 18, 2013; *www.rentrange.com*, accessed March 8, 2015.

### Questions

1. What additional sources of data could RentRange collect to enhance its predictive accuracy? Provide examples to support your answer.
2. What other companies or institutions could utilize RentRange's predictions?

## The Manager's Job and Decision Making

To appreciate how information systems support managers, you first must understand the manager's job. Managers do many things, depending on their position in the organization, the type and size of the organization, the organization's policies and culture, and the personalities of the managers themselves. Despite these variations, however, all managers perform three basic roles (Mintzberg, 1973):[1]

1. *Interpersonal roles:* figurehead, leader, liaison
2. *Informational roles:* monitor, disseminator, spokesperson, analyzer
3. *Decisional roles:* entrepreneur, disturbance handler, resource allocator, negotiator

---

[1] Mintzberg, H. (1973) *The Nature of Managerial Work*, Harper & Row, New York.

Early information systems primarily supported the informational roles. In recent years, however, information systems have been developed that support all three roles. In this chapter, you will focus on the support that IT can provide for decisional roles.

A **decision** refers to a choice among two or more alternatives that individuals and groups make. Decisions are diverse and are made continuously. Decision making is a systematic process. Economist Herbert Simon (1977)[2] described decision making as composed of three major phases: intelligence, design, and choice. Once the choice is made, the decision is implemented. Figure 12.1 illustrates this process, highlighting the tasks that are in each phase. Note that there is a continuous flow of information from intelligence, to design, to choice (bold lines). At any phase, however, there may be a return to a previous phase (broken lines).

This model of decision making is quite general. Undoubtedly, you have made decisions where you did not construct a model of the situation, validate your model with test data, or conduct a sensitivity analysis. The model we present here is intended to encompass *all* of the conditions that might occur when making a decision. For some decisions, some steps or phrases may be minimal, implicit (understood), or completely absent.

**FIGURE 12.1** The process and phases in decision making.

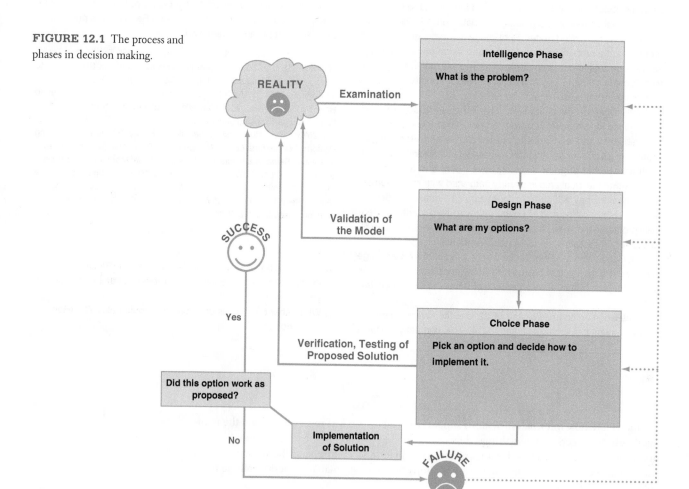

[2] Simon, H.A. (1997) *The New Science of Management Decision*, Prentice-Hall, Englewood Cliffs, NJ.

The decision-making process starts with the *intelligence phase*, in which managers examine a situation and then identify and define the problem or opportunity. In the *design phase*, decision makers construct a model for addressing the situation. They perform this task by making assumptions that simplify reality and by expressing the relationships among all of the relevant variables. Managers then validate the model by using test data. Finally, decision makers set criteria for evaluating all of the potential solutions that are proposed. The *choice phase* involves selecting a solution or course of action that seems best suited to resolve the problem. This solution (the decision) is then implemented. Implementation is successful if the proposed solution solves the problem or seizes the opportunity. If the solution fails, then the process returns to the previous phases. Computer-based decision support assists managers in the decision-making process.

## Why Managers Need IT Support

Making good decisions is very difficult without solid information. Information is vital for each phase and activity in the decision-making process. Even when information is available, however, decision making is difficult due to the following trends:

- The *number of alternatives* is constantly *increasing*, due to innovations in technology, improved communications, the development of global markets, and the use of the Internet and e-business. A key to good decision making is to explore and compare many relevant alternatives. The greater the number of alternatives, the more a decision maker needs computer-assisted searches and comparisons.

- Most decisions must be made *under time pressure*. It often is not possible to manually process information fast enough to be effective.

- Due to increased uncertainty in the decision environment, decisions are becoming more complex. It is usually necessary to *conduct a sophisticated analysis* in order to make a good decision.

- It is often necessary to rapidly access remote information, consult with experts, or conduct a group decision-making session, all without incurring major expenses. Decision makers, as well as the information they need to access, can be situated in different locations. Bringing everything together quickly and inexpensively represents a serious challenge.

These trends create major difficulties for decision makers. Fortunately, as you will see throughout this chapter, a computerized analysis can be of enormous help.

## What Information Technologies are Available to Support Managers?

In addition to discovery, communication, and collaboration tools (Chapter 6) that indirectly support decision making, several other information technologies have been successfully used to support managers. As you saw earlier, these technologies are collectively referred to as *business intelligence*. BI is closely linked to data warehousing, which provides the data needed for BI. You will now learn about additional aspects of decision making that place our discussion of BI in context. First, you will look at the different types of decisions that managers face.

## A Framework for Computerized Decision Analysis

To better understand BI, note that various types of decisions can be placed along two major dimensions: problem structure and the nature of the decision (Gorry and Scott Morton, 1971).[3] Figure 12.2 provides an overview of decision making along these two dimensions.

---

[3] Gorry, G.A. and Scott Morton, M. (1971) "A Framework for Management Information Systems," *Sloan Management Review*, Fall, 21–36.

| | Operational Control | Management Control | Strategic Planning | IS Support |
|---|---|---|---|---|
| **Structured** | Accounts receivable, order entry <br><br> **1** | Budget analysis, short-term forecasting, personnel reports, make-or-buy analysis <br> **2** | **3** | MIS, statistical models (management science, financial, etc.) |
| **Semistructured** | Production scheduling, inventory control <br><br> **4** | Credit evaluation, budget preparation, plant layout, project scheduling, reward systems design <br> **5** | Building a new plant, mergers and acquisitions, planning (product, quality assurance, compensation, etc.) <br> **6** | Decision support systems, business intelligence |
| **Unstructured** | **7** | Negotiating, recruiting an executive, buying hardware, lobbying <br><br> **8** | New technology development, product R&D, social responsibility planning <br> **9** | Decision support systems, expert systems, enterprise resource planning, neural networks, business intelligence, big data |

**FIGURE 12.2** Decision support framework. Technology is used to support the decisions shown in the column at the far right and in the bottom row.

**Problem Structure.** The first dimension is *problem structure*, where decision-making processes fall along a continuum ranging from highly structured to highly unstructured (see the left column in Figure 12.2). *Structured decisions* deal with routine and repetitive problems for which standard solutions exist, such as inventory control. In a structured decision, the first three phases of the decision process—intelligence, design, and choice—are laid out in a particular sequence, and the procedures for obtaining the best (or at least a good enough) solution are known. Two basic criteria used to evaluate proposed solutions are minimizing costs and maximizing profits. These types of decisions are candidates for decision automation.

At the other extreme of complexity are *unstructured decisions*. These decisions are intended to deal with "fuzzy," complex problems for which there are no cut-and-dried solutions. An unstructured decision is one in which there is no standardized procedure for carrying out any of the three phases. In making such a decision, human intuition and judgment often play an important role. Typical unstructured decisions include planning new service offerings, hiring an executive, and choosing a set of research and development (R&D) projects for the coming year. Although BI cannot make unstructured decisions, it can provide information that assists decision makers.

Located between structured and unstructured decisions are *semistructured* decisions, in which only some of the decision process phases are structured. Semistructured decisions require a combination of standard solution procedures and individual judgment. Examples of semistructured decisions are evaluating employees, setting marketing budgets for consumer products, performing capital acquisition analysis, and trading bonds.

**The Nature of Decisions.** The second dimension of decision support deals with the *nature of decisions*. All managerial decisions fall into one of three broad categories:

1. *Operational control*: Executing specific tasks efficiently and effectively.
2. *Management control*: Acquiring and using resources efficiently in accomplishing organizational goals.
3. *Strategic planning*: The long-range goals and policies for growth and resource allocation.

These categories are displayed along the top row of Figure 12.2.

Note that strategic decisions define the context in which management control decisions are made. In turn, management control decisions define the context in which operational control decisions are made.

**The Decision Matrix.** The three primary classes of problem structure and the three broad categories of the nature of decisions can be combined in a decision support matrix that consists of nine cells, as diagrammed in Figure 12.2. Lower level managers usually perform the tasks in cells 1, 2, and 4. The tasks in cell 5 are usually the responsibility of middle managers and professional staff. Finally, the tasks in cells 6, 8, and 9 are generally carried out by senior executives.

**Computer Support for Structured Decisions.** Examples of computer support that might be used for the nine cells in the matrix are displayed in the right-hand column and the bottom row of Figure 12.2. Structured and some semistructured decisions, especially of the operational and management control type, have been supported by computers since the 1950s. Decisions of this type are made in all functional areas, but particularly in finance and operations management.

Problems that lower-level managers encounter on a regular basis typically have a high level of structure. Examples are capital budgeting (e.g., replacing equipment), allocating resources, distributing merchandise, and controlling inventory. For each type of structured decision, prescribed solutions have been developed, which often include mathematical formulas. This approach is called *management science* or *operations research*, and it also is executed with the aid of computers.

# before you go on...

1. Describe the decision-making process proposed by Simon.
2. You are registering for classes next semester. Apply the decision-making process to your decision about how many and which courses to take. Is your decision structured, semistructured, or unstructured?
3. Consider your decision-making process when registering for classes next semester. Explain how information technology supports (or does not support) each phase of this process.

# What is Business Intelligence?

12.2

To provide users with access to corporate data, many organizations are implementing data warehouses and data marts, which you learned about in Chapter 5. Users analyze the data in warehouses and marts using a wide variety of BI tools. Many vendors offer integrated packages of these tools under the overall label of *business intelligence software*. Major BI software vendors include SAS (*www.sas.com*), Hyperion (*www.hyperion.com*, now owned by Oracle), Business Objects (*www.businessobjects.com*, now owned by SAP), Information Builders (*www.informationbuilders.com*), SPSS (*www.spss.com*, now owned by IBM), and Cognos (*www.ibm.com/cognos*).

As you have seen, BI is vital to modern decision making and organizational performance. Let's consider in greater detail the technical foundation for BI and the variety of ways that BI can be used. (Recall our earlier discussion contrasting BI and business analytics, and that we are using the terms interchangeably throughout this chapter.)

The phrase *business intelligence* is relatively new. Business and IT analyst Howard Dresner coined the term in 1989 while he was an analyst at Gartner, a market research firm. The expression is especially popular in industry, where it is used as an umbrella term that encompasses all decision support applications.

BI encompasses not only applications, but also technologies and processes. It includes both "getting data in" (to a data mart or warehouse) and "getting data out" (through BI applications).

In addition, a significant change is taking place within the BI environment. In the past, organizations used BI only to support management. Today, however, BI applications are increasingly available to front-line personnel (e.g., call center operators), suppliers, customers, and even regulators. These groups rely on BI to provide them with the most current information.

## The Scope of Business Intelligence

The use of BI in organizations varies considerably. In smaller organizations, BI may be limited to Excel spreadsheets. In larger ones, BI often is enterprisewide, and it includes applications such as data mining/predictive analytics, dashboards, and data visualization. It is important to recognize that the importance of BI to organizations continues to grow. In fact, it is not an exaggeration to assert that for many firms, BI is now a requirement for competing in the marketplace, as is illustrated in IT's About Business 12.2.

Not all organizations use BI in the same way. For example, some organizations employ only one or a few applications, whereas others utilize enterprisewide BI. In this section, you will examine three specific BI targets that represent different levels of change:

- The development of one or a few related BI applications
- The development of infrastructure to support enterprisewide BI
- Support for organizational transformation

These targets differ in terms of their focus; scope; level of sponsorship, commitment, and required resources; technical architecture; impact on personnel and business processes; and benefits.

**The Development of One or a Few Related BI Applications.** This BI target often is a point solution for a departmental need, such as campaign management in marketing. Sponsorship, approval, funding, impacts, and benefits typically occur at the departmental level. For this target, organizations usually create a data mart to store the necessary data. Organizations must be careful that the data mart—an "independent" application—does not become a "data silo" that stores data that are inconsistent with, and cannot be integrated with, data used elsewhere in the organization.

**The Development of Infrastructure to Support Enterprisewide BI.** This BI target supports both current and future BI needs. A crucial component of BI at this level is an enterprise data warehouse. Because it is an enterprisewide initiative, senior management often provides sponsorship, approval, and funding. In addition, the impacts and benefits are felt throughout the organization.

An example of this target is the 3M Corporation. Traditionally, 3M's various divisions had operated independently, using separate decision support platforms. Not only was this arrangement costly, but it prevented 3M from integrating the data and presenting a "single face" to its customers. For example, sales representatives did not know whether or how business customers were interacting with other 3M divisions. The solution was to develop an enterprise data warehouse that enabled 3M to operate as an integrated company. As an added benefit, the costs of implementing this system were offset by savings resulting from the consolidation of the various platforms.

**Support for Organizational Transformation.** With this target, a company uses BI to fundamentally transform the ways it competes in the marketplace. BI supports a new business model, and it enables the business strategy. Because of the scope and importance of these changes, critical elements such as sponsorship, approval, and funding originate at the highest organizational levels. The impact on personnel and processes can be significant, and the benefits accrue across the organization.

# IT's [about business]

## 12.2 Predicting Airplane Arrivals More Accurately

Air travelers are accustomed to long flight delays and cancellations for any number of reasons. Few customers realize that airlines themselves are not particularly accurate at predicting when a flight will arrive at its destination even when it is ready to leave the gate. Making a pinpoint-accurate prediction on gate arrival times is notoriously tricky, because many factors alter flight times. Weather and wind are the most common, but there are also ground issues, such as the passenger who neglects to board his flight on time, forcing the airline to delay departure while they offload his luggage. As a result, airline predictions are off by an average of seven minutes across the industry.

Flights normally operate according to a flight plan put together a few hours in advance of a flight's scheduled departure. After the flight takes off it is tracked by a dispatcher, who may be monitoring 15 flights simultaneously. So, for example, if headwinds increase, then the pilot must talk to a dispatcher, who may decide to reprogram the "cost index" of the flight, revise the flight plan, and give permission to the pilot to pick up speed (and therefore use more fuel) to arrive on time.

Airlines have been looking to automate these kinds of processes to save costs and also to provide travelers with a better flying experience. Gary Beck, vice president of flight operations for Alaska Airlines, maintains that airlines need to eliminate the human part of these communications in favor of automation.

To encourage this process, Alaska Airlines (*www.alaskaair.com*) and General Electric (GE) (*www.ge.com*) sponsored a Flight Quest contest aimed at developing an algorithm that could help airlines better predict flight arrival times and reduce passenger delays. The contest, which was set up on the contest Web site Kaggle (*www.kaggle.com*), provided contestants with two months of flight data, such as arrivals, departures, weather, and latitudes and longitudes along the routes. Such data are typically not available to the public because they are owned by the airlines and manufacturers.

A team from Singapore won the contest and the $100,000 prize. The winning algorithm produced flight arrival estimates that were nearly 40 percent more accurate than existing estimates. The algorithm could help airlines reduce gate congestion, manage crews more efficiently, and save travelers up to five minutes at the gate. Each minute saved in a flight saves $1.2 million in annual crew costs and $5 million in annual fuel savings for a midsized airline.

A second Flight Quest contest, with a $250,000 prize, challenged data scientists to determine the most efficient flight routes, speeds, and altitudes at any moment, taking into account variables such as weather, wind, and airspace constraints. The winning model proved to be up to 12 percent more efficient when compared with data from past actual flights.

GE plans to develop software and services that incorporate the results of the two Flight Quest contests. It is important to note that GE's goal is not to replace pilot decisions, but to create smart assistants for pilots.

It may take some time, however, before software can be used to fundamentally change how commercial flights operate. For example, Alaska Airlines, which frequently lands planes under difficult weather conditions, has pioneered the use of satellite navigation, as opposed to relying on ground-based instruments. The use of satellite navigation lowers the standard minimum elevations for a plane's approach upon landing. The airline is working with the U.S. Federal Aviation Administration to spread the technique, which also saves fuel, to the lower 48 states. Beck claims that the greatest challenge has been to alter the practices and official handbooks of air traffic controllers, who would no longer need to tell planes where and when to turn. He maintains that satellite navigation systems essentially transform air traffic controllers into air traffic monitors.

*Sources:* Compiled from "Alaska Airlines Could Be Set to Soar," *Nasdaq.com*, January 27, 2014; "How Data Geeks Could Save the Airlines Millions – And Get You Home Quicker," *Bloomberg BusinessWeek*, May 7, 2013; R. Boyle, "Invented: A Much Better Way to Predict Airline Delays," *Popular Science*, April 4, 2013; "GE Flight Quest: Winners Use Algorithms on Flight Data to Help Reduce Delays," *FlightStats*, April 4, 2013; J. Novet, "On Kaggle, GE Finds Data Science Solutions for Patients and Pilots," *GigaOM*, April 3, 2013; J. Leber, "A Data-Crunching Prize to Cut Flight Delays," *MIT Technology Review*, April 3, 2013; J. Bruner, "New Data Competition Tackles Airline Delays," *O'Reilly Radar*, November 29, 2012; *www.ge.com*, *www.alaskaair.com*, *www.kaggle.com*, accessed March 8, 2015.

### Questions
1. Do you think that satellite-based navigation will meet resistance among air traffic controllers? Why or why not?
2. Do you think that pilots will object to having "smart assistants" help them make decisions? Why or why not?
3. Do you think the overall response of the airlines to satellite-based navigation and smart assistants for pilots will be positive or negative? Support your answer.
4. What is the relationship between analytics and smart assistants for pilots?

---

This BI target is closely aligned with corporate performance management. **Corporate performance management (CPM)** is involved with monitoring and managing an organization's performance according to *key performance indicators* (KPIs) such as revenue, return on investment, overhead, and operational costs. For online businesses, CPM includes additional factors such as the number of page views, server load, network traffic, and transactions per second. BI applications allow managers and analysts to analyze data to obtain valuable information and insights concerning the organization's KPIs. This chapter's closing case demonstrates how social sentiment analysis is impacting the performance of two entire industries: the motion picture industry and the television industry. (*Sentiment analysis* refers to the use of natural language processing, text analysis, machine learning, and statistics to identify and extract subjective information in source materials.)

Harrah's Entertainment (a brand of Caesars Entertainment; *www.caesars.com*) provides another good example of this BI target. Harrah's developed a customer loyalty program known as *Total Rewards*. To implement the program, Harrah's created a BI infrastructure (a data warehouse) that collected data from casino, hotel, and special event systems (e.g., wine-tasting weekends) across all the various customer touchpoints (e.g., slot machines, table games, and Internet). Harrah's utilized these data to reward loyal customers and to reach out to them in personal and appealing ways, such as through promotional offers. These efforts helped the company to become a leader in the gaming industry. IT's About Business 12.3 illustrates how Cardlytics uses analytics to predict customer behavior so that merchants can present targeted offers to them through the banks that issue their credit and debit cards.

In Chapter 5, you studied the basics of data warehouses and data marts. In this section, you have seen how important data warehouses and marts are to the different ways that organizations use BI. In the next section, you will learn how the user community can analyze the data in warehouses and marts, how the results of these analyses are presented to users, and how organizations can use the results of these analyses.

# IT's [about business]

## **12.3** Cardlytics Analyzes Customer Buying Behaviors

Card swipe data used to be an untapped source of data for banks. Banks wanted to use that data to increase their revenues and to attract loyalty by targeting deals to their customers. They needed a "middleman," however, to analyze the data and actually deliver the offers.

Many banks have selected Cardlytics (*http://cardlytics.com*) to perform this role. Cardlytics has helped pioneer a data-driven advertising niche called "merchant-funded rewards." The company collects data from the credit and debit card transactions of 70 percent of U.S. bank customers. In 2013 its systems read some 11 billion U.S. transactions, amounting to $500 billion in spending. The company's algorithms present 1 billion ads per month to more than 35 million customers on the Web sites and mobile apps of 400 banks, including Bank of America, PNC, Regents, and Lloyd's of London.

Cardlytics tracks and understands consumer buying behaviors. That is, the company targets people based on what they buy, not on who they are. Cardlytics works on the principle that if you know where and how people are spending money, then you know many things about them even if you can't access their personally identifying information. For example, if a woman is going to McDonald's and then to Target and finally to Babies "R" Us, then she likely is a young mother. Likewise, a man who makes his purchases at bars and Taco Bell is probably single.

Merchants can utilize Cardlytics data analyses based on actual customer buying behaviors to present precisely targeted, relevant advertisements to clients of financial institutions. These ads also include offers to participate in merchant rewards programs. Offers

are distributed via secure bank channels including online banking, mobile banking, secure text, e-mail, and/or ATM machines.

Consider this example. The Sports Authority wants to connect with customers who spend more than $100 per month on sporting goods at its competitors' stores. Cardlytics serves up a Sports Authority offer to those shoppers, and Cardlytics and the banks share a commission from the merchant, typically about 10 percent of any resulting purchases.

Many critics raise privacy concerns about merchant-funded rewards. To address these concerns, the banks prohibit Cardlytics and its competitors from moving data off banks' servers. In fact, banks do not ever share individual customer information with Cardlytics or the merchants. Further, there are limits to what Cardlytics can know or wants to know. The company sees only store-level data, so if customers use their bank cards at a CVS pharmacy, Cardlytics does not know whether they purchased Xanax or chewing gum. Another concern is that the success of merchant-funded rewards could prompt banks and brands to move into sensitive categories such as healthcare and gambling.

Other organizations want to access Cardlytics's analytics. For example, hedge funds want to use the firm's insights to better predict earnings. Further, Cardlytics accumulates enough data to predict whether any retailer's sales will increase or decrease for a particular quarter.

*Sources:* Compiled from E. Chemi, "How Did Americans Spend Their Gas Savings? We Now Know," *CNBC*, January 21, 2015; A. Tanner, "Reading Your Financial Footprints, " *Forbes*, December 16, 2013; D. Gardner, "Cardlytics on HP Vertica Powers Millions of Swiftly Tailored Marketing Offers to Bank Card Customers, " *BriefingsDirect*, November 13, 2013; "Merchant-Funded Rewards Have a Bright Future with U.S. Consumers, Says Auriemma Consulting Group, " *Globe News Wire*, November 12, 2013; P. Britt, "Merchant-Funded Loyalty Programs Poised for Growth, " *Loyalty360. org*, September 6, 2012; S. Zhen, "US Bank Offers Merchant-Funded Rewards via FreeMonee, "*mybanktracker.com*, April 13, 2012; *http://cardlytics.com,* accessed March 4, 2015.

**Questions**

1. Discuss the advantages and disadvantages of Cardlytics's data analyses for the customer. Use specific examples in your answers.
2. Discuss the advantages and disadvantages of Cardlytics's data analyses for the merchants. Use specific examples in your answers.

## before you go on...

1. Define BI.
2. Discuss the breadth of support provided by BI applications to organizational employees.
3. Identify and discuss the three basic targets of BI.

# Business Intelligence Applications for Data Analysis

**12.3**

A good strategy to study the ways in which organizations use business intelligence applications is to consider how the users analyze data, how they present the results of their analyses, and how managers and executives (who can also be users) implement these results. Recall from Chapter 5 that the data are stored in a data warehouse or data mart. The user community analyzes these data employing a variety of BI applications. The results of these analyses can be presented to users via other BI applications. Finally, managers and executives put the overall results to good use. You will become familiar with data analysis, data presentation, and data use in the next three sections.

A variety of BI applications for analyzing data are available. They include multidimensional analysis (also called *online analytical processing*, or *OLAP*), data mining, and decision support systems.

## Multidimensional Analysis or Online Analytical Processing

Some BI applications include **online analytical processing**, also referred to as **multidimensional analysis** capabilities. OLAP involves "slicing and dicing" data stored in a dimensional format, drilling down in the data to greater detail, and aggregating the data.

Consider our example from Chapter 5. Recall Figure 5.6 illustrating the data cube. The product is on the *x*-axis, geography is on the *y*-axis, and time is on the *z*-axis. Now, suppose you want to know how many nuts the company sold in the West region in 2012. You would slice and dice the cube, using *nuts* as the specific measure for product, *West* as the measure for geography, and *2012* as the measure for time. The value or values that remain in the cell(s) after our slicing and dicing is (are) the answer to our question. As an example of drilling down, you also might want to know how many nuts were sold in January 2012. Alternatively, you might want to know how many nuts were sold during 2011–2013, which is an example of aggregation, also called "rollup."

## Data Mining

**Data mining** refers to the process of searching for valuable business information in a large database, data warehouse, or data mart. Data mining can perform two basic operations: (1) predicting trends and behaviors, and (2) identifying previously unknown patterns. BI applications typically provide users with a view of what has happened; data mining helps to explain *why* it is happening, and it predicts what will happen in the future.

Regarding the first operation, data mining automates the process of finding predictive information in large databases. Questions that traditionally required extensive hands-on analysis now can be answered directly and quickly from the data. For example, *targeted marketing* relies on predictive information. Data mining can use data from past promotional mailings to identify those prospects who are most likely to respond favorably to future mailings. Another business problem that uses predictive information is the forecasting of bankruptcy and other forms of default.

Data mining can also identify previously hidden patterns in a single step. For example, it can analyze retail sales data to discover seemingly unrelated products that people often purchase together. The classic example is beer and diapers. Data mining found that young men tend to buy beer and diapers at the same time when shopping at convenience stores.

One significant pattern-discovery operation is detecting fraudulent credit card transactions. Over time a pattern emerges of the typical ways you use your credit card and your typical shopping behaviors—the places in which you use your card, the amounts you spend, and so on. If your card is stolen and used fraudulently, then the usage often varies noticeably from your established pattern. Data mining tools can discern this difference and bring the issue to your attention.

Numerous data mining applications are used in business and in other fields. According to a Gartner report (*www.gartner.com*), most Fortune 1000 companies worldwide currently use data mining, as the following representative examples illustrate. Note that in most cases, the purpose of data mining is to identify a business opportunity in order to create a sustainable competitive advantage.

- *Retailing and sales:* Predicting sales, preventing theft and fraud, and determining correct inventory levels and distribution schedules among outlets. For example, retailers such as AAFES (stores on military bases) use Fraud Watch from SAP (*www.sap.com*) to combat fraud by employees in their 1,400 stores.

- *Banking:* Forecasting levels of bad loans and fraudulent credit card use, predicting credit card spending by new customers, and determining which kinds of customers will best respond to (and qualify for) new loan offers.

- *Manufacturing and production:* Predicting machinery failures, and finding key factors that help optimize manufacturing capacity.

- *Insurance:* Forecasting claim amounts and medical coverage costs, classifying the most important elements that affect medical coverage, and predicting which customers will buy new insurance policies.

- *Policework:* Tracking crime patterns, locations, and criminal behavior; identifying attributes to assist in solving criminal cases. Several cities have teamed up with IBM to analyze crime history and to strategically deploy police officers. Memphis, which reduced its crime rate by 14 percent in 2013, employed this system. Chicago adopted the "predictive policing" system in 2013 in hopes of reducing the city's 500 homicides in 2012. Chicago reported 415 homicides in 2013, but there is disagreement about the causes of the decrease.

- *Healthcare:* Correlating demographics of patients with critical illnesses, and developing better insights on how to identify and treat symptoms and their causes. In March 2013, Microsoft and Stanford University announced that they had mined the search data of millions of users to successfully identify unreported side effects of certain medications.

- *Marketing:* Classifying customer demographics that can be used to predict which customers will respond to a mailing or buy a particular product.

- *Politics:* In his FiveThirtyEight blog, Nate Silver famously analyzed polling and economic data to predict the results of the 2008 presidential election, calling 49 out of 50 states correctly. He then correctly predicted all 50 states in the 2012 presidential election.

- *Weather:* The National Weather Service is predicting weather with increasing accuracy and precision.

- *Higher education:* Desire2Learn (*www.desire2learn.com*) provides an application called Degree Compass that recommends courses based on students' majors, transcripts, and past course success rates. In March 2013, Degree Compass reported a 92 percent accuracy rate across four universities in predicting the grade that a student would receive in a course.

- *Social good:* Datakind (*www.datakind.org*) is an organization that serves as a bridge between social and "mission-driven" organizations that require assistance in interpreting their data and data scientists who provide their talents, usually for free, for noncommercial purposes. For example, Datakind has collaborated with the Sunlight Foundation (*www.sunlightfoundation.com*) in the United States to explore the influence of lobbyists on legislators. This type of research has been conducted before. Nevertheless, by gathering enormous amounts of data—congressional votes, fundraisers, parties, donations, and all of the House of Representatives transcripts going back to the early 1800s—analysts have far more potential to explore and expose relevant issues.

## Decision Support Systems

**Decision support systems (DSSs)** combine models and data to analyze semistructured problems and some unstructured problems that involve extensive user involvement. **Models** are simplified representations, or abstractions, of reality. DSSs enable business managers and analysts to access data interactively, to manipulate these data, and to conduct appropriate analyses.

Decision support systems can enhance learning and contribute to all levels of decision making. DSSs also employ mathematical models. Finally, they have the related capabilities of sensitivity analysis, what–if analysis, and goal-seeking analysis, which you will learn about next. You should keep in mind that these three types of analysis are useful for any type of decision support application. Excel, for example, supports all three.

**Sensitivity Analysis.**   *Sensitivity analysis* is the study of the impact that changes in one or more parts of a decision-making model have on other parts. Most sensitivity analyses examine the impact that changes in input variables have on output variables.

Most models include two types of input variables: decision variables and environmental variables. "What is our reorder point for these raw materials?" is a decision variable (internal to the organization). "What will the rate of inflation be?" is an environmental variable (external to the organization). The output in this example is the total cost of raw materials. Companies generally perform a sensitivity analysis to determine the impact of environmental variables on the result of the analysis.

Sensitivity analysis is extremely valuable because it enables the system to adapt to changing conditions and to the varying requirements of different decision-making situations. It provides a better understanding of the model as well as of the problem that the model purports to describe.

**What–If Analysis.**   A model builder must make predictions and assumptions regarding the input data, many of which are based on the assessment of uncertain futures. The results depend on the accuracy of these assumptions, which can be highly subjective. *What–if analysis* attempts to predict the impact of a change in the assumptions (input data) on the proposed solution. For example, what will happen to the total inventory cost *if* the originally assumed cost of carrying inventories is 12 percent rather than 10 percent? In a well-designed BI system, managers themselves can interactively ask the computer these types of questions as often as they need to.

**Goal-Seeking Analysis.**   *Goal-seeking analysis* represents a "backward" solution approach. It attempts to calculate the value of the inputs necessary to achieve a desired level of output. For example, let's say that an initial BI analysis predicted a profit of $2 million. Management might want to know what sales volume would be necessary to generate a profit of $3 million. To find out, they would perform a goal-seeking analysis.

The managers, however, cannot simply press a button labeled "increase sales." Instead, the company will need to take certain actions to bring about the sales increase. Options include lowering prices, increasing funding for research and development, paying the sales force a higher commission rate, enhancing the advertising program, and, of course, implementing some combination of these actions. Whatever actions the company chooses, they will cost money, and the goal-seeking analysis must take this fact into account.

# before you go on...

1. Describe multidimensional analysis.
2. What are the two basic operations of data mining?
3. What is the purpose of decision support systems?

## 12.4 Business Intelligence Applications for Presenting Results

The results of the types of data analyses you just learned about can be presented with dashboards and data visualization technologies. Today, users are increasingly relying on data that are real time or almost real time. Therefore, you also study real-time BI in this section.

### Dashboards

**Dashboards** evolved from executive information systems, which were information systems designed specifically for the information needs of top executives. Today, however, many employees, business partners, and customers can use digital dashboards.

A dashboard provides easy access to timely information and direct access to management reports. It is user friendly, it is supported by graphics, and, most importantly, it enables managers to examine exception reports and drill down into detailed data. Table 12.1 summarizes the various capabilities common to many dashboards. Moreover, some of the capabilities discussed in this section have been incorporated into many BI products, as illustrated in Figure 12.3.

One outstanding example of a dashboard is the Bloomberg Terminal. Bloomberg LP (*www.bloomberg.com*), a privately held company, provides a subscription service that sells financial data, software to analyze these data, trading tools, and news (electronic, print, TV, and radio). All of this information is accessible through a color-coded Bloomberg keyboard that displays the desired information on a computer screen, either the user's screen or one that Bloomberg provides. Users can also set up their own computers to access the service without a Bloomberg keyboard. The subscription service plus the keyboard is called the Bloomberg Terminal. It

**Table 12.1**
**The Capabilities of Dashboards**

| Capability | Description |
|---|---|
| Drill down | The ability to go to details, at several levels; it can be done by a series of menus or by clicking on a drillable portion of the screen |
| Critical success factors (CSFs) | The factors most critical for the success of business. These can be organizational, industry, departmental, or for individual workers |
| Key performance indicators | The specific measures of CSFs |
| Status access | The latest data available on KPI or some other metric, often in real time |
| Trend analysis | Short-, medium-, and long-term trend of KPIs or metrics, which are projected using forecasting methods |
| Exception reporting | Reports that highlight deviations larger than certain thresholds. Reports may include only deviations |

literally represents a do-it-yourself dashboard, because users can customize their information feeds as well as the look and feel of those feeds (see Figure 12.4).

In another example, a human resources dashboard/scorecard developed by iDashboards, one of the leading BI software vendors. At a glance, users can see employee productivity, hours,

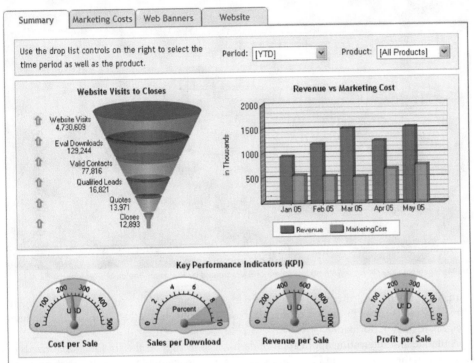

**FIGURE 12.3** Sample performance dashboard.

Image courtesy of Dundas Data Visualization, Inc., 2014 (*www.dundas.com*).

**FIGURE 12.4** A Bloomberg terminal.

Carlos Osario/Zuma Press.

**FIGURE 12.5** Management Cockpit.

The Management Cockpit is a registered trademark of SAP, created by Professor Patrick M. Georges.

team, department, and division performance in graphical, tabular, summary, and detailed form. The selector box to the left enables the user to easily change between specific analyses to compare their performance.

A unique and interesting application of dashboards to support the informational needs of executives is the Management Cockpit. Essentially, a Management Cockpit is a strategic management room containing an elaborate set of dashboards that enable top-level decision makers to pilot their businesses better. The goal is to create an environment that encourages more efficient management meetings and boosts team performance via effective communication. To help achieve this goal, the dashboard graphically displays KPIs and information relating to critical success factors on the walls of a meeting room called the *Management Cockpit Room* (see Figure 12.5). The cockpit-like arrangement of instrument panels and displays helps managers visualize how all of the different factors in the business interrelate.

Within the room, the four walls are designated by color: Black, Red, Blue, and White. The Black Wall displays the principal success factors and financial indicators. The Red Wall measures market performance. The Blue Wall projects the performance of internal processes and employees. Finally, the White Wall indicates the status of strategic projects. The Flight Deck, a six-screen, high-end PC, enables executives to drill down to detailed information. External information needed for competitive analyses can easily be imported into the room.

Board members and other executives hold meetings in the Management Cockpit Room. Managers also meet there with the comptroller to discuss current business issues. The Management Cockpit can implement various what–if scenarios for this purpose. It also provides a common basis for information and communication. Finally, it supports efforts to translate a corporate strategy into concrete activities by identifying performance indicators.

## Data Visualization Technologies

After data have been processed, they can be presented to users in visual formats such as text, graphics, and tables. This process, known as *data visualization*, makes IT applications more attractive and understandable to users. Data visualization is becoming increasingly popular on the Web for decision support. A variety of visualization methods and software packages that support decision making are available. Two particularly valuable applications are geographic information systems and reality mining.

**Geographic Information Systems.** A **geographic information system (GIS)** is a computer-based system for capturing, integrating, manipulating, and displaying data using digitized maps. Its most distinguishing characteristic is that every record or digital object has an identified geographical location. This process, called *geocoding*, enables users to generate information for planning, problem solving, and decision making. In addition, the graphical format makes it easy for managers to visualize the data.

Today, relatively inexpensive, fully functional PC-based GIS packages are readily available. Representative GIS software vendors are ESRI (*www.esri.com*), Intergraph (*www.intergraph.com*), and Pitney Bowes MapInfo (now Pitney Bowes Business Insight; *www.pbinsight.com/welcome/mapinfo*). In addition, both government sources and private vendors provide diversified commercial GIS data. Some of these GIS packages are free, for example, downloadable material from the Environmental Systems Research Institute (ESRI) (*www.esri.com*) and *http://data.geocomm.com*. There are countless applications of GISs to improve decision making in both the public and private sectors. IT's About Business 12.4 focuses on ESRI and illustrates the many uses of GIS. The following example shows how ESRI impacts a huge number of organizations.

# IT's [about business]

## 12.4 Geographic Information Systems Have Many Uses

Founded as the Environmental Systems Research Institute in 1969, ESRI (*www.esri.com*) is an international supplier of geographic information system software and geodatabase management applications. Industry analysts estimate that about 70 percent of GIS users employ ESRI products, particularly one called ArcGIS. Organizations use ArcGIS for many reasons:

- Create and use maps
- Compile geographic data
- Analyze mapped information
- Discover and share geographic information
- Utilize maps and geographic information across a wide range of applications
- Manage geographic information in a database

Essentially, ESRI makes GIS available to people to solve real problems. Let's consider some of the applications where ESRI products are being utilized:

- Consider this scenario, in which a park ranger uses ESRI's ArcGIS software tool. A hiker is missing on one of the trails in a national park. As the head park ranger, your job is to lead a search-and-rescue mission to find him. Sunset is approaching, and in some parts of the park the temperature will fall below freezing in a few hours. What do you do?

Many experienced hikers know that the recommended course of action when you are lost is to follow a stream downhill, which should eventually lead to civilization. However, you cannot assume that the missing hiker is aware of this. He might stay put, or, if he has a phone, he might move *uphill* to find a signal. You also do not know if he is injured.

You open ArcGIS on your computer, and a computer map of the park appears on the screen. You also have access to a database of records from 30,000 lost hiker search-and-rescue missions. You query the database and learn that 66 percent of lost hikers are found within two miles of the spot where they were last seen. You draw a ring on your map reflecting this two-mile perimeter. You then learn that 52 percent of lost hikers are found downhill. You impose an elevation limit on the area with all of the land above the last point seen shaded in one color and the land beneath it shaded in a different color.

Again querying the database, you discover that lost hikers usually quit walking after about three hours. You can now create a predictive model, which describes a priority list of places to search for the lost hiker. When you run the model through ArcGIS, the software provides three concentric circles depicting the hiker's most likely location. The inner circle is the hiker's most likely location, and so on.

Next, you share this map with the public, targeting people who mentioned on Twitter and Facebook that they would be hiking in the park that day. You enable these people to place points on the map where they saw something that might be a clue, such as an article of clothing. You take anything they mention and add it to your predictive model. ArcGIS then produces a new map with new concentric circles, which gives you a reasonable chance to find the hiker before the sun sets.

- A typical utility company serving millions of customers uses GIS to manage its complex infrastructure. Specifically, it employs GIS for customer service, emergency response, electricity and/or water distribution, infrastructure maintenance, automated mapping, network tracing, flow or power analysis, and other aspects of engineering, operations, administration, and finance.

- An irrigation district serves thousands of farmers and maintains hundreds of miles of waterways. It uses GIS for engineering and operations.

- Officials employ GIS to draw attendance boundaries for public schools. For example, a city has to build a new elementary school because the number of elementary-school-aged children has increased. School boards use GIS at public meetings to present the new boundaries to parents.

- Cities use GIS to manage their transportation infrastructures. GIS supports planning, inventory, design, construction, operations, and maintenance.

- More than 80 percent of the information used to manage road, rail, and port facilities has a spatial component. Therefore, facility managers use GIS to design and operate these facilities.

- The telecommunications industry is deploying new broadband networks. The industry utilizes GIS to support the design, implementation, and management of the new network infrastructure.

- GIS is used for the management of coastal resources, including shoreline, aquatic, and terrestrial habitats and biological resources. With GIS and the appropriate scientific database, coastal erosion can be better understood and managed.

- Restaurant companies use GIS to help select optimal locations for new outlets.

- The vast majority of information used in law enforcement is map-based. Agencies must be able to display the location of incidents and to view incidents by categories, time, or date. Advanced GIS capabilities can generate maps that law

enforcement can use to predict the probability that certain crimes will occur.

- State legislatures make extensive use of GIS to redraw congressional districts after each national census.

*Sources:* Compiled from G. Baldwin, "Geospatial Efforts Often Rely on a Single Go-Getter," *Health Data Management*, March 13, 2014; J. Stromberg, "Do You Live Within 50 Miles of a Nuclear Power Plant?" *Smithsonian Magazine*, March 13, 2014; J. Marks, "How Maps Drive Decisions at EPA," *NextGov*, March 12, 2014; "ESRI Maps Offer Geographic Perspective on Third Anniversary of Fukushima Disaster," *The American Surveyor*, March 11, 2014; B. McCann, "GIS Expands into Law Enforcement, Healthcare: ESRI Opens Up," *CivSource*, March 10, 2014; A. Wills, "Crisis in Crimea: A Story Map of the Place Everyone's Watching," *Mashable*, March 6, 2014; J. Tierney, "Mapping the Anxiety About College Admissions," *The Atlantic*, March 6, 2014; S. Postema, "The Future of Journalism: Real-Time Story Maps," *Dutch News Design*, February 27, 2014; P. Tucker, "Mapping the Future with Big Data," *The Futurist*, July/August 2013; *www.esri.com*, accessed March 9, 2015.

**Questions**

1. Describe how your university might use GIS. Provide specific examples in your answer.

2. What are potential disadvantages of GIS? Provide specific examples in your answer.

## Real-Time BI

Until recently, BI focused on the use of historical data. This focus has changed with the emergence of technology for capturing, storing, and using real-time data. Real-time BI enables users to employ multidimensional analysis, data mining, and decision support systems to analyze data in real time. In addition, it helps organizations to make decisions and to interact with customers in new ways.

Figure 12.6 presents a typical support center operations dashboard. The dashboard enables the manager to see, in greater detail, a performance overview of the support center regions as

**FIGURE 12.6** Support Center Operations Dashboard.

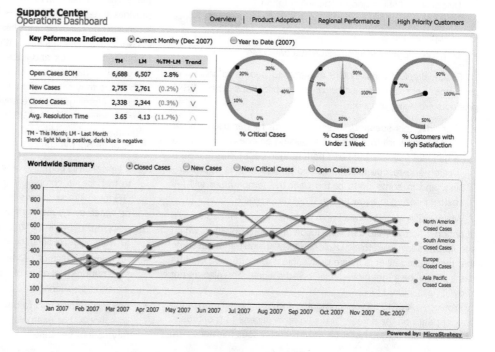

**Powered by: MicroStrategy**

well as specific support centers within those regions. The top visualization is called a micro-chart, which allows the manager to see numerous KPIs at once for all four support regions. The manager can see that all support regions have exceeded their target for cases that were closed in under one week. By selecting a specific support region, the manager can see the historical trend for the past 12 months for the KPIs through the bar chart on the bottom left. In addition, the manager can see certain performance statistics for individual support centers through the bubble chart on the bottom right.

With this dashboard, the manager can quickly understand that the New York support center has generated the most revenue in the North America region. In addition, it appears that the steps that have been taken to address customer satisfaction have been successful, as customer satisfaction has improved in the past few months. Finally, without leaving her screen, the manager can move on to an analysis of the product's performance by clicking the "Product Performance" tab in the upper right-hand corner, making for a more efficient and comprehensive performance analysis.

## before you go on...

1. What is a dashboard? Why are dashboards so valuable to employees?
2. Explain the difference between geographic information systems and reality mining, and provide examples of how each of these technologies can be used by businesses and government agencies.
3. What is real-time BI, and why is this technology valuable to an organization's managers and executives?

---

# What's In IT For Me?

### For the Accounting Major
BI is used extensively in auditing to uncover irregularities. It also is used to uncover and prevent fraud. CPAs use BI for many of their duties, ranging from risk analysis to cost control.

### For the Finance Major
People have been using computers for decades to solve financial problems. Innovative BI applications have been created for activities such as making stock market decisions, refinancing bonds, assessing debt risks, analyzing financial conditions, predicting business failures, forecasting financial trends, and investing in global markets.

### For the Marketing Major
Marketing personnel utilize BI in many applications, from planning and executing marketing campaigns, to allocating advertising budgets, to evaluating alternative routings of salespeople. New marketing approaches such as targeted marketing and database marketing depend heavily on IT in general, and on data warehouses and business intelligence applications in particular.

### For the Production/Operations Management Major
BI supports complex operations and production decisions from inventory control, to production planning, to supply chain integration.

### For the Human Resources Management Major

Human resources personnel use BI for many of their activities. For example, BI applications can find resumes of applicants posted on the Web and sort them to match needed skills and to support management succession planning.

### For the MIS Major

MIS provides the data infrastructure used in BI. MIS personnel are also involved in building, deploying, and supporting BI applications.

## [ Summary ]

1. **Identify the phases in the decision-making process, and use a decision support framework to demonstrate how technology supports managerial decision making.**

   When making a decision, either organizational or personal, the decision maker goes through a three-step process: intelligence, design, and choice. When the choice is made, the decision is implemented.

   Several information technologies have been successfully used to directly support managers. Collectively, they are referred to as *business intelligence information systems*. Figure 12.2 provides a matrix that shows how technology supports the various types of decisions that managers must make.

2. **Describe and provide examples of the three different ways in which organizations use business intelligence.**

   There are three major ways that organizations use BI:

   - The development of one or a few related BI applications. This BI target often is a point solution for a departmental need, such as campaign management in marketing. A data mart usually is created to store necessary data.

   - The development of infrastructure to support enterprisewide BI. This target supports current and future BI needs. A critical component is an enterprise data warehouse.

   - Support for organizational transformation. With this target, BI is used to fundamentally change how a company competes in the marketplace. BI supports a new business model and enables the business strategy.

3. **Specify the BI applications available to users for data analysis, and provide examples of how each one might be used to solve a business problem at your university.**

   Users have a variety of BI applications available to help them analyze data. These applications include multidimensional analysis, data mining, and decision support systems.

   Multidimensional data analysis, also called *online analytical processing*, involves "slicing and dicing" data stored in a dimensional format, drilling down to greater data detail, and aggregating data. Data mining refers to the process of searching for valuable business information in a large database, data warehouse, or data mart. Decision support systems combine models and data in an attempt to analyze semistructured and some unstructured problems with extensive user involvement. (We leave it to you to provide examples of using each application at your university.)

4. **Describe three BI applications that present the results of data analyses to users, and offer examples of how businesses and government agencies can use each of these technologies.**

A dashboard provides easy access to timely information and direct access to management reports. A geographic information system is a computer-based system for capturing, integrating, manipulating, and displaying data using digitized maps. Reality mining analyzes information extracted from the usage patterns of mobile phones and other wireless devices. (Examples of how these technologies might be used by businesses and government agencies, we leave to you.)

## [ Chapter Glossary ]

**business intelligence (BI)** A broad category of applications, technologies, and processes for gathering, storing, accessing, and analyzing data to help business users make better decisions.

**corporate performance management (CPM)** The area of business intelligence involved with monitoring and managing an organization's performance, according to key performance indicators such as revenue, return on investment, overhead, and operational costs.

**dashboard** A BI application that provides rapid access to timely information and direct access to management reports.

**data mining** The process of searching for valuable business information in a large database, data warehouse, or data mart.

**decision** A choice that individuals and groups make among two or more alternatives.

**decision support systems (DSSs)** Business intelligence systems that combine models and data in an attempt to solve semistructured and some unstructured problems with extensive user involvement.

**geographic information system (GIS)** A computer-based system for capturing, integrating, manipulating, and displaying data using digitized maps.

**management** A process by which organizational goals are achieved through the use of resources.

**model (in decision making)** A simplified representation, or abstraction, of reality.

**multidimensional data analysis** See **online analytical processing (OLAP)**.

**online analytical processing (OLAP) (or multidimensional data analysis)** A set of capabilities for "slicing and dicing" data using dimensions and measures associated with the data.

**productivity** The ratio between the inputs to a process and the outputs from that process.

**reality mining** Allows analysts to extract information from the usage patterns of mobile phones and other wireless devices.

## [ Discussion Questions ]

1. Your company is considering opening a new factory in China. List several typical activities involved in each phase of the decision (intelligence, design, and choice).

2. Recall that data mining found that young men tend to buy beer and diapers at the same time when they shop at convenience stores. Now that you know this relationship exists, can you provide a rationale for it?

3. American Can Company announced that it was interested in acquiring a company in the health maintenance organization (HMO) field. Two decisions were involved in this act: (1) the decision to acquire an HMO, and (2) the decision of which HMO to acquire. How can the use of BI assist the company in this endeavor?

4. Discuss the strategic benefits of BI systems.

5. Will BI replace business analysts? (Hint: See W. McKnight, "Business Intelligence: Will Business Intelligence Replace the Business Analyst?" *DMReview*, February 2005.)

## [ Closing Case **Social Sentiment Analysis** ]

### The **Business Problem**

Sentiment analysis refers to the use of natural language processing, text analysis, machine learning, and statistics to identify and extract subjective information in source materials. A basic task in sentiment analysis is classifying whether the expressed opinion in a document, sentence, Web page, online news, Internet discussion group, blog, Facebook post, or tweet is positive, negative, or neutral. Advanced sentiment analysis examines emotional states such as angry, sad, and happy.

The rise of social media in particular has increased interest in sentiment analysis. (We discuss social computing in detail in Chapter 9.) With the proliferation of reviews, ratings, and recommendations, online opinion has become a critical information resource for businesses that want to market their products, identify new opportunities, and manage their reputations. Businesses must understand the conversations, identify relevant content, and take appropriate actions based on these findings.

## The IT Solution

At the University of Southern California's (USC) (*www.usc .edu*) Annenberg Innovation Lab, researchers are using sentiment analysis to analyze, in real time, the sentiment of conversations on a range of topics that thrive on social media. The research analyzes the positive and negative sentiments of 40 million tweets to gain insights into a variety of topics. The researchers hope to help businesses, nonprofit organizations, and government agencies gain new insights from millions of online conversations.

The problem is that most sentiment analysis algorithms use simple terms to express sentiment about a product or a service. However, cultural factors, linguistic nuances, and differing contexts make it very difficult to classify online content as positive, negative, or neutral. Additionally, the fact that humans often disagree on the sentiment expressed in a message demonstrates how difficult it is for algorithms to correctly classify sentiment. Going further, the shorter a piece of text, the more difficult the classification task.

In every subject area—politics, entertainment, technology, and so on—people often use jargon, and sometimes sarcasm, to convey their ideas and opinions. Researchers discovered, for example, that almost 70 percent of tweets on politics are sarcastic. To improve the accuracy of sentiment analytics, researchers must train the software to learn these nuances of language.

As an example, consider the difference between sarcasm and enthusiasm, a distinction that is difficult for sentiment analysis software to discern. The Annenberg Lab assembled a large number of participants both physically and virtually— the latter via Amazon's Mechanical Turk—to examine tweets and assess whether each one was sarcastic. Their findings were used to fine-tune the sentiment analysis software. The research team learned a great deal about sarcasm. For example, they found that if someone puts a word in quotes, then it probably means just the opposite.

## The Results

Let's consider some examples of sentiment analysis at work. First, the Annenberg Lab analyzed social media posts related to new motion picture releases. They looked at this question: "Could you determine how movies would open based on the social buzz?" That is, how much money would a movie make in its opening days? The research found that the ability to understand public sentiment in real time was an excellent predictor of how a movie would open and what types of advertising were effective.

For instance, the researchers discovered that just before the film *Twilight: Breaking Dawn* was released, it received a 90 percent positive sentiment on Twitter. However, soon after its release, this number dropped to 75 percent. Though it appeared that viewers had been disappointed after the initial excitement, a closer analysis revealed that the negative sentiment was not directed against the movie. Rather, *Twilight* fans were "sad" that the series was ending.

In another example, the researchers tracked the DreamWorks' movie *Puss in Boots*, and they found that the Twitter conversations surrounding the film were negative. Responding to this feedback, the movie's marketers created a large television advertising campaign for the film. Within two days, the researchers noticed that *Puss in Boots* not only became the most talked-about movie on social media, but the mentions were overwhelmingly positive. To the marketers, this sentiment shift constituted evidence that the ad campaign had been successful.

These examples indicate that film producers and movie marketers can utilize sentiment analysis to assess popular opinions building up around a film as its release time nears. They can then create a custom message and marketing campaign based on this information. After the film is released, they can predict how well it will do over time.

In television, these insights could change the system by which networks develop shows. Television today is measured the same way it was measured in the 1950s, with the Nielsen ratings (*www.nielsen.com*). The current ratings system reveals only which channel is turned on in 2,500 homes in America. It describes nothing about whether the viewers are engaged and how they feel about the programs.

Today, however, it is possible to examine a million tweets around a piece of television programming. For example, researchers examined the *Oscars* television show to see in real time what people thought about every segment of the show's programming and advertising. The show's producers could actually see where the sentiment became negative in the program (say, at minute 36) and then examine the tweets to learn what viewers did not like.

Sentiment analysis clearly offers significant business opportunities for the media, entertainment, and advertising industries. It can provide marketing managers with near-real-time insight into what consumers are thinking. Marketers can then adjust their strategies and offers while it is still possible to influence the outcomes. Even more compelling, however, are the social implications of sentiment analytics. Sentiment analysis could influence everything from election strategies to public policies to emergency responses.

For example, the Annenberg Lab analyzed tweets during a political debate, where each candidate had a sentiment meter. The debate was literally a real-time, 800,000-person focus group. The researchers observed that when members of the audience perceived that a candidate had made a mistake, the sentiment on the dashboard changed negatively in seconds.

Social sentiment analysis will be valuable to governments as well. People in developing nations use Twitter and Facebook extensively. If government officials in developing nations could monitor a malaria epidemic or a civil conflict by analyzing huge volumes of Twitter data, then they could identify areas where problems are developing and take proactive steps to resolve them.

*Sources:* Compiled from M. Sponder, "The Dollars and Sense of Sentiment," *CMS Wire*, March 7, 2014; I. Lunden, "Thomson Reuters Taps into Twitter for Big Data Sentiment Analysis," *TechCrunch*, February 3, 2014; E. Washington, "Human Sentiment Analysis," *Growing Social Media*, November 6, 2013; R. Munro, "Why Is Sentiment Analysis Hard?" *idibon*, September 6, 2013; "Sentiment Analysis: The New Game Changer for Entertainment Industry," *Shout Analytics*, July 12, 2013; J. Burn-Murdoch, "Social Media Analytics: Are We Nearly There Yet?" *The Guardian*, June 10, 2013; G. Parker, "Tool Developed by USC Annenberg Innovation Lab Explores True Sentiment of Social Media," *USC Annenberg School for Communication and Journalism*, January 30, 2013; "Case Study: Advanced Sentiment Analysis," *Paragon Poll*, 2013; "Case Study: University of Southern California Annenberg Innovation Lab," *IBM Software Information Management*, 2013; J. Taplin, "Social Sentiment Analysis Changes the Game for Hollywood," *Building a Smarter Planet*, November 30, 2012; "USC Annenberg, IBM, and Los Angeles Times Conduct Academy Awards Social Sentiment Analysis," *USC Annenberg School for Communication and Journalism*, February 8, 2012; M. Ogneva, "How Companies Can Use Sentiment Analysis to Improve Their Business," *Mashable*, April 19, 2010; *http://annenberg.usc .edu*, *www.ibm.com*, accessed March 8, 2015.

## Questions

1. Describe areas in which social sentiment analysis would be beneficial for your university. Provide specific examples to support your answer.

2. Describe potential disadvantages that organizations might experience when using social sentiment analysis.

3. What impacts could social sentiment analysis have on television reality shows? Provide specific examples in your answer.

# 13 Acquiring Information Systems and Applications

| [ LEARNING OBJECTIVES ] | [ CHAPTER OUTLINE ] | [ WEB RESOURCES ] |
|---|---|---|
| 1. Discuss the different cost–benefit analyses that companies must take into account when formulating an IT strategic plan. | **13.1 Planning for and Justifying IT Applications** | • Student PowerPoints for note taking **WileyPLUS Learning Space** |
| 2. Discuss the four business decisions that companies must make when they acquire new applications. | **13.2 Strategies for Acquiring IT Applications** | • E-book • Author video lecture for each chapter section |
| 3. Enumerate the primary tasks and the importance of each of the six processes involved in the systems development life cycle. | **13.3 The Traditional Systems Development Life Cycle** | • Practice quizzes • Flash Cards for vocabulary review |
| 4. Describe alternative development methods and the tools that augment these methods. | **13.4 Alternative Methods and Tools for Systems Development** | • Additional "What's in IT for Me?" cases • Video interviews with managers • Lab Manuals for Microsoft Office 2010 and 2013 |

## What's In IT For Me?

### This Chapter Will Help Prepare You To...

| ACCT | FIN | MKT | POM | HRM | MIS |
|---|---|---|---|---|---|
| ACCOUNTING | FINANCE | MARKETING | PRODUCTION OPERATIONS MANAGEMENT | HUMAN RESOURCES MANAGEMENT | MIS |
| Conduct costbenefit analysis on projects | Analyze project ROI | Provide input on customer-related systems | Provide input on supply chain systems | Manage consultants on projects | Support user community in acquiring new systems |

# The Business Problem

Healthcare.gov (*www.healthcare.gov*) is a health insurance exchange Web site operated under the provisions of the 2010 Patient Protection and Affordable Care Act, commonly referred to as "Obamacare." The site was designed to serve the residents of the 36 U.S. states that opted not to create their own state exchanges. Healthcare.gov helps U.S. residents purchase private health insurance plans, and it offers subsidies to people who earn less than four times the federal poverty line. In addition, it assists low-income people who are eligible for Medicaid, and it provides a separate marketplace for small businesses.

The front end, or customer-facing part of the Web site, presents the choices for the consumer and the necessary forms to fill out. The back end contains the databases and services. The Centers for Medicare and Medicaid Services (CMS) oversaw the Web site design. A number of federal contractors, most prominently the CGI Group, built the actual site. CGI received a contract valued at nearly $300 million through 2013 for their work.

Unfortunately, Obama's team paid attention to crafting a healthcare reform policy but not to the details of actually implementing that policy. None of the participants in the White House meetings leading up to the launch of the Web site had any idea as to how well the site would function. Obama's team simply accepted the contractors' assurances that everything was ready to go for the launch. The White House's overriding concern was whether people would visit the exchanges. Unfortunately, they failed to consider what visitors would encounter when they accessed the site. The media concentrated on the marketing and enrollment hurdles as well. The White House maintained this narrow focus despite numerous red flags indicating potential problems with Healthcare.gov that appeared for months prior to the rollout of the site. Federal auditors raised alarms as early as June 2013 when they warned of missed deadlines and unfinished work.

On October 1, 2013, Healthcare.gov was rolled out as planned. However, the launch was marred by serious technological problems, making it difficult (if not impossible) for the public to sign up for health insurance. In fact, the site was unusable to hundreds of thousands of Americans who wanted to enroll. Despite the pledges from Obama administration officials that the "glitches" would be quickly fixed, the list of bugs and problems continued to expand. Millward Brown Digital, a consulting firm, estimated that only 1 percent of the 3.7 million people who tried to register on the exchange in the first week were successful. Further, when people did log on, the site frequently shut down on them.

On October 4, 2013, President Obama publicly attributed the problems with Healthcare. gov to the overwhelming volume of attempted enrollments. The reality, however, was more serious. In fact, the architecture underlying the site was flawed in design, poorly tested, and ultimately nonfunctional. In addition, on the database side of the Web site (as opposed to the public-facing side), the data were garbled and, in some cases, unusable. The nightly reports on new enrollees that the insurance companies received from the federal government contained errors, including incorrect syntax and transposed or duplicate data. In other cases, insurers received multiple enrollments and cancellations from the same individual. Because the documents did not have time stamps, it was impossible to know which form was the most recent. Insurance companies resorted to contacting enrollees directly to obtain correct information, a solution that was possible only because so few people were able to sign up.

Even more alarming were the security flaws. An error message from the Web site relayed personal information over the Internet without encryption. In addition, the e-mail verification system could be bypassed without requiring access to the user's e-mail account.

To address these issues, administration officials put out a call for new contractors, as well as Silicon Valley talent, to fix the project. Unfortunately, these changes did not bring any new transparency to the site's myriad problems. In fact, Obama's aides refused to confirm the existence of any particular bugs or to describe what was wrong. Their primary concern was to maintain at least some public enthusiasm for the insurance marketplace.

On November 13, the government issued its first report on monthly enrollments, covering the disastrous October rollout. The report revealed that fewer than 27,000 people had enrolled through the federal exchange over the entire month. This number represented only 10 percent of the total the administration had been counting on.

## The Solution

With Healthcare.gov in seeming disarray, President Obama and his chief of staff brought in an elite team of programmers from various IT organizations across the country to salvage the site. The team quickly found itself enmeshed in a situation in which multiple contractors were bickering with one another and no one would take ownership of any of the site's many deficiencies. Further, the contractors displayed a total lack of urgency, despite the fact that Healthcare.gov was becoming a national joke and was crippling Obama's healthcare legacy.

One of the team's most shocking discoveries was that the people operating Healthcare.gov had neglected to create a dashboard. As a result, programmers had no reliable method to measure what was actually occurring at the Web site, such as how many people were using it, what response times consumers encountered when they clicked on a feature, and where Web traffic was bottlenecked. The team immediately made implementing a dashboard a top priority.

By observing the dashboard, the team discovered a quick fix to an obvious mistake. Healthcare.gov had been constructed so that every time a user had to obtain information from the site's vast database, the site had to make a query into the database. Well-constructed, high-volume Web sites, particularly e-commerce sites, avoid this problem by storing the most frequently accessed information in a cache. (We discuss cache memory in Technology Guide 1). Queries to the cache are faster and do not tie up connections to the overall database. Not creating and using a cache created a huge, unnecessary bottleneck. The team immediately began to cache the data. As a result of these efforts, the Web site's overall response time—the time it took for a page to load—dropped from eight seconds to two. Although two seconds was still slow, it still represented a significant improvement in the site's performance.

The day after the team successfully cached the data, they announced they could fix Healthcare.gov by the end of November, six weeks away, so that the "vast majority" of visitors could successfully access the site and enroll in a plan.

The team further discovered that the Healthcare.gov developers had made the most basic mistake that developers can make. E-commerce Web sites never open a service to everyone at once. Rather, they introduce it to smaller groups of customers and then expand it. This strategy enables them to monitor how the service functions, fix it if necessary, and then scale it (make it available to larger numbers of customers). The team concluded that Healthcare.gov should have been deployed via this method. Unfortunately, the government failed to adopt this approach.

Consider one particularly difficult problem that the team repaired. The unique identifier that the Web site had to issue to everyone who was trying to enroll was taking too long to generate. In fact, the ID generator had become so overloaded that the Web site was effectively nonfunctional. To resolve this problem, the team worked on a patch (new computer code). The patch was partially successful, but the team learned a few days later that the identifications it was generating did not have the correct number of digits to match the insurance companies' needs. As a result, the team had to remove the patch and restore the old ID generator. Then, in late November, the old generator effectively shut down the entire Web site. The team quickly developed a new patch, this time with the correct number of digits. They then executed a "hot fix," meaning they inserted the patch into the site without testing it. Fortunately for the team, the patch worked.

While these experts were focusing on these immediate problems, other team members worked at a separate office to deal with longer-term issues that the site would face following the November 30 deadline. The most important issue was scale. Would the site be able to handle the volumes of traffic that a functional Healthcare.gov would generate?

# The Results

On December 1, 2013, the team issued a public report card that documented Healthcare.gov's turnaround. A series of hardware upgrades had dramatically increased capacity; the system was now able to accommodate at least 50,000 simultaneous users. The team had performed more than 400 bug fixes. Web site availability had increased from an abysmal 43 percent at the beginning of November to 95 percent. Further, the average response time—originally a disastrous 8 seconds per page and then a slow 2 seconds per page—had decreased to an acceptable 0.343 seconds per page.

One of the key issues in preparing the site to scale was the error rate—the rate at which any click on the site generated a result that it was not supposed to. In October, the error rate had been an astoundingly high 6 percent. The report card indicated that the rate had declined significantly to 0.5 percent. It has since continued to decrease.

On December 23, the Web site handled 83,000 simultaneous users at one point. The result was 129,000 enrollments on that one day, almost 5 times as many as the site had handled in all of October. On Christmas Day, another 93,000 visitors enrolled.

In about one-tenth of the time that a group of Washington contractors had built a Web site that did not work at a cost of more than $300 million, this ad hoc team had rescued the site and, arguably, Obama's chance at a health reform legacy.

As of February 18, 2015, approximately 11.4 million people were enrolled in an insurance plan through healthcare.gov.

Two final notes: In April 2014, Kathleen Sebelius resigned as Secretary of Health and Human Services, in part as a result of the problems with the Healthcare.gov Web site. Also, CMS Administrator Marilyn Tavenner resigned at the end of February, 2015.

*Sources:* Compiled from D. Morgan, "Obamacare's Lead Agency Chief Announces Her Resignation," *Reuters*, January 16, 2015; R. Abelson and K. Thomas, "A Final Push for Healthcare," *The New York Times*, March 25, 2014; L. Nichols, "Healthcare.gov Glitch Fixed Quickly Ahead of Open-Enrollment Deadline," *PR Week*, March 24, 2014; K. Kennedy, "4.2 Million Enrolled in Insurance through February," *USA Today*, March 11, 2014; S. Brill, "Code Red," *Time*, March 10, 2014; A. Aigner-Treworgy and J. Acosta, "Obamacare Enrollment Hits 4 Million, Push Underway to Hit Revised Goal," *Political Ticker*, February 25, 2014; K. Diller, "How Developers Could Have Avoided HealthCare.gov Technical Problems," *SearchSoftwareQuality*, January 30, 2014; P. Wait, "Accenture Jumps into Healthcare.gov Hot Seat," *InformationWeek*, January 14, 2014; D. Talbot, "Diagnosis for Healthcare.gov: Unrealistic Technology Expectations," *MIT Technology Review*, December 2, 2013; M. Scherer, "More Than a Glitch," *Time*, November 4, 2013; E. Scannell, "The IT Fundamentals That Healthcare.gov Ignored," *TechTarget*, November 1, 2013; P. Ford, "The Obamacare Website Didn't Have to Fail; How to Do Better Next Time," *Bloomberg BusinessWeek*, October 16, 2013; *www.healthcare.gov*, accessed February 15, 2015.

## Questions

1. Were the problems with the Healthcare.gov Web site the result of management, technology, or both? Provide specific examples to support your answer.

2. What lessons can you draw from Healthcare.gov about successfully implementing very large information systems projects?

# Introduction

Competitive organizations move as quickly as they can to acquire new information technologies or modify existing ones when they need to improve efficiencies and gain strategic advantage. As you learned from the chapter opening case, problems and pitfalls can arise from the acquisition process.

Today, acquisition goes beyond building new systems in-house, and IT resources involve far more than software and hardware. The old model in which firms built their own systems is being replaced with a broader perspective of IT resource acquisition that provides companies with a number of options. Thus, companies now must decide which IT tasks will remain in-house, and even whether the entire IT resource should be provided and managed by outside organizations. Regardless of which approach an organization chooses, however, it must be able to manage IT projects adeptly.

In this chapter, you learn about the process of acquiring IT resources from a managerial perspective. This means from *your* perspective, because you will be closely involved in all aspects of acquiring information systems and applications in your organization. In fact, when we mention "users" in this chapter, we are talking about you. You will also study the available options for acquiring IT resources and how to evaluate those options. Finally, you will learn how organizations plan and justify the acquisition of new information systems.

# 13.1 Planning for and Justifying IT Applications

Organizations must analyze the need for applications and then justify each purchase in terms of costs and benefits. The need for information systems is usually related to organizational planning and to the analysis of its performance vis-à-vis its competitors. The cost–benefit justification must consider the wisdom of investing in a specific IT application versus spending the funds on alternative projects. This chapter focuses on the formal processes of large organizations. Smaller organizations employ less formal processes, or no processes at all. It is important to note, however, that even if a small organization does not have a formal process for planning and justifying IT applications, the steps of a formal process exist for a reason, and they have value. At the very least, decision makers in small organizations should consider each step when they are planning changes in their information systems.

When a company examines its needs and performance, it generates a prioritized list of both existing and potential IT applications, called the **application portfolio**. These are the applications that have to be added, or modified if they already exist.

## IT Planning

The planning process for new IT applications begins with an analysis of the *organizational strategic plan*, which is illustrated in Figure 13.1. The organization's strategic plan identifies the firm's overall mission, the goals that follow from that mission, and the broad steps required to reach these goals. The strategic planning process modifies the organization's objectives and resources to match its changing markets and opportunities.

**FIGURE 13.1** The information systems planning process.

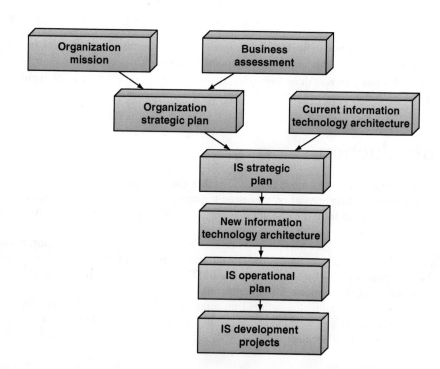

The organizational strategic plan and the existing IT architecture provide the inputs in developing the IT strategic plan. The *IT architecture* delineates the way an organization should utilize its information resources to accomplish its mission. It encompasses both the technical and the managerial aspects of information resources. The technical aspects include hardware and operating systems, networking, data management systems, and applications software. The managerial aspects specify how the IT department will be managed, how the functional area managers will be involved, and how IT decisions will be made.

The **IT strategic plan** is a set of long-range goals that describe the IT infrastructure and identify the major IT initiatives needed to achieve the organization's goals. The IT strategic plan must meet three objectives:

1. *It must be aligned with the organization's strategic plan.* This alignment is critical because the organization's information systems must support the organization's strategies. (Recall the discussion of organizational strategies and information systems in Chapter 2.)

Consider the example of Nordstrom versus Walmart. An application that improves customer service at a small cost would be considered favorably at Nordstrom, but it would be rejected at Walmart. The reason is that the application would fit in favorably (i.e., align) with Nordstrom's service-at-any-cost strategy. However, it would not fit in well with Walmart's low-cost strategy. You see two department stores, same application, same cost and benefits—but different answers to the question "Should we develop the application?"

2. *It must provide for an IT architecture that seamlessly networks users, applications, and databases.*

3. *It must efficiently allocate IS development resources among competing projects so that the projects can be completed on time and within budget and still have the required functionality.*

The existing IT architecture is a necessary input into the IT strategic plan because it acts as a constraint on future development efforts. It is not an absolute constraint, however, because the organization can change to a new IT architecture. Companies prefer to avoid this strategy, however, because it is expensive and time consuming.

Consider this example. You have a Mac (Apple) system, and you need a new software application. You search and find several such packages for both Mac and MS Windows. Unfortunately, the best package runs only on Windows. How much better would this package have to be for you to justify switching from Mac to Windows?

One critical component in developing and implementing the IT strategic plan is the **IT steering committee**. This committee, comprised of a group of managers and staff who represent the various organizational units, is created to establish IT priorities and to ensure that the MIS function is meeting the organization's needs. The committee's major tasks are to link corporate strategy with IT strategy, to approve the allocation of resources for the MIS function, and to establish performance measures for the MIS function and ensure they are met. The IT steering committee is important to you because it ensures that you get the information systems and applications that you need to do your job.

After a company has agreed on an IT strategic plan, it next develops the **IS operational plan**. This plan consists of a clear set of projects that the IS department and the functional area managers will execute in support of the IT strategic plan. A typical IS operational plan contains the following elements:

- *Mission:* The mission of the IS function (derived from the IT strategy).
- *IS environment:* A summary of the information needs of the individual functional areas and of the organization as a whole.
- *Objectives of the IS function:* The best current estimate of the goals of the IS function.
- *Constraints on the IS function:* Technological, financial, personnel, and other resource limitations on the IS function.
- *The application portfolio:* A prioritized inventory of present applications and a detailed plan of projects to be developed or continued during the current year.
- *Resource allocation and project management:* A listing of who is going to do what, how, and when.

## Evaluating and Justifying IT Investment: Benefits, Costs, and Issues

Developing an IT plan is the first step in the acquisition process. Because all companies have limited resources, they must justify investing resources in some areas, including IT, rather than in others. Essentially, justifying IT investment involves calculating the costs, assessing the benefits (values), and comparing the two. This comparison is frequently referred to as cost–benefit analysis. Cost–benefit analysis is not a simple task.

**Assessing the Costs.** Calculating the dollar value of IT investments is not as simple as it may seem. One of the major challenges that companies face is to allocate fixed costs among different IT projects. *Fixed costs* are those costs that remain the same regardless of any change in the company's activity level. Fixed IT costs include infrastructure costs and the costs associated with IT services and IT management. For example, the salary of the IT director is fixed, and adding one more application will not change it.

Another complication is that the costs of a system do not end when the system is installed. Rather, costs for maintaining, debugging, and improving the system can accumulate over many years. This is a critical point because organizations sometimes fail to anticipate these costs when they make the investment.

A dramatic example of unanticipated expenses was the Year 2000 (Y2K) reprogramming projects, which cost organizations worldwide billions of dollars. In the 1960s, computer memory was very expensive. To save money, programmers coded the "year" in the date field 19_ _, instead of _ _ _ _. With the "1" and the "9" hard-coded in the computer program, only the last two digits varied, so computer programs needed less memory. However, this process meant that when the year 2000 rolled around, computers would display the year as 1900. This programming technique could have caused serious problems with financial applications, insurance applications, and countless other apps.

The Y2K example illustrates the point that database design choices tend to affect the organization for a long time. As the 21st century approached, no one still used hardware or software from the 1960s (other than a few legacy applications). Database design choices made in the 1960s, however, were often still in effect decades after the companies implemented them.

**Assessing the Benefits.** Evaluating the benefits of IT projects is typically even more complex than calculating their costs. Benefits may be more difficult to quantify, especially because many of them are intangible — for example, improved customer or partner relations and improved decision making. As an employee, you will probably be asked for input about the intangible benefits that an IS provides for you.

The fact that organizations use IT for multiple purposes further complicates benefit analysis. In addition, to obtain a return from an IT investment, the company must implement the technology successfully. In reality, many systems are not implemented on time, within budget, or with all of the features originally envisioned for them. Also, the proposed system may be "cutting edge." In these cases, there may be no precedent for identifying the types of financial payback the company can expect.

**Conducting the Cost–Benefit Analysis.** After a company has assessed the costs and benefits of IT investments, it must compare them. You have studied, or will study, cost–benefit analyses in more detail in your finance courses. The point is that real-world business problems do not come in neatly wrapped packages labeled "this is a finance problem" or "this is an IS problem." Rather, business problems span multiple functional areas.

There is no uniform strategy for conducting a cost–benefit analysis. Rather, an organization can perform this task in several ways. Here you see four common approaches: (1) net present value, (2) return on investment, (3) breakeven analysis, and (4) the business case approach.

- Analysts use the *net present value (NPV)* method to convert future values of benefits to their present-value equivalent by "discounting" them at the organization's cost of funds. They can then compare the present value of the future benefits with the cost required to achieve those benefits to determine whether the benefits exceed the costs.

- *Return on investment (ROI)* measures management's effectiveness in generating profits with its available assets. ROI is calculated by dividing the net income generated by a project by the average assets invested in the project. ROI is a percentage, and the higher the percentage return, the better.
- *Breakeven analysis* determines the point at which the cumulative dollar value of the benefits from a project equals the investment made in the project.
- In the *business case approach*, system developers write a business case to justify funding one or more specific applications or projects. IS professionals will be a major source of input when business cases are developed because these cases describe what you do, how you do it, and how a new system could better support you.

# before you go on...

**1.** What are some problems associated with assessing the costs of IT?

**2.** Why are the intangible benefits from IT so difficult to evaluate?

**3.** Describe the NPV, ROI, breakeven analysis, and business case approaches.

# Strategies for Acquiring IT Applications                                13.2

After a company has justified an IT investment, it must then decide how to pursue it. As with cost–benefit analyses, there are several options for acquiring IT applications. To select the best option, companies must make a series of business decisions. The fundamental decisions are the following:

- *How much computer code does the company want to write?* A company can choose to use a totally prewritten application (write no computer code), to customize a prewritten application (write some computer code), or to custom-write an entire application (write all new computer code).
- *How will the company pay for the application?* Once the company has decided how much computer code to write, it must decide how to pay for it. With prewritten applications or customized prewritten applications, companies can buy them or lease them. With totally custom applications, companies use internal funding.
- *Where will the application run?* The next decision is whether to run the application on the company's platform or on someone else's platform. In other words, the company can employ either a software-as-a-service vendor or an application service provider. (You will examine these options later in this chapter.)
- *Where will the application originate?* Prewritten applications can be open-source software or they can come from a vendor. The company may choose to customize prewritten open-source applications or prewritten proprietary applications from vendors. Further, it may customize applications in-house, or it can outsource the customization. Finally, it can write totally custom applications in-house, or it can outsource this process.

In the following sections, you will find more details on the variety of options that companies looking to acquire applications can select from. A good rule of thumb is that an organization should consider all feasible acquisition methods in light of its business requirements. You will learn about the following acquisition methods:

- Purchase a prewritten application.
- Customize a prewritten application.
- Lease the application.

- Use application service providers and software-as-a-service vendors.
- Use open-source software.
- Use outsourcing.
- Employ custom development.

## Purchase a Prewritten Application

Many commercial software packages contain the standard features required by IT applications. Therefore, purchasing an existing package can be a cost-effective and time-saving strategy compared with custom-developing the application in-house. Nevertheless, a company should carefully consider and plan the buy option to ensure that the selected package contains all of the features necessary to address the company's current and future needs. Otherwise, these packages can quickly become obsolete. Before a company can perform this process, it must decide which features a suitable package must include.

In reality, a single software package can rarely satisfy all of an organization's needs. For this reason, a company sometimes must purchase multiple packages to fulfill different needs. It then must integrate these packages with one another as well as with its existing software. Table 13.1 summarizes the advantages and limitations of the buy option.

## Customize a Prewritten Application

Customizing existing software is an especially attractive option if the software vendor allows the company to modify the application to meet its needs. However, this option may not be attractive in cases where customization is the *only* method of providing the necessary flexibility to address the company's needs. It also is not the best strategy when the software is either very expensive or likely to become obsolete in a short time. Further, customizing a prewritten application can be extremely difficult, particularly for large, complex applications.

## Lease the Application

Compared with the buy option and the option to develop applications in-house, the lease option can save a company both time and money. Of course, leased packages (like purchased packages) may not exactly fit the company's application requirements. However, as noted,

| **Table 13.1** Advantages and Limitations of the Buy Option | |
|---|---|
| **Advantages** | |
| • Many different types of off-the-shelf software are available<br>• The company can try out the software before purchasing it<br>• The company can save much time by buying rather than building<br>• The company can know what it is getting before it invests in the product<br>• Purchased software may eliminate the need to hire personnel specifically dedicated to a project | |
| **Disadvantages** | |
| • Software may not exactly meet the company's needs<br>• Software may be difficult or impossible to modify, or it may require huge business process changes to implement<br>• The company will not have control over software improvements and new versions<br>• Purchased software can be difficult to integrate with existing systems<br>• Vendors may discontinue a product or go out of business<br>• Software is controlled by another company with its own priorities and business considerations<br>• The purchasing company lacks intimate knowledge about how and why the software functions as it does | |

vendor software generally includes the features that are most commonly needed by organizations in a given industry. Again, the company will decide which features are necessary.

Interested companies commonly apply the 80/20 rule when they evaluate vendor software. Put simply, if the software meets 80 percent of the company's needs, then the company should seriously consider modifying its business processes so that it can utilize the remaining 20 percent. Many times this is a better long-term solution than modifying the vendor software. Otherwise, the company will have to customize the software every time the vendor releases an updated version.

Leasing can be especially attractive to small and medium-sized enterprises (SMEs) that cannot afford major investments in IT software. Large companies may also prefer to lease packages to test potential IT solutions before committing to major investments. In addition, a company that does not employ sufficient IT personnel with the appropriate skills for developing custom IT applications may choose to lease instead of developing software in-house. Even those companies that employ in-house experts may not be able to afford the long wait for strategic applications to be developed in-house. Therefore, they lease (or buy) applications from external resources to establish a quicker presence in the market.

Leasing can be executed in one of three ways. The first way is to lease the application from a software developer, install it, and run it on the company's platform. The vendor can assist with the installation and frequently will offer to contract for the support and maintenance of the system. Many conventional applications are leased this way.

The other two options involve leasing an application and running it on the vendor's platform. Organizations can accomplish this process by using an application service provider or a software-as-a-service vendor.

## Application Service Providers and Software-as-a-Service Vendors

An **application service provider (ASP)** is an agent or a vendor who assembles the software needed by enterprises and then packages it with services such as development, operations, and maintenance. The customer then accesses these applications via the Internet. Figure 13.2 illustrates the operation of an ASP. Note that the ASP hosts both an application and a database for each customer.

**Software-as-a-service (SaaS)** is a method of delivering software in which a vendor hosts the applications and provides them as a service to customers over a network, typically the Internet. Customers do not own the software; rather, they pay for using it. SaaS eliminates the need for customers to install and run the application on their own computers. Therefore, SaaS customers save the expense (money, time, IT staff) of buying, operating, and maintaining the software. For example, Salesforce (*www.salesforce.com*), a well-known SaaS provider for customer relationship management (CRM) software solutions, provides these advantages for its customers.

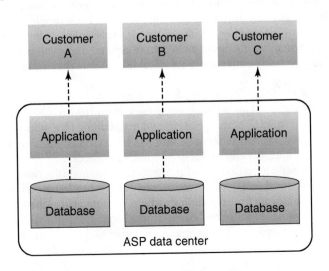

**FIGURE 13.2** Operation of an application service provider.

**FIGURE 13.3** Operation of a software-as-a-service vendor.

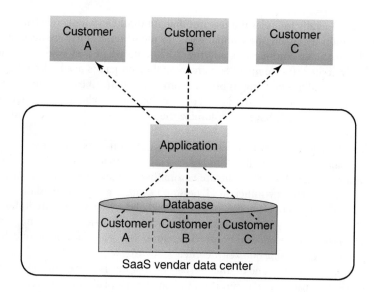

Figure 13.3 displays the operation of a SaaS vendor. Note that the vendor hosts an application that multiple customers can use. The vendor also hosts a database that is partitioned for each customer to protect the privacy and security of each customer's data.

At this point, companies have made the first three decisions and must now decide where to obtain the application. Recall that in general, for prewritten applications, companies can use open-source software or obtain the software from a vendor. For customized prewritten applications, they can customize open-source software or customize vendor software. For totally custom applications, they can write the software in-house, or they can outsource the process.

## Use Open-Source Software

Organizations obtain a license to implement an open-source software product and either use it as is, customize it, or develop applications with it. Unless the company is one of the few that want to tinker with their source code, open-source applications are, basically, the same as a proprietary application except for licensing, payment, and support. Open-source software is really an alternative source of applications rather than a conceptually different development option. (We discuss open-source software in Technology Guide 2.)

## Outsourcing

Acquiring IT applications from outside contractors or external organizations is called **outsourcing**. Companies can utilize outsourcing in many situations. For example, they might want to experiment with new IT technologies without making a substantial up-front investment. They also might use outsourcing to obtain access to outside experts. One disadvantage of outsourcing is that companies frequently must place their valuable corporate data under the control of the outsourcing vendor.

Several types of vendors offer services for creating and operating IT systems, including e-commerce applications. Many software companies, from IBM to Oracle, offer a range of outsourcing services for developing, operating, and maintaining IT applications. IT outsourcers, such as EDS, offer a variety of services. Also, the large CPA companies and management consultants—for example, Accenture—offer outsourcing services.

For example, in September 2014, Philip Morris International (the non-U.S. operation of Philip Morris) outsourced its IT infrastructure management to Indian services firm Wipro. The companies concluded a five-year contract where Wipro manages the tobacco company's applications and IT using Wipro's cloud-based management platform. (We discuss cloud computing in Technology Guide 3.) The contract is reported to be worth some U.S.$35 million U.S. dollars.

Some companies outsource offshore, particularly in India and China. *Offshoring* can save money, but it includes risks as well. The risks depend on which services are being offshored. If a company is offshoring application development, then the major risk is poor communication between users and developers. In response to these risks, some companies are bringing outsourced jobs back in-house, a process called *reverse outsourcing* or *insourcing*.

## Continuous Development

Continuous application development automates and improves the process of software delivery. In essence, a software development project is not viewed as having a defined product, with development stopped when the product is implemented. Rather, a software development project is viewed as constantly changing in response to changing business conditions and in response to user acceptance.

**Continuous application development** is the process of steadily adding new computer code to a software project when the new computer code is ready. Each development team member submits new code when it is finished. Automated testing is performed on the code to ensure that it functions within the software project. Continuous code submission provides developers with immediate feedback from users and status updates for the software on which they are working. IT's About Business 13.1 illustrates continuous development at LinkedIn.

# IT's [about business]

## 13.1 LinkedIn's Fast Development Process Helps Save the Company

MIS

The May 2011 initial public offering (IPO) for the popular business networking site LinkedIn (*www.linkedin.com*) went very well. The stock's share price more than doubled on the first day of trading, giving the company a valuation of $9 billion. Behind the scenes, however, the company's information systems were experiencing problems. In the ensuing months, hundreds of computer programmers struggled to hold the site together with the digital equivalent of duct tape.

By November 2011, LinkedIn noticed that its systems were taxed as the site attracted an increasing number of users. Further, the programmers were burned out. To fix these problems, in February 2012 LinkedIn launched Operation InVersion. The company froze development on new features for two months so that programmers could overhaul the Web site's computing architecture. In the fast-moving world of social computing, such a freeze was sacrilege. It simply was not done.

As risky as the freeze was, it paid off. Today, LinkedIn provides extremely advanced coding tools for its programmers, enabling them to add new features on the fly such as a mobile version of the Web site. (Adding new features on the fly means that LinkedIn programmers code the new features and then insert them while the Web site is actually operating.) This coding agility was a key reason for LinkedIn's $18 billion valuation by mid-2013.

LinkedIn's programmers constantly run tests to identify which language and graphic choices keep users engaged and which tweaks enable mobile pages to load faster. Changes—for example, a fresh look for a menu or a new service—are built into the live Web site almost immediately. LinkedIn updates its site three times a day, in contrast to rivals such as Facebook and Google, who typically update once a day or every few days.

When LinkedIn was founded in 2003, the company used Oracle software for its central database instead of the less expensive, more flexible open-source databases that now dominate Web computing. Immediately after its IPO, LinkedIn switched to NoSQL database software. (We discuss NoSQL database software in detail in Chapter 5.) The company has built its own data storage and messaging systems, both of which are being employed by other companies.

Among the keys to the success of the InVersion project are the artificial intelligence computer code checkers that examine software for any errors introduced by LinkedIn's programmers. Other technology companies have their own algorithmic software tools, but they also dispatch teams of people to oversee the process of adding new code to their company's live Web sites. At LinkedIn, the process is almost entirely automated.

Updating the Web site three times per day has caused at least one problem. Users have noticed that their LinkedIn homepages have become crowded with all types of services and feeds.

LinkedIn believes that its development work has primed the company for its next stage: mining users' economic and job data to spot trends early and to advise people on how to advance their careers. LinkedIn believes it will be able to identify trends such a, which areas welders are migrating to and what skills the successful ones are learning. In short, LinkedIn plans to run information in both directions: from its users, and back to its users.

*Sources:* Compiled from B. Kerschberg, "Why DevOps, Integration, and Continuous Delivery Hold the Key to Enterprise Mobile App Development," *Forbes*, February 4, 2015; M. Nisen, "How LinkedIn Saved Its Engineers from Marathon Late-Night Coding Sessions," *Business Insider*, April 29, 2013; "How LinkedIn's Project Inversion Saved the Company," *Slashdot*,

April 29, 2013; A. Vance, "LinkedIn's Hidden Horsepower," Bloomberg *BusinessWeek*, April 15–21, 2013; A. Vance, "Inside Operation InVersion, the Code Freeze That Saved LinkedIn," *Bloomberg BusinessWeek*, April 10, 2013; P. Houston, "Innovation Lesson: Disrupt Before You're Disrupted," *InformationWeek*, November 9, 2012; *www.linkedin.com*, accessed March 24, 2015.

**Questions**

1. Describe how freezing new feature development on its Web site "saved" LinkedIn.
2. Describe how rapid application development is enabling LinkedIn to add its next feature, mining users' economic and job data.

## Employ Custom Development

Another option is to custom-build an application. Companies can either perform this operation in-house or outsource the process. Although custom development is usually more time consuming and costly than buying or leasing, it often produces a better fit with the organization's specific requirements.

The development process starts when the IT steering committee (discussed previously in this chapter), having received suggestions for a new system, decides it is worth exploring. These suggestions come from users (who will be you in the near future). Understanding this process will help you obtain the systems that you need. Conversely, not understanding this process will reduce your chances, because other people who understand it better will make suggestions that use up available resources.

As the company goes through the development process, its mind-set changes. In systems investigation (the first stage of the traditional systems development life cycle), the organization is trying to decide whether to build something. Everyone knows it may or may not be built. In the later stages of the development process, the organization is committed to building the application. Although a project can be cancelled at any time, this change in attitude is still important.

The basic, backbone methodology for custom development is the systems development life cycle (SDLC), which you will read about in the next section. Section 13.4 examines the methodologies that complement the SDLC: prototyping, joint application development, integrated computer-assisted systems development tools, and rapid application development. You will also consider four other methodologies: agile development, end-user development, component-based development, and object-oriented development.

The SDLC is typically used for large-scale information systems development projects. However, entrepreneurs are also using custom development to deploy much smaller information systems such as mobile apps. IT's About Business 13.2 illustrates how entrepreneurs actually build apps themselves.

## IT's [about business]

### 13.2 Build Your Apps Yourself

The rapid adoption of smartphones and tablets, coupled with the increased bandwidth of 4G wireless networks, has driven an explosion in mobile applications. Unlike large corporations, the independent artist, the mom-and-pop store, and the local pizza parlor do not have the financial and technological resources to develop custom apps. However, entrepreneurs and small businesses can now develop their own mobile apps.

Many online tools, such as Appsme (*www.appsme.com*), AppMakr (*www.appmakr.com*), and Appsbar (*www.appsbar.com*), enable users to build simple apps by incorporating text, images, and other features into a ready-made template. However, these tools may be limited in scope, or they might require any additional features to be coded manually.

To fill in this knowledge gap, mobile developer boot camps now offer intensive do-it-yourself training. Programs such as the

Pragmatic Studio claim that in a matter of weeks they can help turn a novice into a proficient coder, for fees of about $2,700.

Rather than go it alone, other entrepreneurs are using professional developers, who can charge more than $15,000 to produce sophisticated, polished apps. As we discussed earlier in the chapter, these costs can continue to rise after the app is developed. Each update to the operating system and every new device the company installs can affect the ways an app functions.

Let's examine a few examples of how this process functions.

Mike Vichich, a business consultant, had spent several years traveling almost continuously and accumulating many points on his credit cards. Cashing in those points gave him the idea for Glyph (*www.paywithglyph.com*), an iPhone app that tracks and maximizes credit- card rewards. Vichich faced one major obstacle, however: He did not know the first thing about developing a mobile app.

Vichich's case is not unusual. Many entrepreneurs can successfully manage a company in the fast-growing mobile apps market, but they do not possess the technical knowledge to build mobile apps on their own. Fortunately, they have several options to choose from, including (1) using online app-building tools, (2) taking crash courses in computer programming and coding languages, (3) hiring an expensive professional on contract, and (4) recruiting a full-time developer. Vichich combined options 1 and 3 and launched Glyph at the App Store in November 2013.

Michael Perry took 126 hours of training at CodeAcademy (*www.codeacademy.com*), a free online course that teaches a variety of programming languages. His business partner, an app developer who was working part time on their startup, had to devote more time to his other, full-time job. Perry, who had been in charge of business operations, realized he had to learn to code himself to launch the business—an app called GVING (*https://gving.com*) that was designed to help merchants track and reward their customers. The app is available at the App Store, and Perry now has a team of three developers who took over the programming side of the business.

Keith Brown, the owner of Austin Tree Experts in Austin, Texas, combined an online app builder with training to create an app that both employees and customers can use to identify and record details of trees. Austin Tree Experts' Web site and mobile app (*www.austintreeexperts.com*) are used by homeowners, local municipalities, apartment complexes, developers, engineers, architects, and contractors. The company offers many tree services, including trimming, pruning, removal, planting, fertilizing, consulting, and construction site services.

Codiqa (*https://codiqa.com*), an app builder, assisted with the basic code for the app's layout and general function. Because Codiqa was unable to add either a customized GPS feature to pin the location of the trees or a photo-uploading capability to capture images of the trees, Brown turned to W3Schools.com (*www.w3schools.com*) and HTML5rocks.com (*www.html5rocks.com*) for online tutorials. He also submitted questions on StackOverflow.com, a developer forum, whenever he encountered problems. Brown admits that it took him 30 hours of hard work, but he successfully built the app.

*Sources:* Compiled from S. Hirsch, "The Democratization of App Building Has Created a New Paradigm," *Betanews*, March 12, 2014; S. Angeles, "14 Best App Makers of 2014," *Business News Daily*, February 20, 2014; P. Rubens, "DIY Apps and the Rise of 'Citizen Developers'," *BBC News*, February 6, 2014; E. Maltby and A. Loten, "App Building, the Do-It-Yourself Way," *The Wall Street Journal*, March 7, 2013; M. Carney, "New and Improved Glyph: Hack Your Credit Card Utilization," *Pando Daily*, February 13, 2013; S. Perez, "Glyph's New iPhone App Tells You What Credit Cards to Use to Earn Better Rewards," *Tech Crunch*, November 13, 2012; C. Steele, "Do It Yourself: Create Your Own iOS or Android Apps," *PC Magazine*, March 16, 2012.

**Questions**

1. What are the advantages of learning to code so that you can build your own mobile apps? Provide specific examples to support your answer.
2. What are the disadvantages of learning to code so that you can build your own mobile apps? Provide specific examples to support your answer.

# before you go on... 

1. Describe the four fundamental business decisions that organizations must make when acquiring information systems.
2. Discuss each of the seven development methods in this section with regard to the four business decisions that organizations must make.

# The Traditional Systems Development Life Cycle

13.3

The **systems development life cycle** is the traditional systems development method that organizations use for large-scale IT projects. The SDLC is a structured framework that consists of sequential processes by which information systems are developed. For our purposes (see Figure 13.4), we identify six processes, each of which consists of clearly defined tasks:

- Systems investigation
- Systems analysis
- Systems design
- Programming and testing
- Implementation
- Operation and maintenance

**FIGURE 13.4** A six-stage systems development life cycle with supporting tools.

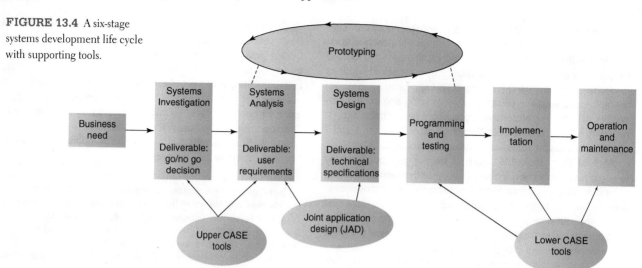

Alternative SDLC models contain more or fewer stages. The flow of tasks, however, remains largely the same. When problems occur in any phase of the SDLC, developers often must go back to previous phases.

Systems development projects produce desired results through team efforts. Development teams typically include users, systems analysts, programmers, and technical specialists. *Users* are employees from all functional areas and levels of the organization who interact with the system, either directly or indirectly. **Systems analysts** are IS professionals who specialize in analyzing and designing information systems. **Programmers** are IS professionals who either modify existing computer programs or write new programs to satisfy user requirements. **Technical specialists** are experts on a certain type of technology, such as databases or telecommunications. The **systems stakeholders** include everyone who is affected by changes in a company's information systems—for example, users and managers. All stakeholders are typically involved in systems development at various times and in varying degrees.

Figure 13.5 indicates that users have high involvement in the early stages of the SDLC, lower involvement in the programming and testing stage, and higher involvement in the later stages. Table 13.2 discusses the advantages and disadvantages of the SDLC.

## Systems Investigation

The initial stage in a traditional SDLC is systems investigation. Systems development professionals agree that the more time they invest in (1) understanding the business problem to be

**FIGURE 13.5** Comparison of user and developer involvement over the SDLC.

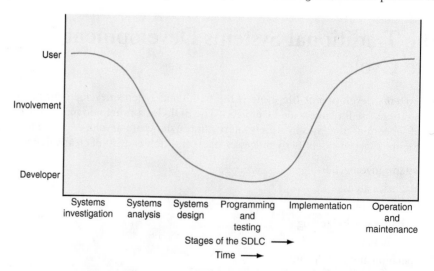

## Table **13.2**
### Advantages and Disadvantages of System Acquisition Methods

**Traditional Systems Development (SDLC)**
*Advantages*
- Forces staff to systematically go through every step in a structured process
- Enforces quality by maintaining standards
- Has lower probability of missing important issues in collecting user requirements

*Disadvantages*
- May produce excessive documentation
- Users may be unwilling or unable to study the approved specifications
- Takes too long to progress from the original ideas to a working system
- Users have trouble describing requirements for a proposed system

**Prototyping**
*Advantages*
- Helps clarify user requirements
- Helps verify the feasibility of the design
- Promotes genuine user participation
- Promotes close working relationship between systems developers and users
- Works well for ill-defined problems
- May produce part of the final system

*Disadvantages*
- May encourage inadequate problem analysis
- Is not practical with large number of users
- User may not want to give up the prototype when the system is completed
- May generate confusion about whether the system is complete and maintainable
- System may be built quickly, which can result in lower quality

**Joint Application Design**
*Advantages*
- Involves many users in the development process
- Saves time
- Generates greater user support for the new system
- Improves the quality of the new system
- The new system is easier to implement
- The new system has lower training costs

*Disadvantages*
- It is difficult to get all users to attend the JAD meeting
- The JAD approach is subject to all of the problems associated with any group meeting

**Integrated Computer-Assisted Software Engineering**
*Advantages*
- Can produce systems with a longer effective operational life
- Can produce systems that closely meet user requirements
- Can speed up the development process
- Can produce systems that are more flexible and adaptable to changing business conditions
- Can produce excellent documentation

*Disadvantages*
- Systems are often more expensive to build and maintain
- The process requires more extensive and accurate definition of user requirements
- It is difficult to customize the end product

**Rapid Application Development**
*Advantages*
- Can speed up systems development
- Users are intensively involved from the start
- Improves the process of rewriting legacy applications

*Disadvantages*
- Produces functional components of final systems, but not the final systems themselves

**End-User Development**
*Advantages*
- Bypasses the IS department and avoids delays
- User controls the application and can change it as needed
- Directly meets user requirements
- Promotes increased user acceptance of new system
- Frees up IT resources

*Disadvantages*
- May eventually require maintenance from IS department
- Documentation may be inadequate
- Leads to poor quality control
- System may not have adequate interfaces to existing systems
- May create lower quality systems

**Object-Oriented Development**
*Advantages*
- Objects model real-world entities
- New systems may be able to reuse some computer code

*Disadvantages*
- Works best with systems of more limited scope (i.e., with systems that do not have huge numbers of objects)

solved, (2) specifying the technical options for the systems, and (3) anticipating the problems they are likely to encounter during development, the greater the chances of success. For these reasons, **systems investigation** addresses *the business problem* (or business opportunity) by means of the feasibility study.

The primary task in the systems investigation stage is the **feasibility study**. Organizations have three basic solutions to any business problem relating to an information system: (1) do nothing and continue to use the existing system unchanged, (2) modify or enhance the existing system, and (3) develop a new system. The **feasibility study** analyzes which of these three solutions best fits the particular business problem. It also provides a rough assessment of the project's technical, economic, and behavioral feasibility, as explained below:

- *Technical feasibility* determines whether the company can develop and/or acquire the hardware, software, and communications components needed to solve the business problem. Technical feasibility also determines whether the organization can use its existing technology to achieve the project's performance objectives.

- *Economic feasibility* determines whether the project is an acceptable financial risk and, if so, whether the organization has the necessary time and money to successfully complete the project. You have already learned about the commonly used methods to determine economic feasibility: NPV, ROI, breakeven analysis, and the business case approach.

- *Behavioral feasibility* addresses the human issues of the systems development project. You will be heavily involved in this aspect of the feasibility study.

After the feasibility analysis is completed, a "go/no-go" decision is reached by the steering committee if there is one or by top management in the absence of a committee. The go/no-go decision does not depend solely on the feasibility analysis. Organizations often have more feasible projects than they can fund. Therefore, the firm must prioritize the feasible projects and pursue those with the highest priority. Unfunded feasible projects may not be presented to the IT department at all. These projects therefore contribute to the *hidden backlog*, which are projects that the IT department is not aware of.

If the decision is no-go, then the project either is put on the shelf until conditions are more favorable or is discarded. If the decision is go, then the project proceeds, and the systems analysis phase begins.

## Systems Analysis

Once a development project has the necessary approvals from all participants, the systems analysis stage begins. **Systems analysis** is the process whereby systems analysts examine the business problem that the organization plans to solve with an information system.

The primary purpose of the systems analysis stage is to gather information about the existing system to determine the requirements for an enhanced system or a new system. The end product of this stage, known as the *deliverable*, is a set of *system requirements*.

Arguably, the most difficult task in systems analysis is to identify the specific requirements that the system must satisfy. These requirements are often called *user requirements*, because users (meaning you) provide them. When the systems developers have accumulated the user requirements for the new system, they proceed to the systems design stage.

## Systems Design

**Systems design** describes how the system will resolve the business problem. The deliverable of the systems design phase is the set of *technical system specifications*, which specify the following:

- System outputs, inputs, and user interfaces
- Hardware, software, databases, telecommunications, personnel, and procedures
- A blueprint of how these components are integrated

When the system specifications are approved by all participants, they are "frozen." That is, they should not be changed. Adding functions after the project has been initiated causes **scope creep**, in which the time frame and expenses associated with the project expand beyond the agreed-upon limits. Scope creep endangers both the project's budget and its schedule. Because scope creep is expensive, successful project managers place controls on changes requested by users. These controls help to prevent runaway projects.

## Programming and Testing

If the organization decides to construct the software in-house, then programming begins. **Programming** involves translating the design specifications into computer code. This process can be lengthy and time consuming, because writing computer code is as much an art as a science. Large-scale systems development projects can involve hundreds of computer programmers who are charged with creating hundreds of thousands of lines of computer code. These projects employ programming teams. The teams often include functional area users, who help the programmers focus on the business problem.

Thorough and continuous testing occurs throughout the programming stage. Testing is the process that assesses whether the computer code will produce the expected and desired results. It is also intended to detect errors, or bugs, in the computer code.

## Implementation

Implementation (or *deployment*) is the process of converting from an old computer system to a new one. The conversion process involves organizational change. Only end users can manage organizational change, not the MIS department. The MIS department typically does not have enough credibility with the business users to manage the change process. Organizations use three major conversion strategies: direct, pilot, and phased.

In a **direct conversion**, the old system is cut off, and the new system is turned on at a certain point in time. This type of conversion is the least expensive. It is also the most risky because, if the new system does not work as planned, there is no support from the old system. Because of these risks, few systems are implemented using direct conversion.

A **pilot conversion** introduces the new system in one part of the organization, such as in one plant or one functional area. The new system runs for a period of time and is then assessed. If the assessment confirms that the system is working properly, then the system is implemented in other parts of the organization.

A **phased conversion** introduces components of the new system, such as individual modules, in stages. Each module is assessed. If it works properly, then other modules are introduced, until the entire new system is operational. Large organizations commonly combine the pilot and phased approaches. That is, they execute a phased conversion using a pilot group for each phase. A fourth strategy is *parallel conversion*, in which the old and new systems operate simultaneously for a time. This strategy is seldom used today. One reason is that parallel conversion is totally impractical when both the old and new systems are online. Imagine that you are completing an order on Amazon, only to be told, "Before your order can be entered here, you must provide all the same information again, in a different form, and on a different set of screens." The results would be disastrous for Amazon. Regardless of the type of implementation process that an organization uses, the new system may not work as advertised. In fact, the new system may cause more problems than the old system that it replaced. IT's About Business 13.3 illustrates how such an implementation caused serious problems at Avon Products.

## Operation and Maintenance

After the new system is implemented, it will operate for a period of time, until (like the old system it replaced) it no longer meets its objectives. Once the new system's operations are stabilized, the company performs audits to assess the system's capabilities and to determine if it is being utilized correctly.

Systems require several types of maintenance. The first type is *debugging* the program, a process that continues throughout the life of the system. The second type is *updating* the system to accommodate changes in business conditions. An example is adjusting to new governmental regulations, such as changes in tax rates. These corrections and upgrades usually do not add any new functions. Instead, they simply help the system to continue to achieve its

# IT's [about business]

### 13.3 Avon Writes Off $125 Million on Failed Software Implementation

Avon Products (Avon) (*www.avon.com*) is a $10 billion U.S. international manufacturer and distributor of beauty, household, and personal care products sold through representatives in more than 140 countries. Avon is the fifth-largest beauty company and the second-largest direct selling enterprise in the world, with 6.4 million independent salespeople or representatives. It is also a multilevel marketing company, in which the sales force is compensated not only for sales they personally generate but also for the sales of the other salespeople whom they recruit. Salespeople are expected to sell products directly to consumers by means of relationship referrals and word-of-mouth marketing.

In 2009, CEO and Chairperson Andrea Jung decided that "Avon ladies" (i.e., Avon sales representatives) should carry iPads so that they could "digitize the sales experience with the customer." Jung wanted her sales team to order Avon products on their iPads so that the company's entire demand-driven supply chain would respond instantly. The Avon ladies would have access to product descriptions and inventories, and they would be able to place orders electronically.

To implement this program, Avon developed a SAP-based order management system. The system combined "back-end" (logistics and order fulfillment) software using SAP ERP modules with "front-end" (customer-facing) software using IBM electronic commerce software. Avon wanted to provide its reps with better insight into inventory as well as a better user experience. In May 2013, Avon launched a pilot system on its Web site in Canada.

When software development projects fail, the end users frequently suffer the most serious consequences. That is the case at Avon in Canada, where, in mid-2014, one independent salesperson was still struggling to cope with the hardships imposed by the company's failed order management system and Web site. She asserted that the system did not work properly when it was launched. Many sales representatives could not log into the new Web site. And, if they did gain access, the system did not accept orders, did not save orders properly, and did not reserve inventory properly. This rep further claimed that the Web site was too complex and required too many steps to place an order. She concluded that the new system "annihilated the business."

Ultimately, more than 100 of the 300 independent sales representatives who reported to her quit. The rep estimates that Avon lost as many as 16,000 representatives across Canada. In light of all the troubles that sales reps encountered using the system, people who were making $50 or $100 per month decided that it simply was not worth their time and effort. The losses among the sales force are devastating to a multilevel marketing company such as Avon, which depends on its independent sale reps to generate revenues.

In late 2013, Avon halted the global deployment of the order management system because the pilot deployment in Canada caused "significant business disruption in that market and did not show a clear return on investment." However, Avon maintained that the new system actually worked, but it was so complicated to use that it drove salespeople from the company in large numbers. Therefore, the usability of the system was not consistent with the experiences that salespeople expect from consumer applications on tablets. Avon stated that it would continue to use the software in Canada despite the problems it caused. In fact, the company took a $125 million write-down for associated software costs after it decided not to deploy the system globally.

In response to the problems Avon experienced with its pilot system, SAP maintained that it was involved only in the back-end applications of Avon's project, so it was not responsible for the front-end, sales-rep-facing application. The company also claimed that the order management system for Avon worked as designed.

The failure of the Avon system is a dramatic example of how usability has become a critical issue in the marketplace. People who are accustomed to using simple, well-designed applications in their personal lives (e.g., from Google, Amazon, and Apple) have no patience for disappointing and confusing applications at work. Essentially, consumer software has become so simple and intuitive to use that people expect business software to follow a similar model. If it does not, then users are much less patient than they were in the past.

As of early 2015, Avon was still performing damage control in Canada. The company's goal has remained the same: to stabilize its Canadian operations by intensifying recruitment and helping its salesforce to utilize the new system.

*Sources:* Compiled from "With Friends Like These . . . Uncovering Responsibility in Avon's Rollout Failure," *Enterprise Applications Consulting,* December 20, 2013; D. Henschen, "Inside Avon's Failed Order-Management Project," *InformationWeek,* December 16, 2013; N. Salerni, "Avon Cancels $125 Million Order Management System; Was the iPad App Too Hard to Use?" *iPhone in Canada,* December 15, 2013; "How NOT to Throw Out 125 Million Dollars," *Useful Usability,* December 12, 2013; D. Henschen, "Avon Pulls Plug on $125 Million SAP Project," *InformationWeek,* December 12, 2013; D. Fitzgerald, "Avon to Halt Rollout of New Order Management System," *The Wall Street Journal,* December 11, 2013; S. Rosenbush, "Avon's Failed SAP Implementation Reflects Rise of Usability," *The Wall Street Journal,* December 11, 2013; *www.avon.com,* accessed March 10, 2015.

### Questions

1. Is the Avon failure the fault of Avon? SAP? IBM? All three? Explain your answer.

2. Recall the discussion of strategic information systems in Chapter 2. Is Avon's new system a strategic information system? Why or why not? Explain your answer.

objectives. In contrast, the third type of maintenance *adds new functions* to the existing system without disturbing its operation.

# before you go on...

1. Describe the feasibility study.
2. What is the difference between systems analysis and systems design?
3. Describe structured programming.
4. What are the four conversion methods?

# Alternative Methods and Tools for Systems Development

13.4

Alternative methods for systems development include joint application design, rapid application development, agile development, and end-user development.

## Joint Application Design

**Joint application design (JAD)** is a group-based tool for collecting user requirements and creating system designs. It is most often used within the systems analysis and systems design stages of the SDLC. JAD involves a group meeting attended by the analysts and all of the users that can be conducted either in person or via the computer. During this meeting, all users jointly define and agree on the systems requirements. This process saves a tremendous amount of time. Table 13.2 lists the advantages and disadvantages of the JAD process.

## Rapid Application Development

**Rapid application development (RAD)** is a systems development method that can combine JAD, prototyping, and integrated computer-assisted software engineering (ICASE) tools (discussed later in this section) to rapidly produce a high-quality system. In the first RAD stage, developers use JAD sessions to collect system requirements. This strategy ensures that users are intensively involved early on. The development process in RAD is iterative; that is, requirements, designs, and the system itself are developed and then undergo a series, or sequence, of improvements. RAD uses ICASE tools to quickly structure requirements and develop prototypes. As the prototypes are developed and refined, users review them in additional JAD sessions. RAD produces the functional components of a final system, rather than prototypes. To understand how RAD functions and how it differs from SDLC, see Figure 13.6. Table 13.2 highlights the advantages and disadvantages of the RAD process.

## Agile Development

**Agile development** is a software development methodology that delivers functionality in rapid iterations, which are usually measured in weeks. To be successful, this methodology requires frequent communication, development, testing, and delivery. Agile development focuses on rapid development and frequent user contact to create software that addresses the needs of business users. This software does not have to include every possible feature the user will require. Rather, it must meet only the user's more important and immediate needs. It can be updated later to introduce additional functions as they become necessary. The core tenet of agile development is to do only what you have to do to be successful right now.

One type of agile development uses the *scrum approach*. A key principle of scrum is that during a project users can change their minds about what they want and need. Scrum acknowledges that a development problem cannot be fully understood or defined from the start.

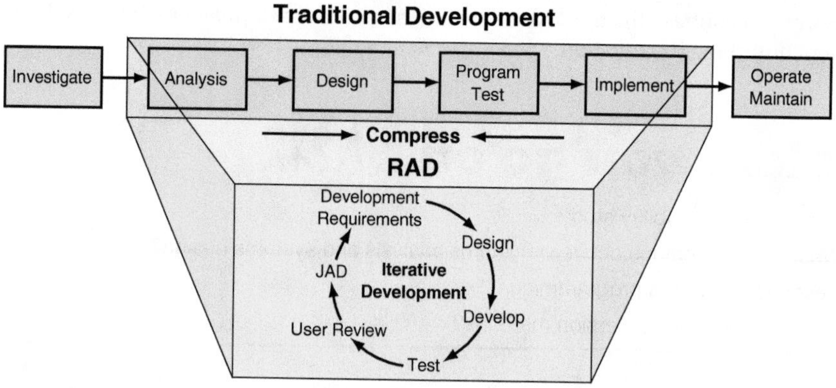

**FIGURE 13.6** A rapid prototyping development process versus SDLC.

datawarehousetraining.com/Methodologies/rapidapplication-development.

Therefore, scrum focuses on maximizing the development team's ability to deliver iterations quickly and to respond effectively to additional user requirements as they emerge.

Scrum contains sets of practices and predefined roles. The primary roles are the following:

- The *Scrum Master*: Maintains the processes (typically replaces a project manager).
- The *Product Owner*: Represents the business users and any other stakeholders in the project.
- The *Team*: A cross-functional group of about seven people who perform the actual analysis, design, coding, implementation, testing, and so on.

Scrum works this way: During each *sprint*—typically a2two- to4four-week period—the team creates a potentially shippable product increment, such as working and tested software. The set of features that goes into each sprint comes from the product backlog, which is a prioritized set of high-level work requirements to be completed.

The sprint planning meeting determines which backlog items will be addressed during a sprint. During this meeting, the Product Owner informs the team of the items in the product backlog that he or she wants to be completed. The team members then determine how many of these projects they can commit to during the next sprint, and they record this information in the sprint backlog.

During a sprint, no one is allowed to change the sprint backlog, which means that the requirements are frozen for the sprint. Each sprint must end on time. If the requirements are not completed for any reason, then they are left out and returned to the product backlog. After each sprint is completed, the team demonstrates how to use the software.

### End-User Development

**End-user development** is an approach in which the organization's end users develop their own applications with little or no formal assistance from the IT department. Table 13.2 lists the advantages and disadvantages of end-user development.

### Tools for Systems Development

Several tools can be used with various systems development methods. These tools include prototyping, integrated computer-assisted software engineering, component-based development, and object-oriented development.

Prototyping.    The **prototyping** approach defines an initial list of user requirements, builds a model of the system, and then refines the system in several iterations based on users' feedback. Developers do not try to obtain a complete set of user specifications for the system at the outset, and they do not plan to develop the system all at once. Instead, they quickly develop a smaller version of the system known as a prototype. A prototype can take two forms. In some cases, it contains only the components of the new system that are of most interest to the users. In other cases, it is a small-scale working model of the entire system.

Users make suggestions for improving the prototype, based on their experiences with it. The developers then review the prototype with the users and utilize their suggestions to refine it. This process continues through several iterations until the users approve the system or it becomes apparent that the system cannot meet the users' needs. If the system is viable, then the developers can use the prototype to build the full system. One typical use of prototyping is to develop screens that a user will see and interact with. Table 13.2 describes the advantages and disadvantages of the prototyping approach.

A practical problem with prototyping is that a prototype usually looks more complete than it is. That is, it may not use the real database, it usually does not have the necessary error checking, and it almost never includes the necessary security features. Users who review a prototype that resembles the finished system may not recognize these problems. Consequently, they might have unrealistic expectations about how close the actual system is to completion.

**Integrated Computer-Assisted Software Engineering Tools.**   **Computer-aided software engineering (CASE)** refers to a group of tools that automate many of the tasks in the SDLC. The tools that are used to automate the early stages of the SDLC (systems investigation, analysis, and design) are called **upper CASE tools**. The tools used to automate later stages in the SDLC (programming, testing, operation, and maintenance) are called **lower CASE tools**. CASE tools that provide links between upper CASE and lower CASE tools are called **integrated CASE (ICASE) tools**. Table 13.2 lists the advantages and disadvantages of ICASE tools.

**Component-Based Development.**   **Component-based development** uses standard components to build applications. Components are reusable applications that generally have one specific function, such as a shopping cart, user authentication, or a catalog. Compared with other approaches, component-based development generally involves less programming and more assembly. Component-based development is closely linked with the idea of Web services and service-oriented architectures, which you will study in Technology Guide 3.

Many startup companies are pursuing the idea of component-based application development. One example is Ning (*www.ning.com*), which allows organizations to create, customize, and share their own social network.

**Object-Oriented Development.**   **Object-oriented development** is based on a different view of computer systems than the perception that characterizes traditional development approaches. Traditional approaches can produce a system that performs the original task but may not be suited for handling other tasks. This limitation applies even when these other tasks involve the same real-world entities. For example, a billing system will handle billing, but it probably cannot be adapted to handle mailings for the marketing department or to generate leads for the sales force. This is true even though the billing, marketing, and sales functions all use similar data, including customer names, addresses, and purchases. In contrast, an *object-oriented (OO) system* begins not with the task to be performed, but with the aspects of the real world that must be modeled to perform that task. Therefore, in our example, if the firm has a good model of its customers and its interactions with them, then it can use this model equally well for billings, mailings, and sales leads.

The development process for an object-oriented system begins with a feasibility study and an analysis of the existing system. Systems developers identify the *objects* in the new system— the fundamental elements in OO analysis and design. Each object represents a tangible, real-world entity, such as a customer, bank account, student, or course. Objects have *properties*, or *data values*. For example, a customer has an identification number, a name, an address, an account number(s), and so on. Objects also contain the *operations* that can be performed on their properties. For example, operations that can be performed on the customer object may include obtain-account-balance, open-account, withdraw-funds, and so on. Operations are also referred to as *behaviors*.

This approach enables OO analysts to define all the relevant objects needed for the new system, including their properties and operations. The analysts then model how the objects interact to meet the objectives of the new system. In some cases, analysts can reuse existing objects from other applications (or from a library of objects) in the new system. This process saves the analysts the time they otherwise would spend coding these objects. In most cases, however, even with object reuse, some coding will be necessary to customize the objects and their interactions for the new system.

You have studied many methods that can be used to acquire new systems. Table 13.2 provides an overview of the advantages and disadvantages of each of these methods.

## before you go on...

1. Describe the tools that augment the traditional SDLC.
2. Describe the alternative methods that can be used for systems development other than the SDLC.

# What's In IT For Me?

### For the Accounting Major

Accounting personnel help perform the cost–benefit analyses on proposed projects. They may also monitor ongoing project costs to keep them within budget. Accounting personnel undoubtedly will find themselves involved with systems development at various points throughout their careers.

### For the Finance Major

Finance personnel are frequently involved with the financial issues that accompany any large-scale systems development project (e.g., budgeting). They also are involved in cost–benefit and risk analyses. To perform these tasks, they need to stay abreast of the emerging techniques used to determine project costs and ROI. Finally, because they must manage vast amounts of information, finance departments are also common recipients of new systems.

### For the Marketing Major

In most organizations, marketing, like finance, involves massive amounts of data and information. Like finance, then, marketing is also a hotbed of systems development. Marketing personnel will increasingly find themselves participating in systems development teams. Such involvement increasingly means helping to develop systems, especially Web-based systems that reach out directly from the organization to its customers.

### For the Production/Operations Management Major

Participation in development teams is also a common role for production/operations people. Manufacturing is becoming increasingly computerized and integrated with other allied systems, from design to logistics to customer support. Production systems interface frequently with marketing, finance, and human resources. In addition, they may be part of a larger, enterprisewide system. Also, many end users in POM either develop their own systems or collaborate with IT personnel on specific applications.

### For the Human Resources Management Major

The human resources department is closely involved with several aspects of the systems acquisitions process. Acquiring new systems may require hiring new employees, changing job descriptions, or terminating employees. Human resources staff performs all of these tasks. Further, if the organization hires consultants for the development project, or outsources it, the human resources department may handle the contracts with these suppliers.

### For the MIS Major

Regardless of the approach that the organization adopts for acquiring new systems, the MIS department spearheads it. If the organization chooses either to buy or to lease the application, the MIS department leads in examining the offerings of the various vendors and in negotiating with the vendors. If the organization chooses to develop the application in-house, then the process falls to the MIS department. MIS analysts work closely with users to develop their information requirements. MIS programmers then write the computer code, test it, and implement the new system.

## [ Summary ]

1. **Discuss the different cost–benefit analyses that companies must take into account when formulating an IT strategic plan.**

    The four common approaches to cost–benefit analysis are the following:

    - *The net present value* method converts future values of benefits to their present-value equivalent by "discounting" them at the organization's cost of funds. They can then compare the present value of the future benefits with the cost required to achieve those benefits to determine whether the benefits exceed the costs.
    - *Return on investment* measures management's effectiveness in generating profits with its available assets. ROI is calculated by dividing net income attributable to a project by the average assets invested in the project. ROI is a percentage, and the higher the percentage return, the better.
    - *Breakeven analysis* determines the point at which the cumulative dollar value of the benefits from a project equals the investment made in the project.
    - In the *business case approach*, system developers write a business case to justify funding one or more specific applications or projects.

2. **Discuss the four business decisions that companies must make when they acquire new applications.**

    - *How much computer code does the company want to write?* A company can choose to use a totally prewritten application (to write no computer code), to customize a prewritten application (to write some computer code), or to customize an entire application (write all new computer code).
    - *How will the company pay for the application?* Once the company has decided how much computer code to write, it must decide how to pay for it. With prewritten applications or customized prewritten applications, companies can buy them or lease them. With totally custom applications, companies use internal funding.
    - *Where will the application run?* Companies must now decide where to run the application. The company may run the application on its own platform or run the application on someone else's platform (use either a software-as-a-service vendor or an application service provider).
    - *Where will the application originate?* Prewritten applications can be open-source software or come from a vendor. Companies may choose to customize prewritten open-source applications or prewritten proprietary applications from vendors. Companies may customize applications in-house or outsource the customization. They can also write totally custom applications in-house or outsource this process.

3. **Enumerate the primary tasks and importance of each of the six processes involved in the systems development life cycle.**

The six processes are the following:

- *Systems investigation:* Addresses the business problem (or business opportunity) by means of the feasibility study; main task in the systems investigation stage is the feasibility study.
- *Systems analysis:* Examines the business problem that the organization plans to solve with an information system; main purpose is to gather information about the existing system in order to determine the requirements for the new system; end product of this stage, known as the "deliverable, " is a set of system requirements.
- *Systems design:* Describes how the system will resolve the business problem; deliverable is the set of technical system specifications.
- *Programming and testing:* Programming translates the design specifications into computer code; testing checks to see whether the computer code will produce the expected and desired results and detects errors, or bugs, in the computer code; deliverable is the new application.
- *Implementation:* The process of converting from the old system to the new system via three major conversion strategies: direct, pilot, and phased; deliverable is properly working application.
- *Operation and maintenance:* Types of maintenance include debugging, updating, and adding new functions when needed.

4. **Describe alternative development methods and tools that augment development methods.**

The following are the alternative methods:

- *Joint application design* is a group-based tool for collecting user requirements and creating system designs.
- *Rapid application development* is a systems development method that can combine JAD, prototyping, and ICASE tools to rapidly produce a high-quality system.
- *Agile development* is a software development methodology that delivers functionality in rapid iterations, which are usually measured in weeks.
- *End-user development* refers to an organization's end users developing their own applications with little or no formal assistance from the IT department.

The following are the tools:

- The *prototyping* approach defines an initial list of user requirements, builds a model of the system, and then improves the system in several iterations based on users' feedback.
- *Integrated computer-aided software engineering* combines upper CASE tools (automate systems investigation, analysis, and design) and lower CASE tools (programming, testing, operation, and maintenance).
- *Component-based development* uses standard components to build applications. Components are reusable applications that generally have one specific function, such as a shopping cart, user authentication, or a catalog.
- *Object-oriented development* begins with the aspects of the real world that must be modeled to perform that task. Systems developers identify the objects in the new system. Each object represents a tangible, real-world entity, such as a customer, bank account, student, or course. Objects have *properties*, or *data values*. Objects also contain the *operations* that can be performed on their properties.

Table 13.2 shows advantages and disadvantages of alternative methods and tools.

# [ Chapter Glossary ]

**agile development** A sof ware development methodology that delivers functionality in rapid iterations, measured in weeks, requiring frequent communication, development, testing, and delivery.

**application portfolio** The set of recommended applications resulting from the planning and justification process in application development.

**application service provider (ASP)** An agent or vendor who assembles the sof ware needed by enterprises and packages them with outsourced development, operations, maintenance, and other services.

**component-based development** A sof ware development methodology that uses standard components to build applications.

**computer-aided software engineering (CASE)** Development approach that uses specialized tools to automate many of the tasks in the SDLC; upper CASE tools automate the early stages of the SDLC and lower CASE tools automate the later stages.

**direct conversion** Implementation process in which the old system is cut off and the new system is turned on at a certain point in time.

**end-user development** Approach in which the organization's end users develop their own applications with little or no formal assistance from the IT department.

**feasibility study** Investigation that gauges the probability of success of a proposed project and provides a rough assessment of the project's feasibility.

**implementation** The process of converting from an old computer system to a new one.

**integrated CASE (ICASE) tools** CASE tools that provide links between upper CASE and lower CASE tools.

**IS operational plan** Consists of a clear set of projects that the IS department and the functional area managers will execute in support of the IT strategic plan.

**IT steering committee** A committee, comprised of a group of managers and staff representing various organizational units, set up to establish IT priorities and to ensure that the MIS function is meeting the needs of the enterprise.

**IT strategic plan** A set of long-range goals that describe the IT infrastructure and major IT initiatives needed to achieve the goals of the organization.

**joint application design (JAD)** A group-based tool for collecting user requirements and creating system designs.

**lower CASE tools** Tools used to automate later stages in the SDLC (programming, testing, operation, and maintenance)

**object-oriented development** A systems development methodology that begins with aspects of the real world that must be modeled to perform a task.

**outsourcing** Use of outside contractors or external organizations to acquire IT services.

**phased conversion** Implementation process that introduces components of the new system in stages, until the entire new system is operational.

**pilot conversion** Implementation process that introduces the new system in one part of the organization on a trial basis; when the new system is working properly, it is introduced in other parts of the organization.

**programmers** IS professionals who modify existing computer programs or write new computer programs to satisfy user requirements.

**programming** The translation of a system's design specifications into computer code.

**prototype** A small-scale working model of an entire system or a model that contains only the components of the new system that are of most interest to the users.

**prototyping** An approach that defines an initial list of user requirements, builds a prototype system, and then improves the system in several iterations based on users' feedback.

**rapid application development (RAD)** A development method that uses special tools and an iterative approach to rapidly produce a high-quality system.

**request for proposal (RFP)** Document that is sent to potential vendors inviting them to submit a proposal describing their sof ware package and how it would meet the company's needs.

**scope creep** Adding functions to an information system after the project has begun.

**service-level agreements (SLAs)** Formal agreements regarding the division of work between a company and its vendors.

**software-as-a-service (SaaS)** A method of delivering sof ware in which a vendor hosts the applications and provides them as a service to customers over a network, typically the Internet.

**systems analysis** The examination of the business problem that the organization plans to solve with an information system.

**systems analysts** IS professionals who specialize in analyzing and designing information systems.

**systems design** Describes how the new system will resolve the business problem.

**systems development life cycle (SDLC)** Traditional structured framework, used for large IT projects, that consists of sequential processes by which information systems are developed.

**systems investigation** The initial stage in the traditional SDLC that addresses the business problem (or business opportunity) by means of the feasibility study.

**systems stakeholders** All people who are affected by changes in information systems.

**technical specialists** Experts on a certain type of technology, such as databases or telecommunications.

**upper CASE tools** Tools that are used to automate the early stages of the SDLC (systems investigation, analysis, and design).

# [ Discussion Questions ]

1. Discuss the advantages of a lease option over a buy option.
2. Why is it important for all business managers to understand the issues of IT resource acquisition?
3. Why is it important for everyone in business organizations to have a basic understanding of the systems development process?
4. Should prototyping be used on every systems development project? Why or why not?
5. Discuss the various types of feasibility studies. Why are they all needed?
6. Discuss the issue of assessing intangible benefits and the proposed solutions.
7. Discuss the reasons why end-user-developed information systems can be of poor quality. What can be done to improve this situation?

# [ Problem-Solving Activities ]

1. Access *www.ecommerce-guide.com*. Find the product review area. Read reviews of three software payment solutions. Assess them as possible components.
2. Use an Internet search engine to obtain information on CASE and ICASE tools. Select several vendors and compare and contrast their offerings.
3. Access *www.ning.com*. Observe how the site provides components for you to use to build applications. Build a small application at the site.
4. Enter *www-01.ibm.com/software*. Find its WebSphere product. Read recent customers' success stories. What makes this software so popular?
5. Enter the Web sites of the Gartner (*www.gartner.com*), the Yankee Group (*www.yankeegroup.com*), and CIO (*www.cio.com*). Search for recent material about ASPs and outsourcing, and prepare a report on your findings.
6. StoreFront (*www.storefront.net*) is a vendor of e-business software. At its site, the company provides demonstrations illustrating the types of storefronts that it can create for shoppers. The site also provides demonstrations of how the company's software is used to create a store.

   a. Run the StoreFront demonstration to see how this is done.

   b. What features does StoreFront provide?

   c. Does StoreFront support smaller or larger stores?

   d. What other products does StoreFront offer for creating online stores? What types of stores do these products support?

# [ Closing Case The Federal Aviation Administration's Next Generation Air Transportation System ]

## The Original Problem

The U.S. air traffic system has achieved an impressive safety record. Nevertheless, many of the network's features are so antiquated that experts blame them for delays and other inefficiencies that cost billions of dollars each year. The Federal Aviation Administration (FAA) (*www.faa.gov*) estimates that if the increasing congestion in the U.S. air transportation system is not addressed, it will cost the nation's economy $22 billion annually in lost economic activity by 2022. Perhaps more seriously, it will also cause increasing safety issues, potentially endangering the flying public.

## The Intended Solution

To resolve these problems, the FAA began to develop the Next Generation Air Transportation System (NextGen) (*www.faa .gov/nextgen*) in 2004. (Development and deployment continue in early 2015.) The purpose of NextGen is to transform America's air traffic control system from a ground-based system to a satellite-based system. NextGen uses global positioning system (GPS) technologies to shorten routes, save time and fuel, reduce traffic delays, increase the number of planes in the air traffic system, and permit controllers to monitor and manage aircraft with greater safety. Planes will be able to fly closer together, take more direct routes, and avoid delays caused when planes remain in holding patterns while they wait for an open runway. To implement NextGen, the FAA will have to transform the nation's entire air transportation system.

The FAA planned for a 20-year, $40 billion project, including upgraded information systems and radar, a new communications network to replace radios, and a satellite-based surveillance system that indicates the locations of nearby planes without relying on air traffic controllers. The goal is to manage planes more precisely and automatically, thereby enabling them to fly closer and with greater safety. The FAA planned to deploy NextGen across the country in stages between 2012 and 2025.

The FAA estimated that by 2018, NextGen will reduce aviation fuel consumption by 1.4 billion gallons, reduce carbon emissions by 14 million tons, and save billions of dollars in costs. Each mile in the air costs an airline about $0.10–0.15 per seat in operating expenses such as flight crew and fuel.

## Problems with NextGen's Implementation

Uneven progress, budget overruns, and conflicts among regulators and airlines demonstrate how extremely challenging the task of modernizing the world's most complex air traffic management network really is. The slow pace of NextGen's implementation has drawn harsh criticism. An April 2013 report by the Government Accountability Office (GAO) found that, although the project exhibited some progress, the implementation has been hindered by bureaucracy, delays designing new navigation procedures, and fear of conflicts with airport neighbors and environmentalists. The report further stated that the FAA had failed to set realistic goals, budgets, or expectations for NextGen. The report raised concerns that NextGen's completion could slip to 2035, and its actual costs could be three times as great as its estimated costs.

FAA Administrator Michael Huerta responded that the agency had met 80 percent of its implementation goals since 2008. He asserted that the FAA will continue to develop NextGen despite government spending cuts.

There were early problems with NextGen. The FAA initially designed new flight paths without much industry input. Airlines, which are responsible for at least $7 billion of NextGen's total cost, have already invested in sophisticated computers and other cockpit equipment to enable pilots to fly more precise paths. Further, various interests have collided frequently. As an example, simply reworking air routes to and from airports can take years, partly as a result of environmental assessments to address local noise concerns.

Difficulties in NextGen implementation have occurred nearly everywhere, from new landing procedures that were impossible for some planes to execute to aircraft tracking software that misidentified planes. Key initiatives are experiencing delays and are at risk of cost overruns. Further, the FAA lacks "an executable plan" for bringing NextGen fully online, according to the GAO.

Some airline officials, frustrated because they have not seen promised money-saving benefits, assert they want better results before they spend more money to equip planes to use NextGen, a vital step to the system's success. Lawmakers are also frustrated. NextGen has enjoyed broad bipartisan support in Congress. With the government facing spending cuts, however, supporters fear the program will not receive the necessary funding to become fully operational. In September 2013, a government–industry advisory committee recommended that, given the likelihood of budget cuts, the FAA should concentrate on just 11 NextGen initiatives that are ready or nearly

ready to come online. The committee concluded that the rest of NextGen's 150 initiatives can wait.

Even the use of GPS-based procedures has been slowed by unforeseen problems. Developing each procedure on an airport-by-airport schedule takes several years. At large airports, new procedures are used only sporadically. During busy periods, controllers do not have time to switch back and forth between the new procedures, which most airliners can use, and older procedures that regional airliners and smaller planes still use. Consequently, all flights use the older procedure because all planes can fly them.

In mid-2014, an internal FAA report projected that NextGen will cost $120 billion to implement, three times more than the original estimate. Further, the FAA estimated that the system will not be fully operational until 2035.

## The Results So Far (Early 2015)

The nations' new information system to reduce airline delays—itself years behind schedule—is finally yielding results. Let's examine a few of them:

- According to the FAA, the implementation of a surface management (taxi) initiative in Boston saved more than 5,000 gallons of aviation fuel and reduced carbon dioxide emissions by 50 tons during one period of heavy congestion.
- A shared surface surveillance system combined with aircraft monitoring techniques reduced taxi-out time by 7,000 hours per year at New York's JFK airport and by 5,000 hours in Memphis, Tennessee.
- NextGen has also been tested in Memphis with Delta Air Lines and FedEx (www.fedex.com).
- The National Air Traffic Controllers Association conducted a demonstration at Dallas/Fort Worth International Airport of a new surveillance display called the Tower Flight Data Manager system that presented surveillance, flight data, weather, airport configuration, and other information critical to controllers.
- Specialized Optimized Profile Descents, also known as Initial Tailored Arrivals, are in operation at airports in San Francisco, Los Angeles, Miami, and Denver.

Let's take a closer look at one specific example, Alaska Air Group (www.alaskaair.com), where the future has arrived. Since Spring 2013, pilots landing at its Seattle–Tacoma International Airport (Sea-Tac) hub no longer descend in steps that require frequent radio contact with air traffic controllers. Instead, they fly smoothly on autopilot, with their engines nearly idle.

One Alaska Air pilot recently demonstrated the new technology in a flight simulator, threading his GPS-guided Boeing 737 through a precise path that cut almost 20 miles from the old route. Significantly, this revised route included a tight turn that would have been impossible with the previous system. The new equipment enables pilots to descend smoothly and to guide planes through narrow bands of airspace. These procedures reduce the number of local residents who are affected by noise. The pilot needed only to monitor his plane's computers to ensure that the plane stayed on track.

Under the old system—which is still employed by planes that lack new equipment and for two arrival tracks that have not been modernized—planes approached Sea-Tac by following radio beacons. Controllers guided in pilots with multiple commands to change direction, altitude, and speed. Those steps frequently consumed extra fuel, and they increased mileage.

Alaska Air—not the FAA—initiated the efforts at Sea-Tac, in 2009. The airline had already been using radar-guided approaches to remote Alaskan airports that are famous for their bad weather. The FAA initially approved the plan; they then took it over a year later. The agency eventually provided nearly $5 million to update two of Sea-Tac's four arrival tracks with GPS guidance technologies.

More than 90 percent of Alaska Airlines pilots now use the two GPS approaches. Alaska Air executives claim that satellite-guided arrivals and departures at Seattle and a handful of other airports saved the carrier $17.6 million and 200,000 gallons of fuel in a single year.

In sum, Alaska Air has successfully deployed some elements of NextGen. Nevertheless, as of early 2015, the success of the entire project remained uncertain.

*Sources:* Compiled from E. Pianin, "Congress Enraged by the FAA's $40B White Elephant," *The Fiscal Times*, November 19, 2014; C. Howard, "NextGen GA Fund Selects Banks to Help Finance General Aviation NextGen Installations, Accelerate FAA's NextGen Implementation," *Avionics Intelligence*, March 14, 2014; W. Bellamy, "NextGen among Top US Transportation Issues for 2014," *Avionics Today*, December 17, 2013; J. Lowy, "The FAA's Next Big Issue Is Acting on Its NextGen Air Traffic Control Dreams," *Associated Press*, November 1, 2013; J. Lowy, "Air Traffic Control Modernization Hits Turbulence," *Associated Press*, October 31, 2013; S. Carey, "The FAA's $40 Billion Adventure," *The Wall Street Journal*, August 19, 2013; W. Jackson, "What's Keeping FAA's NextGen Air Traffic Control on the Runway?" *GCN.com*, July 22, 2013; S. Carey, "The FAA's $40 Billion Adventure," *The Wall Street Journal*, March 20, 2013; J. Mouawad, "Alaska Airlines, Flying above an Industry's Troubles," *The New York Times*, March 2, 2013; J. Hoover, "Problems Plague FAA's NextGen Air Traffic Control Upgrade," *InformationWeek*, October 5, 2011; "Fact Sheet – Next Generation Air Transportation System," *FAA News*, May 27, 2010; *www.faa.gov/nextgen*, *www.faa.gov*, accessed January 30, 2015.

### Questions

1. Describe the many problems that have caused problems with implementing NextGen.

2. In Technology Guide 1, you learned that hardware capabilities double roughly every 18 months (Moore's law). What impact will increases in hardware processing power, with accompanying decreases in size, have on the NextGen system? Support your answer.

3. Recall the discussion of cloud computing in Technology Guide 3. What impact might a cloud computing solution have on the future of the NextGen system? Support your answer.

# 1 Hardware

| [ LEARNING OBJECTIVES ] | [ CHAPTER OUTLINE ] | [ WEB RESOURCES ] |
|---|---|---|

**[ LEARNING OBJECTIVES ]**

1. Identify the major hardware components of a computer system.

2. Discuss strategic issues that link hardware design to business strategy.

3. Describe the various types of computers in the computer hierarchy.

4. Differentiate the various types of input and output technologies and their uses.

5. Describe the design and functioning of the central processing unit.

**[ CHAPTER OUTLINE ]**

TG 1.1 Introduction to Hardware

TG 1.2 Strategic Hardware Issues

TG 1.3 Computer Hierarchy

TG 1.4 Input and Output Technologies

TG 1.5 The Central Processing Unit

**[ WEB RESOURCES ]**

- Student PowerPoints for note taking

**WileyPLUS Learning Space**

- E-book
- Author video lecture for each chapter section
- Practice quizzes
- Flash Cards for vocabulary review
- Additional "IT's About Business" cases
- Video interviews with managers
- Lab Manuals for Microsoft Office 2010 and 2013

## What's In IT For Me?

This Tech Guide Will Help Prepare You To...

| ACCT | FIN | MKT | POM | HRM | MIS |
|---|---|---|---|---|---|
| ACCOUNTING | FINANCE | MARKETING | PRODUCTION OPERATIONS MANAGEMENT | HUMAN RESOURCES MANAGEMENT | MIS |

# Introduction

As you begin this Technology Guide, you might be wondering, why do I have to know anything about hardware? There are several reasons why you will benefit from understanding the basics of hardware. First, regardless of your major (and future functional area in an organization), you will be using different types of hardware throughout your career. Second, you will have input concerning the hardware that you will use. In this capacity, you will be required to answer many questions, such as "Is my hardware performing adequately for my needs? If not, what types of problems am I experiencing?" Third, you will also have input into decisions when your functional area or organization upgrades or replaces its hardware. In addition, some organizations allocate the hardware budget to functional areas or departments. In such cases, you might be responsible for making hardware decisions (at least locally) yourself. MIS employees will act as advisors, but you will provide important input into such decisions.

# TG 1.1 Introduction to Hardware

Recall from Chapter 1 that the term *hardware* refers to the physical equipment used for the input, processing, output, and storage activities of a computer system. Decisions about hardware focus on three interrelated factors: appropriateness for the task, speed, and cost. The incredibly rapid rate of innovation in the computer industry complicates hardware decisions because computer technologies become obsolete more quickly than other organizational technologies.

The overall trends in hardware are that it becomes smaller, faster, cheaper, and more powerful over time. In fact, these trends are so rapid that they make it difficult to know when to purchase (or upgrade) hardware. This difficulty lies in the fact that companies that delay hardware purchases will, more than likely, be able to buy more powerful hardware for the same amount of money in the future. It is important to note that buying more powerful hardware for the same amount of money in the future is a trade-off. An organization that delays purchasing computer hardware gives up the benefits of whatever it could buy today until the future purchase date arrives.

Hardware consists of the following:

- *Central processing unit (CPU):* Manipulates the data and controls the tasks performed by the other components.
- *Primary storage:* Temporarily stores data and program instructions during processing.
- *Secondary storage:* Stores data and programs for future use.
- *Input technologies:* Accept data and instructions and convert them to a form that the computer can understand.
- *Output technologies:* Present data and information in a form people can understand.
- *Communication technologies:* Provide for the flow of data from external computer networks (e.g., the Internet and intranets) to the CPU, and from the CPU to computer networks.

# TG 1.2 Strategic Hardware Issues

For most businesspeople, the most important issues are what the hardware enables, how it is advancing, and how rapidly it is advancing. In many industries, exploiting computer hardware is a key to achieving competitive advantage. Successful hardware exploitation comes from thoughtful consideration of the following questions:

- How do organizations keep up with the rapid price reductions and performance advancements in hardware? For example, how often should an organization upgrade its computers and storage systems? Will upgrades increase personal and organizational productivity? How can organizations measure such increases?

- How should organizations determine the need for the new hardware infrastructures, such as cloud computing? (We discuss cloud computing in Technology Guide 3.)
- Portable computers and advanced communications technologies have enabled employees to work from home or from anywhere. Will these new work styles benefit employees and the organization? How do organizations manage such new work styles?
- How do organizations manage employees who use their own portable devices (e.g., tablets and smartphones) for both personal and work purposes? That is, how do organizations handle the bring-your-own-device (BYOD) phenomenon?

# Computer Hierarchy

TG 1.3

The traditional standard for comparing types of computers is their processing power. This section presents each type of computer, from the most powerful to the least powerful. It describes both the computers themselves and their roles in modern organizations.

## Supercomputers

The term *supercomputer* does not refer to a specific technology. Rather, it indicates the fastest computers available at any given time. At the time of this writing (mid-2015), the fastest supercomputers boasted speeds exceeding 30 petaflops (one petaflop is 1,000 trillion floating point operations per second). A floating point operation is an arithmetic operation involving decimals.

Large organizations use supercomputers to execute computationally demanding tasks involving very large data sets, such as military and scientific applications. In the business environment for example, large banks employ supercomputers to calculate the risks and returns of various investment strategies, and healthcare organizations use them to analyze giant databases of patient data to determine optimal treatments for various diseases.

Laptop computer

## Mainframe Computers

*Mainframes* remain popular in large enterprises for extensive computing applications that are accessed by thousands of users at one time. Examples of mainframe applications are airline reservation systems, corporate payroll programs, Web site transaction processing systems (e.g., Amazon and eBay), and student grade calculation and reporting.

Today's mainframes perform at teraflop (trillions of floating point operations per second) speeds and can handle millions of transactions per day. In addition, mainframes provide a secure, robust environment in which to run strategic, mission-critical applications.

© PhotoEdit/Alamy

Motorola Xoom tablet

## Microcomputers

*Microcomputers* (also called *micros*, *personal computers*, or *PCs*) are small, complete, general purpose computers. It is important to point out that people frequently define a PC as a computer that utilizes the Microsoft Windows operating system. In fact, there are a variety of PCs available, many of which do not use Windows. One well-known example is the Apple Mac, which uses the Mac OS X operating system (discussed in Technology Guide 2).

© Oleksiy Makymenko/Alamy

## Laptop and Notebook Computers

*Laptop and notebook computers* are small, easily transportable, lightweight computers (see Figure TG 1.1). They provide users with access to processing power and data outside an office environment.

Apple iPad tablet

**FIGURE TG 1.1** Laptop, notebook, and tablet computers.

For example, the Google Chromebook is a thin-client laptop that runs Google's Chrome operating system. A **thin client** is a computer that does not offer the full functionality of a fat client. A **fat client** is a computer that has the ability to perform many functions without a network connection. Thin clients are less complex than fat clients because they do not have locally installed software. When thin clients need to run an application, they access it from a server over a network instead from a local disk drive.

A thin client would not have Microsoft Office installed on it. Thus, thin clients are easier and less expensive to operate and support than fat clients. The benefits of thin clients include fast application deployment, centralized management, lower cost of ownership, and easier installation, management, maintenance, and support. The major disadvantage of thin clients is that if the network fails, then users can do very little on their computers. In contrast, if users have fat clients and the network fails, they can still perform some functions because the necessary software, such as Microsoft Office, is installed on their computers.

### Tablet Computers

A *tablet computer*, or simply *tablet*, is a complete computer contained entirely in a flat touch screen that users operate via a stylus, a digital pen, or their fingertip instead of a keyboard or mouse. Examples of tablets are the Apple iPad mini 3 (www.apple.com/ipad), the HP Slate 10 (www.hp.com), the Microsoft Surface Pro 3 (www.microsoft.com), and many others.

### Wearable Computers (Wearables)

*Wearables* are miniature computers that people wear under, with, or on top of their clothing. Key features of wearables are that there is constant interaction between the computer and the users and users can multitask, meaning that they do not have to stop what they are doing to utilize the device. Examples of wearable computers are the Apple Watch (www.apple.com/watch/), the Sony SmartWatch 3 (www.sony.com/SmartWatch), the Samsung Gear S (www.samsung.com/global/microsite/gears/index.html), Google Glass (www.google.com/glass/start/), and the Fitbit (www.fitbit.com) activity tracker.

Google Glass is an excellent example of a wearable computer that provides augmented reality. **Augmented reality** is a live, direct or indirect, view of a physical, real-world environment whose elements are enhanced by computer-generated sensory input such as sound, video, graphics, or GPS data. That is, augmented reality enhances the user's perception of reality. Note that, in contrast, virtual reality replaces the real world with a simulated world.

# IT's Personal: Purchasing a Computer

One day you will purchase a computer for yourself or your job. When that day comes, it will be important for you to know what to look for. Buying a computer can be very confusing if you just read the box. This Technology Guide has explained the major hardware components of a computer. There are more things you need to consider, however, when you purchase a computer: what you plan to do with it, where you plan to use it, and how long you need service from it? Let's look at each question more closely.

- What do you plan to do with your computer? Consider that when you buy a vehicle, your plans for using the vehicle determine the type of vehicle you will purchase. The same

rules apply to purchasing a computer. You need to consider what you currently do with a computer and what you may do before you replace the one under consideration. Although many people simply buy as much as they can afford, they may overpay because they do not consider what they need the computer for.

- Where do you plan to use your computer? If you plan to use it only at home at your desk, then a desktop model will be fine. In general, you can get more computer for your money in a desktop model as opposed to a laptop (i.e., you pay extra for mobility). However, if you think you may want to take the computer with you, then you will need some type of a laptop or tablet computer. When portability is a requirement, you will want to reconsider what you plan to use the computer for because as computers become more portable (smaller), their functionality changes, and you want to ensure the computer will meet your needs.

- How long do you need service from this computer? Today, we anticipate that most of the devices we purchase will become outdated and need to be replaced in a few years. Therefore, the length of service is really more about warranty and the availability of repair services. In some cases, you should base your purchase decision on these issues rather than speed because they can extend the life of your computer.

# Input and Output Technologies

# TG 1.4

Input technologies allow people and other technologies to enter data into a computer. The two main types of input devices are human data-entry devices and source-data automation devices. As their name implies, *human data-entry* devices require a certain amount of human effort to input data. Examples are keyboard, mouse, pointing stick, trackball, joystick, touchscreen, stylus, and voice recognition.

In contrast, *source-data automation* devices input data with minimal human intervention. These technologies speed up data collection, reduce errors, and gather data at the source of a transaction or other event. Barcode readers are an example of source-data automation. Table TG 1.1 describes the various input devices.

## Table **TG 1.1**
### Input Devices

| Input Device | Description |
| --- | --- |
| *Human Data-Entry Devices* | |
| Keyboards | Most common input device (for text and numerical data). |
| Mouse | Handheld device used to point the cursor at a point on screen, such as an icon; the user clicks a button on the mouse, instructing the computer to take some action. |
| Optical mouse | The mouse is not connected to computer by a cable; rather, it uses camera chip to take images of surface it passes over, comparing successive images to determine its position. |
| Trackball | User rotates a ball built into top of device to move the cursor (rather than moving an entire device such as a mouse). |
| Pointing stick | Small button-like device; the cursor moves in the direction of the pressure the user places on the stick. Located between the keys near the center of the keyboard. |
| Touchpad | User moves the cursor by sliding a finger across a sensitized pad and then can tap the pad when the cursor is in (also called a trackpad) the desired position to instruct the computer to take action (also called glide-and-tap pad). |
| Graphics tablet | A device that can be used in place of, or in conjunction with, a mouse or trackball; it has a flat surface for drawing and a pen or stylus that is programmed to work with the tablet. |
| Joystick | The joystick moves the cursor to the desired place on the screen; commonly used in video games and in workstations that display dynamic graphics. |

## Table TG 1.1 (Continued)

| Input Device | Description |
| --- | --- |
| Touchscreen | Users instruct computer to take some action by touching a particular part of the screen; commonly used in information kiosks such as ATM machines. Touchscreens now have gesture controls for browsing through photographs, moving objects around on a screen, flicking to turn the page of a book, and playing video games. For example, see the Apple iPhone. |
| Stylus | Pen-style device that allows user either to touch parts of a predetermined menu of options or to handwrite information into the computer (as with some PDAs); works with touch-sensitive screens. |
| Digital pen | Mobile device that digitally captures everything you write; built-in screen confirms that what you write has been saved; also captures sketches, figures, and so on with on-board flash memory |
| Web camera (Webcam) | A real-time video camera whose images can be accessed via the Web or instant messaging. |
| Voice recognition | Microphone converts analog voice sounds into digital input for a computer; critical technology for physically challenged people who cannot use other input devices. |

*Gesture-Based Input*

Gesture recognition refers to technologies that enable computers to interpret human gestures. These technologies would be the first step in designing computers that can understand human body language. This process creates a richer interaction between machines and humans than has been possible via keyboards, graphical user interfaces, and the mouse. Gesture recognition enables humans to interact naturally with a computer without any intervening mechanical devices. With gesture-based technologies, the user can move the cursor by pointing a finger at a computer screen. These technologies could make conventional input devices (the mouse, keyboards, and touchscreens) redundant. Examples of gesture-based input devices are the Nintendo Wii (*www.nintendo.com/wii*), the Microsoft Kinect (*www.xbox.com/kinect*), and the Leap Motion Controller (*www.leapmotion.com*).

| | |
| --- | --- |
| Wii | A video game console produced by Nintendo. A distinguishing feature of the Wii is its wireless controller, which can be used as a handheld pointing device and can detect movement in three dimensions. |
| Microsoft Kinect | A device that enables users to control and interact with the Xbox 360 through a natural interface using gestures and spoken commands. Kinect eliminates the need for a game controller. |
| Leap Motion Controller | A motion-sensing, matchbox-sized device placed on a physical desktop. Using two cameras, the device "observes" an area up to a distance of about three feet. It precisely tracks fingers or items such as a pen that cross into the observed area. The Leap can perform tasks such as navigating a Web site, using pinch-to-zoom gestures on maps, performing high-precision drawing, and manipulating complex three-dimensional visualizations. The smaller observation area and higher resolution of the device differentiates it from the Microsoft Kinect, which is more suitable for whole-body tracking in a space the size of a living room. |

*Source-Data Automation Input Devices*

| | |
| --- | --- |
| Automated teller machine (ATM) | A device that includes source-data automation input in the form of a magnetic stripe reader; human input via a keyboard; and output via a monitor, printer, and cash dispenser. |
| Magnetic stripe reader | A device that reads data from a magnetic stripe, usually on the back of a plastic card (e.g., credit and debit cards). |

## Table **TG 1.1** (Continued)

| Input Device | Description |
|---|---|
| Point-of-sale terminals | Computerized cash registers that also may incorporate touchscreen technology and barcode scanners to input data such as item sold and price. |
| Barcode scanners | Devices that scan black-and-white barcode lines printed on merchandise labels. |
| Optical mark reader | Scanner for detecting the presence of dark marks on a predetermined grid, such as multiple-choice test answer sheets. |
| Magnetic ink character reader | A device that reads magnetic ink printed on checks that identify the bank, checking account, and check number. |
| Optical character recognition | Software that converts text into digital form for input into computer. |
| Sensors | Devices that collect data directly from the environment and input data directly into computer; examples are vehicle airbag activation sensors and radio-frequency identification tags. |
| Cameras | Digital cameras capture images and convert them into digital files. |
| Radio-frequency identification (RFID) | Uses technology that contains active or passive tags (transmitters) to wirelessly transmit product information to electronic readers. (We discuss RFID in detail in Chapter 8.) |

The output generated by a computer can be transmitted to the user via several output devices and media. These devices include monitors, printers, plotters, and voice. Table TG 1.2 describes the various output devices.

## Table **TG 1.2**
### Output Devices

| Output Device | Description |
|---|---|
| *Monitors* | |
| Cathode ray tubes | Video screens on which an electron beam illuminates pixels on a display screen. |
| Liquid crystal displays (LCDs) | Flat displays that have liquid crystals between two polarizers to form characters and images on a backlit screen. |
| Flexible displays | Thin, plastic, bendable computer screens. |
| Organic light-emitting diodes (OLEDs) | Displays that are brighter, thinner, lighter, cheaper, faster, and take less power to run than LCDs. |
| Retinal scanning displays | Project image directly onto a viewer's retina; used in medicine, air traffic control, and controlling industrial machines. |
| Heads-up displays | Any transparent display that presents data without requiring the user to look away from his or her usual viewpoint; for example, see Microvision (*www.microvision.com*). |

## Table **TG 1.2** (Continued)

| Output Device | Description |
|---|---|
| *Printers* | |
| Laser | Use laser beams to write information on photosensitive drums; produce high-resolution text and graphics. |
| Inkjet | Shoot fine streams of colored ink onto paper; usually less expensive to buy than laser printers but can be more expensive to operate; can offer resolution quality equal to laser printers. |
| Thermal | Produce a printed image by selectively heating coated thermal paper; when the paper passes over the thermal print head, the coating turns black in the areas where it is heated, producing an image. |
| *Plotters* | Use computer-directed pens for creating high-quality images, blueprints, schematics, drawing of new products, and so on. |
| *Voice output* | A speaker/headset that can output sounds of any type; voice output is a software function that uses this equipment. |
| *Electronic book reader* | A wireless, portable reading device with access to books, blogs, newspapers, and magazines. On-board storage holds hundreds of books (e.g., Amazon Kindle, Sony Reader). |
| *Pocket projector* | A projector in a handheld device that provides an alternative display method to alleviate the problem of tiny display screens in handheld devices. Pocket projectors will project digital images onto any viewing surface (e.g., see the Pico Projector). |

**Multimedia technology** is the computer-based integration of text, sound, still images, animation, and digitized motion video. It usually consists of a collection of various input and output technologies. Multimedia merges the capabilities of computers with televisions, CD players, DVD players, video and audio recording equipment, and music and gaming technologies. High-quality multimedia processing requires powerful microprocessors and extensive memory capacity, including both primary and secondary storage.

## TG 1.5 The Central Processing Unit

The **central processing unit** performs the actual computation or "number crunching" inside any computer. The CPU is a **microprocessor** (e.g., Intel's Core i3, i5, and i7 chips with more to come) made up of millions of microscopic transistors embedded in a circuit on a silicon wafer or *chip*. For this reason, microprocessors are commonly referred to as chips.

As shown in Figure TG 1.2, the microprocessor has different parts, which perform different functions. The **control unit** sequentially accesses program instructions, decodes them, and controls the flow of data to and from the arithmetic logic unit (ALU), the registers, the caches, primary storage, secondary storage, and various output devices. The **arithmetic logic unit** performs the mathematical calculations and makes logical comparisons. The registers are high-speed storage areas that store very small amounts of data and instructions for short periods.

**The microprocessor**

| Control unit | Arithmetic-logic unit |
|---|---|
| Registers | |

Input →

Output

↓ Primary storage (main memory) ↑

Communication devices

↓ Secondary storage ↑

**FIGURE TG 1.2** Parts of a microprocessor.

## How the CPU Works

In the CPU, inputs enter and are stored until they are needed. At that point, they are retrieved and processed, and the output is stored and then delivered somewhere. Figure TG 1.3 illustrates this process, which works as follows:

- The inputs consist of data and brief instructions about what to do with the data. These instructions come into the CPU from random access memory (RAM). Data might be entered by the user through the keyboard, for example, or read from a data file in another part of the computer. The inputs are stored in registers until they are sent to the next step in the processing.
- Data and instructions travel in the chip via electrical pathways called *buses*. The size of the bus—analogous to the width of a highway—determines how much information can flow at any time.
- The control unit directs the flow of data and instructions within the chip.
- The ALU receives the data and instructions from the registers and makes the desired computation. These data and instructions have been translated into **binary form**—that is, only 0s and 1s. A "0" or a "1" is called a **bit**. The CPU can process only binary data. All types of data, such as letters, decimal numbers, photographs, music, and so on, can be converted to a binary representation, which can then be processed by the CPU.

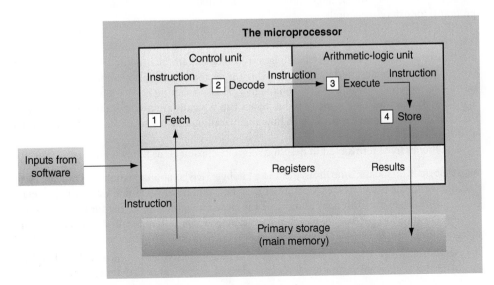

**FIGURE TG 1.3** How the CPU works.

- The data in their original form and the instructions are sent to storage registers and then are sent back to a storage place outside the chip, such as the computer's hard drive. Meanwhile, the transformed data go to another register and then on to other parts of the computer (e.g., to the monitor for display or to storage).

Intel offers excellent demonstrations of how CPUs work: Search the web for "Intel" with "Explore the Curriculum" to find their demos. This cycle of processing, known as a *machine instruction cycle*, occurs billions of times per second.

## Advances in Microprocessor Design

Innovations in chip designs are coming at a faster and faster rate, as described by **Moore's law**. In 1965, Gordon Moore, a cofounder of Intel Corporation, predicted that microprocessor complexity would double approximately every 18 months. His prediction has been amazingly accurate.

The advances predicted from Moore's law arise mainly from the following changes:

- Producing increasingly miniaturized transistors.
- Placing multiple processors on a single chip. Chips with more than one processor are called *multicore* chips. For example, the Cell chip, produced by a consortium of Sony, Toshiba, and IBM, contains nine processors. Intel (*www.intel.com*) and AMD (*www.amd .com*) offer multicore chips (e.g., quadcore chips with four CPUs).
- Intel's three-dimensional (3D) chips require less power than Intel's current chips while improving performance. These chips enhance the performance of all computers. However, they are particularly valuable in handheld devices, because they extend the device's battery life.

In addition to increased speeds and performance, Moore's law has had an impact on costs. For example, in 1997, a desktop computer with a Pentium II microprocessor, 64 megabytes of random access memory, a 4-gigabyte hard drive, and a 17-inch monitor cost $4,000. In early 2015, a desktop computer with an Intel i7 quad-core processor, 12 gigabytes of random access memory, a 2-terabyte hard drive plus 32 gigabytes of solid-state storage, and a 27-inch touch-screen cost less than $2,000.

## Computer Memory

The amount and type of memory that a computer possesses has a great deal to do with its general utility. A computer's memory also determines the types of programs that the computer can run, the work it can perform, its speed, and its cost. There are two basic categories of computer memory. The first is *primary storage*. It is called "*primary*" because it stores small amounts of data and information that the CPU will use immediately. The second category is *secondary storage*, which stores much larger amounts of data and information (e.g., an entire software program) for extended periods.

*Memory Capacity.* As you have seen, CPUs process only binary units—0s and 1s—which are translated through computer languages into bits. A particular combination of bits represents a certain alphanumeric character or a simple mathematical operation. Eight bits are needed to represent any one of these characters. This 8-bit string is known as a **byte**. The storage capacity of a computer is measured in bytes. Bits typically are used as units of measure only for telecommunications capacity, as in how many million bits per second can be sent through a particular medium.

The hierarchy of terms used to describe memory capacity is as follows:

- *Kilobyte*: Kilo means "one thousand," so a kilobyte (KB) is approximately 1,000 bytes. Actually, a kilobyte is 1,024 bytes. Computer designers find it convenient to work with powers of 2: 1,024 is 2 to the 10th power, and 1,024 is close enough to 1,000 that for kilobyte people use the standard prefix *kilo*, which means exactly 1,000 in familiar units such as the kilogram or kilometer.
- *Megabyte*: Mega means "one million," so a megabyte (MB) is approximately 1 million bytes. Most personal computers have hundreds of megabytes of RAM memory.

- *Gigabyte*: Giga means "one billion," so a gigabyte (GB) is approximately 1 billion bytes.
- *Terabyte*: A terabyte is approximately 1 trillion bytes. The storage capacity of modern personal computers can be several terabytes.
- *Petabyte*: A petabyte is approximately 1,000 terabytes.
- *Exabyte*: An exabyte is approximately 1,000 petabytes.
- *Zettabyte*: A zettabyte is approximately 1,000 exabytes.

To get a feel for these amounts, consider the following example: If your computer has one terabyte of storage capacity on its hard drive (a type of secondary storage), it can store approximately 1 trillion bytes of data. If the average page of text contains about 2,000 bytes, then your hard drive could store approximately 10 percent of all the print collections of the Library of Congress. That same terabyte can store 70 hours of standard-definition compressed video.

**Primary Storage.**    **Primary storage**, or **main memory**, as it is sometimes called, stores three types of information for very brief periods of time: (1) data to be processed by the CPU, (2) instructions for the CPU as to how to process the data, and (3) operating system programs that manage various aspects of the computer's operation. Primary storage takes place in chips mounted on the computer's main circuit board, called the *motherboard*. These chips are located as close as physically possible to the CPU chip. As with the CPU, all the data and instructions in primary storage have been translated into binary code.

The four main types of primary storage are (1) register, (2) cache memory, (3) random access memory, and (4) read-only memory (ROM). You learn about each type of primary storage next.

**Registers** are part of the CPU. They have the least capacity, storing extremely limited amounts of instructions and data only immediately before and after processing.

**Cache memory** is a type of high-speed memory that enables the computer to temporarily store blocks of data that are used more often and that a processor can access more rapidly than main memory (RAM). Cache memory is physically located closer to the CPU than RAM. Blocks that are used less often remain in RAM until they are transferred to cache; blocks used infrequently remain in secondary storage. Cache memory is faster than RAM because the instructions travel a shorter distance to the CPU.

*Random access memory* is the part of primary storage that holds a software program and small amounts of data for processing. Compared with the registers, RAM stores more information and is located farther away from the CPU. However, compared with secondary storage, RAM stores less information and is much closer to the CPU.

RAM is temporary and, in most cases, *volatile*—that is, RAM chips lose their contents if the current is lost or turned off, as from a power surge, brownout, or electrical noise generated by lightning or nearby machines.

Most of us have lost data at one time or another due to a computer "crash" or a power failure. What is usually lost is whatever is in RAM, cache, or the registers at the time, because these types of memory are volatile. Therefore, you need greater security when you are storing certain types of critical data or instructions. Cautious computer users frequently save data to nonvolatile memory (secondary storage). In addition, most modern software applications have autosave functions.

**Read-only memory** is the place—actually, a type of chip—where certain critical instructions are safeguarded. ROM is nonvolatile, so it retains these instructions when the power to the computer is turned off. The read-only designation means that these instructions can only be read by the computer and cannot be changed by the user. An example of ROM is the instructions needed to start or "boot" the computer after it has been shut off.

**Secondary Storage.**    **Secondary storage** is designed to store very large amounts of data for extended periods. Secondary storage has the following characteristics:

- It is nonvolatile.
- It takes more time to retrieve data from it than from RAM.
- It is cheaper than primary storage (see Figure TG 1.4).
- It can utilize a variety of media, each with its own technology.

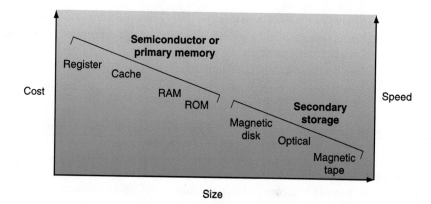

One secondary storage medium, magnetic tape, is kept on a large open reel or in a smaller cartridge or cassette. Although this is an old technology, it remains popular because it is the cheapest storage medium, and it can handle enormous amounts of data. As a result, many organizations (e.g., the U.S. Government Social Security Administration) use magnetic tape for archival storage. The downside is that it is the slowest method for retrieving data because all the data are placed on the tape sequentially. This process means that the system might have to run through the majority of the tape before it comes to the desired piece of data.

**Magnetic disks** (or hard drives or **fixed disk drives**) are the most commonly used mass storage devices because of their low cost, high speed, and large storage capacity. Hard disk drives read from, and write to, stacks of rotating (at up to 15,000 rpm) magnetic disk platters mounted in rigid enclosures and sealed against environmental and atmospheric contamination (see Figure TG 1.5). These disks are permanently mounted in a unit that may be internal or external to the computer.

**Solid-state drives** (**SSDs**) are data storage devices that serve the same purpose as a hard drive and store data in memory chips. Whereas hard drives have moving parts, SSDs do not. SSDs use the same interface with the computer's CPU as hard drives and are therefore a seamless replacement for hard drives. SSDs offer many advantages over hard drives. They use less power, are silent and faster, and produce about one-third the heat of a hard drive. The major disadvantage of SSDs is that they cost more than hard drives.

Unlike magnetic media, **optical storage devices** do not store data via magnetism. Rather, a laser reads the surface of a reflective plastic platter. Optical disk drives are slower than magnetic hard drives, but they are less fragile and less susceptible to damage from contamination.

In addition, optical disks can store a great deal of information, both on a routine basis and when combined into storage systems. Types of optical disks include compact disk read-only memory and digital video disk.

*Compact disk read-only memory* (CD-ROM) storage devices feature high capacity, low cost, and high durability. However, because a CD-ROM is a read-only medium, it cannot be written on. CD-R can be written on, but once this is done, what was written on it cannot be

Homiel / iStockphoto

© Krzysztof Krzyscin/iStockphoto

changed later. That is, CD-R is writable, while CD-ROM is not, but it is not rewritable, which CD-RW (compact disk, rewritable) is. There are applications where not being rewritable is a plus, because it prevents some types of accidental data destruction. CD-RW adds rewritability to the recordable compact disk market.

The digital video disk (*DVD*) is a 5-inch disk with the capacity to store about 135 minutes of digital video. DVDs can also perform as computer storage disks, providing storage capabilities of 17 gigabytes. DVD players can read current CD-ROMs, but current CD-ROM players cannot read DVDs. The access speed of a DVD drive is faster than that of a typical CD-ROM drive.

A dual-layer *Blu-ray disc* can store 50 gigabytes, almost three times the capacity of a dual-layer DVD. Development of Blu-ray technology is ongoing, with three- and four-layered Blu-ray discs available.

**Flash memory devices** (or *memory cards*) are nonvolatile electronic storage devices that contain no moving parts and use 30 times less battery power than hard drives. Flash devices are also smaller and more durable than hard drives. The trade-offs are that flash devices store less data than hard drives. Flash devices are used with digital cameras, handheld and laptop computers, telephones, music players, and video game consoles.

One popular flash memory device is the **thumb drive** (also called *memory stick, jump drive,* or *flash drive*). These devices fit into Universal Serial Bus (USB) ports on personal computers and other devices, and they can store many gigabytes. Thumb drives have replaced magnetic floppy disks for portable storage.

## before you go on...

1. Decisions about hardware focus on which three factors?
2. What are the overall trends in hardware?
3. Define hardware and list the major hardware components.
4. Describe the different types of computers.
5. Distinguish between human data-input devices and source-data automation.
6. Briefly describe how a microprocessor functions.
7. Distinguish between primary storage and secondary storage.

---

# What's In IT For Me?

### For All Business Majors

The design of computer hardware has profound impacts for businesspeople. Personal and organizational success can depend on an understanding of hardware design and a commitment to knowing where it is going and what opportunities and challenges hardware innovations will bring. Because these innovations are occurring so rapidly, hardware decisions both at the individual level and at the organizational level are difficult.

At the *individual level*, most people who have a home or office computer system and want to upgrade it, or people who are contemplating their first computer purchase, are faced with the decision of *when* to buy as much as *what* to buy and at what cost. At the *organizational level*, these same issues plague IS professionals. However, they are more complex and more costly. Most organizations have many different computer systems in place at the same time. Innovations may come to different classes of computers at different times or rates. Therefore, managers must decide when old hardware *legacy systems* still have a productive role in the organization and when they should be replaced. A legacy system is an old computer system or application that continues to be used, typically because it still functions for the users' needs, even though newer technology is available.

# [ Summary ]

1. **Identify the major hardware components of a computer system.**

Modern computer systems have six major components: the central processing unit (CPU), primary storage, secondary storage, input technologies, output technologies, and communications technologies.

2. **Discuss the strategic issues that link hardware design to business strategy.**

Strategic issues linking hardware design to business strategy include the following: How do organizations keep up with the rapid price/performance advancements in hardware? How often should an organization upgrade its computers and storage systems? How can organizations measure benefits gained from price/performance improvements in hardware?

3. **Describe the various types of computers in the computer hierarchy.**

Supercomputers are the most powerful computers, designed to handle intensive computational demands. Organizations use mainframes for centralized data processing and managing large databases. Microcomputers are small, complete, general purpose computers. Laptop or notebook computers are small, easily transportable computers. Tablet computers are complete computers contained entirely in a flat touch screen that uses a stylus, digital pen, or fingertip as an input device instead of a keyboard or mouse. Wearable computers are miniature computers that people wear under, with, or on top of their clothing.

4. **Differentiate the various types of input and output technologies and their uses.**

Principal human data-entry input technologies include the keyboard, mouse, optical, mouse, trackball, touchpad, joystick, touch screen, stylus, and voice-recognition systems. Principal source-data automation input devices include ATMs, POS terminals, barcode scanners, optical mark readers, magnetic ink character readers, optical character readers, sensors, cameras, radio-frequency identification, and retinal scanning displays. Common output technologies include various types of monitors, impact and nonimpact printers, plotters, and voice output.

5. **Describe the design and functioning of the central processing unit.**

The CPU is made up of the arithmetic logic unit, which performs the calculations; the registers, which store minute amounts of data and instructions immediately before and after processing; and the control unit, which controls the flow of information on the microprocessor chip. After processing, the data in their original form and the instructions are sent back to a storage location outside the chip.

# [ Glossary ]

**arithmetic logic unit (ALU)** Portion of the CPU that performs the mathematical calculations and makes logical comparisons.

**augmented reality** A live, direct or indirect, view of a physical, real-world environment whose elements are enhanced by computer-generated sensory input such as sound, video, graphics, or GPS data.

**binary form** The form in which data and instructions can be read by the CPU—only 0s and 1s.

**bit** Short for *binary digit* (0s and 1s), the only data that a CPU can process.

**byte** An 8-bit string of data, needed to represent any one alphanumeric character or simple mathematical operation.

**cache memory** A type of high-speed memory that enables the computer to temporarily store blocks of data that are used more often and that a processor can access more rapidly than main memory (RAM).

**central processing unit (CPU)** Hardware that performs the actual computation or "number crunching" inside any computer.

**control unit** Portion of the CPU that controls the flow of information.

**fat clients** Computers that offer full functionality without having to connect to a network.

**flash memory devices** Nonvolatile electronic storage devices that are compact, are portable, require little power, and contain no moving parts.

**gesture recognition** An input method that interprets human gestures, in an attempt for computers to begin to understand human body language.

**magnetic disks (or hard drives or fixed disk drives)** A form of secondary storage on a magnetized disk divided into tracks and sectors that provide addresses for various pieces of data.

**magnetic tape** A secondary storage medium on a large open reel or in a smaller cartridge or cassette.

**microprocessor** The CPU, made up of millions of transistors embedded in a circuit on a silicon wafer or chip.

**Moore's law** Prediction by Gordon Moore, an Intel cofounder, that microprocessor complexity would double approximately every two years.

**multimedia technology** Computer-based integration of text, sound, still images, animation, and digitized full-motion video.

**optical storage devices** A form of secondary storage in which a laser reads the surface of a reflective plastic platter.

**primary storage (also called main memory)** High-speed storage located directly on the motherboard that stores data to be processed by the CPU, instructions telling the CPU how to process the data, and operating system programs.

**random access memory (RAM)** The part of primary storage that holds a software program and small amounts of data when they are brought from secondary storage.

**read-only memory (ROM)** Type of primary storage where certain critical instructions are safeguarded; the storage is nonvolatile and retains the instructions when the power to the computer is turned off.

**registers** High-speed storage areas in the CPU that store very small amounts of data and instructions for short periods.

**secondary storage** Technology that can store very large amounts of data for extended periods.

**sequential access** Data access in which the computer system must run through data in sequence to locate a particular piece.

**server** Computers that support networks, enabling users to share files, software, and other network devices.

**solid-state drives (SSDs)** Data storage devices that serve the same purpose as a hard drive and store data in memory chips.

**thin client** A computer that does not offer the full functionality of a fat client.

**thumb drive** Storage device that fits into the USB port of a personal computer and is used for portable storage.

## [ Discussion Questions ]

1. What factors affect the speed of a microprocessor?
2. If you were the Chief information officer (CIO) of a firm, what factors would you consider when selecting secondary storage media for your company's records (files)?
3. Given that Moore's law has proved itself over the past two decades, speculate on what chip capabilities will be in 10 years. What might your desktop PC be able to do?
4. If you were the CIO of a firm, how would you explain the workings, benefits, and limitations of using thin clients as opposed to fat clients?
5. Where might you find embedded computers at home, at school, and/or at work?
6. What does this statement mean: "Hardware is useless without software."

## [ Problem-Solving Activities ]

1. Access the Web sites of the major chip manufacturers— for example, Intel (*www.intel.com*), Motorola (*www.motorola.com*), and Advanced Micro Devices (*www.amd.com*)—and obtain the latest information on new and planned chips. Compare performance and costs across these vendors. Ensure to take a close look at the various multicore chips.

2. Access "The Journey Inside" on Intel's Web site at *http://www.intel.com/content/www/us/en/education/k12/the-journey-inside.html*. Prepare a presentation of each step in the machine instruction cycle.

# 2 Software

| [ LEARNING OBJECTIVES ] | [ CHAPTER OUTLINE ] | [ WEB RESOURCES ] |
|---|---|---|

**[ LEARNING OBJECTIVES ]**

1. Discuss the major software issues that confront modern organizations.
2. Describe the general functions of the operating system.
3. Identify the major types of application software.

**[ CHAPTER OUTLINE ]**

TG 2.1 Software Issues

TG 2.2 Systems Software

TG 2.3 Application Software

**[ WEB RESOURCES ]**

- Student PowerPoints for note taking

**WileyPLUS Learning Space**

- E-book
- Author video lecture for each chapter section
- Practice quizzes
- Flash Cards for vocabulary review
- Additional "IT's About Business" cases
- Video interviews with managers
- Lab Manuals for Microsoft Office 2010 and 2013

## What's In IT For Me?

### This Tech Guide Will Help Prepare You To...

| ACCT | FIN | MKT | POM | HRM | MIS |
|---|---|---|---|---|---|
| ACCOUNTING | FINANCE | MARKETING | PRODUCTION OPERATIONS MANAGEMENT | HUMAN RESOURCES MANAGEMENT | MIS |

# Introduction

As you begin this Technology Guide, you might be wondering, why do I have to know anything about software? There are several reasons why you will benefit from understanding the basics of software. First, regardless of your major (and future functional area in an organization), you will be using different types of software throughout your career. Second, you will have input concerning the software that you will use. In this capacity, you will be required to answer many questions, such as "Does this software help me do my job?" "Is this software easy to use?" "Do I need more functionality and, if so, what functionality would be most helpful to me?" Third, you will also have input into decisions when your functional area or organization upgrades or replaces its software. In addition, some organizations allocate the software budget to functional areas or departments. In such cases, you might be responsible for making software decisions (at least locally) yourself. MIS employees will act as advisors, but you will provide important input into such decisions.

Computer hardware is only as effective as the instructions you give it. Those instructions are contained in **software**. The importance of computer software cannot be overestimated. The first software applications for computers in business were developed in the early 1950s. At that time, software was less costly. Today, software comprises a much larger percentage of the cost of modern computer systems because the price of hardware has dramatically decreased, while both the complexity and the price of software have dramatically increased.

The ever-increasing complexity of software has also increased the potential for errors, or *bugs*. Large applications today may contain millions of lines of computer code, written by hundreds of people over the course of several years. Thus, the potential for errors is huge, and testing and debugging software is expensive and time consuming.

In spite of these overall trends—increasing complexity, cost, and numbers of defects—software has become an everyday feature of our business and personal lives. Your examination of software begins with definitions of some fundamental concepts. Software consists of computer programs, which are sequences of instructions for the computer. The process of writing or coding programs is called **programming**. Individuals who perform this task are called *programmers*.

Computer programs include documentation, which is a written description of the program's functions. Documentation helps the user operate the computer system, and it helps other programmers understand what the program does and how it accomplishes its purpose. Documentation is vital to the business organization. Without it, the departure of a key programmer or user could deprive the organization of the knowledge of how the program is designed and how it functions.

The computer can do nothing until it is instructed by software. Computer hardware, by design, is general purpose. Software enables the user to instruct the hardware to perform specific functions that provide business value. There are two major types of software: systems software and application software. Figure TG 2.1 illustrates the relationship among hardware, systems software, and application software.

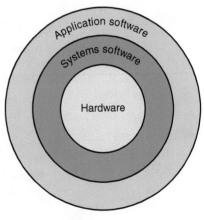

**FIGURE TG 2.1** Systems software serves as an intermediary between hardware and functional applications.

# Software Issues

The importance of software in computer systems has brought new issues to the forefront for organizational managers. These issues include software defects (bugs), licensing, open systems, and open-source software.

### Software Defects

All too often, computer program code is inefficient, poorly designed, and riddled with errors. The Software Engineering Institute (SEI) at Carnegie Mellon University defines good software as usable, reliable, defect-free, cost-effective, and maintainable. As our dependence on computers and networks increases, the risks associated with software defects are becoming more serious.

The SEI maintains that, on average, professional programmers make between 100 and 150 errors in every 1,000 lines of code they write. Fortunately, the software industry recognizes this problem. Unfortunately, however, the problem is enormous, and the industry is taking only initial steps to resolve it. One critical step is better design and planning at the beginning of the development process (discussed in Chapter 13).

## Software Licensing

Many people routinely copy proprietary software. However, making copies without the manufacturer's explicit permission—a practice known as *piracy*—is illegal. The Business Software Alliance (BSA) (*www.bsa.org*), a nonprofit trade association dedicated to promoting a safe and legal digital world, collects, investigates, and acts on software piracy tips. The BSA has calculated that piracy costs software vendors around the world billions of dollars annually. Most of the tips the BSA receives come from current and past employees of offending companies.

To protect their investment, software vendors must prevent their products from being copied and distributed by individuals and other software companies. A company can copyright its software, which means that the U.S. Copyright Office grants the company the exclusive legal right to reproduce, publish, and sell that software.

The number of computing devices in organizations continues to grow, and businesses continue to decentralize, so IS managers are finding it increasingly difficult to supervise their software assets. In fact, the majority of chief information officers (CIOs) are not confident that their companies were in compliance with software licensing agreements. For example, one medium-size company was fined $10,000 for unknowingly using Microsoft Exchange mailbox licenses that had not been purchased. Worse, the company was also fined $100,000 for not having the necessary licenses for Autodesk, Inc.'s AutoCAD design software.

To help companies manage their software licenses, new firms have arisen that specialize in tracking software licenses for a fee. For example, Express Metrix (*www.expressmetrix.com*) will track and manage a company's software licenses to ensure they are in compliance with U.S. copyright laws.

## Open Systems

The **open systems** concept refers to a group of computing products that work together. In an open system, the same operating system (OS) with compatible software is installed on all computers that interact within an organization. A complementary approach is to employ application software that will run across all computer platforms. Where hardware, operating systems, and application software are all designed as open systems, users can purchase the best software, called *best of breed*, for a job without worrying whether it will run on particular hardware.

## Open-Source Software

Organizations today are increasingly selecting open-source software rather than proprietary software. **Proprietary software** is purchased software that has restrictions on its use, copying, and modification. Companies that develop proprietary software spend money and time developing their products, which they then sell in the marketplace. This software is labeled *proprietary* because the developer keeps the source code—the actual computer instructions—private (just as Coca-Cola does with its formula). Therefore, companies that purchase the software can utilize it in their operations, but they cannot change the source code themselves.

In contrast, the source code for **open-source software** is available at no cost to both developers and users. This software is distributed with license terms that ensure that its source code will always be available.

Open-source software is produced by worldwide "communities" of developers who write and maintain the code. Inside each community, however, only a small group of developers, called *core developers*, is allowed to modify the code directly. All the other developers must submit their suggested changes to the core developers.

There are advantages to implementing open-source software in an organization. According to OpenSource (*www.opensource.org*), open-source development produces high-quality, reliable, low-cost software. This software is also flexible, meaning that the code can be changed to meet users' needs. In many cases, open-source software can be more reliable than proprietary software. Because the code is available to many developers, more bugs are discovered early and quickly, and they are fixed immediately. Technical support for open-source software is also available from firms that offer products derived from the software. An example is Red Hat (*www.redhat.com*), a major Linux vendor that supplies solutions to problems associated with open-source technology. Specifically, Red Hat provides education, training, and technical support, for a fee.

Open-source software, however, also has disadvantages. The major drawback is that companies that use open-source software depend on the continued goodwill of an army of volunteers for enhancements, bug fixes, and so on, even if they have signed a contract that includes support. Some companies will not accept this risk, although as a practical matter the support community for Linux, Apache, and Firefox is not likely to disappear. Further, organizations that do not have in-house technical experts will have to purchase maintenance–support contracts from a third party. In addition, open-source software poses questions concerning ease of use, the time and expense needed to train users, and compatibility with existing systems either within or outside the organization.

There are many examples of open-source software, including the GNU (GNU's Not UNIX) suite of software (*www.gnu.org*) developed by the Free Software Foundation (*www.fsf.org*); the Linux operating system (see *www.linux-hq.com*); Apache Web server (*www.apache.org*); sendmail SMTP (Send Mail Transport Protocol) e-mail server (*www.sendmail.org*); the Perl programming language (*www.perl.org*); the Firefox browser from Mozilla (*www.mozilla.com*); and Sun's StarOffice applications suite (*www.sun.com/software/star/staroffice/index.jsp*). In fact, more than 150,000 open-source projects from around the world are under way at SourceForge (*www.sourceforge.net*), the popular open-source hosting site.

Open-source software is moving to the mainstream, as you see by the many major companies that use this type of software. For example, Japan's Shinsei Bank (*www.shinseibank.com*) uses Linux on its servers; SugarCRM (*www.sugarcrm.com*) for certain customer relationship management tasks; and MySQL (*www.mysql.com*) open-source database management software. Further, the *Los Angeles Times* uses Alfresco (*www.alfresco.com*) to manage some of the images and video for its Web site.

# Systems Software

## TG 2.2

Systems software is a set of instructions that serves primarily as an intermediary between computer hardware and application programs. Systems software performs many functions:

- It controls and supports the computer system and its information-processing activities.
- It enables computer systems to perform self-regulatory functions by loading itself when the computer is first turned on.
- It provides commonly used sets of instructions for all applications.
- It helps users and IT personnel program, test, and debug their own computer programs.
- It supports application software by directing the computer's basic functions.

The major type of systems software with which we are concerned is the operating system. The **operating system** is the "director" of your computer system's operations. It supervises the overall operation of the computer by monitoring the computer's status, scheduling operations, and managing input and output processes. Well-known desktop operating systems include Microsoft Windows (*www.microsoft.com*), Apple Mac OS X (*www.apple.com*), Linux (*www.linuxhq.com*), and Google Chrome (*www.google.com/chrome*). When a new version with new features is released, the developers often give the new version a new designation. For example, in early 2015, the latest version of Windows was Windows 10, and the latest version of OS X was Yosemite.

The operating system also provides an interface between the user and the hardware. This user interface hides the complexity of the hardware from the user. That is, you do not have to know how the hardware actually operates; you simply have to know what the hardware will do and what you need to do to obtain the desired results.

The ease or difficulty of the interaction between the user and the computer is determined to a large extent by the **graphical user interface (GUI)**. The GUI allows users to directly control the hardware by manipulating visible objects (such as icons) and actions that replace complex commands. Microsoft Windows provides a widely recognized GUI.

GUI technology incorporates features such as virtual reality, head-mounted displays, speech input (user commands) and output, pen and gesture recognition, animation, multimedia, artificial intelligence, and cellular/wireless communication capabilities. These new interfaces, called *natural user interfaces* (NUIs), will combine social, haptic, and touch-enabled gesture-control interfaces. (A *haptic interface* provides tactile feedback through the sense of touch by applying forces, vibrations, or motions to the user.)

A **social interface** guides the user through computer applications by using cartoon-like characters, graphics, animation, and voice commands. The cartoon-like characters can be puppets, narrators, guides, inhabitants, or *avatars* (computer-generated human-like figures). Social interfaces are hard to create without being corny. For example, the assistant "Clippy" was so annoying to users of Microsoft Office 97 that it was eliminated from Office 2003 and all subsequent versions.

*Motion control gaming consoles* are another type of interface. Three major players currently offer this interface: the Xbox 360 Kinect, the PS3 PlayStation Move, and the Nintendo Wii.

- Kinect tracks your movements without a physical controller, has voice recognition, and accommodates multiple players.

- The PlayStation Move uses a physical controller with motion-sensing electronics, making it the technological "cross" between Kinect and Wii. Move requires each player to use a wand.

- Wii uses a physical controller. Compared with Kinect and Move, Wii has been on the market longer, it has the biggest library of motion-sensing games, and it is the least expensive. On the negative side, Wii has the least accurate motion sensing of the three systems, and, unlike Kinect and Move, it is not available in high definition.

Touch-enabled gesture-control interfaces enable users to browse through photos, "toss" objects around a screen, "flick" to turn the pages of a book, play video games, and watch movies. Examples of this type of interface are Microsoft Surface and the Apple iPhone. Microsoft Surface is used in casinos such as Harrah's iBar in Las Vegas and in some AT&T stores. A very visible use of Surface was the touch wall used by the major television networks during their coverage of various elections.

# TG 2.3 Application Software

Application software is a set of computer instructions that provides specific functionality to a user. This functionality may be broad, such as general word processing, or narrow, such as an organization's payroll program. Essentially, an application program applies a computer to a certain need. As you will see, modern organizations use many different software applications.

Application software may be developed in-house by the organization's information systems personnel, or it may be commissioned from a software vendor. Alternatively, the software can be purchased, leased, or rented from a vendor that develops applications and sells them to many organizations. This "off-the-shelf" software may be a standard package, or it may be customizable. Special-purpose programs or "packages" can be tailored for a specific purpose, such as inventory control and payroll. A **package, or software suite**, is a group of programs with integrated functions that has been developed by a vendor and is available for purchase in a prepackaged form. Microsoft Office is a well-known example of a package, or software suite.

General-purpose, off-the-shelf application programs designed to help individual users increase their productivity are referred to as **personal application software**. Table TG 2.1 lists some of the major types of personal application software.

**Speech-recognition software**, also called *voice recognition*, is an input technology, rather than strictly an application, that enables users to provide input to systems software and application software. As the name suggests, this software recognizes and interprets human speech, either one word at a time (*discrete speech*) or in a conversational stream (*continuous speech*). Advances in processing power, new software algorithms, and better microphones have enabled developers to design extremely accurate speech-recognition software. Experts predict that, in

## Table TG 2.1
### Personal Application Software

| Category of Personal Application Software | Major Functions | Examples |
| --- | --- | --- |
| Spreadsheets | Use rows and columns to manipulate primarily numerical data; useful for analyzing financial information and for what–if and goal-seeking analyses | Microsoft Excel, Corel Quattro Pro, Apple iWork Numbers |
| Word processing | Allow users to manipulate primarily text with many writing and editing features | Microsoft Word, Apple iWork Pages |
| Desktop publishing | Extend word processing software to allow production of finished, camera-ready documents, which may contain photographs, diagrams, and other images combined with text in different fonts | Microsoft Publisher, QuarkXPress |
| Data management | Allow users to store, retrieve, and manipulate related data | Microsoft Access, FileMaker Pro |
| Presentation | Allow users to create and edit graphically rich information to appear on electronic slides | Microsoft PowerPoint, Apple iWork Keynote |
| Graphics | Allow users to create, store, and display or print charts, graphs, maps, and drawings | Adobe PhotoShop, Corel DRAW |
| Personal information management | Allow users to create and maintain calendars, appointments, to-do lists, and business contacts | IBM Lotus Notes, Microsoft Outlook |
| Personal finance | Allow users to maintain checkbooks, track investments, monitor credit cards, and bank and pay bills electronically | Quicken, Microsoft Money |
| Web authoring | Allow users to design Web sites and publish them on the Web | Microsoft FrontPage, Macromedia Dreamweaver |
| Communications | Allow users to communicate with other people over any distance | Novell Groupwise |

the near future, voice recognition systems will be built into almost every device, appliance, and machine that people use. Applications for voice recognition technology abound. Consider these examples:

- Call centers are using this technology. The average call costs $5 if it is handled by an employee, but only 50 cents with a self-service, speech-enabled system. The online brokerage firm E-Trade Financial uses Microsoft's Tellme (*www.microsoft.com/en-us/tellme*) to field about 50,000 calls per day, thereby saving at least $30 million annually.
- Apple's OS X and Microsoft's Windows 10 operating systems come with built-in voice technology.
- Nuance's Dragon NaturallySpeaking (*www.nuance.com*) enables accurate voice-to-text and e-mail dictation.

# before you go on...

1. What does the following statement mean? "Hardware is useless without software."
2. What are the differences between systems software and application software?
3. What is open-source software, and what are its advantages? Can you think of any disadvantages?
4. Describe the functions of the operating system.

# What's In IT For Me?

### For the Accounting Major

Accounting application software performs the organization's accounting functions, which are repetitive and performed in high volumes. Each business transaction (e.g., a person hired, a paycheck produced, an item sold) produces data that must be captured. Accounting applications capture these data and then manipulate them as necessary. Accounting applications adhere to relatively standardized procedures, handle detailed data, and have a historical focus (i.e., what happened in the past).

### For the Finance Major

Financial application software provides information about the firm's financial status to persons and groups inside and outside the firm. Financial applications include forecasting, funds management, and control applications. Forecasting applications predict and project the firm's future activity in the economic environment. Funds management applications use cash flow models to analyze expected cash flows. Control applications enable managers to monitor their financial performance, typically by providing information about the budgeting process and performance ratios.

### For the Marketing Major

Marketing application software helps management solve problems that involve marketing the firm's products. Marketing software includes marketing research and marketing intelligence applications. Marketing applications provide information about the firm's products and competitors, its distribution system, its advertising and personal selling activities, and its pricing strategies. Overall, marketing applications help managers develop strategies that combine the four major elements of marketing: product, promotion, place, and price.

### For the Production/Operations Management Major

Managers use production/operations management (POM) application software for production planning and as part of the physical production system. POM applications include production, inventory, quality, and cost software. These applications help management operate manufacturing facilities and logistics. Materials requirements planning (MRP) software also is widely used in manufacturing. This software identifies which materials will be needed, how much will be needed, and the dates on which they will be needed. This information enables managers to be proactive.

### For the Human Resources Management Major

Human resources management application software provides information concerning recruiting and hiring, education and training, maintaining the employee database, termination, and administering benefits. HRM applications include workforce planning, recruiting, workforce management, compensation, benefits, and environmental reporting subsystems (e.g., equal employment opportunity records and analysis, union enrollment, toxic substances, and grievances).

### For the MIS Major

If your company decides to develop its own software, the MIS function is responsible for managing this activity. If the company decides to buy software, the MIS function deals with software vendors in analyzing their products. The MIS function also is responsible for upgrading software as vendors release new versions.

## [ Summary ]

1. **Discuss the major software issues that confront modern organizations.**

   Computer program code often contains errors. The industry recognizes the enormous problem of software defects, but only initial steps are being taken to resolve it. Software licensing is yet another issue for organizations and individuals. Copying proprietary software is illegal. Software vendors copyright their software to protect it from being copied. As a result, companies must license vendor-developed software to use it.

2. **Describe the general functions of the operating system.**

   Operating systems manage the actual computer resources (i.e., the hardware). They schedule and process applications (jobs); manage and protect memory; manage the input and output functions and hardware; manage data and files; and provide security, fault tolerance, graphical user interfaces, and windowing.

3. **Identify the major types of application software.**

   The major types of application software are spreadsheet, data management, word processing, desktop publishing, graphics, multimedia, communications, speech recognition, and groupware. Software suites combine several types of application software (e.g., word processing, spreadsheet, and data management) into an integrated package.

## [ Chapter Glossary ]

**application software** The class of computer instructions that directs a computer system to perform specific processing activities and provide functionality for users.

**computer programs** The sequences of instructions for the computer, which comprise software.

**documentation** Written description of the functions of a software program.

**graphical user interface (GUI)** Systems software that allows users to have direct control of the hardware by manipulating visible objects (such as icons) and actions, which replace command syntax.

**open-source software** Software made available in source-code form at no cost to developers.

**open systems** Computing products that work together by using the same operating system with compatible software on all the computers that interact in an organization.

**operating system (OS)** The main system control program, which supervises the overall operations of the computer, allocates CPU time and main memory to programs, and provides an interface between the user and the hardware.

**package** Common term for an integrated group of computer programs developed by a vendor and available for purchase in prepackaged form.

**personal application software** General-purpose, off-the-shelf application programs that support general types of processing, rather than being linked to any specific business function.

**programming** The process of writing or coding programs.

**proprietary software** Software that has been developed by a company and has restrictions on its use, copying, and modification.

**social interface** A user interface that guides the user through computer applications by using cartoon-like characters, graphics, animation, and voice commands.

**software** A set of computer programs that enable the hardware to process data.

**software suite** See **package**.

**speech-recognition software** Software that recognizes and interprets human speech, either one word at a time (discrete speech) or in a stream (continuous speech).

**systems software** The class of computer instructions that serve primarily as an intermediary between computer hardware and application programs; provides important self-regulatory functions for computer systems.

# [ Discussion Questions ]

1. You are the CIO of your company, and you have to develop an application of strategic importance for your firm. What are the advantages and disadvantages of using open-source software?

2. What does this statement mean: "Hardware is useless without software."

# [ Problem-Solving Activities ]

1. A great deal of free software is available over the Internet. Go to *http://www.pcmag.com/article2/0, 2817, 2381528, 00.asp*, and observe all the software available for free. Choose a software program, and download it to your computer. Prepare a brief discussion about the software for your class.

2. Enter the IBM Web site (*www.ibm.com*), and perform a search on the term "software." Click on the drop box for Products, and notice how many software products IBM produces. Is IBM only a hardware company?

3. Compare the following proprietary software packages with their open-source software counterparts. Prepare your comparison for the class.

| Proprietary | Open Source |
| --- | --- |
| Microsoft Office | Google Docs, OpenOffice |
| Adobe Photoshop | Picnik.com, Google Picasa |

# 3 Cloud Computing

| [ LEARNING OBJECTIVES ] | [ TECHNOLOGY GUIDE OUTLINE ] | [ WEB RESOURCES ] |
|---|---|---|

**[ LEARNING OBJECTIVES ]**

1. Describe the problems that modern information technology departments face.

2. Describe the key characteristics and advantages of cloud computing.

3. Describe each of the four types of clouds.

4. Explain the operational model of each of the three types of cloud services.

5. Identify the key benefits of cloud computing.

6. Discuss the concerns and risks associated with cloud computing.

7. Explain the role of Web services in building a firm's IT applications, providing examples.

**[ TECHNOLOGY GUIDE OUTLINE ]**

TG 3.1 Introduction to Cloud Computing

TG 3.2 What Is Cloud Computing?

TG 3.3 Different Types of Clouds

TG 3.4 Cloud Computing Services

TG 3.5 The Benefits of Cloud Computing

TG 3.6 Concerns and Risks with Cloud Computing

TG 3.7 Web Services and Service-Oriented Architecture

**[ WEB RESOURCES ]**

- Student PowerPoints for note taking

**WileyPLUS Learning Space**

- E-book
- Author video lecture for each chapter section
- Practice quizzes
- Flash Cards for vocabulary review
- Additional "IT's About Business" cases
- Video interviews with managers
- Lab Manuals for Microsoft Office 2010 and 2013

# What's In **IT** For Me?

## This Tech Guide Will Help Prepare You To...

| ACCT | FIN | MKT | POM | HRM | MIS |
|------|-----|-----|-----|-----|-----|
| ACCOUNTING | FINANCE | MARKETING | PRODUCTION OPERATIONS MANAGEMENT | HUMAN RESOURCES MANAGEMENT | MIS |

We devote this Technology Guide to a vital topic: cloud computing. A working knowledge of cloud computing will enhance your appreciation of what technology can and cannot do for a business. In addition, it will enable you to make an immediate contribution by analyzing how your organization manages its IT assets. Going further, you will be using these computing resources in your career, and you will have input into decisions about how your department and organization can best utilize them. Additionally, cloud computing can be extremely valuable if you decide to start your own business.

This Technology Guide defines **cloud computing** as a type of computing that delivers convenient, on-demand, pay-as-you-go access for multiple customers to a shared pool of configurable computing resources (e.g., servers, networks, storage, applications, and services) that can be rapidly and easily accessed over the Internet. Cloud computing allows customers to acquire resources at any time and then delete them the instant they are no longer needed. We present many examples of how the cloud can be used for business purposes. In addition, the cloud provides you with personal applications. Therefore, this guide can help you plan for your own use of the cloud. For a more detailed discussion of how you can utilize the cloud, see the section titled IT's Personal: "The Cloud."

# TG 3.1 Introduction to Cloud Computing

You were introduced to the concept of IT infrastructure in Chapter 1. Recall that an organization's *IT infrastructure* consists of IT components—hardware, software, networks, and databases—and IT services—developing information systems, managing security and risk, and managing data. (It is helpful to review Figure 1.3 here.) The organization's IT infrastructure is the foundation for all of the information systems that the organization uses.

Modern IT infrastructure has evolved through several stages since the early 1950s, when firms first began to apply information technology to business applications. These stages are as follows:

- *Stand-alone mainframes*: Organizations initially used mainframe computers in their engineering and accounting departments. The mainframe was typically housed in a secure area, and only MIS personnel had access to it.

- *Mainframe and dumb terminals*: Forcing users to go to wherever the mainframe was located was time consuming and inefficient. As a result, firms began placing so-called "dumb terminals"—essentially electronic typewriters with limited processing power—in user departments. This arrangement enabled users to input computer programs into the mainframe from their departments, a process called *remote job entry*.

- *Stand-alone personal computers*: In the late 1970s, the first personal computers appeared. The IBM PC's debut in 1981 legitimized the entire personal computer market. Users began bringing personal computers to the workplace to improve their productivity—for example, by using spreadsheet and word processing applications. These computers were not initially supported by the firm's MIS department. However, as the number of personal computers increased dramatically, organizations decided to support these devices, and they established policies as to which PCs and software they would support.

- *Local area networks (client/server computing)*: When personal computers are networked, individual productivity increases. For this reason, organizations began to connect personal computers into local area networks (LANs) and then connect these LANs to the mainframe, a type of processing known as *client/server computing*.

- *Enterprise computing*: In the early 1990s, organizations began to use networking standards to integrate different kinds of networks throughout the firm, thereby creating enterprise computing. As the Internet became widespread after 1995, organizations began using the TCP/IP networking protocol to integrate different types of networks. All types of hardware were networked, including mainframes, personal computers, smartphones, printers, and many others. Software applications and data now flow seamlessly throughout the enterprise and between organizations.

- *Cloud computing and mobile computing*: Today, organizations and individuals can use the power of cloud computing. As you will see in this Technology Guide, cloud computing provides access to a shared pool of computing resources, including computers, storage, applications, and services, over a network, typically the Internet.

Keep in mind that the computing resources in each stage can be cumulative. For instance, most large firms still use mainframe computers (in addition to all the other types of computing resources) as large servers to manage operations that involve millions of transactions per day.

To appreciate the impacts of cloud computing, you first need to understand traditional IT departments in organizations and the challenges they face. Traditionally, organizations have utilized **on-premise computing**. That is, they own their IT infrastructure (their software, hardware, networks, and data management) and maintain it in their data centers.

On-premise computing incurs expenses for IT infrastructure, the expert staffs needed to build and maintain complex IT systems, physical facilities, software licenses, hardware, and staff training and salaries. Despite all of this spending, however, organizations typically do not use their infrastructure to its full capacity. The majority of these expenses are typically applied to maintaining the existing IT infrastructure, with the remainder being allocated to developing new systems. As a result, on-premise computing can actually inhibit an organization's ability to respond quickly and appropriately to today's rapidly changing business environments.

As you will see in the next section, cloud computing can help organizations manage the problems that traditional IT departments face with on-premise computing. The next section defines cloud computing and describes its essential characteristics.

# before you go on... 

**1.** Describe the stages in the evolution of today's IT infrastructure.

**2.** Describe the challenges that traditional IT departments face.

# TG 3.2 What Is Cloud Computing?

Information technology departments have always been tasked to deliver useful IT applications to business users. For a variety of reasons, today's IT departments are facing increased challenges in delivering useful applications. As you study cloud computing, you will learn how it can help organizations manage the problems that occur in traditional IT departments. You will also discover why so many organizations are utilizing cloud computing.

## Cloud Computing Characteristics

The cloud computing phenomenon has several important characteristics. We take a closer look at them in this section.

**Cloud Computing Provides On-Demand Self-Service.** A customer can access needed computing resources automatically. This characteristic gives customers *elasticity* and *flexibility*. That is, customers can increase (scale up) or decrease (scale down) the amount of computing they need.

Consider retailers. During the Christmas buying season, these firms need much more computational capacity than at other times of the year. Therefore, if they used cloud computing, they would scale up during peak periods of business activity and scale down at other times.

**Cloud Computing Encompasses the Characteristics of Grid Computing.** **Grid computing** pools various hardware and software components to create a single IT environment with shared resources. Grid computing shares the processing resources of many geographically dispersed computers across a network.

- Grid computing enables organizations to utilize their computing resources more efficiently.
- Grid computing provides fault tolerance and redundancy, meaning that there is no single point of failure, so the failure of one computer will not stop an application from executing.
- Grid computing makes it easy to *scale up*—that is, to access increased computing resources (i.e., add more servers)—to meet the processing demands of complex applications.
- Grid computing makes it easy to *scale down* (remove computers) if extensive processing is not needed.

Consider Oxford University's (United Kingdom) Diagnostic Mammography National Database (eDiaMoND; *www.ediamond.ox.ac.uk/*) project. The project aims to improve breast cancer screening and reduce the rate of erroneous diagnoses. The users of the system are radiologists, doctors, and technicians who want to query, retrieve, process, and store patients' breast images and diagnostic reports. These images tend to be large, requiring fast access, high quality, and rigid privacy.

The system utilizes a large distributed database that runs on a grid computing system. The grid is formed in a collaborative way, by sharing resources (CPU cycles and data) among different organizations. The database contains digital mammographies with explanatory notes and comments about each image. Because medical and university sites have different equipment, the images and reports are standardized before they are stored in the database.

The system enables individual medical sites to store, process, and manage mammograms as digital images and to enable their use through data mining and sharing of these mammography archives. Radiologists can collaborate on diagnoses without being in the same physical location.

With this system in place, the institutions involved have improved their collaboration resulting in quicker and more accurate diagnoses. By pooling their resources, each institution gained access to a much larger and more sophisticated set of resources, without increasing their costs proportionately.

Cloud Computing Encompasses the Characteristics of Utility Computing. In **utility computing**, a service provider makes computing resources and infrastructure management available to a customer as needed. The provider then charges the customer for its specific usage rather than a flat rate. Utility computing enables companies to efficiently meet fluctuating demands for computing power by lowering the costs of owning the hardware infrastructure.

Cloud Computing Utilizes Broad Network Access. The cloud provider's computing resources are available over a network, accessed with a Web browser, and they are configured so that they can be used with any computing device.

Cloud Computing Pools Computing Resources. The provider's computing resources are available to serve multiple customers. These resources are dynamically assigned and reassigned according to customer demand.

Cloud Computing Often Occurs on Virtualized Servers. Cloud computing providers have placed hundreds or thousands of networked servers inside massive data centers called **server farms** (see Figure TG 3.1). Recall that a *server* is a computer that supports networks, thus enabling users to share files, software, and other network devices. Server farms require massive amounts of electrical power, air-conditioning, backup generators, and security. They also need to be located fairly closely to fiber-optic communications links (Figure TG 3.2).

Media Bakery

**FIGURE TG 3.1** A server farm. Notice the ventilation in the racks and ceiling.

Going further, Gartner estimates that typical utilization rates on servers are very low, generally from 5 to 10 percent. That is, most of the time, organizations are utilizing only a small percentage of their total computing capacity. Chief information officers (CIOs) tolerate this inefficiency to make certain that they can supply sufficient computing resources to users in case demand should spike. To alleviate this problem, companies and cloud computing providers are turning to virtualization.

**Server virtualization** uses software-based partitions to create multiple virtual servers—called *virtual machines*—on a single physical server. The major benefit of this system is that each server no longer has to be dedicated to a particular task. Instead, multiple applications can run on a single physical server, with each application running within its own software environment. As a result, virtualization enables companies to increase server utilization. In addition, companies realize cost savings in two areas. First, they do not have to buy additional servers to meet peak demand. Second, they reduce their utility costs because they are using less energy. The following example illustrates the benefits of virtualization for Amerijet International (*www.amerijet.com*).

When commercial and personal shippers need to move cargo quickly and reliably, they often turn to Amerijet International. The company carries more than 200 million pounds of freight annually to more than 550 destinations worldwide. Amerijet is experiencing continued global growth, but the firm's existing information systems were inadequate to support that growth. Amerijet's current systems could not provide maximum availability for critical applications. Moreover, the company had run out of space in its data center to add additional hardware.

Amerijet's worldwide cargo transportation services depend on a reliable IT infrastructure. Furthermore, the carrier needed to change its approach to IT management to support both new application development and its rapid business growth. In short, Amerijet had to turn its IT infrastructure into a business enabler.

Amerijet decided to virtualize the servers in its data center. As a result, the carrier was able to run more than 120 virtual machines on just 14 physical servers. The entire

**FIGURE TG 3.2**

Organizational server farms in relation to the Internet.

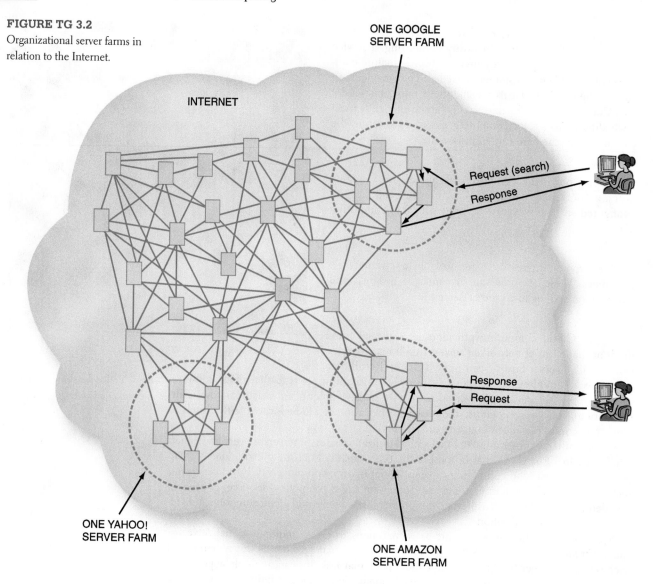

conversion process to virtualized servers took a total of just 10 hours. The benefits were compelling:

- Amerijet is able to file a flight plan for a particular aircraft in 2 minutes versus 45 minutes prior to virtualization. This faster process enables the firm to get planes in the air faster and to meet more customs cutoff times for international freight clearance. As a result, Amerijet's customers do not have to wait an extra day to receive their shipments.

- Amerijet has realized a 60 percent reduction in data center energy costs.

- Amerijet managers receive cargo inventory reports in seconds versus 30–40 minutes prior to virtualization.

- Amerijet has experienced no unplanned downtime since deployment of its virtualized servers.

With cloud computing, setting up and maintaining an IT infrastructure need no longer be a challenge for an organization. Businesses do not have to scramble to meet the evolving needs of developing applications. In addition, cloud computing reduces upfront capital expenses and operational costs, and it enables businesses to better utilize their infrastructure and to share it from one project to the next. In general, cloud computing eases the difficult tasks of procuring, configuring, and maintaining hardware and software environments. In addition, it allows enterprises to get their applications up and running faster, with easier manageability and less maintenance. It also enables IT to adjust IT resources (e.g., servers, storage, and networking) more rapidly to meet fluctuating and unpredictable business demand.

Businesses are increasingly employing cloud computing for important and innovative work. Let's take a look at Lionsgate's (*www.lionsgate.com*) use of Amazon Web Services.

Lionsgate is a global entertainment corporation that produces feature films and television shows, which they distribute worldwide. Their products include the television show *Mad Men* and the movie *Hunger Games*. Their productions appear in theaters, on TV, and online. As a successful media and entertainment company, Lionsgate faced IT challenges that included need for additional IT infrastructure capacity, leading to increased costs; increasing enterprise application workloads; and faster time-to-market requirements.

As a result, the company turned to Amazon Web Services (AWS; *http://aws.amazon.com*) for development and test workloads, production workloads for enterprise applications, and backup, archive, and disaster recovery strategies. Lionsgate's objectives were to reduce costs, increase flexibility, and increase operational efficiency. Lionsgate decided to use Amazon Simple Storage Service and Amazon Elastic Compute Cloud.

Lionsgate has experienced many benefits from using AWS. The firm has reduced the time required to deploy infrastructure from weeks to days or hours. Further, testing and development for its SAP applications also requires less time. AWS has increased the speed of building servers, improved disaster recovery and systems backup, and increased systems availability. The company avoided acquiring additional data center space, saving an estimated $1 million over three years. Overall, Lionsgate believes that moving to AWS saved the company about 50 percent compared to a traditional hosting facility.

These benefits have helped Lionsgate become more agile and more responsive to rapidly changing conditions in the marketplace. AWS has also contributed to helping the company maintain its systems security. Lionsgate is able to use its existing hardware policies and procedures for a secure, seamless, and scalable computing environment that requires few resources to manage.

In the next section, you learn about the various ways in which customers (individuals and organizations) can implement cloud computing. Specifically, you will read about public clouds, private clouds, hybrid clouds, and vertical clouds.

## before you go on...

1. Describe the characteristics of cloud computing.
2. Define server virtualization.

# Different Types of Clouds

# TG 3.3

There are three major types of cloud computing that companies provide to customers or groups of customers: public clouds, private clouds, and hybrid clouds. A fourth type of cloud computing is called vertical clouds (Figure TG 3.3).

## Public Cloud

**Public clouds** are shared, easily accessible, multicustomer IT infrastructures that are available nonexclusively to any entity in the general public (individuals, groups, and/or organizations). Public cloud vendors provide applications, storage, and other computing resources as services over the Internet. These services may be free or offered on a pay-per-usage model. Samba Tech (*www.sambatech.com*) provides an example of a young company using the public cloud.

International media companies such as Viacom (*www .viacom.com*), Bloomberg (*www.bloomberg.com*), and ESPN (*www.espn.com*) rely on Samba Tech to deliver video content

**FIGURE TG 3.3** Public clouds, private clouds, and hybrid clouds.

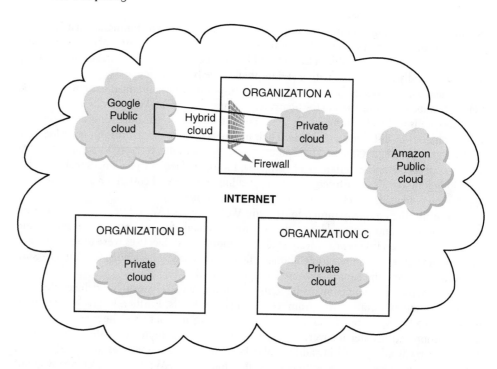

to online viewers across Latin America. As a result of its rapid growth, Samba decided to utilize cloud computing. The firm's chief technology officer noted that buying and managing complex IT (i.e., on-premise computing) was never part of the company's strategy.

Samba turned to Rackspace (*www.rackspace.com*), a public cloud provider, to help it with its huge IT capacity demands. In 2009, Samba needed Rackspace to host about 1 terabyte of data. In 2015, Rackspace hosts over 100 terabytes of Samba's data. Further, when Samba needs additional processing power—to deliver videos for a new marketing campaign, or to coincide with a large sporting event—Rackspace provides that power quickly and affordably.

## Private Cloud

**Private clouds** (also known as *internal clouds* or *corporate clouds*) are IT infrastructures that can be accessed only by a single entity or by an exclusive group of related entities that share the same purpose and requirements, such as all of the business units within a single organization. Private clouds provide IT activities and applications as a service over an intranet within an enterprise. Enterprises adopt private clouds to ensure system and data security. For this reason, these systems are implemented behind the corporate firewall. As an example of a private cloud, let's take a look at the National Security Agency (NSA; *www.nsa.gov*).

The NSA was running out of storage space for hundreds of different databases that contain information needed to run the agency as well as to produce intelligence on foreign matters. As a result, NSA analysts had to access many different databases to do their jobs. Questions that spanned more than one database had to be manually integrated by the analyst. The agency had to consolidate its databases to make its analysts more efficient and effective.

At first, the NSA decided to simply add more storage capacity. However, this approach actually added to the problem, so the agency decided to implement a private cloud. By putting all its different databases in one private cloud, analysts had to interface with only one system, making their jobs much easier.

The private cloud contains data that the agency acquires and uses for its missions. The cloud has strict security protocols and strong encryption, and has a distributed architecture across multiple geographic areas. In addition, the cloud provides a way to track every instance of every individual accessing data as specific as a single word or name in a file. This tracking includes when the data arrived, who can access them, who did access them, and who downloaded them, copied them, printed them, forwarded them, modified them, or deleted them.

Further, if the data have legal requirements, such as they must be purged at the five-year point, a notice will automatically tell NSA staff that the data need to be purged. One agency staff member noted that if the NSA had had this ability at the time, it is unlikely that U.S. soldier Bradley Manning would have succeeded in obtaining classified documents in 2010.

After implementation of the private cloud, analysts can perform tasks in minutes that once took days, overall data management costs have decreased, and the security of the data has been greatly enhanced.

## Hybrid Cloud

**Hybrid clouds** are composed of public and private clouds that remain unique entities, but are nevertheless tightly integrated. This arrangement offers users the benefits of multiple deployment models. Hybrid clouds deliver services based on security requirements, the mission-critical nature of the applications, and other company-established policies. For example, customers may need to maintain some of their data in a private cloud for security and privacy reasons while storing other, less-sensitive data in a public cloud because it is less expensive. Let's examine two examples of hybrid cloud computing.

Boeing (*www.boeing.com*) is among the world's largest aircraft manufacturers. The company has developed two hybrid cloud computing applications.

The first application enables Boeing to track all of the flight paths that planes take around the world. Boeing's sales staff uses the app to help sell aircraft by demonstrating how a newer, faster plane could improve operations. The app incorporates both historical and real-time data, which creates some computationally heavy workloads. Therefore, the app requires huge amounts of processing power to collect the data, analyze them, and present them in a user-friendly format.

The application was running on five connected, synchronized laptop computers. When Boeing's IT team wanted to migrate the app to the cloud, they needed approval from Boeing's internal security and legal teams.

In order to protect proprietary data in the app, Boeing uses a process it calls "shred and scatter." Boeing takes the data it plans to put in the cloud and breaks them up into the equivalent of puzzle pieces. Those pieces are then encrypted and sent to Microsoft's Azure Cloud, where they are stored and processed. To gather any actionable information, however, the user must reassemble the data on Boeing's cloud behind the company's firewall.

In the second application, Boeing uses Amazon's Web Services cloud along with on-premise Boeing software to create a hybrid application. The app is essentially a Digital Toolbox that allows mechanics around the world to research, conduct, and verify maintenance and repairs performed on Boeing aircraft. It combines data that Boeing hosts itself about its own planes with repair information from other aircraft manufacturers. The app automatically and seamlessly routes users to information inside Boeing's data centers if it is stored there, or to Amazon's Web Services cloud if the information is from another airline. The app has been a success because many of the large airlines work with multiple aircraft manufacturers (e.g., Boeing and Airbus), but they can go to Boeing to get the Digital Toolbox information from a variety of manufacturers.

## Vertical Clouds

It is now possible to build cloud infrastructure and applications for different businesses — the construction, finance, or insurance businesses, for example — thus building vertical clouds (see *www.vertical-cloud.com*).

# before you go on...

1. What is a public cloud?
2. What is a private cloud?
3. What is a hybrid cloud?
4. What is a vertical cloud?

# TG 3.4 Cloud Computing Services

Cloud computing services are based on three models: infrastructure-as-a-service (IaaS), platform-as-a-service (PaaS), and software-as-a-service (SaaS). These models represent the three types of computing generally required by consumers: infrastructure to run software and store data (IaaS), platforms to develop applications (PaaS), and software applications to process their data (SaaS). Figure TG 3.4 illustrates the differences among the three models.

As you examine the figure from left to right, note that the customer manages the service less and less, and the vendor manages it more and more.

Although each model has its distinctive features, all three share certain characteristics. First, customers rent them instead of buying them. This arrangement shifts IT from a capital expense to an operating expense. Second, vendors are responsible for maintenance, administration, capacity planning, troubleshooting, and backups. Finally, obtaining additional computing resources—that is, scale from the cloud—is usually fast and easy. Examples are more storage from an IaaS vendor, the ability to handle more PaaS projects, and more users of a SaaS application.

## Infrastructure-as-a-Service

With the **infrastructure-as-a-service (IaaS) model**, cloud computing providers offer remotely accessible servers, networks, and storage capacity. They supply these resources on demand from their large resource pools, which are located in their data centers.

IaaS customers are often technology companies with IT expertise. These companies want access to computing power, but they do not want to be responsible for installing or maintaining it. Companies use the infrastructure to run software or simply to store data.

To deploy their applications, IaaS users install their operating system and their application software on the cloud computing provider's computers. They can deploy any software on this infrastructure, including different operating systems, applications, and development platforms. Each user is responsible for maintaining their operating system and application software. Cloud providers typically bill IaaS services on a utility computing basis—that is, the cost reflects the amount of resources the user consumes.

Amazon is a well-known IaaS provider. The company sells the spare capacity of its vast IT infrastructure to its customers in a cloud environment. These services include its Simple Storage Service (S3) for storing their customers' data and its Elastic Compute Cloud (EC2) service

**FIGURE TG 3.4** Comparison of on-premise software, infrastructure-as-a-service, platform-as-a-service, and software-as-a-service.

| ON-PREMISE SOFTWARE | INFRASTRUCTURE-AS-A-SERVICE | PLATFORM-AS-A-SERVICE | SOFTWARE-AS-A-SERVICE |
|---|---|---|---|
| Applications | Applications | Applications | Applications |
| Data | Data | Data | Data |
| Operating system | Operating system | Operating system | Operating system |
| Servers | Servers | Servers | Servers |
| Virtualization | Virtualization | Virtualization | Virtualization |
| Storage | Storage | Storage | Storage |
| Networking | Networking | Networking | Networking |
| Examples | Amazon, IBM, Google, Microsoft, Rackspace | Microsoft Windows Azure, Google App Engine, Force.com | Salesforce.com, Google Apps, Dropbox, Apple iCloud, Box.net |

On-premise software: CUSTOMER MANAGES all.
Infrastructure-as-a-service: CUSTOMER MANAGES Applications, Data, Operating system; VENDOR MANAGES Servers, Virtualization, Storage, Networking.
Platform-as-a-service: CUSTOMER MANAGES Applications, Data; VENDOR MANAGES Operating system, Servers, Virtualization, Storage, Networking.
Software-as-a-service: VENDOR MANAGES all.

for operating their customers' applications. Customers pay only for the amount of storage and computing they use.

To illustrate IaaS, let's examine Courtagen Life Sciences (*www.courtagen.com*). This firm operates a DNA sequencing laboratory. To analyze one person's genome, Courtagen runs a workload that is computationally intensive for two to three hours, requiring 15–16 Amazon virtualized server instances or virtual machines. (A server instance, or virtual machine, is a software partition of a physical server. Recall our discussion of virtualization in TG 3.2.) The analysis employs Courtagen's Ziphyr bioinformatics software to examine the patient's genome sequence and search medical journals and online patient forums. The software then integrates the results and creates a report for doctors that combines an individual's genomic information with the most relevant, recent research. Courtagen's goal is to find subtle inferences in the data that are currently missing from the medical system.

Courtagen operates without a supporting data center. Instead, the company relies on Amazon Web Services infrastructure-as-a-service. (We discuss Web services later in this Technology Guide.) One critical feature that influenced Courtagen's decision to select Amazon was the option to buy cloud computing at bargain rates in the middle of the night or on weekends, when demand is lower. Amazon offers set prices for on-demand services, set prices for reserved virtual machines, and spot prices for virtual machines that vary with demand. Amazon's spot marketplace allows companies to bid a rate at which they would run a computing job, and Amazon decides if it has the capacity to perform the operation at that price. Courtagen's staff watches for dropping prices on Amazon Spot Instances to find the right price to bid.

Courtagen asserts that Amazon meets its business IT needs—the capacity to handle effectively computationally intensive tasks, adequate security to safely handle personal information, and minimal operating costs. In mid-2014, Courtagen was analyzing about 200 people's genomes per month, and the company was growing roughly 20 percent per month.

## Platform-as-a-Service

In the **platform-as-a-service (PaaS) model**, customers rent servers, operating systems, storage, a database, software development technologies such as Java and .NET, and network capacity over the Internet. The PaaS model allows the customer both to run existing applications and to develop and test new applications. PaaS offers customers several advantages, which include the following:

- Application developers can develop and run their software solutions on a cloud platform without the cost and complexity of buying and managing the underlying hardware and software layers.
- Underlying computing and storage resources automatically scale to match application demand.
- Operating system features can be upgraded frequently.
- Geographically distributed development teams can work together on software development projects.
- PaaS services can be provided by diverse sources located throughout the world.
- Initial and ongoing costs can be reduced by the use of infrastructure services from a single vendor rather than maintaining multiple hardware facilities that often perform duplicate functions or suffer from incompatibility problems.

As an example of an entity that employed PaaS to improve its performance, consider Novartis International AG (*www.novartis.com*), a pharmaceutical company based in Basel, Switzerland. The company employs approximately 100,000 people in 140 countries and has core businesses in pharmaceuticals, vaccines and diagnostics, and consumer health.

Novartis needed an alternative to its systems development process. The process was inflexible, expensive, and delivered new functionality much too slowly. These problems meant that the company was limited in the number of new development projects it could undertake. Novartis needed to reduce systems development effort and cost, while delivering systems with required functionality more quickly.

As a result, Novartis turned to Dell Boomi AtomSphere (*www.boomi.com*) for its platform-as-a-service product. Using this PaaS product, Novartis was able to reduce development efforts, and deliver twice the amount of new functionality in one-sixth the time than was possible earlier.

### Software-as-a-Service

With the **software-as-a-service (SaaS) delivery model**, cloud computing vendors provide software that is specific to their customers' requirements. SaaS is the most widely utilized service model, and it provides a broad range of software applications. SaaS providers typically charge their customers a monthly or yearly subscription fee.

SaaS applications reside in the cloud instead of on a user's hard drive or in a data center. The host manages the software and the infrastructure that runs this software and stores the customer's data. The customers do not control either the software, beyond the usual configuration settings, or the infrastructure, beyond changing the resources they use, such as the amount of disk space required for their data. This process eliminates the need to install and run the application on the user's computers, thereby simplifying maintenance and support.

What differentiates SaaS applications from other applications is their ability to scale. As a result, applications can run on as many servers as is necessary to meet changing demands. This process is transparent to the user.

To reduce the risk of an infrastructure outage, SaaS providers regularly back up all of their customers' data. Customers can also back up their data on their storage hardware.

To understand how SaaS operates, consider the case of AAA Northern California, Nevada, and Utah (AAA NCNU) (*http://calstate.aaa.com*), formerly known as the California State Automobile Association, which is one of the largest motor clubs in the American Automobile Association (AAA) National Federation. The club needed to replace its old human resource (HR) management and financial management (FM) systems. For example, the FM system alone contained 6,000 charts of accounts. Furthermore, the club had overcustomized its HR and FM systems, which made them difficult to maintain and enhance in order to respond to changing business conditions.

The club chose Workday (*www.workday.com*) for its new IT platform for its FM and HR systems. Workday provides software-as-a-service offerings for enterprisewide HR and FM systems. In addition to the benefits of SaaS offerings, the Workday system tightly integrates the HR and FM systems, thereby enhancing real-time visibility into the business. For instance, the ability to immediately identify how a change in the number of employees at any of the nearly 100 field offices might affect that location's profit-and-loss statement has taken managerial capabilities to a new level. After one year, the club has reduced the total cost of ownership of its FM and HR systems—including IT support, maintenance, and licensing—by 60 percent. Additionally, those 6,000 charts of accounts now number just 80. This dramatic reduction has greatly simplified administrative tasks while improving reporting and analysis.

As we previously discussed, a major concern related to cloud computing is security. In the case of AAA NCNU, the company's CIO realized she was taking risks as she handed over her company's HR and FM computing tasks to Workday. What would happen, for example, if Workday lost sensitive employee and/or financial data? Fortunately, the company's employee information has remained secure.

## IT's Personal: "The Cloud"

This Technology Guide defines the cloud as distributed computing services, and it presents many examples of how the cloud can be used for both personal and business purposes. This IT's Personal is intended to help you differentiate between the business and personal applications of the cloud and to help you plan for your own use of the cloud.

First, you need to understand that there is no single "cloud." Rather, almost all businesses refer to their Internet-based services as "cloud services." Basically, anything you do over the Internet that you used to do on a local computer is a form of cloud computing. When you store files on Dropbox, create a document using Google Docs, use iCloud to store purchases or sync documents, or use OnLive on your iPad, you are using cloud-based services that are intended for personal use.

Infrastructure-as-a-service is an important application of the cloud for personal purposes. Dropbox is one of the most prominent companies in this area. In the past, users had to carry around a USB drive, a CD, an external hard drive, or (way back in the day) floppy disks to store their personal information. Today, users can employ Dropbox for this purpose. At the time of this writing, a free Dropbox account offered 2 GB of online storage. Not only does Dropbox offer you a place to store your files (eliminating the need for a personal infrastructure of removable storage), but it also provides synchronization across computers and access from mobile devices!

Virtualization is gaining ground. If you have an iPad, you should look up the app called "OnLive" and give it a test run. OnLive allows you to log into a virtual computer that is running Windows 7 or Windows 8. Here, your iPad is simply providing the input/output, and the server is "serving up" a virtual operating system. It is very likely that one day your home computer will be virtual as well.

Software-as-a-service has been a popular option for quite some time. For example, Google Docs offers Internet-based word processing, spreadsheet, presentation, forms, and drawing tools. Recently, Microsoft has moved into the game with their Microsoft Office 365 product. Basically, each of these services allows you to use a computer program without having to install it on your computer or mobile device. You simply access the entire program (and your saved files) over the Internet.

Google has combined a couple of these cloud services with Google Drive, a service that offers the same services as Dropbox in addition to Google Docs' online editing and file-sharing capabilities. This also crosses over with SaaS because of the added benefit of Google Docs. It is very likely that one day Google will merge virtualization, infrastructure, and software into a single cloud-based service. If this technology becomes available, then all you will need as a consumer is an Internet-connected device, and you will be able to store, access, edit, and share your files from the cloud. You will also be able to choose apps to run on your "virtual machine" much the way you currently purchase applications for your mobile devices from a vendor-approved store.

So, what is the point? Simply, cloud-based services are here to stay. The rise of ubiquitous Internet access has engendered a new world of possibilities.

A word of caution, however. Along with its seemingly endless possibilities, cloud computing raises many critical security and privacy issues. Because your files, apps, and editing capability will no longer be stored on a local machine, they are only as safe as the company to which you have entrusted them makes them. So, when you select a cloud provider, make sure you choose wisely!

A subset of SaaS is the *desktop-as-a-service* (DaaS) model, also known as a *cloud desktop* or *desktop in the cloud*. In this model, a SaaS provider hosts a software environment for a desktop personal computer, including productivity and collaboration software—spreadsheets, word processing programs, and so on—such as Google Apps, Microsoft 365, and other products. The DaaS model can be financially advantageous for consumers because they do need to purchase a fully configured personal computer, or fat client. In addition, this model makes the PC environment simpler to deploy and administer.

# before you go on...

1. Describe infrastructure-as-a-service.
2. Describe platform-as-a-service.
3. Describe software-as-a-service.

# The Benefits of Cloud Computing                   TG 3.5

Cloud computing offers benefits for both individuals and organizations. It allows companies to increase the scale and power of their IT and the speed at which it can be deployed and accessed. It eliminates administrative problems and it operates across locations, devices, and organizational boundaries.

Nearly half of the respondents in a recent CIO Economic Impact survey indicated that they evaluate cloud computing options first—before traditional IT approaches—before making any new IT investments. IBM predicts that the global cloud computing market will grow 22 percent annually to $241 billion by 2020. Next we examine three major benefits that cloud computing provides to individuals and organizations.

### Benefit 1: Cloud Computing Has a Positive Impact on Employees

Cloud computing enables companies to provide their employees with access to all the information they need no matter where they are, what device they are using, or with whom they are working. Consider this example.

The attorneys of one multistate law firm needed to access documents and data on a constant basis. Since 2000, the firm's data volume had expanded from 30 gigabytes to more than 40 terabytes. Moreover, all of these data have to be stored and accessed securely. In the past, attorneys often had to manually copy case-relevant data onto external hard drives and USB devices, and then ship these devices back and forth among themselves and the firm's headquarters. These processes were nonsecure, time consuming, and expensive.

To address these needs, the law firm turned to cloud computing for data storage, offsite disaster recovery, and multisite access within a highly secure public cloud. Rather than maintaining a massive inventory of extra storage as required by its old IT infrastructure, the firm can now increase storage capacity on demand. The cloud provides attorneys with constant access via encrypted communication channels. Furthermore, the cloud facilitates collaboration among distributed teams of attorneys, thereby increasing their overall productivity. The cloud environment has made the firm's attorneys much more efficient and the firm's IT expenses have declined by 60 percent.

### Benefit 2: Cloud Computing Can Save Money

Over time, the cost of building and operating an on-premise IT infrastructure will typically be more expensive than implementing the cloud computing. Cloud providers purchase massive amounts of IT infrastructure (e.g., hardware and bandwidth) and gain cost savings by buying in large quantity. As a result, these providers continually take advantage of Moore's law (discussed in Technology Guide 1). For example, the Amazon cloud, known as Amazon Web Services, reduced its prices many times over the last 10 years.

As a result, cloud computing can reduce or eliminate the need to purchase hardware, build and install software, and pay software licensing fees. The organization pays only for the computing resources it needs, and then only when it needs them. This pay-for-use model provides greater flexibility and it eliminates or reduces the need for significant capital expenditures.

For example, State Street Bank (*www.statestreet.com*) in Boston creates its own highly customized software to manage its assets. In fact, the bank spends some 25 percent of its annual IT budget on software development. In addition, State Street's data center contains a broad array of best-of-breed systems. Integrating these systems, a job the State Street traditionally has performed in-house, is quite expensive. Consequently, State Street is implementing a private cloud to achieve approximately $600 million in cost savings from reduced amounts of software development and a reduced need for systems integration.

### Benefit 3: Cloud Computing Can Improve Organizational Flexibility and Competitiveness

Cloud computing allows organizations to use only the amount of computing resources they need at a given time. Therefore, companies can efficiently scale their operations up or down as needed to meet rapidly changing business conditions. Cloud computing is also able to deliver computing services faster than the on-premise computing.

Consider PAC2000A (*http://www.pac2000a.it/*), a large Italian retailer. The company had been using a custom-developed, in-house application to manage shelf prices across more than 1,000 outlets. The pricing application was not able to incorporate consumer demand into its algorithms, whether on a national or a local scale. When the retailer implemented a SaaS-based price optimization system, it gained sophisticated analytical capabilities on very detailed cost and competitors' data. This process led to more precise localized pricing decisions, more accurate forecasts, and a 2.4 percent increase in comparable store sales.

# before you go on...

1. Describe how cloud computing can help organizations expand the scope of their business operations.
2. Describe how cloud computing can help organizations respond quickly to market changes.

# Concerns and Risks with Cloud Computing    TG 3.6

Gartner predicts that cloud computing will grow at an annual rate of 19 percent through the year 2015. Even if this prediction is accurate, however, cloud computing will still account for less than 5 percent of total worldwide IT spending that year. Why is this percentage so low? The reason is that there are serious concerns with cloud computing. These concerns fall into six categories: legacy IT systems, reliability, privacy, security, the legal and regulatory environment, and criminal use of cloud computing.

## Concern 1: Legacy IT Systems

Historically, organizational IT systems have accumulated a diversity of hardware, operating systems, and applications. When bundled together, these systems are called "legacy spaghetti." These systems cannot easily be transferred to the cloud because they must first be untangled and simplified. Furthermore, many IT professionals have vested interests in various legacy systems, and they resist efforts to exchange these systems for cloud computing.

## Concern 2: Reliability

Many skeptics contend that cloud computing is not as reliable as a well-managed, on-premise IT infrastructure. Although cloud providers are improving the redundancy and reliability of their offerings, outages still occur. Consider the examples of Dropbox and Google.

On January 10, 2014, file-sharing service Dropbox (*www.dropbox.com*) went offline for about two days. Although hackers tried to claim credit for the crash, Dropbox said that the outage was its own fault. According to the company, during routine maintenance a programming error applied software upgrades to the operating systems of operational computers. Engineers attempted to restore the systems from backups, but thanks to the sheer size of Dropbox's databases, it took two days to get back to normal. The company maintained that no user data were damaged or compromised.

Then, on March 14, 2014, Dropbox service stopped working for about one hour. Users received errors when attempting to access the Dropbox Web site or mobile apps. The company acknowledged the outage on Twitter, describing it only as a "service issue." Forty minutes after that first tweet, Dropbox said that the issue had been resolved. The company never went into detail about what exactly happened with this outage.

When Gmail, Google Calendar, Google Docs, and Google+ go offline, people notice. On January 24, 2014, these Google services went down for some 25 minutes. Google says a software bug on its end caused the glitch. According to engineers, a system that controls the services sent faulty configurations to a variety of servers, which resulted in widespread errors. Google had everything back up and running for most folks in about 25 minutes, but for some users, it took 30 minutes to an hour for services to get back online.

Then, on March 17, 2014, several Google services went down for about three and one-half hours, including Google Hangouts, Google Voice, and parts of Google Drive. Once again, Google blamed maintenance problems. The company said that routine procedures redirected traffic to the wrong set of servers, causing a cycle of overloaded machines trying to handle more requests than they could manage.

## Concern 3: Privacy

Privacy advocates have criticized cloud computing for posing a major threat to privacy because the providers control, and thus lawfully or unlawfully monitor, the data and communication stored between the user and the host company. For example, AT&T and Verizon collaborated with NSA to use cloud computing to record more than 10 million phone calls between American citizens. In addition, providers could accidentally or deliberately alter or even delete some information.

Using a cloud computing, provider also complicates data privacy because of the extent to which cloud processing and cloud storage are used to implement cloud services. The point is that customer data may not remain on the same system or in the same data center. This situation can lead to legal concerns over jurisdiction.

There have been efforts to address this problem by integrating the legal environment. One example is the US-EU Safe Harbor, a streamlined process for U.S. companies to comply with the European Union directive on the protection of personal data.

## Concern 4: Security

Critics also question how secure cloud computing really is. Because the characteristics of cloud computing can differ widely from those of traditional IT architectures, providers need to reconsider the effectiveness and efficiency of traditional security mechanisms. Security issues include access to sensitive data, data segregation (among customers), privacy, error exploitation, recovery, accountability, malicious insiders, and account control.

The security of cloud computing services is a contentious issue that may be delaying the adoption of this technology. Security issues arise primarily from the unease of both the private and public sectors with the external management of security-based services. The fact that providers manage these services provides great incentive for them to prioritize building and maintaining strong security services.

Another security issue involves the control over who is able to access and utilize the information stored in the cloud. (Recall our discussion of least privilege in Chapter 4.) Many organizations exercise least-privilege controls effectively with their on-premise IT infrastructures. Some cloud computing environments, in contrast, cannot exercise least-privilege controls effectively. This problem occurs because cloud computing environments were originally designed for individuals or groups, not for hierarchical organizations in which some people have both the right and the responsibility to exercise control over other people's private information. To address this problem, cloud computing vendors are working to incorporate administrative, least-privilege functionality into their products. In fact, many have already done so.

Consider Panama City, Florida as an example. Panama City was one of the first cities in the United States to adopt Google Apps for Government. The city was searching for a way to gain visibility into who was using Google Apps and how users were collaborating both inside and outside the city's IT domain. Further, the city had to have the ability to control and enforce data-sharing policies where necessary. The city decided to adopt CloudLock (*www .cloudlock.com*).

CloudLock provides a security system to protect its clients' information assets located in public cloud applications such as Google Apps. CloudLock provides key data management issues such as the following:

- *Data inventory*: how many information assets exist and what are their types?
- Which information assets are shared with the public or over the Internet?
- Who has access to what information asset and what information asset is accessible to whom?

Using CloudLock, Panama City was able to notify data owners of policy violations or exposed documents containing potentially sensitive information; change or revoke excessive privilege; and audit permissions changes. Further, the city's IT manager was able to designate department leaders to manage their respective organizational unit's data policies and usage by giving them access to the CloudLock application.

## Concern 5: The Regulatory and Legal Environment

There are numerous legal and regulatory barriers to cloud computing, many of which involve data access and transport. For example, the European Union prohibits consumer data from being transferred to nonmember countries without the consumers' prior consent and approval. Companies located outside the European Union can overcome this restriction by demonstrating that they provide a "safe harbor" for the data. Some countries, such as Germany, have enacted even more restrictive data export laws. Cloud computing vendors are aware of these regulations and laws, and they are working to modify their offerings so that they can assure customers and regulators that data entrusted to them are secure enough to meet all of these requirements.

To obtain compliance with regulations such as the Federal Information Security Management Act (FISMA), the Health Insurance Portability and Accountability Act (HIPAA), and the Sarbanes-Oxley Act in the United States, the Data Protection Directive in the European Union, and the credit card industry's Payment Card Industry's Data Security Standard (PCI DSS), cloud computing customers may have to adopt hybrid deployment modes that are typically more expensive and may offer restricted benefits. This process is how, for example, Google is able to "manage and meet additional government policy requirements beyond FISMA," and Rackspace (*www.rackspace.com*) is able to claim PCI compliance. FISMA requires each federal agency to develop, document, and implement a program to provide information security for the information and information systems that support the operations of the agency, including those provided by contractors. PCI DSS is a set of requirements designed to ensure that all companies that process, store, or transmit credit card information maintain a secure environment.

## Concern 6: Criminal Use of Cloud Computing

The cloud opens up a world of possibilities for criminal computing. Cloud computing makes available a well-managed, generally reliable, scalable global infrastructure that is, unfortunately, as well suited to illegal computing activities as it is to legitimate business activities.

The huge amount of information stored in the cloud—including, most likely, your credit card and Social Security numbers—makes it an attractive target for data thieves. Additionally, the very nature of cloud computing makes it difficult to catch criminals.

The biggest problem, however, is that the cloud puts immense computing power at the disposal of anyone. Cloud criminals have access to easy-to-use encryption technology and anonymous communication channels that make it less likely that their activities will be intelligible to, or intercepted by, authorities. When law enforcement pursues criminals, the wrongdoers can rapidly shut down computing resources in the cloud, thus greatly decreasing the chances that there will be any clues left for forensic analysis.

One of the most straightforward options criminals are employing is simply to register for an account (with an assumed name, of course) and "legitimately" procure services for illegal purposes. Criminals are using Gmail or the text-sharing Web site Pastebin (*www.pastebin.com*) to plan crimes and share stolen information with near impunity. Although such uses are prohibited by most company's terms-of-service agreements, policing the cloud is expensive and not very rewarding for cloud providers.

Criminals with greater computing needs are using stolen credit cards to purchase access to computers and storage in the cloud. One emerging criminal use of cloud computing is brute-force password cracking. To break into encrypted files, attackers run programs that repeatedly try different passwords until the program finds the correct one. Today, attackers can rent time on hundreds of servers at once by employing services such as Amazon's Elastic Computing Cloud. German security specialist Thomas Roth calculated that he could use Amazon's cloud to crack the encryption keys used to protect Wi-Fi networks in six minutes. The cost of doing so would be $1.68.

In addition to creating opportunities for cybercriminals, the cloud can make it difficult for authorities or companies to track digital crimes. One reason is the rise of server virtualization, where users rent instances or virtual machines from cloud vendors. When users no longer need the virtual machine and shut it down, other clients of the cloud vendor immediately reuse the storage and computational capacity allocated to that machine. Therefore, the criminal information is overwritten by data from legitimate customers. Although incident response and law enforcement officials can forensically recover useful data from an operating virtual machine, it is nearly impossible to recover any data after the machine has been "de-provisioned." In a real sense, that virtual machine no longer exists, nor does any evidence that it may have held.

Criminals may also disappear in another way. Many cloud vendors offer geographical diversity—that is, virtual machines that are located in different physical locations. Criminals can use this feature to attack computers in the United States from computers in, say, Asia, or vice versa. Such transnational attacks typically place political and technical obstacles in the way of authorities seeking to trace a cyberattack back to its source.

Another weakness exploited by criminals arises from the Web-based applications, or SaaS offerings, provided by cloud vendors. With millions of users commingling on tens of thousands of servers, a criminal can easily mix in among legitimate users.

Even more complicated for authorities and victims, cyberattacks can originate within cloud programs that we use and trust. For instance, researchers at the security firm F-Secure reported that they had detected several phishing sites hosted within Google Docs. What made the attacks possible is a feature within Google's spreadsheet system that lets users create Web-based forms, with titles such as "Webmail Account Upgrade" and "Report a Bug." These forms, located on a Google server, were authenticated with Google's encryption certificate. Significantly, they requested sensitive information such as the user's full name, username, Google password, and so on, according to the F-Secure researchers.

## before you go on...

**1.** Discuss the various risks of cloud computing.

**2.** In your opinion, which risk is the greatest? Support your answer.

---

# TG 3.7 Web Services and Service-Oriented Architecture

Thus far, we have explained how cloud computing can deliver a variety of functionality to users in the form of services (think IaaS, PaaS, and SaaS). We conclude by examining Web services and service-oriented architecture.

**Web services** are applications delivered over the Internet (the cloud) that MIS professionals can select and combine through almost any device, from personal computers to mobile phones. By using a set of shared standards, or protocols, these applications permit different systems to "talk" with one another—that is, to share data and services—without requiring human beings to translate the conversations. Web services have enormous potential because they can be employed in a variety of environments: over the Internet, on an intranet inside a corporate firewall, or on an extranet set up by business partners. In addition, they perform a wide variety of tasks, from automating business processes to integrating components of an enterprisewide system to streamlining online buying and selling.

Web services provide numerous benefits for organizations:

- The organization can utilize the existing Internet infrastructure without having to implement any new technologies.

- Organizational personnel can access remote or local data without having to understand the complexities of this process.

- The organization can create new applications quickly and easily.

The collection of Web services that are used to build a firm's IT applications constitutes a **service-oriented architecture**. Businesses accomplish their processes by executing a series of these services. One of the major benefits of Web services is that they can be reused across an organization in other applications. For example, a Web service that checks a consumer's credit could be used with a service that processes a mortgage application or a credit card application.

Web services are based on four key protocols: XML, SOAP, WSDL, and UDDI. **Extensible markup language (XML)** is a computer language that makes it easier to exchange data among a variety of applications and to validate and interpret these data. XML is a more powerful and flexible markup language than **hypertext markup language (HTML)**. HTML is a page-description language for specifying how text, graphics, video, and sound are placed on a Web page document. HTML was originally designed to create and link static documents composed primarily of text (Figure TG 3.5). Today, however, the Web is much more social and interactive, and many Web pages have multimedia elements, such as images, audio, and video. To integrate these rich media into Web pages, users had to rely on third-party plug-in applications such as Flash, Silverlight, and Java. Unfortunately for users, these add-ons require both additional programming and extensive computer processing.

The next evolution of HTML, called **HTML5**, solves this problem by enabling users to embed images, audio, and video directly into a document without the add-ons. HTML5 also makes it easier for Web pages to function across different display devices, including mobile devices and desktops. HTML5 also supports offline data storage for apps that run over the Web.

(a) html

```
<!DOCTYPE HTML PUBLIC "-//W3C//DTD XHTML 1.0 Transitional//EN" http://www.wiley.com/college/gisslen/0470179961/video/
video111
<html xmlns="http://www.wiley.com/college/rainer/0470179061/video/video111.html><head>
<meta http-equiv="content-Type" content="text/html; charset=ISO-8859-1">
<title>CSS Text Wrapper</title>
<link type="text/css" rel="stylesheet" href="css/stylesheet.css">
</head><body id="examples">

<div id="container">
        <div class="wrapper">
                <div class="ex">
                        <script type="text/javascript">shapewrapp
er("15","7.5,141,145|22.5,89,89|37.5,68,69|52.5,46,50|67.5,3
height: 15px; width: 39px;"></div><div style="float: left; clear: left; height: 15px; width: 27px;"></div><div style="float:
15px; width: 4px;"></div><div style="float: left; clear: left; height: 15px; width: 6px;"></div><div style="float:
right; cle
width: 43px;"></div><div style="float: left; clear: left; height: 15px; width: 57px;"></div><div style="float: right; clear:
                        <span style="font-size: 13px;" class=c">
```

(b) XML

```
<feature numbered="no" xml:id="c08-fea-0001">
    <titleGroup>
        <title type="featureName">OPENING CASE</title>
        <title type="main">Tiger Tans and Gifts</title>
    </titleGroup>
    <section xml:id="c08-sec-0002">
        <p>
            <blockFixed onlyChannels="print" type="graphic">
                <mediaResource alt="p0310" copyright="John Wiley &amp; Sons, Inc." eRights="yes"
                    href="urn:x-wiley:9781118443590:media:rainer9781118443590c08:p0310" pRights="yes"/>
            </blockFixed>
            Lisa Keiling owns & tanning salon in Wedowee, Alabama, that does very well from January to May....
        </p>
    </section>
</feature>
```

**FIGURE TG 3.5** (a) Screenshot of an HTML wrapper. This wrapper gives instructions on how to open a video associated with this book. (b) Example of XML tagging done in Chapter 9 of this book.

Web pages will execute more quickly, and they will resemble smartphone apps. HTML5 is used in a number of Internet platforms, including Apple's Safari browsers, Google Chrome, and Firefox browsers. Google's Gmail and Google Reader also use HTML5. Web sites listed as "iPad ready" are using HTML5 extensively. Examples of such sites are CNN, *The New York Times*, and CBS.

Whereas HTML is limited to describing how data should be presented in the form of Web pages, XML can present, communicate, and store data. For example, in XML a number is not simply a number. The XML tag also specifies whether the number represents a price, a date, or a ZIP code. Consider this example of XML, which identifies the contact information for Jane Smith.

```
<contact-info>
<name>Jane Smith</name>
<company>AT&T</company>
<phone>(212) 555-4567</phone>
</contact-info>
```

*Simple object access protocol (SOAP)* is a set of rules that define how messages can be exchanged among different network systems and applications through the use of XML. These rules essentially establish a common protocol that allows different Web services to interoperate. For example, Visual Basic clients can use SOAP to access a Java server. SOAP runs on all hardware and software systems.

The *Web services description language (WSDL)* is used to create the XML document that describes the tasks performed by the various Web services. Tools such as VisualStudio.Net automate the process of accessing the WSDL, reading it, and coding the application to reference the specific Web service.

*Universal description, discovery, and integration (UDDI)* allows MIS professionals to search for needed Web services by creating public or private searchable directories of these services. In other words, UDDI is the registry of descriptions of Web services.

Examples of Web services abound. As one example, the Food and Nutrition Service (FNS) within the U.S. Department of Agriculture (USDA) uses Amazon Web Services successfully. The FNS administers the department's nutrition assistance programs. Its mission is to provide children and needy families with improved access to food and a healthier diet through its food assistance programs and comprehensive nutrition education efforts.

The Supplemental Nutrition Assistance Program, or SNAP, is the cornerstone of the USDA's nutrition assistance mission. More than 47 million people—most of them children—receive SNAP benefits each month. To help recipients, in 2010 the FNS created a Web application called the SNAP Retail Locator. Faced with limited budget and time to implement the solution, the FNS selected Amazon Web Services to host the application. As its name suggests, the SNAP Retail Locator, which receives 30,000 visitors per month, helps SNAP recipients find the closest SNAP-authorized store and also provides driving directions to the store. The application has been available 100 percent of the time since it was launched. In addition, by employing Amazon, the FNS saved 90 percent of the cost it would have incurred had it hosted the application on-premises.

# before you go on...

**1.** What are Web services?

**2.** What is a service-oriented architecture?

**For All Business Majors**

As with hardware (see Technology Guide 1), the design of enterprise IT architectures has profound impacts for businesspeople. Personal and organizational success can depend on an understanding of cloud computing and a commitment to knowing the opportunities and challenges they will bring.

At the organizational level, cloud computing has the potential to make the organization function more efficiently and effectively, while saving the organization money. Web services and SOA make the organization more flexible when deploying new IT applications.

At the individual level, you might utilize cloud computing yourself if you start your own business. Remember that cloud computing provides startup companies with world-class IT capabilities at a very low cost.

# [ Summary ]

**1. Describe the problems that modern information technology departments face.**

Traditional IT departments (on-premise computing) face many problems:

- They spend huge amounts on IT infrastructure and expert staffs to build and maintain complex IT systems. These expenses include software licenses, hardware, and staff training and salaries.
- They must manage an infrastructure that often is not used to its full capacity.
- They spend the majority of their budgets on maintaining existing IT infrastructure, with the remainder being spent on developing new systems.
- They have difficulty capturing, storing, managing, and analyzing all these data.
- They can actually inhibit an organization's ability to respond quickly and appropriately to rapidly changing dynamic environments.
- They are expensive.

**2. Describe the key characteristics and advantages of cloud computing.**

*Cloud computing* is a type of computing that delivers convenient, on-demand, pay-as-you-go access for multiple customers to a shared pool of configurable computing resources (e.g., servers, networks, storage, applications, and services) that can be rapidly and easily accessed over the Internet. The essential *characteristics* of cloud computing include the following:

- Cloud computing provides on-demand self-service.
- Cloud computing includes the characteristics of grid computing.
- Cloud computing includes the characteristics of utility computing.
- Cloud computing utilizes broad network access.
- Cloud computing pools computing resources.
- Cloud computing typically occurs on virtualized servers.

**3. Describe each of the four types of clouds.**

*Public clouds* are shared, easily accessible, multicustomer IT infrastructures that are available nonexclusively to any entity in the public (individuals, groups, and/or organizations). *Private clouds* (also known as *internal clouds* or *corporate clouds*) are IT infrastructures that are accessible only by a single entity, or by an exclusive group of related entities that share the same purpose and requirements, such as all the business units within a single organization. *Hybrid clouds* are composed of public and private clouds that remain unique entities but are bound together, offering the benefits of multiple deployment models. *Vertical clouds* serve specific industries.

4. **Explain the operational model of each of the three types of cloud services.**

   With the *infrastructure-as-a-service* model, cloud computing providers offer remotely accessible servers, networks, and storage capacity. In the *platform-as-a-service* model, customers rent servers, operating systems, storage, a database, software development technologies such as Java and .NET, and network capacity over the Internet. With the *software-as-a-service* delivery model, cloud computing vendors provide software that is specific to their customers' requirements.

5. **Identify the key benefits of cloud computing.**

   The benefits of cloud computing include making individuals more productive; facilitating collaboration; mining insights from data; developing and hosting applications; cost flexibility; business scalability; improved utilization of hardware; market adaptability; and product and service customization.

6. **Discuss the concerns and risks associated with cloud computing.**

   Cloud computing does raise concerns and have risks, which include legacy spaghetti, cost, reliability, privacy, security, and the regulatory and legal environment.

7. **Explain the role of Web services in building a firm's IT applications, providing examples.**

   *Web services* are applications delivered over the Internet that MIS professionals can select and combine through almost any device, from personal computers to mobile phones. A *service-oriented architecture* makes it possible for MIS professionals to construct business applications using Web services.

# [ Chapter Glossary ]

**cloud computing** A technology in which tasks are performed by computers physically removed from the user and accessed over a network, in particular the Internet.

**extensible markup language (XML)** A computer language that makes it easier to exchange data among a variety of applications and to validate and interpret these data.

**grid computing** A technology that applies the unused processing resources of many geographically dispersed computers in a network to form a virtual supercomputer.

**HTML5** A page-description language that makes it possible to embed images, audio, and video directly into a document without add-ons. Also makes it easier for Web pages to function across different display devices, including mobile devices as well as desktops. Supports the storage of data offline.

**hybrid clouds** Clouds composed of public and private clouds that remain unique entities but are bound together, offering the benefits of multiple deployment models.

**hypertext markup language (HTML)** A page-description language for specifying how text, graphics, video, and sound are placed on a Web page document.

**infrastructure-as-a-service (IaaS) model** A model with which cloud computing providers offer remotely accessible servers, networks, and storage capacity.

**on-premise computing** A model of IT management where companies own their IT infrastructure (their software, hardware, networks, and data management) and maintain it in their data centers.

**platform-as-a-service (PaaS) model** A model with which customers rent servers, operating systems, storage, a database, software development technologies such as Java and .NET, and network capacity over the Internet.

**private clouds** (also known as *internal clouds* or *corporate clouds*) IT infrastructures that are accessible only by a single entity or by an exclusive group of related entities that share the same purpose and requirements, such as all the business units within a single organization.

**public clouds** Shared, easily accessible, multicustomer IT infrastructures that are available nonexclusively to any entity in the general public (individuals, groups, and/or organizations).

**server farms** Massive data centers, which may contain hundreds of thousands of networked computer servers.

**server virtualization** A technology that uses software-based partitions to create multiple virtual servers (called *virtual machines*) on a single physical server.

**service-oriented architecture** An IT architecture that makes it possible to construct business applications using Web services.

**software-as-a-service (SaaS) delivery model** A delivery model with which cloud computing vendors provide software that is specific to their customers' requirements.

**utility computing** A technology whereby a service provider makes computing resources and infrastructure management available to a customer as needed.

**Web services** Applications delivered over the Internet that IT developers can select and combine through almost any device, from personal computers to mobile phones.

## [ Discussion Questions ]

1. What is the value of server farms and virtualization to any large organization?
2. If you were the chief information officer of a firm, how would you explain the workings, benefits, and limitations of cloud computing?
3. What is the value of cloud computing to a small organization?
4. What is the value of cloud computing to an entrepreneur who is starting a business?

## [ Problem-Solving Activities ]

1. Investigate the status of cloud computing by researching the offerings of the following leading vendors: Dell (*www.dell.com*), Oracle (*www.oracle.com*), IBM (*www.ibm.com*), Amazon (*www.amazon.com*), Microsoft (*www.microsoft.com*), and Google (*www.google.com*). Note any inhibitors to cloud computing.

# 4   Intelligent Systems

| [ LEARNING OBJECTIVES ] | [ TECHNOLOGY GUIDE OUTLINE ] | [ WEB RESOURCES ] |
|---|---|---|
| 1. Explain the potential value and the potential limitations of artificial intelligence. | TG 4.1 Introduction to Intelligent Systems | • Student PowerPoints for note taking |
| 2. Provide examples of the benefits, applications, and limitations of expert systems. | TG 4.2 Expert Systems | **WileyPLUS Learning Space** |
| 3. Provide examples of the use of neural networks. | TG 4.3 Neural Networks | • E-book |
| 4. Provide examples of the use of fuzzy logic. | TG 4.4 Fuzzy Logic | • Author video lecture for each chapter section |
| 5. Describe the situations in which genetic algorithms would be most useful. | TG 4.5 Genetic Algorithms | • Practice quizzes |
| 6. Describe the use case for several major types of intelligent agents. | TG 4.6 Intelligent Agents | • Flash Cards for vocabulary review |
| | | • Additional "IT's About Business" cases |
| | | • Video interviews with managers |
| | | • Lab Manuals for Microsoft Office 2010 and 2013 |

What's In **IT** For **Me?**

This Tech Guide Will Help Prepare You To...

**ACCT** — ACCOUNTING    **FIN** — FINANCE    **MKT** — MARKETING    **POM** — PRODUCTION OPERATIONS MANAGEMENT    **HRM** — HUMAN RESOURCES MANAGEMENT    **MIS** — MIS

# Introduction to Intelligent Systems

TG 4.1

This Technology Guide focuses on information systems that can make decisions by themselves. These systems are called **intelligent systems**. The major categories of intelligent systems are expert systems, neural networks, fuzzy logic, genetic algorithms, and intelligent agents. You will learn about each of these systems in the following sections.

The term intelligent systems describes the various commercial applications of artificial intelligence. **Artificial intelligence (AI)** is a subfield of computer science that studies the thought processes of humans and recreates the effects of those processes via machines, such as computers and robots.

One well-publicized definition of AI is "behavior by a machine that, if performed by a human being, would be considered *intelligent*." This definition raises the question, "What is *intelligent behavior*?" The following capabilities are considered to be signs of intelligence: learning or understanding from experience, making sense of ambiguous or contradictory messages, and responding quickly and successfully to new situations.

The ultimate goal of AI is to build machines that mimic human intelligence. A widely used test to determine whether a computer exhibits intelligent behavior was designed by Alan Turing, a British AI pioneer. The **Turing test** proposes a scenario in which a woman or a man and a computer both pretend to be women or men, and a human interviewer has to identify which is the real human. Based on this standard, the intelligent systems exemplified in commercial AI products are far from exhibiting any significant intelligence.

We can better understand the potential value of AI by contrasting it with *natural (human) intelligence*. AI has several important commercial advantages over natural intelligence, but it also displays some limitations, as outlined in Table TG 4.1.

## Table TG 4.1
### Comparison of the Capabilities of Natural Versus Artificial Intelligence

| Capabilities | Natural Intelligence | Artificial Intelligence |
|---|---|---|
| Preservation of knowledge | Perishable from an organizational point of view | Permanent |
| Duplication and dissemination | Difficult, expensive, takes time | Easy, fast, and inexpensive once in a computer |
| Total cost of knowledge | Can be erratic and inconsistent, incomplete at times | Consistent and thorough |
| Documentability of process and knowledge | Difficult, expensive | Fairly easy, inexpensive |
| Creativity | Can be very high | Low, uninspired |
| Use of sensory experiences | Direct and rich in possibilities | Must be interpreted first; limited |
| Recognizing patterns and relationships | Fast, easy to explain | Machine learning still not as good as people in most cases, but in some cases better than people |
| Reasoning | Making use of wide context of experiences | Good only in narrow, focused, and stable domains |

Intelligent systems show up in a number of places, some of them surprising, as the following examples illustrate:

- A good session player is hard to find, but ujam (*www.ujam.com*) is always ready to rock. This Web app doubles as a studio band and a recording studio. It analyzes a melody and then produces sophisticated harmonies, bass lines, drum tracks, horn parts, and more.

  Before ujam can produce accompaniment, the app must figure out which notes the user is singing or playing. Once ujam recognizes these notes, its algorithms (an **algorithm** is a problem-solving method expressed as a finite sequence of steps) use a mix of statistical techniques and programmed musical rules to search for chords to match the tune.

- To the human eye, an X-ray is a murky puzzle. But to a machine, an X-ray—or a CT scan or MRI scan—is a dense data field that can be assessed down to the pixel level. AI techniques currently are being applied aggressively in the field of medical imaging.

  New software gathers high-resolution image data from multiple sources—X-rays, MRI scans, ultrasounds, and CT scans—and then groups together biological structures that share hard-to-detect similarities. For instance, the software can examine several images of the same breast to measure tissue density. The software then color-codes tissues of similar densities so that humans can observe the pattern as well.

  The software finds and indexes pixels that share certain properties, even pixels that are far apart in one image or in a different image altogether. This process enables medical personnel to identify hidden features of diffuse structures as well as features within a region of tissue.

- For years, electric utilities manually collected data from meters in homes and businesses. The companies analyzed those data to bill their customers for usage. Utility planners analyzed those data to better estimate future usage and plan new facilities. This system has always had problems. For instance, many regions of the United States are subject to brownouts when the utilities cannot meet peak power demands during heat waves. The utilities typically appealed to customers over the radio and television to try and get them to lower their use of air-conditioning.

  The shortcomings of that system highlight the benefits of intelligent systems. A developing solution is to use an intelligent meter's real-time information about each customer's usage during peak times, share details about temperature conditions with customers, and try to entice them to take action. Ideally, utilities would like to be able to send a message to each customer telling them that the utility will charge more per kilowatt hour in those periods of peak demand. The customer could then decide whether to pay more or use less. With such an intelligent system, a utility would be able to save the cost of buying electricity on the spot market at a much higher rate to meet peak demands, thereby reducing the number of brownouts and delivering better customer service.

- Building a model to run a major railroad is a complex task. One of the nation's largest freight carriers, Norfolk Southern (*www.nscorp.com*), uses an intelligent system, the Princeton Locomotive and Shop Management System (PLASMA), to manage its huge operation. PLASMA uses algorithms to analyze the railroad's operations by tracking thousands of variables to predict the impact of changes in fleet size, maintenance policies, transit time, and other factors. The key breakthrough was refining PLASMA so that it could mimic the complex behavior of the company's dispatch center in Atlanta, Georgia. PLASMA examines vast amounts of historical data contained in the railroad's databases. It then uses this analysis to model the dispatch center's collective human decision making and suggest improvements.

- South Jersey Healthcare (*www.inspirahealthnetwork.org*) deployed an intelligent medication distribution system, which provides easy access to its pharmaceutical inventory, medical records, and patient billing. The system is managing over 700,000 doses of medication per month and has delivered quantifiable benefits. With the system, the healthcare company has been able to make more effective ordering decisions based on real-time inventory information. As a result, the firm has reduced medication inventory by almost 40 percent. Furthermore, the system helps nurses and pharmacists deliver medicine to patients faster. Medication distribution time has been cut from 2 hours to 18 minutes, on average.

- Nakajima USA (*www.nakajimausa.com*) is a manufacturer of licensed plush, collectible, and seasonal toys, lifestyle goods, and trendy character merchandise. The firm has developed an intelligent, real-time inventory control system, instead of relying on periodic inventory reports. This process is critical for the firm because its products come from overseas and have a long replenishment cycle. (A replenishment cycle is the time between when an order for inventory is placed until the time the next order for inventory is placed.) The intelligent system gives the company faster and better visibility into which of its core products are selling and need to be restocked, therefore allowing more efficiency in managing inventory in stores. The system also allows the company to capture more customer information at checkout.

- Vertical, or topic-specific, search is gaining popularity in areas from travel and electronics to books, films, and more. Vertical search occurs when a person goes directly to a site such as IMDB or Kayak rather than through a general search engine such as Google or Bing. Vertical search uses semantic analysis, text classification, feature extraction, and advanced big data analytics, combined with other artificial intelligence algorithms. Google has noted the threat and is putting a lot of effort into vertical search in an effort to deliver more relevant, focused, tailored search results. However, vertical search does present an opportunity to get an edge on Google by incorporating human logic and knowledge into specific vertical topics. An example is Zite (*www.zite.com*), an app that offers relevant news articles by learning behavior. The app uses several AI technologies to make news delivery much more intelligent than a simple Google News feed.

## before you go on...

**1.** What is artificial intelligence?

**2.** Differentiate between artificial and human intelligence.

# Expert Systems

## TG 4.2

When an organization has to make a complex decision or solve a problem, it often turns to experts for advice. These experts possess specific knowledge and experience in the problem area. They can offer alternative solutions and predict whether the proposed solutions will succeed. At the same time, they can calculate the costs that the organization may incur if it does not resolve the problem. Companies engage experts for advice on such matters as mergers and acquisitions, advertising strategy, and purchasing equipment. The more unstructured the situation, the more specialized and expensive the advice.

*Expertise* refers to the extensive, task-specific knowledge acquired from training, reading, and experience. This knowledge enables experts to make better and faster decisions than non-experts in solving complex problems. Expertise takes a long time (often many years) to acquire, and it is distributed unevenly across organizations.

Expert systems (ESs) are computer systems that attempt to mimic human experts by applying expertise in a specific domain. Expert systems can either *support* decision makers or completely *replace* them. Expert systems are the most widely applied and commercially successful intelligent systems. A fascinating example of an expert system is IBM's Watson (see Chapter 2 closing case).

Human resources management uses expert systems to analyze applicants for available positions. These systems assign "scores" to candidates, lessening the workload for HR managers in the hiring process. HR managers still make the final decision, but the expert system provides useful information and recommendations.

An ES is typically decision-making software that can perform at a level comparable to a human expert in certain specialized problem areas. Essentially, an ES transfers expertise from a domain expert (or other source) to the computer. This knowledge is then stored in the computer, which users can call on for specific advice as needed. The computer can make inferences and arrive at conclusions. Then, like a human expert, it offers advice or recommendations. In addition, it can explain the logic behind the advice. Because ESs can integrate and manipulate enormous amounts of data, they sometimes perform better than any single expert can.

An often overlooked benefit of expert systems is that they can be embedded in larger systems. For example, credit card issuers use expert systems to process credit card applications.

The transfer of expertise from an expert to a computer and then to the user involves four activities:

1. *Knowledge acquisition*: Knowledge is acquired from domain experts or from documented sources.

2. *Knowledge representation*: Acquired knowledge is organized as rules or frames (object-oriented) and stored electronically in a knowledge base.

3. *Knowledge inferencing*: The computer is programmed so that it can make inferences based on the stored knowledge.

4. *Knowledge transfer*: The inferenced expertise is transferred to the user in the form of a recommendation.

The above examples demonstrate the usefulness of expert systems in a relatively narrow domain. Overall, however, expert systems may not be as useful as users would like. Consider the Microsoft® Windows troubleshooting software located in the Help section in the taskbar menu. Microsoft has designed this expert system to provide solutions, advice, and suggestions for common errors that users encounter in the operating system. We have all found, however, that in some cases the Help section does not provide particularly useful advice.

## The Components of Expert Systems

An expert system contains the following components: knowledge base, inference engine, user interface, blackboard (workplace), and explanation subsystem (justifier). In the future, ESs will include a knowledge-refining component as well. You will learn about all these components below. In addition, Figure TG 4.1 shows the relationships among these components.

The *knowledge base* contains knowledge necessary for understanding, formulating, and solving problems. It comprises two basic elements: (1) *facts*, such as the problem situation,

**FIGURE TG 4.1** Structure and process of an expert system.

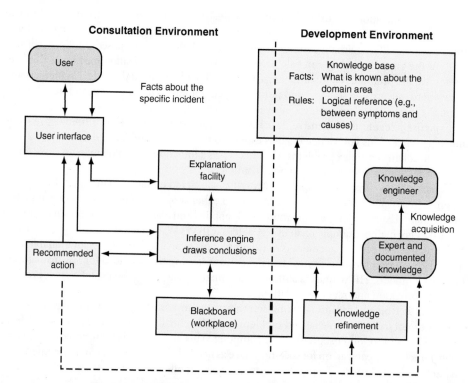

and (2) *rules* that direct the use of knowledge to solve specific problems in a particular domain.

The *inference engine* is essentially a computer program that provides a methodology for reasoning and formulating conclusions. It enables the system to make inferences based on the stored knowledge. The inference engine is considered the "brain" of the ES.

Here is an example of the inference engine for a medical expert system for lung cancer treatment:

IF lung capacity is high
AND X-ray results are positive
AND patient has fever
AND patient has coughing
THEN surgery is necessary.
IF tumor has spread
OR contraindications to surgery exist
THEN surgery cannot be performed.

The *user interface* enables users to communicate with the computer. The communication is carried out in a natural language, usually a question-and-answer format, and in some cases is supplemented by graphics. The dialogue between the user and the computer triggers the inference engine to match the problem symptoms with the knowledge contained in the knowledge base and then generate advice.

The *blackboard* is an area of working memory set aside for the description of a current problem, as specified by the input data. Thus, it is a kind of database.

Unique to an ES is its ability to *explain* its recommendations. This function is performed in a subsystem called the *explanation subsystem* or *justifier*. The explanation subsystem interactively answers questions such as the following: *Why* did the ES ask a certain question? *How* did the ES reach a particular conclusion? *What* is the plan to reach the solution?

Human experts have a *knowledge-refining* system; that is, they can analyze their own performance, learn from it, and improve it for future consultations. This type of evaluation is necessary in computerized learning as well so that the program can be improved by analyzing the reasons for its success or failure. Unfortunately, such a component is not available in commercial expert systems at the moment; however, it is being developed in experimental systems.

## Applications, Benefits, and Limitations of Expert Systems

Today, expert systems are found in all types of organizations. They are especially useful in the 10 generic categories shown in Table TG 4.2.

| Category | Problem Addressed |
| --- | --- |
| Interpretation | Inferring situation descriptions from observations |
| Prediction | Inferring likely consequences of given situations |
| Diagnosis | Inferring system malfunctions from observations |
| Design | Configuring objects under constraints |
| Planning | Developing plans to achieve goal(s) |
| Monitoring | Comparing observations to plans, flagging exceptions |
| Debugging | Prescribing remedies for malfunctions |
| Repair | Executing a plan to administer a prescribed remedy |
| Instruction | Diagnosing, debugging, and correcting student performance |
| Control | Interpreting, predicting, repairing, and monitoring systems behavior |

**Table**

# TG 4.2

**Ten Generic Categories of Expert Systems**

During the past few years, thousands of organizations worldwide have successfully applied ES technology to problems ranging from researching AIDS to analyzing dust in mines. Why have ESs become so popular? The answer is, because they provide such a large number of capabilities and benefits. Table TG 4.3 lists the major benefits of ESs.

Despite all of these benefits, expert systems present some problems as well. The following difficulties are involved with using expert systems:

- Transferring domain expertise from human experts to the expert system can be difficult because people cannot always explain *how* they know what they know. Often they are not aware of their complete reasoning process.

- Even if the domain experts can explain their entire reasoning process, automating that process may not be possible. The process might be either too complex or too vague, or it might require too many rules.

- In some contexts, there is a potential liability from the use of expert systems. Humans make errors occasionally, but they are generally "let off the hook" if they took reasonable care and applied generally accepted methods. An organization that uses an expert system, however, may lack this legal protection if problems arise later. The usual example of this issue is medical treatment, but it can also arise if a business decision driven by an expert system harms someone financially.

**Table TG 4.3**
**Benefits of Expert Systems**

| Benefit | Description |
|---|---|
| Increased output and productivity | ESs can configure components for each custom order, increasing production capabilities. |
| Increased quality | ESs can provide consistent advice and reduce error rates. |
| Capture and dissemination of scarce expertise | Expertise from anywhere in the world can be obtained and used. |
| Operation in hazardous environments | Sensors can collect information that an ES interprets, enabling human workers to avoid hot, humid, or toxic environments. |
| Accessibility to knowledge and help desks | ESs can increase the productivity of help desk employees, or even automate this function. |
| Reliability | ESs do not become tired or bored, call in sick, or go on strike. They consistently pay attention to details. |
| Ability to work with incomplete or uncertain information | Even with an answer of "don't know," an ES can produce an answer, although it may not be a definite one. |
| Provision of training | The explanation facility of an ES can serve as a teaching device and a knowledge base for novices. |
| Enhancement of decision-making and problem-solving capabilities | ESs allow the integration of expert judgment into analysis (e.g., diagnosis of machine malfunction and even medical diagnosis). |
| Decreased decision-making time | ESs usually can make faster decisions than humans working alone. |
| Reduced downtime | ESs can quickly diagnose machine malfunctions and prescribe repairs. |

In the case of medical treatment, consider a physician who consults with a medical expert system when treating a patient. If the patient's care goes poorly, then the question arises, who is liable? The physician? The expert system? The vendor of the expert system?

## before you go on... 

**1.** What is an expert system?

**2.** Describe the benefits and limitations of using expert systems.

# Neural Networks

# TG 4.3

A **neural network** is a system of programs and data structures that simulates the underlying functions of the biological brain. A neural network usually involves a large number of processors operating in parallel, each with its own small sphere of knowledge and access to data in its local memory (see Figure TG 4.2). Typically, a neural network is initially "trained" or fed large amounts of data and rules about data relationships.

Neural networks are particularly adept at recognizing subtle, hidden, and newly emerging patterns within complex data, as well as interpreting incomplete inputs. Neural networks can help users solve a wide range of problems, from airline security to infectious disease control. They are the standard for combating fraud in the credit card, healthcare, and telecom industries, and they are becoming increasingly important in today's stepped-up international efforts to prevent money laundering.

Neural networks are used in a variety of ways, as illustrated by the following examples.

- The Bruce nuclear facility in Ontario, Canada, has eight nuclear reactors, making it the largest facility in North America and the second largest in the world. The plant uses a neural network in its checkpoint X-ray screening system to detect weapons concealed in personal belongings. The system also identifies biologically dangerous liquids.

- Neural networks are used in research into diseases like Alzheimer's, Parkinson's, and epilepsy. Researchers build robots with simulated rat brains that mimic the rats' neural activity. The researchers then can study the brain's function and its reaction to stimuli.

- Investors employ neural networks to forecast the performance of stock index futures, currencies, natural gas and oil stocks, T-bond futures, gold stocks, and other major investments.

- In banking systems, neural networks help detect fraud in credit card transactions and insurance claims, fight crime, and gauge customer satisfaction.

**FIN**

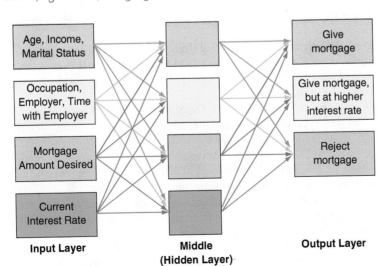

**FIGURE TG 4.2** Neural network.

Figure TG 4.2 illustrates how a neural network might process a typical mortgage application. Note that the network has three levels of interconnected nodes (similar to the human brain): an input layer; a middle, or hidden, layer; and an output layer. When the neural network is trained, the strengths, or *weights*, of its connections change. In our example, the input nodes are age, income, occupation, marital status, employer, length of time with that employer, the desired amount of the mortgage, and the current interest rate. The neural network has already been trained with data input from many mortgage applications, successful and unsuccessful. That is, the neural network has established a pattern as to which input variables are necessary for a successful mortgage application. Interestingly, the neural network can adjust as both mortgage amounts and interest rates increase or decrease.

Machine learning systems often use neural networks. **Machine learning systems** are artificial intelligence systems that learn from data. For instance, a machine learning system can be trained on e-mail messages to learn to distinguish between spam and nonspam messages. After learning, the system can then be used to classify new e-mail messages into spam and nonspam folders. The following are other examples of machine learning:

- *Optical character recognition*: Printed, handwritten characters are recognized automatically based on previous examples.
- *Face recognition*: Identify faces in images.
- *Topic identification*: Categorize news articles as to whether they are about politics, sports, entertainment, and so on.
- *Fraud detection*: Identify credit card transactions that may be fraudulent.
- *Customer segmentation*: Identify which customers may respond positively to a particular promotion.

Because neural networks are difficult to set up and use, two researchers at the University of Vienna (Austria) have created a system called N2Sky. N2Sky helps to set up neural networks in the cloud so that their services can be shared. The two researchers want to make neural networks available as a shared resource so that anyone, anywhere can use them easily for the problem that they have at hand.

## before you go on...

**1.** What are neural networks?

**2.** Describe how neural networks function.

## TG 4.4 Fuzzy Logic

**Fuzzy logic** is a branch of mathematics that deals with uncertainties by simulating the processes of human reasoning. The rationale behind fuzzy logic is that decision making is not always a matter of black or white, or true or false. Rather, it frequently involves gray areas where the term *maybe* is more appropriate.

A computer programmed to use fuzzy logic precisely defines subjective concepts that humans do not define precisely. For example, for the concept "income," descriptive terms such as "high" and "moderate" are subjective and imprecise. Using fuzzy logic, however, a computer could define "high" incomes as those exceeding $200,000 per year, and "moderate" incomes as those ranging from $150,000 to $200,000 per year. A loan officer at a bank might then use these values when considering a loan application.

Fuzzy logic has also been used in financial analysis and Internet searches. In accounting and finance, fuzzy logic allows you to analyze assets expressed in imprecise values (e.g., intangible ones like goodwill). As an example, Google uses fuzzy logic to locate answers to your search terms, based on your perception of the topic as reflected in how you phrase your query, which determines the relevance of the Web pages that Google delivers to you.

## before you go on...

**1.** What is fuzzy logic?

**2.** Give some examples where fuzzy logic is used.

# Genetic Algorithms

TG 4.5

Recall that an algorithm is a problem-solving method expressed as a finite sequence of steps. A **genetic algorithm** mimics the evolutionary, "survival-of-the-fittest" process to generate increasingly better solutions to a problem. That is, a genetic algorithm is an optimizing method that finds the combination of inputs that produces the best outputs. Genetic algorithms have three functional characteristics:

- *Selection (survival of the fittest)*: The key to selection is to give preference to better and better outcomes.
- *Crossover*: Combining portions of good outcomes in the hope of creating an even better outcome.
- *Mutation*: Randomly trying combinations and evaluating the success (or failure) of an outcome.

Genetic algorithms are best suited to decision-making environments in which thousands or millions of solutions are possible. Genetic algorithms can find and evaluate solutions intelligently, and they can process many more possibilities more thoroughly and quickly than a human can. (Users do have to tell the genetic algorithm what constitutes a "good" solution, which could be low cost or high return, or any number of other results.) Let's look at some examples:

- Boeing uses genetic algorithms to design aircraft parts such as the fan blades on its 777 jet. Rolls Royce and Honda also use genetic algorithms in their design processes.
- Retailers such as Marks and Spencer, a British chain with 320 stores, use genetic algorithms to manage their inventories more effectively and to optimize their store displays.
- Air Liquide, a producer of industrial gases, uses genetic algorithms to find optimal production schedules and distribution points in its supply chain. The company, which has 40 plants and 8,000 client sites, must consider factors such as power prices and projections of customer demand, as well as the power costs and efficiency of each plant.

## before you go on...

**1.** What is a genetic algorithm?

**2.** Give examples of the use of genetic algorithms.

# Intelligent Agents

TG 4.6

An **intelligent agent** is a software program that assists you, or acts on your behalf, in performing repetitive, computer-related tasks. Intelligent agents often use expert systems and fuzzy logic behind the scenes to create their seemingly intelligent behavior.

You may be familiar with an early type of intelligent agent—the paper clip (Clippy) that popped up in early versions of Microsoft Word. For example, if your document appeared as though it was going to be a business letter—that is, if you typed in a date, name, and address—the animated paper clip would offer helpful suggestions on how to proceed. Users objected so strenuously to this primitive intelligent agent that Microsoft eliminated it from subsequent versions.

There are many intelligent agents (also called *bots*) used for a wide variety of tasks. You can view the many different types of available agents by visiting BotSpot (*www.botspot.com*) and

SmartBot (*www.smartbot.com*). The following sections examine three types of agents: information agents, monitoring and surveillance agents, and user or **personal agents**.

## Information Agents

**Information agents** search for information and display it to users. The best known information agents are buyer agents. A **buyer agent**, also called a **shopping bot**, helps customers find the products and services they need on a Web site. There are many examples of information agents. We present here a few illustrative cases.

- The information agents for Amazon.com display lists of books and other products that customers might like, based on past purchases.

- Google and Ask.com use information agents to find information, and not just when you request it. Google, for example, sends out Googlebots to surf all the Web sites in Google's index. These bots copy individual pages to Google's repository, where Google's software indexes them. Therefore, whenever you perform a Google search, the search engine builds a list of all the pages that have the keywords you specify, and it presents them to you in PageRank order. Google's PageRank algorithm sorts Web pages based on the number of links on the Web that point to each page. That is, the more the Web links that point to a particular page, the higher that page will be on the list.

- The Federal Electronic Research and Review Extraction Tool (FERRET) was developed jointly by the Census Bureau and the Bureau of Labor Statistics. You can use FERRET to find information on employment, healthcare, education, race and ethnicity, health insurance, housing, income and poverty, aging, and marriage and the family.

## Monitoring and Surveillance Agents

**Monitoring and surveillance agents**, also called **predictive agents**, constantly observe and report on some item of interest. There are many examples of predictive agents. Consider the following:

- Allstate uses monitoring and surveillance agents to manage its large computer networks 24/7/365. Every five seconds, the agent measures 1,200 data points. It can predict a system crash 45 minutes before it happens. The agent also watches to detect electronic attacks early so that they can be prevented.

- Monitoring and surveillance agents can watch your competitors and notify you of price changes and special offers.

- Predictive agents can monitor Internet sites, discussion groups, and mailing lists for stock manipulations, insider trading, and rumors that might affect stock prices.

- These agents can search Web sites for updated information on topics of your choice, such as price changes on desired products (e.g., airline tickets).

## User Agents

**User agents**, also called personal agents, take action on your behalf. Let's look at what these agents can do (or will be able to do shortly).

- Check your e-mail, sort it according to your priority rules, and alert you when high-value e-mails appear in your inbox.

- Automatically fill out forms on the Web for you. They will also store your information for future use.

## before you go on...

1. Define intelligent agents, information agents, monitoring and surveillance agents, and user agents.

2. Explain the uses of each type of intelligent agent.

### For the Accounting Major

Intelligent systems are used extensively in auditing to uncover irregularities. They are also used to uncover and prevent fraud. Today's CPAs use intelligent systems for many of their duties, ranging from risk analysis to cost control. Accounting personnel also use intelligent agents for mundane tasks such as managing accounts and monitoring employees' Internet use.

### For the Finance Major

People have been using computers for decades to solve financial problems. Innovative intelligent applications have been developed for activities such as making stock market decisions, refinancing bonds, assessing debt risks, analyzing financial conditions, predicting business failures, forecasting financial trends, and investing in global markets. Often, intelligent systems can facilitate the use of spreadsheets and other computerized systems used in finance. Finally, intelligent systems can help reduce fraud in credit cards, stocks, and other financial services.

### For the Marketing Major

Marketing personnel use intelligent systems in many applications, from allocating advertising budgets to evaluating alternative routings of salespeople. New marketing approaches such as targeted marketing and marketing transaction databases are heavily dependent on IT in general and on intelligent systems in particular. Intelligent systems are especially useful for mining customer databases and predicting customer behavior. Successful applications appear in almost every area of marketing and sales, from analyzing the success of one-to-one advertising to supporting customer help desks. With customer service becoming increasingly important, the use of intelligent agents is critical for providing fast response.

### For the Production/Operations Management Major

Intelligent systems support complex operations and production decisions, from inventory to production planning. Many of the early expert systems in the production/operations management field were developed for tasks ranging from diagnosing machine failures and prescribing repairs to complex production scheduling and inventory control. Some companies, such as DuPont and Kodak, have deployed hundreds of ESs in the planning, organizing, and control of their operational systems.

### For the Human Resources Management Major

Human resources personnel employ intelligent systems for many applications. For example, recruiters use these systems to find applicants' resumes on the Web and sort them to match needed skills. Expert systems are also used in evaluating candidates (tests, interviews). HR personnel use intelligent systems to train and support employees in managing their fringe benefits. In addition, they use neural networks to predict employee job performance and future labor needs.

### For the MIS Major

The MIS function develops (or acquires) and maintains the organization's various intelligent systems, as well as the data and models that these systems use. In addition, MIS staffers sometimes interact with subject area experts to capture the expertise used in expert systems.

# What's In
# IT For
# Me?

# [ Summary ]

1. **Explain the potential value and the potential limitations of artificial intelligence.**

   Table TG 4.1 differentiates between artificial and human intelligence on a number of characteristics.

2. **Provide examples of the benefits, applications, and limitations of expert systems.**

   Expert systems are computer systems that attempt to mimic human experts by applying expertise in a specific domain. Tables TG 4.2 and TG 4.3 offer examples of expert systems.

3. **Provide examples of the use of neural networks.**

   A neural network is a system of programs and data structures that simulates the underlying concepts of the human brain. Neural networks are used to detect weapons concealed in personal belongings, in research on various diseases, for financial forecasting, to detect fraud in credit card transactions, to fight crime, and in many other applications.

4. **Provide examples of the use of fuzzy logic.**

   Fuzzy logic is a branch of mathematics that deals with uncertainties by simulating the process of human reasoning. Fuzzy logic is used in financial analysis, the manufacture of antilock brakes, measuring intangible assets like goodwill, and finding responses to search terms in Google.

5. **Describe the situations in which genetic algorithms would be most useful.**

   A genetic algorithm is an intelligent system that mimics the evolutionary, survival-of-the-fittest process to generate increasingly better solutions to a problem. Genetic algorithms are used to design aircraft parts such as fan blades, to manage inventories more effectively, to optimize store displays, and to find optimal production schedules and distribution points.

6. **Describe the use case for several major types of intelligent agents.**

   An intelligent agent is a software program that assists you, or acts on your behalf, in performing repetitive, computer-related tasks. Intelligent agents are used to display lists of books or other products that customers might like, based on past purchases; to find information; to manage and monitor large computer networks 24/7/365; to detect electronic attacks early so that they can be stopped; to watch competitors and send notices of price changes and special offers; to monitor Internet sites, discussion groups, and mailing lists for stock manipulations, insider trading, and rumors that might impact stock prices; to check e-mail, sort it according to established priority rules, and alert recipients when high-value e-mails appear in their inbox; and to automatically fill out forms on the Web.

# [ Chapter Glossary ]

**algorithm** A problem-solving method expressed as a finite sequence of steps.

**artificial intelligence (AI)** A subfield of computer science that is concerned with studying the thought processes of humans and recreating the effects of those processes via machines, such as computers.

**buyer agent (or shopping bot)** An intelligent agent on a Web site that helps customers find products and services that they need.

**expert systems (ESs)** Computer systems that attempt to mimic human experts by applying expertise in a specific domain.

**fuzzy logic** A branch of mathematics that deals with uncertainties by simulating the processes of human reasoning.

**genetic algorithm** An approach that mimics the evolutionary, "survival-of-the-fittest" process to generate increasingly better solutions to a problem.

**information agent** A type of intelligent agent that searches for information and displays it to users.

**intelligent agent** A software program that assists you, or acts on your behalf, in performing repetitive, computer-related tasks.

**intelligent systems** A term that describes the various commercial applications of artificial intelligence.

**machine learning systems** Artificial intelligence systems that learn from data.

**monitoring and surveillance agents** (or **predictive agents**) Intelligent agents that constantly observe and report on some item of interest.

**neural network** A system of programs and data structures that simulates the underlying concepts of the human brain.

**personal agents** See **user agents**.

**predictive agents** See **monitoring and surveillance agents**.

**shopping bot** See **buyer agent**.

**Turing test** A test in which a woman or a man and a computer both pretend to be women or men, and the human interviewer has to decide which is the real human.

**user agents** (or **personal agents**) Intelligent agents that take action on your behalf.

## [ Discussion Questions ]

1. Explain how your university could employ an expert system in its admission process. Could it use a neural network?

   What might happen if a student were denied admission to the university and his/her parents discovered that an expert system was involved in the admission process?

2. One difference between a conventional business intelligence system and an expert system is that the former can explain *how* questions, whereas the latter can explain both *how* and *why* questions. Discuss the implications of this statement.

## [ Problem-Solving Activities ]

1. You have decided to purchase a new video camcorder. To purchase it as inexpensively as possible and still get the features you want, you use a shopping bot. Visit several of the shopping bot Web sites that perform price comparisons for you. Begin with MySimon (*www.mysimon.com*), BizRate. com (*www.bizrate.com*), and Google Product Search.

   Compare these shopping bots in terms of ease of use, number of product offerings, speed in obtaining information, thoroughness of information offered about products and sellers, and price selection. Which site or sites would you use, and why? Which camcorder would you select and buy? How helpful were these sites in making your decision?

2. Access the MyMajors Web site (*www.mymajors.com*). This site contains a rule-based expert system to help students find majors. The expert system has more than 300 rules and 15,000 possible conclusions. The site ranks majors according to the likelihood that a student will succeed in them, and it provides 6 possible majors from among 60 alternative majors that a student might consider.

   Take the quiz, and see if you are in the "right major" as defined by the expert system. You must register to take the quiz.

3. Access Exsys (*www.exsys.com*), and click on the Corvid Demo (www.exsyssoftware.com/CORVID52/corvidsr? KBNAME=../Download2/DownloadForm.cvR). Provide your e-mail address, and click on the link for "Student—Needed for Class." Try the various demos, and report your results to the class.

# Index

*Page numbers in **bold** indicate end of chapter glossary terms.*
*Page numbers in italic indicate figures.*